Section 1

GENERAL INFORMATION

	Page
MAIN SPECIFICATIONS OF ENGINES	5
MAIN SPECIFICATIONS OF VEHICLES	5
PERFORMANCES	7
CAPACITIES	7
UNIT IDENTIFICATION DATA	8
JACKING UP AND TOWING THE CAR	9
ORDERING SPARE PARTS	9
SERVICE HINTS	10
CAR KEYS	10

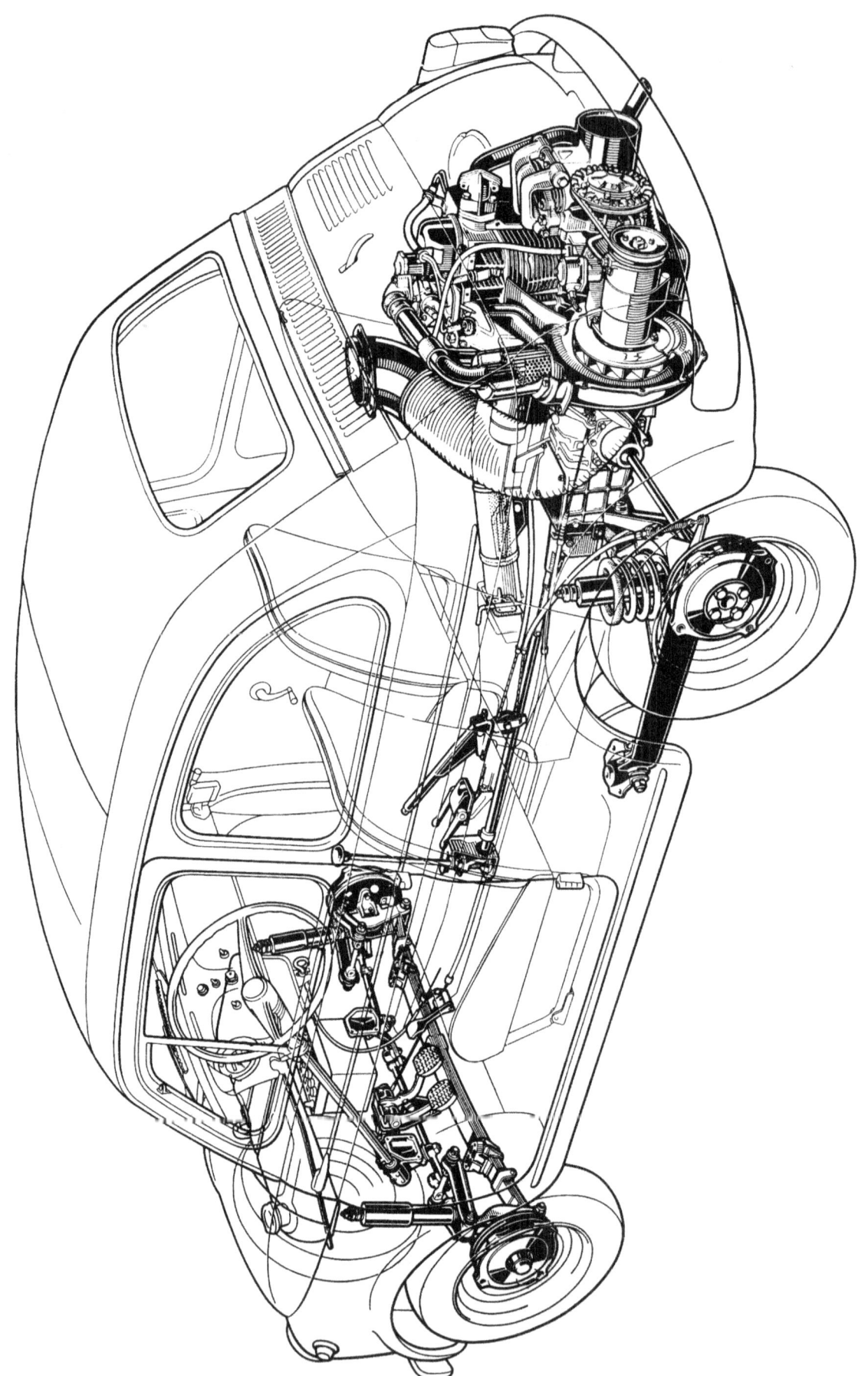

Fig. 1 - Phantom view of mechanical components.

NEW 500 - 500 D

500 (110 F)

500 S.W. - 500 L

SHOP MANUAL

DIREZIONE ASSISTENZA TECNICA AUTOVEICOLI

SECTION INDEX

Section	Section Page
GENERAL	1 — 3
ENGINE	2 — 11
FUEL SYSTEM — LUBRICATION — COOLING	3 — 67
CLUTCH - GEARBOX DIFFERENTIAL	4 — 89
FRONT SUSPENSION AND WHEELS	5 — 125
REAR SUSPENSION AND WHEELS SHOCK ABSORBERS	6 — 143
STEERING GEAR AND LINKAGE	7 — 159
BRAKES WHEELS AND TIRES	8 — 173
AIR CONDITIONING CHASSIS TIGHTENING REFERENCE	9 — 189
ELECTRICAL	10 — 195
BODY	11 — 265
MAINTENANCE TOOL EQUIPMENT VEHICLE SPECIFICATIONS	12 — 285
MODEL 500 D - 500 TYPE 110 F 500 STATION WAGON - 500 L	13 — 297

IMPORTANT

All the dimensions in metric units shown in this publication are the official ones.

Dimensions are also given in British and American units for prompt reference, and they have been calculated to a degree of approximation according to the need for accuracy in individual measurements.

GENERAL INFORMATION

The « New 500 » Model is manufactured in the following versions:

— Convertible;
— Sun Roof;
— Sports (Convertible and Metal Top);
— Version 140 (U.S.A. and Canada - Convertible and Sun Roof);
— Version 144 (U.S.A. and Canada - Sports Convertible and Metal Top).

Servicing directions in this manual are referred to above types. For parts particular to single versions, descriptions are preceded by applicable wording:
Convertible, Sun Roof, Sports, Version 140 or Version 144.
Whenever no special mention is made, data are intended to be common.

MAIN SPECIFICATIONS OF ENGINES

	500	500 Sports
Engine type	110.000 ([1])	110.004 ([2])
Number of cylinders, in line	2	2
Bore	2.5984" (66 mm)	2.6535" (67,4 mm)
Stroke	2.7559" (70 mm)	2.7559" (70 mm)
Displacement	29.23 cu. in. (479 cm^3)	30.48 cu. in. (499,5 cm^3)
Compression ratio	7	8.6
Maximum power (with fan, without exhaust silencer)	16.5 H.P.	21 H.P.
Maximum power, S.A.E. standards	21 H.P.	25 H.P.
Maximum torque (with fan, without exhaust silencer)	20.25 ft.lbs (280 kgcm)	25.32 ft.lbs (350 kgcm)
at	3,500 r.p.m.	3,500 r.p.m.

([1]) Engine to suit Version 140 is the type 110.040.
([2]) Engine to suit Version 144 is the type 110.044.

MAIN SPECIFICATIONS OF VEHICLES

Dimensions.	
Length, overall, with bumpers	116.93" (2,970 m) ([1])
Width, overall	52.05" (1,322 m)
Height, no load	52.16" (1,325 m)
General Data.	
Wheelbase	72.44" (1,840 m)
Tread, front	44.13" (1,121 m)
Tread, rear	44.69" (1,135 m)
Ground clearance	5.31" (0,135 m)
Turning radius	16.93" (4,300 m)

([1]) « Version 140 and 144 » = 121.06" (3,075 m).

(continued)

Main Specifications of Vehicles (continued).

Weights.	
Curb weight (with replenishments, spare wheel, tool kit and accessories):	
Sun Roof	1102 lbs (500 kg)
Convertible	1080 lbs (490 kg)
Sports Car	1124 lbs (510 kg)
Sun Roof - Version 140	1113 lbs (505 kg)
Convertible - Version 140	1091 lbs (495 kg)
Sports Car - Version 144	1135 lbs (515 kg)
Useful load	4 people ([1])
Total weight, full load:	
Sun Roof	1720 lbs (780 kg)
Convertible	1698 lbs (770 kg)
Sports Car	1587 lbs (720 kg)
Sun Roof - Version 140	1731 lbs (785 kg)
Convertible - Version 140	1709 lbs (775 kg)
Sports Car - Version 144	1598 lbs (725 kg)

([1]) « Sports Car » = 2 people plus 154 lbs (70 kg) luggage.

MAIN DIMENSIONS OF VEHICLES

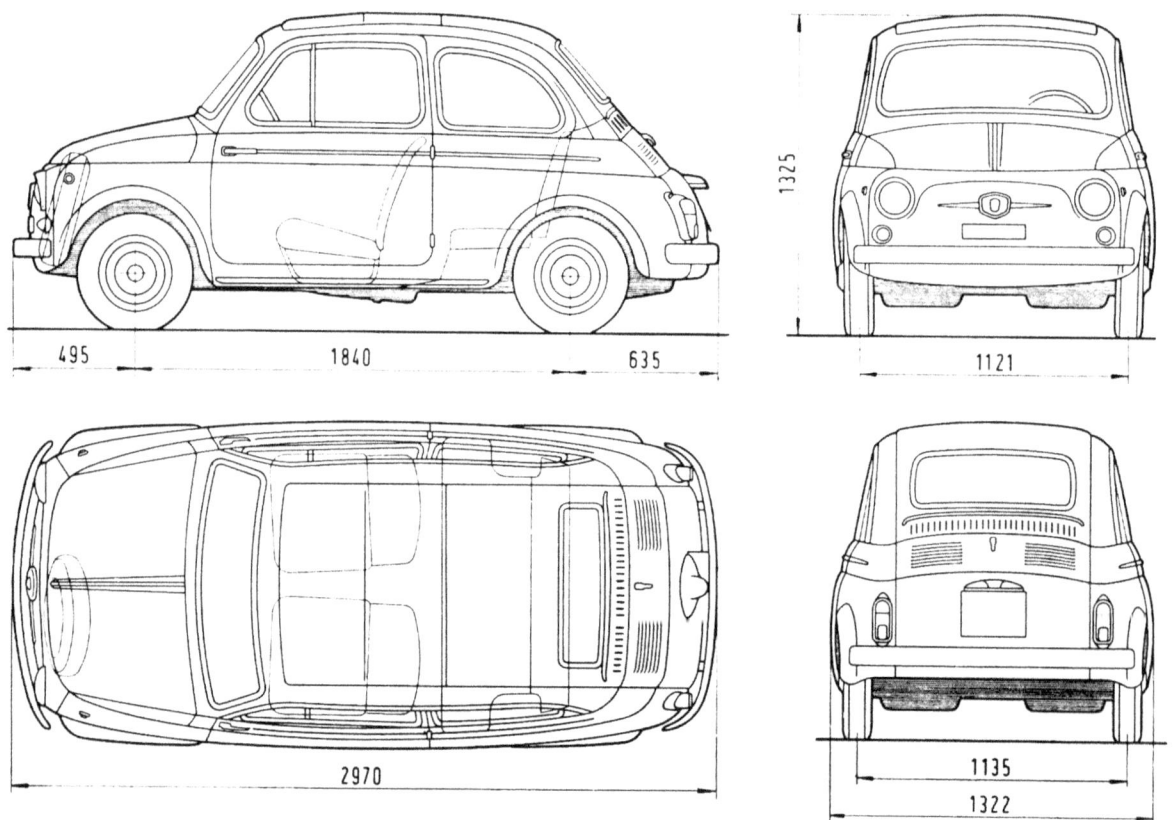

Fig. 2 - Main dimensions.

The height is intended with unladen cars:

495 = 19.49"	635 = 25.00"	1121 = 44.13"	1135 = 44.69"
1840 = 72.44"	1325 = 52.16"	2970 = 116.93"	1322 = 52.05"

GENERAL INFORMATION

PERFORMANCES

	500	500 Sports
Speeds.		
Maximum speed, on level, after run-in period (1,800 miles - 3.000 km):		
low gear	15.5 m.p.h. (25 km/h)	16.2 m.p.h. (26 km/h)
2nd gear	24.9 m.p.h. (40 km/h)	27.3 m.p.h. (44 km/h)
3rd gear	40.4 m.p.h. (65 km/h)	43.5 m.p.h. (70 km/h)
high gear	59 m.p.h. (95 km/h)	above 65.2 m.p.h. (105 km/h)
Climbable gradient,		
fully laden car:		
low gear, abt	20 %	28 %
2nd gear, abt	12 %	17 %
3rd gear, abt	6.5 %	9 %
high gear, abt	3.5 %	5 %

CAPACITIES

UNIT	QUANTITY				Fill in
	Imp. Units	U.S. Units	lt.	kg.	
Fuel tank (reserve supply - .8 to 1.1 Imp. gals - .9 to 1.3 U.S. gals - 3,5 to 5 lt)	4.6 gals	5.5 gals	21	—	Gasoline: «500» 83 Oct. Rat. «Sports» 92 (Res. Method)
Oil pan	1.54 qts (¹)	1.85 qts (¹)	1,75	1,6 (¹)	FIAT oil (²)
Gearbox and differential	.97 qts	1.16 qts	1,1	1,00	FIAT W 90 oil (SAE 90 EP)
Steering gear	.105 qts	.124 qts	0,12	0,11	
Hydraulic brake circuit	.194 qts	.232 qts	0,22	0,22	FIAT blue label brake fluid for hydraulic brakes
Hydraulic shock absorbers:					
— front, each	.112 qts	.137 qts	0,13	0,12	FIAT S.A.I. oil
— rear, each	.088 qts	.104 qts	0,10	0,09	FIAT S.A.I. oil

(¹) Total capacity of oil pan, lines, filter and crankshaft: 1.85 Imp. qts - 2.22 U.S. qts (1,900 kg).
(²) Recommended oil grades:

LOWEST ANTICIPATED OUTDOOR TEMPERATURE	FIAT SERVICE MS (*) (API) OIL	FIAT MULTIGRADE OIL (*)
Below —15° C (5° F) (minimum)	VS 10 W (SAE 10 W)	—
Between 0° and —15° C (32° to 5° F) (minimum)	VS 20 (SAE 20)	10 W - 30
Above 0° C (32° F) (minimum)	VS 30 (SAE 30)	10 W - 30
Above 30° C (86° F) (average)	VS 40 (SAE 40)	20 W - 40

(*) WARNING. - Do not top up with oils of other grades or Make (see page 307).

UNIT IDENTIFICATION DATA

The vehicle is fully identified by two numbers: the engine number and the chassis number.

To order parts a third number should be quoted: the « Number for Spares ».

Engine Number.

This number is punched on a pad cast on crankcase rear end, to the left of power plant rear support.

The engine number is preceded by the FIAT name and engine type (fig. 3).

Fig. 3 - Location of engine number on cranckase

Chassis or Integral Body Number.

As shown in fig. 4, this number is punched on front compartment rear wall, under the identification plate.

Number for Spares.

Stamped on lower edge of identification plate (see fig. 4).

Unit Identification Plate.

Unit identification plate, giving Engine and Chassis Numbers and Number for Spares, is located on

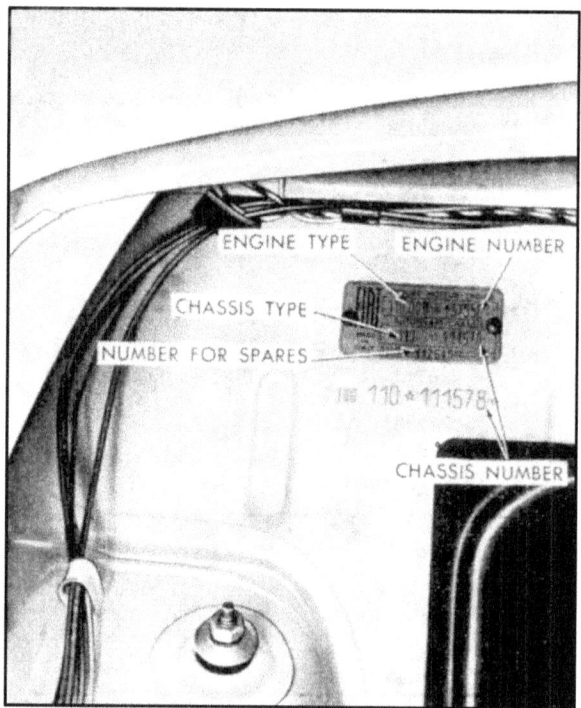

Fig. 4 - Location of chassis number and of identification plate.

front compartment rear wall, right hand top side, above Chassis Number (fig. 4).

NOTE - As far as 140 and 144 Version cars are concerned, unit identification plate specifies also body paint number.

This plate is shown in fig. 5.

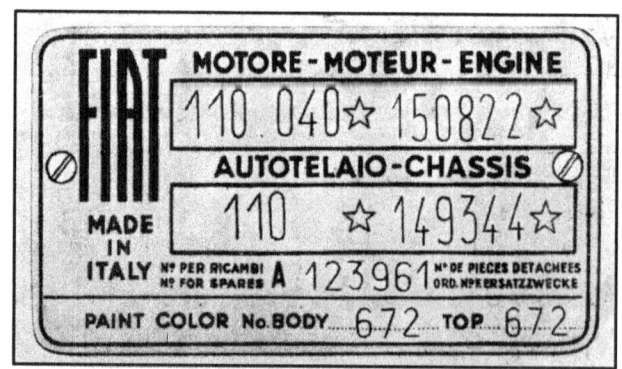

Fig. 5 - Unit identification plate, 140 Version.

GENERAL INFORMATION

JACKING UP AND TOWING THE CAR

To raise car front or rear ends, use hydraulic garage jack **Arr. 2027** with cross member **Arr. 2072**.

At front, place cross member under the leaf spring (fig. 8); at rear, place cross member under the swinging arms.

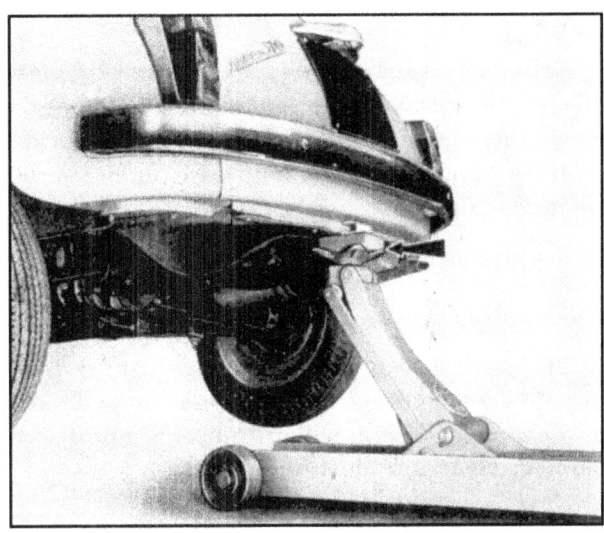

Fig. 7 - Detail of car raised by jack.
The arrow points to the wooden block that must always be interposed between jack and bracket.

Fig. 6 - Using hydraulic jack Arr. 2027 under floor bracket to raise car at front end.

Should cross member **Arr. 2072** be unavailable, proceed as follows:

At front: place jack head under the bracket mounted at center of floor front cross beam; this bracket serves also to accomodate the tow rope when necessary (fig. 6).

At rear: a wooden block at least $1^{3}/_{16}''$ (3 cm) thick must always be interposed between jack head and the bracket welded to body floor rear cross beam (fig. 7).

For some particular servicing of car raise and rest it on stands **Arr. 2002 bis**.

Fig. 8.
Raising the front end with garage jack Arr. 2027 and cross member Arr. 2072.

Prior to jacking up the car, always lock rear wheels through the parking brake.

NOTE - When the vehicle is raised with the column type jack, interpose the cross member I. 36055/1 between jack head and car contact area.

ORDERING SPARE PARTS

Wenn ordering spare parts, quote: Car Model, Engine Number, Chassis Number, Number for Spares and Catalogue Number of the part on order.

SERVICE HINTS

Before attempting any repair, adjustment, check, removal or installation of any part, take the necessary precautions to prevent damages to inner trim or body varnish by protecting parts involved with some suitable covering.

To ensure best possible results when servicing the different units of the car, aside from the skill of repairmen, it is essential to do the job in well-lighted, clean and dust-free shops.

The Shop must have available the general and special tools designed for the job and the type of car being serviced. To this end, consult the « Tool Catalogue » issued by the FIAT Service Department.

The importance of washing carefully all engine components and of freeing lubrication ducts from possible obstructions when disassembling or overhauling, cannot be over-emphasized.

An adequate lubrication of units and parts before re-assembly, is essential to eliminate the risk of seizure during the initial period of operation.

When disassembling an engine or other units, proceed with order, do not mix up parts and handle them carefully.

When a unit has received proper care and best possible servicing, it must again operate as if it were new.

Use exclusively original FIAT spares: in fact, only these will restore the units to perfect efficiency.

Follow strictly the techniques outlined on succeeding pages and keep within the tabulated allowances, wear limits and torque specifications.

Remember that if an operation is not performed according to best shop practice, the unit serviced cannot give satisfactory results. In this case, it would require a second disassembly to remedy any trouble, with a deriving time waste and cost increase before it can be restored to full efficiency.

To obtain best results, without unnecessary wastes of material and time, perform each servicing operation methodically, with order, care and proper equipment.

CAR KEYS

Each new car is delivered with two sets of keys to suit:
— ignition;
— door, driver's side.

These keys bear an identification number stamped on key head.
To have car key duplications made through the cutting machine Ap. 5013, identify keys quoting code number and applicable use.

Section 2
ENGINE

	Page
DESCRIPTION OF COMPONENTS	13
MISCELLANEOUS OPERATIONS	14
CRANKCASE AND CYLINDERS	19
PISTONS - PINS - RINGS	25
CONNECTING RODS - ROD BEARINGS AND BUSHINGS	28
CRANKSHAFT AND MAIN BEARINGS	33
CYLINDER HEAD - VALVES - GUIDES AND SPRINGS	39
TIMING GEAR	47
SPECIFICATIONS - REPAIR AND REBUILD STANDARDS	52
TIGHTENING REFERENCE	57
ENGINE BENCH TEST	58
TROUBLES AND CORRECTIONS	60

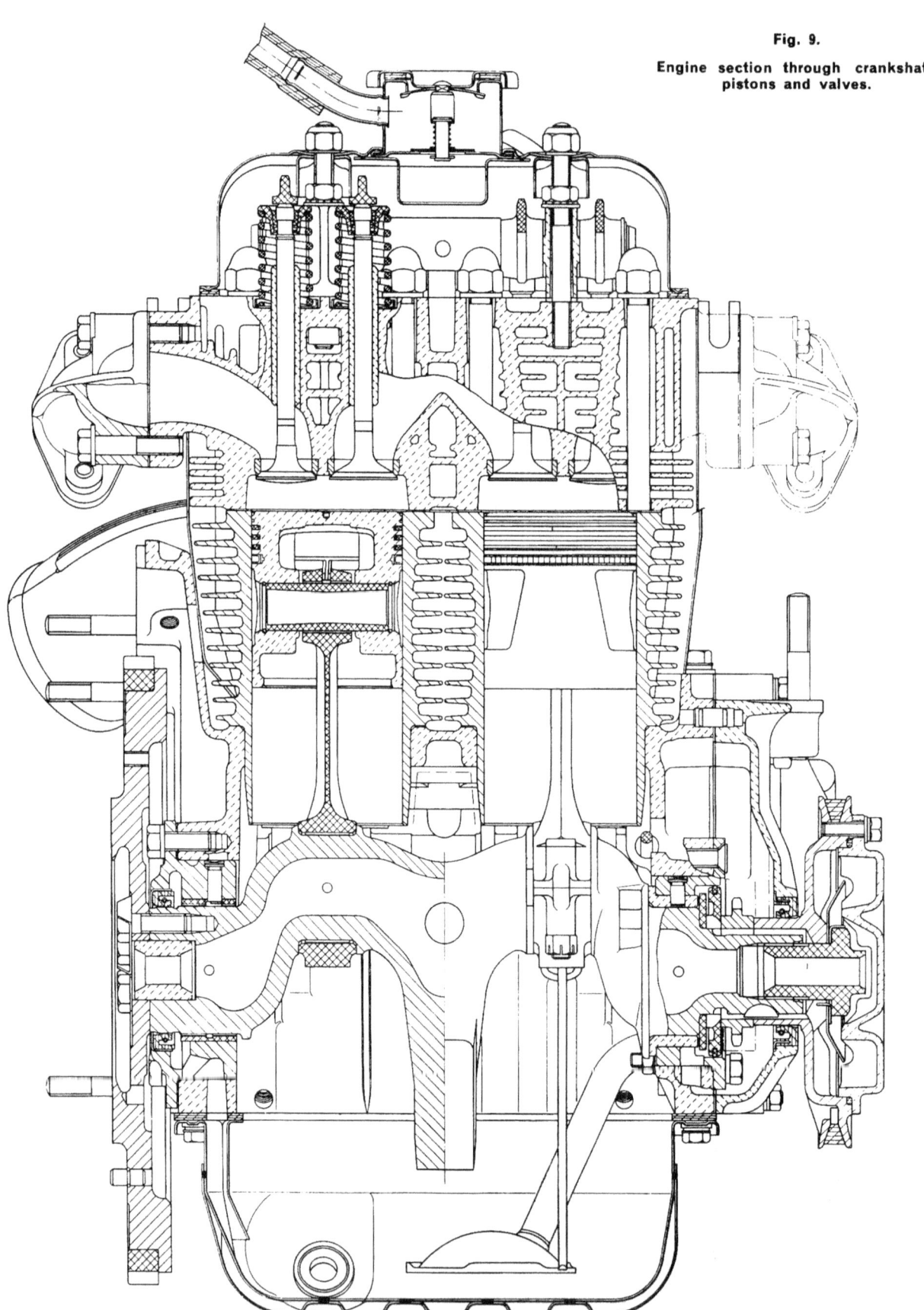

Fig. 9.
Engine section through crankshaft, pistons and valves.

ENGINE

Description of Components.

The « New 500 » is powered by a four-stroke, Otto cycle, rear mounted twin-cylinder gasoline engine.

This arrangement offers many advantages, among which:

— improved load distribution on axles, especially under extreme service conditions such as one person alone or car under full load;

— better exploitation of space available in favor of roominess and luminosity;

— elimination of propeller shaft with less vibrations and reduction in repair costs.

The **cylinder block** is formed by two cast-iron cylinders with cooling fins. The bottom of cylinders fits into proper seats machined in crankcase which is of aluminum and carries 8 studs on which are inserted the **cylinders** and the aluminum **cylinder head** with cast-iron valve seat inserts.

Crankshaft is of special cast iron and is supported by two bush-type bearings. At center the crankshaft is provided with a counterweight and is hollow to provide a passage for the lube oil.

Connecting rods are of steel with thin wall **bearing halves** on big end and bronze **bushes** in small end.

Pistons, of light alloy, are taper-oval-shaped with maximum diameter at bottom of skirt, along the axis perpendicular to piston pin. Pistons are fitted with four rings of which: one compression at top, two standard oil scrapers and one side-slotted oil scraper.

Piston pin is of steel and retained in piston bosses by two circlips. The piston pin bore is .0984" (2,5 mm) off center with respect to piston centerline, on the side opposite the skirt expansion slot.

Overhead valves controlled by chain-driven camshaft through pushrods and rockers.

Cylinder head is finned to provide a larger heat dissipation surface and carries the **intake and exhaust manifolds**. Intake manifolds join into a single central flange which mounts the carburetor. Exhaust manifolds are almost parallel to engine axis.

The carburetor is of the downdraft type with starting device (choke) controlled by lever located on floor tunnel. Pleated paper element air cleaner with silencer on carburetor air intake.

Mechanical, diaphragm type **fuel pump** actuated through a pushrod by a cam on camshaft.

Forced lubrication by gear pump mounted within timing gear cover and drawing oil from sump. Lube oil is cleaned by a centrifugal filter and pressure is governed by a regulating valve mounted on pump body.

Fig. 10 - Engine assembly, viewed from generator end.

Crankcase is vented through a rubber hose connected to rocker cover.

Engine air cooling. A centrifugal blower, mounted on generator shaft, and housed in a specially designed spiral cowling, conveys air to and around engine.

The temperature of air conveyed on to the engine is governed by a thermostat on engine cowling.

This thermostat operates a shutter which, in open position, allows exhaust of engine-heated air.

With shutter in closed position, air is recirculated in engine cowling.

Warmed air flowing out from engine cowling can be used for car interior heating purposes, by operating a control lever on heating system tunnel.

Ignition is by battery, coil and distributor driven by a gear keyed on camshaft.

Engine starting is by electric motor mounted on gearbox casing and controlled by a lever located behind gearshift lever.

Power plant suspension is obtained by a spring support mounted at center of rear cross member and by two rubber pads mounted laterally to gearbox.

MISCELLANEOUS OPERATIONS

ENGINE REMOVAL AND INSTALLATION	page 14
ENGINE DISASSEMBLY	» 15
ENGINE ASSEMBLY	» 17

ENGINE REMOVAL AND INSTALLATION

Raise the car tail with the hydraulic jack and rest it on stands **Arr. 2002 bis** placed under the suitable body brackets.

In front compartment: raise the lid, disconnect battery positive clamp and disinsert the line for fuel delivery from tank to fuel pump.

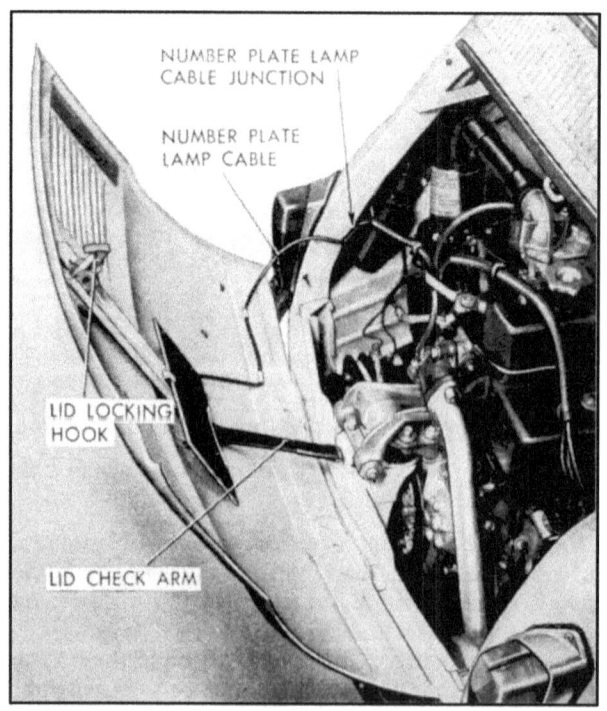

Fig. 11 - Engine compartment lid open.

Fig. 12 - Engine removal using the jack with cross member Arr. 2074.

In rear compartment: open lid, disconnect number plate lamp cable and, from the trapezoidal slot, remove the engine compartment lid check strap and remove the lid from hinges (fig. 11).

Disconnect ignition coil cables.

Disconnect the cables on generator and starter, and remove the starter control tie rod. Disconnect the oil pressure indicator cable, the fuel line on pump, the accelerator and starting device controls

ENGINE: DISASSEMBLY

Take off the hoses of the heating and cooling system (one for air arrival to blower and one for car heating system).

Remove side aprons.

Remove starter.

Place the jack, provided with cross member **Arr. 2074**, under the engine (fig. 12).

Undo the nuts securing gearbox to engine and the flywheel protection apron.

Remove the bolts fixing the elastic support to cross member.

Remove rear cross member mounting nuts on

NOTES

During removal and installing operations, engine can be supported by hook Arr. 2077 (fig. 13).

This hook has two slots to fit the hoist chain link.

To lift engine only, set link on the first slot. Shift the link to the second slot if the power plant complete is to be raised.

The installation of engine does not involve any particular difficulty. Reverse the procedure outlined for removal. Utmost care must be taken in joining engine to gearbox-differential unit: the clutch shaft must be inserted into splined hub of driven member.

Fig. 13 - Engine removal by the hoist with hook Arr. 2077.

one of which is fixed the ground cable and take off the cross member.

Slide the engine away from gearbox.

Lower the jack and remove the engine from below car.

ENGINE DISASSEMBLY

Remove exhaust silencer (two collars for attachment to engine and two connections for exhaust pipe, one on either side of cylinder head).

Place the engine on rotating stand **Arr. 2204** and secure by the clamping arms **Arr. 2205/11** (fig. 15) (one on the four studs for exhaust silencer attachment to crankcase and the other on the two studs for crankcase attachment to gearbox).

Drain lube oil by removing the sump plug.

Take off the tappet cover.

Remove the connection for air delivery to sump cooling ducts.

Remove air cleaner (two bolts on air cowling and two nuts for connection to carburetor).

Remove generator drive belt by taking off the three nuts securing the semi-pulley to generator.

Remove all bolts securing air conveyor to cylinder head, to crankcase and to the engine cowling assembly, opposite to air conveyor.

Disconnect accelerator control tie rod.

Take off the air conveyor complete with gener-

Fig. 14 - Removing crankshaft sprocket with puller A. 46020.

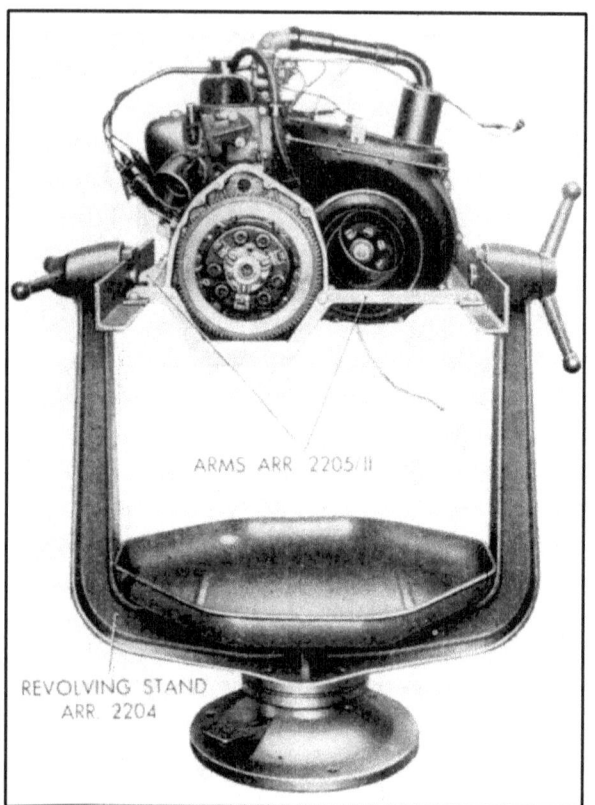

Fig. 15 - Engine on revolving stand, secured by arms Arr. 2205/II.

ator after removing the clamp fixing the generator to crankcase.

Take off the ignition distributor.

Remove all mounting bolts of the engine cowling and take off the assembly.

Take off the carburetor and relevant drip tray.

Take off rockers assembly (two nuts).

Disinsert rocker pushrods.

Slacken the four central cap nuts and the four standard cylinder hold down nuts; remove head using, if necessary, puller **A. 40014** (fig. 67).

Remove the four sleeves for pushrods and the casing containing the oil duct to rockers.

Remove fuel pump.

Remove fuel pump control push rod.

Remove centrifugal filter cover-pulley (six screws).

Remove centrifugal filter mounting flange by unscrewing crankshaft central bolt. Remove timing cover containing the oil pump gears and the oil regulating valve.

Take off the sprocket on camshaft by undoing the four mounting screws and removing the chain.

Using puller **A. 46020** remove crankshaft sprocket (fig. 14).

Remove rocker pushrod tappets.

Pull out camshaft.

Remove flywheel from crankshaft (6 screws with lockplates).

On two central studs of cylinders, mount tool **A. 60156** to hold cylinders in place (fig. 16).

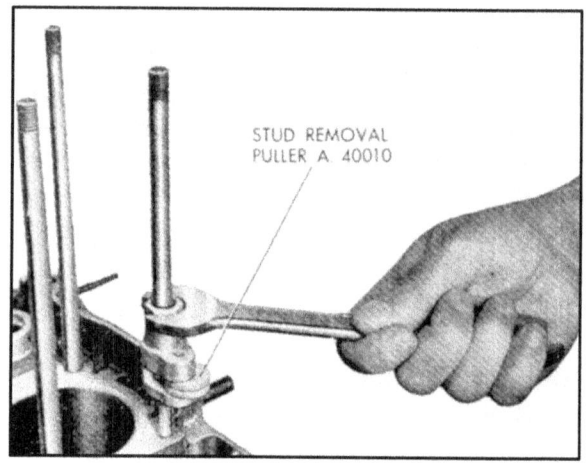

Fig. 17 - Removal of stud from crankcase by puller A. 40010.

Turn engine upside down on rotating stand.

Remove oil sump and suction scoop.

Remove connecting rod caps.

Remove tool **A. 60156**.

Take off connecting rod-piston-cylinder assemblies from crankcase.

Take off the rear main bearing housing by removing the six mounting screws on crankcase.

Take off front main bearing housing by removing the six screws on crankcase.

Remove crankshaft from crankcase by setting it diagonally during withdrawal.

NOTE - Withdrawal of cylinder mounting studs from crankcase is made with use of puller **A. 40010** (fig. 17).

Fig. 16 - Cylinder hold-down tool A. 60156.

ENGINE ASSEMBLY

To assemble engine, proceed as follows.

Thoroughly wash crankcase with studs in place and blow dry with compressed air.

Position crankcase on stand **Arr. 2204** and secure with clamping arms **Arr. 2205/2**, then operate as outlined here below.

Install cylinder, piston and connecting rod assemblies with paper gaskets between cylinders and crankcase seats.

Fit big end bearing shells, which have been cleaned from any oil residues.

Slide crankshaft into crankcase, lubricate crankshaft journals, place a paper gasket between supporting member and crankcase, flywheel end, then install supporting member and bearing assemblies.

Secure supporting members with screws and toothed washers.

Seat connecting rods on crankpin journals and secure to connecting rods, rod bearing cap and shell assemblies, which have been oiled liberally. Draw up bearing cap nuts with 23.9 ft.lbs (3.300 kgmm) of torque.

NOTE

For clearance inspection of connecting rod bearing halves to crankpin journals, and of main bearings to bearing journals, proceed as outlined under « Connecting Rods » and « Crankshaft ».

Install camshaft and check bearing bores on crankcase for complete absence of burrs. Should burrs be found, remove them using a scraper wetted with oil.

Fit timing gear cover paper gasket.

Install the outer thrust ring, inner thrust ring, shoulder washer, fit the camshaft drive drive sprocket and lock with Woodruff key. Install the timing chain and driven sprocket so that timing marks on sprocket are indexing. Secure driven sprocket with screws and lockplates and bend down lockplates, using pliers.

Install the timing gear cover, oil pump, oil pressure relief valve and seal assembly, and secure with nuts, toothed washers and plain washers (no plain washers are needed to lock nuts 10 x 1,25).

Position oil pump suction horn and secure with nuts and toothed washers.

Install flywheel, which is secured with screws and lockplates. After the flywheel has been firmly

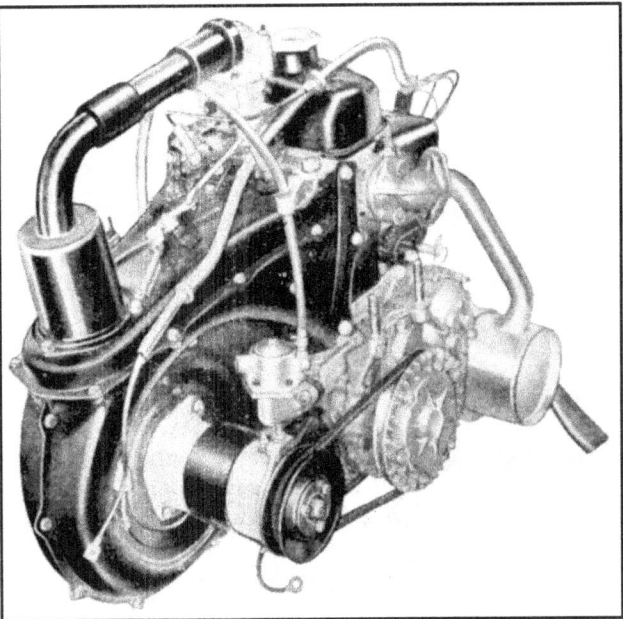

Fig. 18 - Engine assembly, generator and fuel pump side.

held with tool **A. 60161** (fig. 19), tighten screws with 23.1 ft.lbs (3.200 kgmm) of torque, then bend down lockplates, using pliers.

Install the centrifugal oil filter mounting flange, the oil slinger, the mounting screw on crankshaft and screw lockplate. Draw up the screw with 108½ ft.lbs (15.000 kgmm) of torque and bend down the lockplate.

Install the clutch assembly and secure to flywheel using screws and toothed washers.

Fig. 19 - Using tool A. 60161 to lock flywheel in position.

Position the oil pan cork gasket, install the oil pan and secure with screws, toothed washers and lockplates, which are bent down on screw heads.

Install oil cooling air conveyor on oil pan and secure with screws and toothed washers.

Turn over the engine on revolving stand and fit the centrifugal filter mounting flange rubber seal. Next place the oil filter cover and secure with screws, plain and toothed washers. Screw tightening torque: 5.8 ft.lbs (800 kgmm).

Install the cylinder head gasket, slide in tappets, sleeves, push rods, oil delivery line to rocker arm shaft and the casing with seal ring. Then go over the cylinder head, including valves, cups, springs and exhaust manifold, and install it in place.

Secure the cylinder head with four cap nuts internally and four standard nuts externally, and fit plain washers.

Draw up nuts with 23,9 ft.lbs (3.300 kgmm) of torque (fig. 96) in the sequence shown in fig. 95.

Install the rocker arm shaft and arm assembly and both supports. Tighten rocker arm supports with screws, plain and toothed washer to 15.2 ft.lbs (2.100 kgmm) of torque. Check valve-to-rocker arm clearance as outlined on page 50.

Temporarily plug intake duct hole, to avoid possible admission of foreign matter.

Install spark plugs and seals.

Install the engine cowling and air exhaust throttle valve assembly, which should be secured: on up side with two nuts, two plain washers and two toothed washers; on down side with two screws and two toothed washers; centrally with one screw and one spring washer.

Fit toothed washers on spark plug end, then screw up terminals with relevant rubber boots.

Install fan, generator and ground cable assembly and secure to crankcase and warmed air intake shrouding.

Tighten generator-to-fan nuts.

Install both lower exhaust silencer mounting brackets on crankcase, but do not secure them.

Install air conveyor and secure to engine cowling with six screws, six toothed washers, one nut and one toothed washer.

Join the two sections of air conveyor and secure with seven screws, seven toothed washers and five nuts.

Install the fuel pump, after sliding the control rod into seat. Interpose insulator and graphite gaskets which have been wetted with flax oil; secure the fuel pump to crankcase with nuts and toothed washers.

Install the air conveyor cover, complete with accelerator control relay lever and rod. To secure, tighten eight mounting screws, eight toothed washers, eight plain washers and eight nuts.

Install fuel line retaining clip, which is secured with one of air conveyor upper screws.

Install generator and fan drive pulley, after placing four adjusting rings between pulley halves and a thrust ring on the outside. Secure pulley to generator shaft with three screws and three toothed washers.

Install generator and fan drive belt.

To install the carburetor, position: bakelite heat shield, crankcase-to-heat shield graphite gasket and heat shield-to-carburetor body graphite gasket. Secure carburetor with two copper washers and two self-locking nuts.

Install exhaust silencer and secure to exhaust manifolds with nuts and spring washers after placing two graphite gaskets in between.

Install both exhaust silencer upper mounting brackets and secure them on up side to brackets already in place with nuts and toothed washers and on down side with screws and toothed washers.

Position the ignition distributor and set it on 10° advance. Secure distributor with nut, plain washer and spring washer.

Install fuel pump-to-carburetor line, complete with mounting bracket rubber lining, and secure line with two clamps.

NOTE - For easier positioning of fuel line into fuel pump and carburetor funnels, it is good practice heating line end before installation.

Install air cleaner elbow and rubber hose assembly on carburetor, with a graphite gasket in between, and secure it with nuts, plain washers and spring washers.

Position the air cleaner, line and hose assembly and connect it to elbow. Secure cleaner to air conveyor cover with screws and toothed washers.

Install spark plug cables, complete with rubber grommet for cable mounting bracket on engine cowling and connect cables to ignition distributor and spark plugs.

Install oil gauge sending unit and gasket.

Install cylinder head cover and oil breather pipe assembly, with cork gasket in between, and secure with self-locking nuts and fiber washers.

Tie the accelerator control relay lever rod to carburetor, by means of clip.

Fill the oil pan with the proper amount of oil and slide in the dip stick.

CRANKCASE AND CYLINDERS

CLEANING	page	19
CHECKING CYLINDER WEAR	»	19
HONING AND REAMING CYLINDERS	»	20
CHECKING CYLINDER HEIGHT	»	22
CHECKING WEAR OF TAPPET SEATS	»	23

The crankcase is an aluminum casting suitably ribbed.

There are directly cast main bearing bores and camshaft bearing bores. On crankcase are also machined or cast cylinder and tappet seats, gearbox companion flange, timing gear cover mounting flange, in addition to bosses, flanges and seatings to provide attachment for sundry engine accessories (fuel pump, air conveyor, muffler, etc.).

Cast iron, radial-finned, separate cylinders are located symmetrically on crankcase.

Cylinder finning has been designed to increase cooling area.

Cylinders are installed by sliding into crankcase bores and are held is place through head tightness.

Cleaning.

When the engine has been disassembled, clean the crankcase by immersing it for some twenty minutes in a washing tank containing a water and soda solution which has been heated to 176° to 185° F (80° to 85° C).

Next raise the assembly and, using a spray pump, submit the engine to a heavy jet of this

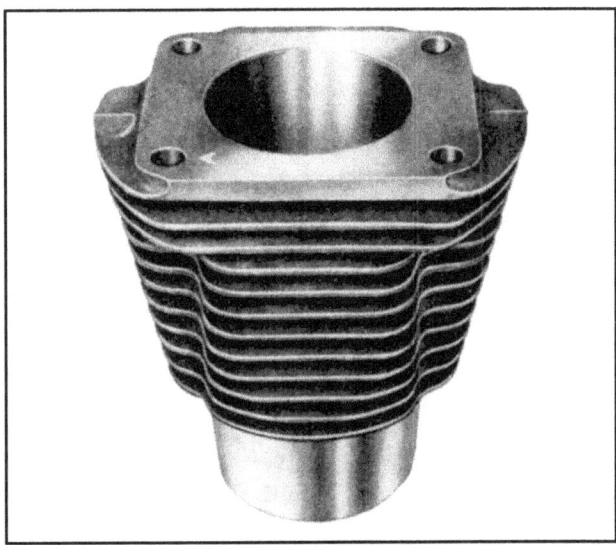

Fig. 21 - Finned cylinder.

Letter A stamped on cylinder indicates the class to which cylinder belongs, as referred to its inside diameter.

solution to remove all hardened deposits and foreign matter from oil galleries.

Thoroughly blow the cylinder block, especially internal oil passages, with compressed air.

Checking Cylinder Wear.

Inspect cylinder inner walls and hone away any slight scoring marks, if detected.

After this operation, check if the clearance between piston maximum diameter and cylinder bore is still within the maximum permissible limit of .0059" (0,15 mm).

Diameter measurements must be taken at two different heights in cylinder, along both the longitudinal and transverse axes (fig. 24). To bring dial indicator to zero, use ring gauge C. 672 (fig. 22).

If wear or ovalization are between .0059" (0,15 mm) and .0079" (0,20 mm), the cylinder may be simply honed; otherwise, if the limit of .0079" (0,20 mm) is exceeded, rebore must be made using a reamer.

Fig. 20 - Engine crankcase bottom view.

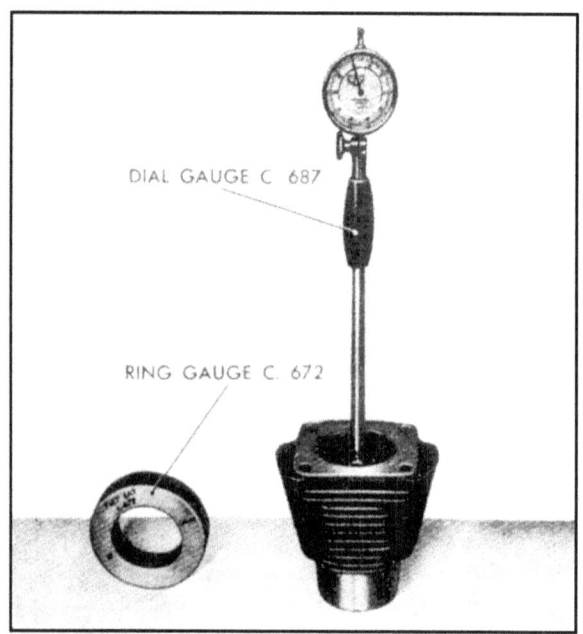

Fig. 22 - Checking cylinder diameter by dial gauge C. 687 brought to zero with ring gauge C. 672.

Honing and Reaming Cylinders.

Honing or reaming operations must bring bore to the measures corresponding to the oversizes of spare pistons, in order to obtain the correct fit clearance of .00079" to .00158" (0,020 to 0,040 mm) between piston and cylinder, as tabulated on page 21.

As shown in the table, cylinders are divided into three classes depending on their diameters.

Fig. 23 - Grinding a cylinder on stationary grinder, using tool A. 60000 and hone A. 11209.

Letters A, B and C identifying said classes are stamped on cylinder mating face with cylinder

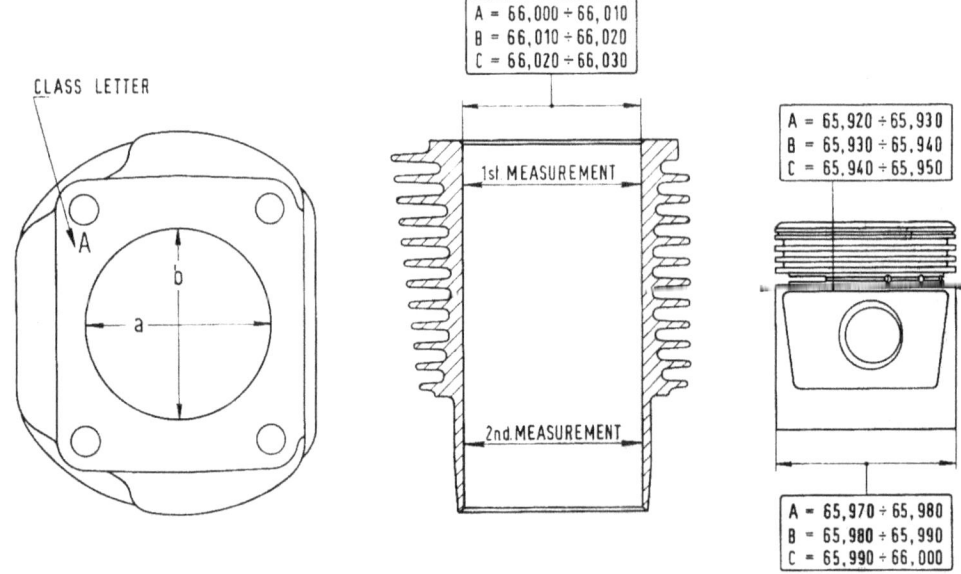

Fig. 24 - Cylinder and piston main data (engine to suit « 500 » car).

NOTE - Specifications of cylinders and pistons as fitted to « 500 Sports » car engine, are given on table page 22 and in fig. 33.

ENGINE: CRANKCASE AND CYLINDERS

head (fig. 24). Accordingly, also pistons are divided into three classes as the cylinders and, therefore, the piston and the cylinder of a set must belong to the same class.

NOTE - Pistons and rings to suit Model 500 Sports engine, do not come for replacement in oversize dimensions. During engine overhaul, should above parts prove to be worn beyond permissible limits, they must be substituted.

If cylinders require honing or reaming, their diameter must be brought to a dimension corresponding to one of the three classes of oversize pistons, following the data of said Table. Of course, the class letter originally stamped on cylinders shall be replaced with the letter identifying the class of the oversize piston being installed.

Honing is performed on stationary machine using honer **A. 11209** (fig. 23) provided with medium or extra-coarse grain hones.

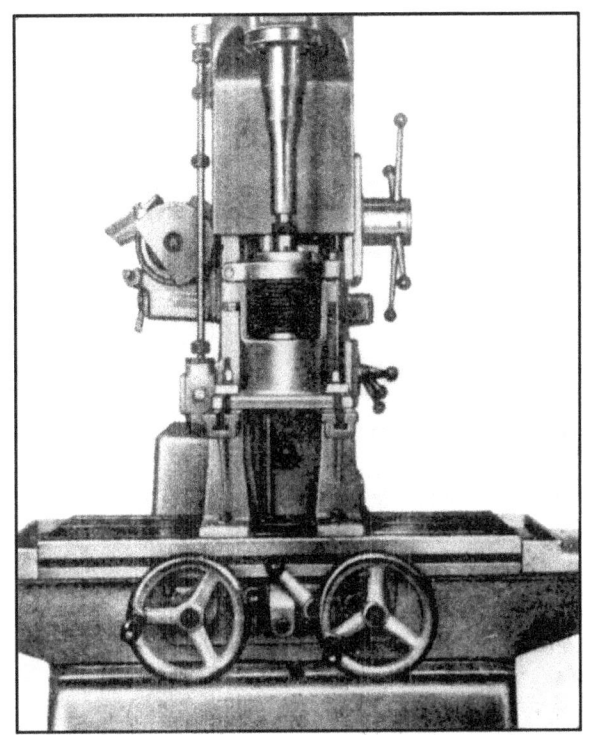

Fig. 25 - Reaming a cylinder on stationary boring machine with tool A. 60000.

TABLE OF CYLINDER DIAMETERS TO OVERSIZE PISTON DIAMETERS
Model «500»

OVERSIZES		CLASS	PISTON DIAMETER (at skirt bottom, square to pin axis)		CYLINDER DIAMETER		FITS OF NEW PARTS	
in.	mm		in.	mm	in.	mm	in.	mm
Standard		A	2.5972 to 2.5976	65,970 to 65,980	2.5984 to 2.5988	66,000 to 66,010	.0008 to .0016	0,020 to 0,040
		B	2.5976 to 2.5980	65,980 to 65,990	2.5988 to 2.5992	66,010 to 66,020		
		C	2.5980 to 2.5984	65,990 to 66,000	2.5992 to 2.5996	66,020 to 66,030		
.0079	0,2	A	2.6051 to 2.6055	66,170 to 66,180	2.6063 to 2.6067	66,200 to 66,210	.0008 to .0016	0,020 to 0,040
		B	2.6055 to 2.6059	66,180 to 66,190	2.6067 to 2.6071	66,210 to 66,220		
		C	2.6059 to 2.6063	66,190 to 66,200	2.6071 to 2.6075	66,220 to 66,230		
.0157	0,4	A	2.6130 to 2.6134	66,370 to 66,380	2.6142 to 2.6146	66,400 to 66,410	.0008 to .0016	0,020 to 0,040
		B	2.6134 to 2.6138	66,380 to 66,390	2.6146 to 2.6150	66,410 to 66,420		
		C	2.6138 to 2.6142	66,390 to 66,400	2.6150 to 2.6154	66,420 to 66,430		
.0236	0,6	A	2.6209 to 2.6213	66,570 to 66,580	2.6220 to 2.6224	66,600 to 66,610	.0008 to .0016	0,020 to 0,040
		B	2.6213 to 2.6217	66,580 to 66,590	2.6224 to 2.6228	66,610 to 66,620		
		C	2.6217 to 2.6221	66,590 to 66,600	2.6228 to 2.6232	66,620 to 66,630		

TABLE OF CYLINDER DIAMETERS TO OVERSIZE PISTON DIAMETERS
Model «500 Sports»

CLASS	PISTON DIAMETER (at skirt bottom, square to pin axis)		CYLINDER DIAMETER		FITS OF NEW PARTS	
	in.	mm	in.	mm	in.	mm
A	2.6516 to 2.6520	67,350 to 67,360	2.6535 to 2.6539	67,400 to 67,410	.0016 to .0024	0,040 to 0,060
B	2.6520 to 2.6524	67,360 to 67,370	2.6539 to 2.6543	67,410 to 67,420	.0016 to .0024	0,040 to 0,060
C	2.6524 to 2.6528	67,370 to 67,380	2.6543 to 2.6547	67,420 to 67,430	.0016 to .0024	0,040 to 0,060

Reaming may be performed either on the stationary machine (fig. 25) or portable reamer **M. 111** (fig. 26). To secure cylinders to the work table of the stationary machine, use fixture **A. 60000**; when using the portable machine, the fixture must be secured on a metal base as shown in fig. 26.

Maximum permissible limit for reaming in relation to piston oversizes is .0236" (0,6 mm).

Checking Cylinder Height.

The height of cylinders measured from seating face on crankcase to top surface is 3.5433"±.0006" (90±0,015 mm). Check this height.

If it is found to be less than specified, replace the cylinder to prevent that possible carbon deposits (on piston top and on underside of compression chamber) reduce the clearance to the extent where piston strikes the head.

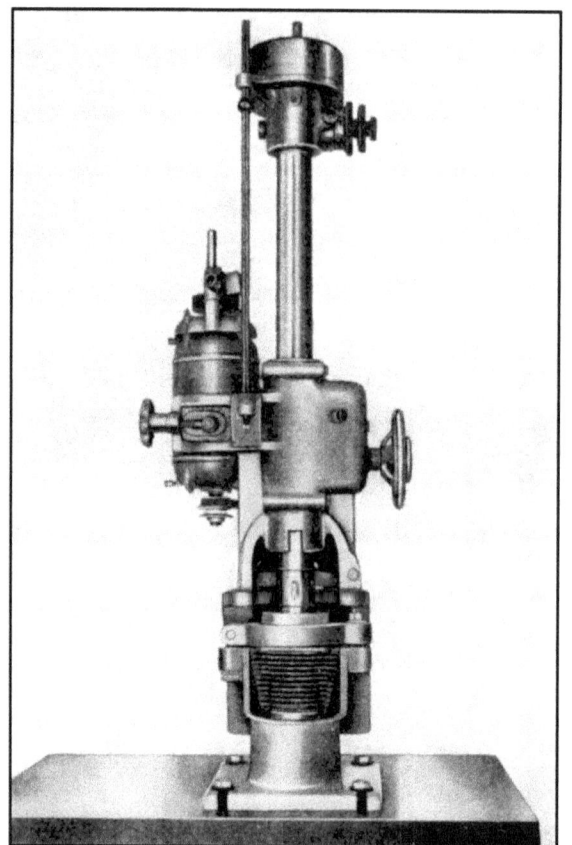

Fig. 26 - Reaming a cylinder on portable machine M. 111 with tool A. 60000.

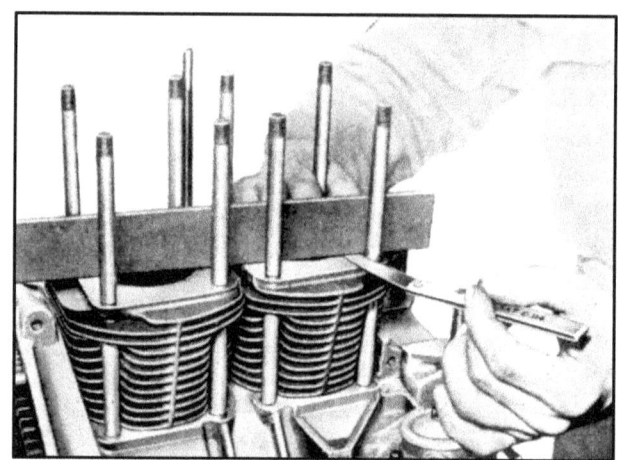

Fig. 27 - Checking cylinder head mating face for level

Out-of-true should not exceed .00315" (0,08 mm).

Insert a .0079"±.00197" (0,2±0,05 mm) thick oiled paper gasket between crankcase and cylinder bottom face and a .0236" to .0275" (0,6 to 0,7 mm) thick graphitized asbestos (Klingerite) gasket between cylinder and cylinder head. The squeezing of gaskets will take up any small possible departure from coplanarity of the cylinder-to-cylinder head mating surfaces.

ENGINE: CRANKCASE AND CYLINDERS

Checking Wear of Tappet Seats.

Check that the clearance between tappets and their seats does not exceed .00315" (0,05 mm). If clearance is greater, ream the seat with reamer U. 0338/1 (1st oversize) or U. 0338/2 (2nd oversize) and replace tappets with corresponding oversize spares (fig. 28).

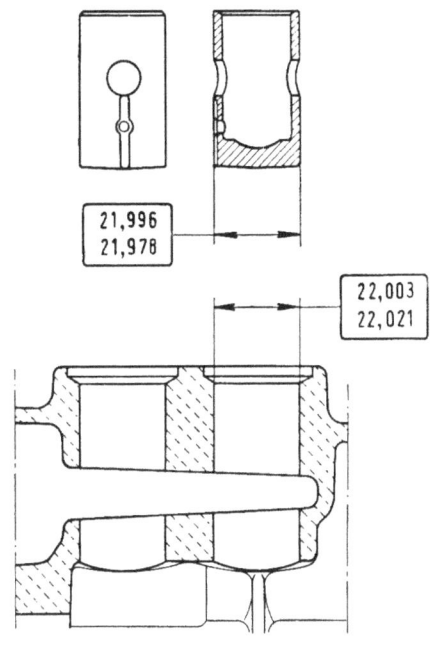

Fig. 29 - Tappet and seat diameters.

Fig. 28 - Reaming tappet seats in crankcase with reamer U. 0338/1 or U. 0338/2.

Spare tappets are supplied in the .00197" and .00394" (0,05 and 0,10 mm) diameter oversizes.

TAPPET-TO-SEAT FIT DATA

OVERSIZES	SEAT I.D.	TAPPET O.D.	FIT CLEARANCE
Standard	.8670" to .8662" (22,021 to 22,003 mm)	.8660" to .8652" (21,996 to 21,978 mm)	.00028" to .00169" (0,007 to 0,043 mm)
.00197" (0,05 mm)	.8689" to .8682" (22,071 to 22,053 mm)	.8680" to .8672" (22,046 to 22,028 mm)	.00028" to .00169" (0,007 to 0,043 mm)
.00394" (0,10 mm)	.8709" to .8702" (22,121 to 22,103 mm)	.8700" to .8692" (22,096 to 22,078 mm)	.00028" to .00169" (0,007 to 0,043 mm)

NOTE - When rebuilding the engine, take care to thoroughly clean all cylinder parts, especially cooling fin grooves.
As a matter of fact, gum deposits on fins as resulting from dust, oil and gasoline mixture, are apt to sensibly reduce the cylinder area exposed to cooling air draft.
There is no need to outline the damages which poor cylinder cooling may bring about. The same care for cleaning should be devoted also to cylinder head.

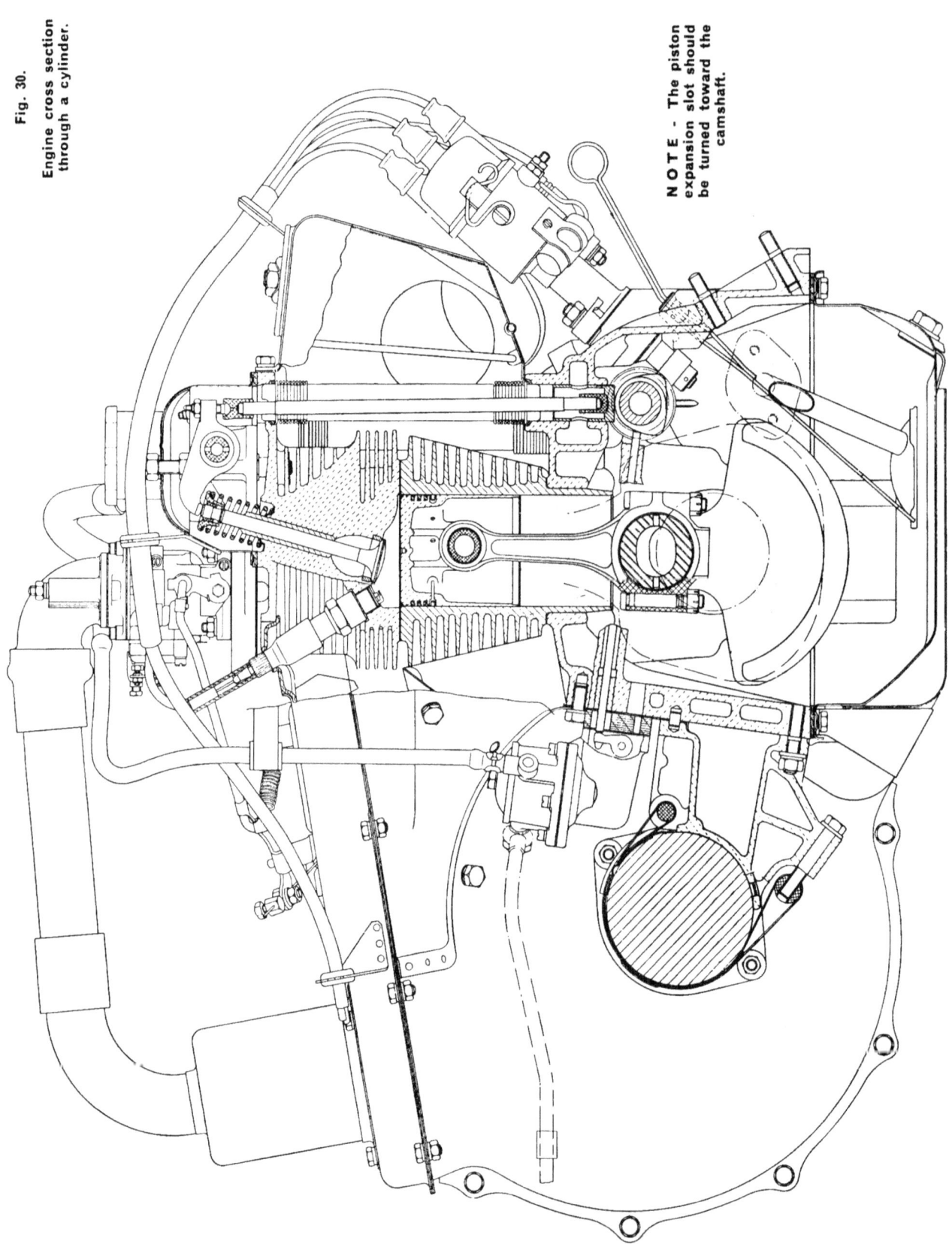

Fig. 30. Engine cross section through a cylinder.

NOTE - The piston expansion slot should be turned toward the camshaft.

PISTONS - PINS - RINGS

CLEANING, INSPECTION AND REPAIR . . . . page 25
ASSEMBLY . . . . » 26

Also pistons are subdivided into three classes based on skirt diameter: A, B and C; pistons must always be fitted in cylinders of the same class; fit clearance between cylinder and piston:

— at skirt top
 { Model «500» .0028" to .0035" (0,070 to 0,090 mm)
 { Model «500 Sports» .0035 to .0043" (0,090 to 0,110 mm)

— at skirt bottom
 { Model «500» .0008" to .0016" (0,020 to 0,040 mm)
 { Model «500 Sports» .0016 to .0024" (0,040 to 0,060 mm)

First compression ring, as well as second and third oil rings are of special cast iron. Fourth radial-slotted oil scraper ring is of steel.

Steel piston pin.

Cleaning, Inspection and Repair.

When servicing pistons, always decarbonize piston tops, ring grooves and rings; check cylinder-to-piston clearances which must never exceed .0059" (0,15 mm) for model «500» and .0079" (0,20 mm) for Model «500» Sports, at skirt bottom, measured square to pin axis. If clearance is greater, in which

Fig. 31 - Using feeler gauge C. 316 to check piston-to-cylinder wall clearance.

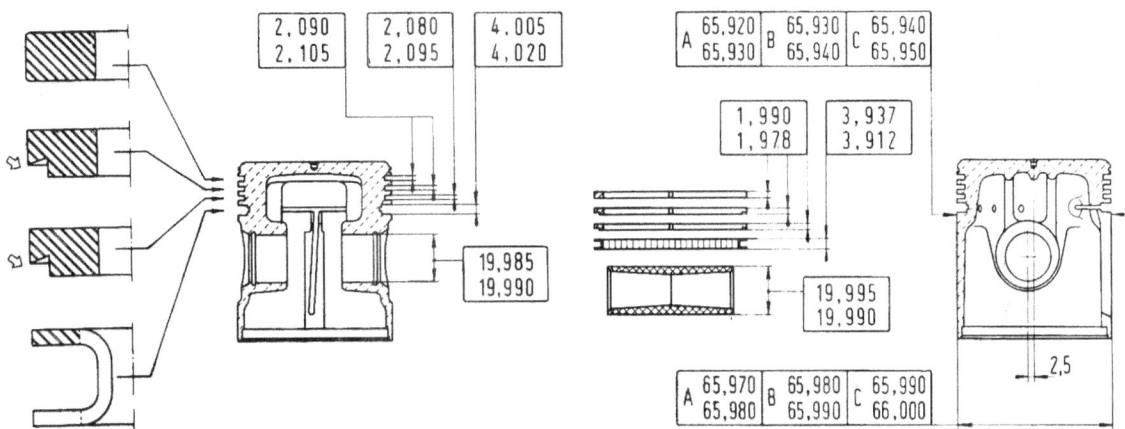

Fig. 32 - Piston, piston pin and rings main data, Model «500».

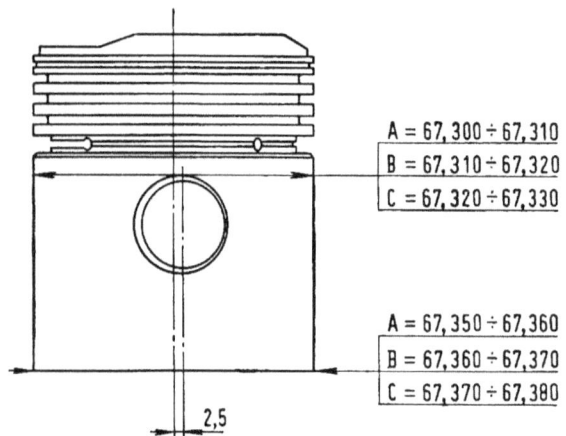

Fig. 33 - Piston main data, Model « 500 Sports ».

case cylinders need reboring, install oversize pistons (model « 500 » only).

As spares, pistons are supplied in the following oversize classes:

.0079" .0157" .0236"
(0,2 mm) (0,4 mm) (0,6 mm)

NOTE - Pistons and piston rings of Model « 500 Sports » engine do not come for replacement in oversize dimensions. Should piston-to-cylinder wall clearance prove to be in excess of wear limit, cylinders, pistons and rings must be replaced.

If pistons need not be replaced, check ring-to-groove clearance after decarbonizing and make sure it still falls within the values tabulated on page 27.

Before fitting rings on pistons, with the specially designed installer **A. 10114** (fig. 36), it is essential to place rings in cylinder to check gap clearance which must result as tabulated on page 27 (see

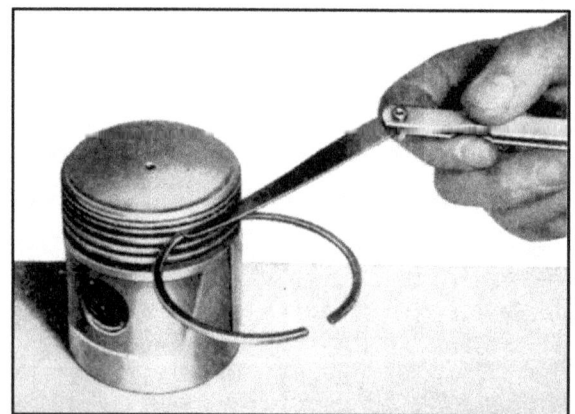

Fig. 34 - Checking piston ring-to-land clearance.

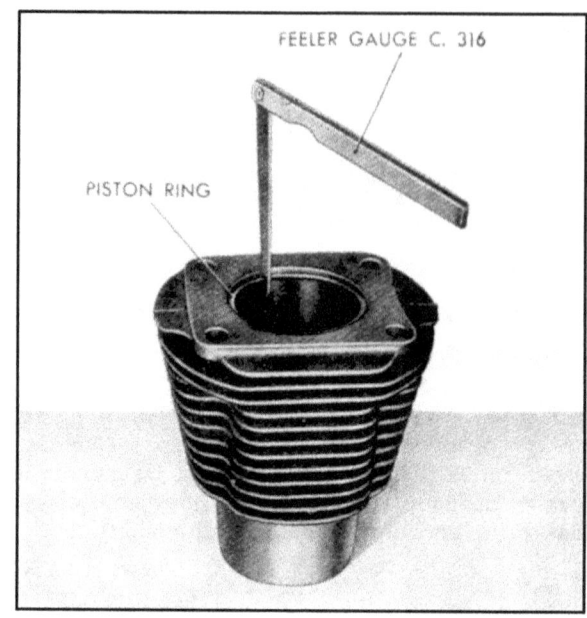

Fig. 35 - Checking ring gap (ring in cylinder).

fig. 35); otherwise recondition using hand grinder **A. 10650** or, if necessary, replace.

Rings are supplied as spares in the same oversize classes as pistons:

.0079" .0157" .0236"
(0,2 mm) (0,4 mm) (0,6 mm)

Piston rings should be installed on piston with the gap on the opposite side to the piston slot.

Ring gaps should not be in line but scattered around the piston.

Check that piston pin-to-boss is a pinch fit assembly. Should a clearance be found, restore bore roundness using expansible reamer **U. 0307** to adapt bore to the oversize of piston pin being installed.

Piston pins are supplied as spares in standard size and oversized on outer diameter by .0079" (0,2 mm).

Pin-to-bore pinch fit must be .0000" to .00039" (0,000 to 0,010 mm).

Install pins after heating pistons in an oven or in hot water at 176° F (80° C) to expand the bore and facilitate pin insertion.

To install and remove pins, use special tool **A. 60157**.

Pistons must always be installed with expansion slot turned toward the camshaft.

Assembly.

Installation of piston pin and rod assemblies in cylinders must always be carried out on bench, inserting same from crankcase end of cylinders (fig. 37). The installation of pistons is facilitated by using piston installer **A. 60154** which keeps rings tight in their grooves (fig. 37).

ENGINE: PISTONS - PINS - RINGS

SIZES	PISTON PIN DIAMETER	PISTON BOSS DIAMETER
Standard	.7872" to .7870" (19,995 to 19,990 mm)	.7868" to .7870" (19,985 to 19,990 mm)
.0079" (0,2 mm) oversize . .	.7951" to .7949" (20,195 to 20,190 mm)	.7947" to .7949" (20,185 to 20,190 mm)

To match pistons with connecting rods, see instructions under « Piston-Connecting Rod Assembly and Installation » (page 32). The piston-connecting rod assembly must be checked for correct alignment

Fig. 36 - Piston ring installer-and-remover A. 10114.

on fixture **C. 627**; if any incorrectness is found, check connecting rod ends center-to-center parallelism as directed on page 31.

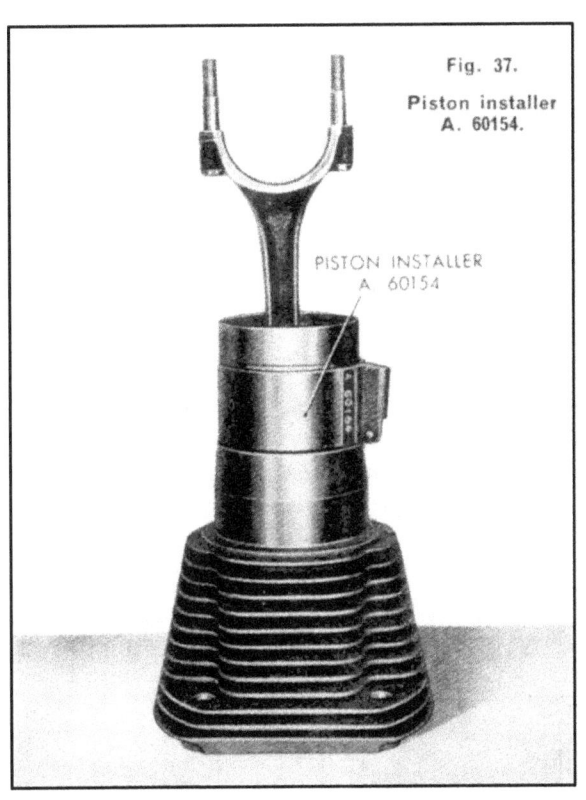

Fig. 37. Piston installer A. 60154.

FIT DATA OF PISTONS - CYLINDERS - PISTON PINS - PISTON RINGS

PISTONS - CYLINDERS - PISTON PINS - PISTON RINGS		FITS OF NEW PARTS	WEAR LIMITS
Piston-to-cylinder, square to pin axis:			
— Model « 500 »	at skirt top	.0028" to .0035" (0,070 to 0,090 mm)	.0098" (0,25 mm)
	at skirt bottom	.0008" to .0016" (0,020 to 0,040 mm)	.0059" (0,15 mm)
— Model « 500 Sports »	at skirt top	.0035" to .0043" (0,090 to 0,110 mm)	.0098" (0,25 mm)
	at skirt bottom	.0016" to .0024" (0,040 to 0,060 mm)	.0079" (0,20 mm)
Piston pin-to-boss bore		Pinch fit at all times 0 to .0004" (0 to 0,01 mm)	Pinch fit at all times
Ring-to-piston groove land:			
— 1st groove		.0039" to .0050" (0,100 to 0,127 mm)	.0079" (0,20 mm)
— 2nd groove		.0039" to .0050" (0,100 to 0,127 mm)	.0079" (0,20 mm)
— 3rd groove		.0035" to .0046" (0,090 to 0,117 mm)	.0059" (0,15 mm)
— 4th groove		.0027" to .0043" (0,068 to 0,108 mm)	.0059" (0,15 mm)
Ring gap (rings in cylinder):			
— 1st, 2nd and 3rd ring		.0098" to .0138" (0,25 to 0,35 mm)	.0197" (0,50 mm)
— 4th radial-slotted ring		none	none

CONNECTING RODS
ROD BEARINGS AND BUSHINGS

CHECKING BEARING INSERTS AND CRANKPIN JOURNALS	page	28
CHECKING BEARING INSERT-TO-CRANKPIN JOURNAL CLEARANCE	»	29
INSTALLATION OF BEARING INSERTS	»	30
CHECKING BUSHINGS	»	30
CHECKING CONNECTING ROD WEIGHT	»	31
CHECKING ALIGNMENT	»	31
PISTON - CONNECTING ROD ASSEMBLY AND INSTALLATION	»	32

Connecting rods must be checked for:

— condition of bearings and clearance of bearings to crankpins;

— condition of bushings and clearance of bushings to piston pins;

— weight;

— alignment of big end to small end bores.

Fig. 39 - Connecting rod components.

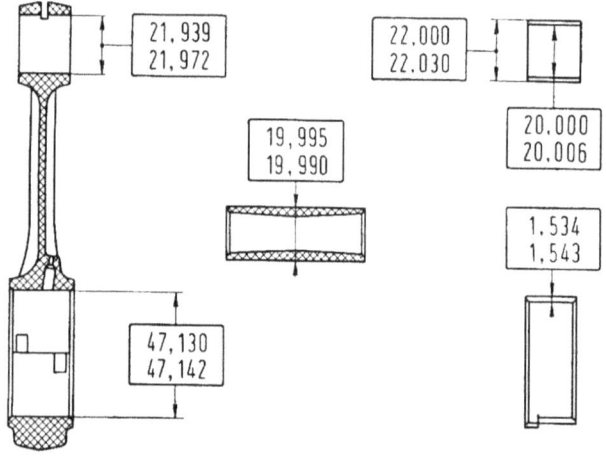

Fig. 38 - Main data for connecting rod, bearing, bush and pin.

class of undersize bearing halves will have to be fitted after regrinding of crankpins.

Undersize classes of bearing halves are:

.01"	.02"	.03"	.04"
(0,254 mm)	(0,508 mm)	(0,762 mm)	(1,016 mm)

Checking Rod Bearing Inserts and Crankpin Journals.

Bearing halves are of the babbit-lined thin-wall type and cannot be reworked or adapted. Therefore, if scoring or scuffing marks, or excessive wear are detected, bearings must be replaced.

Normally, when replacing bearing halves the crankpins must be reground.

Before regrinding, measure each crankpin in the spot of maximum wear to determine which

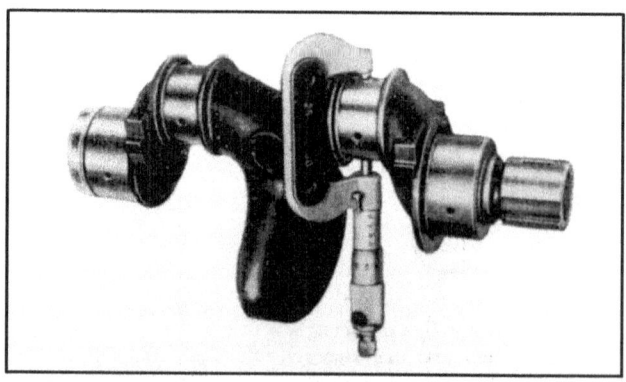

Fig. 40 - Measuring crankpin diameter by micrometer.

ENGINE: CONNECTING RODS - ROD BEARINGS AND BUSHINGS

Crankpin regrind operation is described on page 33 under « Bearing and Crankpin Journals ». However, the table of the diameters to which crankpins must be ground in order to install undersize diameter bearings is repeated here below.

Bearing-half-to-crankpin clearance is .00043″ to .00240″ (0,011 to 0,061 mm). This clearance is inspected as outlined on next paragraph.

CRANKPIN DIAMETERS

Standard	UNDERSIZES			
	.01″ (0,254 mm)	.02″ (0,508 mm)	.03″ (0,762 mm)	.04″ (1,016 mm)
from 1.7328″ (44,013 mm) to 1.7336″ (44,033 mm)	from 1.7228″ (43,759 mm) to 1.7236″ (43,779 mm)	from 1.7128″ (43,505 mm) to 1.7136″ (43,525 mm)	from 1.7028″ (43,251 mm) to 1.7036″ (43,271 mm)	from 1.6928″ (42,997 mm) to 1.6936″ (43,017 mm)

Checking Rod Bearing Insert-to-Crankpin Journal Clearance.

Rod bearing bore diameters are: 1.8555″ to 1.8560″ (47,130 to 47,142 mm).

Thicknesses of standard and undersize bearing halves are as tabulated (page 30).

Assembly clearance is .00043″ to .00240″ (0,011 to 0,061 mm), wear limit .0059″ (0,15 mm).

The bearing half-to-crankpin clearance must be checked before crankshaft installation.

Install the connecting rod with its bearing halves on crankpin; tighten cap nut to 23.9 ft.lbs (3300 kgmm) and swing connecting rod around crankpin.

This brings parts in the correct relationship for subsequent checks. Again take down connecting rod and proceed as outlined hereafter.

A new method of bearing clearance inspection has been lately introduced in workshop procedure, namely the « Plastigage » calibrated strip, for replacement of cigarette paper method.

Clearance is determined through the amount of strip flattening.

« Plastigage » calibrated strip is supplied in several diameters according to the value of clearance under inspection. Strip is contained in proper envelopes (fig. 45) on which the following data are stamped: the type of strip, the clearance range and the graduation scale of the flattened strip at its widest point, to determine the amount of clearance.

To check clearance, proceed as follows:

— wipe the oil from all crankpin journals and rod bearing inserts;

— install bearing inserts on connecting rods and rod caps;

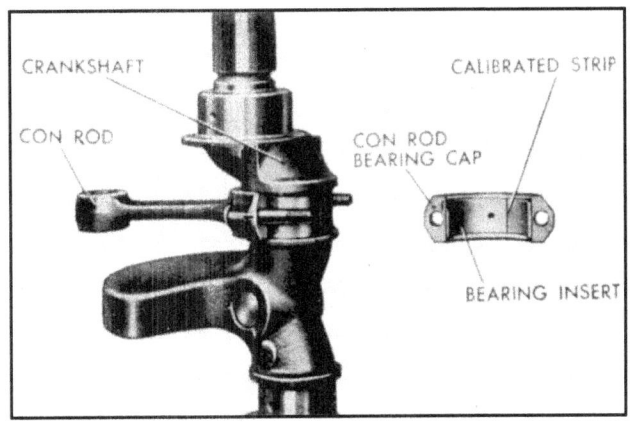

Fig. 41 - « Plastigage » position for bearing insert-to-crankpin journal clearance inspection.

— match connecting rods with crankpin journals, according to their identification numbers;

— place a piece of « Plastigage type PG-1 » the full width of the bearing insert, along the crankshaft longitudinal axis (fig. 41);

— fit the bearing cap and draw up the nuts with 23.9 ft.lbs (3.300 kgmm) of torque, using a torque indicating wrench;

— remove the bearing cap. The « Plastigage » will be found adhering to either the bearing shell or the crankpin and it will have developed a rectangular section as it was flattened from tightening action.

— to determine the actual clearance between crankpin and bearing shell, compare the width of the flattened « Plastigage » at its widest point with the graduations on the envelope (fig. 42). The number within the graduation on the envelope indicates the bearing clearance in millimeters.

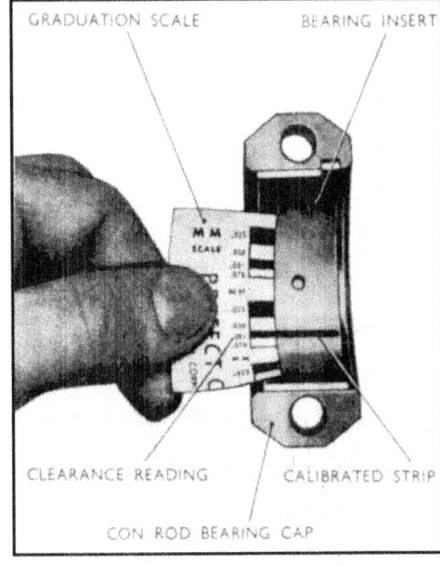

Fig. 42 - Checking bearing insert-to-crankpin journal clearance by comparing width of flattened « Plastigage ».

If clearance is within the tolerance range of .00043" to .00240" (0,011 to 0,061 mm) which is the assembly clearance, or it reads less than .0059" (0,15 mm), max. wear limit, bearing shells can still be used without touching crankpin journals.

Conversely, should clearance be in excess of the above, bearing inserts must be replaced by undersized ones and crankpin journals ground as outlined on page 36.

The same inspection should be repeated at the other connecting rod.

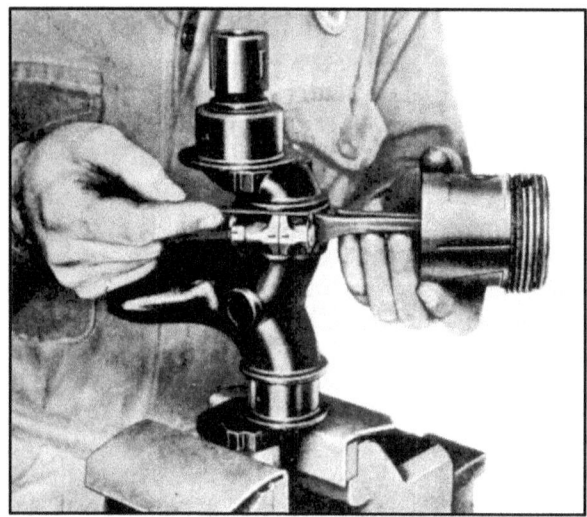

Fig. 43 - Checking crankshaft land-to-connecting rod shoulder clearance.

NOTICE

«Plastigage type PG-1» enables clearance inspection up to .0030" (0,076 mm). Therefore, should inspection indicate no flattening of «Plastigage» strip, the procedure should be repeated using «Plastigage type PR-1», which enables clearance inspection up to .0060" (0,152 mm).

It will be thus possible to determine whether actual wear is or not in excess of .0059" (0,15 mm) limit.

Installation of Rod Bearing Inserts.

During assembly:

— never touch up the bearing half-to-connecting rod mounting faces;

— make sure all parts are perfectly clean before assembly;

— check that bearing location lug is radially free in its seat (if this is not the case, a forcing on crankshaft will result in the area of contact with the bearing half);

— since bearing half circumference is greater than that of seats in rod and cap, bearings must be fitted in such a way as to project of an equal amount with respect to the two parting planes.

THICKNESS OF CONNECTING ROD BEARING HALVES

Standard	FOR DIAMETER UNDERSIZED BY			
	.01" (0,254 mm)	.02" (0,508 mm)	.03" (0,762 mm)	.04" (1,016 mm)
.0604" (1,534 mm)	.0654" (1,661 mm)	.0704" (1,788 mm)	.0754" (1,915 mm)	.0804" (2,042 mm)
.0607" (1,543 mm)	.0657" (1,670 mm)	.0707" (1,797 mm)	.0757" (1,924 mm)	.0807" (2,051 mm)

Checking Bushings.

Small end bush must be firmly fitted and must not show deep scoring, scuffing or excessive wear marks.

If necessary, bushes must be reamed with expansible reamer **U. 0307** (fig. 44) so that their I.D.

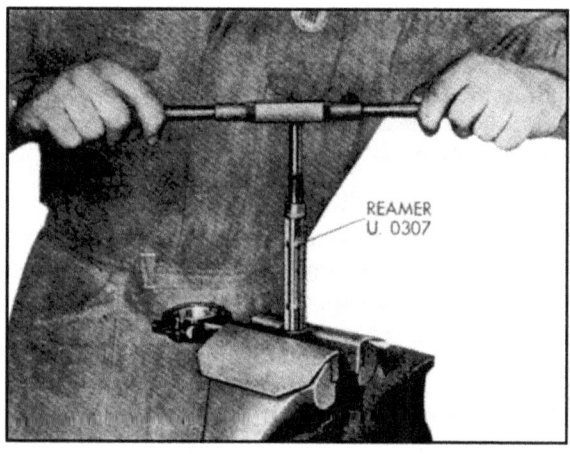

Fig. 44 - Reaming connecting rod bushing with reamer U. 0307.

CALIBRATED STRIP

Fig. 45 - «Plastigage» calibrated strip for bearing insert-to-crankpin journal clearance inspection, and envelope with graduation scale.

ENGINE: CONNECTING RODS - ROD BEARINGS AND BUSHINGS

BUSH-TO-PISTON PIN FIT DATA

	I. D. OF PRESS FITTED AND REAMED BUSH	PISTON PIN DIAMETER	BUSH-TO-PIN FIT CLEARANCE
Standard	.7874" to .7876" (20,000 to 20,006 mm)	.7870" to .7872" (19,990 to 19,995 mm)	.00020" to .00063" (0,005 to 0,016 mm)
.0079 (0,2 mm) oversize	.7953" to .7955" (20,200 to 20,206 mm)	.7949" to .7951" (20,190 to 20,195 mm)	.00020" to .00063" (0,005 to 0,016 mm)

permits to fit .0079" (0,2 mm) oversize piston pins (see table above).

Preparatory to small end bush reaming operation, clamp the big end with tool **A. 60077** and secure the tool in a vise.

Bush-to-piston pin clearance must be .00020" to .00063" (0,005 to 0,016 mm).

In case bushes need replacement, operate as follows:

Take off old bush using remover **A. 60155**.

With the same tool install new bush. Interference between bush O. D. and small end bore must be .0011" to .0036" (0,028 to 0,091 mm).

Mill a slot in bush, in correspondence with the groove machined at top on connecting rod small end: this will ensure a good lubrication between bush and piston pin.

Use a cutter having a diameter of 2.1654" (55 mm) and a width of .1181" (3 mm) (see fig. 46) whose center, during the milling operation, is at 1.3780" (35 mm) from small end bore axis.

Using reamer **U. 0307**, ream bush I. D. to .7874" to .7876" (20,000 to 20,086 mm). With such an I. D. a standard piston pin may be fitted.

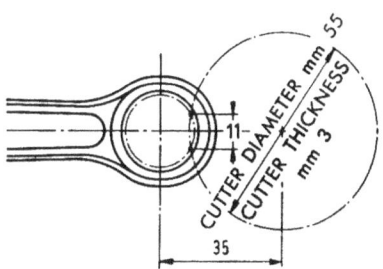

Fig. 46 - Data for bush milling.

Checking Alignment.

Use fixture **C. 627**. Insert connecting rod big end on stub shaft of fixture, insert piston pin in small end bore and then rest checking square on piston pin.

Misalignment is revealed by the gap existing between square and vertical plane of fixture (fig. 48).

If connecting rod is found misaligned, straighten by clamping the rod in a vise and using forked lever **A. 10029** (fig. 47). Replace connecting rod if misalignment is excessive.

Before installing connecting rods in engine, it is advisable to check the connecting rod-piston assembly by the same fixture used to check alignment of connecting rod alone.

BUSH-TO-SMALL END FIT DATA

SMALL END BORE diameter	BUSH O. D.	PINCH FIT
.8637" to .8650" (21,939 to 21,972 mm)	.8661" to .8673" (22,000 to 22,030 mm)	.0011" to .0036" (0,028 to 0,091 mm)

Checking Connecting Rod Weight.

Both connecting rods of an engine must have the same weight.

This condition must be checked on a double-scale, central-zero balance.

Maximum permissible weight difference between lighter and heavier connecting rod is .212 oz. (6 grams).

Fig. 47 - Straightening a connecting rod stem using forked lever A. 10029.

Fig. 48 - Checking connecting rod alignment on fixture C. 627.

Piston-Connecting Rod Assembly and Installation.

As far as the orientation of connecting rod identification number in rod-piston assemblies is concerned, the mating of said two parts would be unconsequential since connecting rods are symmetrical; however, to ensure correct installation of piston - whose expansion slot must be positioned on the camshaft side-it becomes essential to proceed as follows (see also fig. 49):

— mate the rod and piston sets in such a way

Fig. 50 - Connecting rod-piston assembly.

Note position of expansion slot in piston with respect to connecting rod numbering.

that the cylinder identification number stamped on connecting rod stem and cap faces the expansion slot side in piston;

— install the rod-piston assembly with identification numbers facing on the opposite side to the camshaft.

If one or both connecting rods must be replaced, the new connecting rod cap and body must be stamped with the number identifying the cylinder in which connecting rod must be installed. Stamping must be carried out as shown in fig. 50.

Connecting rod cap nuts must be tightened to 23.9 ft.lbs (3300 kgmm).

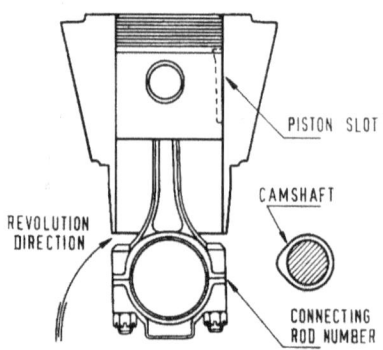

Fig. 49 - Diagram for connecting rod-piston assembly installation on engine.

Fig. 51 - Tightening connecting rod cap nuts with torque wrench.

(Tightening torque = 23.9 ft.lbs - 3300 kgmm).

CRANKSHAFT AND MAIN BEARINGS

SOUNDNESS	page 33
CHECKING AND GRINDING CRANKSHAFT BEARING AND CRANKPIN JOURNALS	» 33
CHECKING MAIN BEARING-TO-BEARING JOURNAL CLEARANCE	» 36
TIGHTENING INSTRUCTIONS FOR NUTS AND SCREWS	» 38
OIL SEALS	» 38
CLUTCH SHAFT PILOT BUSHING	» 39
FLYWHEEL AND RING GEAR	» 39

Crankshaft is of special cast-iron and is hollow to provide the necessary passage for lube oil. It is supported on its ends and is provided with two cranks and a central counterweight.

This shaft has also a particular function in the lubrication system since its cavity provides a passage for the oil coming from centrifugal filter.

Particular care must be exercised in inspecting this item during overhauls.

Wash crankshaft carefully and inspect for:

— soundness;
— roundness and wear of journal and crankpins;
— cleanliness of oil galleries.

Soundness.

Replace shaft if cracked in any point. As a matter of fact crankshaft soundness is an essential requisite for safe and good engine operation.

Checking and Grinding Crankshaft Bearing and Crankpin Journals.

Inspect journals and crankpins: if light scoring marks are noticed, reface by a very fine grade stone (carborundum); if remarkable out-of-round or deep scoring marks are noticed, regrind journals and crankpins and fit suitable undersize bearings.

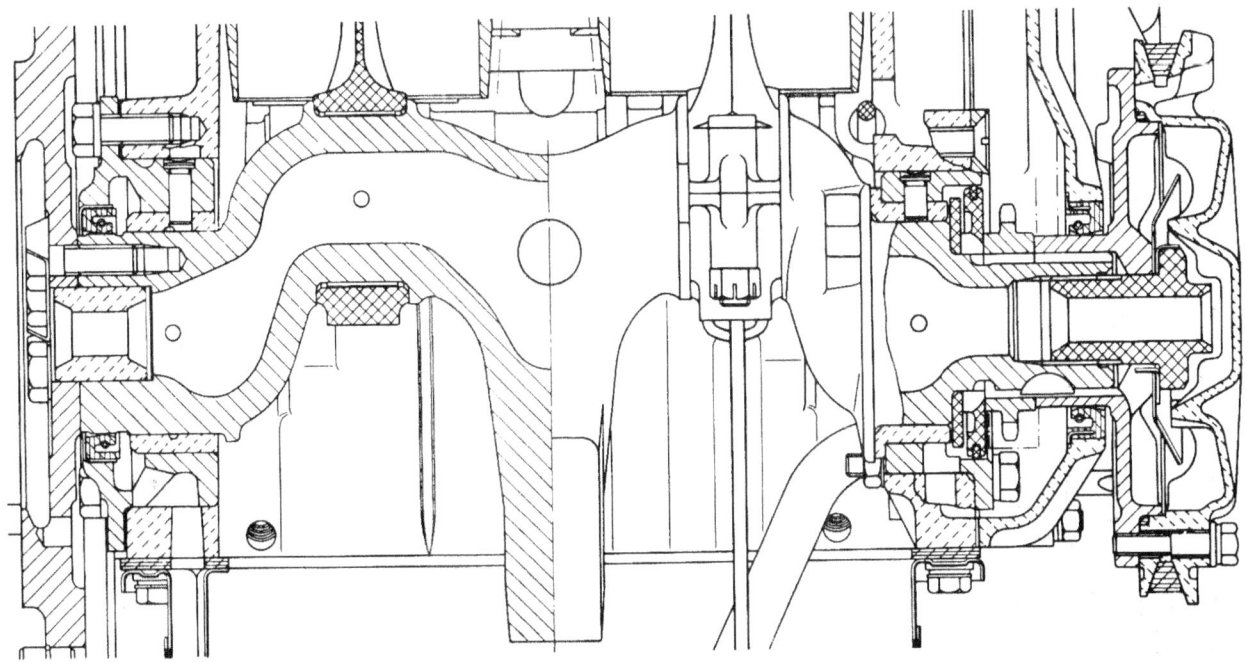

Fig. 52 - Detail of engine longitudinal section through crankshaft.

CRANKSHAFT RADII DATA

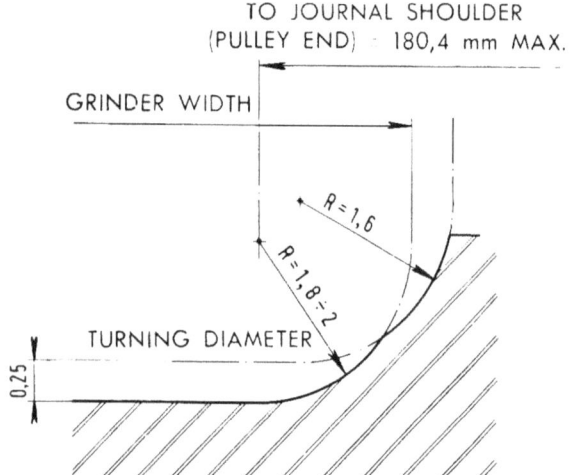

Fig. 53 - Radii on crankshaft flywheel end shoulder.

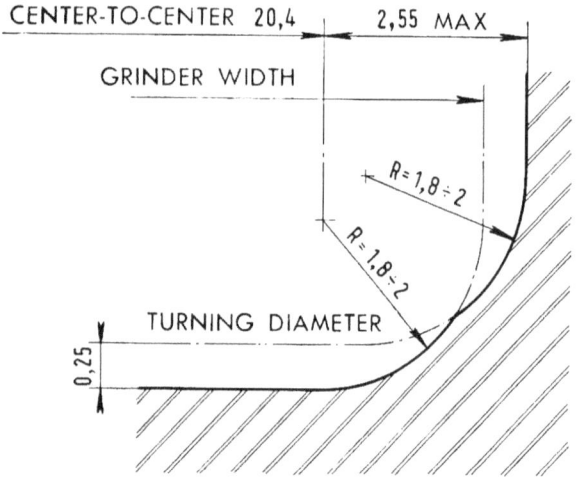

Fig. 54 - Radii on crankpin shoulders.

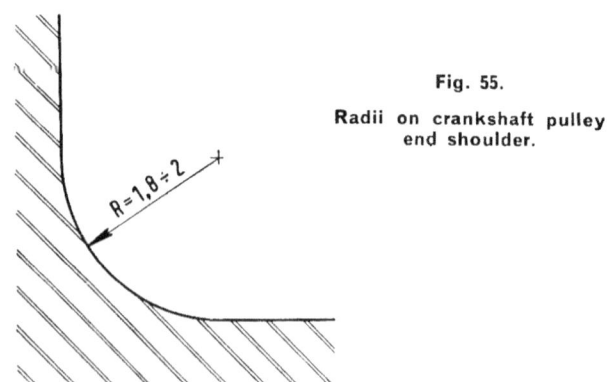

Fig. 55.
Radii on crankshaft pulley end shoulder.

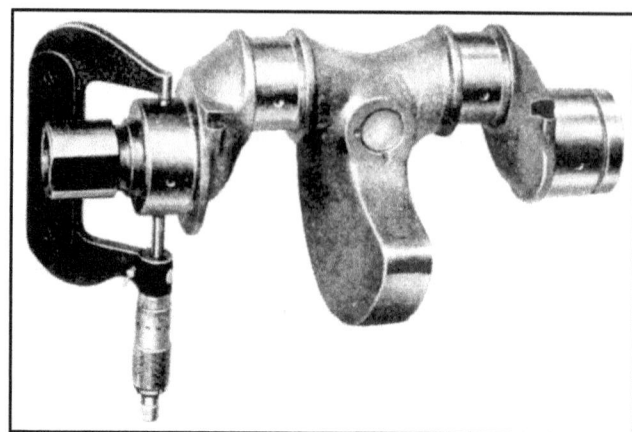

Fig. 56 - Measuring crankshaft journals with micrometer.

Undersize main bearing classes are:

.0079"   .0157"   .0236"   .0314"   .0394"
(0,2 mm) (0,4 mm) (0,6 mm) (0,8 mm) (1 mm)

Main bearings, both front and rear, are supplied also without supports but in a single .0394" (1 mm) I. D. undersize.

Undersize connecting rod bearing half classes are:

.01"   .02"   .03"   .04"
(0,254 mm) (0,508 mm) (0,762 mm) (1,016 mm)

As already said, before regrinding measure each journal and crankpin in the point of maximum wear to determine which class of undersize bearings will have to be fitted after regrinding of journals and crankpins.

Fit clearances are:

— Journal-to-main bearing:
   .00079" to .00256" (0,020 to 0,065 mm).

— Crankpin-to-connecting rod bearing half:
   .00043" to .0024" (0,011 to 0,061 mm).

Before loading on grinder, crankshaft must be fitted with flange and bush **A. 60162** to obtain a correct installation on the machine (figs. 57, 58, 60).

While grinding, be careful not to alter the journal and crankpin shoulder radii (figs. 53, 54, 55).

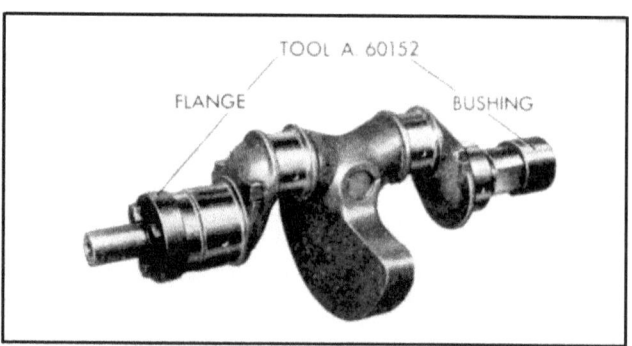

Fig. 57 - Crankshaft and adapters for mounting on grinder.

ENGINE: CRANKSHAFT AND MAIN BEARINGS

CRANKSHAFT JOURNAL DIAMETERS

Standard	UNDERSIZES				
	.0079" (0,2 mm)	.0157" (0,4 mm)	.0236" (0,6 mm)	.0315" (0,8 mm)	.0394" (1 mm)
from 2.1248" (53,970 mm)	from 2.1169" (53,770 mm)	from 2.1091" (53,570 mm)	from 2.1012" (53,370 mm)	from 2.0933" (53,170 mm)	from 2.0854" (52,970 mm)
to 2.1260" (54,000 mm)	to 2.1181" (53,800 mm)	to 2.1102" (53,600 mm)	to 2.1024" (53,400 mm)	to 2.0945" (53,200 mm)	to 2.0866" (53,000 mm)

MAIN BEARING I. D.

Standard	UNDERSIZES				
	.0079" (0,2 mm)	.0157" (0,4 mm)	.0236" (0,6 mm)	.0315" (0,8 mm)	.0394" (1 mm)
2.1268" (54,020 mm) 2.1274" (54,035 mm)	2.1189" (53,820 mm) 2.1195" (53,835 mm)	2.1110" (53,620 mm) 2.1116" (53,635 mm)	2.1031" (53,420 mm) 2.1037" (53,435 mm)	2.0953" (53,220 mm) 2.0959" (53,235 mm)	2.0874" (53,020 mm) 2.0880" (53,035 mm)

Standards and undersizes of journals, crankpins and bearings are tabulated here above and on next page.

To obtain a correct alignment of journals and crankpins, it is essential that centering of crankshaft on machine be very accurate.

Grinding must be performed with a fine grain wheel so that ground surfaces are given a high finish within the tolerance limits specified in the tables.

After grinding, wash carefully the shaft with gasoline.

Particularly the oil ducts must be flushed repeatedly with gasoline under pressure.

Fig. 58 - Grinding main bearing journals on grinding machine.

CRANKPIN DIAMETERS

Standard	UNDERSIZES			
	.01″ (0,254 mm)	.02″ (0,508 mm)	.03″ (0,762 mm)	.04″ (1,016 mm)
from 1.7328″ (44,013 mm) to 1.7336″ (44,033 mm)	from 1.7228″ (43,759 mm) to 1.7236″ (43,779 mm)	from 1.7128″ (43,505 mm) to 1.7136″ (43,525 mm)	from 1.7028″ (43,251 mm) to 1.7036″ (43,271 mm)	from 1.6928″ (42,997 mm) to 1.6936″ (43,017 mm)

CONNECTING ROD HALF BEARING THICKNESS

Standard	UNDERSIZE			
	.01″ (0,254 mm)	.02″ (0,508 mm)	.03″ (0,762 mm)	.04″ (1,016 mm)
.0604″ (1,534 mm)	.0654″ (1,661 mm)	.0704″ (1,788 mm)	.0754″ (1,915 mm)	.0804″ (2,042 mm)
.0607″ (1,543 mm)	.0657″ (1,670 mm)	.0707″ (1,797 mm)	.0757″ (1,924 mm)	.0807″ (2,051 mm)

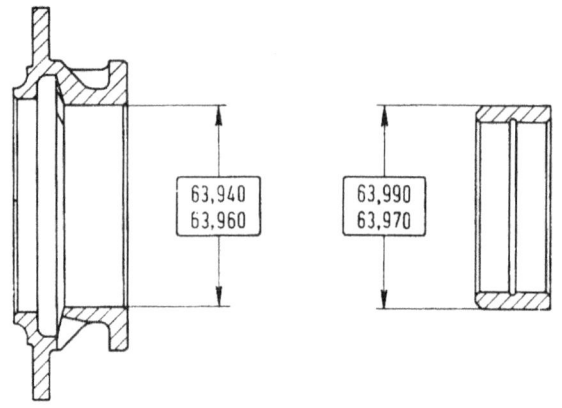

Fig. 59 - Crankshaft main bearing and support - Flywheel end.
Pinch fit between main bearings and supports (front and rear) is .00039″ to .00197″ (0,010 to 0,050 mm).

Checking Main Bearing-to-Bearing Journal Clearance.

The clearance between main bearings and journals must be checked before installing crankshaft in engine.

Measure maximum main bearing I.D. and minimum journal diameters using a micrometer caliper. If

Fig. 60 - Grinding connecting rod bearing journals on grinding machine.

ENGINE: CRANKSHAFT AND MAIN BEARINGS

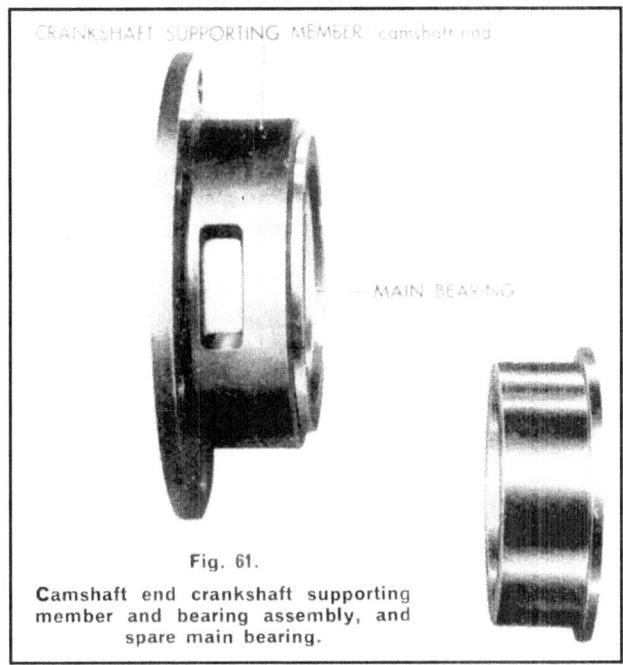

Fig. 61.
Camshaft end crankshaft supporting member and bearing assembly, and spare main bearing.

Fig. 63 - Checking crankshaft end play.

End play of a new crankshaft, measured between flywheel end bearing and crankshaft shoulder, should be .0118" to .0173" (0,30 to 0,44 mm).

clearance exceeds .0039" (0,10 mm), replace bearings and regrind journals to the diameters tabulated on page 35 and corresponding to the undersizes of the new bearings.

Bearings are supplied as spares in the standard and undersize diameter classes, as tabulated, complete with their housings. Therefore they need not be adapted, provided the journals have been ground to the value of the required undersize class.

However, also bearings with .0394" (1 mm) stock on I.D. are supplied, which must be adapted after installation in their supports.

Bearings with .0394" (1 mm) stock on I.D. are also supplied as spares; however, the diameter of this type of bearing must be adapted to the corresponding crankpin undersize and then press-fitted in its support, specified pinch fit being .00039" to .00197" (0,010 to 0,050 mm) (fig. 59).

After press-fitting, drill in bearings a hole in line with the location dowel seat in the support, next trim with reamer U. 0334 (fig. 62). At this point press fit the location dowels: the hollow dowel must be placed on the flywheel end support.

N. B. - After press-fitting the bearing and dowel, and before proceeding with the facing and reaming operations, heat the complete support to 302° F (150° C) for an hour in oven or engine oil bath.

Finally, ream the bearings fitted in supports on a parallel lathe; this operation must be carried out at room temperature.

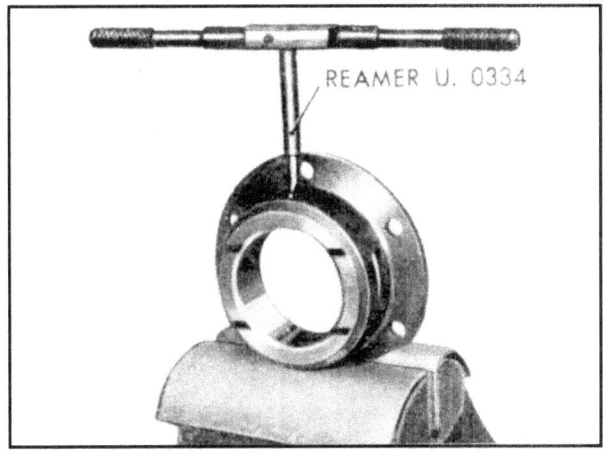

Fig. 62 - Trimming hole in support for bearing location dowel seat - Timing gear end.

Fig. 64 - Using a torque wrench to tighten crankshaft supporting member screws (camshaft end).

Tightening Instructions for Nuts and Screws.

Tightening of cap self-locking nuts and of main bearing screws must be performed with a torque wrench; tighten smoothly, gradually and steadily up to the specified torque which must not be exceeded.

Cleanliness of all seating faces and threads is an essential condition. No lubricant must be present on threads and on nuts.

OIL SEALS

Two inner-spring rubber seals - one in a special seat in timing gear cover and the other on crankshaft support (flywheel end) - have been fitted to provide oil tightness (figs. 52 and 66).

During overhauls, check that these seals are properly seated, that their inner surface is not worn and that their contact is perfect, respectively, on fan and generator drive pulley hub and on crankshaft. Replace if required.

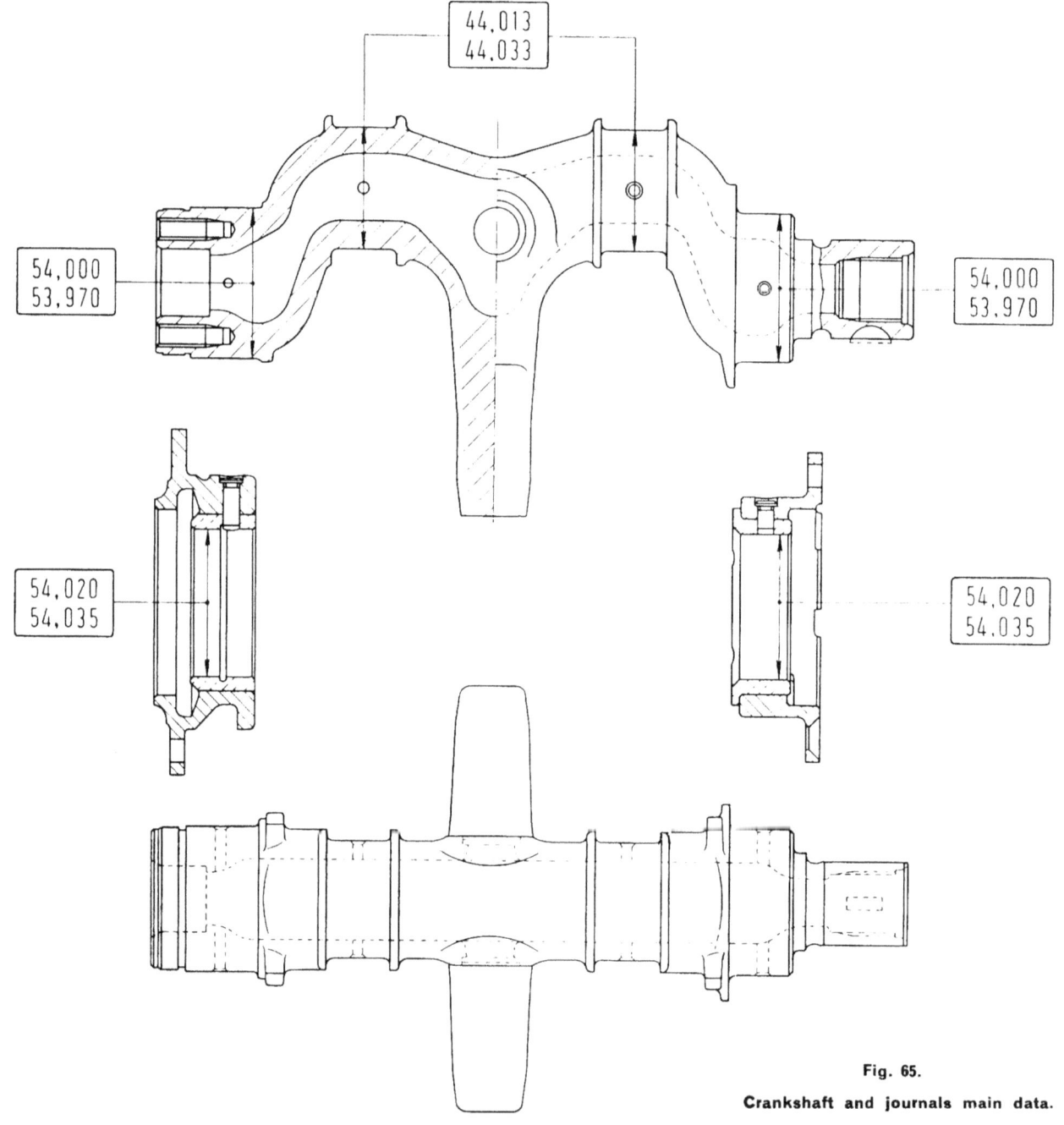

Fig. 65.
Crankshaft and journals main data.

ENGINE: CYLINDER HEAD - VALVES - GUIDES AND SPRINGS

CLUTCH SHAFT PILOT BUSHING

A self-lubricating, bronze bush (fig. 66) is fitted in crankshaft for clutch shaft support. Replace said bush if found excessively worn, using special puller **A. 40006/1/2** for its removal.

FLYWHEEL AND RING GEAR

Check the contact surfaces of flywheel on crankshaft and on clutch driven plate: they must be perfectly flat and mirror-like.

Check ring gear conditions: if excessive wear or tooth damage is noticed, replace the ring gear.

To facilitate installation on flywheel, ring gear must be heated in oil bath to 176° F (80° C); then, with a press, install the slightly expanded ring as taken directly from the bath.

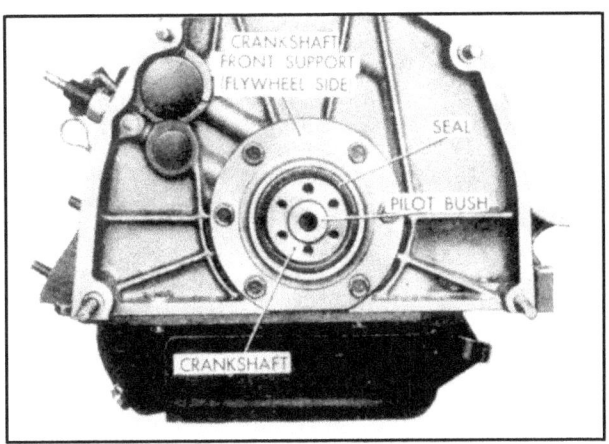

Fig. 66 - View of engine front end without flywheel.

Use all-purpose puller A. 40006/1/2 to remove clutch shaft pilot bushing from crankshaft seat.

CYLINDER HEAD
VALVES - GUIDES AND SPRINGS

REMOVAL AND DISASSEMBLY OF CYLINDER HEAD	page	39
CYLINDER HEAD INSPECTION AND SERVICING	»	40
VALVE GUIDE INSPECTION AND SERVICING	»	41
VALVE SEAT INSPECTION AND SERVICING	»	43
VALVE INSPECTION AND SERVICING	»	44
INSPECTING VALVE SPRINGS	»	45
VALVE SEALING TEST	»	45
CYLINDER HEAD ASSEMBLY AND INSTALLATION	»	46

Cylinder head is an aluminum casting suitably finned to increase cooling surface. Thru bolts secure the head and the cylinders to crankcase.

Valves are controlled by camshaft through tappets, pushrods and rockers. Connection between head and crankcase for passage of pushrods, lube oil and vented gases is ensured by five resilient sleeves mounted directly between cylinder head and crankcase.

Removal and Disassembly of Cylinder Head.

Cylinder head should be removed and disassembled whenever compression losses are experienced due to leaky valves or, after a certain period of operation, when carbon deposits must be scraped off from compression chambers.

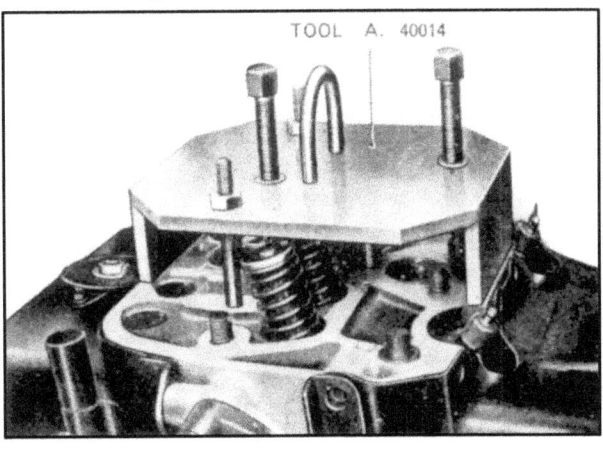

Fig. 67 - Tool A. 40014 for cylinder head removal.

Fig. 68. Engine components: crankcase, cylinder, head, timing sprockets cover.

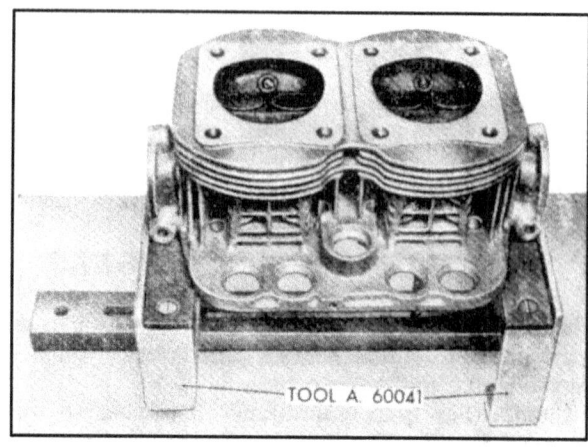

Fig. 70 - Tool A. 60041 for cylinder head bench overhauling.

To remove cylinder head, operate as follows.

Take out: air cleaner, carburetor, rockers cover, screws securing the blower conveyor to cylinder head, the two side exhaust manifolds and spark plug cables.

Remove cylinder hold down nuts and take off the head using puller A. 40014 (fig. 67).

Disassembly of cylinder head is not particularly difficult; however, the following chapters will deal with this operation, indicating also the required tooling.

Cylinder head disassembly must be performed on bench after securing the head with supporting fixture A. 60041 (fig. 70) and wooden base plate A. 60158.

Place cylinder head on base plate A. 60158 and, using tool A. 60084, depress the upper cup so as to free the valves by removing their locks.

Remove also snap rings.

Cylinder Head Inspection and Servicing.

First, remove carbon deposits using wire brush A. 11416 driven by an electric, portable drill.

Check that seating plane is not deformed, proceeding as follows:

— Coat a surface plate with a film of lampblack.

— Place cylinder head on surface plate, slide it back and forth and check the streaks left by the lampblack.

If surface results irregular, recondition with planishing stake M. 30 or, if this is not available, with

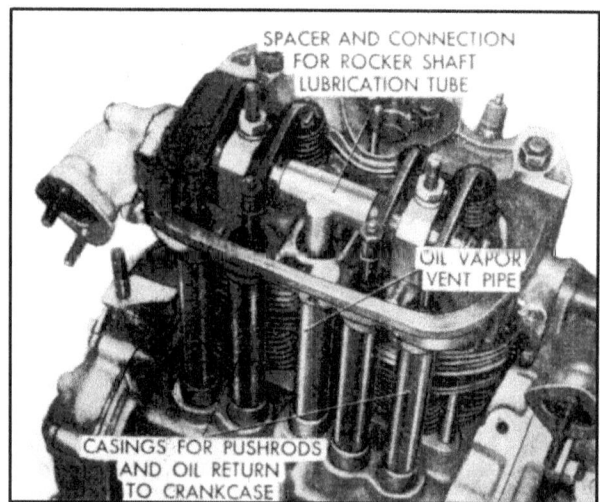

Fig. 69 - Engine without blower cowling and cylinder head cover.

Fig. 71 - Tool A. 60084 for valve and valve spring removal.

ENGINE: CYLINDER HEAD - VALVES - GUIDES AND SPRINGS

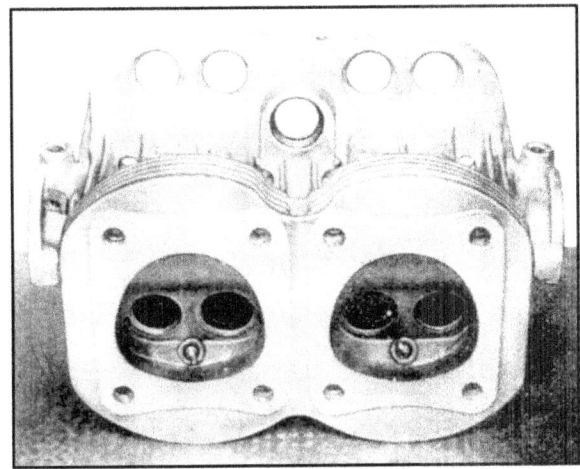

Fig. 72 - Cylinder head on surface plate.

a file. Be careful to remove the least possible amount of material so as not to alter the compression ratio appreciably.

After flattening, clean carefully by washing to remove all traces of abrasive material.

Valve Guide Inspection and Servicing.

Clean carefully valve guides and recondition with brush **A. 11417 bis** (fig. 73) and reamer **U. 0310**.

Valve guides are press fitted with a .00134" to .00244" (0,034 to 0,062 mm) pinch fit.

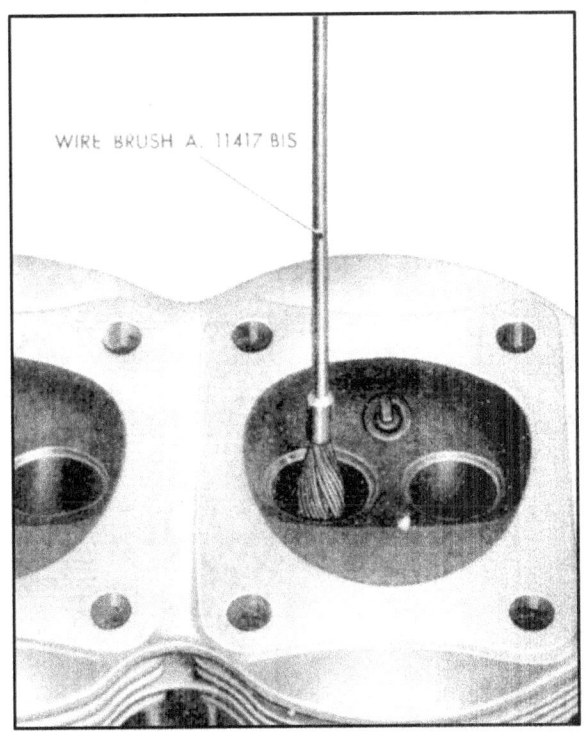

Fig. 73 - Cleaning valve guides with wire brush A. 11417 bis.

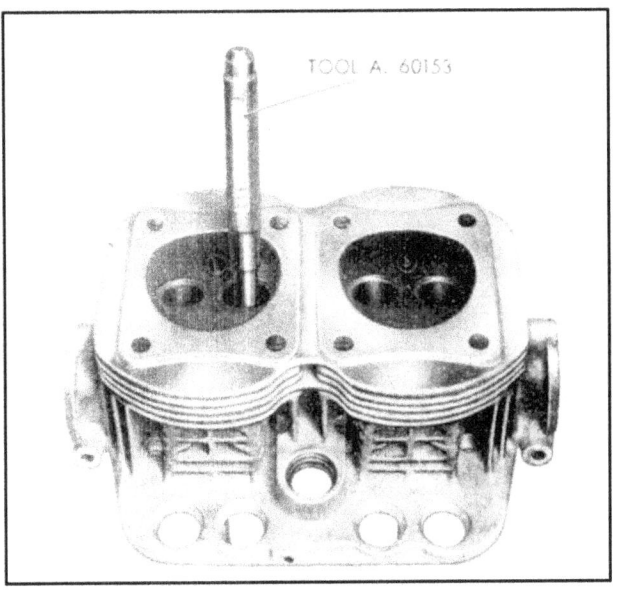

Fig. 74 - Removing a valve guide with tool A. 60153.

VALVE GUIDE-TO-SEAT FIT DATA

VALVE GUIDE SEAT DIAMETER	VALVE GUIDE O. D.	PINCH FIT
.5118" to .5125" (13,00 to 13,018 mm)	.5139" to 5143" (13,052 to 13,062 mm)	.00134" to .00244" (0,034 to 0,062 mm)

To remove and install valve guides, use punch **A. 60153** (fig. 74).

Since valve guides have no stop ring, during press-fitting the depth of insertion is determined by the pilot bush equipping tool **A. 60153** (fig. 75).

Replace valve guides when clearance between valve and guide is excessive and replacement of

Fig. 75 - Installing a valve guide using tool A. 60153 provided with pilot bush.

VALVE - VALVE GUIDE AND SEAT MAIN SPECIFICATIONS - «New 500»

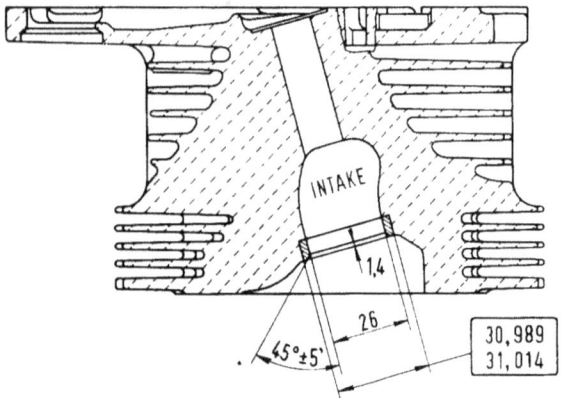

Fig. 76 - Main specifications of cylinder head intake valve seats.

VALVE - VALVE GUIDE AND SEAT MAIN SPECIFICATIONS - «New 500 Sports»

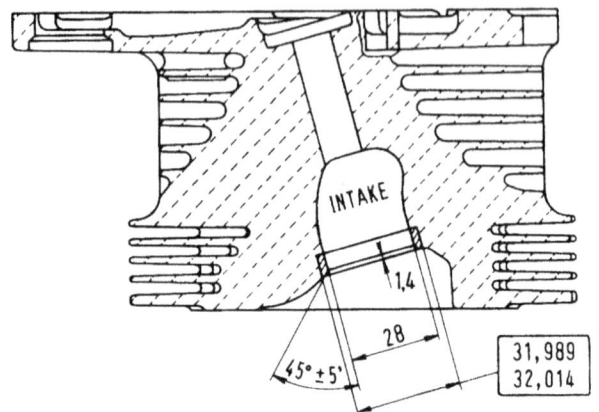

Fig. 79 - Main specifications of cylinder head intake valve seats.

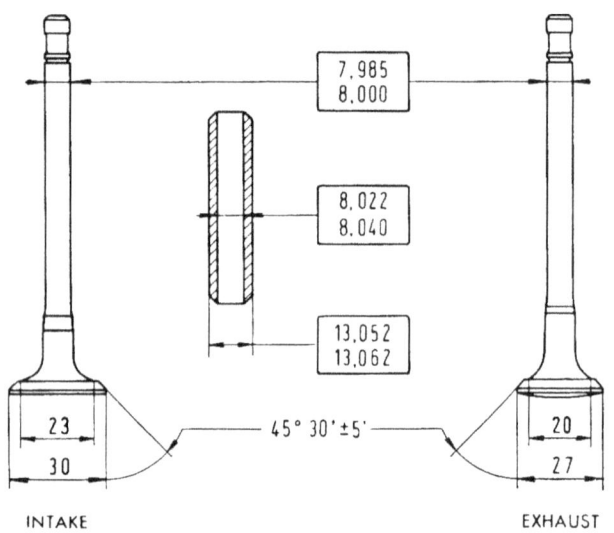

Fig. 77 - Main specifications of intake and exhaust valves and valve guides.

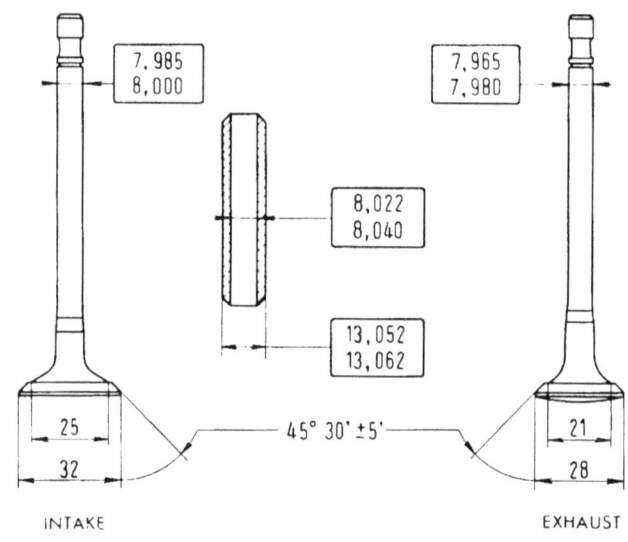

Fig. 80 - Main specifications of intake and exhaust valves and valve guides.

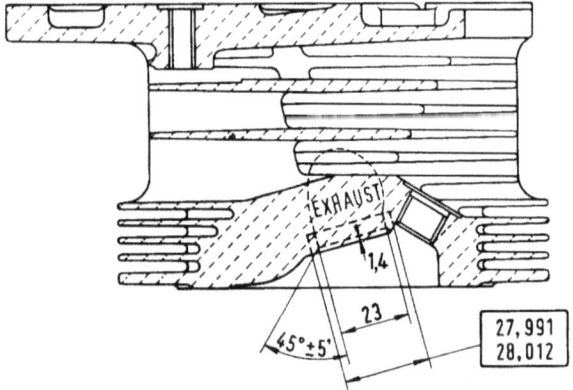

Fig. 78 - Main specifications of cylinder head exhaust valve seats.

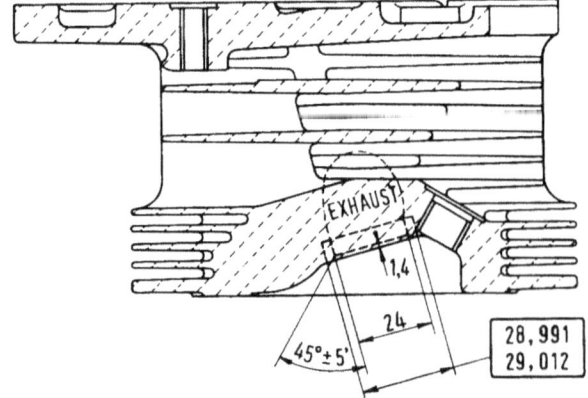

Fig. 81 - Main specifications of cylinder head exhaust valve seats.

ENGINE: CYLINDER HEAD - VALVES - GUIDES AND SPRINGS

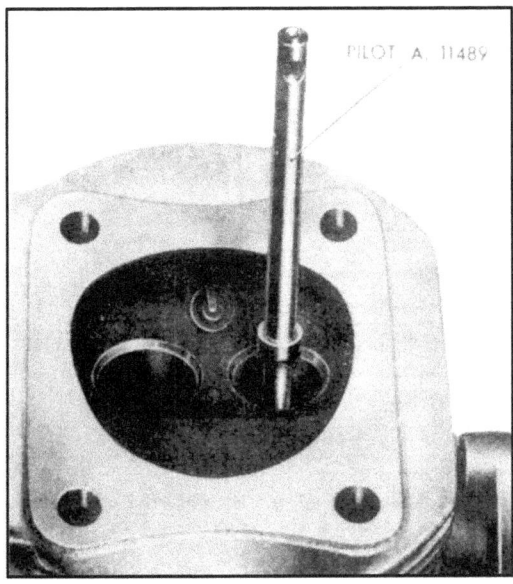

Fig. 82 - Pilot A. 11489 for valve seat refacing.

valve alone is not sufficient to overcome the trouble. Fit clearance between valve stem and guide is .00087" to .00217" (0,022 to 0,055 mm); maximum permissible wear limit is .0059" (0,15 mm).

Valve Seat Inspection and Servicing.

Recondition valve seats in cylinder head, after decarbonizing.

Seat angle must be 45° ± 5'.

To recondition seats (both of intake and exhaust valves), use cutters **A. 11479** (having an inclination of 20°) and **A. 60159** (with an inclination of 75°); one removes material at top, the other at bottom.

Insert pilot **A. 11489** (fig. 82) in valve guide and then apply the cutter, driving it by spindle **A. 11482** (fig. 83). Pilot **A. 11489** must be selected from the three allotted, so as to obtain the correct matching to valve guide with the least possible clearance.

Fig. 83 - Cutter A. 60159 (75°) for valve seat reduction.

VALVE AND VALVE SEAT REFACING DIAGRAMS

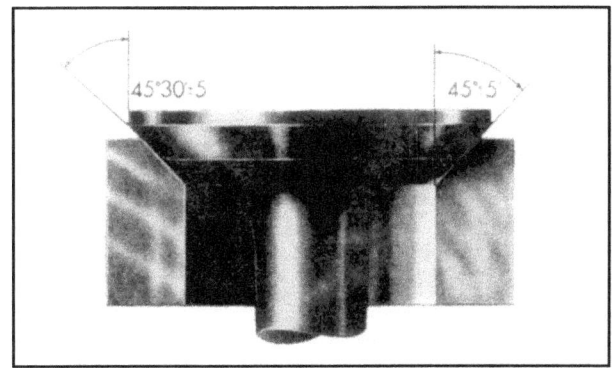

Fig. 84 - Inclination angles on valve head and seat.

Fig. 85 - Reconditioning valve seat top with 20° cutter.

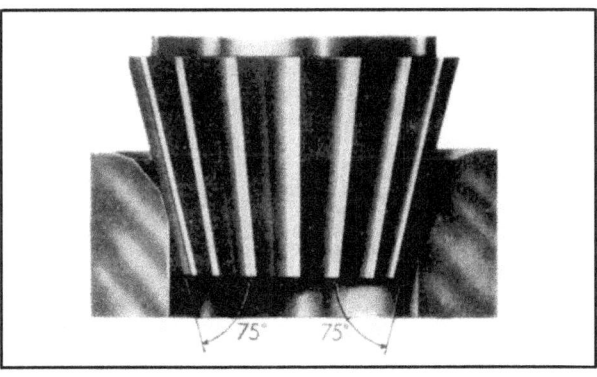

Fig. 86 - Reconditioning valve seat bottom with 75° cutter.

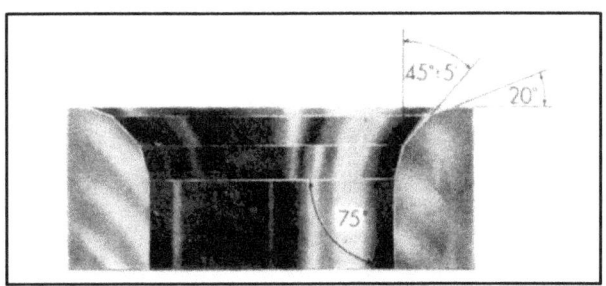

Fig. 87 - Specimen of finished seat.

Fig. 88 - Refacing valve seats with the Vibrocentric tool and grinder A. 11478.

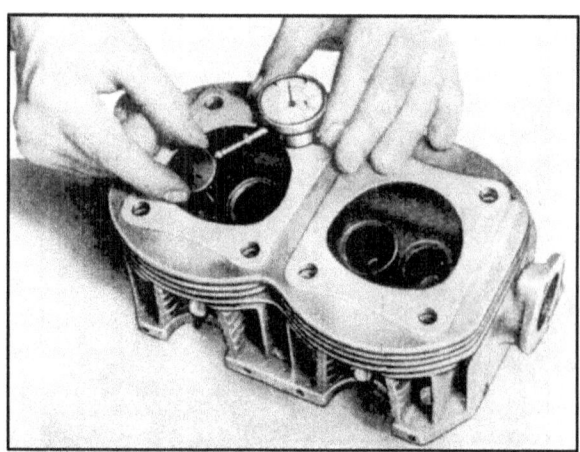

Fig. 90 - Checking valve stem-to-guide clearance.

After reconditioning, grind seats with taper grinder **A. 11478**, using the Vibrocentric fixture **A. 11460** and spindle **A. 11475** (fig. 88); the grinder must be fitted on pilot **A. 11489**, same as for the cutters.

Much care must be exercised in grinding valve seats; the grinder must remain in contact with the seat for short instants and during this time the current to the Vibrocentric fixture must be switched off to prevent vibrations which might lead to incorrect grinding.

To obtain a good work, dress quite often the grinder with a diamond point dresser, installing grinder on fixture **A. 11480** (fig. 89).

The above tool serves also to restore grinder to correct taper of 45°±5'.

When grinding seats, wet grinder slightly with a few drops of kerosene.

Valve Inspection and Servicing.

Check valve soundness and then the clearance between stem and guide; specified clearance is .00087" to .00217" (0,022 to 0,055 mm) and maximum permissible wear limit .0059" (0,15 mm).

Valve cleaning should be performed using wire brush **A. 11419**.

Recondition valve seating face after having checked that stem is not distorted. Replace if necessary. Introduce valve stem in self-centering spindle of universal grinder **A. 11401** and position support so that valve will have an inclination, with respect to grinder wheel, such that the correct refacing angle is ensured: 45° 30'±5'.

Check to see that after reconditioning valves the head margin is not less than .0197" (0,5 mm).

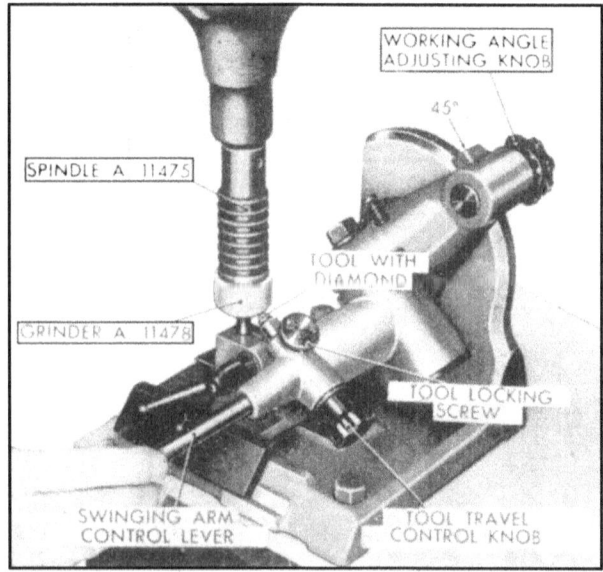

Fig. 89 - Dressing the grinder on tool A. 11480.

Fig. 91 - Refacing valve faces with universal grinder A. 11401.

ENGINE: CYLINDER HEAD - VALVES - GUIDES AND SPRINGS

VALVE-TO-GUIDE FIT DATA

VALVE GUIDE I.D.	VALVE STEM DIAMETER	FIT CLEARANCE	WEAR LIMIT
.3158" to .3165" (8,022 to 8,040 mm)	.3144" to .3150" (7,985 to 8,000 mm)	.00087" to .00217" (0,022 to 0,055 mm)	.0059" (0,15 mm)

Inspecting Valve Springs.

Check that valve springs are not cracked or have not weakened.

Spring flexibility should be checked with tester **A. 11493** comparing the load and give-in characteristics recorded with the data tabulated for new springs in fig. 93.

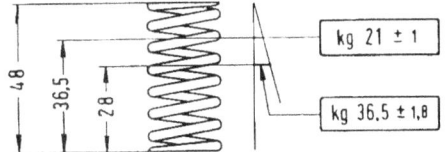

Fig. 93 - Valve spring check data, **Model «500»**.

For specifications of Model «500 Sports» valve springs, see covering table on page bottom.

Valve Sealing Test.

After reconditioning valves and valve seats, run a sealing test using fixture **A. 60017**, after blanking spark plug seats with plug **A. 60018** (fig. 94).

Fixture **A. 60017**, which must be placed over valve seats of each cylinder, consists of:

— a compression chamber;
— a rubber sealing lining;
— a rubber bulb;
— a pressure gauge.

Compress air with rubber bulb until pointer in gauge moves close to scale end.

If matching between valve and seat is not perfect, escaping air will immediately be revealed by pointer which will move back toward zero.

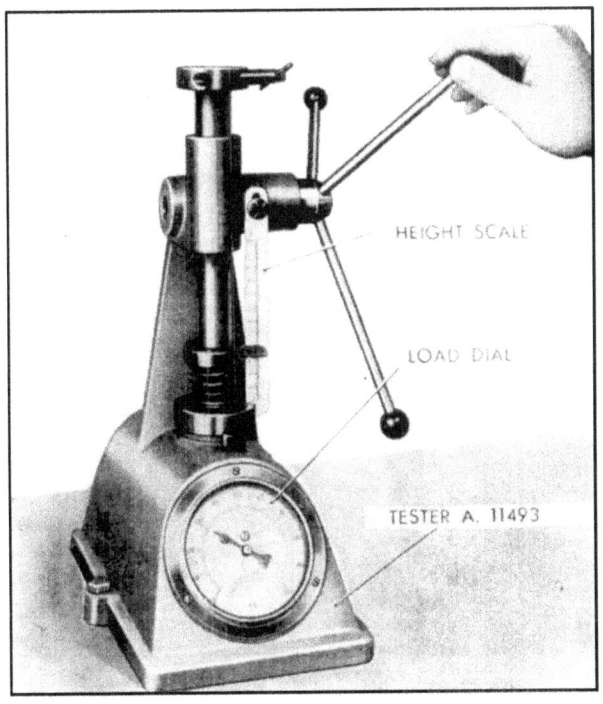

Fig. 92 - Tester **A. 11493** for checking the valve and clutch springs flexibility.

VALVE SPRINGS

ENGINE Type	WORKING Coils N°	INSIDE Diameter	WIRE Diameter	A	B		C		MINIMUM PERMISSIBLE Load to B
110.000 110.040	5.25	.7321" (18,6 mm)	.1260" (3,2 mm)	1.8898" (48 mm)	1.4370" (36,5 mm)	46.3 lbs (21 kg)	1.1024" (28 mm)	80.5 lbs (36,5 kg)	37.5 lbs (17 kg)
110.004 110.044	7.25	.7598" (19,3 mm)	.1260" (3,2 mm)	2.2519" (57,2 mm)	1.5945" (40,5 mm)	52 lbs (23,6 kg)	1.2598" (32 mm)	78.5 lbs (35,6 kg)	43 lbs (19,5 kg)

A = Height, free spring.   B = Height, seated spring.   C = Height, minimum, working spring.

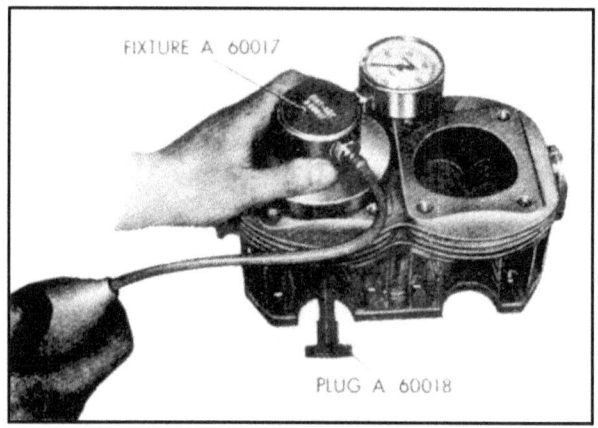

Fig. 94 - Valve seal test using fixture A. 60017 and plug A. 60018.

Cylinder Head Assembly and Installation.

Place the head, complete with valves and springs, on the cylinders after interposing the gasket.

Insert in their seats on head the sleeves for rocker pushrods and for rocker shaft lubrication pipe with relevant gaskets and rings. Then, fit the washers and nuts and tighten slightly.

Many engine troubles are originated by defective conditions of valves. It is therefore absolutely necessary that valve sealing be perfect and that valve stem-to-guide clearance be within specified limits.

Using a torque wrench, tighten nuts to 23.9 ft.lbs (3300 kgmm) following the tightening sequence illustrated in fig. 95.

Tightening of nuts must be performed in two stages:

— 1st: to a torque of about 18.1 ft.lbs (2500 kgmm);

— 2nd: to the recommended torque of 23.9 ft.lbs (3300 kgmm).

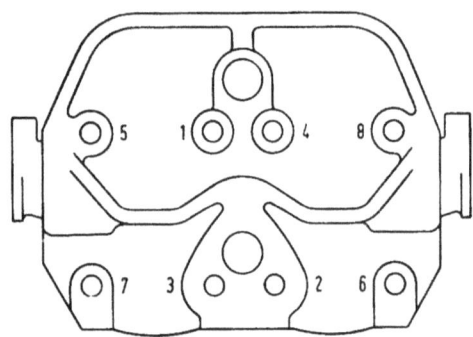

Fig. 95 - Cylinder head hold-down nuts tightening sequence.

Fig. 96 - Tightening cylinder head hold-down nuts with torque wrench.

NOTE ON SELF-LOCKING NUTS

When the threads, on which self-locking nuts of the nylon ring insert type must be screwed, are in good condition (free from burrs, rust traces, indents), or when they are not cross milled from the factory assembly process, self-locking nuts may be screwed on and off more than once until practicable. However, it is advisable to watch the loosening torque and replace nuts when this tends to decrease.

Loosening torque can be rated at some 20% less than the tightening torque specified for each nut.

Conversely, should the threads, which are to receive the nylon ring type self-locking nuts, show cross mills, or just only burrs, rust pits or indents nuts must be replaced every time, as the nylon ring is liable to be damaged with consequent loss of self-locking ability.

If, when service is in progress, the necessity arises to screw nuts on and off threads having milled slits or being in conditions as above, it is good practice temporarily using standard type nuts, which will be replaced by self-locking nuts as soon as service operations are terminated.

Self-locking nuts of the castellated type can be screwed on and loosened indefinitely as their particular design affords an unrestrained locking ability.

TIMING GEAR

CAMSHAFT AND CAMSHAFT SEATS ON CRANKCASE	page	47
Valve Gear Data	»	47
Inspection	»	49
TAPPETS	»	49
PUSHRODS	»	49
ROCKERS	»	50
TAPPET-TO-ROCKER CLEARANCE ADJUSTMENT	»	50
VALVE TIMING	»	51

CAMSHAFT AND CAMSHAFT SEATS ON CRANKCASE

The cast-iron camshaft is located in crankcase and is supported at both ends. Camshaft seats are machined directly in crankcase and no bushes are interposed. The chain-driven camshaft takes the drive from crankshaft and, in turn, operates the valves through tappets, pushrods and rockers. Tappet seats are machined in crankcase.

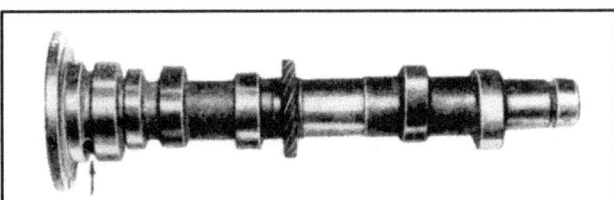

Fig. 97 - Camshaft.
The arrow points to the lube oil outlet port.

Valve Gear Data.

Intake:	500	500 Sports
— opens, B.T.D.C.	9°	25°
— closes, A.B.D.C.	70°	51°
Exhaust:		
— opens, B.B.D.C.	50°	64°
— closes, A.T.D.C.	19°	12°

These data are referred to the following rocker arm-to-valve stem adjustment clearances:

Model « 500 » { intake .0177" (0,45 mm)
exhaust .0150" (0,38 mm)

Model « 500 Sports » - intake and exhaust .0154" (0,39 mm).

Final tappet operation clearance, with cold engine, for both intake and exhaust valves: .0059" (0,15 mm).

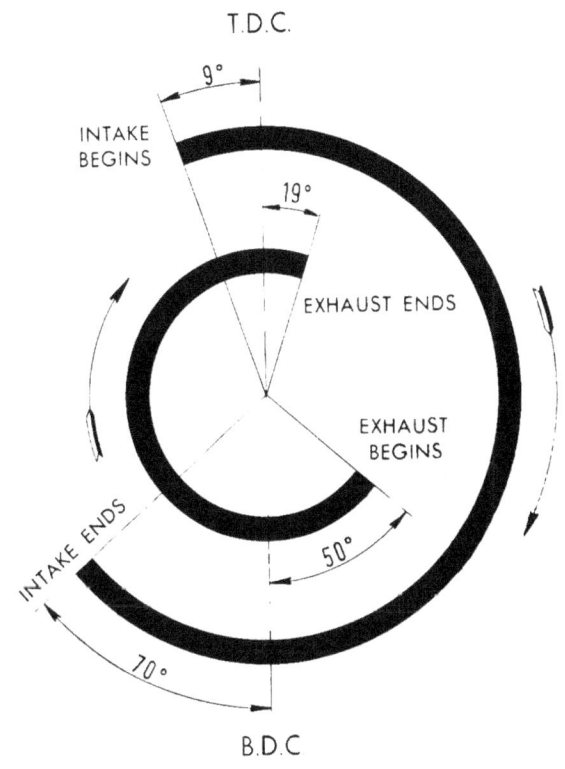

Fig. 98 - Valve timing diagram (Model « 500 » engine).

NOTE - Up to engine No. 033069, from engine No. 033074 to No. 033308, from engine No. 033377 to No. 033384 and from engine No. 033431 to No. 033434, valve gear data, as referred to .0177" (0,45 mm) rocker arm-to-valve stem adjustment clearance, were as follows:

Intake	{ opens, B.T.D.C.	20°
	closes, A.B.D.C.	50°
Exhaust	{ opens, B.B.D.C.	50°
	closes, A.T.D.C.	20°

Final tappet operation clearance, cold engine: intake and exhaust .0039" (0,10 mm).

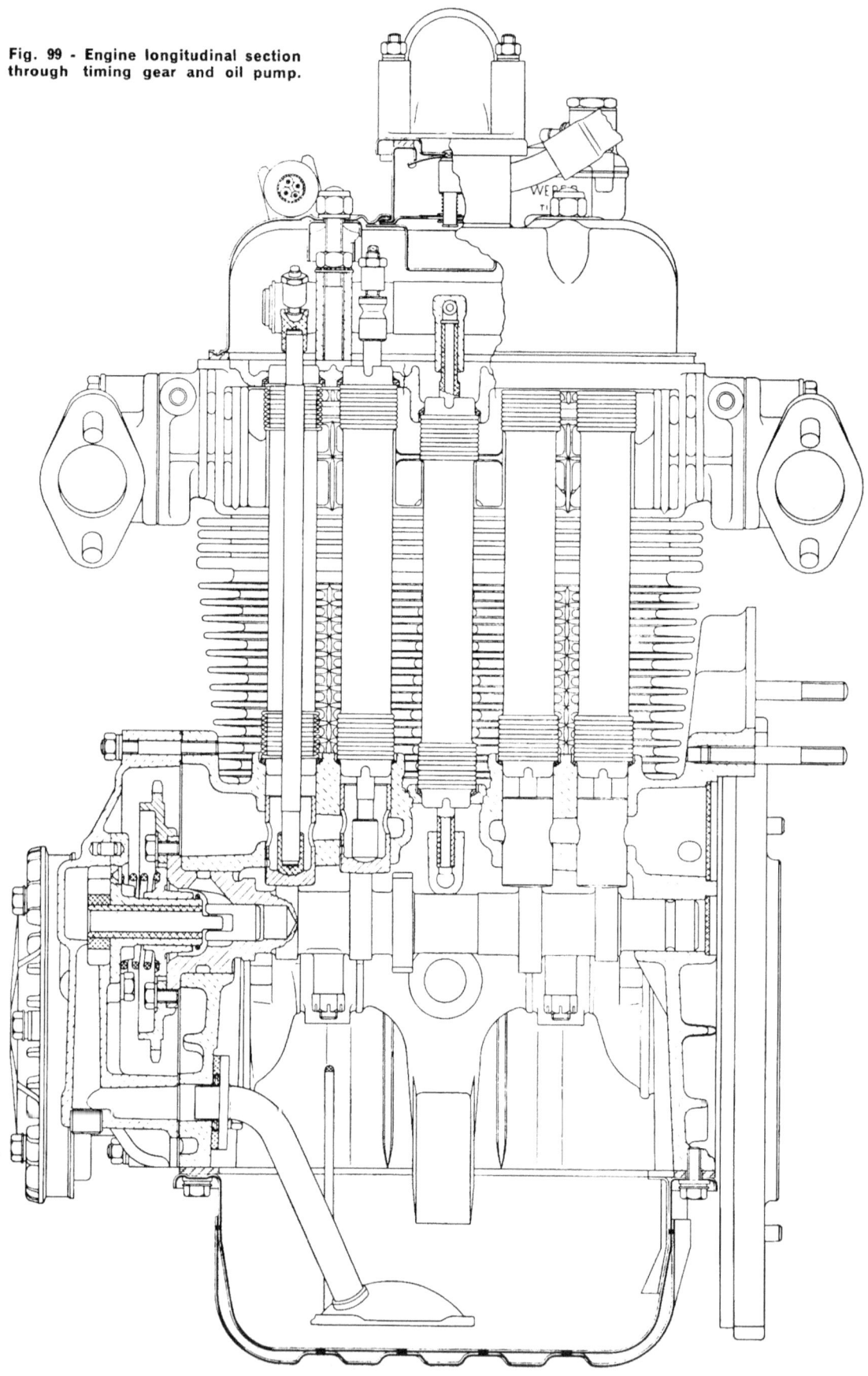

Fig. 99 - Engine longitudinal section through timing gear and oil pump.

ENGINE: TIMING GEAR

CAMSHAFT AND CAMSHAFT SEATS DATA

	CAMSHAFT JOURNAL DIAMETER	SEAT DIAMETER	FIT CLEARANCE
Timing gear end	1.6919" to 1.6929" (42,975 to 43,000 mm)	1.6939" to 1.6954" (43,025 to 43,064 mm)	.00098" to .00350" (0,025 to 0,089 mm)
Flywheel end	.8653" to .8661" (21,979 to 22,000 mm)	.8669" to .8682" (22,020 to 22,053 mm)	.00079" to .0029" (0,020 to 0,074 mm)

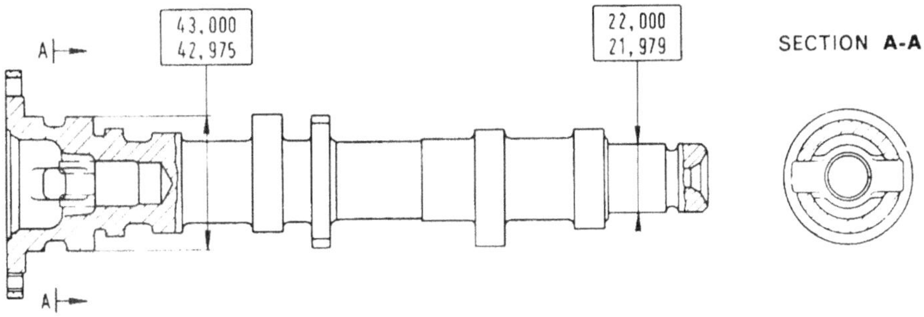

Fig. 100.
Camshaft data
(Model « 500 » engine).

SECTION A-A

Inspection.

All camshaft journal and cam surfaces must be mirror like. If any scoring mark or sign of seizure is found, the camshaft should be replaced.

However, when nicks are very slight, they may be remedied using a fine grain hone.

It is advisable to check also the condition of ignition distributor drive gear: if tooth wear is excessive, replace the camshaft. Camshaft journal-to-seat clearances are tabulated above.

TAPPETS

For tappet and tappet seat checking instructions refer to page 23 under « Crankcase ».

The tappet end surface in contact with camshaft cams must always be as smooth as possible; any evidence of slight scratches may be remedied using a fine grain hone.

Make sure tappet seat surface is free from scoring marks.

Assembly data are given in the table below (see also fig. 29).

PUSHRODS

Pushrods must not show any deformation. Their end surfaces in contact with rocker setscrew and tappet seats must not show any evidence of seizure or roughness. Replace parts if necessary.

Pushrods are contained in special, axially-resilient sleeves compressed between cylinder head and crankcase. Through these sleeves sump is vented and receives the oil returning from cylinder head.

Two rubber seals, one upper and one lower, are fitted on each sleeve to ensure oil-tightness.

Check sleeves and seals; replace parts as required.

TAPPET AND TAPPET-SEAT DATA

OVERSIZES	TAPPET DIAMETER	SEAT DIAMETER	FIT CLEARANCE
Standard	.8660" to .8652" (21,996 to 21,978 mm)	.8670" to .8662" (22,021 to 22,003 mm)	.00028" to .00169" (0,007 to 0,043 mm)
.0020" (0,05 mm)	.8680" to .8672" (22,046 to 22,028 mm)	.8689" to .8682" (22,071 to 22,053 mm)	.00028" to .00169" (0,007 to 0,043 mm)
.0040" (0,10 mm)	.8700" to .8692" (22,096 to 22,078 mm)	.8709" to .8702" (22,121 to 22,103 mm)	.00028" to .00169" (0,007 to 0,043 mm)

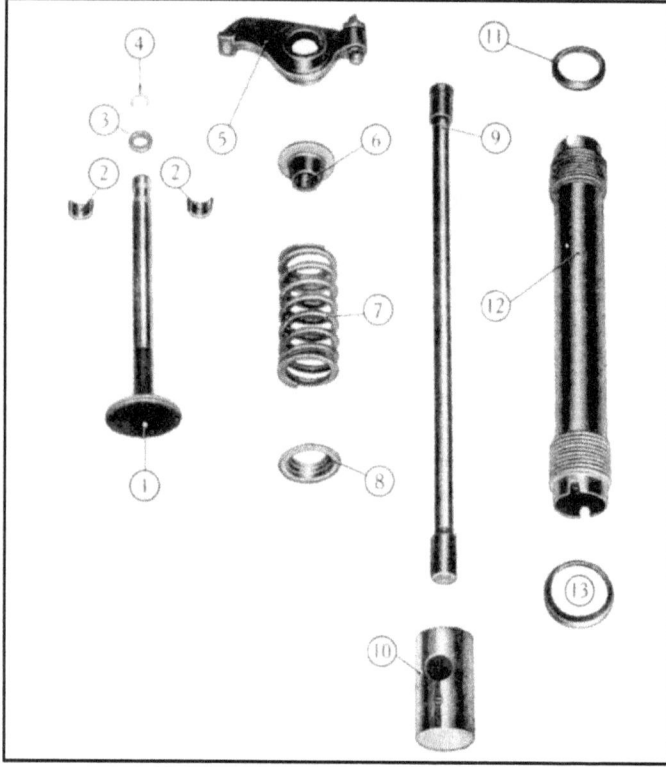

Fig. 101 - Valve tappet assembly.

1. Intake valve. - 2. Upper cup lock. - 3. Oil shield (for intake valves only). - 4. Snap ring. - 5. Rocker. - 6. Upper spring cup. - 7. Valve spring. - 8. Lower spring cup. - 9. Pushrod. - 10. Tappet. - 11. Oil seal ring. - 12. Pushrod sleeve. - 13. Seal ring.

ROCKERS

During overhauls, check the rocker shaft-to-bore clearance: fit clearance is .00063" to .00217" (0,016 to 0,053 mm), while maximum allowable wear is .0059" (0,15 mm).

If necessary, replace the more worn of the two parts, or both.

Check also that contacting surfaces are neither scored nor scuffed.

Replace parts as required.

Accurately check the conditions of rocker-to-valve and rocker ball head-to-pushrod contact surfaces which must be polished to a mirror-like finish.

Assembly clearance of rocker arm shaft-to-shaft support: .00020" to .00138" (0,005 to 0,035 mm); wear limit: .0039" (0,10 mm).

TAPPET-TO-ROCKER CLEARANCE ADJUSTMENT

This clearance must be kept reasonably constant and accurately adjusted in order not to alter the recommended timing gear data.

In fact, if clearance is excessive, noises will develop; while, if much less than specified, valves will keep on staying a bit open, with detrimental consequences to valves and their seats.

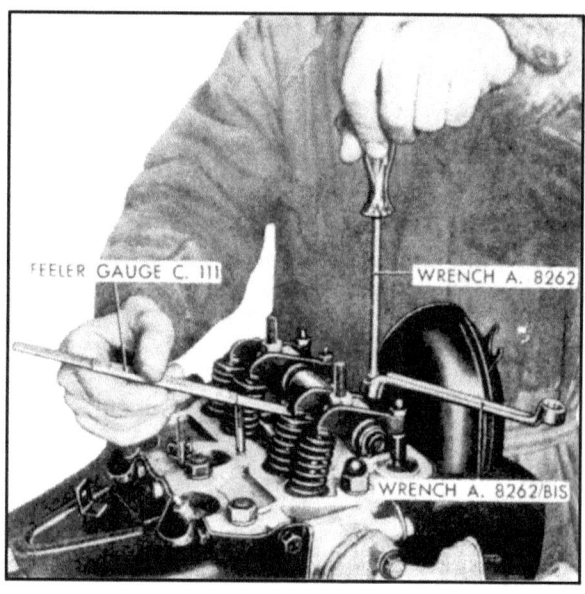

Fig. 103 - Adjusting rocker clearance by wrenches A. 8262, A. 8262/bis and feeler gauge C. 110 (.0059" - 0,15 mm) or C. 111 (.0039" - 0,10 mm).

Adjustments must be made using the recommended wrenches: **A. 8262** and **A. 8262/bis** (fig. 103); rocker-to-valve stem clearance, when cold, must be .0059" (0,15 mm) both for intake and exhaust valves. Check with feeler gauge **C. 110**.

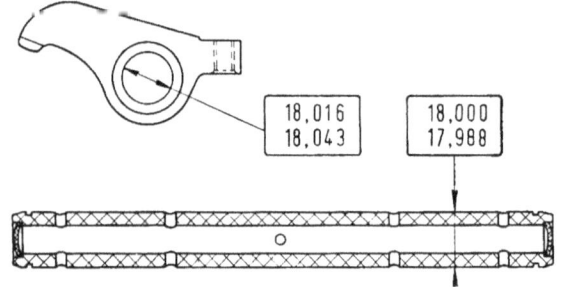

Fig. 102 - Rocker and rocker shaft data.

NOTE - Cold clearance of rocker arms to valve stems on engines having pre-modification camshaft should be: .0039" (0,10 mm), intake and exhaust. Check with feeler gauge **C. 111**.

ENGINE: TIMING GEAR

VALVE TIMING

Reference marks are ground on valve gears for timing purposes, as follows:

— drive gear on crankshaft bears a line at a gear tooth;

— driven gear on camshaft bears a point at a gear tooth space.

When valve timing is correct, above two marks are lined up as shown in fig. 105 and engine cylinder No. 1 ist at top dead center in the intake stroke.

If, for any reason, the camshaft has been uncoupled from crankshaft (for instance, when chain has been taken down), to re-time the valve gear proceed as follows:

Turn crankshaft until reference line on its sprocket is oriented toward camshaft sprocket centre. Next, turn camshaft until reference point on its sprocket registers with crankshaft sprocket mark (fig. 105).

Finally, leave sprockets undisturbed and mount the chain.

If valve timing procedure stages should be checked with the engine down from car, operate as follows:

— fit graduated sector **C. 673** (fig. 104);

— temporarily adjust valve stem-to-rocker arm clearance of cylinder No. 1 at .0177" (0,45 mm) for intake valve and at .0150" (0,38 mm) for exhaust valve (Model « 500 » engine), or at .0154" (0,39 mm) both valves (Model « 500 Sports » engine);

— turn about the crankshaft and set the flywheel mark at 0° on graduated sector;

— make sure that gear marks are lined up, in this position.

If the engine is being assembled, proceed as follows to install the driven gear:

a) set the timing mark on drive gear toward the center of camshaft;

b) position the driven gear on camshaft mounting flange with four screw holes in line, and tighten two mounting screws only;

c) turn about the camshaft until the driven gear mark registers with the reference line on drive gear;

d) take down the driven gear without moving the camshaft, install the timing chain and replace the driven gear;

Fig. 104 - Graduated sector C. 673 for valve gear timing.

e) draw up the driven gear screws with 6.5 ft.lbs (900 kgmm) of torque, using a torque wrench;

— check on graduated sector that all advance and retard angles are as specified on page 47;

— after this, adjust the valve stem-to-rocker arm clearance to the final operation value as outlined on page 50.

Fig. 105 - Timing marks on sprockets.

SPECIFICATIONS
REPAIR AND REBUILD STANDARDS

CYLINDERS AND CRANKCASE

		in.	mm
Cylinder barrel diameter:			
— Model « 500 »	Class A	2.5984 to 2.5988	66,000 to 66,010
	Class B	2.5988 to 2.5992	66,010 to 66,020
	Class C	2.5992 to 2.5996	66,020 to 66,030
— Model « 500 Sports »	Class A	2.6535 to 2.6539	67,400 to 67,410
	Class B	2.6539 to 2.6543	67,410 to 67,420
	Class C	2.5643 to 2.6547	67,420 to 67,430
Camshaft seat diameter — Timing gear end		1.6939 to 1.6954	43,025 to 43,064
Flywheel end		.8669 to .8682	22,020 to 22,053
Valve tappet crankcase seat diameter		.8670 to .8662	22,021 to 22,003

CONNECTING RODS - BEARING INSERTS - BUSHINGS

	in.	mm
Connecting rod bearing bore diameter	1.8555 to 1.8560	47,130 to 47,142
Connecting rod small end bushing bore diameter	.8637 to .8650	21.939 to 21,972
Standard con rod bearing half thickness	.0604 to .0675	1,534 to 1,543
Replacement connecting rod bearing half undersize range	.0100 - .0200 .0300 - .0400	0,254 - 0,508 0,762 - 1,016
Connecting rod small end bushing O. D.	.8661 to .8673	22,000 to 22,030
Connecting rod small end bushing I. D. (bushing in place)	.7874 to .7876	20,000 to 20,006
Piston pin-small end bushing fit: — assembly clearance — wear limit	.00020 to .00083 .0020	0,005 to 0,016 0,05
Small end bushing-to-bushing bore	pinch fit at all times .0011 to .0036	0,028 to 0,091
Con rod bearing half-to-con rod journal fit: — assembly clearance — wear limit	.00043 to .00240 .0059	0,011 to 0,061 0,15
Maximum misalignment of connecting rod axes: — 4 $^{59}/_{64}$" (125 mm) apart from rod centerline	± .0020	± 0,05
Weight tolerance in the same set of connecting rods	± .1 oz	± 3 gr

ENGINE: SPECIFICATIONS - REPAIR AND REBUILD STANDARDS

PISTONS - PISTON PINS - PISTON RINGS

		in.	mm
Standard piston diameter, square to pin axis:			
Model «500» — at skirt top	Class A	2.5953 to 2.5957	65,920 to 65,930
	Class B	2.5957 to 2.5961	65,930 to 65,940
	Class C	2.5961 to 2.5965	65,940 to 65,950
Model «500» — at skirt bottom	Class A	2.5972 to 2.5976	65,970 to 65,980
	Class B	2.5976 to 2.5980	65,980 to 65,990
	Class C	2.5980 to 2.5984	65,990 to 66,000
Model «500 Sports» — at skirt top	Class A	2.6496 to 2.6500	67,300 to 67,310
	Class B	2.6500 to 2.6504	67,310 to 67,320
	Class C	2.6504 to 2.6508	67,320 to 67,330
Model «500 Sports» — at skirt bottom	Class A	2.6516 to 2.6520	67,350 to 67,360
	Class B	2.6520 to 2.6524	67,360 to 67,370
	Class C	2.6524 to 2.6528	67,370 to 67,380
Piston pin bore diameter		.7868 to .7870	19,985 to 19,990
Piston ring groove height — 1st groove		.0823 to .0829	2,090 to 2,105
— 2nd groove		.0823 to .0829	2,090 to 2,105
— 3rd groove		.0819 to .0825	2,080 to 2,095
— 4th groove		.1577 to .1583	4,005 to 4,020
Piston pin diameter, standard		.7872 to .7870	19,995 to 19,990
Replacement piston pin oversizes		.0079	0,2
Piston ring thickness:			
— first compression ring and second and third oil rings		.0783 to .0779	1,990 to 1,978
— fourth radial-slotted oil ring		.1550 to .1540	3,937 to 3,912
Piston-to-cylinder barrel fit, measured square to pin axis:			
Model «500»			
— at skirt top	assembly clearance	.0028 to .0035	0,070 to 0,090
	wear limit	.0098	0,25
— at skirt bottom	assembly clearance	.0008 to .0016	0,020 to 0,040
	wear limit	.0059	0,15
Model «500 Sports»			
— at skirt top	assembly clearance	.0035 to .0043	0,090 to 0,110
	wear limit	.0098	0,25
— at skirt bottom	assembly clearance	.0016 to .0024	0,040 to 0,060
	wear limit	.0079	0,20
Piston pin-to-pin boss fit		pinch fit at all times 0 to .0004	0 to 0,01

(continued)

Pistons - Piston Pins - Piston Rings (continued).

		in.	mm
Piston ring-to-groove land fit (vertically):			
— first compression ring and second oil ring	assembly clearance wear limit	.0039 to .0050 .0079	0,100 to 0,127 0,20
— third oil ring	assembly clearance wear limit	.0035 to .0046 .0059	0,090 to 0,117 0,15
— fourth radial-slotted oil ring .	assembly clearance wear limit	.0027 to .0043 .0059	0,068 to 0,108 0,15
Gap of piston rings in cylinder barrel:			
— first, second and third rings .	assembly clearance wear limit	.0098 to .0138 .0197	0,25 to 0,35 0,50
— fourth ring		touch fit at all times	
Piston oversize range (Model « 500 » only)		.0079 .0157 - .0236	0,2 - 0,4 - 0,6
Piston ring oversize range (Model « 500 » only):			
— first, second and third rings		.0079 .0157 - .0236	0,2 - 0,4 - 0,6
— fourth ring		.0157	0,4

CRANKSHAFT - MAIN BEARING INSERTS

	in.	mm
Con rod journal diameter, standard	1.7328 to 1.7336	44,013 to 44,033
Main bearing journal diameter, standard	2.1260 to 2.1248	54,000 to 53,970
I. D. of standard main bearings in supporting members, camshaft and flywheel ends	2.1268 to 2.1274	54,020 to 54,035
Undersize range of main bearings in supporting members, camshaft and flywheel ends	.0079-.0157-.0236 .0315-.0394	0,2 - 0,4 - 0,6 0,8 - 1,00
Main bearing-to-bearing journal fit: — assembly clearance .... — wear limit	.00079 to .00256 .0039	0,020 to 0,065 0,10
Crankshaft end play	.0118 to .0173	0,30 to 0,44

ENGINE: SPECIFICATIONS - REPAIR AND REBUILD STANDARDS

CYLINDER HEAD - VALVES - GUIDES - SPRINGS

	in.	mm
Valve guide cylinder head seat diameter	.5118 to .5125	13,000 to 13,018
Valve guide O. D.	.5139 to .5143	13,052 to 13,062
Valve guide I. D., valves in head	.3158 to .3165	8,022 to 8,040
Valve guide-to-cylinder head fit	pinch fit at all times .00134 to .00244	0,034 to 0,062
Valve stem diameter: — intake and exhaust, Model « 500 » and intake, Model « 500 Sports » — exhaust, Model « 500 Sports »	.3144 to .3150 .3136 to .3142	7,985 to 8,000 7,965 to 7,980
Valve-to-valve guide fit: — assembly clearance { intake and exhaust, Model « 500 » and intake, Mod. « 500 Sports » exhaust, Model « 500 Sports » . — wear limit	.00087 to .00217 .00165 to .00295 .0059	0,022 to 0,055 0,042 to 0,075 0,15
Valve seat angle	45° ± 5'	
Valve face angle	45° 30' ± 5'	
Valve head diameter - Face bottom end: Model « 500 » { intake exhaust	1.1811 1.0630	30 27
Model « 500 Sports » { intake exhaust	1.2598 1.1024	32 28
Maximum run-out of valve turning on stem, with dial plunger on center of outside face	.00079	0,02
Valve seat height	.0551	1,4
Valve seat smaller diameter: Model « 500 » { intake { I. D. O. D. exhaust { I. D. O. D.	.9055 1.1020 to 1.1029 1.0236 1.2200 to 1.2211	23 27,991 to 28,012 26 30,989 to 31,014
Model « 500 Sports » { intake { I. D. O. D. exhaust { I. D. O. D.	.9449 1.1414 to 1.1422 1.1024 1.2594 to 1.2604	24 28,991 to 29,012 28 31,989 to 32,014
Valve spring I. D. { Model « 500 » Model « 500 Sports »	.7321 .7598	18,6 19,3
Free spring height { Model « 500 » Model « 500 Sports »	1.8898 2.2519	48 57,2
Spring height under 46.3 lbs (21 kg) of load (valves closed) Model « 500 »	1.4370	36,5
Spring height under 52 lbs (23,6 kg) of load (valves closed) Model « 500 Sports »	1.5945	40,5

(continued)

Cylinder Head - Valves - Guides - Springs (continued).

	in.	mm
Spring height under 80.5 lbs (36,5 kg) of load (valves open) Model «500»	1.1024	28
Spring height under 78.5 lbs (35,6 kg) of load (valves open) Model «500 Sports»	1.2598	32
Axial lift of valves — Model «500» intake	.3260	8,28
Axial lift of valves — Model «500» exhaust	.3244	8,24
Axial lift of valves — Model «500 Sports»: intake and exhaust	.3602	9,15
Minimum load for spring height of 1.4370" (36,5 mm) Model «500»	37.5 lbs	17 kg
Minimum load for spring height of 1.5945" (40,5 mm) Model «500 Sports»	43 lbs	19,5 kg

CAMSHAFT AND CAMSHAFT SEATS

	in.	mm
Camshaft journal diameter:		
— timing gear end	1.6919 to 1.6929	42,975 to 43,000
— flywheel end	.8653 to .8661	21,979 to 22,000
Camshaft seat diameter:		
— timing gear end	1.6939 to 1.6954	43,025 to 43,064
— flywheel end	.8669 to .8682	22,020 to 22,053
Camshaft journal-to-seat fit clearance:		
— timing gear end	.00098 to .0035	0,025 to 0,089
— flywheel end	.00079 to .0029	0,020 to 0,074

TAPPETS - ROCKER ARMS - ROCKER ARM SHAFT AND SUPPORTS

	in.	mm
Valve tappet crankcase seat diameter	.8662 to .8670	22,003 to 22,021
Valve tappet O. D., standard	.8660 to .8652	21,996 to 21,978
Valve tappet oversize range	.00197 - .00394	0,05 - 0,10
Valve tappet-to-tappet seat fit: assembly clearance	.00028 to .00169	0,007 to 0,043
Valve tappet-to-tappet seat fit: wear limit	.00315	0,08
Rocker arm shaft support bore diameter	.7089 to .7096	18,005 to 18,023
Rocker arm shaft diameter	.7087 to .7082	18,000 to 17,988
Rocker arm shaft support-to-rocker arm shaft fit: assembly clearance	.00020 to .00138	0,005 to 0,035
Rocker arm shaft support-to-rocker arm shaft fit: wear limit	.0039	0,10
Rocker arm bore diameter	.7093 to .7104	18,016 to 18,043
Rocker arm-to-rocker shaft fit: assembly clearance	.00063 to .00217	0,016 to 0,055
Rocker arm-to-rocker shaft fit: wear limit	.0059	0,15

ENGINE TIGHTENING REFERENCE

ITEM	Drwg. or Std. Part No.	Thread	Material	Tightening torque ft.lbs	Tightening torque kgmm
Main bearing-to-crankcase screw ...	1/11003/21	8 MA (x1,25)	R 80 Cdt	15.2	2100
Flywheel-to-crankshaft screw	1/47500/30	8 MA (x1,25)	R 100	23.1	3200
Cap-to-connecting rod self-locking nut	1/25664/20	8 MB (x 1)	R 80 bolt R 100	23.9	3300
Rocker shaft-to-head nut	1/17016/11	8 MA (x1,25)	R 50 Cdt stud R 80	15.2	2100
Cylinder head hold-down nut	1/21647/11	10 x 1,25 M	R 50 Cdt stud R 100 Cdt	23.9	3300
Cylinder head hold-down nut	1/40549/11	10 x 1,25 M	R 50 Cdt stud R 100 Cdt	23.9	3300
Gear-to-camshaft screw	1/09794/21	6 MA (x 1)	R 80 Cdt	6.5	900
Generator and fan drive pulley hub screw	987109	24 MC (x1,5)	R 50	108.5	15000
Generator and fan drive pulley-to-hub screw	1/42904/21	6 MA (x 1)	R 80 Cdt	5.8	800
Fan-to-generator self-locking nut ...	1/25756/11	10 x 1,25 M	R 50 Cdt shaft R 80	25.3	3500
Pulley-to-generator self-locking nut ...	1/25756/11	10 x 1,25 M	R 50 Cdt shaft R 80	14.5	2000

IMPORTANT NOTICE ON THE USE OF TORQUE WRENCHES

Remember that screws and nuts must be drawn up to the prescribed torque, using torque wrenches, in a dry condition, namely without oiling either threads or seating faces (screw head seating face, lockplates, washers, etc.), which should be accurately cleaned of any sign of rust, dirt, or other foreign matter.

ENGINE BENCH TEST

INSTALLING ENGINE ON TEST BENCH . . . . page	58
PRELIMINARY OPERATIONS . . . . »	58
TEST PROCEDURE . . . . »	58
INSPECTION AFTER BENCH TEST . . . . »	59

After overhauling, the engine must be bench and brake tested.

Installing Engine on Test Bench.

Place engine on stands and secure by bracket I. 31781/A on flywheel end and bracket I. 31781/B on generator-fan pulley end.

Connect: exhaust silencer to flanged pipe I. 31782, flywheel to bench input shaft by flange I. 31763/A or I. 31763/B, according to the type of test bench used.

Connect fuel lines.

Connect ignition distributor and generator cables on bench control board.

Preliminary Operations.

Check oil in sump for correct level.
Open the fuel cock.
Send current to ignition system.
Start engine.

Test Procedure.

After starting the engine see if:

— oil and fuel leaks occur at faying surfaces, connections and gaskets;

— oil circulates correctly and test bench oil gauge installed in place of the oil gauge sending unit reads the specified pressure of 35.5 to 42.6 psi (2,5 to 3 kg/cm^2);

— engine runs correctly.

In case of operation troubles, stop engine at once and remedy as required before resuming the test.

It should be noted, however, that during the initial test period engine operation is still rough due to friction between contact surfaces of the newly installed parts which still need some breaking-in.

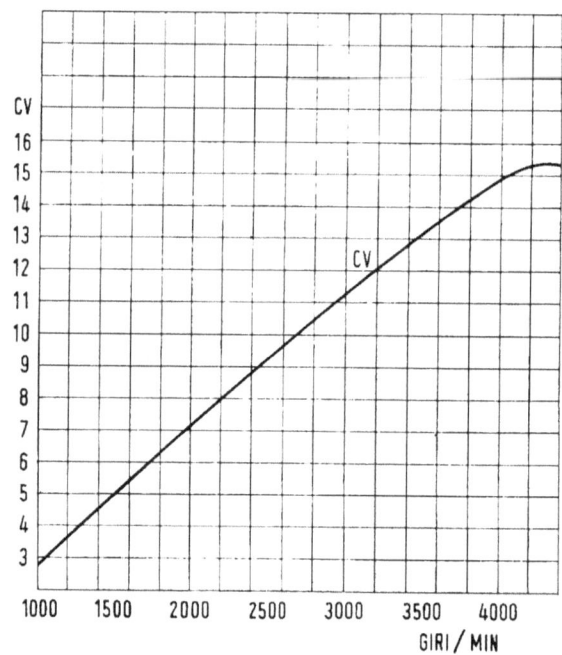

Fig. 106 - Power curve of the 110.000 and 110.040 engines.

Data are the minimum for a fully run-in engine and are intended with fan, without exhaust silencer.

GIRI/MIN = R. p. m. — CV = HP

This generally occurs when the engine under test has newly fitted pistons, main and connecting rod bearings as this calls for a regrinding of crankpins and journals and a reboring of cylinders.

For this reason the engine must be submitted to the following testing range.

ENGINE: BENCH TEST

Test Speed Rate - r.p.m.	Time - Min.	Brake Load
500	15'	no load
2,000	15'	half load
2,000	5'	full load
Grand total	35 minutes	

NOTE - When bench testing a rebuilt engine, do not race it to top speed in an effort to reach values shown in power curve.

Engine break-in will be completed by the Owner who is bound not to drive the car beyond the speed rates specified for the initial use.

Engine braking is obtained by adjusting the water flow in hydraulic brake turbine or by acting on the generator or on the impeller blades, depending on the type of brake used.

To rate the power developed by engine at the different speeds, the formula is:

$$HP = 0.001 \cdot P \cdot N$$

where:

HP = Power;

P = Load in kg (reading of dynamometer or weight applied on brake arm end);

N = R. P. M. (tachometer reading);

0.001 = Constant for a brake arm length of 28.189" (0,716 m).

For brakes with arm length of 56.378" (1,432 m) the formula is:

$$HP = 0.002 \cdot P \cdot N$$

Gasoline used during tests: O. N. 83 minimum (Research Method), Model «500» engine; O. N. 92 minimum, Model «500 Sports» engine.

Inspection after Bench Test.

Engine disassembly for inspection and overhaul will be necessary only if operation troubles have developed during test.

After remedying troubles and reassembling the engine, repeat bench test and make sure engine operates smoothly.

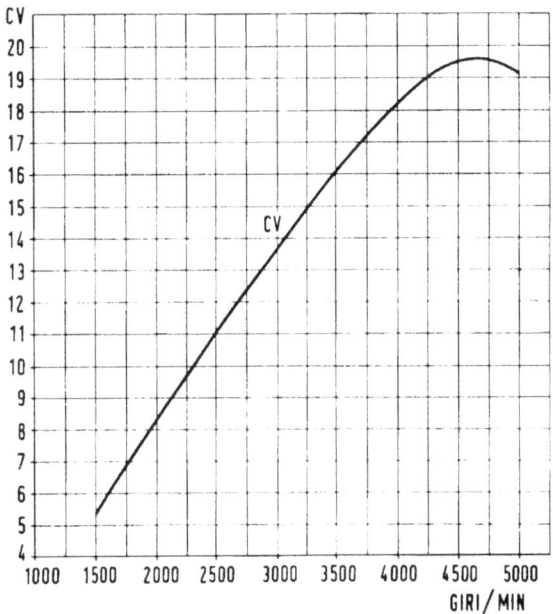

Fig. 107 - Power curve of the 110.004 and 110.044 engines.

Data are the minimum for a fully run-in engine and are intended with fan, without exhaust silencer.

GIRI/MIN = R. p. m. — CV = HP.

ENGINE TROUBLE DIAGNOSIS AND CORRECTIONS

Engine Will Not Start.

POSSIBLE CAUSES	REMEDIES
1) Weak battery.	1) Check and re-charge battery as recommended under « Battery ».
2) Corroded or loose battery terminal connections.	2) Clean, examine and tighten cable clamps to battery terminals, as recommended under « Battery ». Replace cables and clamps if they are too much corroded.
3) Weak coil.	3) Check coil and replace by a new one.
4) Loose or broken ignition cables from coil to distributor and from distributor to spark plugs.	4) Examine and re-set circuit or replace faulty cables.
5) Cracked distributor cap.	5) Replace cap.
6) Moisture or dirt deposits on distributor cap contact points.	6) Wipe and clean points.
7) Distributor breaker contact points dirty, oxidized or blackened; pitted points or excessive point gap.	7) Clean contacts and adjust point gap as recommended under « Ignition Distributor ».
8) Distributor rotor cracked, or showing signs of burning or wet.	8) Clean or replace rotor, if necessary.
9) Center distributor cap contact worn or broken or with distorted pressure spring.	9) Replace contact and contact spring.
10) Shorted condenser or with poor insulation.	10) Bench test condenser and replace it, if defective.
11) Fouled spark plugs or excessive spark plug gap.	11) Clean spark plugs and set gap as recommended under « Spark Plugs ».
12) Improper timing (ignition).	12) Check and set timing as recommended under « Ignition Timing ».
13) Defective starting motor.	13) Locate failure and correct as recommended under « Starting Motor ».
14) Carburetor flooded: a) due to too long starting with inserted choke without using accelerator. b) due to carburetor defect.	14) Proceed as follows: a) remove and wipe spark plugs or wait some minutes and start engine with choke out and all open throttle; b) remove and rebuild carburetor as recommended in covering chapter.
15) Dirt or water in fuel line or carburetor.	15) Remove and thoroughly clean carburetor; if trouble recurs, flush and blow fuel tank and lines.
16) Incorrect fuel level in carburetor bowl.	16) Check fuel level in bowl and adjust it, if necessary, as recommended under « Carburetor ».

(continued)

ENGINE: TROUBLE DIAGNOSIS AND CORRECTIONS

Engine Will Not Start (continued).

POSSIBLE CAUSES	REMEDIES
17) Defective fuel pump.	17) Remove and rebuild fuel pump as recommended under « Fuel Pump ».
18) Poor compression.	18) Check compression (99.6 to 106.7 p.s.i. - 7 to 7,5 kg/cm², Model « 500 » and 106.7 to 113.8 - 7,5 to 8 kg/cm², Model « 500 Sports »), using a pressure gauge; service valve seats and rebuild engine if compression is too low.
19) Engine overheating.	19) Check generator and fan drive belt tension and air outlet shutter control thermostat operation. If faults are as outlined under « Cooling », follow directions in this chapter to remove them.

Engine Stalls.

POSSIBLE CAUSES	REMEDIES
1) Idling speed too low.	1) Increase throttle opening slightly and adjust mixture rating as recommended under « Carburetor ».
2) Idle mixture too lean or too rich.	2) Adjust mixture rating as recommended under « Carburetor ».
3) Carburetor flooding:	3) Proceed as follows:
a) due to too long starting with inserted choke without using accelerator;	a) remove and wipe spark plugs or wait some minutes and start engine with choke out and all open throttle;
b) due to carburetor defect.	b) remove and rebuild carburetor as recommended in covering chapter.
4) Needle valve in carburetor stuck.	4) Rebuild as recommended under « Carburetor ».
5) Dirt or water in fuel line or carburetor.	5) Remove and thoroughly clean carburetor; if trouble recurs, flush and blow fuel tank and lines.
6) Incorrect fuel level in carburetor bowl.	6) Check and adjust fuel level as recommended under « Carburetor ».
7) Incorrect use of choke device.	7) Operate as recommended in covering paragraph of chapter « Carburetor ».
8) Loose or corroded battery terminals.	8) Clean terminals and tighten nuts as recommended under « Battery ». Replace cables and terminal clamps if they are too much worn.
9) Loose ignition cables from coil to distributor and from distributor to spark plugs.	9) Examine and re-set circuit.
10) Loose ignition switch connections.	10) Examine and re-set circuit.
11) Spark plugs dirty, damp or gaps set too wide.	11) Clean spark plugs and set gap as recommended under « Spark Plugs ».

(continued)

Engine Stalls (continued).

POSSIBLE CAUSES	REMEDIES
12) Distributor breaker contact points dirty, oxidized or blackened; pitted points or excessive point gap.	12) Clean contacts and adjust point gap as recommended under «Ignition Distributor».
13) Distributor rotor contact worn.	13) Replace distributor rotor.
14) Distributor advance not operating.	14) Rebuild ignition distributor as recommended in covering chapter.
15) Defective coil and condenser.	15) Inspect and replace both of them, if necessary. Operate as recommended under «Ignition Coil» and «Ignition Distributor».
16) Exhaust system restricted.	16) Thoroughly clean exhaust silencer, exhaust piping and manifolds.
17) Incorrect valve tappet clearance.	17) Adjust tappet clearance as recommended under «Timing Gear».
18) Burned valves.	18) Replace valves.
19) Poor compression.	19) Check compression (99.6 to 106.7 p.s.i. - 7 to 7,5 kg/cm^2, Model «500» and 106.7 to 113.8 p.s.i. - 7,5 to 8 kg/cm^2, Model «500 Sports»), using a pressure gauge; rebuild engine if compression is too low.
20) Engine overheating.	20) Check generator and fan drive belt for a loose condition and the air outlet shutter control thermostat on engine cowling for defective operation; proceed as required, following recommendations under «Cooling».

Engine Has No Power.

POSSIBLE CAUSES	REMEDIES
1) Incorrect ignition timing.	1) Inspect and set ignition as recommended under «Ignition Timing».
2) Weak coil or condenser.	2) Bench test coil and condenser as recommended under «Ignition Coil» and «Ignition Distributor». Replace both parts, if necessary.
3) Reduced accelerator pedal travel.	3) Locate failure and correct it.
4) Distributor rotor contact worn.	4) Replace distributor rotor.
5) Defective centrifugal or vacuum advance (distributor).	5) Rebuild ignition distributor and vacuum advance, as recommended in covering chapter.
6) Excessive play in distributor shaft.	6) Rebuild distributor and replace damaged parts.
7) Weak spring in breaker movable contact.	7) Replace distributor breaker arm, spring and point assembly.
8) Distributor cam worn.	8) Replace cam body.
9) Insufficient distributor point dwell.	9) Adjust point dwell angle as recommended under «Ignition Distributor».

(continued)

ENGINE: TROUBLE DIAGNOSIS AND CORRECTIONS

Engine Has No Power (continued).

POSSIBLE CAUSES	REMEDIES
10) Spark plugs dirty, damp or gaps incorrectly set.	10) Clean spark plugs and set gap as recommended under « Spark Plugs ».
11) Low grade fuel.	11) Use fuel with 83 Oct. Rating (Research Method) on Model « 500 » Sun Roof and Convertible, and 92 Oct. Rating on Model « 500 Sports ».
12) Weak valve springs.	12) Check spring pressure on tester A. 11493 and compare figures with those tabulated under « Valve Springs ».
13) Valves sticking when hot, burned or twisted.	13) Overhaul valves and valve guides as recommended under « Cylinder Head »; replace as required.
14) Incorrect valve tappet clearance.	14) Adjust tappet clearance as recommended under « Timing Gear ».
15) Worn camshaft lobes.	15) Replace camshaft.
16) Valve timing incorrect.	16) Time valves as recommended in covering chapter.
17) Insufficient engine bench running-in.	17) If necessary, remove engine from car and test it on bench.
18) Poor compression.	18) Check compression (99.6 to 106.7 p.s.i. - 7 to 7,5 kg/cm^2, Model « 500 » and 106.7 to 113.8 p.s.i. - 7,5 to 8 kg/cm^2, Model « 500 Sports »), using a pressure gauge; if pressure is too low, locate failure and rebuild engine.
19) Blown cylinder head gasket.	19) Remove cylinder head, check cylinder head and block for even mating surfaces, replace head gasket.
20) Defective fuel pump.	20) Rebuild fuel pump and replace worn parts.
21) Too rich or lean fuel mixture.	21) Adjust carburetor.
22) Carburetor in poor condition.	22) Clean carburetor, blow jets and adjust carburetor as recommended.
23) Dirt or water in gas line or carburetor.	23) Remove and thoroughly clean carburetor; if trouble recurs, flush and blow fuel tank and lines.
24) Incorrect fuel level in carburetor bowl.	24) Check fuel level in bowl and adjust as recommended under « Carburetor ».
25) Engine overheating.	25) Check generator and fan drive belt for a loose condition and the air outlet shutter control thermostat on engine cowling for defective operation; proceed as required, following recommendations under « Cooling ».
26) Clutch slipping.	26) Check throwout mechanism for correct operation, driven disk linings for absence of oil or grease, or wear. Operate as required (see chapter « Clutch »).
27) Tight wheel bearings.	27) Locate origin of failure; replace as required and adjust correctly as recommended under « Front and Rear Suspension and Wheels ».
28) Brakes dragging.	28) Inspect and adjust brakes.

Engine « Lopes » or Misses at Idle.

POSSIBLE CAUSES	REMEDIES
1) Incorrect carburetor idle adjustment.	1) Adjust idle as recommended under « Carburetor ».
2) Dirty jets or plugged passages in carburetor.	2) Remove and clean jets; if necessary, remove carburetor and rebuild it thoroughly.
3) Dirt or water in fuel line or carburetor.	3) Remove and thoroughly clean carburetor; if trouble recurs, flush and blow fuel tank and lines.
4) Carburetor flooding: a) due to long starting with inserted choke without using accelerator; b) due to carburetor defect.	4) Proceed as follows: a) remove and wipe spark plugs or wait some minutes and start engine with choke out and all open throttle; b) remove and rebuild carburetor as recommended in covering chapter.
5) Leaking gasket between carburetor and intake manifold spacer.	5) Check mating surfaces for level, replace gasket and tighten nuts properly.
6) Blown cylinder head gasket.	6) Check mating surfaces for level, replace gasket and tighten screws at specified torque.
7) Incorrect valve tappet clearance.	7) Adjust clearance as recommended under « Timing Gear ».
8) Burned, warped or pitted valves.	8) Rebuild cylinder head.
9) Worn camshaft lobes.	9) Replace camshaft.
10) Worn timing chain.	10) Replace chain.
11) Uneven compression rates.	11) Using pressure gauge, check compression in each cylinder (99.6 to 106.7 p.s.i. - 7 to 7,5 kg/cm^2, Model « 500 » and 106.7 to 113.8 p.s.i. - 7,5 to 8 kg/cm^2, Model « 500 Sports »), and rebuild engine, if required.
12) Engine overheating.	12) Check generator and fan drive belt for a loose condition and the air outlet shutter control thermostat on engine cowling for defective operation; proceed as required, following recommendations under « Cooling ».
13) Weak battery.	13) Check state of charge of battery and recharge.
14) Incorrect ignition timing.	14) Set ignition timing.
15) Leaks in ignition wiring.	15) Locate leak and correct as necessary.
16) Moisture on electrical system wires.	16) Wipe cable terminals, if damp. If the whole cable insulation is soaked, replace the cable.
17) Defective centrifugal ignition advance mechanism.	17) Rebuild ignition distributor as recommended under « Ignition Distributor ».
18) Excessive play in distributor shaft.	18) Rebuild ignition distributor and replace worn parts.
19) Distributor cam worn.	19) Rebuild ignition distributor and replace cam body.
20) Spark plugs damp, dirt or the gaps set too wide.	20) Clean spark plugs and adjust gap as recommended under « Spark Plugs ».

ENGINE: TROUBLE DIAGNOSIS AND CORRECTIONS

Engine Misses at High Speed.

POSSIBLE CAUSES	REMEDIES
1) Dirty jets in carburetor, especially the main jet and emulsion well.	1) Remove jets and blow them clean.
2) Dirt or water in fuel line or carburetor.	2) Remove and thoroughly clean carburetor; if trouble recurs, flush and blow fuel tank and lines.
3) Incorrect ignition timing.	3) Set ignition timing as recommended in covering chapter.
4) Weak coil or condenser.	4) Bench test coil and condenser and replace by new ones, if necessary.
5) Distributor breaker points dirty or incorrectly spaced.	5) Clean and adjust points.
6) Distributor rotor contact worn.	6) Replace distributor rotor.
7) Loose ignition wiring.	7) Check wiring cables for secure fastening on nuts and spark plug inserts.
8) Excessive play in distributor shaft.	8) Rebuild ignition distributor and replace worn parts.
9) Spark plugs dirty, damp or the gaps set too wide.	9) Clean spark plugs and adjust gap as recommended under « Spark Plugs ».
10) Weak distributor point contact.	10) Smooth distributor points and adjust gap.
11) Insufficient spring tension on contact breaker arm.	11) Replace breaker arm assembly.
12) Distributor cam lobe worn.	12) Rebuild ignition distributor and replace cam body.
13) Detonation or preignition.	13) Check spark advance and set ignition timing, where necessary. Make sure that spark plugs are the Factory recommended type and in serviceable condition. If pistons and combustion chambers are carboned up, use higher grade fuel.
14) Weak valve springs.	14) Remove, inspect and replace springs, if required.
15) Worn camshaft lobes.	15) Check valve timing and compare data with those in valve timing diagram as shown under « Valve Timing »; replace camshaft, if necessary.
16) Badly worn diaphragm in fuel pump.	16) Remove fuel pump and replace diaphragm as recommended under « Fuel Pump ».
17) Engine overheating.	17) Check generator and fan drive belt for a loose condition and the air outlet shutter control thermostat on engine cowling for defective operation; proceed as required following recommendations under « Cooling ».
18) Low grade fuel.	18) Use fuel with 83 Oct. Rating (Research Method) on Model « 500 » Sun Roof and Convertible, and 92 Oct. Rating on Model « 500 Sports ».

Engine Misses While Idling.

POSSIBLE CAUSES	REMEDIES
1) Spark plugs dirty, damp or the gaps set too wide.	1) Clean spark plugs and adjust gap as recommended under « Spark Plugs ».
2) Broken or loose ignition wires.	2) Check wiring cables for secure fastening on nuts and spark plug inserts.
3) Burned or pitted breaker contact points, or set with insufficient gap.	3) Overhaul and adjust contact points as recommended under « Ignition Distributor ».
4) Coil or condenser defective.	4) Bench test coil and condenser and replace them, if required.
5) Weak battery.	5) Check battery state of charge using a hydrometer and recharge battery, if necessary. Proceed as recommended under « Battery ».
6) Distributor cap cracked.	6) Replace cap.
7) Distributor rotor contact worn.	7) Replace distributor rotor.
8) Moisture on electrical system wires.	8) Wipe cable terminals, if damp. If the whole cable insulation is soaked, replace the cable.
9) Excessive play in distributor shaft or distributor cams worn.	9) Rebuild ignition distributor and replace worn parts.
10) Burned, warped or pitted valves.	10) Overhaul cylinder head and replace valves. Proceed as recommended under « Cylinder Head ».
11) Incorrect valve tappet clearance.	11) Adjust clearance as recommended under « Rocker Arms ».
12) Incorrect carburetor idle adjustment.	12) Adjust idle speed as recommended under « Carburetor ».
13) Improper carburetor float level.	13) Check and adjust float as recommended under « Carburetor ».
14) Poor compression.	14) Check compression using a pressure gauge; if pressure is too low (below 99.6 to 106.7 p.s.i. - 7 to 7,5 kg/cm^2, **Model « 500 »** and 106.7 to 113.8 p.s.i. - 7,5 to 8 kg/cm^2, **Model « 500 Sports »**), locate causes and remove them.

NOTE

When checking compression rating of each cylinder (99.6 to 106.7 ft.lbs - 7 to 7,5 kg/cm^2 for Model « 500 » and 106.7 to 113.8 ft.lbs - 7,5 to 8 kg/cm^2 for Model « 500 Sports »), see that the following conditions are strictly complied with: carburetor throttle valve all open, battery charged and engine cranked by starting motor at 360 to 400 r.p.m.

Section 3

FUEL SYSTEM
LUBRICATION SYSTEM
COOLING SYSTEM
POWER PLANT MOUNTINGS

	Page
FUEL SYSTEM	69
FUEL PUMP	69
AIR CLEANER	70
FUEL TANK	71
WEBER 26 IMB 1 AND 26 IMB 3 CARBURETORS	72
LUBRICATION SYSTEM	78
CENTRIFUGAL OIL FILTER	79
OIL PUMP	81
LOW OIL PRESSURE INDICATOR SENDING UNIT	83
COOLING SYSTEM	84
AIR OUTLET THERMOSTAT AND SHUTTER	85
GENERATOR AND FAN DRIVE BELT	86
POWER PLANT MOUNTINGS	87
ENGINE SERVICE EQUIPMENT	88

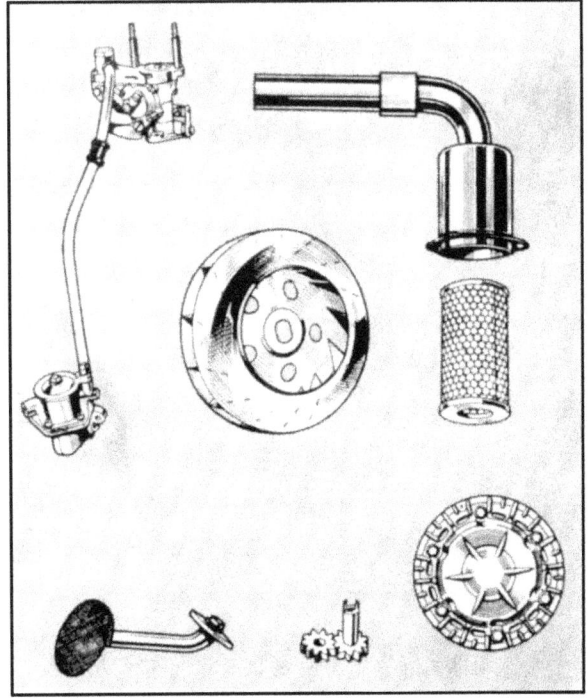

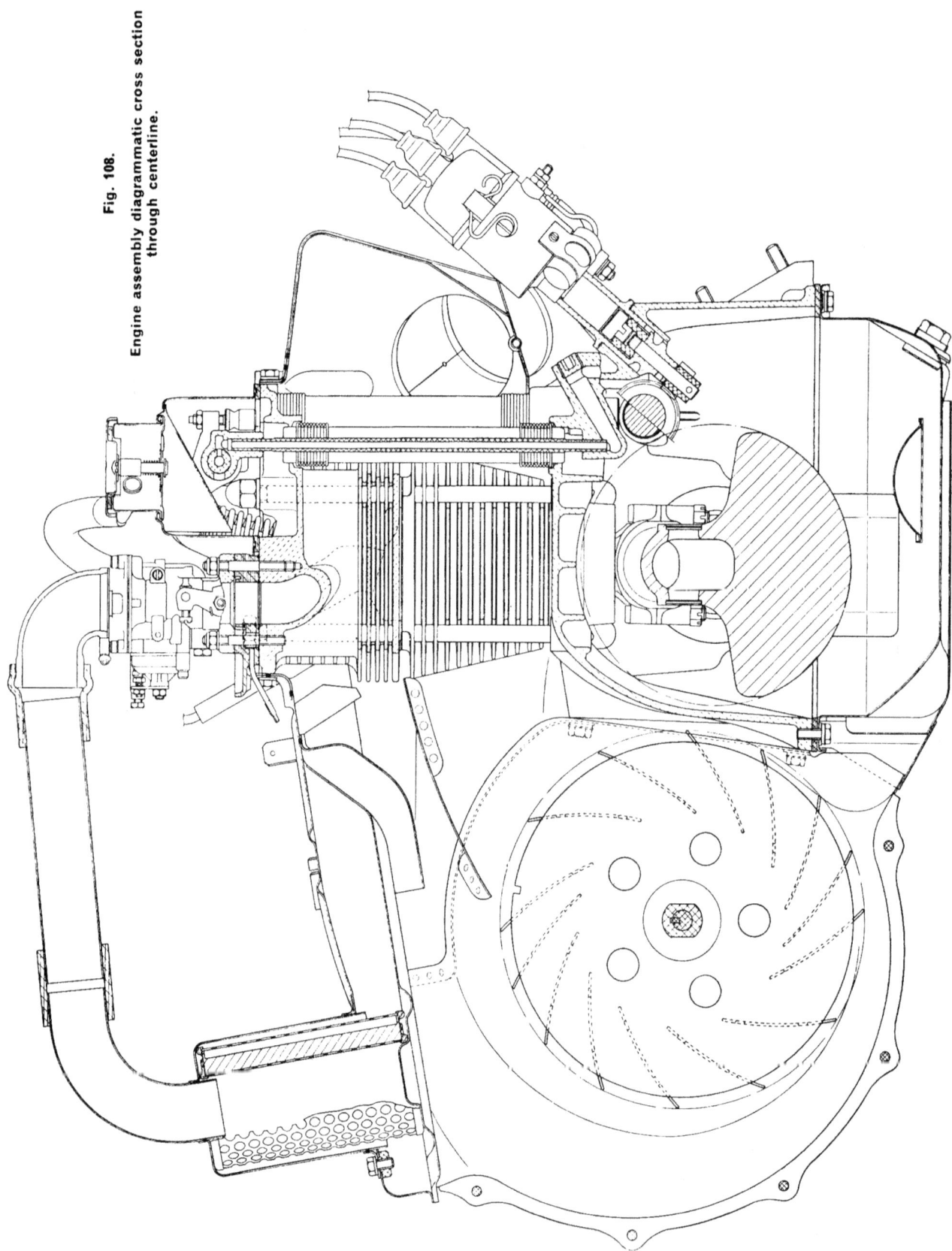

Fig. 108.
Engine assembly diagrammatic cross section through centerline.

FUEL SYSTEM

FUEL PUMP	page	69
AIR CLEANER	»	70
FUEL TANK	»	71
WEBER 26 IMB 1 AND 26 IMB 3 CARBURETORS	»	72

The engine is fed by a diaphragm pump which sucks fuel from fuel tank in front compartment and sends it on to carburetor.

Fuel Pump.

Fuel pump is mounted on engine crankcase, generator side (fig. 110), and is operated by an eccentric of camshaft through a pushrod which in turn actuates the diaphragm control rocker (fig. 110).

The pump, which draws fuel from the tank arranged in front compartment and sends it to the carburetor, consists of two joined parts. The upper portion houses the fuel bowl (which serves also for pump priming), the strainer and the inlet and outlet valves.

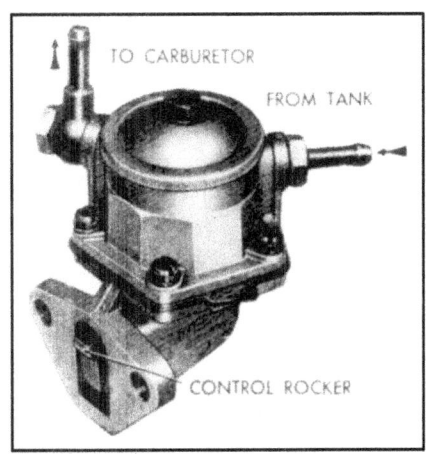

Fig. 109 - Fuel pump.
Arrows point to fuel inlet and outelt.

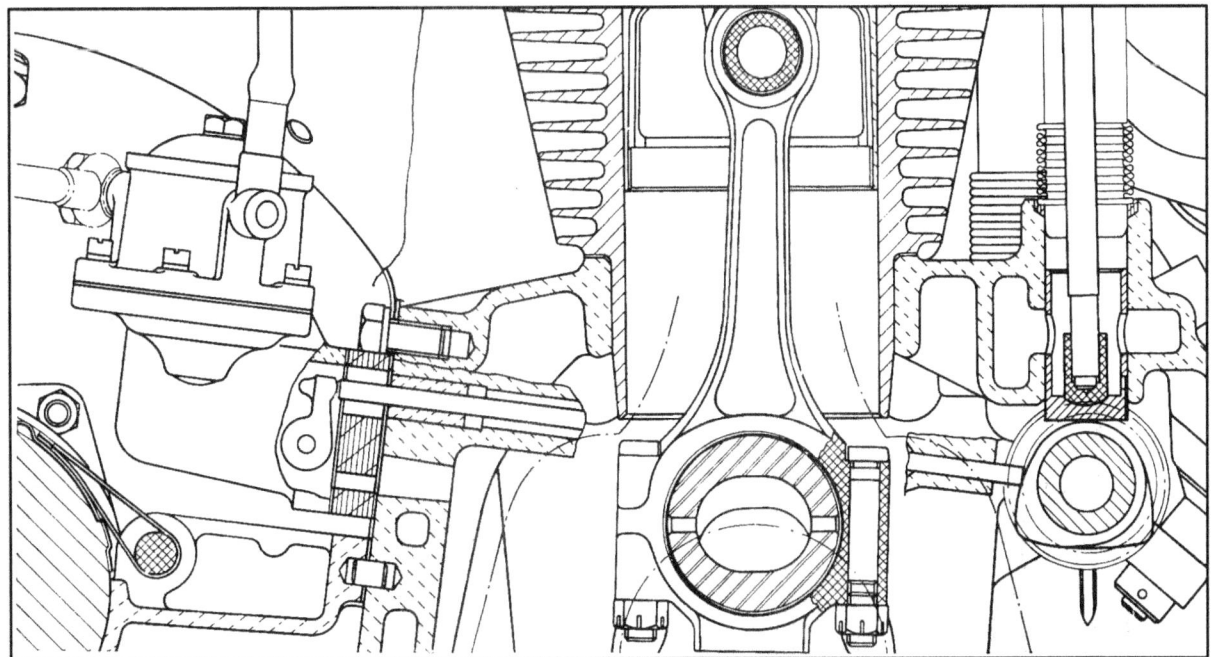

Fig. 110 - Detail of engine cross section through fuel pump control.

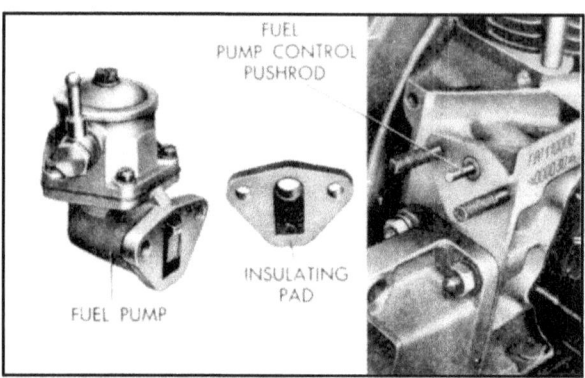

Fig. 111 - Fuel pump and control.

The lower portion houses the diaphragm and relevant control rocker (fig. 109).

The fuel pump requires no particular attention. Nevertheless, a periodical check is recommended.

By taking off pump cover, the sludge deposited in fuel bowl or on strainer may be removed.

The disassembly of inlet and outlet valves is performed afer removing the retaining plate. Wash these valves in gasoline. Replace if found damaged.

The inlet chamber diaphragm control mechanism must be washed in kerosene and wetted with some thin oil.

Fuel pump seals, even if slightly damaged, must be replaced. Apply grease sparingly on new seals before assembly.

If a new diaphragm has to be fitted, keep it in kerosene for at least fifteen minutes before assembly.

When no gasoline reaches carburetor, check to see if this condition is due to one of the following possible causes:

 a) empty tank;
 b) loose fuel pump cover screws;
 c) leaky pipes or connections;
 d) bent or flattened pipes;
 e) dirty strainer;
 f) dirty or distorted valves;
 g) weak spring;
 h) fuel pump control pushrod excessively worn, shortened or seizing in its seat.

Correct the condition by eliminating the cause of trouble.

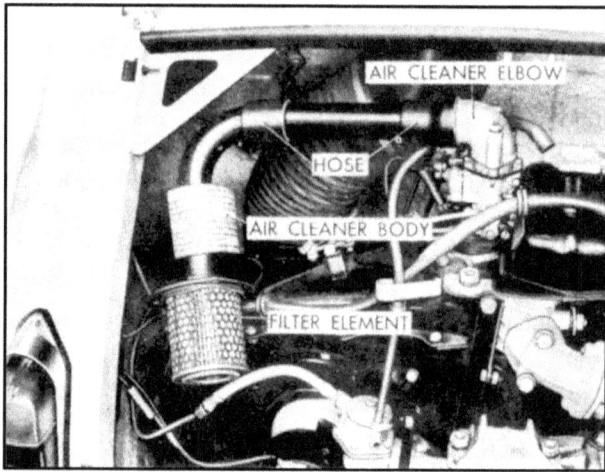

Fig. 113 - Taking out the filter element.

Air Cleaner.

Air cleaner is of the pleated paper type with perforated shell and plastic ends (figs. 113 and 148).

It is contained in a casing housed in a recess of a silencing chamber provided in blower conveyor. Connection between cleaner and carburetor is by a pipe. The silencing chamber is specially designed to dampen out the intake noise and carburetor hiss and communicates with blower conveyor interior in a location warranting the drawing of the purest possible air.

High and constant efficiency of the cleaner is essential for positive protection of engine. In fact, if dust or any other foreign matter - suspensed in the air drawn in by the engine - succeeds in flowing past the cleaner and reaching the engine inner components, dirt will mix with the lube oil and form a strongly abrasive compound that will accelerate wear and shorten engine life.

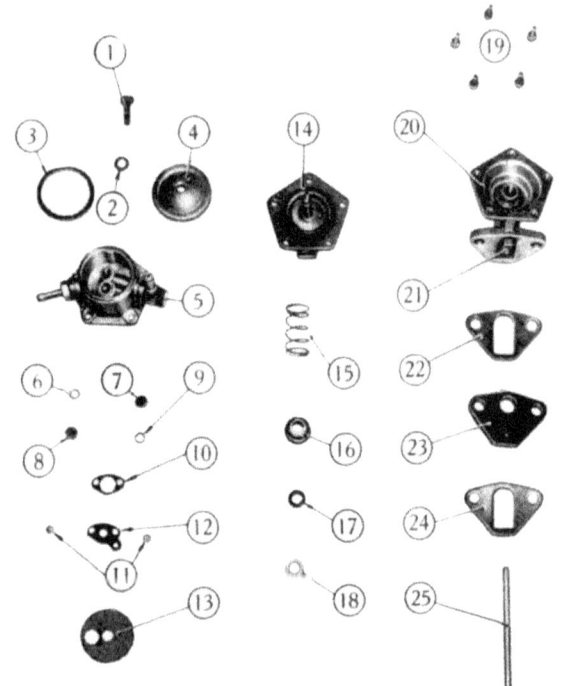

Fig. 112 - Fuel pump components.

1. Cover screw. - 2. Screw gasket. - 3. Cover gasket. - 4. Cover. - 5. Upper body. - 6. Spring for inlet valve. - 7. Inlet valve. - 8. Outlet valve. - 9. Spring for outlet valve. - 10. Plate gasket. - 11. Plate screws. - 12. Valve retaining plate. - 13. Filter gauze. - 14. Diaphragm, complete with tie rod. - 15. Return spring. - 16. Spring thrust cup. - 17. Felt. - 18. Washer for felt. - 19. Connection screws. - 20. Lower body. - 21. Rocker. - 22-24. Gaskets. - 23. Insulating pad. 25. Pump control pushrod.

ENGINE: FUEL SYSTEM

Replace filtering element every 6,000 miles (10.000 km). When dusty conditions of operation prevail, replace cartridge more often.

NOTE - Oversized air cleaners are supplied whenever particular requirements must be met, as for hot weather countries and prevailingly dusty areas.

Fuel Tank.

The tank is located in front compartment.

It carries: the filler union with cap, fuel reserve supply indicator sending unit and the connection (with filter) for fuel suction plastic pipe.

To remove tank for cleaning purposes or for repairs, proceed as follows:

— remove spare wheel and tool bag;

— disconnect fuel delivery line to pump;

— disconnect the cable to fuel reserve supply indicator;

— remove the four screws with clips fixing the tank to body;

— take off tank.

Carefully drain tank before cleaning or repairing.

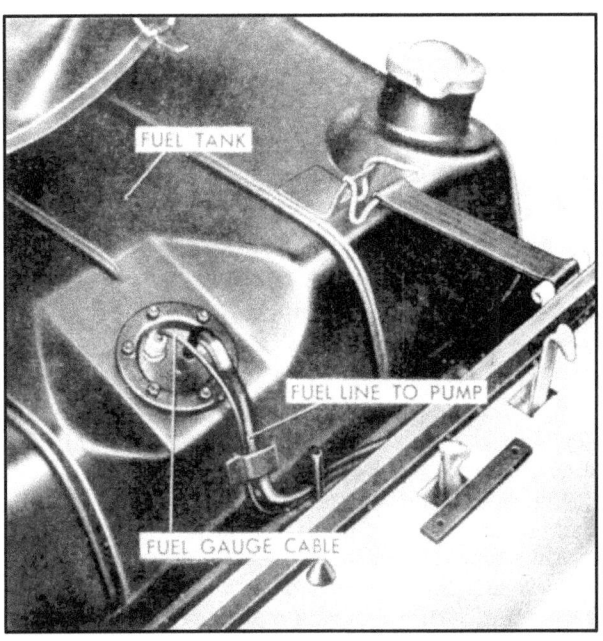

Fig. 114 - Fuel tank in front compartment.

The fuel reserve supply indicator (red light) glows when fuel amount in tank is less than .8 to 1.1 Imp. gals - .9 to 1.3 U. S. gals (3,5 to 5 lt).

Fig. 115.

Power plant (air conveyor and cylinder head cover removed).

NOTE - Before removing pump and relevant lines for cleaning and inspection, disconnect plastic pipe on tank to prevent the flow of fuel from tank through syphoning.

WEBER CARBURETORS TYPE 26 IMB 1 AND 26 IMB 3

Operation	page	72
Starting Device	»	73
Idle Speed Adjustment	»	75
Carburetor Trouble Shooting Instructions	»	75
Carburetor Servicing Instructions	»	76
Carburetor Cleaning Instructions	»	77
Setting Data of Weber 26 IMB 1 (Sedan) and 26 IMB 3 (Sports Car) Carburetors	»	77

The Weber 26 IMB1 carburetor is a downdraft, single body carburetor with 1.0236" (26 mm) diameter throat at the height of throttle shaft.

The fuel mixture rating system consists of a throttle valve controlled by accelerator pedal through a cable which operates a lever secured to throttle valve shaft. This carburetor is fitted with a progressive-action starting device which enables the driver to suit the mixture richness to the most varied conditions of starting, until the engine has reached the rated operation temperature.

The dampened needle valve ensures a smooth engine running since, thanks to its dampening device, it is not affected by vibrations and, therefore, keeps steadily constant the level in carburetor bowl.

Secondary Venturi diameter is .8268" (21 mm) and is in a single casting with carburetor body. A fuel strainer is incorporated in carburetor cover.

Operation.

Referring to the diagram (fig. 116) the air from above, flows through Venturi (24) where it mixes with the fuel issuing from nozzle (25) and is then conveyed to cylinders through primary Venturi (21) and throat, where throttle (19) is adjusting the flow.

From fuel line, joined to carburetor by connection (8), the fuel flows across filter gauze (7), through needle valve (10) into bowl (16) where float (12) hinged to pivot (11) controls the opening of needle (10) and maintains a constant fuel level.

From bowl (16) - via metered main jet (15) - fuel reaches emulsion well (23) whence, after having been mixed with the air coming from metered air corrector screw (1), through emulsion orifices (22) and spray nozzle (25), it finally reaches the Venturis where it blends with the air stream promoted by engine suction and is then drawn into cylinders.

The purpose of secondary Venturi (24) is to increase the vacuum around nozzle (25) and to carry the air/fuel mixture to the center of primary Venturi (21).

While idling, through an appropriate passage fuel is carried from well (23) to idle speed jet (13) where it is mixed with the air coming from air inlet (5). Through duct (3) and idle speed orifice (18) - adjustable by taper-point screw (17) - the fuel reaches carburetor throat past throttle (19) where it is further mixed with the air stream drawn in by engine vacuum through the gap around the throttle in idling speed position.

From duct (3) the mixture can also reach the carburetor throttle chamber through transition hole (20), located in exact relation to the throttle; the purpose of this progression hole is to permit a smooth acceleration of engine from idling speed, proportionately to the increase in throttle opening.

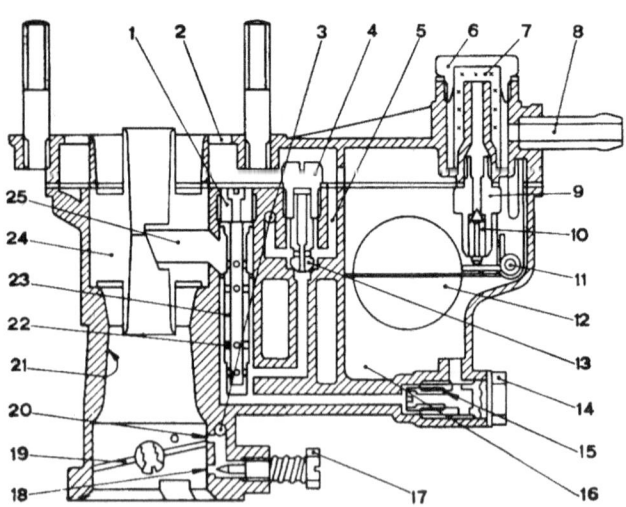

Fgi. 116.

Diagrammatic section of Weber 26 IMB1 carburetor.

1. Air corrector jet. - 2. Air inlet. - 3. Idle speed mixture duct. - 4. Idle speed jet holder. - 5. Idle speed air orifice. - 6. Filter cover. - 7. Filter. - 8. Fuel inlet connection. - 9. Needle valve seat. - 10. Needle. - 11. Float pivot. - 12. Float. - 13. Idle speed jet. - 14. Main jet holder. - 15. Main jet. - 16. Bowl. - 17. Idle speed mixture adjustment screw. - 18. Idle speed mixture orifice. - 19. Throttle. - 20. Transition hole. - 21. Primary Venturi (not interchangeable). - 22. Emulsion orifices. - 23. Emulsion well. - 24. Secondary Venturi (not interchangeable). - 25. Main nozzle.

ENGINE: FUEL SYSTEM

Starting Device (fig. 117).

This device has the function of ensuring proper engine cold starting. It is controlled by means of the lever placed behind the gearbox lever and must be progressively set back to rest position as engine is reaching the rated operation temperature. The starting device is made up of valve (33, fig. 117) actuated by the lug of rocker (36) connected, through a suitable shaft, to control lever (38). By pulling the device control to stroke end, through lever (38) and rocker (36), valve (33) is lifted from its seat and brought in the « fully open » position (diagram « A », figure 117). Under these conditions valve (33) closes air hole (27) and mixture hole (29) and uncovers mixture orifices (30) (32) [which communicate with starting jet (46) through duct (26)] and air holes (35). With valve (33) partially opened, hole (29) may communicate with carburetor throat, through the valve central slot, duct (28) and hole (31) drilled in Venturi (21) in correspondence with the restriction.

With throttle in idling speed position, the vacuum of engine cranked by the starter causes the fuel contained in the recess of jet (46), in the jet and in reserve well (45) to be emulsioned with the air coming from holes (43) and (44). Through duct (26) and holes (30) and (32) the mixture arrives - simultaneously with air from holes (35) - past the throttle through duct (34), thus permitting prompt starting of the engine.

After engine firing the device delivers a mixture whose fuel/air ratio is such as to permit regular running of engine while still cold. But, as the engine warms up, this mixture would be excessive and too rich; therefore, it becomes necessary to exclude gradually the device as the engine is reaching the rated operation temperature. During this maneuver, valve (33) slowly uncovers hole (27) which permits a greater amount of air to enter through spring guide hole (42) (to weaken the mixture) while, by closing progressively holes (30) and (32) and air holes (35) also the amount of mixture is reduced (see diagram « B », fig. 117).

Hole (29), duct (28), and hole (31), drilled in Venturi (21), have the task of permitting a regular progression of acceleration also with cold engine. By opening throttle (19) to speed up the engine, the vacuum acting on duct (34) is reduced. This would cause a reduction in the amount of fuel delivered through said duct (34), with consequent irregular running of the engine, but, through hole (31), duct (28) and hole (29) (from which air is drawn when throttle is closed), some mixture is sucked in by the vacuum formed in the restriction of the Venturi consequent to the opening of the throttle, and this compensates for the reduction in delivery through duct (34).

When the starting device is excluded, valve (33) covers also hole (29) and prevents the entrance of mixture (diagram « C », fig. 117).

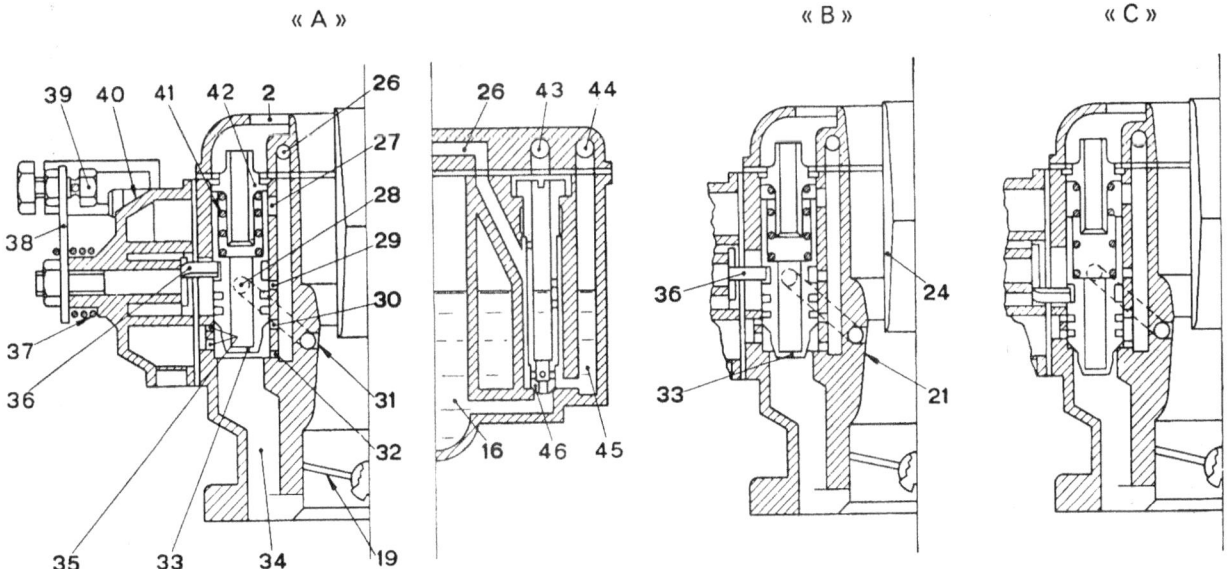

Fig. 117 - Starting device (choke) diagrammatic section.

« A »: Device fully inserted. - « B »: Device partially inserted. - « C »: Device disinserted.

2. Air inlet. - 16. Bowl. - 19. Throttle. - 21. Primary Venturi. - 24. Secondary Venturi. - 26. Mixture duct. - 27. Mixture leaning air orifice. - 28. Transition duct. - 29. Transition mixture orifice. - 30. Starting mixture orifice. - 31. Transition orifice. - 32. Starting mixture orifice. - 33. Starting valve. - 34. Mixture duct. - 35. Starting device air orifices. - 36. Rocker. - 37. Lever return spring. - 38. Starting device control lever. - 39. Control wire screw. - 40. Cover with support for starting device control bowden. - 41. Starting valve spring. - 42. Spring casing. 43. Starting jet emulsion air orifice. - 44. Air emulsion reserve well orifice. - 45. Starting reserve well. - 46. Starting jet.

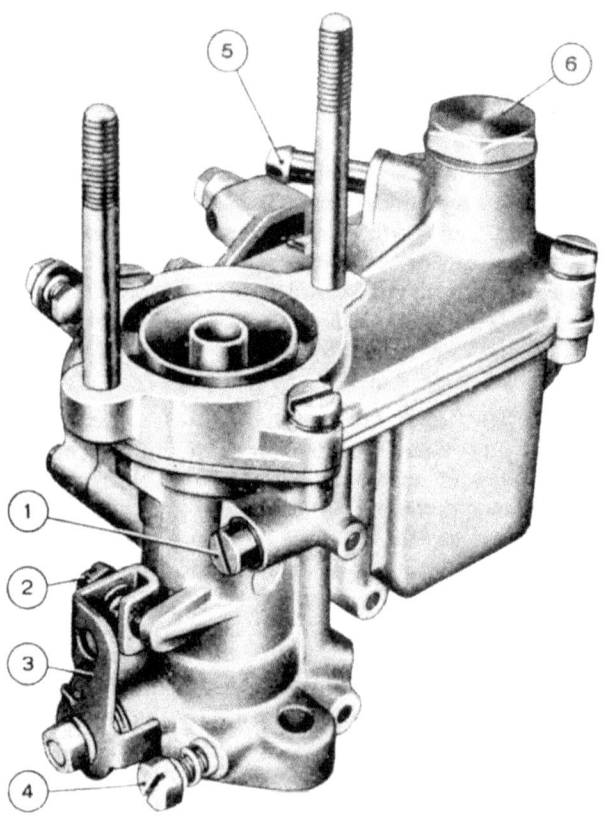

Fig. 118 - Weber 26 IMB 1 carburetor.

1. Idle speed jet holder. - 2. Slow running adjustment screw. - 3. Throttle control lever. - 4. Idle speed mixture adjustment screw. - 5. Fuel inlet connection. - 6. Strainer plug.

CHOKE USE DIRECTIONS

To avail of all the advantages the progressive-action starting device may offer, use it as follows:

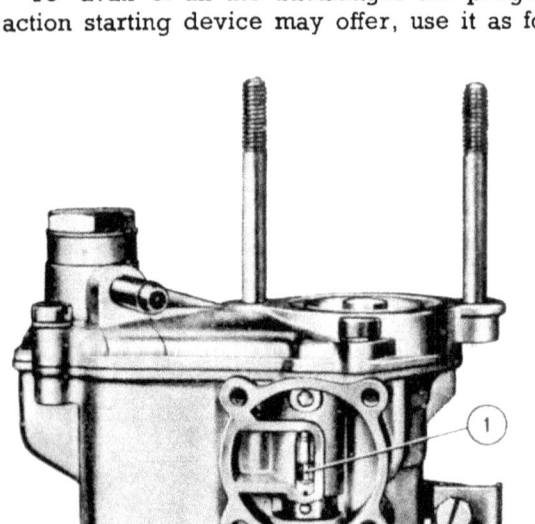

Engine Starting.

Cold starts - fully throw in the device (position A, fig. 119); after engine fires push the control part way in.

Warm starts - throw in the device only partially (position B, fig. 119).

Engine Warm-up.

During engine warming-up period, even with car running, push home gradually the starting device lever through successive stages so as to supply the engine with a supplementary amount of mixture as strictly necessary for a regular and smooth engine operation (position B, fig. 119).

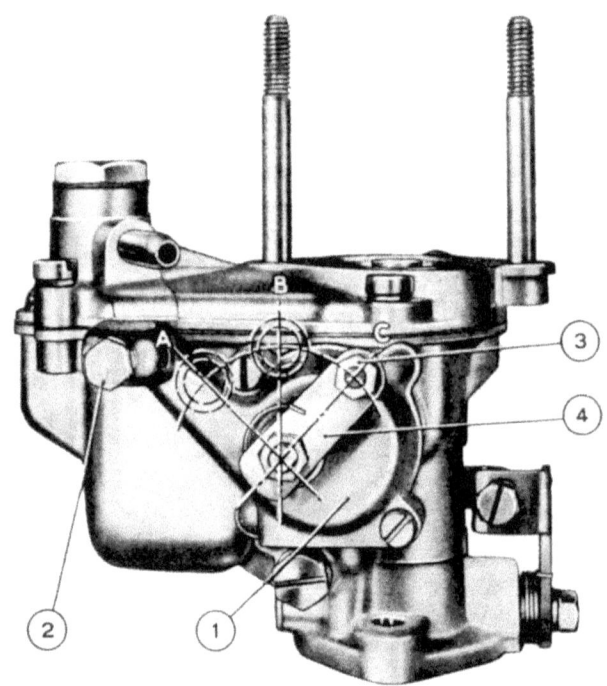

Fig. 119 - Weber 26 IMB 1 carburetor, starting device (choke) end.

1. Choke device cover. - 2. Bowden mounting screw. - 3. Nut and screw, choke bowden wire. - 4. Choke control lever.

A. Position of lever 4 for « fully inserted » choke. - B. « Partially inserted » choke. - C. « Disinserted » choke.

Fig. 120.

Weber 26 IMB 1 carburetor, with choke device cover removed.

1. Choke valve. - 2. Choke device cover. - 3. Choke valve shaft.

ENGINE: FUEL SYSTEM

Normal Car Driving.

As soon as the engine has reached the rated operation temperature, exclude completely the starting device by bringing the control lever to position C (fig. 119).

Idle Speed Adjustment (fig. 121).

Idling speed is adjusted by throttle setscrew (fig. 121) and mixture setscrew. Throttle screw allows of adjusting the throttle opening; conical mixture setscrew has the purpose of metering the amount of mixture coming from idling speed passage, which will then blend with the air flowing past the throttle that, in idle speed setting, leaves a gap between its edges and the throat walls.

This makes possible a rating of mixture best suited to engine requirements and smooth operation.

Always adjust idling speed with engine running and warm by first setting throttle to minimum opening by throttle setscrew so as to ensure steady operation.

Next, by turning mixture setscrew in or out, set mixture richness to the most suitable ratio for said throttle opening, thus accomplishing a fast and steady idling; reduce minimum throttle opening some more, by throttle setscrew, until best idling speed is obtained.

Carburetor Trouble Shooting Instructions.

Carburetor should be serviced only if carburetion is definitely at fault.

Some possible causes may be:

Flooded carburetor: improperly seated needle valve.

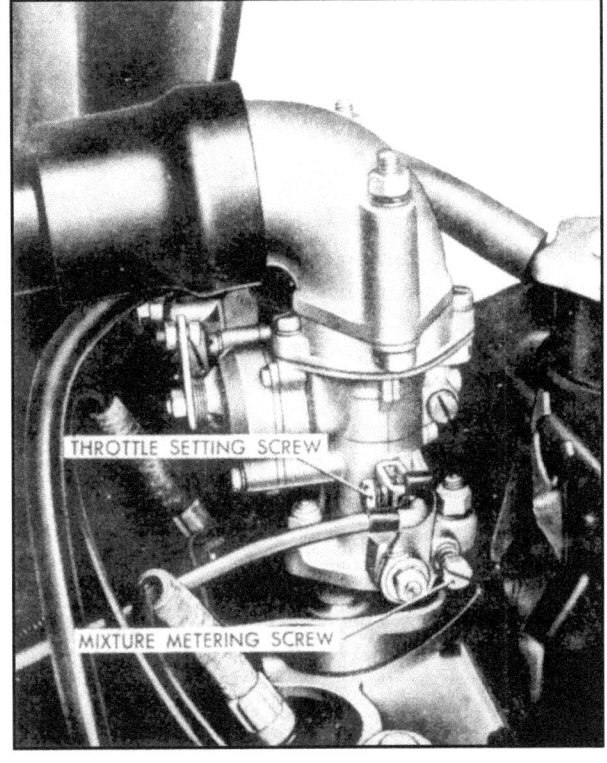

Fig. 121 - Weber 26 IMB 1 carburetor in place on engine.

Idle speed is adjusted by working respectively on throttle setting screw and mixture metering screw.

Engine does not start when cold: starting device operation is irregular because starting jet is obstructed or starting device control travel has shortened.

Engine does not start when warm: clogged jets or passages, misadjusted idle speed circuit.

Engine does not idle: clogged jets or passages, misadjusted idle speed circuit.

Fig. 122.
Weber 26 IMB 1 carburetor, open.

1. Emulsion well with air bleed jet. - 2. Secondary Venturi. - 3. Nozzle tube. - 4. Spring retainer and guide. - 5. Choke valve spring lock ring. - 6. Gasket and carburetor cover. - 7. Cover locating dowel. - 8. Fuel bowl. - 9. Choke jet. - 10. Float.

Engine pick up is poor: obstructed main jet or emulsion orifices.

Excessive gasoline consumption: foreign matter in emulsion well calibrated orifices.

Carburetor Servicing Instructions.

FUEL LEVEL IN BOWL

The needle valve seat and float are easily accessible for inspection by removing the carburetor cover.

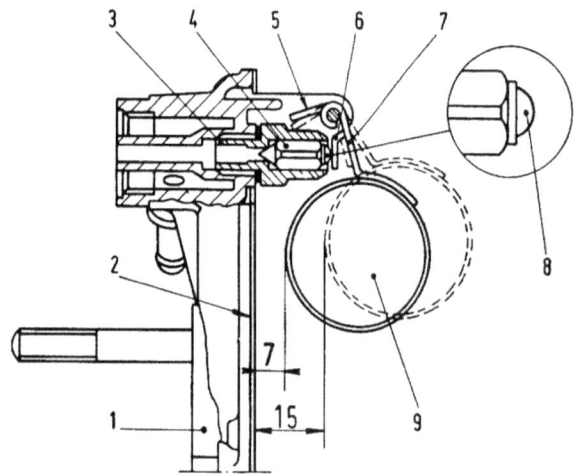

Fig. 123 - Float adjustment data.

1. Carburetor cover. - 2. Cover gasket. - 3. Needle valve seat. - 4. Needle. - 5. Lug. - 6-7. Arms. - 8. Needle ball. - 9. Float.
7 = .2756" - 15 = .5906"

Before checking level in bowl, see that:

— needle valve seat is well screwed in and gasket is in place;

— calibrated orifice in valve seat is unobstructed and not worn;

— the needle slides freely in its guide.

In case sealing is imperfect, replace the valve assembly:

— the float is not distorted or broken and moves on its pivot without drag or excessive play; replace if these conditions are not met.

Next, check the level and proceed as directed hereafter (fig. 123):

a) Check that needle valve (3) is screwed tight in its seat.

b) Keep carburetor cover (1) upright or else the weight of float (9) would lower ball (8) fitted on needle (4).

c) Check that with cover held vertical and float arm (6) in slight contact with ball (8) of needle (4), the float is .2756" (7 mm) away from cover with gasket (2) flat against cover face.

d) Check that float travel is .3150" (8 mm); if necessary, bend lug (5) as required.

e) If float (9) is not correctly positioned, bend float arms (7) until the correct adjustment is obtained. See that arm (6) is perpendicular to needle axis and does not show rough spots or indents which might impair free sliding of the needle.

f) Check that float (9) rotates freely around ist pivot pin.

As a rule, the above adjustment operations must be performed every time a new float is installed.

CAUTION - Should replacement of the needle valve be required, make sure first that the new valve seat is screwed tight in its lodging with a new seal interposed. This will mean that the level check must be repeated.

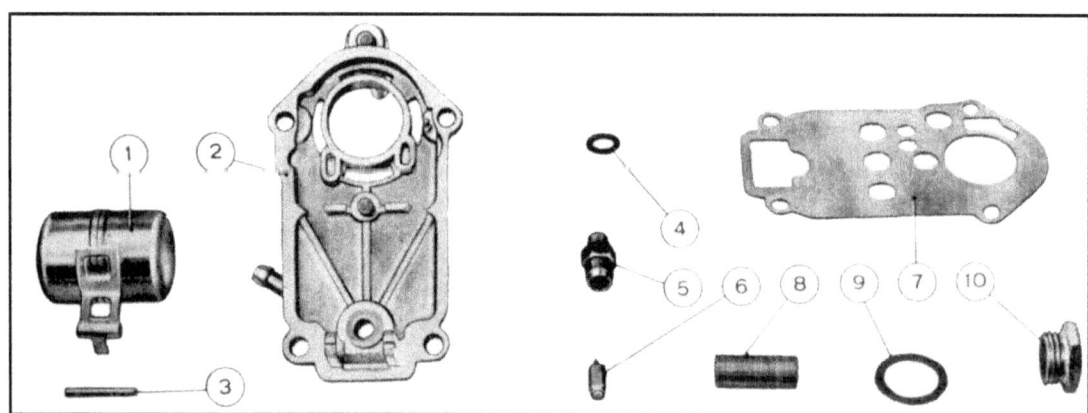

Fig. 124 - Weber 26 IMB 1 carburetor cover components.

1. Float. - 2. Carburetor cover. - 3. Float pivot. - 4. Needle valve for gasket. - 5-6. Needle valve seat and needle valve. - 7. Cover gasket. 8. Filter strainer. - 9. Gasket. - 10. Filter inspection plug.

ENGINE: FUEL SYSTEM

THROTTLE VALVE COMPONENTS

Throttle valve shaft should rotate freely in its guides even when engine is very warm. Excessive clearances caused by wear and throttle valve distortions must not be tolerated, as they are liable to cause irregular engine operation especially at idling speed.

Should above conditions be experienced, replace throttle valve and shaft assembly and seal rings.

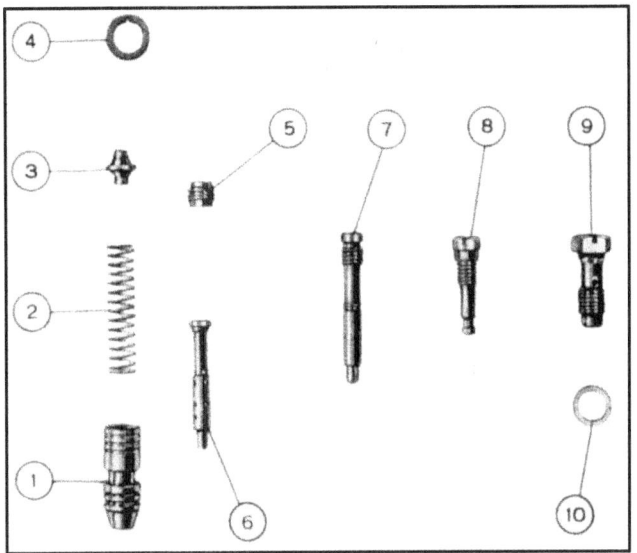

Fig. 126 - Jets, jet holders and choke valve.

1. Choke valve. - 2. Spring. - 3. Spring retainer and guide. - 4. Lock ring. - 5. Air bleed jet. - 6. Emulsion well. - 7. Choke jet. - 8. Idling jet holder and jet. - 9. Main jet holder and jet. - 10. Main jet holder gasket.

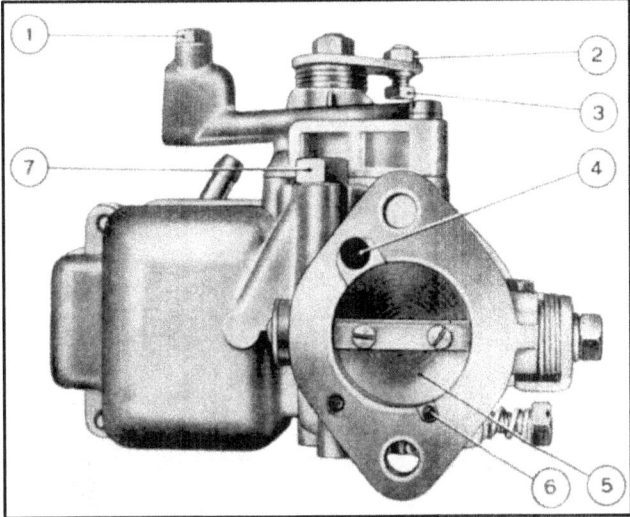

Fig. 125 - Weber 26 IMB 1 carburetor.

1. Bowden mounting screw. - 2-3. Nut and screw, choke bowden wire. - 4. Starting mixture duct. - 5. Throttle. - 6. Idle speed passage. 7. Main jet holder.

Carburetor Cleaning Instructions.

For thorough cleaning of carburetor, proceed as follows:

Passages. - All fuel passages have a diameter that is the most appropriate to insure best operating conditions: it is therefore essential to remove any dirt or scale deposited by fuel, which would alter undesirably the conditions of operation. Clean with gasoline and blow dry with compressed air all passages in castings. Do not pass drills or other metal points through jets and passages because these would be altered in their calibrated diameters.

Calibrated parts. - Idling and main jet holders, and relevant bayonet-coupled jets, are easily removed by using a wrench or a screwdriver.

To clean the different calibrated parts, wash in gasoline and blow with a compressed air blast. We strongly advise against the use of metallic points or other unsuitable tools which may irreparably upset the pre-established calibration of orifices.

Should it be necessary to disassemble carburetor adjustment components for inspection of some parts, make sure that after re-assembly parts are again well tight in their seats to avoid possible operating troubles.

Strainer. - To clean the strainer, unscrew and take off its plug, with gasket, on carburetor cover and then pull out the strainer.

Clean strainer seat carefully. Wash strainer in gasoline and blow clean with an air blast.

SETTING DATA OF WEBER 26 IMB 1 (SEDAN) AND 26 IMB 3 (SPORTS CAR) CARBURETORS

	500		Sports Car	
	in	mm	in	mm
Throat diameter	1.0236	26	1.0236	26
Primary Venturi diameter	.8268	21	.8661	22
Main jet diameter	.0441	1,12	.0433	1,25
Idling jet diameter	.0177	0,45	.0177	0,45
Choke jet diameter	.0354 F 5	0,90 F 5	.0354 F 5	0,90 F 5
Main air jet diameter	.0925	2,35	.0925	2,35
Needle seat (dampened) diameter	.0492	1,25	.0492	1,25

LUBRICATION SYSTEM

Description	page	78
CENTRIFUGAL OIL FILTER	»	79
Inspection and Cleaning	»	80
OIL PUMP	»	81
Disassembly	»	81
Inspection	»	82
Reassembly	»	83
LOW OIL PRESSURE INDICATOR SENDING UNIT	»	83

Description.

Engine is pressure-lubricated through a gear-type pump, incorporated in timing gear cover and axially driven by camshaft via a front dog clutch engagement (figs. 131-138).

The pump draws oil from sump through a suction scoop (1, fig. 131) provided with filtering screen, fixed to crankcase in corrispondence with hole (2) communicating with duct (3) in timing gear cover (4) and hence with pump.

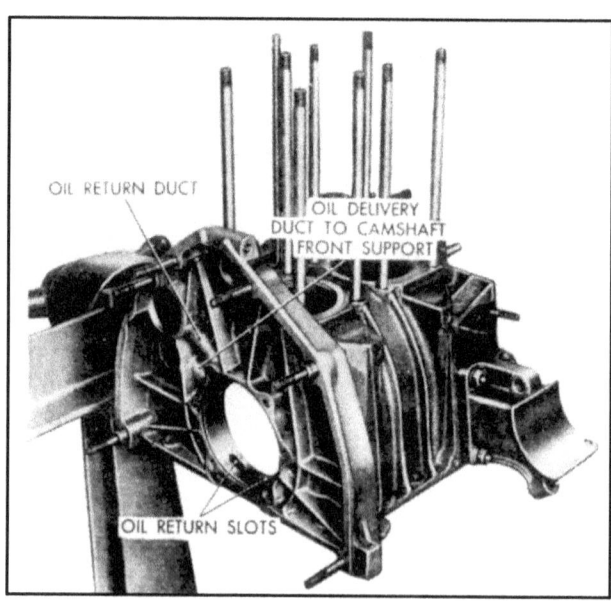

Fig. 128 - Engine crankcase - flywheel end - with indication of lubrication ducts.

Fig. 127 - View of engine bottom with oil pump suction scoop.

From camshaft rear seat the oil passes on to crankshaft rear support whence it flows into an adjacent chamber; from here, through suitable groovings in crankshaft front end it reaches the centrifugal filter.

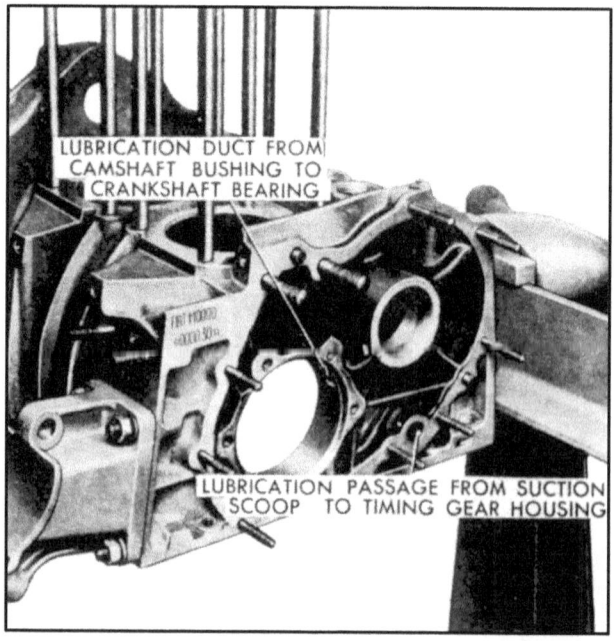

Fig. 129 - Engine crankcase - timing gear drive end - with indication of lubrication ducts.

ENGINE: LUBRICATION SYSTEM

The centrifugal filter rotates integrally with crankshaft and performs also as a pulley for generator and blower drive.

From filter, the oil enters a passage in crankshaft, lubricates main and connecting rod bearings, and, through a groove in front main bearing and ducts rifled in crankcase, it reaches the insufficient oil pressure sending unit and the delivery pipe for lubrication of rocker supports (see fig. 142).

The four pushrod sleeves provide the return of oil from cylinder head to two cavities machined in crankcase (tappets have a lateral hole to permit the passage of oil).

Said cavities communicate: one with the timing gear housing, and the other with crankshaft front support drain.

Oil pressure is controlled by a relief valve (5, fig. 131) coaxially mounted with respect to camshaft rear end.

It consists of a hubbed disc sliding on guide (6) of oil pump drive shaft (7). Under the load imposed by spring (9) the valve disc circumferentially closes an annular chamber communicating with the lubrication circuit.

Excessive oil pressure will cause the disc to uncover the chamber.

Fig. 130 - Engine without cylinder head cover.
The tube carrying oil to rockers passes inside the central casing.

CENTRIFUGAL OIL FILTER

The oil filter is of the centrifugal type and is formed by two flanges and an oil slinger. The filter is installed on crankshaft rear end.

Fig. 131 - Detail of engine longitudinal section through oil pump.

1. Suction scoop. - 2. Hole in crankcase. - 3. Duct in timing sprocket cover. - 4. Timing sprocket cover. - 5. Oil pressure relief valve. - 6. Drive shaft guide and oil pump cover. - 7. Oil pump driving gear shaft. - 8. Camshaft. - 9. Oil pressure relief valve spring.

Shaft (7) for oil pump drive gear is controlled, as shown in the figure, by a front teeth coupling and by a sleeve press fitted in camshaft. Furthermore, the shaft is hollow to permit the passage of lube oil to camshaft rear seat.

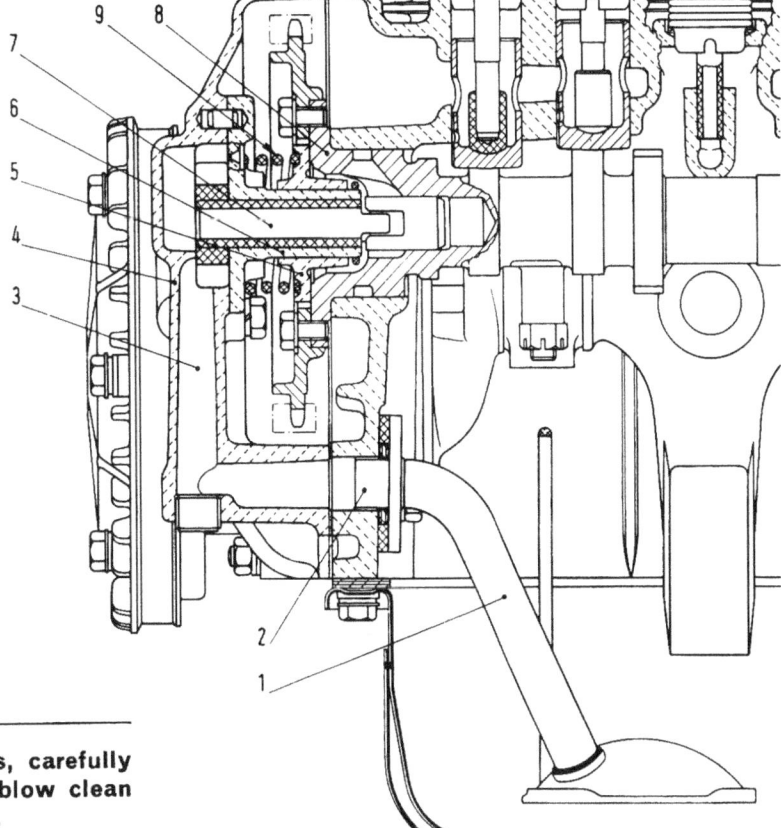

NOTE - While overhaul is in progress, carefully wash all oil ducts and passages and blow clean with a strong blast of compressed air.

Fig. 132 - Pulley-centrifugal filter assembly and oil suction ducts, on partially cut-away engine.

Fig. 134 - Engine detail showing lube oil passages.

1. Splines in crankshaft for oil passage to filter. - 2. Oil inlet into circuit from filter. - 3. Hole for oil passage to main bearing.

The diameter of the slinger (fig. 133) is smaller than that of the flanges but is sufficient to sling the oil into an area where the centrifugal force separates the dirt.

The radial vanes provided on outer flange inner face retain the dirt and convey the oil towards the center of filter.

The oil, coming from the side splines (1, fig. 134) of crankshaft is forced by the slinger to the periphery of filter, where it is cleaned, then returning to the filter center and hence into crankshaft (2, fig. 134).

The inner flange, or hub, and the slinger are secured to crankshaft by a hollow screw (fig. 133); the outer flange is fixed to hub by six peripheral screws.

A groove is machined on the outer flange periphery to adapt the generator and blower drive belt.

Inspection and Cleaning.

Check the conditions of outer-to-inner flange seal gaskets.

Replace the gaskets if oil leaks are noticed.

On account of its obvious importance in ensuring the satisfactory lubrication of engine components,

Fig. 133 - Hub for generator-blower drive pulley and for centrifugal filter.

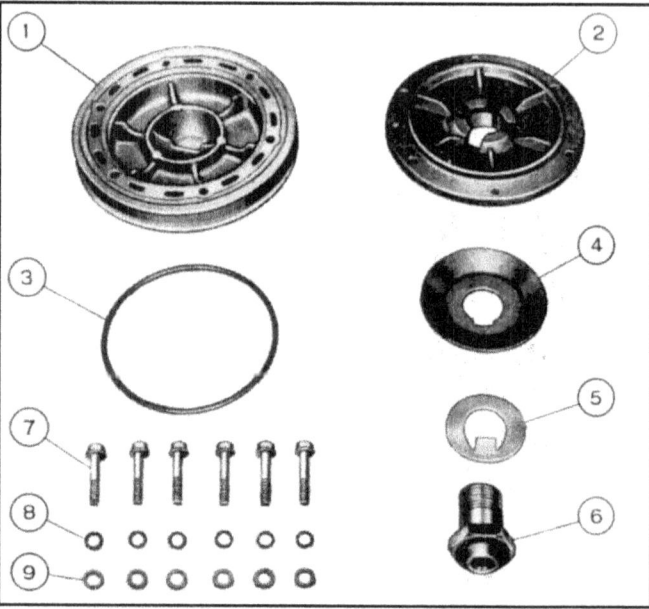

Fig. 135 - Centrifugal oil filter components.

1. Drive pulley. - 2. Rotor hub. - 3. Seal ring. - 4. Oil slinger. - 5. Lock plate. - 6. Hub-to-crankshaft hollow screw. - 7-8-9. Pulley-to-hub mounting screws, toothed washers and plain washers.

ENGINE: LUBRICATION SYSTEM

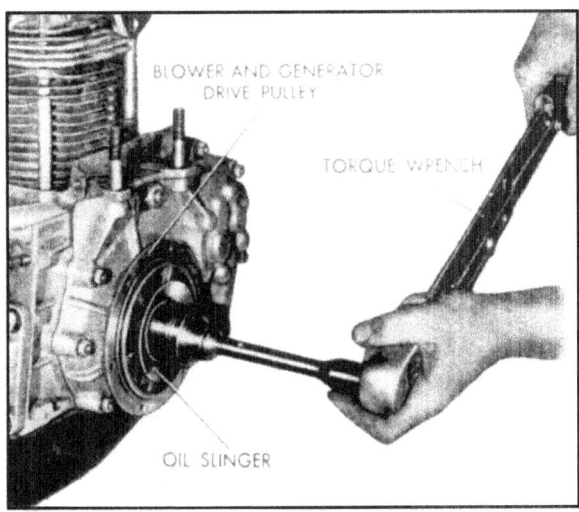

Fig. 136 - Tightening crankshaft pulley screw with torque wrench.

(Tightening torque of 108.5 ft.lbs - 15.000 kgmm).

the oil filter must receive particular cleaning care. Filter should therefore be cleaned everytime engine is overhauled.

To clean filter, take down the cover-pulley and accurately scrape its inner surface to remove any possible trace of sludge accumulated on and between the vanes.

Cover removal is very easy (see fig. 135 for centrifugal oil filter components).

NOTE - The filter-to-crankshaft hollow mounting screw must be tightened with a torque wrench to 108.5 ft.lbs (15.000 kgmm); the cover-to-mounting flange fixing screws must instead be tightened to 5.8 ft.lbs (800 kgmm).

Fig. 137 - Engine rear end with generator pulley, and centrifugal filter pulley.

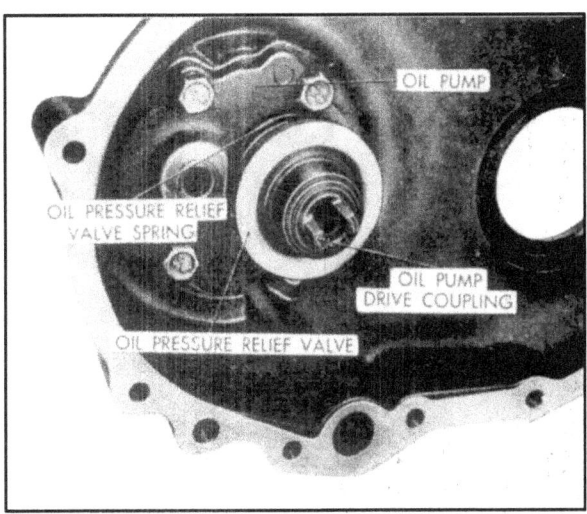

Fig. 138 - Oil pump and pressure relief valve installed on timing sprocket cover.

OIL PUMP

The helical-spur gear type pump is camshaft-driven through a front dog clutch engagement.

Pump gears are located in a special housing in timing gear cover where they are held by a cover plate; bossed through-holes are machined in cover plate for gear shafts passage. On drive gear shaft guide is mounted the pressure relief valve.

The pump suction scoop, provided with filtering screen, is secured in crankcase and communicates with a duct in timing gear case (fig. 132).

Disassembling the Pump.

To take pump down from engine proceed as follows:

Disassemble the engine rear central support from timing gear casing.

Take off the filter cover pulley and remove the V-belt.

Fig. 139 - Timing sprocket cover with oil pump casing.

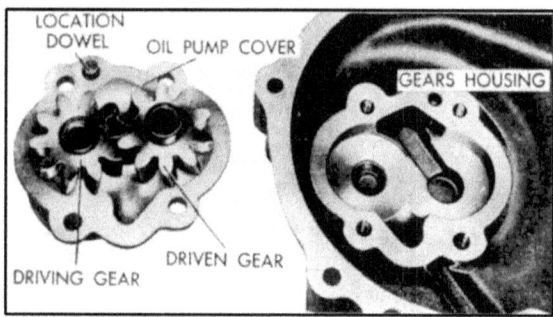

Fig. 140 - Gears, cover and housing of oil pump.

Back out the hollow screw fixing the slinger and mounting flange of filter on crankshaft.

Unscrew the nuts fixing timing gear cover to crankcase.

Take off the timing gear cover and, with it, also the oil pump assy and the pressure relief valve will come off.

Take out pump suction scoop (with screen) from sump.

To disassemble the pump components:

Remove lock ring and disinsert the pressure relief valve and spring.

Take off pump cover-plate and pull out the gears and shafts.

Inspection.

After disassembly, accurately wash all components and blow clean with a compressed air blast. Then:

1) Inspect the timing gear cover carefully:
— no cracks must be noticed; if any, replace the cover;
— inner duct for oil delivery to pump must be unobstructed; send in a strong blow of compressed air to provide good cleaning.

2) Check oil pump gear teeth.

If any trace of damage or excessive wear is found, replace the gears.

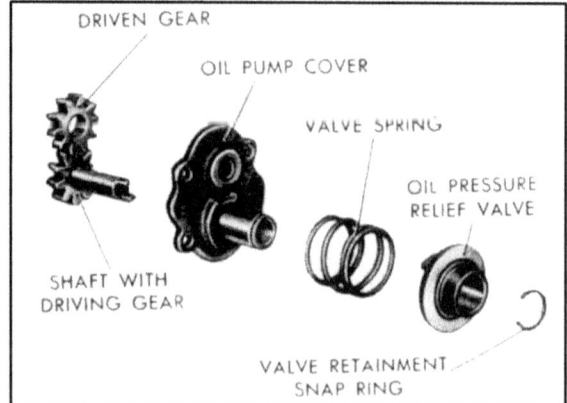

Fig. 141 - Disassembled oil pump and pressure relief valve.

Specified backlash is .0059'' (0,15 mm). If lash is greater than .0079'' (0,20 mm) gears should be replaced, because this is the maximum allowable limit for backlash.

3) Check the clearance between gear teeth and housing walls in timing gear cover: specified clearance is .0012'' to .0035'' (0,03 to 0,09 mm). Generally, this clearance never increases appreciably. However, should it exceed .0047'' (0,12 mm) (max. allowable limit) after a long period of operation, replace the gears and, if necessary, also the timing gear cover.

4) Check that drive gear is solidly press-fitted on its shaft. Specified pinch fit is .0016'' to .0031'' (0,04 to 0,08 mm).

5) Driven gear-to-shaft fit clearance is instead of .00079'' to .00236'' (0,02 to 0,06 mm). Check that it doesn't exceed the maximum allowable limit of .0039'' (0,10 mm).

6) Check the drive and driven gear widths using a micrometer. When new, specified width is .3937'' to .3928'' (10,000 to 9,978 mm). Should this value result less than .3917'' (9,95 mm), replace the gears.

The spare drive gear is supplied complete with its shaft.

7) Check the drive gear shaft-to-seat fit clearance, which is .00063'' to .00276'' (0,016 to 0,070 mm); if clearance exceeds the maximum wear limit of .0059'' (0,15 mm), replace the most worn part or both, as required.

8) The driven gear shaft is instead press-fitted in its seat in cover plate. Pinch fit is .0016'' to .0039'' (0,04 to 0,10 mm).

If any clearance is found, replace the shaft.

9) On pump cover plate, check with a micrometer the outer diameter of the drive gear shaft guide boss on which the oil pressure relief valve slides.

This diameter, when new, is .7874'' to .7866'' (20,000 to 19,979 mm) while the inner diameter of valve is .7882'' to .7895'' (20,000 to 20,053 mm): the clearance between these parts is thus of .00079'' to .00291'' (0,020 to 0,074 mm).

If clearance is greater than the wear limit of .0059'' (0,15 mm), replace the most worn part or both, as required.

The cover plate is supplied as a spare complete with driven gear shaft and location dowel.

10) Inspect the filtering screen of pump suction scoop: remove any obstruction in the mesh and check for integrity. Replace if torn.

11) Check that the pump drive dog clutch is press-fitted strongly on camshaft and that wear of dogs, if any, is not excessive to the extent where transmission of the drive to pump shaft is compromised. Should this transmission not be as desired, change the clutch or the shaft - or both - as required.

ENGINE: LUBRICATION SYSTEM

Reassembling the Pump.

No particular instructions are necessary to reassemble the pump; just reverse the operations described for disassembly, minding that for correct location of pump cover plate on timing gear cover a dowel is provided.

LOW OIL PRESSURE INDICATOR SENDING UNIT

The sending unit is located on the right-hand side of cylinder block and, by electric cable, is connected to the optical indicator in instrument cluster on dashboard.

The indicator lights up (2.5-Watt red bulb) only when ignition is turned ON and goes OUT when oil pressure is sufficient for adequate lubrication.

With hot engine running below 1,000 r. p. m., the indicator may light up although everything is right.

The indicator signals when oil pressure drops as low as 14 to 8.5 psi (1 to 0,6 kg/cm^2).

NOTE - An accidental short circuit involving, for instance, the indicator bulb, may cause damage to the sending unit.

Have this point in mind in case of inoperative sending unit. Of course, the short circuit should be corrected before replacing the sender.

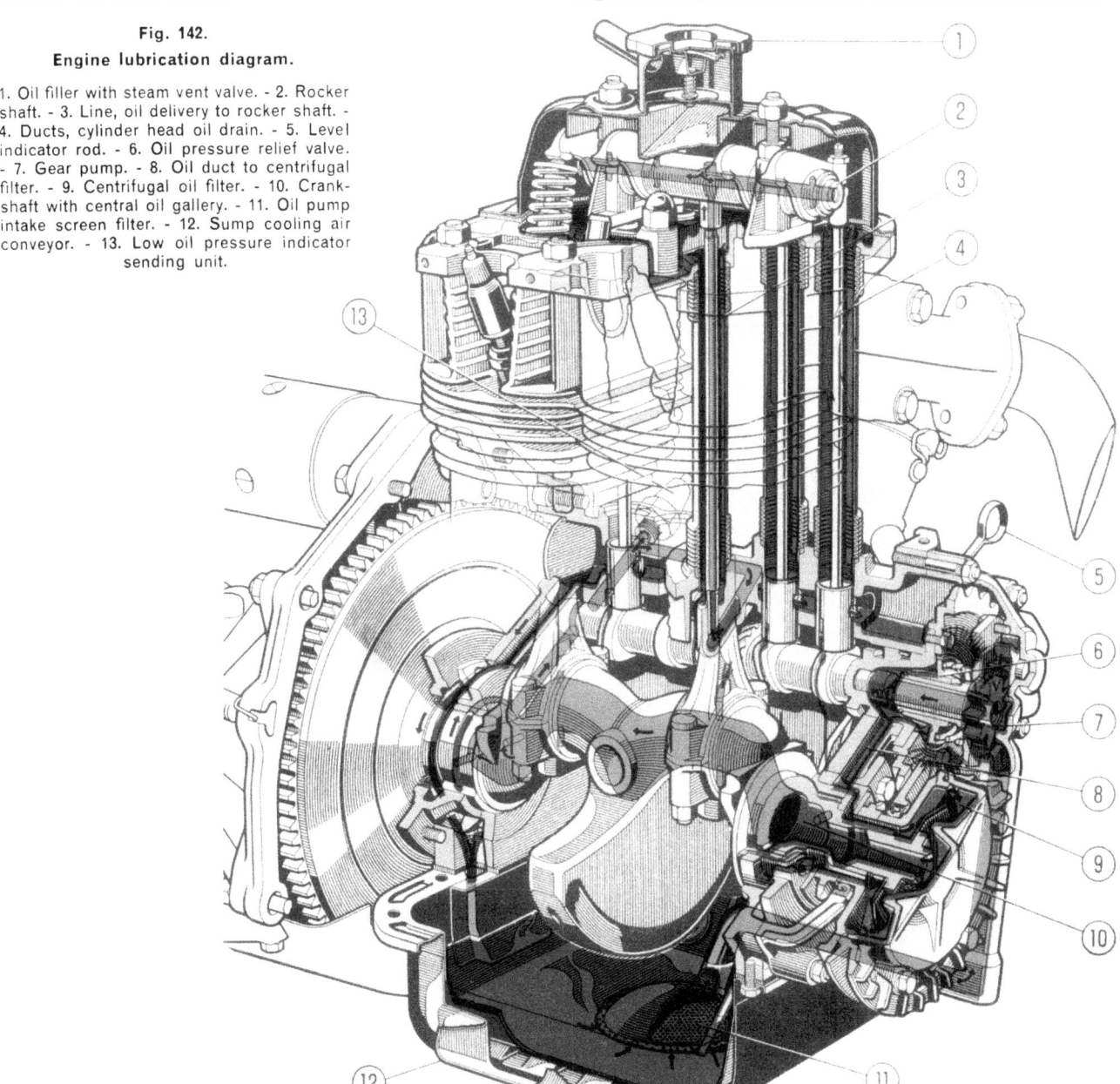

Fig. 142.
Engine lubrication diagram.

1. Oil filler with steam vent valve. - 2. Rocker shaft. - 3. Line, oil delivery to rocker shaft. - 4. Ducts, cylinder head oil drain. - 5. Level indicator rod. - 6. Oil pressure relief valve. - 7. Gear pump. - 8. Oil duct to centrifugal filter. - 9. Centrifugal oil filter. - 10. Crankshaft with central oil gallery. - 11. Oil pump intake screen filter. - 12. Sump cooling air conveyor. - 13. Low oil pressure indicator sending unit.

COOLING SYSTEM

Description . . . . page 85
AIR OUTLET THERMOSTAT AND SHUTTER . . . . » 85
ADJUSTING THE TENSION OF GENERATOR AND FAN DRIVE BELT . . . . » 86

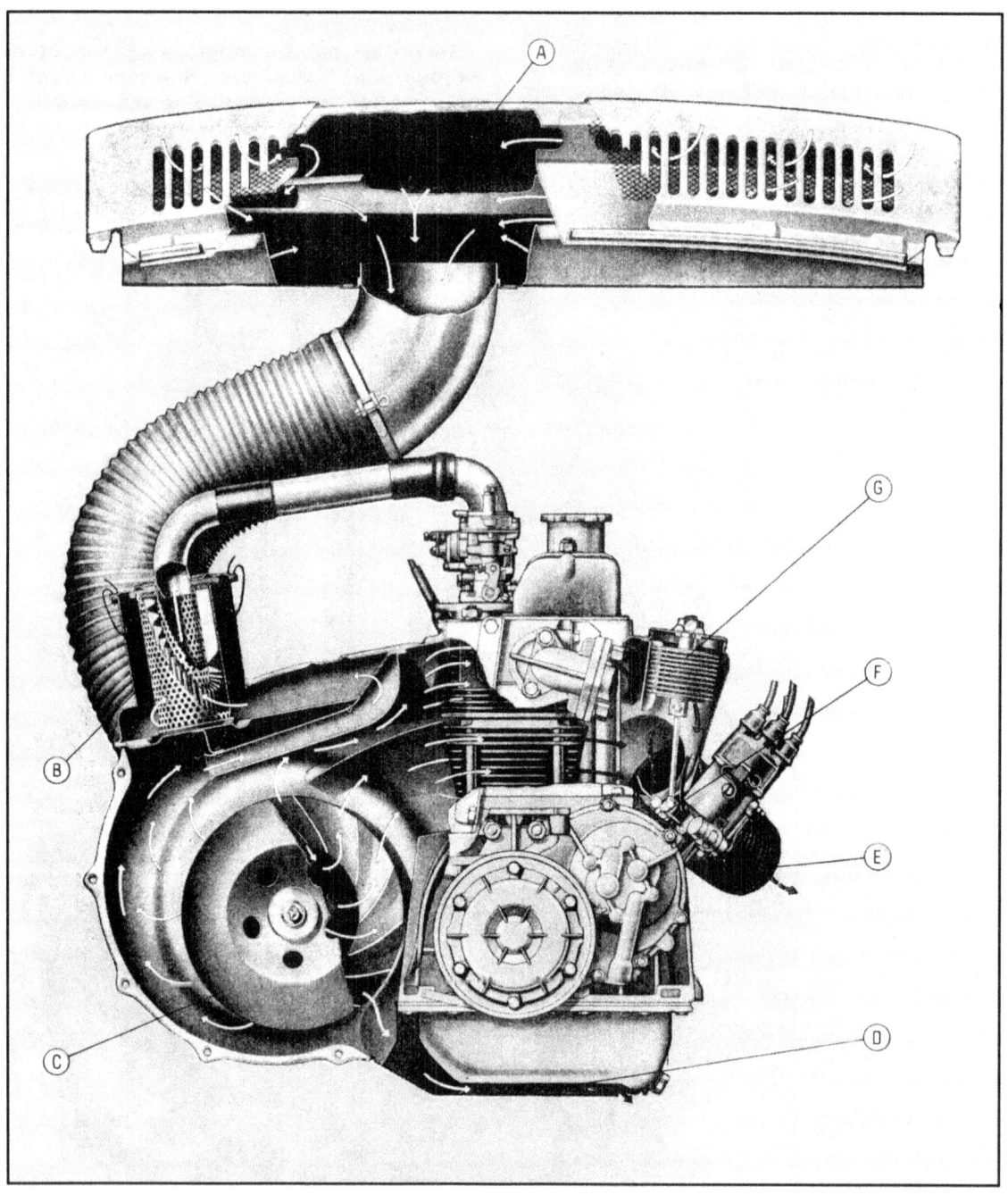

Fig. 143 - Engine cooling air circulation system.

A. Engine cooling air intake. - B. Carburetor air suction cleaner. - C. Centrifugal fan and air conveyor. - D. Oil pan cooling air passage. E. Warmed air admission hose to car interior. - F. Engine air outlet control shutter, wide open position (at 178° to 189° F - 81° to 87° C). G. Air outlet thermostat.

ENGINE: COOLING SYSTEM

Fig. 144 - Cooling blower mounted on generator shaft extension.

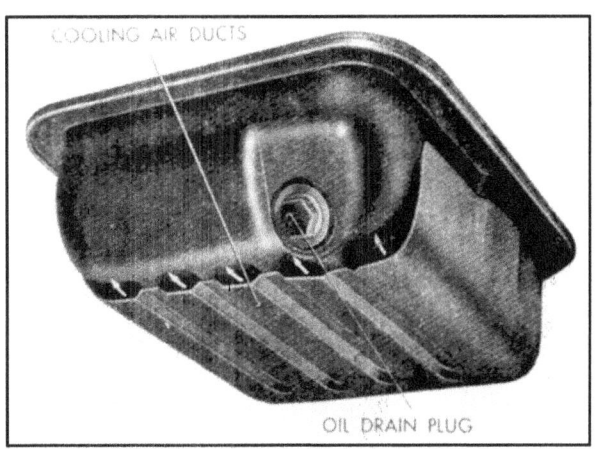

Fig. 146 - Oil sump with blower cowling.
Arrows indicate air outlets.

Description.

Engine is cooled by a forced air circulation promoted by a fan having 14 vanes arranged at different angles to reduce high-speed humming.

The fan is mounted on generator shaft output end.

Cooling system components are:

— an air intake chamber at rear end of body;

— an elbow pipe for admittance of incoming air; a tie hose to conveyor is secured to pipe through a clip.

— a spiral air conveyor containing the centrifugal fan; in air duct to cylinders, downstream of main air flow, there is an intake through which air is drawn for carburetion; specially designed ducts in sump, communicating with conveyor, serve to cool the sump (figures 143, 146, 147);

— a cowling on the opposite side to the conveyor is to collect engine air. A bellows thermostat on cowling operates a butterfly shutter which controls air outlet from engine.

NOTE - By operating the heater lever on center tunnel at rear seat, warmed air from engine cowling is admitted inside the car for heating and windshield demisting purposes.

Outlet Thermostat and Shutter.

The thermostat (G, fig. 143), located on right hand side cowling of engine, should start opening the engine heated air outlet shutter (F) with air at a temperature of 158° to 165° F (70° to 74° C). The shutter should be wide open when the air is as warm as 178° to 189° F (81° to 87° C).

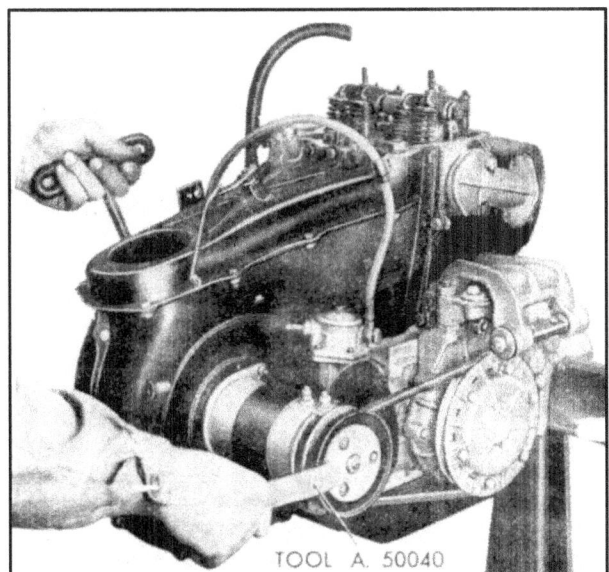

Fig. 145 - Tool A. 50040 to hold the generator shaft when removing the blower.

Fig. 147 - Oil sump with blower cowling.

Fig. 148 - View of engine assembly, partly cut-away.

Provided the engine cowling is not distorted and above conditions are favourably experienced, set the tension of thermostat-to-shutter link by varying the quantity of shims (1 to 4) which are located between thermostat upper shank and cover shoulder washer.

Remove any hindrances to shutter swiveling travel and replace the return spring, if unserviceable.

During removal and installing operations of engine shroud, or cowling, and air conveyor, utmost care should be taken to avoid the danger of distortions, which would entail air leaks on engine operation and abnormal stresses of related parts.

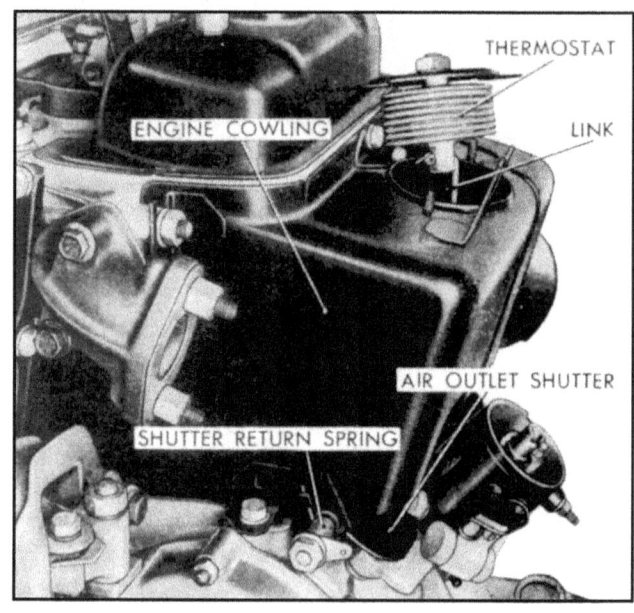

Fig. 149 - Location of cooling air outlet thermostat and shutter.

When servicing the engine cooling air control system, see that:

— the edge of the shutter in closed position mates perfectly with the cowling outline;

— the shutter can swivel freely;

— initial thermostat pulling power is .0197" to .0394" (0,5 to 1 mm).

ADJUSTING THE TENSION OF GENERATOR AND FAN DRIVE BELT

Fig. 150 - Checking the generator and blower drive belt tension.
A = Normal give-in: about 13/32" (1 cm) under a 22 lbs (10 kg) pressure; B = Nuts securing the pulley halves with spacer rings.

The generator and centrifugal fan are V-belt-driven through pulleys: the centrifugal oil filter cover/pulley on crankshaft transmits the drive to the pulley on generator.

Belt tension is correct when, under a hand pressure of about 22 lbs (10 kg), the belt sags .13/32" (1 cm) (fig. 150).

A slackened belt slips and will not drive the generator and centrifugal fan at the required speed. Under these conditions the belt will wear rapidly. Conversely, a too-tight belt induces an abnormal strain on generator bearings.

To permit the adjustment of belt tension, the pulley on generator is demountable in two halves between which spacer rings are squeezed. Tension is increased or reduced by reducing or increasing the number of spacer rings, respectively.

Place the spacer rings removed from between the pulley halves on pulley outer face so that rings may be re-inserted when fitting a new belt.

ENGINE: POWER PLANT MOUNTINGS

POWER PLANT MOUNTINGS

The power plant and differential assembly is elastically mounted on two supports.

At front the plant rests on a cross member secured under car floor through two rubber-block mountings bolted to gearbox casing (fig. 155). Position of rubber blocks on cross member is adjustable to ensure proper alignment of the assembly.

At rear the engine crankcase is sprung on body rear cross member through an articulated swinging arm that compresses a coil spring (see figs. 151, 152 and 153).

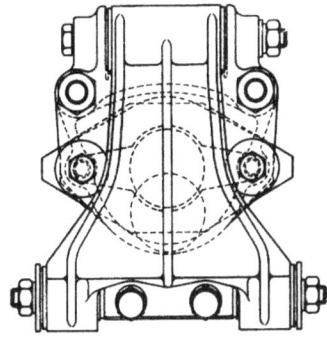

Fig. 151.

Engine rear suspension arm top view.

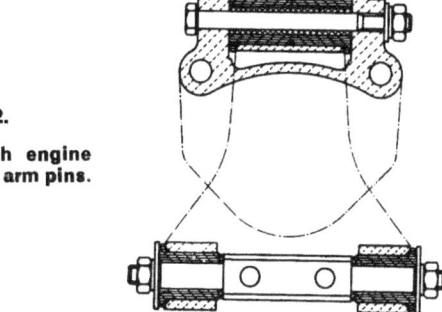

Fig. 152.

Section through engine rear suspension arm pins.

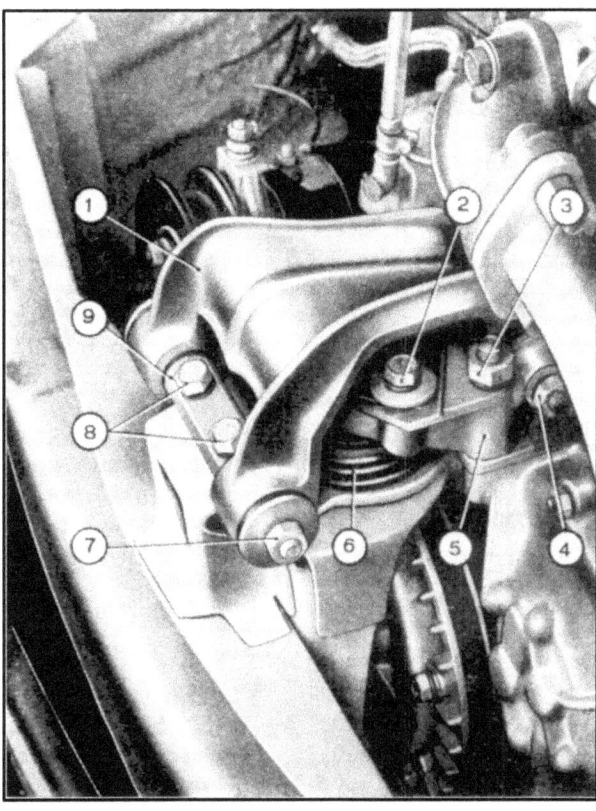

Fig. 154 - Power plant rear suspension.

1. Suspension arm. - 2. Screw, rubber pad to bracket. - 3. Bracket-to-engine nut. - 4. Nut, arm to bracket. - 5. Arm bracket. - 6. Spring. - 7. Arm pin-to-support nut. - 8. Screws, pin to support. - 9. Pin arm to support.

A rubber bumper pad is mounted inside the spring.

When servicing the engine, check the condition of rubber-mounting parts: replace any worn or damaged parts.

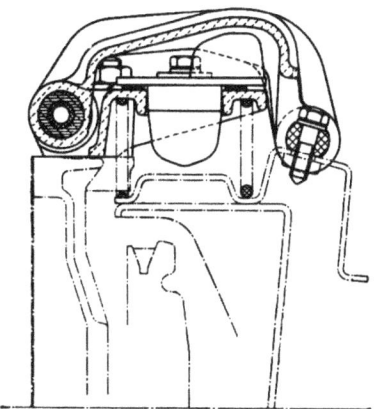

Fig. 153 - Rear support cross section.

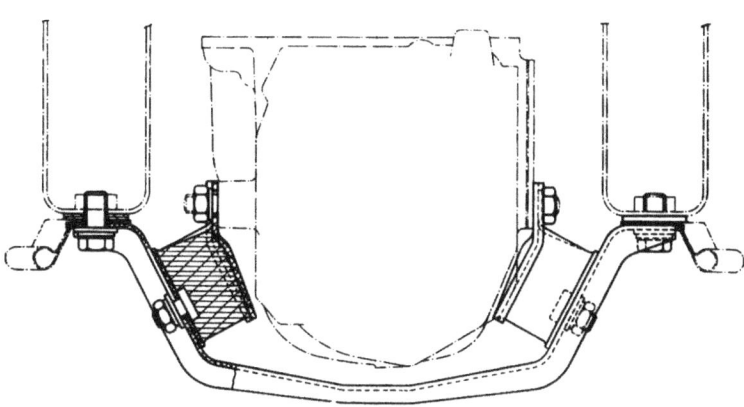

Fig. 155 - Power plant front support cross section.

ENGINE SERVICE EQUIPMENT

Catalogue Number		DESCRIPTION
Early	Late	
Arr. 2074	A. 60512	Adapter, engine and engine-gearbox-differential unit removing and installing.
Arr. 2077	A. 60516	Hook, engine and engine-gearbox-differential unit lifting and moving.
Arr. 2205/2	Arr. 22205/2	Arms, engine mounting on rotating stand.
A. 8262	A. 50033	Wrench, valve-to-rocker clearance adjustment.
A. 8262/bis	A. 50053	Wrench, rocker adjustment screw locknuts.
A. 10114	A. 60182	Piston ring installer and remover.
A. 11475	A. 94069	Grinding stone carrier spindle, valve seat grinding.
A. 11478	A. 94056	Grinding stone, valve seats.
A. 11479	A. 94057	20° cutter, intake and exhaust valve seat refacing.
A. 11482	A. 94058	Cutter carrier spindle, valve seat refacing.
A. 11489	A. 94059	Set of pilots, valve seat refacing cutters.
A. 40006/1/2	A. 40006/1/2	Puller, clutch pilot bushing.
A. 40014	A. 40014	Puller, cylinder head.
A. 50022	A. 50022	Wrench, spark plugs.
Ap. 5030	Ap. 5030	Tool, engine timing.
Ap. 5030/1	Ap. 5030/1	Fixture, ignition timing.
A. 50040	A. 50040	Wrench, pulley retainment during generator installation.
A. 50089	A. 50089	Socket (13 mm), rocker arm support nuts locking.
A. 60000	A. 60027	Tool, cylinder reaming (modified).
A. 60017	A. 60017	Tester, valve seat tightness.
A. 60018	A. 60018	Plug, spark plug seat blanking during valve tightness test.
A. 60041	A. 60041	Fixture, cylinder head support during decarbonizing.
A. 60077	A. 60077	Reamer, small end bushing.
A. 60084	A. 60084	Remover and installer, engine valve.
A. 60152	A. 60152	Fixture and bush, crankshaft mounting on grinder.
A. 60153	A. 60153	Punch, valve guide installation and removal.
A. 60154	A. 60154	Installer, pistons.
A. 60155	A. 60155	Fixture, connecting rod bush installation and removal.
A. 60156	A. 60156	Tool, cylinder retainment (engine on rotating stand).
A. 60157	A. 60157	Tool, piston pin installer and remover.
A. 60158	A. 60158	Base plate, wooden - cylinder head support during valve installation and removal.
A. 60159	A. 60159	75° cutter, intake and exhaust valve seats refacing.
A. 60161	A. 60161	Tool, flywheel retainment during installation on crankshaft.
A. 60162	A. 60162	Gauge, with connection, engine oil pressure.
A. 68001	A. 76001	Installer, spark plugs.
A. 72020 bis	D. 15166	Covers, engine protection during car wash.
C. 110	A. 95110	Feeler gauge, tappet clearance adjustment (.0039" - 0,10 mm).
C. 111	A. 95111	Feeler gauge, tappet clearance adjustment (.0059" - 0,15 mm).
C. 316	A. 95316	Feeler gauges, set of, piston-to-cylinder clearance inspection.
C. 645	A. 95645	Fixture, engine dead center inspection.
C. 672	A. 95672	Ring gauge, cylinder bore dial indicator calibration.
C. 673	A. 95673	Graduated sector, engine timing checks.
U. 0307	A. 90307	Expansible reamer, piston pin bore and connecting rod small end bush.
U. 0310	A. 90310	Reamer, valve guide bore.
U. 0334	A. 90334	Reamer, crankshaft support dowel holes.
U. 0338/1	A. 90338/1	Reamer, tappet guide bore (1st oversizing).
U. 0338/2	A. 90338/2	Reamer, tappet guide bore (2nd oversizing).
—	—	New dial for fixture C. 645, engine top dead center inspection.

Section 4

CLUTCH
GEARBOX
DIFFERENTIAL

	Page
CLUTCH	90
CLUTCH SERVICING INSTRUCTIONS	91
CLUTCH WITHDRAWAL MECHANISM	94
GEARBOX-DIFFERENTIAL UNIT	99
GEARBOX	103
DIFFERENTIAL AND FINAL DRIVE	111
SWING AXLE SHAFTS AND SLIP JOINTS	120
GEARSHIFT CONTROL MECHANISM	122

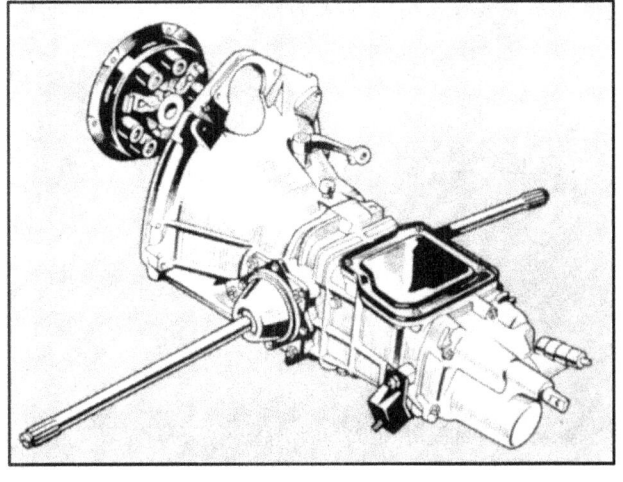

CLUTCH

Description	page	91
SERVICING INSTRUCTIONS	»	91
Removal and Installation	»	91
Pilot Bushing	»	91
Disassembly	»	92
Pressure Springs	»	92
Withdrawal Lever Carrier Ring Retaining Springs	»	92
Withdrawal Levers	»	92
Pressure Spring Specifications	»	93
Withdrawal Lever Carrier Ring Spring Specifications	»	93
Pressure Plate	»	93
Driven Plate	»	93
Assembly and Adjustment	»	93
WITHDRAWAL MECHANISM	»	94
CLUTCH SPECIFICATIONS	»	95
CLUTCH SERVICE EQUIPMENT	»	95
CLUTCH TROUBLE DIAGNOSIS AND CORRECTIONS	»	96

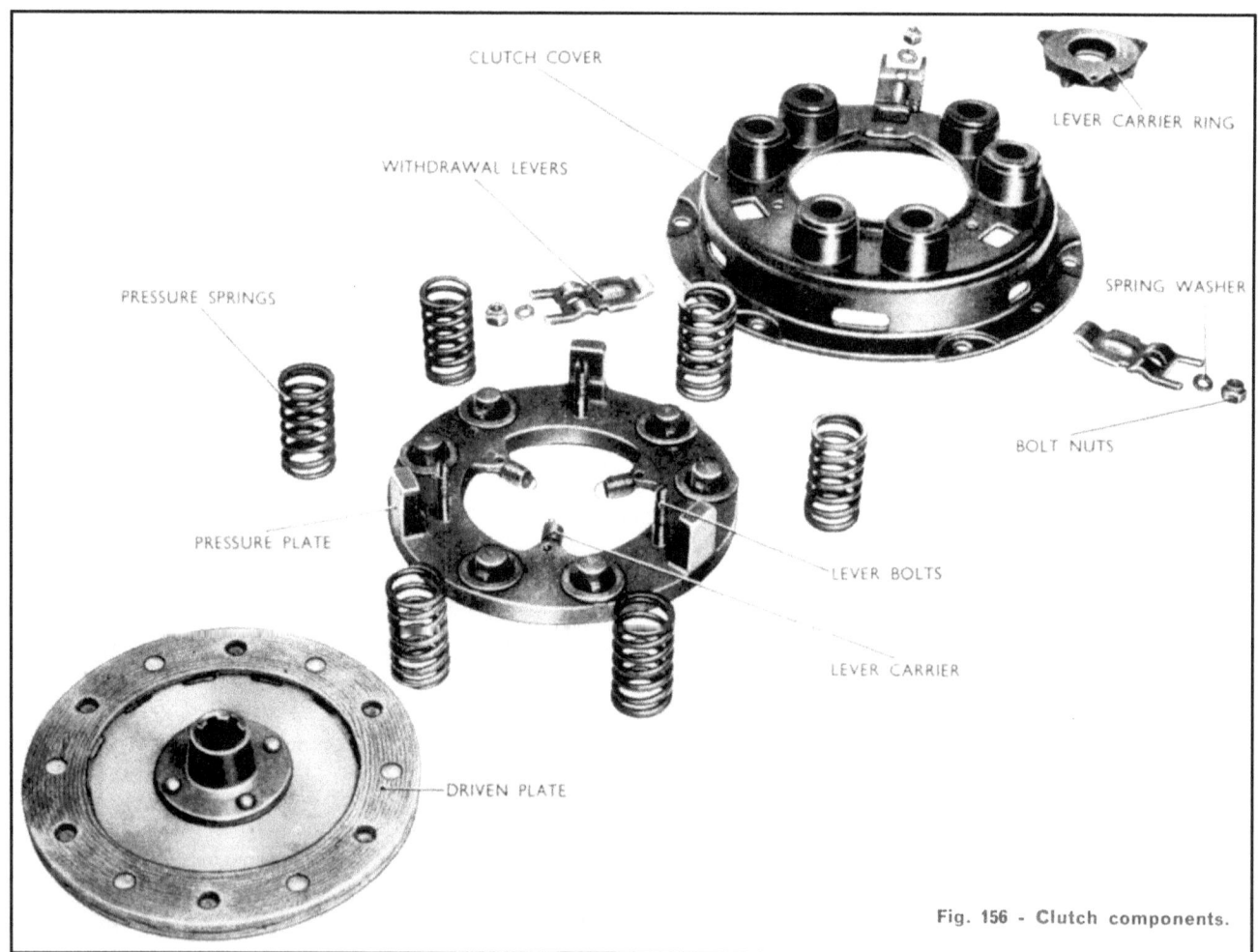

Fig. 156 - Clutch components.

CLUTCH

Description.

The clutch installed on the « New 500 » is of the single-plate, dry type.

A sheet metal cover, fixed by six screws to flywheel, encloses the clutch driven plate, pressure plate, and the six springs with respective cups.

Inserted in their bolts on clutch cover are three withdrawal levers whose inner ends are attached to a carrier ring through three springs which hold levers and carrier ring against pressure plate (fig. 157).

Driven plate release is obtained through a throwout ring with central thrust carbon ring, acting on the withdrawal levers carrier ring, and is controlled by clutch pedal through a suitable shaft, tie rod and fork linkage.

When clutch pedal is pressed, the throwout ring (with its carbon ring) is pushed towards flywheel, thus exerting a pressure on withdrawal levers carrier ring and hence on lever inner tips. Consequently, the lever outer tips lift the pressure plate and hence disengage the clutch.

Each withdrawal lever is mounted on a bolt, with adjustment nut, inserted in pressure plate. Levers are kept in their seats by a guide which is a part of the pressure plate.

Adjustment of release lever height is recommended only when the clutch is rebuilt. As a matter of fact lever mounting nuts connot get loose on operation as they are clenched down on mounting bolts.

However it is possible to set the position of clutch release sleeve whenever the clutch pedal free travel is in excess of prescribed value, or $1\frac{3}{8}''$ to $1\frac{9}{16}''$ (35 to 40 mm), due to the wear of driven plate facings.

Pedal free travel adjusting procedure is outlined on page 94.

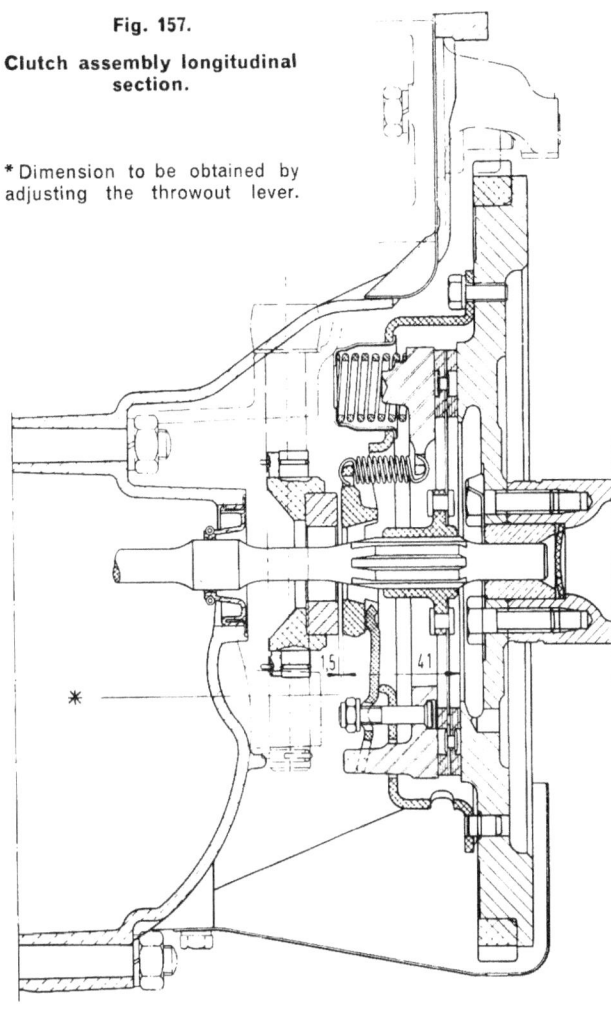

Fig. 157.

Clutch assembly longitudinal section.

* Dimension to be obtained by adjusting the throwout lever.

SERVICING INSTRUCTIONS

Removal and Installation.

To remove clutch from car, first disconnect gearbox from engine (see pertinent instructions given on page 103) and then take off the screws securing clutch to flywheel.

This also frees the driven plate.

To install clutch on flywheel, use as a guide flywheel locating dowels.

Prior to tightening down clutch mounting screws, align driven plate using tool **A. 62023** (fig. 158).

Pilot Bushing.

Whenever clutch unit is disassembled, it is essential to check that pilot bush on crankshaft - for

Fig. 158 - Installing the clutch on flywheel using pilot A. 62023 to center the driven plate.

Fig. 159 - Clutch assembly installed on engine.

clutch shaft rear support - is not damaged or excessively worn.

Clutch shaft tang on bush end must also be found in good condition.

Max. clearance between clutch shaft tang and bush must not be greater than .0059" (0,15 mm), otherwise pilot bush must be replaced.

For pilot bush removal use puller **A. 40006/1/2**.

Disassembly.

Place unit on fixture **A. 62038**, as shown in fig. 165, and lock cover by the studs provided.

Unhook the withdrawal lever carrier ring springs and take out the ring.

Fig. 160 - Location dowels on flywheel for clutch centering.

Unscrew the withdrawal lever fixing nuts on bolts and remove the levers and washers; slacken gradually the three T-handles to relieve pressure of clutch springs.

Next, take off clutch cover, springs and lever mounting bolts.

Pressure Springs.

When servicing the clutch, always check springs for perfect efficiency. In case springs are excessively weak - i. e., the spring length of .9646" (24,5 mm), corresponding to the actual assembly value, is obtained with a load of less than 43 lbs (19,5 kg) - replace the springs.

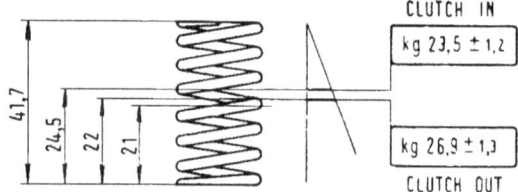

Fig. 161 - Pressure spring specifications.

Withdrawal Lever Carrier Ring Retaining Springs.

The length of closed springs, under rated clutch load, is .7677" (19,5 mm) while the length of expanded springs (under a load of 4.85 ± .44 lbs - (2,2 ± 0,2 kg) should be 1.1811" (30 mm). If an excessive weakening of springs is noticed, replace the springs.

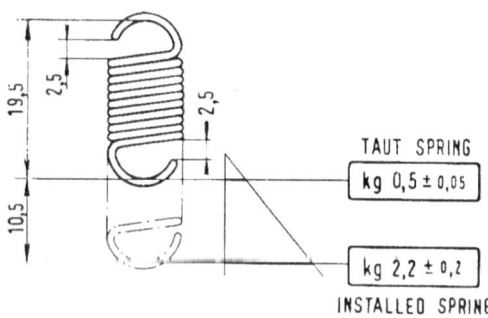

Fig. 162 - Withdrawal lever carrier ring retaining spring specifications.

Withdrawal Levers.

Check the withdrawal levers and their bolts for excessive wear, and replace if necessary.

Throroughly clean the inside end of levers, so to remove any sign of contact with carrier ring.

CLUTCH

PRESSURE SPRING SPECIFICATIONS

PART Number	WIRE Dia.	OUTSIDE Dia.	WORKING COILS No.	TOTAL COILS No.	HEIGHT, FREE SPRING	SEATED SPRING Length	SEATED SPRING Corresponding Load	SEATED SPRING Minimum Load
891312	.1102" (2,8 mm)	.9134" (23,2 mm)	6	7.5	1.6417" (41,7 mm)	.9646" (24,5 mm)	51.8 ± 2.6 lbs (23,5 ± 1,2 kg)	43 lbs (19,5 kg)

WITHDRAWAL LEVER CARRIER RING SPRING SPECIFICATIONS

PART Number	WIRE Dia.	OUTSIDE Dia.	WORKING COILS No.	TAUT SPRING Length	TAUT SPRING Corresponding Load	SEATED SPRING Length	SEATED SPRING Corresponding Load
891319	.0394" (1 mm)	.3740" (9,5 mm)	10.5	.7677" (19,5 mm)	1.1 ± .11 lbs (0,5 ± 0,05 kg)	1.1811" (30 mm)	4.85 ± .44 lbs (2,2 ± 0,2 kg)

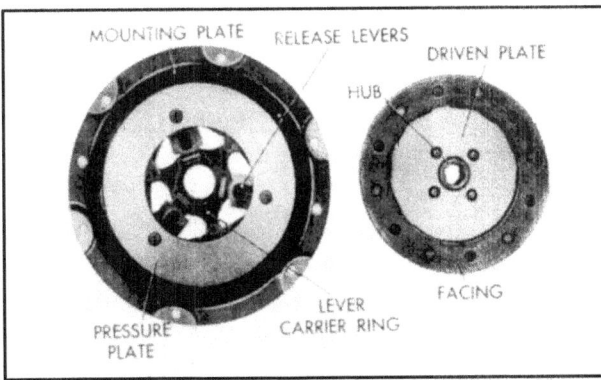

Fig. 163 - Clutch assembly with separate driven plate, viewed from pressure plate side.

Pressure Plate.

Check plate for absence of cracks and for perfect flatness of its contact face with driven plate. Otherwise, clutch will develop noises.

If deformations or nicks found are not too severe, the trouble may either be remedied by a slight lapping on planishing stake or turning of the contact face.

Similarly, check also the flywheel friction surface, as described on page 39.

Driven Plate.

Whenever clutch driven plate facings are worn, fit new ones. Rivet upsetting must be perfect and rivet heads must be flush with facings, otherwise flywheel and pressure plate working surfaces will be scored.

Check proper balancing and centering of driven plate.

If balance needs correction, grind plate peripherally on the heavier spots.

Centering checks are easily accomplished by first inserting driven plate on a splined shaft, then verifying with a scriber that, during rotation, out-of-center on sides or warping are not greater than .0118" (0,3 mm).

To prevent rattling: clutch shaft splines should not have any lengthwise clearance in excess of .0039" (0,10 mm) and side clearance of .0118" (0,30 mm) with respect to driven plate hub.

Ensure a free sliding of driven plate on shaft splines, since undue plate drag would cause a grabbing clutch and lead to subsequent gearshift troubles.

Assembly and Adjustment.

Proceed as follows:

Place the pressure plate, complete with carrier ring bolts and springs, on fixture **A. 62038** (fig. 165).

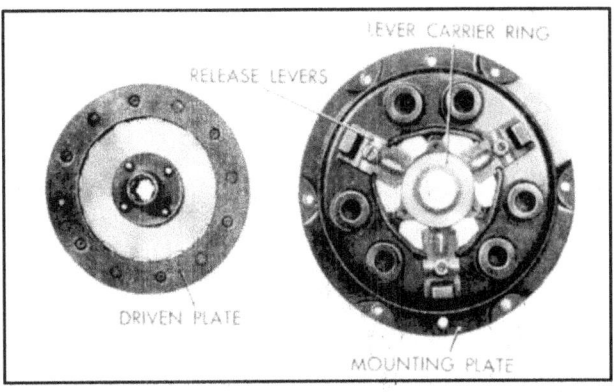

Fig. 164 - Clutch assembly with separate driven plate.

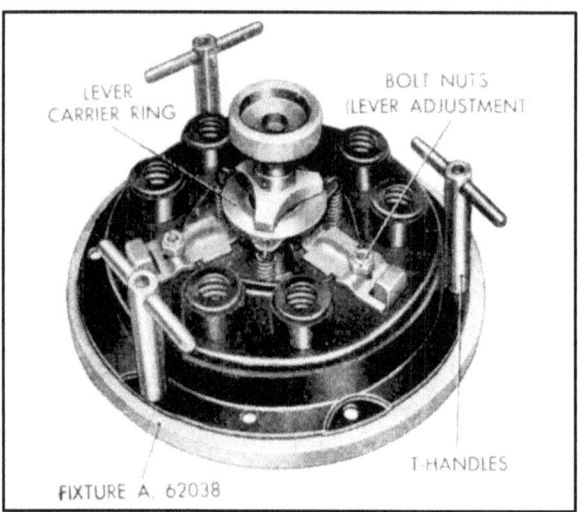

Fig. 165 - Fixture A. 62038 for clutch disassembly, reassembly and adjustment.

Fit the six pressure springs in their respective seats on pressure plate.

Insert the cups on springs and install the cover.

Using fixture **A. 62038,** compress the clutch cover making sure that the withdrawal lever supporting bolts are properly guided into their holes in cover.

On bolts, install the three withdrawal levers with relevant nuts and washers.

Place the carrier ring on levers and hook up the retainment springs.

Tighten up fully the T-handles and adjust the clearance between the carrier ring and its central shoulder: by means of adjustment nuts, set withdrawal levers stroke to .0039'' (0,10 mm). Check with gauge **C. 110.** After this, caulk the adjustment nuts.

Clutch pressure plate and cover must be installed in the same position as before disassembly, not to compromise the balance of the assembly.

WITHDRAWAL MECHANISM

This mechanism consists of:

— a forked lever, integral with a shaft (passing through clutch housing) on which the outer operating lever is keyed (fig. 166);

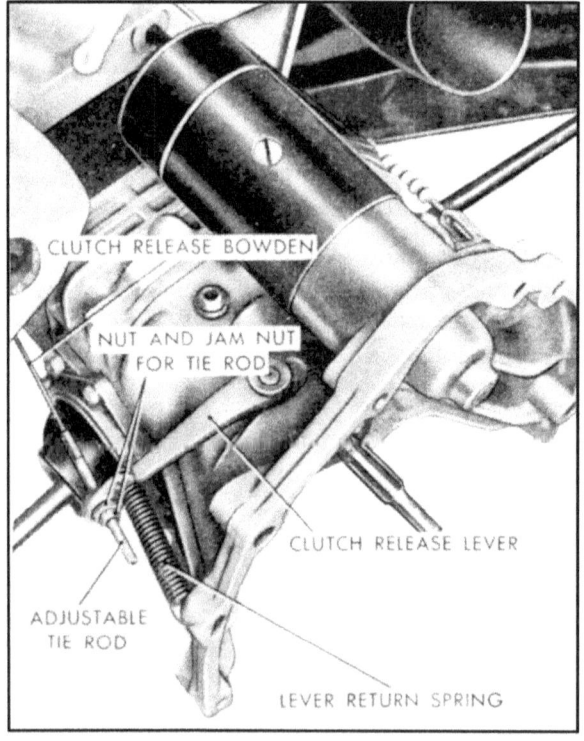

Fig. 166 - Clutch controls and adjusting mechanism.

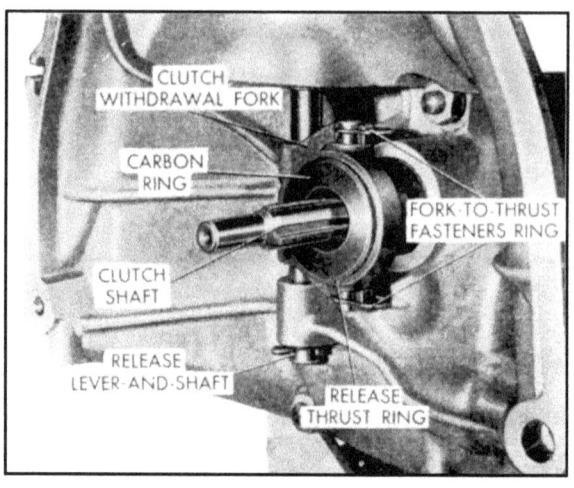

Fig. 167 - Clutch throwout mechanism.

— a return spring, connected to outer operating lever and anchored on gearbox casing. When in normal position, this spring keeps the central thrust carbon ring away from withdrawal levers carrier ring. The carbon ring is pressed against carrier ring by the throwout ring connected to forked lever (fig. 167).

Clutch pedal must have a free travel of $1^{3}/_{8}''$ to $1^{9}/_{16}''$ (35 to 40 mm). Should any correction be required, turn in or out the release lever control tie rod, which is adjustable.

After adjustment, lock by nut and jam nut (see fig. 166).

CLUTCH SPECIFICATIONS

Type	Single plate, working dry
Driven plate with facings of	Ferodo
Facing O. D.	5.51″ (140 mm)
Facing I. D.	3.78″ (96 mm)

Clutch springs:
     Part. No. ....
     Wire diameter ....
     Spring O. D. ....
     Number of working coils ....
     Total number of coils ....
     Free length ....
     Seated length ....
     Corresponding load ....
     Minimum load ....
	
	 891312
	 .1102″ (2,8 mm)
	 .9134″ (23,2 mm)
	 6
	 7 $\frac{1}{2}$
	 1.6417″ (41,7 mm)
	 .9646″ (24,5 mm)
	 51.80 ± 2.65 lbs (23,5 ± 1,2 kg)
	 43 lbs (19,5 kg)

Lever carrier ring springs:
     Part No. ....
     Wire diameter ....
     Spring O. D. ....
     Number of working coils ....
     Length, taut spring under 1.1 ± .11 lbs
     (0,5 ± 0,05 kg) of load ....
     Mounting length ....
     Corresponding load ....
	
	 891319
	 .0394″ (1 mm)
	 .3740″ (9,5 mm)
	 10 $\frac{1}{2}$
	
	 .7677″ (19,5 mm)
	 1.1811″ (30 mm)
	 4.85 ± .44 lbs (2,2 ± 0,2 kg)

Pedal free travel	$1\frac{3}{8}$″ to $1\frac{9}{16}$″ (35 to 40 mm)
Clearance between center lobes of fixture A. 62038 and lever carrier ring	.0039″ (0,10 mm)
Driven plate facing max. permissible out-of-true	.0059″ to 0.118″ (0,15 to 0,30 mm)

Clearance between clutch shaft and clutch hub splines:
     longitudinally ....
     crosswise ....
	
	 .0020″ to .0039″ (0,05 to 0,10 mm)
	 .0059″ to .0118″ (0,15 to 0,30 mm)

CLUTCH SERVICE EQUIPMENT

Catalogue Number		DESCRIPTION
Early	Late	
A. 62023	A. 70023	Pilot for driven plate centering at assembly of clutch on flywheel.
A. 62038	A. 70038	Fixture for clutch assembly, disassembly and adjustment.
A. 40006/1/2	A. 40006/1/2	Puller for pilot bush.

CLUTCH TROUBLE DIAGNOSIS AND CORRECTIONS

Noises when Clutch Pedal is Depressed.

POSSIBLE CAUSES	REMEDIES
1) Throwout thrust sleeve or ring excessively worn, damaged or broken.	1) Replace sleeve and ring.
2) Seizure of thrust ring and withdrawal levers.	2) Replace thrust ring. Clean lever ends with metal brush and smooth out bearing contact faces with felt polishers.
3) Insufficient pedal free play.	3) Set pedal free play at $1^{3}/_{8}''$ to $1^{9}/_{16}''$ (35 to 40 mm). To do so, work on withdrawal lever control rod as directed on page 94.
4) Pedal return spring broken, weak or unhooked.	4) Replace spring or hook it up and check for correct position.
5) Forked lever return spring broken, weak or unhooked.	5) Replace spring or hook it up carefully.
6) Excessive play of driven plate hub to clutch shaft causes rattles.	6) Replace the driven plate and check that clearance between hub of new driven plate and clutch shaft is within .0039'' (0,10 mm) endwise and .0118'' (0,30 mm) crosswise. Should clearance exceed above limits, replace also the clutch shaft.

The Clutch Grabs.

POSSIBLE CAUSES	REMEDIES
1) Oil or grease on flywheel, pressure plate and driven plate facings.	1) Remove cause of leakage, clean flywheel and pressure plate thoroughly, replace driven plate facings.
2) Loose driven plate facings due to poor rivet tightness.	2) If facings are not worn, replace defective rivets. Otherwise, replace facings and clench rivets securely.
3) Driven plate hub does not slide freely on clutch shaft.	3) Remove any foreign matter or dirt deposits from shaft splines. Should trouble still be present, replace damaged part.
4) Pressure plate deeply cracked or broken.	4) Replace pressure plate.
5) Improper adjustment of withdrawal levers.	5) Adjust withdrawal levers as specified on page 93, under « Assembly and Adjustment of Clutch. »
6) Misalignment.	6) Locate the defective point and, if possible, reset alignment or replace distorted parts.
7) Stiffened throwout mechanism.	7) Locate stiff point and replace parts, if necessary.
8) Driven plate facings worn out.	8) Install new facings and make sure that the driven plate, pressure plate and flywheel are not damaged.

CLUTCH

Noises when Clutch Pedal is Released.

POSSIBLE CAUSES	REMEDIES
1) Misalignment of driven plate to flywheel causes slight movement of driven plate hub in respect of facings. This noise is particularly audible with engine idling or running at low speed.	1) Set level of driven plate. With driven plate locked on clutch shaft, set it under slight rotation and check for no runout in excess of .0118" (0,3 mm), using a scriber.
2) Insufficient pedal free play.	2) Set clutch pedal free play at $1^{3}/_{8}$" to $1^{9}/_{16}$" (35 to 40 mm) as directed on page 94.
3) Pedal return spring broken, weak or unhooked.	3) Replace the spring or hook it up carefully.
4) Forked lever return spring broken, weak or unhooked.	4) Replace the spring or hook it up and check for correct position.

The Clutch Slips.

POSSIBLE CAUSES	REMEDIES
1) Insufficient clutch pedal return travel, due to the flexible cable being stuck or the pedal return spring being too weak.	1) Locate cause of failure and replace spring or eliminate sticking of control cable.
2) Damaged throwout mechanism.	2) Overhaul throwout mechanism; also clutch, if required.
3) Clutch pressure springs weak or broken.	3) Overhaul clutch and replace springs.
4) Oil or grease on driven plate facings.	4) Remove cause of oil leakage and replace facings, if they cannot be reconditioned by rubbing with turpentine and metal brush.
5) Driven plate facings worn or burned.	5) Replace facings.

Excessive Facing Wear.

POSSIBLE CAUSES	REMEDIES
1) Insufficient pedal free play.	1) Set clutch pedal free play at $1^{3}/_{8}$" to $1^{9}/_{16}$" (35 to 40 mm) as directed on page 94.
2) Driver steps unnecessarily on pedal; this causes facing wear and damage to throwout ring.	2) Advise driver to discontinue wrong practice and step on clutch pedal only when necessary.
3) Pressure springs weak or broken.	3) Check pressure springs for tension as specified on page 93 and replace springs, if they are unserviceable.
4) Driven plate facings installed incorrectly.	4) Replace facings by new ones and install them correctly. Check driven plate for center.

The Clutch Drags.

POSSIBLE CAUSES	REMEDIES
1) Excessive pedal free play.	1) Set free play at $1^3/_8''$ to $1^9/_{16}''$ (35 to 40 mm) as directed on page 94.
2) Driven plate warped.	2) Set level of driven plate, if possible. Maximum plate runout: .0118'' (0,3 mm).
3) Roughness on driven plate facings.	3) Rub facings with a metal brush or replace them, if necessary.
4) Driven plate facings improperly fitted, loose or broken.	4) Replace facings. Facing rivets should be clenched, to avoid damage to pressure plate and flywheel.
5) Driven plate hub forcing on clutch shaft.	5) Locate cause of trouble and remove it, if possible. Otherwise replace the driven plate.
6) Damaged clutch shaft splines prevent the driven plate from sliding.	6) Replace the clutch shaft; also the driven plate, if required.
7) Oil or grease on driven plate facings.	7) Replace facings.

Fig. 168.
Clutch-gearbox-differential unit partial cutaway.

GEARBOX-DIFFERENTIAL UNIT

Description of Components . . . . page	99
Gearbox and Road Wheel Ratios . . . . »	103
Removal of Gearbox-Differential Unit . . . . »	103
Installation of Gearbox-Differential Unit . . . . »	120
Unit Adjustment and Tightening Reference . . . . »	123
Service Equipment . . . . »	123
Technical Specifications . . . . »	124
GEARBOX . . . . »	103
Disassembly . . . . »	103
Inspecting Disassembled Components . . . . »	105
Assembly . . . . »	106
Trouble Diagnosis and Corrections . . . . »	109
DIFFERENTIAL AND FINAL DRIVE . . . . »	111
Noise Diagnosis and Remedies . . . . »	111
Disassembly . . . . »	112
Inspection and Repair of Parts . . . . »	112
Installing and Adjusting Final Drive Gear Set . . . . »	114
Determining Pinion Shim Pack Thickness . . . . »	115
Assembly . . . . »	117
Ring Gear-to-Pinion Backlash Adjustment and Differential Bearing Rotation Torque Inspection . . . . »	119
Checking and Adjusting Tooth Contact Between Pinion and Ring Gear . . . . »	120
SWING AXLE SHAFTS AND SLIP JOINTS . . . . »	120
Description and Repair . . . . »	120
GEARSHIFT CONTROL MECHANISM . . . . »	122
Adjustment . . . . »	122
Removal . . . . »	122
Disassembly and Inspection of Gearshift Lever Components . . . . »	122

Description of Components.

The gearbox and the differential are in a single unit, contained in an aluminum casing in two halves parting along differential centerline.

The drive is transmitted to rear wheels by two half axle shafts coupled to wheel shafts through slip joints.

The gearbox provides four speeds forward and a reverse, the fourth gear being an overdrive. Constant mesh 2nd, 3rd and 4th speed gears with driving gears provided with front teeth for quick engagement.

The gearbox-differential casing is fixed to engine by six studs of crankcase (two of which mount also the starter) and rests on a support with rubber pads secured to body floor.

The unit consists of the following three detachable parts:

— support for connection of gearbox to engine: performs as half-cover for the differential front end and a clutch/flywheel housing at rear;

— a central body divided into two compartments: the front compartment houses the 1st, 3rd, 4th and reverse gears with primary shaft, layshaft and reverse shaft, as well as the striker rods and forks;

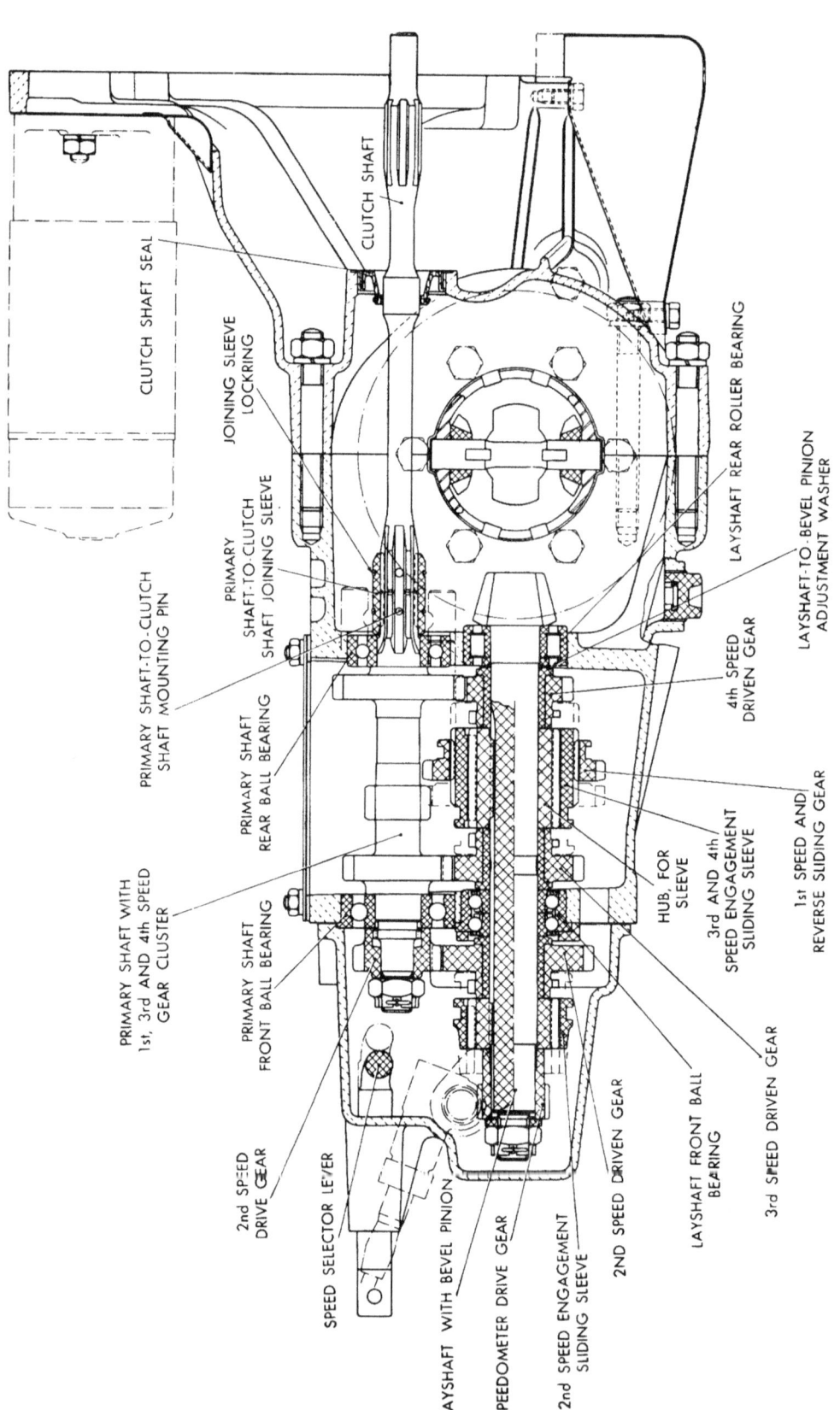

Fig. 169 - Gearbox-differential unit longitudinal section.

GEARBOX-DIFFERENTIAL UNIT

the rear compartment performs as half-cover for the differential unit;

— gearbox casing cover containing the 2nd speed gears and relevant forks, the gear selection rod and the speedometer drive gears.

The central body is provided with a top inspection cover; the support for connection of gearbox to engine has a recess for the starter.

The primary shaft is coupled to clutch shaft through a sleeve and two pins retained by rings. Primary shaft and 1st, 3rd and 4th driving gears form a cluster. On the primary shaft extension outside the central body is mounted the 2nd speed driving gear. The primary shaft is supported at its ends by ball bearings, while the clutch shaft rotates in a bronze bush press fitted in crankshaft output end.

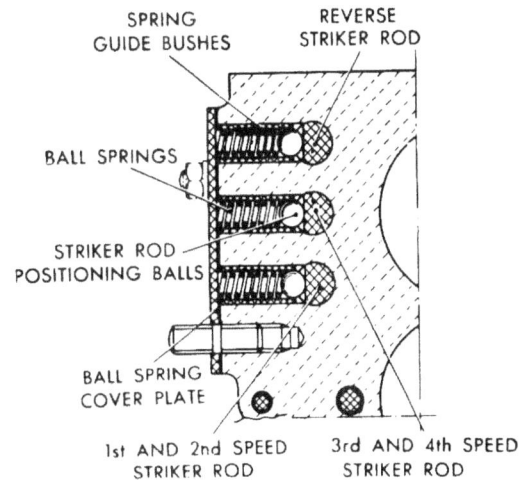

Fig. 171 - Detail of gearbox section through striker rod positioning ball springs.

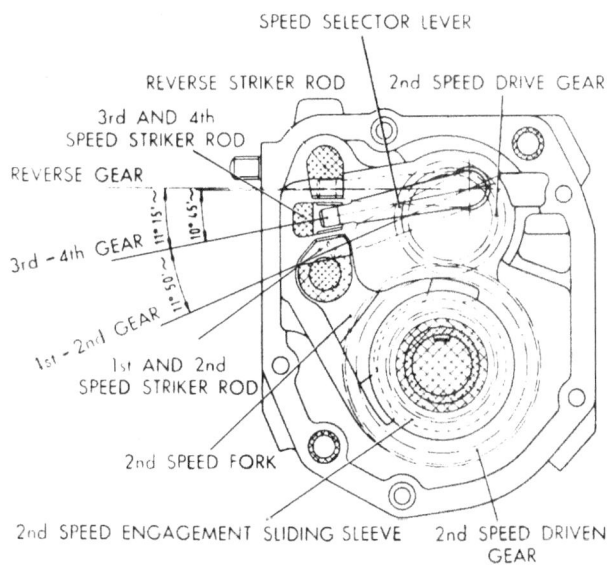

Fig. 170 - Cross section of gearbox through striker rods with the indication of the gear selector lever angular displacement.

An oil seal is fitted in the clutch shaft passage seat in connection support.

The layshaft with drive pinion is supported at front by a ball bearing retained by a plate; at rear it revolves on a roller bearing.

The layshaft carries: the pinion adjustment shim, the 4th speed driven gear and bushing, the hub and relevant engagement sleeve for 3rd and 4th speed with 1st speed and reverse gear, the 3rd speed gear and bushing and, outside the casing, the 2nd speed gear and bushing, the hub with relevant 2nd speed engagement sleeve and the speedometer driving gear.

Gears are shifted by means of a hand lever mounted on tunnel, between the seats, which,

through a rod, actuates the selector and shifting mechanism housed in the casing cover.

Positioning of the striker rods is ensured by a spring loaded poppet ball (fig. 171). The risk of shifting two gears at the same time is prevented by three rollers sliding in suitable seats machined in the rods (see fig. 172).

The differential unit and the final drive gear set are housed in the two semi-covers previously described; the final drive pinion is integral with layshaft.

The differential case may be split in two halves: the bevel gear is fitted on one of the halves and is secured by the same screws joining the two halves.

The differential side gears have an inner splining in which the splined axle shaft ends slide by means of a specially designed slip joint.

The differential case is supported by two taper roller bearings secured in position by adjuster rings.

Two rubber oil boots are inserted on swing axle shafts and fit over side gear extensions.

The Gleason final drive couple ratio is 8 to 41 (Model «500») or 8 to 39 (Model «500 Sports»).

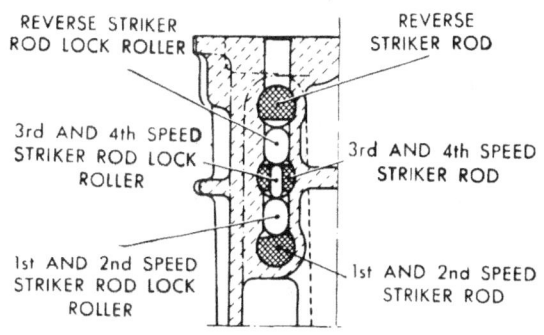

Fig. 172 - Detail of gearbox section through striker rod location rollers.

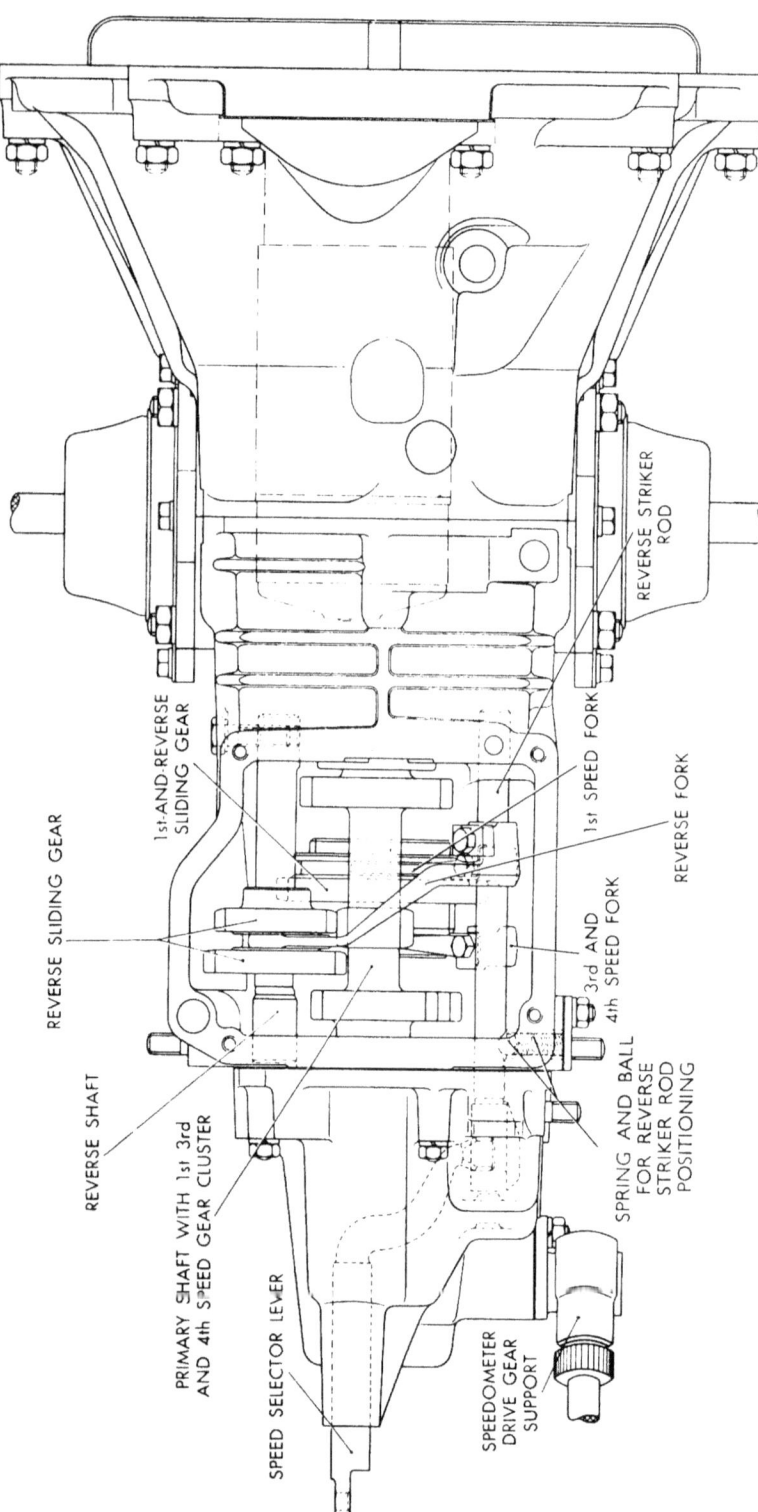

Fig. 173 - Top view of gearbox-differential unit without gear inspection lid.

NOTICE

Gearbox rebuild involves necessarily also dismantling of differential carrier and axle shaft assembly, inasmuch as the bevel pinion should be removed to strip the layshaft gear cluster.

In turn, differential rebuild will entail disassembly of gearbox. As a matter of fact, for a perfect meshing of final drive gear set teeth the procedure requires the bevel pinion-layshaft unit to be taken down.

GEARBOX AND ROAD WHEEL RATIOS

SPEEDS	1st (*)	2nd	3rd	4th	Reverse (*)
Gear ratios ..	$\frac{36}{11} = 3.27$	$\frac{31}{15} = 2.06$	$\frac{26}{20} = 1.30$	$\frac{21}{24} = .87$	$\frac{24}{11} \times \frac{36}{19} = 4.13$
Ratio to wheels, 8 to 41 final drive ratio	16.77	10.59	6.66	4.48	21.18
Ratio to wheels, 8 to 39 final drive ratio	15.95	10.07	6.33	4.26	20.15

(*) See covering note on page 108.

REMOVAL OF GEARBOX-DIFFERENTIAL UNIT

Disconnect positive clamp from battery post.
Raise the car rear end on stands.
Disconnect: the starter cables at starter, the control tie rod and remove the starter, the clutch control tie rod, the reaction spring and the clip securing the sheath on gearbox casing.
Remove the three screws securing the axle shaft splined sleeves to the flexible joint on wheels and take off the inner spring. Place a hydraulic jack provided with support **Arr. 2076** under the gearbox-differential unit.
Remove the nuts securing the unit to engine.
Detach the unit support from body floor and, pushing the unit forward, disinsert the clutch shaft from its seat on crankshaft.
Lower the jack and remove the unit.

GEARBOX

Disassembly.

Before disassembling the gearbox, carry out the following preliminary operations:

— disconnect front support and remove upper cover;
— remove sump bottom plug and drain oil;
— wash the unit.

Next, disassemble the unit proceeding as follows:

— place the unit on rotating stand **Arr. 2204**, fixing it to support **Arr. 2206/7** (fig. 174);
— remove the speedometer drive support with gears;
— take off the front cover with relevant gasket and the gear selector rod.

For complete dismantling of the gearbox, detach first the gearbox casing from the mounting-on-engine support and remove the differential unit operating as follows:

— snap off the lockring and slide the splined sleeves off the axle shafts;

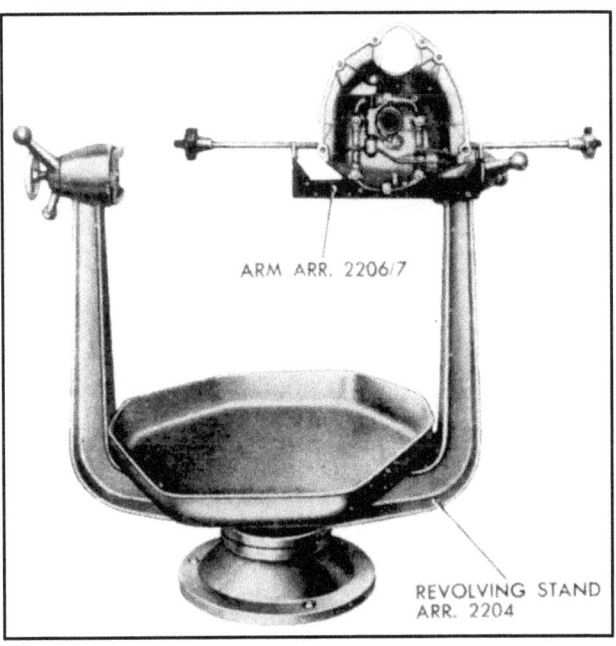

Fig. 174 - Gearbox-differential unit on revolving-type service stand.

Fig. 175 - Gearbox with top cover removed.

1. Primary shaft. - 2. 4th speed driving gear. - 3. 1st speed gear fork. - 4. Reverse fork. - 5. 3rd and 4th speed gear fork. - 6. Reverse striker rod. - 7. 3rd speed driving gear. - 8. Reverse shaft. - 9. Reverse gears. - 10. 1st speed gear and reverse driving gear. - 11. 1st speed and reverse sliding driven gear.

— take off the two roller bearing housings with relevant rubber boot fastening covers, the boots and the adjuster ring lockrings;

— detach the mounting-on-engine support and remove the differential case assembly complete with ring gear and axle shafts.

Then, proceed in gearbox dismantling as follows:

— open the fasteners and undo the selector fork-to-striker rod fixing screws;

— lock the primary shaft and layshaft by engaging two gears contemporaneously;

— remove cotter pins and undo the primary shaft and layshaft nuts;

— remove the retaining cover and withdraw the striker rod positioning balls and springs;

— pull off the upper rod and the reverse selector fork, the intermediate rod with relevant safety roller and the 3rd and 4th gear fork;

— from layshaft remove the plain washer and the speedometer drive driving gear;

— take off the second gear engagement sliding sleeve with fork and rod, the sliding sleeve hub, the second speed driven gear with relevant bush and the 1st gear engagement fork (take care not to drop the safety rollers while pulling out the striker rods);

— from the primary shaft remove the 2nd speed driving gear;

— undo the reverse shaft retainment screw, remove the shaft and relevant gear;

— demount layshaft front bearing retainment plate;

— by sliding the bearings off their seats, move the primary shaft forward so that the primary shaft-to-clutch shaft coupling sleeve is brought in correspondence with casing top opening. In this position it will be possible to take off a ring and a connection pin and to withdraw the clutch shaft with sleeve (1-2, fig. 177);

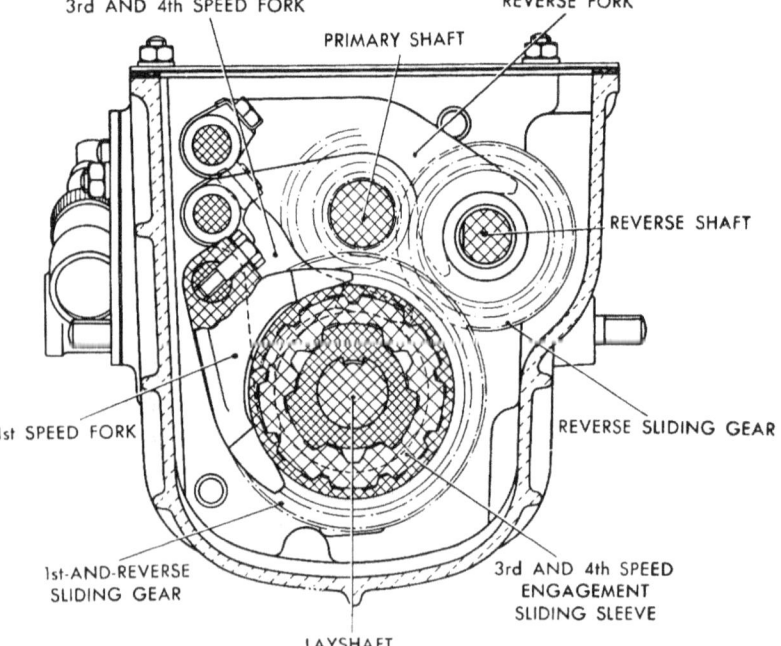

Fig. 176.

Gearbox cross section through 3rd and 4th speed engagement sleeve.

NOTE - When the gearbox is being rebuilt, it is good practice to go over the gear forks for engagement of first, second, third and fourth, and reverse speed, and check them for the absence of distortions and a snug fit in relevant gear or sliding sleeve seats.

GEARBOX-DIFFERENTIAL UNIT

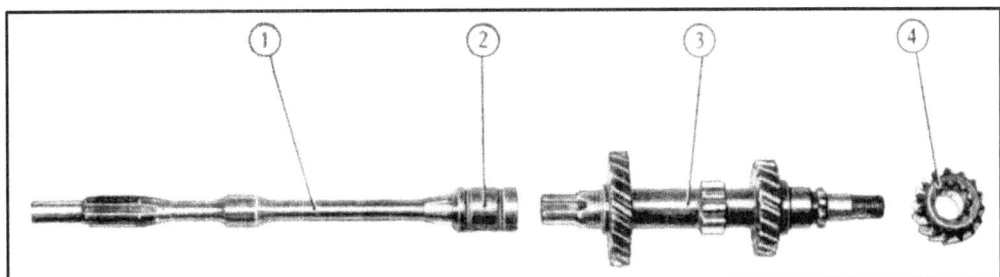

Fig. 177.
Gearbox components.

1. Clutch shaft. - 2. Clutch shaft-to-primary shaft coupling sleeve. - 3. Primary shaft. - 4. 2nd speed driving gear.

— from primary shaft remove front bearing;

— by properly tilting the primary shaft in the casing, pull it out and then remove the rear bearing;

— withdraw the layshaft with final drive pinion and roller bearing inner race;

— from inside the casing, take off the adjustment shim, the 3rd and 4th speed driven gears with relevant bushes, the hub with sliding sleeve; the 1st speed and reverse driven gear; drive out from their seats the front bearing and the bevel pinion rear bearing outer race;

— by an arbor press and tool **A. 42013**, drive out the drive pinion roller bearing inner race.

Inspecting Disassembled Components.

After properly washing all components, check that:

a) Gearbox casing is not cracked and bearing seats are neither worn nor damaged, to prevent bearing outer ring rotation during operation.

b) Ball bearings are in perfect conditions and both axial and radial play is not excessive.

Maximum permissible bearing play is the following:

— front bearings of primary shaft layshaft:
   a) sidewise .00177" (0,045 mm);
   b) endwise .01772" (0,450 mm);

— primary shaft rear bearing:
   a) sidewise .00157" (0,040 mm);
   b) endwise .01575" (0,40 mm).

Hold the bearings firmly by outer race and, at the same time, rock the inner race back and forth: sliding must be free and noiseless. If sliding is rough, replace bearings. Check roller bearings inspecting the condition of rollers and outer and inner races.

Always replace bearings even if their efficiency is just slightly unsatisfactory.

c) Primary shaft and layshaft checked between centers and dial gauge are perfectly centered, the out-of-true reading for bearing seats being less than .0008" (0,02 mm); splines must not be indented.

d) Reverse shaft is perfectly smooth.

e) Gear teeth show no sign of damage or excessive wear. Teeth of each pair in mesh must mate on their entire length. Contact surfaces are smooth and show no indent marks.

Backlash between gears is not greater than .0039" (0,10 mm); maximum wear limit is .0079" (0,20 mm).

Quick engagement front teeth of 2nd, 3rd and 4th speed gears are not excessively worn or damaged.

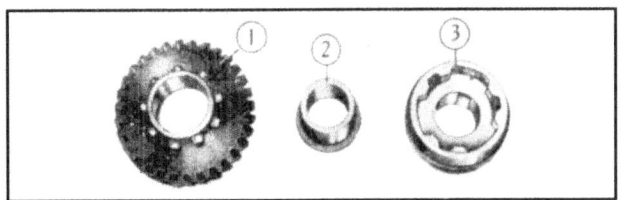

Fig. 178 - Layshaft gear for 2nd speed engagement.

1. 2nd speed driven gear. - 2. Gear bush. - 3. 2nd speed gear engagement hub and sliding sleeve.

f) Sliding sleeves and relevant hubs are perfectly smooth on working surfaces and clearance between mating parts is not greater than .0059" (0,15 mm).

Meshing teeth are in good condition.

g) Gear shifting selector forks are not distorted and striker rods slide freely in their seats in casing.

Fig. 179 - Layshaft gears for engagement of 1st, 3rd and 4th speed.

1. 4th speed driven gear. - 2. Gear bush. - 3. 3rd and 4th speed gear engagement sliding sleeve and hub. - 4. Gear bush. - 5. 3rd speed driven gear. - 6. 1st speed and reverse sliding driven gear.

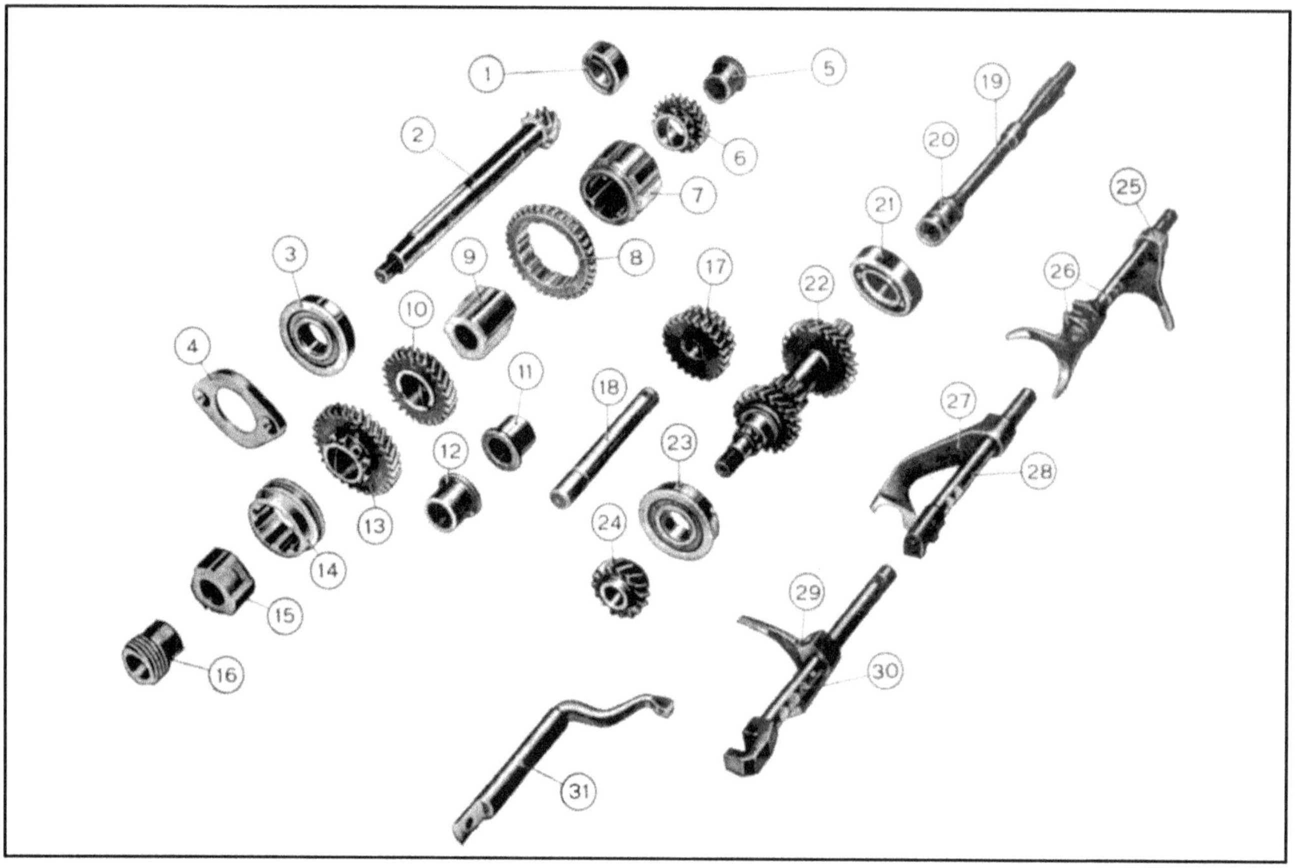

FIAT - NEW 500

Fig. 180 - Gearbox gears, forks and striker rods.

1. Rear roller bearing. - 2. Layshaft with bevel pinion. - 3. Front ball bearing. - 4. Front bearing plate. - 5. Bushing. - 6. 4th speed driven gear. - 7. 3rd and 4th speed sliding sleeve. - 8. 1st and reverse sliding gear. - 9. Sliding sleeve hub. - 10. 3rd speed driven gear. - 11. Bushing. - 12. Bushing. - 13. 2nd speed driven gear. - 14. 2nd speed sliding sleeve. - 15. 2nd speed sliding sleeve hub. - 16. Speedo drive gear. 17. Reverse sliding gear. - 18. Reverse sliding gear shaft. - 19. Clutch shaft. - 20. Clutch shaft-to-primary shaft sleeve. - 21. Primary shaft rear ball bearing. - 22. Primary shaft with 1st and reverse, 3rd and 4th gear train. - 23. Primary shaft front ball bearing. - 24. 2nd speed drive gear. - 25. 1st gear fork. - 26. 1st and 2nd gear striker rod with 2nd gear fork. - 27. Reverse gear fork. - 28. Reverse gear striker rod. 29. 3rd and 4th gear fork. - 30. 3rd and 4th striker rod. - 31. Gear selector and engagement lever.

h) Oil seals are in perfect condition: replace as required.

i) Striker rod locking balls and safety rollers slide freely in their seats. Their improper operation could cause troubles in the engagement and disengagement of gears. Check also ball load spring efficiency.

Assembly.

Place gearbox casing on rotation stand **Arr. 2204** and secure to support **Arr. 2206/7**.
Install rear roller bearing on layshaft.

Fig. 181 - Layshaft and final drive pinion complete with gears, bearings and sliding sleeves.

NOTE - If no item in layshaft assembly from bevel pinion to front bearing has been replaced, thickness of pinion shim should not vary.

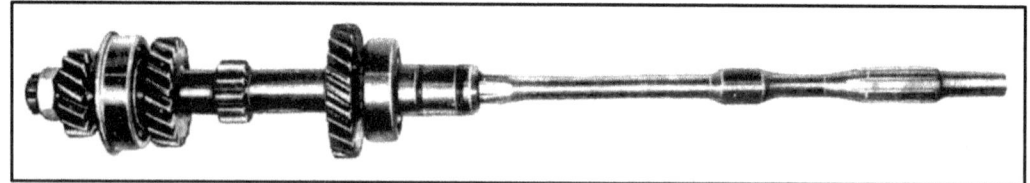

Fig. 182 - Clutch shaft and primary shaft with driven gears and ball bearings.

GEARBOX-DIFFERENTIAL UNIT

Install layshaft in the casing and, at the same time, fit the adjustment shim, the 4th speed driven gear with bush, the sleeve and hub for 3rd and 4th gear engagement, the 1st speed and reverse driven gear and the 3rd speed driven gear with hub.

Install front layshaft ball bearing, secure the bearing retainment plate with screws and caulk the screws.

Insert the primary shaft (with 1st, 3rd and 4th driving gear train); fit rear ball bearing. Move the shaft forward, insert the clutch shaft provided with coupling sleeve and connect it to the primary shaft by retainment ring and pin. Position the shaft and insert the rear bearing in its seat. Fit front bearing and slide it in its seat on casing.

On layshaft insert the 2nd speed driven shaft and bush, the 2nd speed engagement sliding sleeve and hub; at the same time insert the 2nd speed striker rod and the 1st speed fork. Fit the safety roller in its seat.

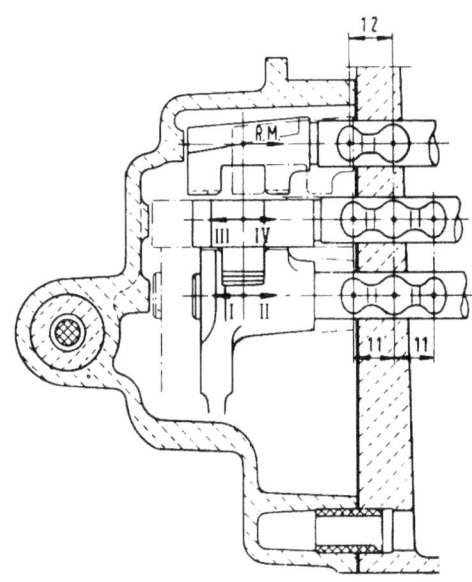

Fig. 184 - Detail of gearbox section with indication of striker rod stroke.

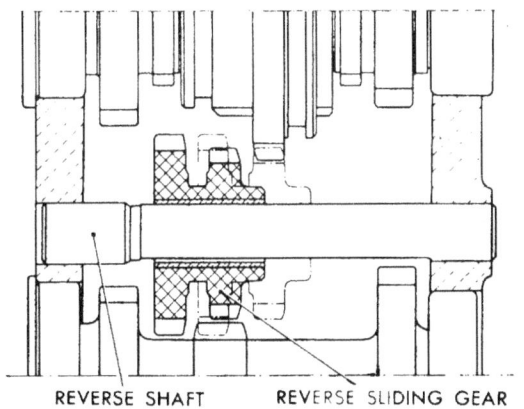

Fig. 183 - Detail of gearbox section through reverse sliding gear.

Install the three positioning balls on the striker rods and secure by spring and cap.

Install the casing front cover, with relevant gasket. At the same time insert the speed selector rod which shall engage the striker rod dogs.

Install the speedometer drive support on gearbox casing.

Install upper cover.

For the subsequent differential assembly and adjustment operations, see the following chapters.

Fill up the gearbox and differential casing with FIAT W 90 (SAE 90 EP) oil.

Casing capacity: 1.16 U. S. qts - .97 Imp. qts (1,110 lt - 1 kg).

Slide the 2nd speed driving gear primary shaft.

Place engagement fork on 3rd and 4th speed engagement sliding sleeve, insert the striker rod, lock the relevant fork and fit the safety roller.

Fit the third safety roller; install the reverse shaft and insert the relevant gear. Lock reverse shaft with the proper screw.

Install the reverse striker rod with relevant fork.

Slide the speedometer driving gear on layshaft.

Using a torque wrench, draw up with 18.1 to 25.3 ft.lbs (2.500 to 3.500 kgmm) and with 28.9 to 36.2 ft.lbs (4.000 to 5.000 kgmm) respectively, the nuts on the primary shaft and layshaft ends (interposing the plain washer between speedometer driving gear and nut). Lock by cotter pin.

To hold the shafts fast while tightening the nuts, engage two gears.

Lock the forks on striker rods by screws and fasteners.

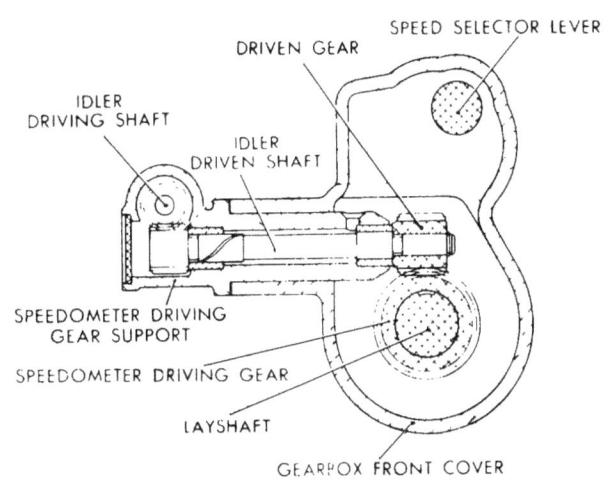

Fig. 185 - Detail of gearbox section through speedometer drive gears.

Fig. 186 - Gearbox-differential unit longitudinal section.

NOTE - Starting from engine No. 173487, first and reverse gear ratios have been modified as follows:

	EARLY RATIO	LATE RATIO
1st gear	$\dfrac{36}{11} = 3.27$	$\dfrac{37}{10} = 3.70$
Reverse	$\dfrac{24}{11} \times \dfrac{36}{19} = 4.13$	$\dfrac{25}{10} \times \dfrac{37}{18} = 5.14$

GEARBOX-DIFFERENTIAL UNIT

TRANSMISSION TROUBLE DIAGNOSIS AND CORRECTIONS

Noisy Transmission.

POSSIBLE CAUSES	REMEDIES
1) Excessive backlash of gears in mesh due to gear wear.	1) Rebuild transmission and replace worn gears.
2) Gears, bearings or gear bushings damaged.	2) Rebuild transmission and replace worn parts.
3) Shafts misaligned or out of center due to loose mounting nuts.	3) Disassemble transmission and check components, repair and replace as required. On reassembly, tighten nuts to specified torque (page 123).
4) Dirt or metal chips in the lubricant.	4) Disassemble transmission, clean all components and make sure that they are sound. Replace lubricant.
5) Insufficient oil level in transmission case.	5) Add FIAT W 90 (SAE 90 EP) oil up to lower brim of filler plug seat.

Transmission Jumps out of Gear or Gearshifting is Irregular.

POSSIBLE CAUSES	REMEDIES
1) Improper shifting.	1) Be sure the gears are completely engaged before releasing the clutch pedal.
2) Gearshift lever mounting bracket out of adjustment.	2) Adjust as outlined on page 122.
3) Incorrect assembly or damage of striker rod positioning balls and springs.	3) Remove cover and overhaul parts. Assemble the proper way.
4) Striker rod rollers worn or assembled incorrectly.	4) Disassemble and replace worn parts and assemble the correct way as outlined on page 107.

Oil Leakage.

POSSIBLE CAUSES	REMEDIES
1) Overfilled transmission case.	1) Check oil level for lower brim of filler plug seat.
2) Front extension, upper cover and clutch housing nuts loose.	2) Check tension and tighten nuts where required. Clutch housing nuts should be drawn up with 27 $^1/_2$ ft.lbs (3.800 kgmm) of torque, using a torque wrench.
3) Speed selector and engagement lever seal at front extension damaged.	3) Remove extension and lever, replace gasket and install on extension.
4) Faulty bell housing gasket.	4) Remove and replace gasket by a new one.
5) Gaskets: upper cover-to-case, front extension-to-case, damaged.	5) Replace gaskets which do not warrant oil tightness.

Transmission Shifts Hard.

POSSIBLE CAUSES	REMEDIES
1) Defective link of gearshift lever to internal front lever.	1) Disassemble gearshift mechanism and inspect lever ball cap, inner cup and spring. Replace damaged parts.
2) Internal front lever rubber bushing and plates damaged.	2) Disassemble gearshift mechanism and replace bushing and plates.
3) Speed selector and engagement lever control rod twisted.	3) Remove rod and straighten.
4) Control rod-to-speed selector and engagement lever joint damaged.	4) Remove and replace flexible joint.
5) Speed selector and engagement lever worn.	5) Remove front extension and replace lever.
6) Stiffened striker rods in case seats.	6) Remove rods, locate cause of stiffening and repair as required.
7) Sliding sleeves and gears bound in their seats due to the presence of dirt in splines.	7) Locate cause of binding and clean parts thoroughly.
8) Improper quality of transmission lubricant.	8) Drain case and clean thoroughly. Refill with FIAT W 90 (SAE 90 EP) oil.
9) Misadjusted clutch linkage and clutch make declutching impossible.	9) Rebuild clutch throwout mechanism and check height of clutch fingers. Adjust as directed under « Clutch » (page 94).

Fig. 187.
Power plant and rear suspension.

Also visible are the gearshift control rod and gearbox-differential unit front support.

DIFFERENTIAL AND FINAL DRIVE

To facilitate the location of differential unit troubles, follow the directions outlined below which make possible a methodical diagnosis of operations troubles.

NOISE DIAGNOSIS AND REMEDIES

The following tests are essential to establish whether noises are actually located in differential unit or caused by some other unit.

Locating Noise.

Test No. 1. - Drive car at a speed of about 12 m.p.h. (20 km/h) to determine the nature of noises present. Then, gradually increase the speed to about 37 m.p.h. (60 km/h). As the car picks up speed, record any noises that might develop at the different speeds as well as the moment in which they are audible and in which they fade away. Release the accelerator and, without braking, let the car come to a dead stop.

During this deceleration, check once more every change in the noises noticed and the speeds at which noises are more marked.

In all probability, all noises will appear and disappear at the same speeds both when accelerating and decelerating.

Test No. 2. - Run the car up to 44 m.p.h. (70 km/h). After this, shift to neutral, switch off ignition, and coast until car comes to a dead stop. Again, record all noises heard at the different deceleration speeds.

All noises noticed in test No. 1 and still present in test No. 2 cannot be attributed to the differential inasmuch as this unit, not being under load, cannot originate any noise other than that due to bearings.

On the contrary, any noise recorded in the first test but absent in the second, may be ascribed to rear axle.

These noises may be singled out by the following test:

Test No. 3. - Park the car, apply brake, and start the engine. Next, increase engine r.p.m. gradually. Compare all noises appearing in this test with the ones recorded during tests No. 1 and 2.

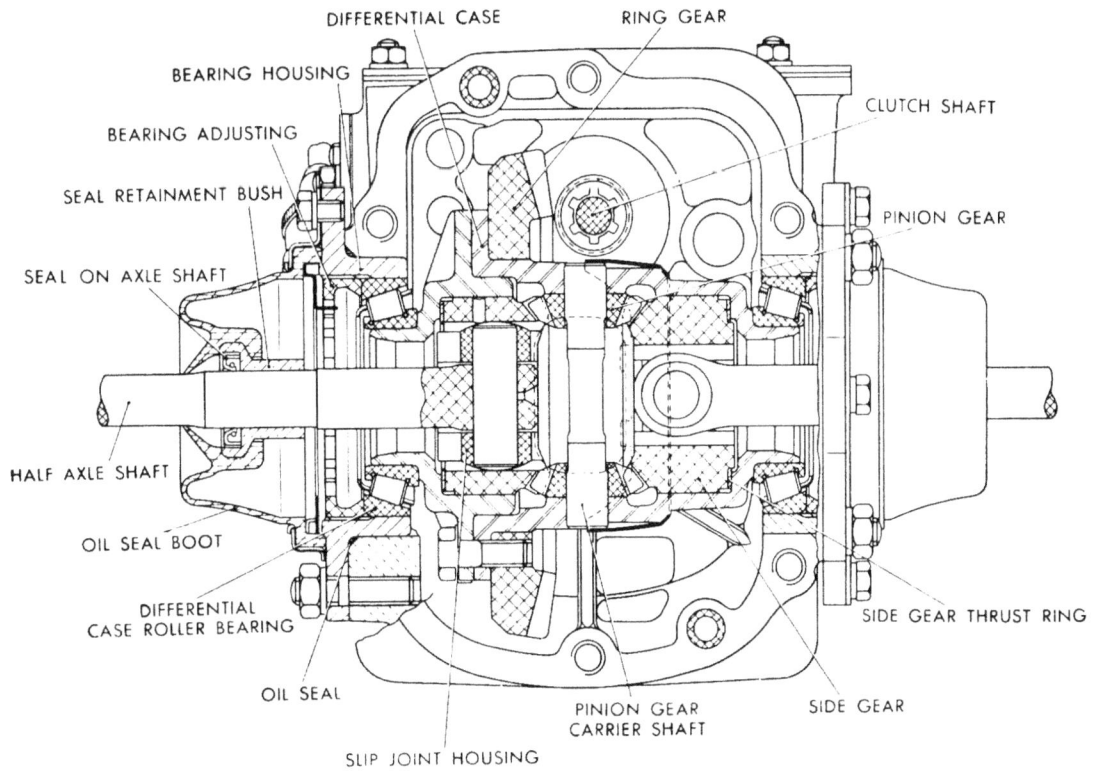

Fig. 188 - Gearbox-differential section through axle shafts.

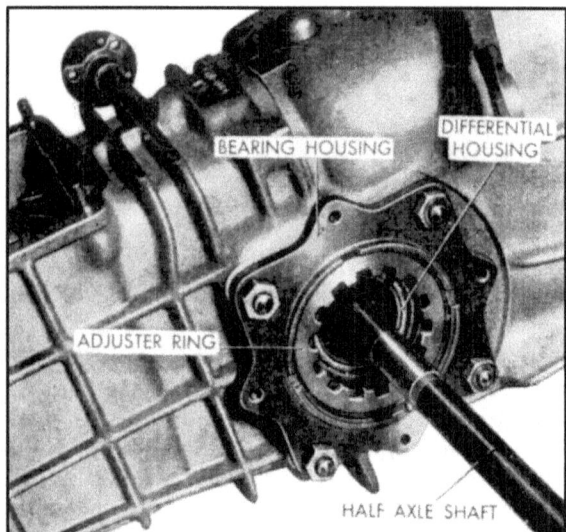

Fig. 189 - Scrap view of gearbox-differential unit.

Any noise that developed in test No. 1 and is still present can be disregarded. Such noises are due to units which have nothing to do with the rear axle, such as the air cleaner, exhaust silencer, engine or body.

Test No. 4. - Noises experienced in test No. 1 which, by elimination, are still present in the two further tests (2 and 3), may be attributed to the differential.

To check this assumption, raise rear wheels clear of ground, run engine and engage direct drive. It will now be possible to ascertain whether the noises ascribed to rear axle are actually caused by it.

Elimination of Noises.

Gear noise on pull.

Check adjustment of differential case bearings.
Check ring gear-to-pinion backlash.

Gear noise on coast.

Check meshing depth of bevel pinion teeth. The pinion may need to be moved away from or toward the ring gear.

Thumping.

Make sure that no gear teeth or bearing races are chipped or excessively worn.

Noises due to excessive play.

Inspect ring gear and pinion for excessive backlash.
Make sure bevel pinion axial play is not excessive.

Noise on turns.

Check that: idle pinions are not too tightly fitted on their shaft, idle pinion shaft surface is perfectly smooth, side gears are not too tightly fitted on their supports, all gears are neither chipped nor damaged in any other way, and wear of differential unit gears and thrust washers is not excessive.

SERVICING INSTRUCTIONS

Disassembly.

For differential removal from gearbox, refer to the directions given on page 103.

For differential disassembly (operation to be performed on bench), proceed as follows:

Remove lockring (2, fig. 191) retaining the splined sleeve (4) and take off the sleeve.

Remove the retaining covers (7) and oil boots (11), with bushes and seals, adjuster ring lockrings (13), adjuster ring housings (14) with bearing adjusters and roller bearing outer races.

Undo the screws joining the two case halves (5-12) and securing the ring gear (16).

Remove the idle pinion carrier shaft retaining cup (15).

Remove idle pinions (10) by disinserting the shaft.
Take off the two axle shafts (1).

Remove side gears (6) and relevant thrust rings (8).
Pull roller bearing inner races out of half-cases.

Inspection and Repair of Differential Parts.

After disassembly, the components of differential unit must be accurately checked for proper efficiency and to determine the presence of wear, damages or other irregularities. The idle pinion carrier shaft, which is heavily stressed when car negotiates turns, must be carefully checked for undesirable roughness.

If clearance to idle pinions exceeds .0059" (0,15 mm), replace the shaft. The ring gear and pinion set, the side gears and idle pinions must be checked for broken, chipped or excessively worn teeth.

GEARBOX-DIFFERENTIAL UNIT

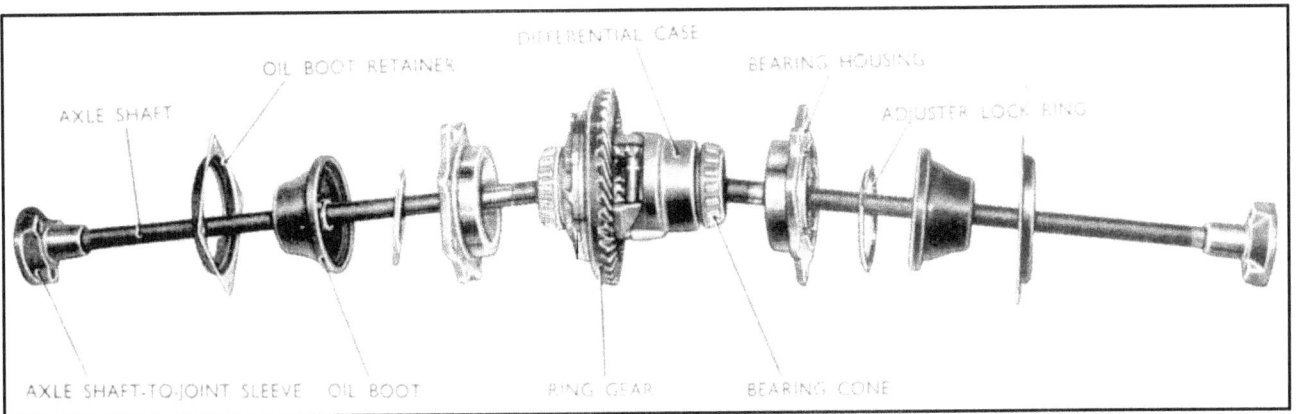

Fig. 190 - Differential unit complete with axle shafts.

Check the condition of ball and roller bearings: rollers, balls and races must not be damaged or worn.

If damages to side pinion thrust ring contact surfaces are slight, recondition rings; when damages are too heavy, replace the rings with new ones or with rings oversized in thickness, as required.

Thrust rings are supplied as spares in the following thicknesses:

— Standard . . . . .0394" (1 mm)
— Oversize   .0512" to .0591" (1,3 to 1,5 mm)

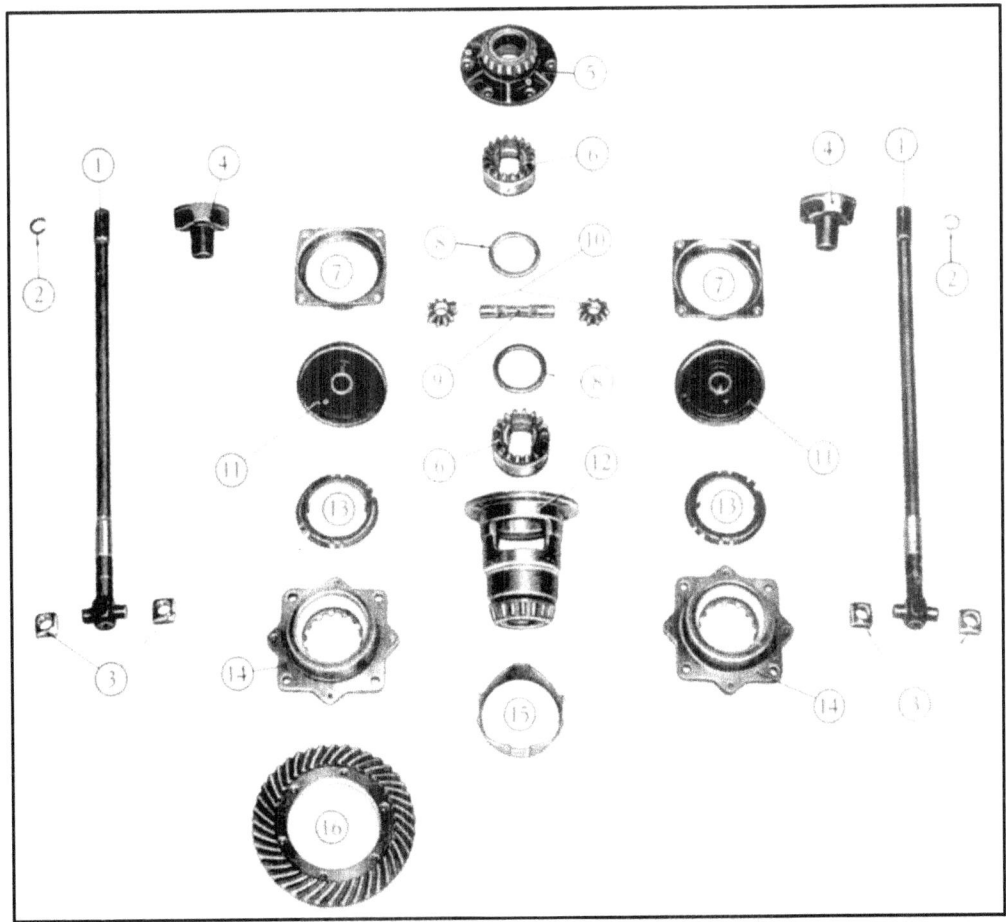

Fig. 191 - Differential components.

1. Axle shafts. - 2. Sleeve retainment lockrings. - 3. Slip joint casings. - 4. Axle shaft-to-wheel shaft coupling sleeve. - 5. Differential case cover with bearing inner race. - 6. Side gears. - 7. Oil boot retainment cover. - 8. Side gear thrust ring. - 9. Idle pinion shaft. - 10. Idle pinions. - 11. Oil boots. - 12. Differential case with bearing inner race. - 13. Adjuster retainment ring. - 14. Bearing housings with retaining nuts and outer races. - 15. Idle pinion shaft retainment cup. - 16. Bevel gear.

INSTALLING AND ADJUSTING FINAL DRIVE GEAR SET

Installation and adjustment of the final drive gear set require particular care.

If specific rules are not followed, the unit will have to be disassembled again and a new adjustment made.

In order to establish the correct meshing of the two gears, their relative position is accurately set during assembly in the Factory.

On the pinion stem (fig. 192) is stamped the centesimal value (millimeters) of the difference between the nominal mating clearance and the actual mating clearance (fig. 199). Such difference may be either positive or negative (plus or minus) and, therefore, the figure shall be preceded by signs + or —.

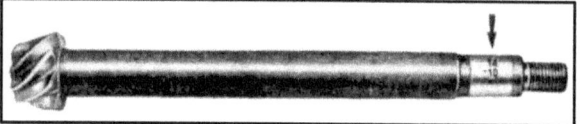

Fig. 192 - Layshaft with final drive pinion.

The arrow points to the number (14) for correct mating with ring gear and to the centesimal figure (— 10) for accurate mating position of pinion and gear.

At assembly the pinion must be set in the pre-established position.

However, in view of the machining tolerances of the case and of the wear of the components mounted on the case itself, suitable measurements shall be made before installing the pinion, in order to establish the correct value of pinion adjustment shim thickness.

In fact, it is the thickness of this shim, mounted between rear roller bearing and 4th speed driven gear bushing (fig. 169), that determines the correct backlash.

Specific tools and fixtures have been designed to facilitate the calculations and measurements, supplying also a simplified shim thickness determination formula, i. e.:

$$S = 0.90 + a - (b + c)$$

where:

S = Shim thickness;

0.90 = Standard coefficient (determined as explained on page 116);

a = Value read on the dial indicator applied to fixture **A. 62036** (fig. 194);

b = Value stamped on pinion stem (fig. 192);

c = Value read on dial indicator (fig. 196) corresponding to the difference between height of tool **A. 62037** (fig. 197) and the sum of the thicknesses of the items to be installed on pinion and included between front bearing inner shoulder and rear bearing outer shoulder.

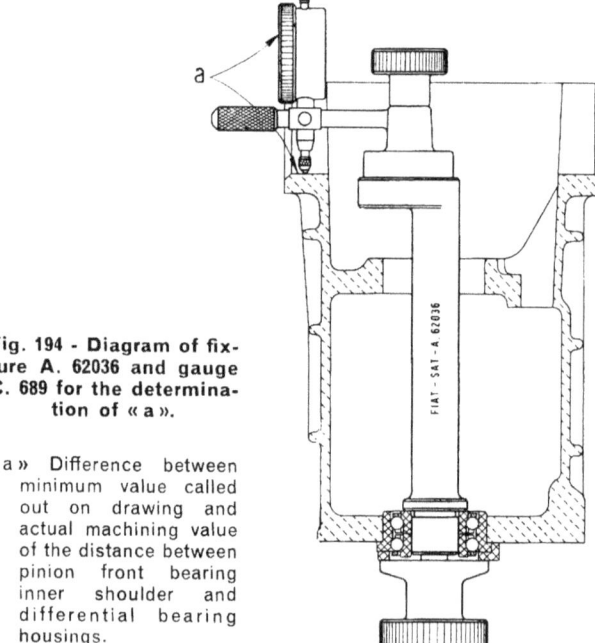

Fig. 194 - Diagram of fixture A. 62036 and gauge C. 689 for the determination of «a».

«a» Difference between minimum value called out on drawing and actual machining value of the distance between pinion front bearing inner shoulder and differential bearing housings.

The following chapter lists the operations to be performed, while on page 116 is indicated the specific function of each tool and is demonstrated the formula mentioned above. Said formula is stamped on tool **A. 62036** so as to be easily seen by the operator.

After installing the drive pinion and the differential assembly, adjust backlash as described on page 119.

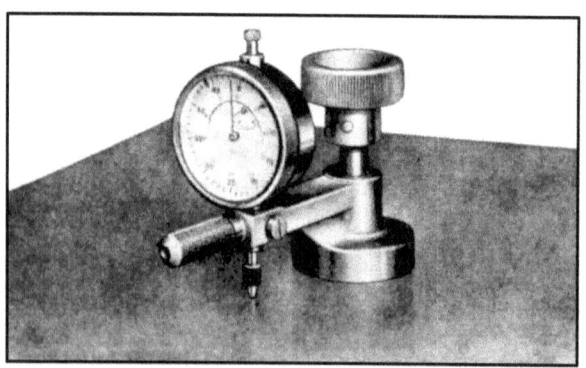

Fig. 193 - Bringing fixture C. 689 dial indicator to zero on surface plate.

GEARBOX-DIFFERENTIAL UNIT

Determining Pinion Shim Pack Thickness.

1) Install gearbox-differential casing on rotating stand **Arr. 2204** and secure to support **Arr. 2206/7**.

Press fit in its seat on casing the front ball bearing; install the retainment plate and tighten the securing screws.

Install fixture **A. 62036** (fig. 194) and lock it in position on front bearing retainment plate by means of the knurled knob.

On a surface plate (fig. 193), set centesimal and millimetrical scales of dial gauge **C. 689** to zero. Next, fit dial gauge on fixture (fig. 194) and make sure that gauge plunger rests on roller bearing housing seat (fig. 195).

Fig. 196 - Reading value « c » on dial indicator.

Fig. 195 - Reading value « a » on gauge C. 689 to determine drive pinion shim thickness.

Move back and forth horizontally the gauge support and note the indication of dial pointers; block dial gauge in position where pointers indicate the maximum values.

The reading represents « a » and shall be recorded before performing the subsequent operation.

2) On a surface plate, place tool **A. 62037** (dummy shaft) and insert on it the following items:
— 3rd speed driven gear bush, 3rd and 4th speed gear engagement sleeve hub, 4th speed driven gear bush and drive pinion roller bearing inner race (fig. 196).

On the surface plate, place a dial gauge and set it to zero on tool **A. 62037** (fig. 197); then, rest the dial gauge plunger on roller bearing inner race and take a reading at the dial (fig. 196).

The reading represents « c » and shall be recorded.

3) Read coefficient « b » on pinion stem (fig. 192).

All the factors required to establish the shim thickness will thus be known.

Substitute the numerical values in formula:

$$S = 0.90 + a - (b + c)$$

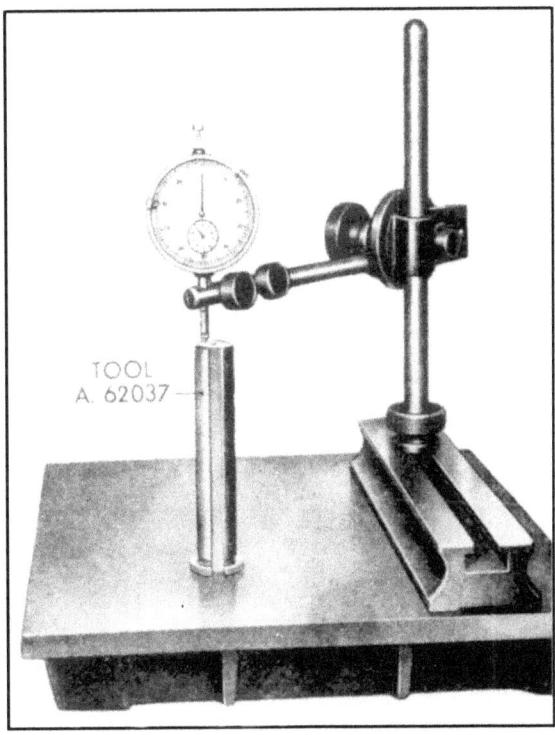

Fig. 197 - Setting dial indicator to zero on tool A. 62037.

By solving the formula the shim thickness will be found.

Shims are supplied in the following thicknesses: .0039" (0,10 mm) and .0059" (0,15 mm). One or more shims can be used for adjustment.

NOTE - 0.90 is a constant coefficient and has been determined as explained below.

METHOD FOLLOWED IN DETERMINING COEFFICIENT 0.90 AND FUNCTION OF TOOLS

The initial formula used to determine the required thickness of pinion shim is:

$$S = A - (B + C)$$

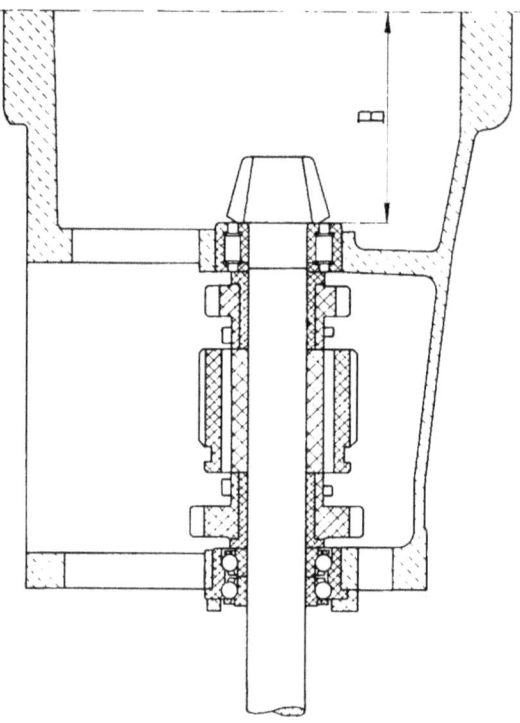

Fig. 199 - Graphic demonstration of value « B ».

« B » Distance between pinion shoulder and axis passing through the center of bearing housings.

Value « b » stamped on the pinion indicates the difference between nominal value (2.9528" - 75 mm) and actual mating value (B).

where:

A = distance between pinion front bearing inner shoulder and centerline of bearing housing seats (fig. 198);

B = distance between centerline of bearing housing seats and pinion shoulder on roller bearing (fig. 199);

C = sum of the height of items included between front ball bearing and pinion shoulder, excepting the adjustment shim (figure 200).

In consideration of the difficulties that might be met in carrying out such a measurement, special tools have been developed permitting a remarkable simplification of the several operations involved.

Tool A. 62036 (fig. 198).

Is used to determine « A ».

Tool height, from surface in contact with ball bearing inner race to surface in contact with dial indicator, is 5.9268" (150,54 mm). This is the minimum value called out on drawings for the distance between ball bearing inner race and bearing housing seats.

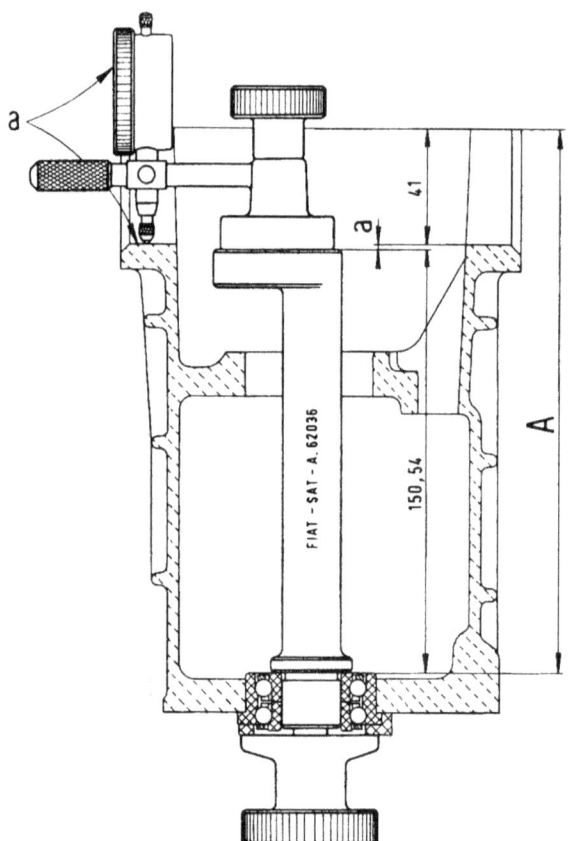

Fig. 198 - Graphic demonstration of values « A » and « a ».

« A » Distance between pinion front bearing inner shoulder and the axis passing through the differential bearing housing center.

« a » Difference between the minimum value called out on drawing (5.9268" - 150,54 mm) and actual machining value of the distance between pinion front bearing inner shoulder and differential bearing housings.

GEARBOX-DIFFERENTIAL UNIT

To obtain «A», 5.9268" (150,54 mm) must be summed with the bearing housing seat radius 1.6142" (41,000 mm) and dial indicator reading (as measured in fig. 198 and marked «a»).

$$A = 150{,}54 + 41{,}000 + a$$

Determination of «B».

Add algebrically 2.9528" (75 mm) (corresponding to the drawing call-out for the distance between centerline of bearing housing seats and pinion shoulder) and centesimal coefficient «b» stamped on pinion stem.

$$B = 75 + b$$

Tool A. 62037 (fig. 200).

Is used to determine «C».

Height of tool is 4.5527" (115,64 mm), which corresponds to the sum of the minimum drawing call-outs for the individual heights of all parts mounted between front ball bearing and pinion shoulder, excepting the shim.

To obtain «C», the tool height of 4.5527" (115,64 mm) must be summed with the dial indicator reading (as measured in fig. 196 and marked «c»).

$$C = 115{,}64 + c$$

We have now determined all values needed to solve formula.

$$S = A - (B + C).$$

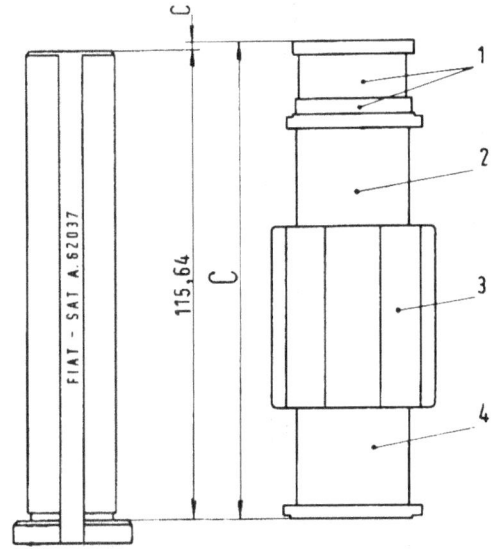

Fig. 200 - Graphic demonstration of «C» and «c».

1. Bevel pinion rear roller bearing inner race. - 2. Bush, 4th speed driven gear. - 3. Hub, 3rd and 4th speed engagement sleeve. - 4. Bush, 3rd speed driven gear.

«C» Total height of items 1, 2, 3 and 4 which must be mounted on final drive pinion.

«c» Difference between actual height «C» and the minimum drawing call-out 4.5527" (115,64 mm) represented by tool A. 62037.

By substitution we shall have:

$$S = 150{,}54 + 41{,}000 + a - (75 + b + 115{,}64 + c);$$
$$S = 150{,}54 + 41{,}000 - 75 - 115{,}64 + a - (b + c).$$

$$S = 0{,}90 + a - (b + c)$$

The formula thus obtained allows the elimination of some fixed numerical values, hence remarkably simplifying the computation work required to determine shim thickness, as described on page 114.

ASSEMBLY

Before proceeding with the reassembly of differential case, from gearbox casing remove tool **A. 62036** used for the determination of final drive pinion shim thickness.

Assemble the pinion and the items it carries as directed under gearbox «Assembly» on page 106.

Tighten nut with torque wrench to 28.9 to 36.2 ft.lbs (4.000 to 5.000 kgmm).

Differential case must be reassembled on bench and operations required are:

Fit on case (12, fig. 191) the roller bearing inner race and, internally, the thrust ring and side gear.

From inside case, insert the axle shaft complete with pivot and runners forming the slip joint.

Install the idle pinions and carrier shaft.

Insert the ring gear on case and install idle pinions carrier shaft retaining cup.

On cover (5, fig. 191), install the roller bearing inner race and, internally, the thrust ring and side gear; then, insert the axle shaft complete with slip joint.

Join case halves and tighten the screws securing the case halves and ring gear with torque wrench to 23.1 ft.lbs (3200 kgmm); secure screws by lockplates.

Using tool **A. 62028** (fig. 201), place outer races in bearing housings; fit oil seals.

On the two axle shafts, insert the bearing housings with adjuster rings.

Install the assembly thus obtained in gearbox casing.

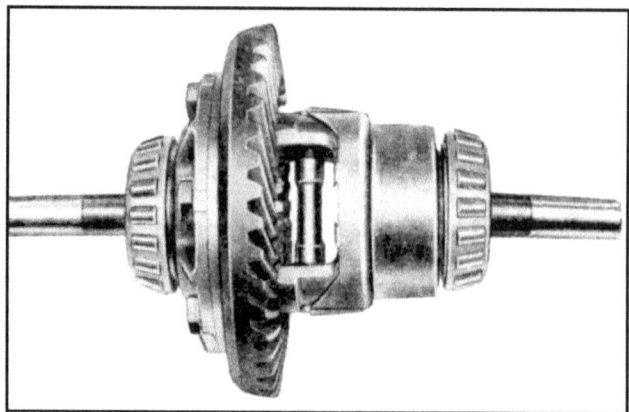

Fig. 202 - **Differential unit.**
The retaining cup on idle pinion shaft is visible.

Fig. 201 - Using tool A. 62028 to install or remove differential roller bearing outer races from their seats.

Join the front support to gearbox casing and tighten the six mounting nuts to 27.5 ft.lbs (3.800 kgmm), using a torque wrench.

Place bearing housings in their seats and tighten the mounting nuts with torque wrench to 13 ft.lbs (1800 kgmm).

NOTE - After the gearbox and differential assembly has been made and all necessary adjusting and inspecting operations have been completed, refill gearbox and differential case with **1.14 (U.S.)** or **.94 (Imp.) quarts (1,075 liters - 1 kg)** of **FIAT W 90 (SAE 90 EP) oil.**

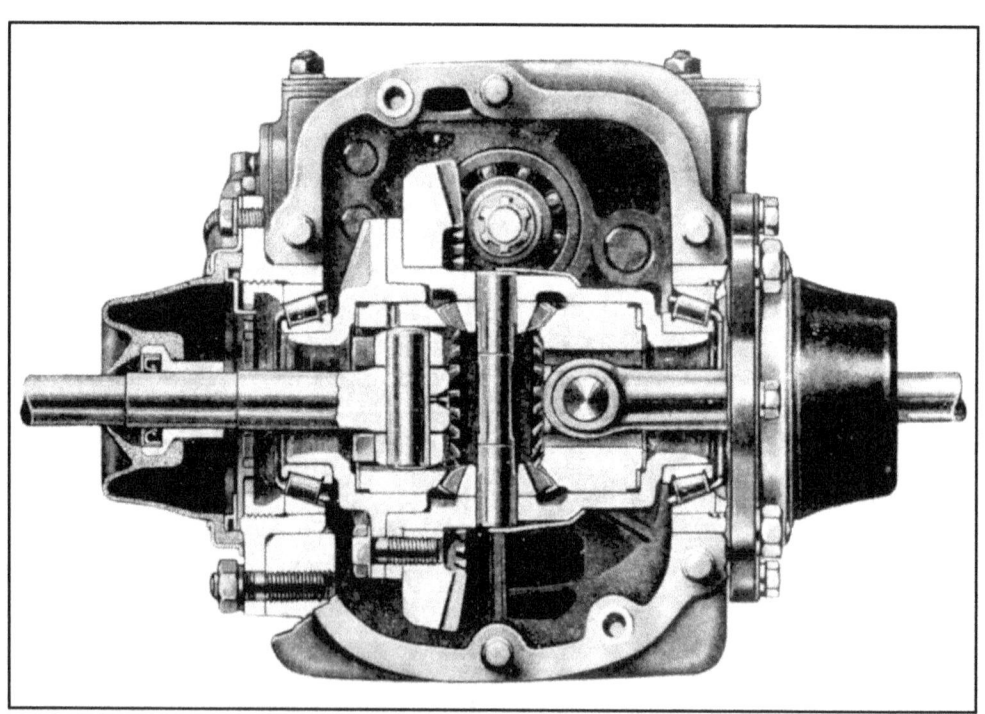

Fig. 203 - Gearbox-differential section through axle shafts.

RING GEAR-TO-PINION BACKLASH ADJUSTMENT AND DIFFERENTIAL BEARING ROTATION TORQUE INSPECTION

To check ring gear-to-pinion backlash, install fixture **A. 62039** which is fixed to the two lower mounting holes in gearbox front support flange.

The fixture is equipped with dial indicator whose plunger is brought in contact with ring gear through clutch shaft passage hole (fig. 204).

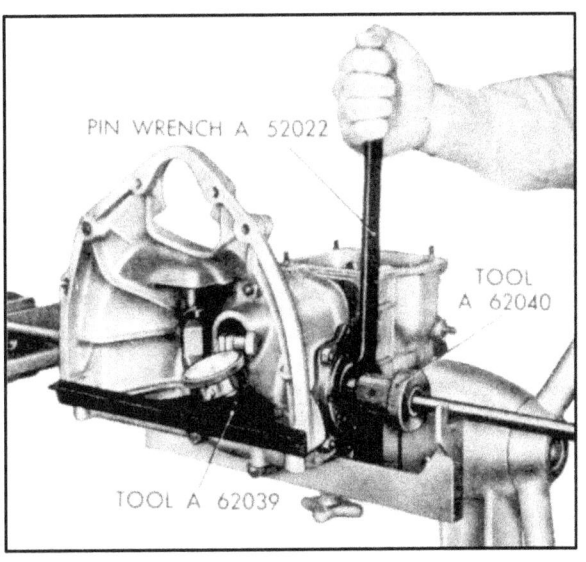

Fig. 205 - Adjusting ring gear-to-pinion backlash and differential bearing play, using special wrench A. 52022.

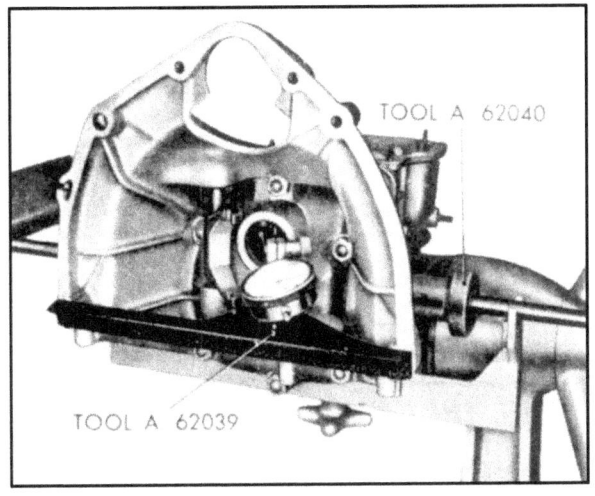

Fig. 204 - Checking ring gear-to-pinion backlash, using dial gauge of fixture A. 62039.

Tool A. 62040 fixes axle shaft to ring gear.

Screw in adjusters until they contact their respective bearings.

On one of the axle shafts mount tool **A. 62040** (fig. 204), which will lock the shaft against differential case; lock final drive pinion rotation using tool **A. 62041**; manually rotate axle shaft (now become integral with ring gear) as far as permitted by the backlash, which will hence be read on dial indicator: it must be .0031" to .0047" (0,08 to 0,12 mm).

If the reading is either lower or greater than specified, move the ring gear respectively in or out from the pinion by tightening one of the adjusters and slackening the other of the same amount, using pin wrench **A. 52022** (fig. 207).

After obtaining the specified backlash, remove tool **A. 62041** and then, using support **A. 62040**, mount dynamometer **A. 95697** (fig. 206) on axle shaft.

First set bearings by rotating axle shaft a few turns and then check, with the dynamometer, the

Fig. 206.

Checking differential case roller bearing rotation torque, using dynamometer A. 95697 mounted on tool A. 62040.

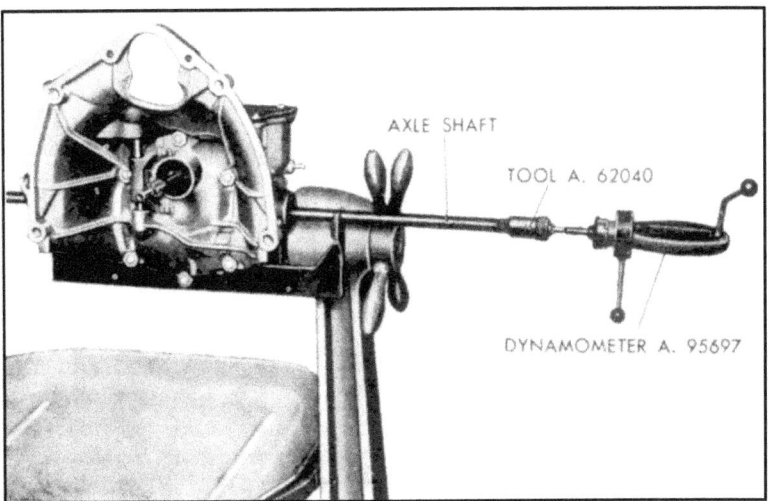

Rotation (not starting) torque, should be 1.01±.07 ft.lbs (140±10 kgmm).

rotation torque; if required, tighten adjusters until the specified torque of 1.01±.07 ft.lbs (140±10 kgmm) is obtained.

This is an operation that must receive the utmost care, because if one adjuster is set differently with respect to the other, a variation in ring gear-to-pinion backlash may take place resulting in a variation of rotation torque.

Therefore, after adjustments, always check up on ring gear-to-pinion backlash and, if required, restore to specified value and repeat the rotation torque check.

CHECKING AND ADJUSTING TOOTH CONTACT BETWEEN PINION AND RING GEAR

The final inspection of tooth contact pattern must be carried out as follows:

Paint some of the ring gear teeth with red lead, then start the differential into rotation while braking the axle shafts, so as to have the unit working under load.

A contact impression will be left on ring gear teeth and contact will be correct when the drive pinion tooth contact pattern is evenly distributed on the ring gear teeth (fig. 207).

Should tooth contact be improper, the following cases, as shown in figures 208 through 211, may be met:

1) **Excessive contact on tooth flank** (fig. 208): too deep meshing. - Move pinion out from ring gear by reducing thickness of shim.

2) **Excessive contact on tooth heel** (fig. 209): too slight meshing. - Move pinion in towards ring gear by increasing thickness of shim.

3) **Excessive contact on tooth face** (fig. 210): too slight meshing. - Move pinion in towards ring gear by increasing thickness of shim.

4) **Excessive contact on tooth toe** (fig. 211): too deep meshing. - Move pinion out from ring gear by reducing thickness of shim.

In all the above mentioned cases, to adjust pinion by replacing the shim, the differential unit and drive pinion shaft must again be disassembled.

Consequently, when unit will be reassembled after tooth contact adjustments, the backlash and bearing rotation torque must be rechecked.

SWING AXLE SHAFTS AND SLIP JOINTS

Description and Repair.

The two axle shafts are connected to differential through slip joints which allow shafts to swing and slide in a specially designed splined housing in differential side gear.

At the other end, axle shafts are connected to wheel drive shaft flexible joints with the intermediary of a sliding sleeve.

While servicing the assembly, check the condition of slip joint sliding surfaces and housing in differential side gears: if clearance has become greater than .0079" (0,20 mm) on account of wear, replace slip joints and - if necessary - also differential side gears.

Check also the clearance between slip joint pivots and runners; if found excessive, replace the axle shafts (joint pivot is not supplied as a spare) and runners.

Axle shaft-to-sliding sleeve spline clearance must not exceed .0059" (0,15 mm).

Observe the sliding sleeve snap ring for snug fit in its groove-seat on shaft.

It is essential to check the condition of boots, bushings and oil seals: replace any damaged part.

INSTALLATION OF GEARBOX-DIFFERENTIAL UNIT

Raise car rear end and rest on stands.

Using pilot **A. 62023**, check that clutch driven disc hub is aligned with clutch shaft pilot bush.

Support gearbox-differential unit assembly by a garage jack equipped with arm **Arr. 2076**. Raise the assembly and, by pushing it in towards engine, insert clutch shaft in driven disc hub splines and into pilot bush.

Couple gearbox rear housing to engine crankcase by the studs, around two of which are concentrically placed the location dowels.

Partially screw in the gearbox/differential-to-body front support mounting screws, interposing the fiber washers. Lower hydraulic garage jack and pull it out from under car.

Screw in the four lower mounting nuts and tighten with torque wrench to 18.1 to 21.7 ft.lbs (2500 to 3000 kgmm).

Fully tighten the front support screws.

Connect: gearshift control rod to speed selector lever and the speedometer drive bowden.

Insert springs between axle shafts and wheel

GEARBOX-DIFFERENTIAL UNIT

ADJUSTING THE RING GEAR-TO-PINION TOOTH CONTACT

Pinion is moved in toward or out from ring gear by increasing or decreasing the thickness of shim pack on pinion shaft.

NOTE - If the procedure to determine pinion shim thickness has been followed correctly, there will be hardly any need for a new disassembly and adjustment of differential, due to defective tooth contact.

Fig. 207 - Correct tooth contact.

Excessive contact on tooth flank:

move pinion out from ring gear by reducing thickness of shim.

Fig. 208.

Excessive contact on tooth heel:

move pinion in towards ring gear by increasing thickness of shim.

Fig. 209.

Excessive contact on tooth face:

move pinion in towards ring gear by increasing thickness of shim.

Fig. 210.

Excessive contact on tooth toe:

move pinion out from ring gear by reducing thickness of shim.

Fig. 211.

drive shaft and tighten the three mounting screws of each splined sleeve on flexible joint to 20.3 ft.lbs (2800 kgmm).

Install flywheel housing cover.

Fit in place starter motor with relevant cover and tighten the two mounting nuts to 18.1 to 21.7 ft.lbs (2500 to 3000 kgmm). Install starter control tie rod; connect the two starter cables; fit clutch control tie rod; hook up the return spring and secure clutch control bowden retainment bracket on gearbox casing. Reconnect the cable to battery positive post.

GEARSHIFT CONTROL MECHANISM

Adjustment.

When an unsatisfactory engagement of gears is detected, the gearshifting control mechanism needs some adjustment.

Operations to perform are:

Undo the screws fixing cover to tunnel and raise cover along gearshift lever stem.

Slacken the lever support mounting screws; slots have been machined in tunnel to allow longitudinal displacement of support.

Push support forward, if first and third speed engagement is improper, and backward if 2nd, 4th and reverse speed engagements need adjustment.

Next, tighten the mounting screws.

After adjustment, install components back in their original position.

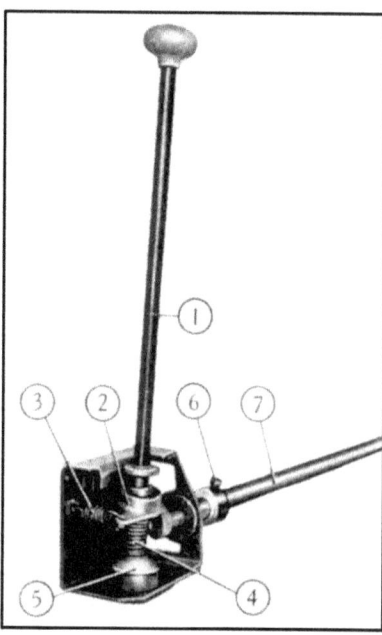

Fig. 213 - Gearshift control mechanism.

1. Hand lever. - 2. Inner lever. - 3. Lever return spring. - 4. Hand lever spring. - 5. Ball seat. - 6. Inner lever - to - rod mounting screw. - 7. Gearshift control rod.

Disconnect gearshift control rod at speed engagement control lever.

From front end, pull out the assembly.

Disassembly and Inspection of Gearshift Lever Components.

Gearshift hand lever is removed by backing out the lever-to-support mounting self-locking nut (figure 214).

Observe that lever ball and socket are in good condition.

The inner lever return spring and the hand lever spring must still have the required flexibility; if found excessively weak, replace as required.

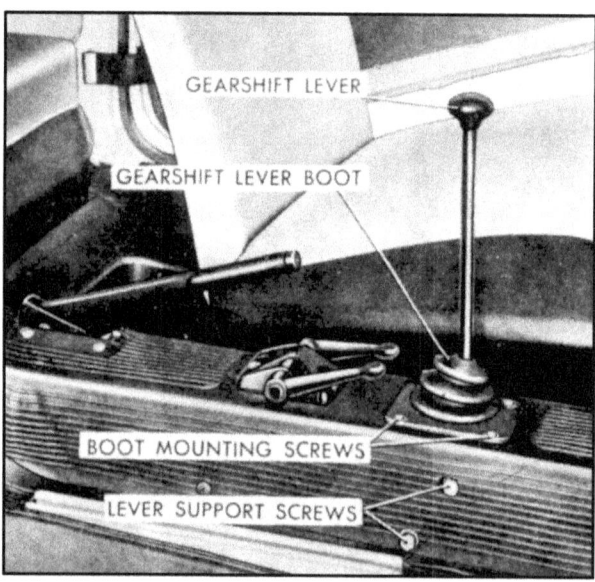

Fig. 212 - Location of gearshift lever on control passage tunnel.

Removal.

To remove this assembly from car, proceed as follows:

Unscrew the gearshift control lever knob, then, the cover fixing screws and slide cover out of hand lever.

Remove the screws fixing the assembly on tunnel.

Take off tunnel front cover.

Fig. 214.

Gearshift hand lever assembly.

Arrow points to hand lever - to - support self-locking mounting nut.

GEARBOX-DIFFERENTIAL ADJUSTMENT AND TIGHTENING REFERENCE

ITEM	Drwg. or Std. Part No.	Thread	Material	Tightening Torque
Primary shaft gear nut	1/08019/11	14 MC (x1)	R 50 (Shaft 14CN5 Cmt 5)	18.1 to 25.3 ft.lbs (2.500 to 3.500 kgmm)
Layshaft gear nut	1/07934/11	14 MB (x1,5)	R 50 Cdt (Shaft 14CN5 Cmt 5)	28.9 to 36.2 ft.lbs (4.000 to 5.000 kgmm)
Ring gear-to-differential case screw	891596	8 MA (x1,25)	R 100	23.1 ft.lbs (3.200 kgmm)
Differential bearing housing-to-gearbox casing nut	1/61008/11	8 MA (x1,25)	R 50 Cdt (Stud R 50)	13.0 ft.lbs (1.800 kgmm)
Gearbox casing and support-to-engine nut	1/21647/11	10 x 1,25 M	R 50 Cdt (Stud R 50 Cdt)	27.5 ft.lbs (3.800 kgmm)
Gearbox differential support assembly-to-engine nut	1/61008/11	8 MA (x1,25)	R 50 Cdt (Stud R 100)	18.1 to 21.7 ft.lbs (2.500 to 3.000 kgmm)
Axle shaft sleeve-to-flexible joint screw	1/60446/21	8 MA (x1,25)	R 80 Cdt	20.3 ft.lbs (2.800 kgmm)
Differential roller bearing rotation torque (not break-away) Final drive pinion-to-gear backlash				1.01 ± 0.07 ft.lbs (140 ± 10 kgmm) .0031" to .0047" (0,08 to 0,12 mm)

GEARBOX-DIFFERENTIAL SERVICE EQUIPMENT

- A. 42013 — Puller - final drive pinion roller bearing inner ring.
- A. 52022 — Wrench - differential bearing adjuster rings.
- A. 62028 — Tool - remover and installer, differential case roller bearing outer ring.
- A. 62036 — Fixture - drive pinion shim thickness determination (to be used with C. 689).
- A. 62037 — Shaft - final drive pinion and bearing assembly measurement to determine pinion adjustment shim thickness.
- A. 62039 — Tool - pinion-to-ring gear backlash check-up.
- A. 62040 — Tool - differential case bearing rotation torque check-up, with support for attachment of dynamometer A. 95697.
- A. 62041 — Tool - bevel pinion retainment.
- A. 95697 — Dynamometer - differential bearing rotation torque determination.
- Arr. 2076 — Support - to be mounted on garage jack for gearbox-differential installation and removal.
- Arr. 2206/7 — Support - gearbox-differential unit retainment on rotating stand Arr. 2204.
- C. 689 — Fixture, with dial gauge, shim thickness determination (use with A. 62036).

GEARBOX-DIFFERENTIAL TECHNICAL SPECIFICATIONS

Speeds	4 forward and reverse
Primary shaft	integral with 1st, 3rd, 4th and reverse speeds drive gear cluster
Bearings	two
Type	ball
Layshaft	integral with final drive pinion
Bearings front	ball type, double row
rear	cylindrical roller
Type of gears:	
drive, 2nd, 3rd, 4th speed	helical, constant mesh
driven, 2nd, 3rd, 4th speed	with dogs for quick engagement
drive and driven, 1st and reverse	straight spur gears
Gear ratios (*):	
1st gear	3.27 to 1
2nd gear	2.06 to 1
3rd gear	1.30 to 1
4th gear	0.87 to 1
Reverse	4.13 to 1
Spiral bevel final drive gear ratio «500»	8 to 41
«500 Sports»	8 to 39

Ratio to wheels:	«500»	«500 Sports»
1st gear	16.77 to 1	15.95 to 1
2nd gear	10.59 to 1	10.07 to 1
3rd gear	6.66 to 1	6.33 to 1
4th gear	4.48 to 1	4.26 to 1
Reverse	21.18 to 1	20.15 to 1

Differential case bearings	2
Type	taper roller
Adjustment	by adjusters
Rotation torque	1.01 ± .07 ft.lbs (140 ± 10 kgmm)
Final drive pinion and ring gear (mated):	
backlash	.0031" to .0047" (0,08 - 0,12 mm)
adjustment	by shims
pinion shim thickness	.0039" to .0059" (0,10 - 0,15 mm)
Lube oil:	
grade	FIAT W 90 (SAE 90 EP)
quantity lt.	1,075
kg	1,000
qts.	(U.S.) 1.14 - (Imp.) .94

(*) See note page 108.

Section 5
FRONT SUSPENSION AND WHEELS

	Page
REMOVAL AND DISASSEMBLY	127
LEAF SPRING	128
SWINGING ARMS	130
KINGPIN HOUSING	131
STEERING KNUCKLE AND WHEEL HUB	132
ASSEMBLY AND INSTALLATION	135
CHECKING AND ADJUSTING FRONT WHEEL CAMBER AND CASTER	136
TIGHTENING REFERENCE	139
SERVICE EQUIPMENT	139
SPECIFICATIONS	140
TROUBLE DIAGNOSIS AND CORRECTIONS	141

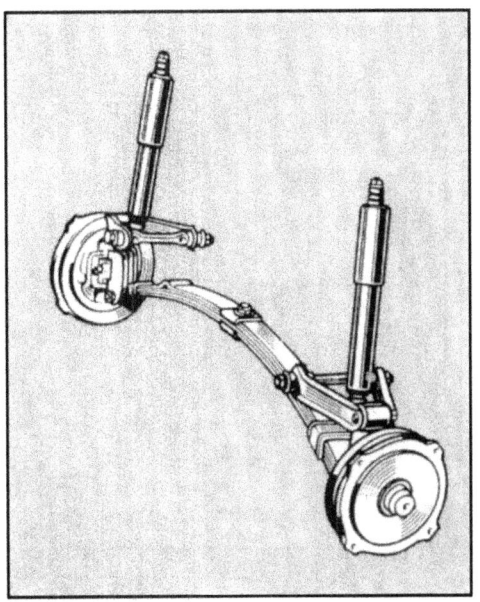

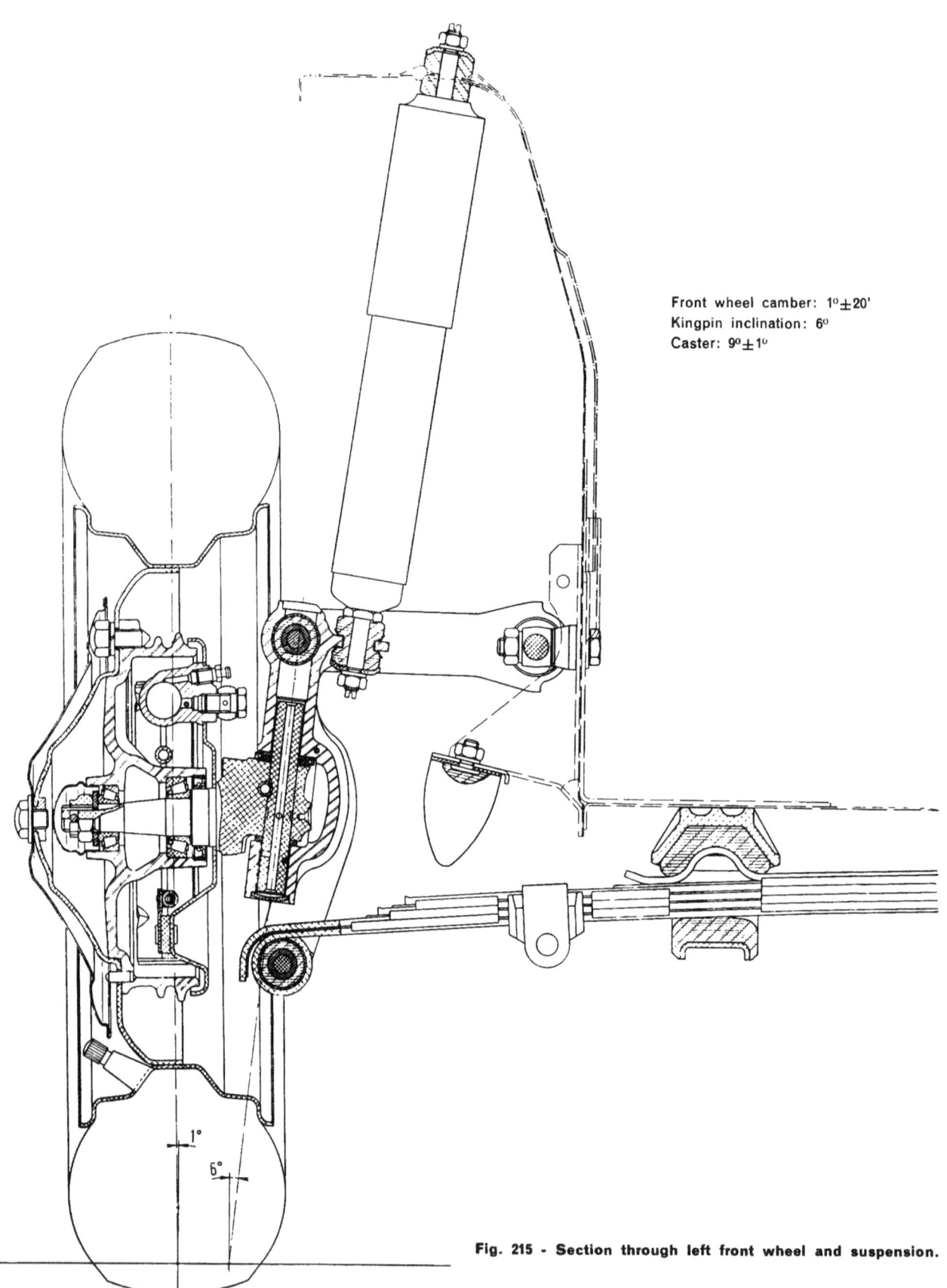

Front wheel camber: 1°±20'
Kingpin inclination: 6°
Caster: 9°±1°

Fig. 215 - Section through left front wheel and suspension.

FRONT SUSPENSION AND WHEELS

Description.

The independent-wheel front suspension of the « New 500 » consists of a transversal leaf spring anchored to body through two rubber mountings and to kingpins through « estendblocks » (fig. 215).

The leaf spring performs also as stabilizer.

Upper articulation of kingpins in swinging arms is obtained by « estendblocks »; half-arms are in turn anchored on body (fig. 226) and swing on their pin through rubber bushes.

The suspension system includes hydraulic shock absorbers whose top end is connected to body and lower end to kingpin housing.

Two rubber buffers, secured to body-mounted brackets, limit leaf spring oscillations; spring center bolt is provided with rubber pad.

Front Suspension Removal and Disassembly.

Using hydraulic jack, raise front of car on stands.
Remove wheels.
Disconnect steering linkages from Pitman arm, drag link and steering knuckle arms.

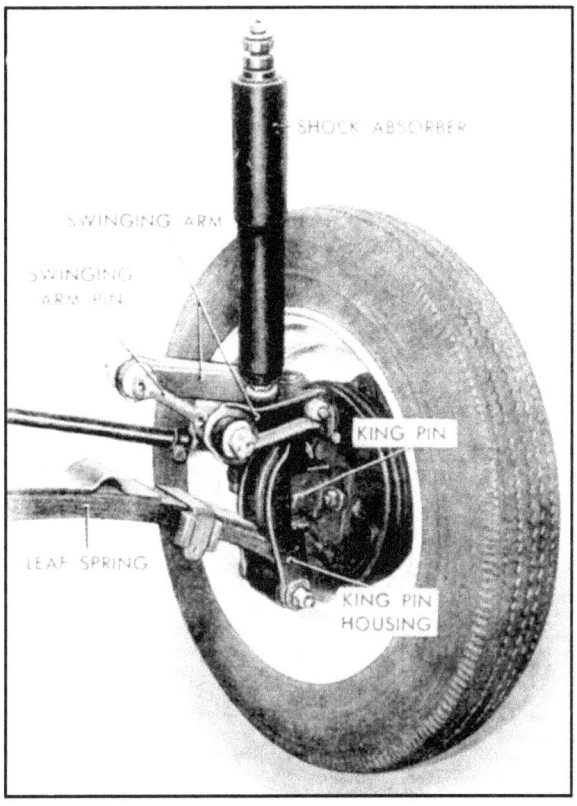

Fig. 217 - Right front suspension.

Fig. 216 - Left front suspension, on car.

Also visible are the two swinging arm-to-body stud mounting nuts.

Back out shock absorber upper mounting nut and push down the outer cylinder.

Disconnect brake lines at wheel cylinders; before doing this, blank brake fluid reservoir outlet by inserting a suitable wooden peg through reservoir filler opening.

Fit cross beam **Arr. 2072** under leaf spring and support by hydraulic garage jack **Arr. 2027**.

Remove self-locking nut securing leaf spring to kingpin housing and take off spring mounting bolt.

Remove nuts securing swinging arm pin to studs on body and remove swinging arm assembly.

Remove adjusting shims and spacers from studs.

Remove nuts securing leaf spring elastic mounting to body (fig. 219); lower hydraulic jack slowly and take off the spring.

Disconnect hydraulic shock absorber from kingpin housing using wrench **A. 56030**.

Back out swinging arm pin mounting nuts and disinsert pin.

Fig. 218 - Front suspension, bottom view.

Spring mountings are secured to body floor.

To remove kingpin, operate as follows:

Drive the « estendblock » out of kingpin housing using drift rod **A. 66056**.

By a punch, drive off lockpin of kingpin.

Remove lower plug and take off kingpin.

LEAF SPRING

Description.

The spring consists of a main leaf and four other leaves. Polyethylene insulating strips are sandwiched between leaves.

Leaves are held together by a center bolt and two elastically-mounted side clips.

For attachment to kingpin housings, « estendblocks » are fitted in main leaf eyes.

A rubber buffer is mounted on spring center bolt.

Spring data is given in tables on page 129 and in figs. 221 and 222.

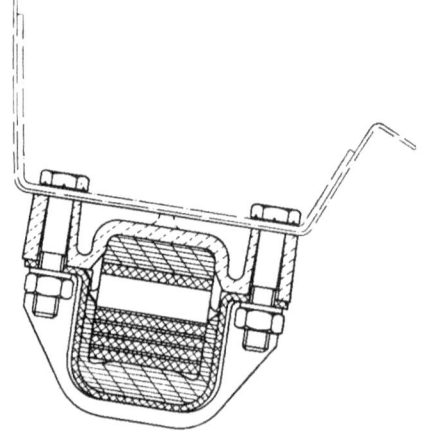

Fig. 219 - Section through one of the two spring mountings.

Inspection and Repair of Leaf Spring and « Estendblocks ».

Disassemble leaf spring by taking off the side clips and center bolt. Next, wash all parts carefully.

Check the following:

a) Leaves are not broken or cracked; replace if required.

The third spring leaf does not come for replacement. In case of damage of this leaf, the whole spring should be replaced.

b) No paint is present between leaves; remove any trace of paint.

c) Mating faces of leaves must be perfectly smooth and clean; with a file or other suitable means, eliminate any indentation or rough areas.

d) Camber of leaves; if necessary, restore the required camber (see the setting data given for reassembled springs in the following tables).

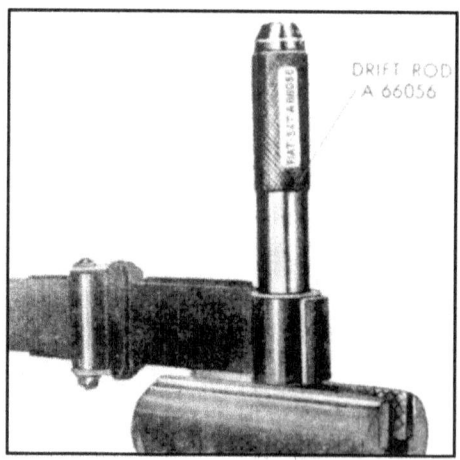

Fig. 220 - Drift rod A. 66056 for installation and removal of « estendblock » in spring main leaf eye.

e) Condition of « estendblocks » force-fitted in main leaf eyes. Some of the troubles they cause (noise or squeaks) are detectable when spring is mounted on car.

If the above troubles are noticed, or excessive wear, traces of seizure and dryness of rubber parts, replace the « estendblocks ».

Removal and installation of « estendblocks » is done using drift rod **A. 66056** (fig. 220).

f) Good condition of all rubber pads, center buffer and polyethylene linings. Replace parts as required.

FRONT SUSPENSION AND WHEELS

LEAF SPRING SPECIFICATIONS

Position	Load P		Camber		Elastic give-in from pos. 2		Flexibility, between pos. 2 and pos. 3	
	lbs	kg	in	mm	in	mm	in/100 lbs	mm/100kg
2	220.5	100	5.3936±.2362	137±6	—	—	2.23±.10	125±6
3	440.9*	200*	—	—	4.9212±.2362	125±6		

FRONT LEAF SPRING, LOADED AT CENTER

* When testing the spring never exceed 440.9 lbs (200 kg) load.

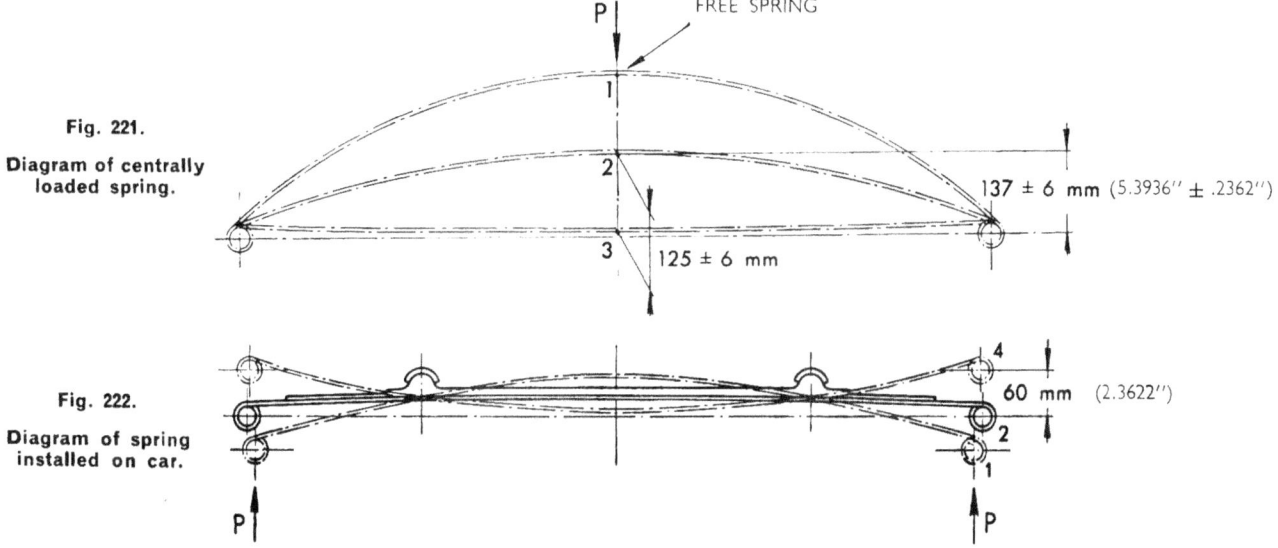

Fig. 221. Diagram of centrally loaded spring.

Fig. 222. Diagram of spring installed on car.

Position	Load P		Camber		Elastic give-in from pos. 1		Flexibility between pos. 1 and pos. 3	
		lbs	kg	in	mm	in	mm	in/100 lbs	mm/100 kg
1	Initial load for flexibility check-up	220.5	100	—	—	—	—		
2	Static load	297.6	135	1.1023 ±.1181	28±3	—	—	1.55±.07	87±5
3	Final load for flexibility check-up	330.7	150	—	—	1.7125±.0984	43,5±2,5		
4	Metal-to-metal deflection load	451.9	205	—	—	—	—		

FRONT LEAF SPRING, INSTALLED ON CAR

Spring specifications are intended at assembly conditions, i. e., with pre-compressed rubber pads and without bumpers. Give-in check-up must be carried out by loading both eyes simultaneously.

SWINGING ARMS

Description.

Consisting of two pressed sheet steel half-arms (fig. 223) joined, at assembly, by two pins: one on king pin housing and one on body.

Rubber bushes (« Flanblocks ») are press-fitted in half-arms for the attachment of swinging arm pin to body (fig. 226).

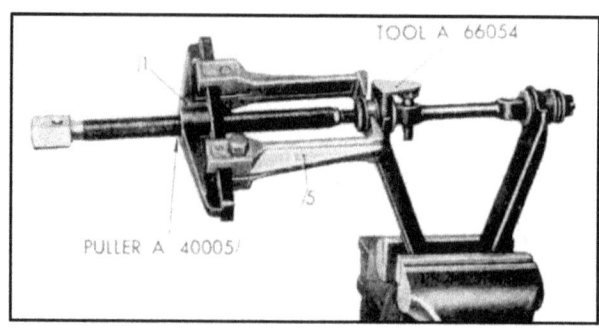

Fig. 224 - Removal of rubber bushes by universal puller A. 40005 and arm retainer tool A. 66054.

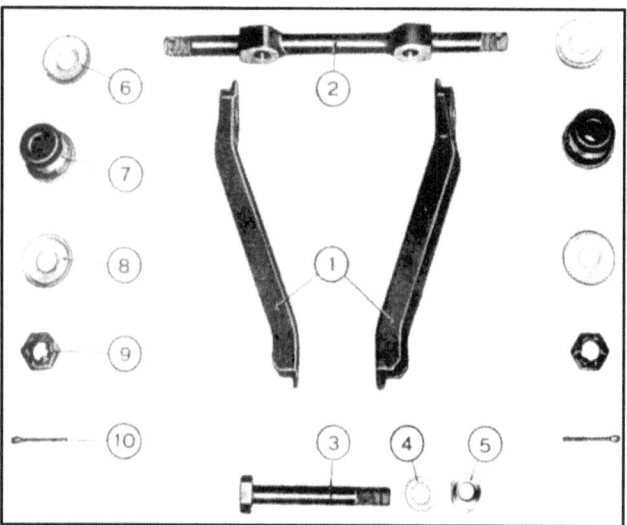

Fig. 223 - Swinging arm components.

1. Half-arms. - 2. Pin, arm to body mounting. - 3. Pin, arm to kingpin housing mounting. - 4 and 5. Washer and nut. - 6 and 8. Cups, rubber bushes. - 7. Rubber bushes. - 9 and 10. Split pins and nuts, mounting, pin (2) to arms.

b) The surface of pin in contact with camber and caster adjustment shims should not show any sign of indents or roughness such as to prejudice adjustment accuracy; if not too marked, smoothen out irregularities; otherwise replace the pin.

c) Check the condition of half-arm bushes; inner surface must not show signs of seizure and clearance to pin must be greater than .0157" (0,40 mm) (fit clearance: .00059" to .0059" - 0,015 to 0,150 mm).

Observe that rubber parts of bush are not torn, cracked or weak and replace as required.

Installation of rubber bushes in arms is carried out using tool **A. 66058** (fig. 225).

Disassembly.

Clamp swinging arm in a vise and fit tool **A. 66054** (fig. 224) for half arms-to-pin retainment.

Remove split pin and nut securing the half-arms on their pin.

Fit universal puller **A. 40005**/, using bridge piece /1, the two arms /5, and pull out the rubber bushes (fig. 224).

Pull out tool **A. 66054** and insert it on the other half-arm.

Also on this side, repeat the operations performed for bush removal on the first half-arm.

Inspection of Arm, Rubber Bushes and Pin.

a) Inspect half-arms which must be undistorted; straighten out, if necessary. Make sure they have the same inclination and that holes are properly aligned.

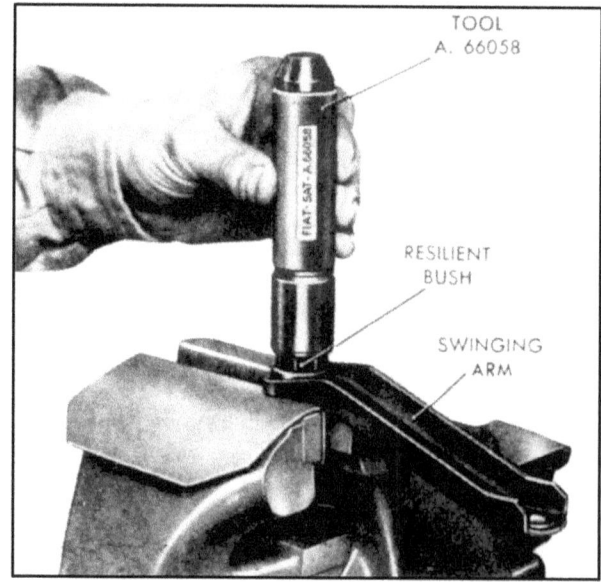

Fig. 225 - Installation of rubber bush in half-arm, using tool A. 66058.

NOTICE

Tightening of the two swinging arm pin mounting nuts (5, fig. 226) must be carried out while keeping the axes of swinging arm and of pin hole (for screws 7, fig. 226) on the same plane.

FRONT SUSPENSION AND WHEELS

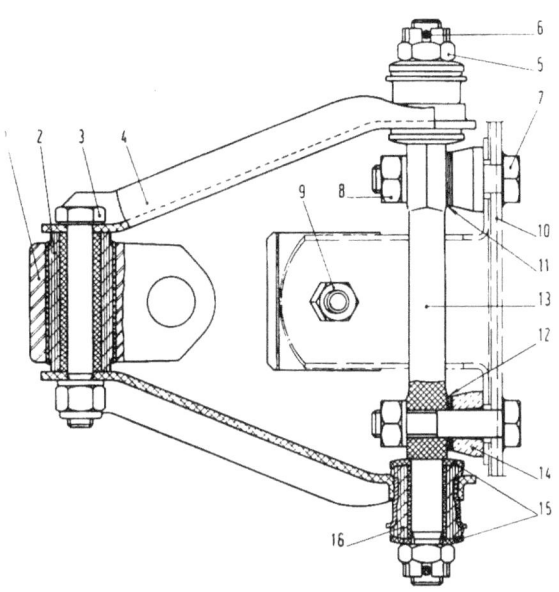

Fig. 226 - Section through left swinging arm.

1. Kingpin housing. - 2. Estendblock. - 3. Pin, swinging arm to kingpin housing. - 4. Half-arm. - 5 and 6. Nut and split pin. - 7. Screw, welded on body. - 8. Nut, mounting, pin 13 to body. - 9. Rubber buffer mounting nut. - 10. Body panel. - 11 and 12. Camber and caster adjustment shims. - 13. Pin, swinging arm to body. - 14. Spacer. - 15. Cups, for rubber bush. - 16. Rubber bush.

KINGPIN HOUSING

Inspection and Repair of « Estendblock », Kingpin Housing and Kingpin Bushings.

As already mentioned on page 128, the removal of « estendblock » is performed using tool **A. 66056** (fig. 227) which also serves for its installation.

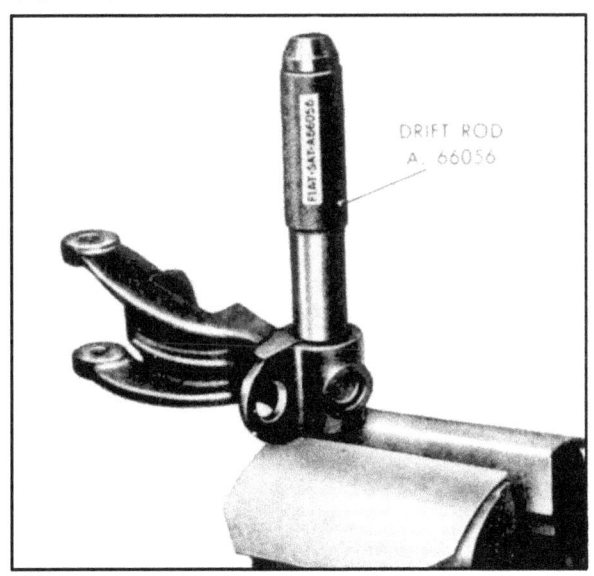

Fig. 227 - Drift rod **A. 66056** for kingpin housing « estendblock » removal and installation.

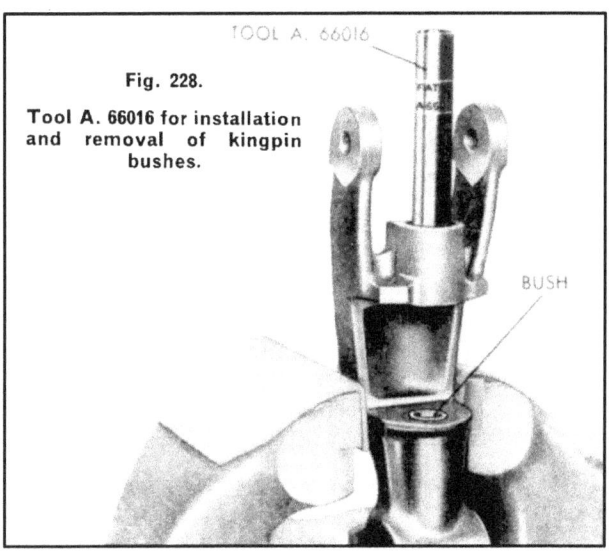

Fig. 228.

Tool **A. 66016** for installation and removal of kingpin bushes.

Make sure the « estendblock » is not worn, that is, it has no sign of seizure on its inner surface or its rubber has not hardened. Replace, if required.

Check that kingpin-to-bush clearance is not greater than .0079" (0,20 mm) (fit clearance, when new, is .00063" to .00213" - 0,016 to 0,054 mm).

If clearance is excessive, replace the two bushes and, if necessary, also the kingpin.

Kingpin bush installation and removal are carried out using tool **A. 66016** (fig. 228); after assembly, bushes must be accurately smoothened with reamer **A. 90316** (fig. 229) to a diameter of .5912" to .5922" (15,016 to 15,043 mm).

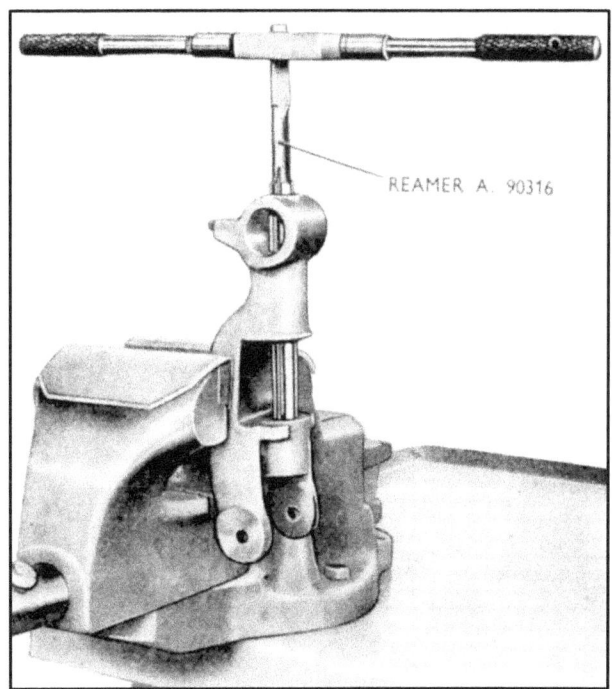

Fig. 229 - Smoothening inner surfaces of kingpin bushes with reamer **A. 90316**.

Using fixture **C. 1004**, check that kingpin housing has not been distorted, proceeding as follows:

a) Place pin (1, fig. 230) in kingpin housing upper hole and lower pin (2) with square (3) in lower holes.

— Check that square tip just contacts upper pin (1).

— Repeat this operation on the other side. This will check kingpin housing alignment.

If misaligned, on one side the square tip will clear pin (1) with a wide gap, while on the other it will force against the pin.

If this is the case, replace the housing.

b) Remove upper pin (1), and in its place, insert bar 4 (fig. 231). If kingpin housing is in good condition, the lower end of bar (4) should place itself tangentially to lower pin (2).

Should this not be the case, i. e., if the gap between the two parts is excessive or the parts strike each other, the kingpin housing is evidently distorted; the kingpin could not possibly assume, after assembly, the exact inclination prescribed of 6º (fig. 215).

If this is the case, replace the housing.

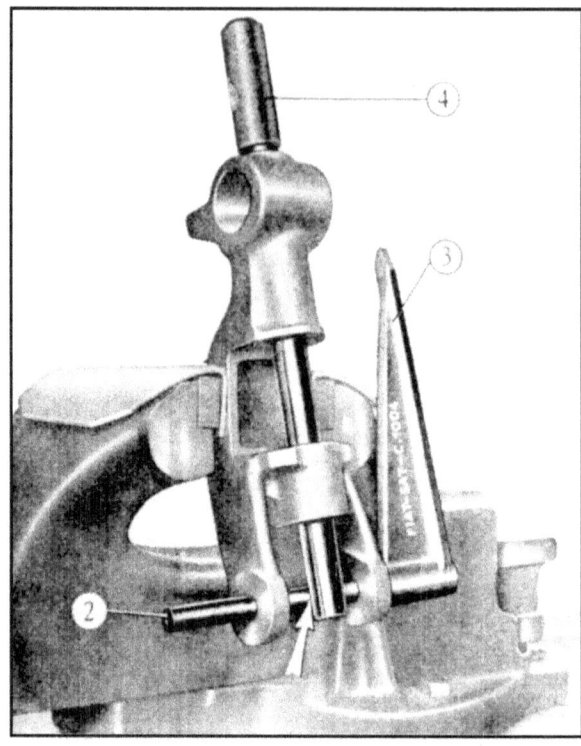

Fig. 231 - Checking kingpin housing inclination with fixture C. 1004.

2. Lower pin with square 3. - 4. Bar.

Arrow points to bar 4 which must be tangential to pin 2.

NOTE - To prevent abnormal torsion of the « estendblock » press-fitted in kingpin housing, the housing-to-swinging arm pin nut must be tightened arranging the parts so that the angle between swinging arm plane and housing axes is about 95º (fig. 235).

While servicing progresses, check also kingpin lubricator squirt hole which must be unobstructed; clean if required.

STEERING KNUCKLE AND WHEEL HUB

Disassembly.

Use remover **A. 46023** (fig. 232) to drive off wheel hub caps and tool **A. 66059** (fig. 234) for their installation.

To remove the wheel hub/drum assembly, after removal of hub cap, split pin and nut, use universal puller **A. 40005** with bridge piece /1 and arms /9 (fig. 233).

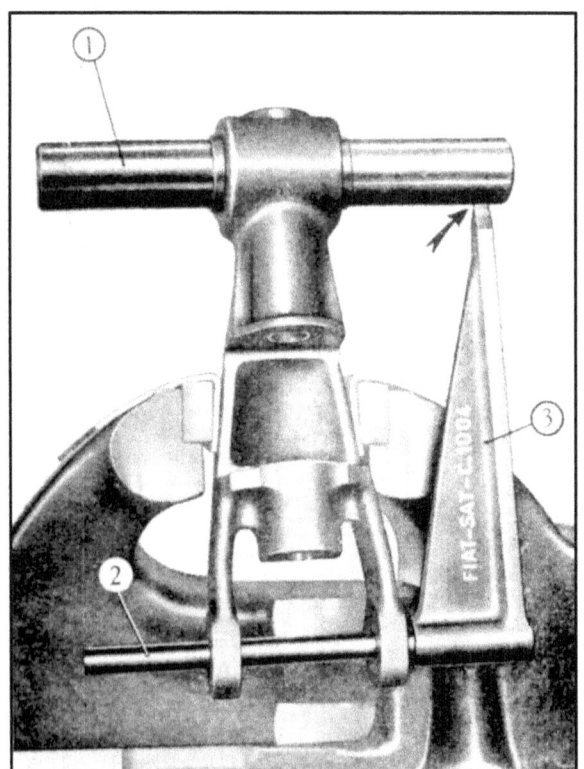

Fig. 230 - Checking parallelism of kingpin housing axes with fixture C. 1004.

1. Upper pin. - 2. Lower pin with square 3.

Arrow points to square tip which must barely contact pin 1.

FRONT SUSPENSION AND WHEELS

From drum, remove the outer roller bearing, oil seal and inner roller bearing outer race.

Pull out the steering knuckle inner roller bearing inner ring using puller **A. 46000**.

Back out the drum-to-steering knuckle mounting nuts (two) and remove the complete brake housing flange.

The removal of steering knuckle from kingpin housing is carried out as follows (see page 128):

— remove the « estendblock » from kingpin housing using drift rod **A. 66056** (fig. 227);

— drive off the lockpin from kingpin by means of a punch;

— remove the lower plug and slide off the kingpin.

The steering knuckle is thus disengaged, along with snap ring, both thrust washers and shoulder ring.

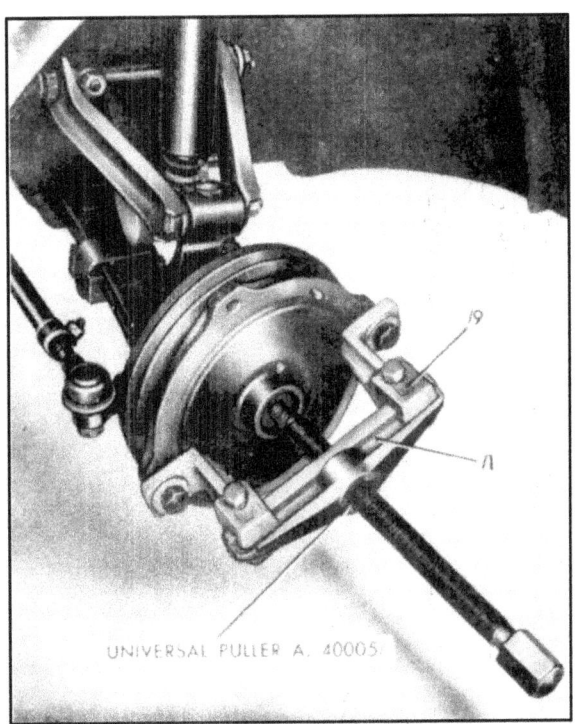

Fig. 233 - Removing left front wheel brake drum by puller A. 40005.

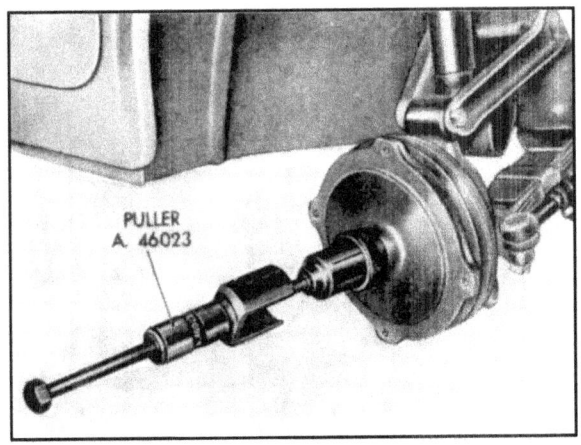

Fig. 232 - Removing right front wheel hub cap by remover A. 46023.

Inspection.

Inspect carefully all components. Particularly:

a) See that steering knuckle and steering arm are not cracked, otherwise replace.

b) Inspect steering knuckle surfaces in contact with roller bearing inner races, which must not show any scoring or seizure signs.

c) Inspect the condition of the two upper thrust rings and of lower packing ring. Replace, if worn.

Spare lower packing rings are supplied in the thicknesses tabulated in the opposite column.

After reassembly, no appreciable clearance must result between steering knuckle and kingpin housing. This is obtained by installing the lower packing ring of the proper thickness.

d) Check that seats on drums for roller bearing outer races are perfectly smooth. No clearance is

RING		STAND	OVERSIZES						UNDER-SIZES	
	in.	.002	.004	.006	.008	.010	.012	.002	.004
	mm	0,05	0,10	0,15	0,20	0,25	0,30	0,05	0,10
Thkss	in.	.0977	.0979	.1016	.1036	.1056	.1076	.1095	.0957	.0938
	mm	2,482	2,487	2,582	2,632	2,782	2,632	2,782	2,432	2,382
	in.	.098	.100	.102	.104	.106	.108	.110	.096	.094
	mm	2,50	2,55	2,60	2,65	2,70	2,75	2,80	2,45	2,40

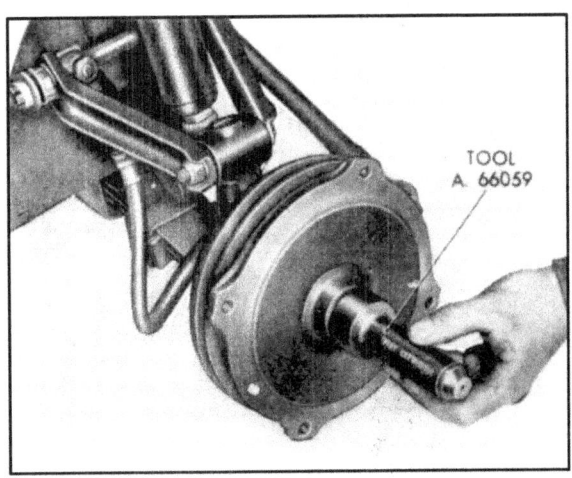

Fig. 234 - Installing right front wheel hub cap by tool A. 66059.

CAMBER AND CASTER CHECK AND ADJUSTMENT DATA

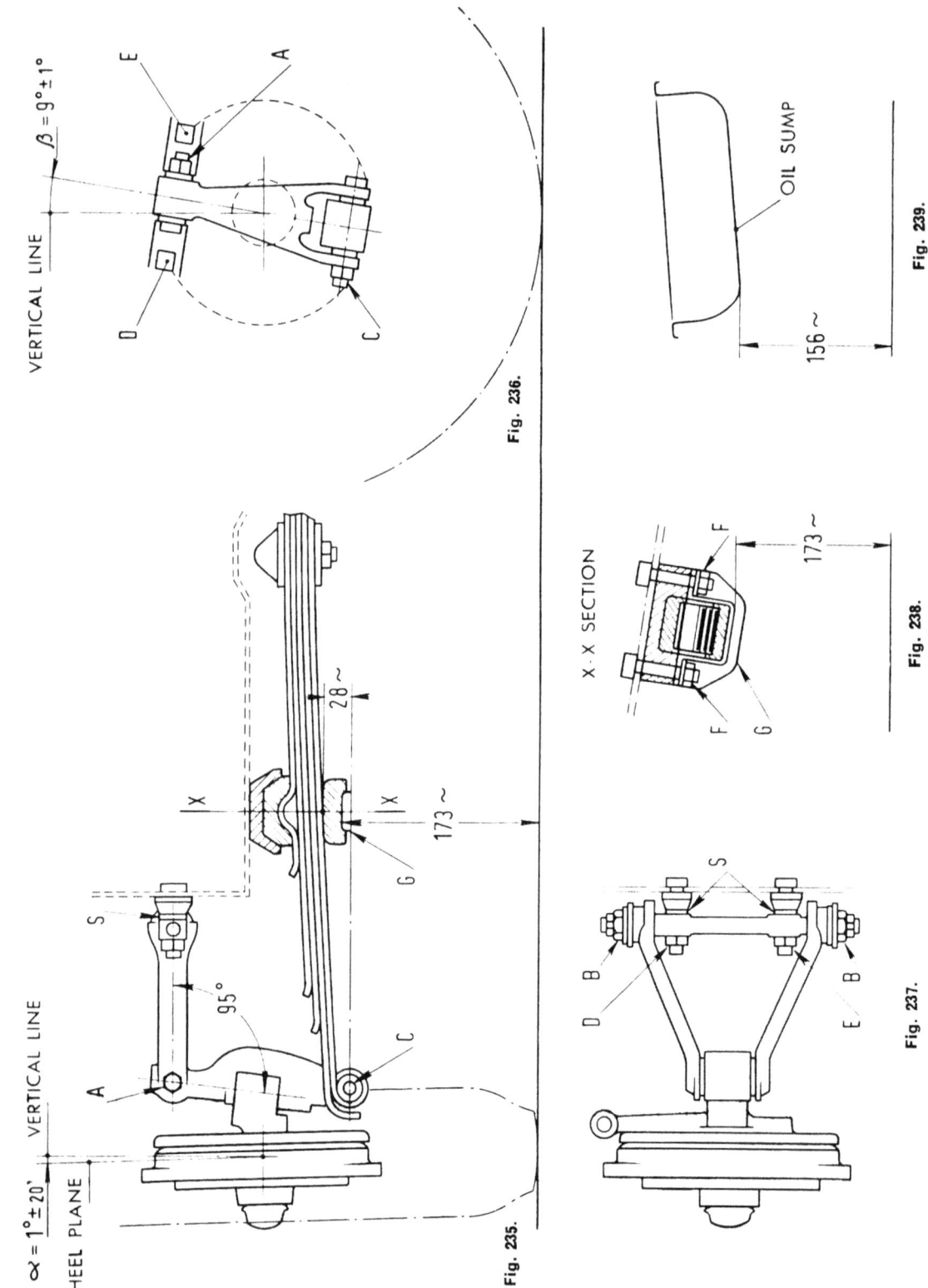

Fig. 235.
Fig. 236.
Fig. 237.
Fig. 238.
Fig. 239.

FRONT SUSPENSION AND WHEELS

permitted between races and seats. See that bearing cages and rollers are not chipped or broken.

e) The seal must not be torn and must adhere perfectly to both drum and steering knuckle.

NOTE - See page 154 for front and rear hydraulic shock absorber servicing.

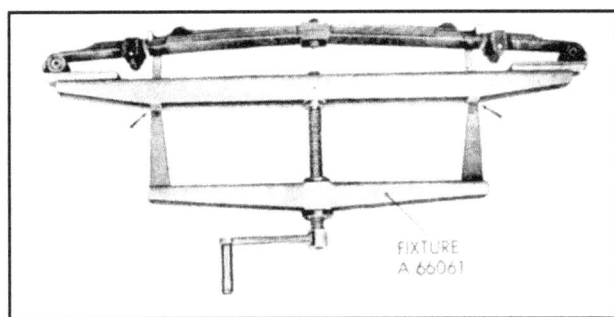

Fig. 241 - Leaf spring position under «full static load» on fixture A. 66061.

Arrows point to the reference indexes for correct spring compression.

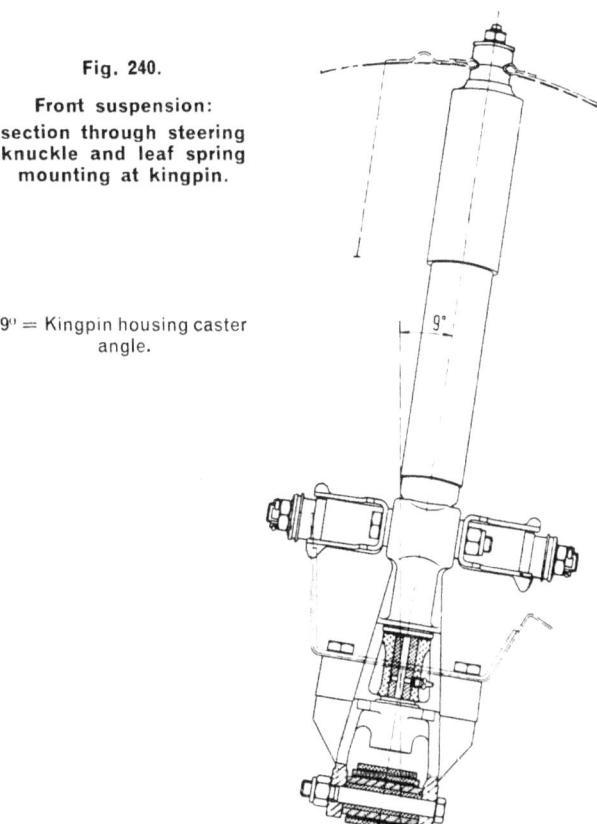

Fig. 240.

Front suspension: section through steering knuckle and leaf spring mounting at kingpin.

9° = Kingpin housing caster angle.

On bench, assemble:

— the brake housing flange on steering knuckle and tighten nuts to 14.5 ft.lbs (1200 kgmm);

— the roller bearings and seal on drum hub; pack liberally with FIAT MR grease the pocket between the two bearings;

— the nut with washer securing the wheel hub to steering knuckle; tighten nut to 21.7 ft.lbs (3000 kgmm). Then, back out nut of at least 60° and insert cotter pin into steering knuckle opening.

FRONT SUSPENSION ASSEMBLY AND INSTALLATION

Install the spring on fixture **A. 66061** (fig. 241) and load it with the proper screw of the fixture until the index «Nuova 500» appears below cross beam lower edge.

In this position the spring attains the «full static load» setting, same as on car; the sag in correspondence with plane X-X (fig. 235) is approximately 1.10″ (28 mm).

Insert the spring so set and provided with upper elastic supports on the studs projecting from body bottom.

Fit the two support lower caps with elastic pads and screw on the stud nuts to a torque of 28.9 ft.lbs (4.000 kgmm).

NOTE

Starting from car No. 043624, the right steering knuckle nut has a counterclockwise threading and is identified by a circle groove on outside face.

Conversely, the left steering knuckle nut is still threading clockwise and brings no identification mark.

Above variation has been introduced as a prudential measure, like what already existing at left hand steering knuckles, to avoid that, should wheel bearings seize accidentally, right hand steering knuckle nuts are dragged to lock bearings and, consequently, road wheels.

This should be borne in mind when servicing front hubs, so that right hand steering knuckle nuts be not inadvertently screwed out by counterclockwise rotation, thus causing overtightness on the nut.

— the cap to hub using tool **A. 66059** (fig. 234);

— the steering knuckle to kingpin housing interposing the two upper thrust rings, the snap ring and lower packing ring whose thickness shall be selected as specified on page 133, to take up any play between knuckle and kingpin housing. Secure steering knuckle pin with elastic cotter.

Connect now the swinging arm to the wheel assembly by bolt and nut.

The nut must be screwed onto the bolt (A, figure 235) by arranging the parts in such a way that between the arm plane and the kingpin housing the angle results about 95° (fig. 235). By this provision the swinging arm-to-kingpin housing coupling will be perfectly elastic and undue torsional stresses on kingpin housing « estendblock » during operation will be prevented. Tightening torque is 39.8 to 43.4 ft.lbs (5500 to 6000 kgmm).

Insert the swinging arm pin on the two studs welded on body sides so as to support the suspension/wheels assembly.

Connect kingpin housing to spring eye by inserting the bolt and tightening the self-locking nut to 28.9 ft.lbs (4000 kgmm). During this operation the spring must be kept always « set » by fixture **A. 66061** to ensure correct assembly and to prevent abnormal stresses on the « estendblocks ».

Slide off the swinging arm and insert spacers and shims (S, fig. 237) on studs, seeing that the resulting thickness is the same as found at disassembly; again attach the swinging arm.

Screw on the nuts securing the pin to body and tighten to 28.9 ft.lbs (4000 kgmm).

Install shock absorber and secure it to kingpin housing and to body, inserting the plain washer between rubber pad and toothed washer.

Remove fixture **A. 66061**, connect steering rods, brake fluid pipes and install wheels. Remove plug from brake fluid tank inlet opening. Raise car by hydraulic jack **Arr. 2027**, remove stands and lower car to ground.

After installing both right and left suspensions, adjust front end geometry according to the directions contained in the following chapter.

CHECKING AND ADJUSTING FRONT WHEEL CAMBER AND CASTER

Front wheel alignment adjustment becomes necessary when an excessive tire wear or irregular steering performance (stiffening, etc.) is noticed.

Values of front end setting, as referred to « static load » conditions (corresponding to an orderly load of four passengers), should be as follows:

— camber: 1°±20′;
— caster: 9°±1°.

Fig. 243.

Front wheel alignment checking gauge.

Camber angle value is read on « camber » scale. Caster angle value is read on « caster » scale.

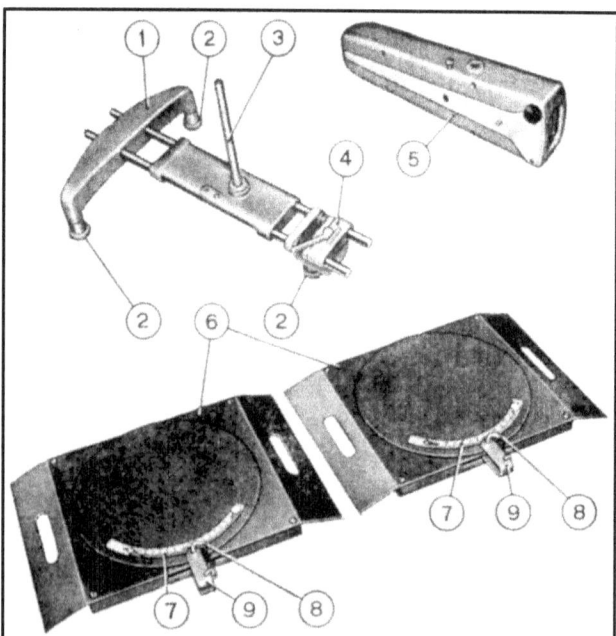

Fig. 242 - Fixture **C. 694**.

1. Holding bracket. - 2. Screw clamps for fastening fixture to wheel rim. - 3. Gage holding pin. - 4. Clamping skid. - 5. Gage. - 6. Turntable disc. - 7. Graduated sector. - 8. Turntable plate lock pin. - 9. Reference index.

Camber (α, fig. 235) and caster (β, fig. 236) adjustments are performed by interposing shims (S, fig. 237) between swinging arm pin and spacers on studs welded to body (at points D and E, fig. 247).

Spare shim thickness is .0197″ (0,5 mm).

Camber and caster are checked using fixture **C. 694** (fig. 242); toe-in by gauge **C. 692** (see page 166).

Fixture **C. 694** consists of:

— 1 gauge;
— 1 gauge holder bracket with means for clamping to wheel rim;
— 2 graduated turntables.

The gauge is made up of a pendulum goniometer whose dial has two scales (fig. 243): one

FRONT SUSPENSION AND WHEELS

fixed and the other movable (to permit zeroing by a knob).

The first scale is used to determine camber angle magnitude, the second is for caster measurements.

The holder bracket consists of a frame having a special device for clamping to wheel rim and a pin for gauge mounting.

Turntables (on which wheels rest and swivel) are made up of a sheet metal quadrangular base carrying the turntable disc. Besides around its axis, the turntable disc may move in any horizontal direction by means of a system of roller plates sliding orthogonally to each other.

The disc carries also an adjustable, graduated sector which may be set to zero on an index of the turntable (fig. 242).

Use of the Fixture.

First, inspect all car components involved in front end geometry so as to correct any possible slight defect likely to lead to erroneous readings during checks and adjustments.

Check:

— tire pressure: which should be 17.1 p.s.i. (1,20 kg/cm²) for front wheels, and 26.3 p.s.i. (1,85 kg/cm²) for rear wheels;

— play in wheel bearings: adjust, if necessary;

— play between pin and bushes of kingpin housing: replace parts, if worn;

— backlash of worm-to-sector gear set; adjust, if necessary (see page 163);

— play in steering rod articulation heads: replace heads, if necessary;

— shock absorber efficiency: replace or service shock absorbers, as required.

After performing the above checks:

— Place the car under « static load » (corresponding to an orderly load of four passengers); under this condition, the height of spring supports (G, figure 238) above ground must be about 6.811" (173 mm) (fig. 238) and the height of oil sump lowest point about 6.142" (156 mm) (fig. 239).

— Set steering wheel in mid-travel position, with spokes horizontal.

— Place two wooden blocks having the same thickness as fixture C. 694 turntables, under rear wheels.

— Raise front wheels and rest them at center of turntables. This way wheels can be easily set at various angles as required for caster inspection.

— Set the turntable pointer to zero on the sector scale (fig. 244).

— Install the holding bracket and the fixture gauge.

— Install gauge of fixture C. 694 on the wheel under check.

— Adjust screws on bracket so that clamping on rim is possible.

— Rest the two screws on rim edge and slide skid along the two guides until also skid screw may clamp the rim.

— Secure the fixture to rim by rotating the handle on skid. Check fixture for fastness by pulling it outwards and set the gauge.

Checking Camber.

With fixture clamped to wheel and gauge set normally to car centerline (fig. 244) read value of camber angle on the « Camber » scale of gauge, which should be $1° \pm 20'$.

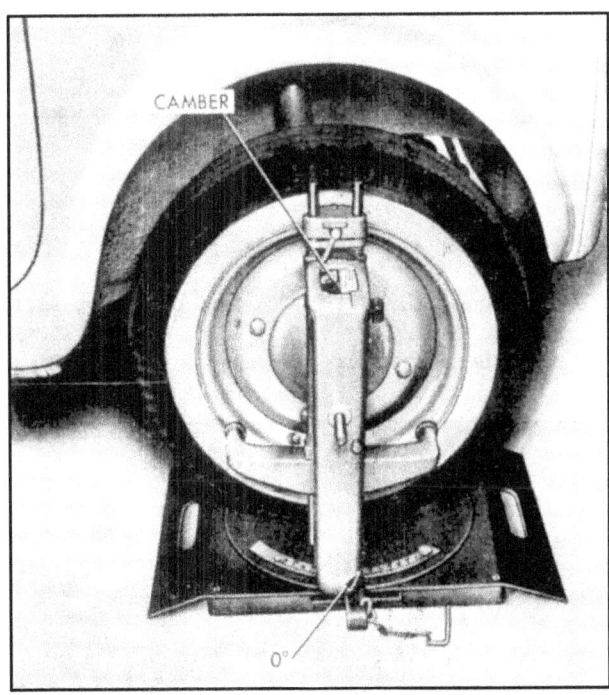

Fig. 244 - Checking front wheel camber.

The wheel must be in straightahead position; graduated sector must be set at 0°. Camber scale must read 1° (tolerance is ± 20').

NOTE - To compensate for a possible small out-of-true of the wheel, deriving from slight differences in thickness of rim sheet, or stress warpage of the rim itself, it is advisable to repeat the check after rotating wheel 180°. Should a different reading be had, take the average of the two readings to ensure correct results.

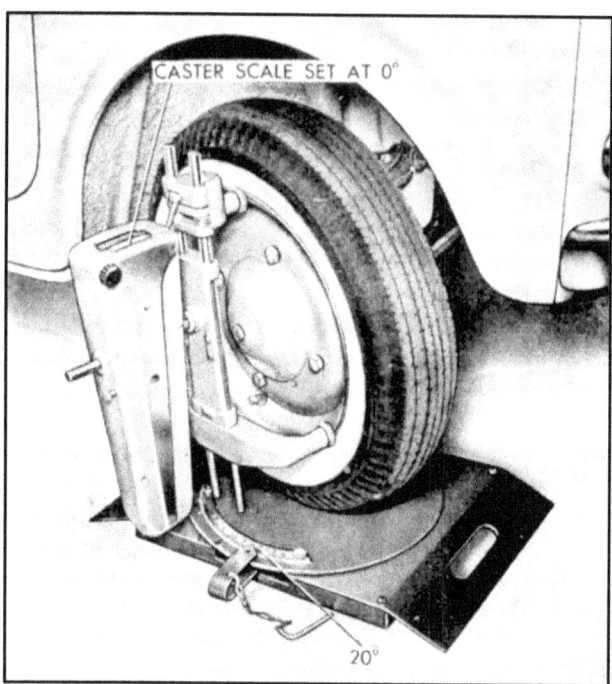

Fig. 245 - Checking front wheel caster.

1) With wheel steered 20° out, set « Caster » scale at zero.

Checking Caster.

To check caster angle, set gauge normally to car centerline.

Steer wheel 20° out and bring caster scale to « zero » (fig. 245).

Steer wheel 20° in and read « caster » angle

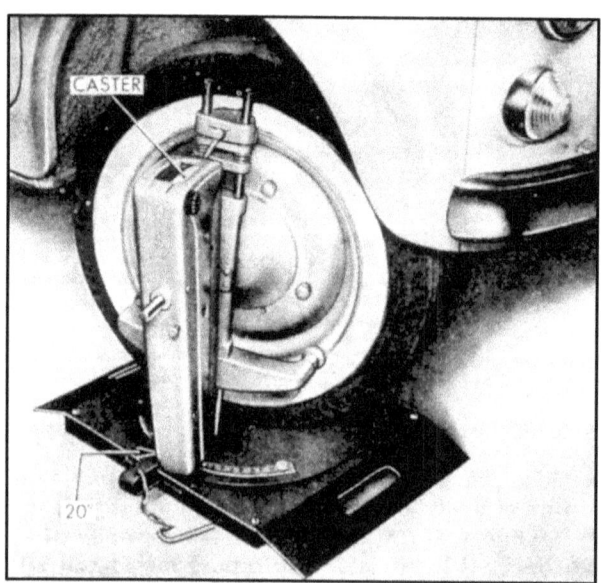

Fig. 246 - Checking front end caster.

2) With wheel steered 20° in, the « Caster » scale must read 9°; tolerance ± 1°.

value on « caster » scale: reading should be 9°±1° (fig. 246).

Should caster and camber not comply with specified values, adjust as follows:

Setting Front End Caster and Camber.

Caster.

Slacken the two nuts securing swinging arm pin to body:

— **if caster angle must be increased** (β, fig. 236), move shims (S, fig. 237) from rear screw (E) to front screw (D, fig. 247);

— **if caster angle must be reduced** (β, fig. 236), move shims from front screw (D) to rear screw (E, fig. 247).

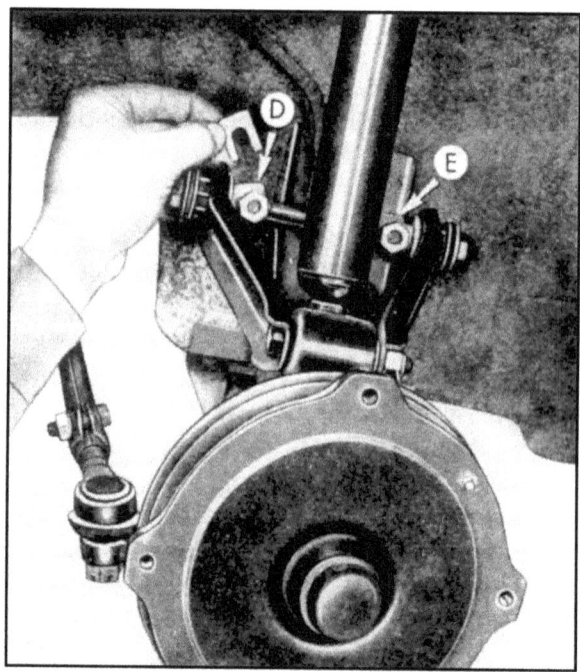

Fig. 247 - Adjusting front wheel camber and caster.

D and E: points where shims must be installed.

Camber.

Slacken the two nuts securing swinging arm pin to body:

— **if camber angle must be increased** (α, figure 235), add the same number of shims (S, fig. 237), on both screws (D and E, fig. 247);

— **if camber angle must be reduced** (α, fig. 235), remove the same number of shims from both screws (D and E, fig. 247).

The addition or removal of shims in points D and E permits camber adjustment without disturbing caster.

FRONT SUSPENSION AND WHEEL TIGHTENING REFERENCE

ITEM	Drwg. or Std. Part No.	Thread	Material	Tightening Torque ft.lbs (kgmm)
Front swinging arm-to-body mounting pin rubber bushing nut . . .	1/07933/11	12 MB (x1,5)	R 50 Cdt (Pin C 40 Bon)	28.9 to 36.2 ft.lbs (4.000 to 5.000 kgmm)
Leaf spring-to-body nut	1/21647/11	10 x 1,25 M	R 50 Cdt (Screw C 21 R)	28.9 ft.lbs (4.000 kgmm)
Kingpin housing-to-swinging arm nut	1/25745/11	10 x 1,25 M	R 50 Cdt (Screw R 80 Cdt)	39.8 to 43.4 ft.lbs (5.500 to 6.000 kgmm)
Brake housing flange-to-steering knuckle nut	1/61008/11	8 MA (x1,25)	R 50 Cdt (Screw R 50)	14.5 ft.lbs (2.000 kgmm)
Leaf spring-to-kingpin housing nut .	1/25745/11	10 x 1,25 M	R 50 Cdt (Screw R 80 Cdt)	28.9 ft.lbs (4.000 kgmm)
Swinging arm-to-body nut	1/21647/11	10 x 1,25 M	R 50 Cdt (Screw C 21 R)	28.9 ft.lbs (4.000 kgmm)
Bearing-on-steering knuckle nut . .	980498 4042887	14 MB (x1,5)	R 50 (steering knuckle 38 NCD 4 Bon)	21.7 ft.lbs (3.000 kgmm) see page 135
Wheel-to-hub screw	990166	10 MA (x1,5)	C 35 R (Bon Cdt)	32.5 to 39.8 ft.lbs (4.500 to 5.500 kgmm)

FRONT SUSPENSION AND WHEEL SERVICE EQUIPMENT

A.	10228	Tool device - aiding installation of shock absorber.
A.	40005/1/5	Puller - swinging arm rubber bushes (use with A. 66054).
A.	40005/1/9	Puller - wheel drums.
A.	46023	Puller - wheel hub cap remover.
A.	56024	Wrench - shock absorber plug.
A.	56030	Wrench - hydraulic shock absorber removal and installation.
A.	66016	Installer and remover - bushes on kingpin housing.
A.	66054	Tool - swinging arm retainment during rubber bush removal (use with A. 40005/1/5).
A.	66056	Tool - kingpin housing « estendblock » removal and installation.
A.	66058	Installer - bushes on swinging arm.
A.	66059	Installer - wheel hub caps.
A.	66061	Fixture - leaf spring flexing to static load setting.
A.	90316	Reamer - kingpin housing bushes.
Arr.	2072	Cross beam - car front end lifting with hydraulic jack Arr. 2027.
C.	692	Gauge - wheel toe-in check-up.
C.	694	Fixture - wheel alignment check-up.
C.	1004	Fixture - kingpin housing alignment check-up.

FRONT SUSPENSION AND WHEEL SPECIFICATIONS

Leaf Spring	1
Leaves	1 main and 4 auxiliary
Sag, with set spring	1.1023″ ± .1181″ (28 ± 3 mm) under a 297.6 lbs (135 kg) load
Bushes for connection to kingpin housing	« estendblock »
Connection to body bottom	by 2 supports with rubber pads
Position of spring to tighten the nut of pin for connection to kingpin housing	static load setting
Swinging Arms	2 (4 half-arms)
Connection to body	by pin and rubber bushes
Position of arm and of pin hole axes for pin nut tightening	on the same plane
Kingpin Housings.	
Connection to leaf spring and to swinging arm . .	by « estendblock »
Kingpin angle	6°
Caster	9° ± 1°
Caster adjustment	by shims .0197″ (0,5 mm thk)
Position of kingpin housing with respect to swinging arm plane for tightening the pin nut	95°
Steering Knuckles.	
Steering knuckle-to-kingpin housing play adjustment	by packing rings: thkss .0977″ to .098″ (2,482 to 2,50 mm) oversize rates: .002″ - .004″ - .006″ - .008″ - .010″ - .012″ (0,05 - 0,10 - 0,15 - 0,20 - 0,25 - 0,30 mm) undersize rates: .002″ - .004″ (0,05 - 0,10 mm)
Wheels.	
Camber	1° ± 20′
Camber adjustment	by shims .02″ (0,5 mm) thk
Toe-in	.0″ to .0787″ (0 to 2 mm)
Toe-in adjustment	by adjustable sleeves on track rods
Bearing lubrication	FIAT MR grease
Hydraulic Shock Absorbers	2
Type	telescopic
Diameter (outer cylinder)	1.063″ (27 mm)
Fluid	FIAT S. A. I. oil
Capacity	.112 Imp. qts - .137 U.S. qts 7.93 ± .3 cu in. (130 ± 5 cc - 0,120 kg)

TROUBLE DIAGNOSIS AND CORRECTIONS
FRONT SUSPENSION AND WHEELS

Wheel Bounce.

POSSIBLE CAUSES	REMEDIES
1) Tire cracked.	1) Repair tire, if possible, or replace it by a new one.
2) Uneven tire pressure.	2) Check tire pressure and inflate correctly.
3) Unbalanced wheel rim or tires.	3) Proceed as recommended on page 187.
4) Semi-elliptic spring mounting worn.	4) Replace mounting and upper rubber pad.
5) Inoperative shock absorber.	5) Check shock absorber on test equipment and overhaul it. Proceed as recommended on page 156.
6) Wheel rim or tire misaligned.	6) Proceed as recommended on page 187.

Suspension Noise.

POSSIBLE CAUSES	REMEDIES
1) Lack of lubrication.	1) Lubricate: kingpin housings, tie rods and wheel bearings, following lubrication chart in Section « Maintenance » (page 286).
2) Noisy or inoperative shock absorbers.	2) Overhaul shock absorbers and refill with **FIAT S.A.I.** fluid as recommended on page 156.
3) Worn or loose wheel bearings.	3) Remove wheels and wheel hub drum and check bearing operation. Replace and lubricate as required and reassemble as outlined on page 135.

Pull to One Side.

POSSIBLE CAUSES	REMEDIES
1) Low or uneven tire pressure.	1) Check tire pressure and inflate correctly.
2) Incorrect front wheel alignment.	2) Check and adjust: caster, camber and toe-in.
3) Suspension arms distorted.	3) Check amount of distortion and replace arms if they are distorted beyond repair.
4) Inoperative shock absorbers.	4) Disassemble, overhaul and refill with **FIAT S.A.I.** fluid.
5) Brake binding.	5) Service and adjust brakes as directed on page 178.

Excessive Tire Wear.

POSSIBLE CAUSES	REMEDIES
1) Failure to rotate tires.	1) For uniform tire wear, interchange tires crosswise every 3,000 miles (5.000 km).
2) Incorrect camber.	2) Check camber angle and adjust as recommended on page 137.
3) Incorrect toe-in.	3) Check toe-in and adjust as recommended on page 166.
4) Improper tire inflation.	4) Proceed as directed on page 187.
5) Turning corners too fast.	5) Advise owner to negotiate curves at moderate speed to reduce tire wear.
6) Pick-ups too quick.	6) Advise gradual acceleration.
7) Sustained high-speed driving on gravel roads.	7) Advise moderate speed on roads of this kind.
8) Too much play at wheel bearings.	8) Adjust clearance and lubricate bearings as outlined on page 135.
9) Wheel wobble.	9) Locate origin of failure as outlined under the following heading and proceed as required.
10) Stiffened suspension arms.	10) Disassemble suspension arms and replace damaged rubber bushings.
11) Brakes out of adjustment.	11) Set brake shoe-to-drum clearance as directed on page 178.

Wheel Wobble.

POSSIBLE CAUSES	REMEDIES
1) Uneven tire pressure.	1) Inflate to correct pressure.
2) Loose or worn wheel bearings.	2) Remove, inspect and replace bearings as required. Lubricate and reassemble as outlined on page 135.
3) Inoperative shock absorbers.	3) Disassemble, overhaul and refill with FIAT S.A.I. fluid.
4) Loose steering knuckle or kingpin housing.	4) Remove and replace: kingpin housing bushings, if worn; the kingpin and washers or shims as outlined on pages 131 and 133.
5) Incorrect front wheel alignment.	5) Check and adjust: caster, camber, and toe-in.
6) Control arm rubber bushings, or kingpin housing and semi-elliptic spring «estendblocks», worn.	6) Check and replace bushings as directed in covering chapters.

Section 6

REAR SUSPENSION AND WHEELS SHOCK ABSORBERS

	Page
DESCRIPTION	145
REMOVAL	145
SWINGING ARMS	146
COIL SPRINGS	149
INSTALLATION	149
CHECKING AND ADJUSTING REAR WHEEL TOE-IN	151
SERVICE EQUIPMENT	152
TIGHTENING REFERENCE	153
SPECIFICATIONS	153
HYDRAULIC SHOCK ABSORBERS	154
TROUBLE DIAGNOSIS AND CORRECTIONS	157

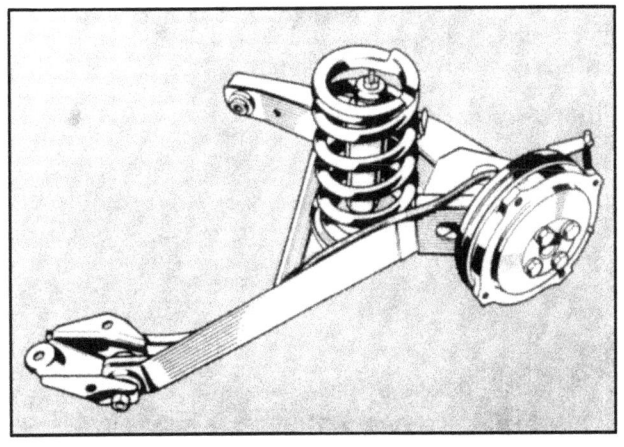

NOTE - Nuts securing swinging arm to front and rear supports must be tightened with wheel set vertically.

This will prevent «estendblocks» being stress-twisted during operation.

To set wheel plane vertical, use fixture A. 66062.

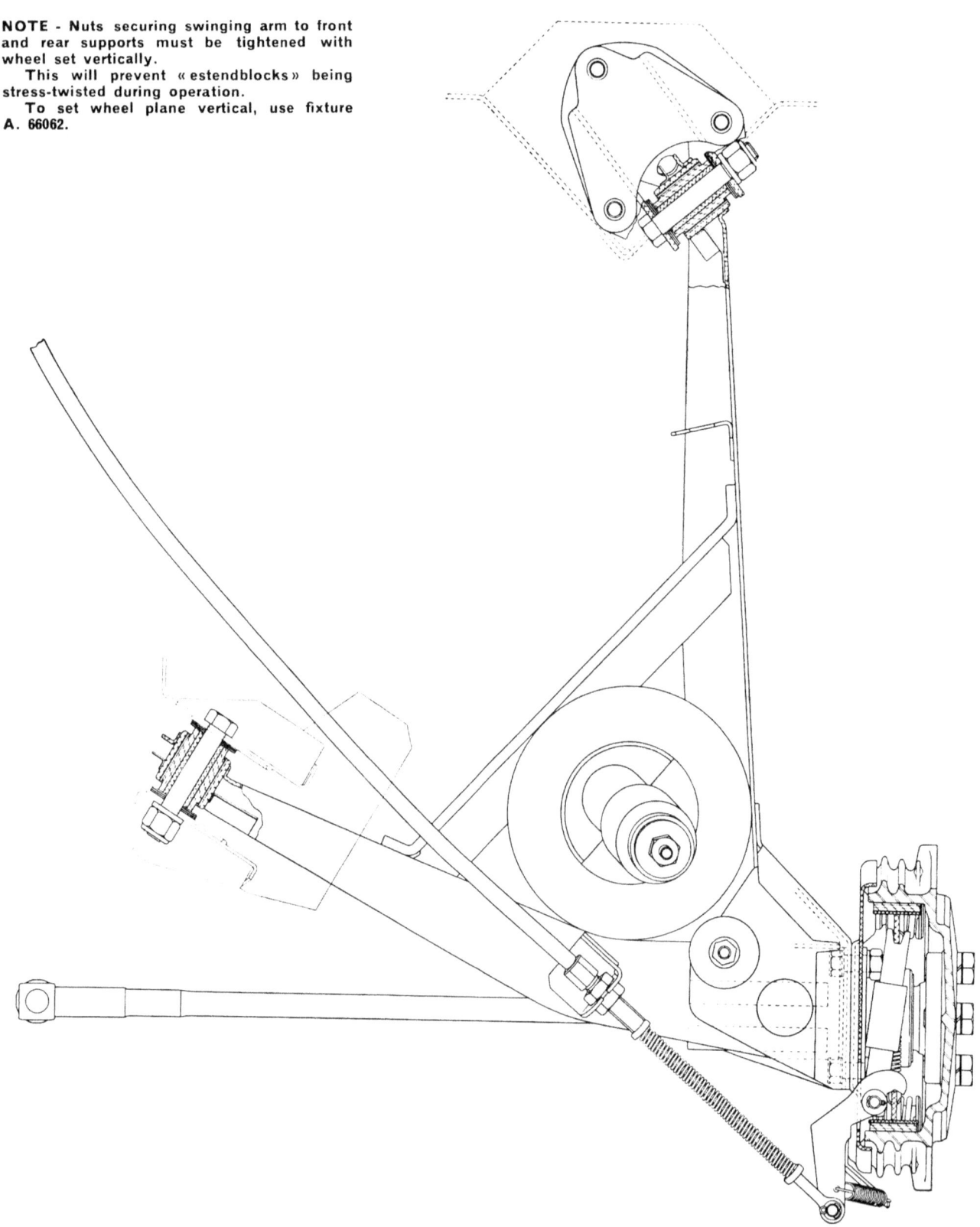

Fig. 248 - Right rear suspension assembly, sectioned through brake drum and arm mountings.

REAR SUSPENSION AND WHEELS

DESCRIPTION	page 145
REMOVAL OF REAR SUSPENSION ASSEMBLY	» 145
SWINGING ARMS	» 146
Disassembly, Inspection and Repair	» 146
Assembly	» 148
Wheel Bearing Adjustment	» 148
Swinging Arm Adjustment	» 148
COIL SPRINGS	» 149
Inspection	» 149
INSTALLATION OF REAR SUSPENSION ASSEMBLY	» 149
CHECKING AND ADJUSTING REAR WHEEL TOE-IN	» 151
SERVICE EQUIPMENT	» 152
TIGHTENING REFERENCE	» 153
SPECIFICATIONS	» 153

Description.

Rear wheels are independently sprung, with swinging arms, coil springs and telescopic, double acting, hydraulic shock absorbers.

Swinging arms are mounted on floor by « estend-blocks ».

Coil springs are provided at both ends with insulator rings.

Shock absorbers are of the same type as for front suspension.

At its vertex, the swinging arm carries the bearing housing secured by nuts (which also performs as a hub for wheel drive shaft) and the brake housing flange.

Externally, wheel shaft carries the brake drum; at the inner end, it is coupled to axle shaft through a splined flexible joint.

Removal of Rear Suspension Assembly.

Raise car on stands and take off wheel on side of suspension to be removed.

Support swinging arm by placing a hydraulic jack underneath.

Inside car, remove rear wheelhousing linings and unscrew the shock absorber mounting nut on floor.

Unhook the parking brake shoe control lever return spring.

Undo the three screws of sleeve coupling the flexible joint to differential shaft, pull back sleeve and take off inner spring.

Remove brake fluid reservoir cap, take out filtering screen, blank delivery hole as specified on page 180, and then disconnect brake line at connection on body floor. Disconnect parking brake control tie rod as follows:

— remove cotter pin and disinsert wire eye from pin on shoe control lever;

— undo wire adjustment nuts and free wire from fairlead on swinging arm.

Fig. 249 - Left rear suspension detail.

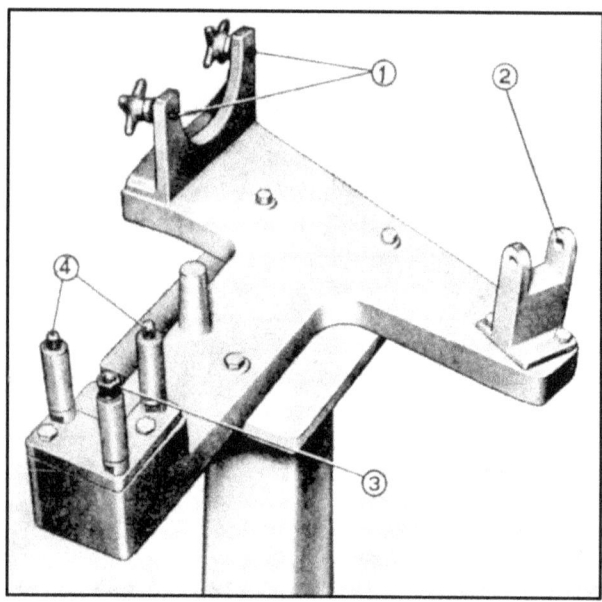

Fig. 250 - Fixture **A. 66064**, for swinging arm inspection and adjustment.

1. Clamp screws, securing wheel shaft on fixture. - 2. Alignment bracket, swinging arm member check-up. - 3. Swinging arm external support centering pins. - 4. Nut, to secure swinging arm external support on fixture stud.

With hydraulic jack, lower the swinging arm, press in shock absorber by telescoping-in the outer cylinder and pull out coil spring together with its mounting rubber rings.

Back out the self-locking nut securing swinging arm to internal support welded on floor. Disinsert mounting pin, and note the number and arrangement of « estendblock » side shims.

Next, remove the three swinging arm external support fixing screws and take off swinging arm.

Between support and floor there is a rubber pad.

SWINGING ARMS

Disassembly, Inspection and Repair.

After disconnecting the shock absorber, install swinging arm on fixture **A. 66064**.

If swinging arm has not been distorted, its installation on fixture should be easily carried out by proceeding as follows:

— Tighten the clamp screws (1, fig. 250) on wheel drum.

Fig. 251 - Rear suspension assembly.

1. Brake shoe control cable and sheath. - 2. Coil spring. - 3. Oil boot. - 4. Axle shaft. - 5. Bumper. - 6. Flexible joint. - 7. Swinging arm. - 8. Cable adjusting nut. - 9. Swinging arm-to-front bracket mounting pin. - 10. Swinging arm front bracket-to-underbody mounting screw. - 11. Engine front support cross member. - 12. Swinging arm rear self-locking nut. - 13. Shock absorber-to-swinging arm lower nut. - 14. Sleeve screws. - 15. Axle shaft-to-flexible joint sleeve.

— Couple swinging arm inner member to seat (2, fig. 250) on fixture.

— Fit swinging arm external support holes on fixture pins (3, fig. 250).

If somehow these three operations cannot be performed, the swinging arm needs straightening at distortion point.

NOTE - Replace fixture pins (3, fig. 250) to external support holes and install suspension arm right side up (fig. 253) or upside down (fig. 254), according to whether the right or left hand arm is involved.

Swinging arm components are disassembled as follows:

— Take off cotter pin and back out nut fixing flexible joint to wheel shaft; disinsert plain washer and joint.

— Pull out wheel shaft and brake drum using universal puller **A. 40005/1/9**, then the two oil seals, both outer and inner bearing inner rings, thrust ring of joint and resilient spacer.

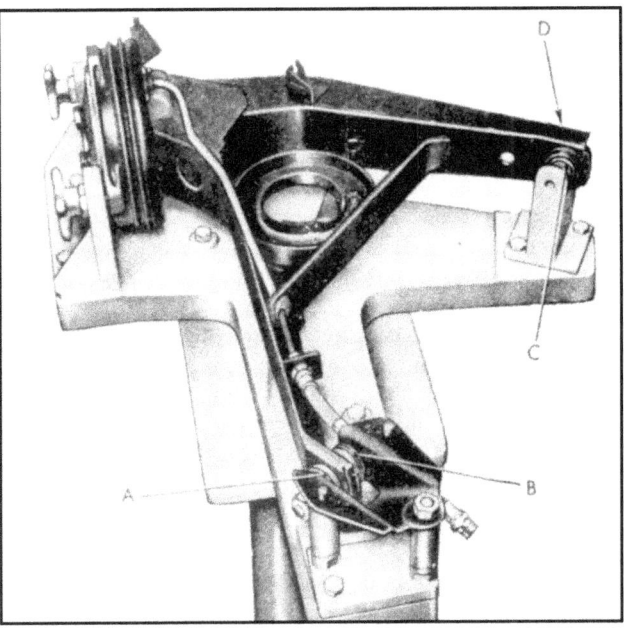

Fig. 253 - Adjusting right rear suspension swinging arm on fixture A. 66064.

A and B. Swinging arm external support adjustment shims.
C and D. Swinging arm internal support adjustment shims.

c) oil seals fit snugly on wheel shaft, on joint spacer or shoulder ring and on hub seats;

d) resilient spacer is not permanently distorted;

Fig. 252 - Swinging arm assembly, on adjustment fixture A. 66064.

— Remove the two bearing outer rings using puller **A. 6511** (fig. 255).

If necessary, remove swinging arm external support, disconnect brake line at wheel cylinder, then the bearing housing and brake housing flange.

Check that:

a) « estendblocks » are a tight fit in their respective seats in swinging arm and mounting pins slide in freely without any appreciable play: if « estendblocks » must be replaced, use tool **A. 66056** which is suitable for their installation and removal;

b) inner and outer bearing outer rings have no play in their seats and that rollers and cages are not broken or worn;

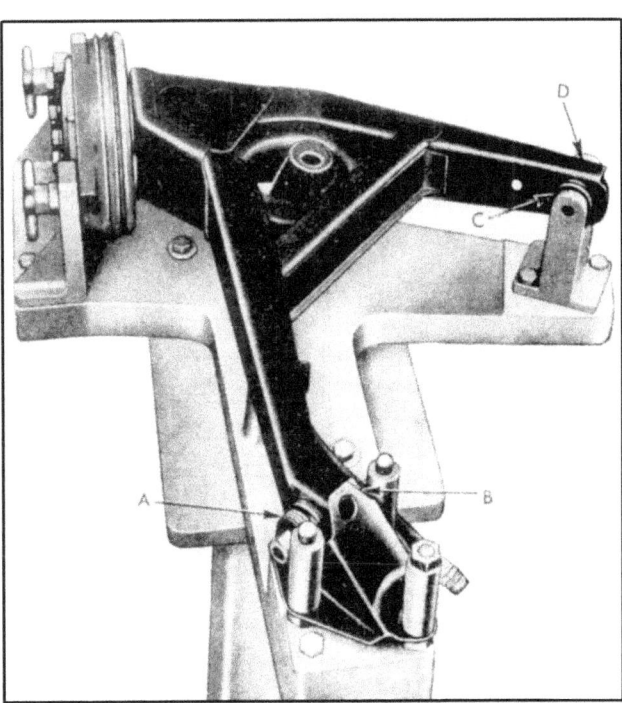

Fig. 254 - Adjusting left rear suspension swinging arm on fixture A. 66064.

A and B. Swinging arm external support adjustment shims. - C and D. Swinging arm internal support adjustment shims.

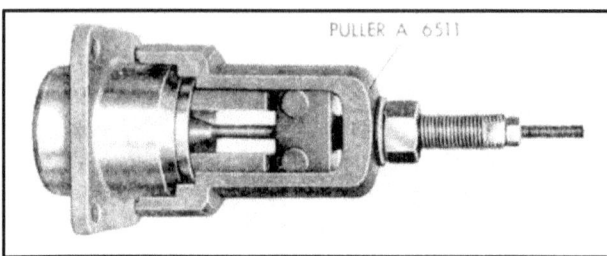

Fig. 255 - Rear wheel outer bearing outer ring removal.

whenever new bearings or bearing housings are fitted, always install a new spacer;

e) the mating surface of bearing inner rings on wheel shaft is perfectly smooth; shaft splines-to-flexible joint splines lash must never exceed .0059" (0,15 mm);

f) flexible joint is not damaged to the point where metal-to-rubber bonding is compromised.

Assembly.

To assemble swinging arm, reverse the disassembly operations with the following provisions:

— Use tool **A. 66056** to install « estendblock » on swinging arm.

— The bearing housing and brake housing flange mounting nuts must be tightened with a torque wrench to 43.4 ft.lbs (6000 kgmm).

— During assembly, pack bearings with FIAT MR grease.

— Preload the bearings and adjust the swinging arm as directed on opposite column.

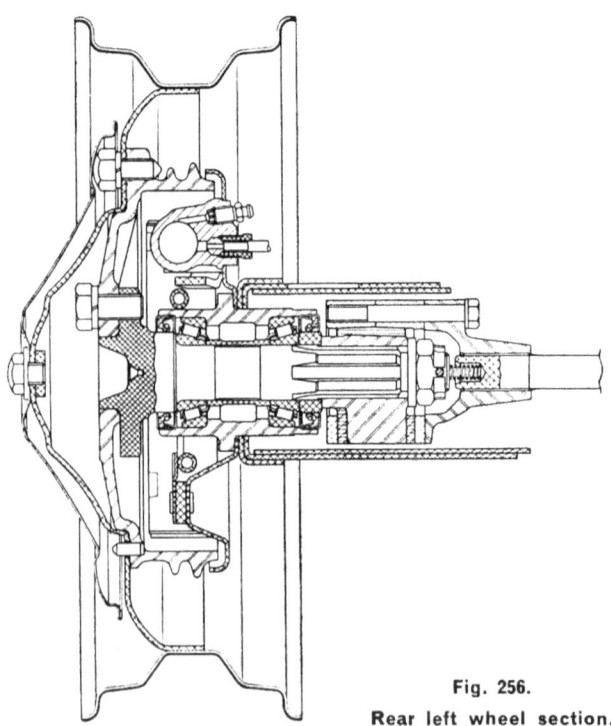

Fig. 256.
Rear left wheel section.

NOTE - If the axle shaft-to-flexible joint tie sleeve has been removed, coat the mating splines with **FIAT B 2 G** grease on reinstallation.

Wheel Bearing Adjustment.

To assure steady bearing adjustment and taper down sagging danger on operation, wheel bearings should be preloaded.

Tighten wheel shaft nut gradually, so that rotation torque will not exceed .36 ft.lbs (50 kgmm).

To check the rotation torque, proceed as follows.

Install support **A. 95697/2** on wheel drum. Insert the shank (2, fig. 257) of dynamometer **A. 95697** in support and grasp lever (3).

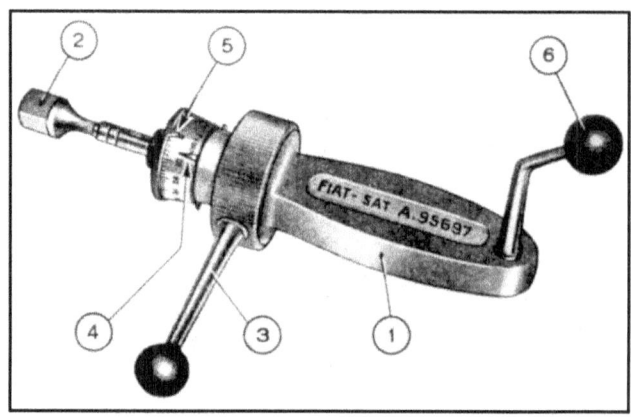

Fig. 257 - Bearing rotation torque dynamometer.

1. Dynamometer A. 95697. - 2. Dynamometer shank to insert in item A. 95697/2, fitted to wheel drum. - 3. Dynamometer grip lever. 4. Rotation torque setting index. - 5. Adjustable needle. - 6. Dynamometer operating lever.

Move the needle (5) to register .36 ft.lbs (50 kgmm) on dynamometer scale, as shown in fig. 257 and, using the lever (6), rotate the dynamometer and the wheel shaft some turns, clockwise.

During rotation, check that the needle (5) does not exceed the setting index (4).

If the rotation torque proves to be over .36 ft.lbs (50 kgmm), which indicates high bearing preload, remove the wheel shaft and replace the resilient spacer by a new one.

Next repeat the rotation torque test.

Swinging Arm Adjustment.

To adjust the swinging arm, use fixture **A. 66064** (fig. 253).

At points A and B (fig. 253), between the « estendblock » and the swinging arm-to-body front mounting bracket, fit six shims, three on each side. For shim centering use alignment bar **A. 66057**; next, while

REAR SUSPENSION AND WHEELS

removing the alignment bar, slip in the mounting pin and screw in the nut. After rear wheel geometry adjustment this nut shall be tightened with 43.4 to 50.6 ft.lbs (6000 to 7000 kgmm) of torque.

Then, at points C and D (fig. 253), insert the number of shims required to fill in the gap between the « estendblock » and the two fixture shoulders.

The number of shims, so determined - both at C and D - must later be fitted between the « estendblock » and the shoulders on the swinging arm-to-body mounting bracket.

COIL SPRINGS

Spring specifications:

— wire diameter   .5315″ ± .0019″ (13,5 ± 0,05 mm)
— working coils . . . .   4 ¼
— free height . . . . 8.70″ (221 mm)
— height under a load of
  904 ± 44 lbs (410 ± 20 kg) 5.94″ (151 mm)
— height under a load of
  1268 ± 64 lbs (575 ± 29 kg) 4.24″ (123 mm)
— solid height . . . . 3.67″ (93 mm)
— flexibility . . .3034 in/100 lbs (17 mm/100 kg)

Inspection.

Inspect springs carefully to check on their efficiency. If any cracks are found, replace springs.

Check condition of insulator rings: replace, if damaged.

INSTALLATION OF REAR SUSPENSION ASSEMBLY

Proceed as follows:

Insert swinging arm inner end in the mounting bracket welded on body floor; place between the « estendblock » and bracket the number of adjustment shims determined previously on fixture **A. 66064**. Then, insert the alignment bar **A. 66057** through « estendblock » and shims, aligning them with holes in mounting bracket. Next, holding firmly the entire assembly, while removing the alignment bar, slip in the mounting pin.

Screw in nut which, after checking rear wheel geometry, must be tightened to 43.4 to 50.6 ft.lbs (6000 to 7000 kgmm) with a torque wrench.

Screw in - without tightening - the three swinging arm external bracket-to-body floor mounting screws, plain and spring washers; screws will have to be tightened to specified torque, or 28.9 to 36.2 ft.lbs (4000 to 5000 kgmm) only after having adjusted rear wheel geometry.

Seat properly, on swinging arm, the coil spring lower insulator ring; insert spring on shock absorber (previously secured to arm) and position spring in its seat on arm.

Place the upper insulator ring on spring. Raise suspension assembly by means of a hydraulic jack or fixture **A. 66062** and insert spring in its seat under body floor.

Make sure shock absorber-to-floor rubber ring has been fitted, then extend shock absorber until its upper mounting pin protrudes into car through the hump in floor, and secure shock absorber by its mounting nut and lock washer after having inter-

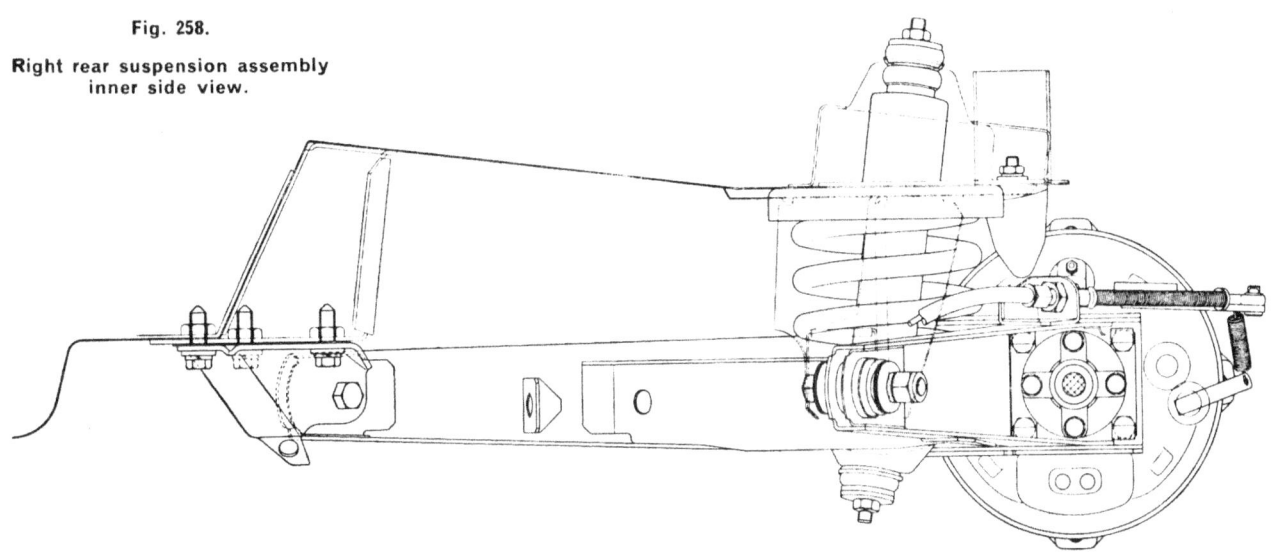

Fig. 258.
Right rear suspension assembly inner side view.

posed rubber ring and plain washer. Use wrench **A. 56030** to secure shock absorber.

Refit the rear wheelhousing lining in place.

Connect brake line to the connection on body floor.

Remove the wooden peg from brake fluid reservoir.

Bleed brake system.

Between axle shaft and wheel shaft, insert the inner spring; then couple the splined sleeve to the joint and tighten the screws to 20.3 ft.lbs (2800 kgmm).

Connect parking brake tie rod and adjust tension by the two stretchers.

Install wheels and draw up mounting screws with 32.5 to 39.8 ft.lbs (4500 to 5500 kgmm) of torque.

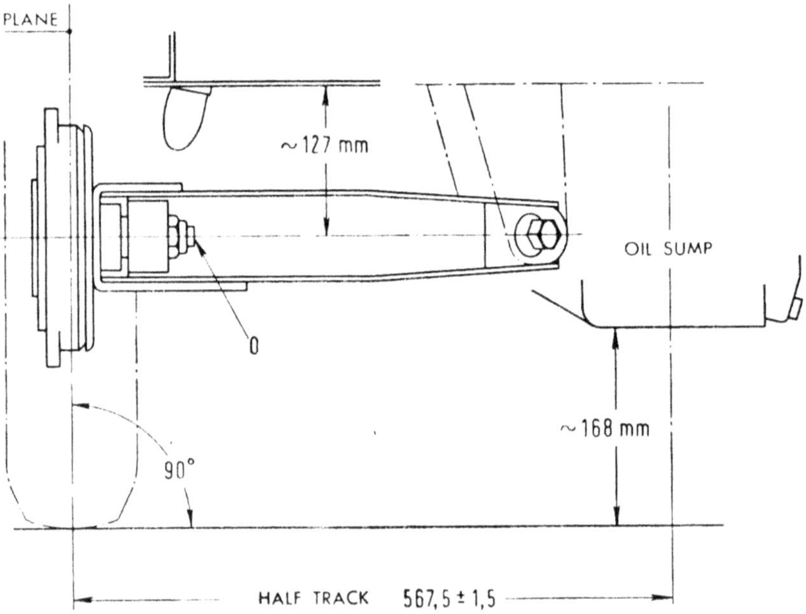

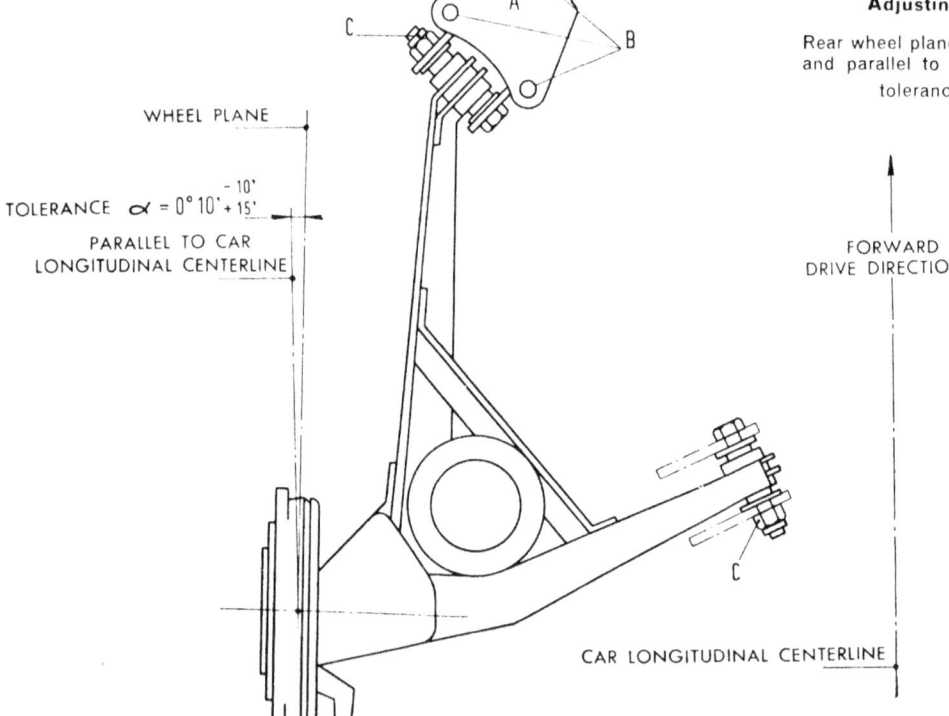

Fig. 259.

Position of rear suspension components for rear wheel toe-in inspection and adjustment.

Fig. 260.

Adjusting rear wheel toe-in angle.

Rear wheel plane must be perpendicular to ground and parallel to car longitudinal centerline with a tolerance of $0° 10' {}^{-10'}_{+15'}$ toe-in.

To adjust rear wheel geometry, move suitably the swinging arm outer support. Slight movements are permitted by the play existing between the support holes A and the mounting screws. Screws B must be tightened to 28.9 to 36.2 ft.lbs (4000 to 5000 kgmm). Nuts C must be tightened to 43.4 to 50.6 ft.lbs (6000 to 7000 kgmm), after adjustment has been carried out.

CHECKING AND ADJUSTING REAR WHEEL TOE-IN

After the rear suspension has been installed, check and adjust the rear wheel toe-in.

To do so, the rear wheels must be set with their plane:

— perpendicular to ground;

— tilted to car longitudinal centerline, by an angle of $0° 10'\,^{-10'}_{+15'}$ (α, fig. 260) toeing-in at front;

— 22.342''±.059'' (567,5±1,5 mm) apart from car longitudinal centerline (half track, fig. 259).

To adjust rear wheel geometry, move suitably the swinging arm outer support.

Slight movements are permitted by the play existing between the support holes (A, fig. 260) and the mounting screws (B).

It should be noted that to a toe-in angle variation of $0° 10'$ (α, fig. 260) corresponds a displacement of about .216'' (5,5 mm) measured at 72.441'' (1,84 m) from wheel center (distance equal to car wheelbase).

To check and adjust rear wheel geometry:

a) Place the car on stands and remove front and rear wheels.

b) Install fixtures **A. 66062** for spring compression and wheel retainment in vertical position (figure 261).

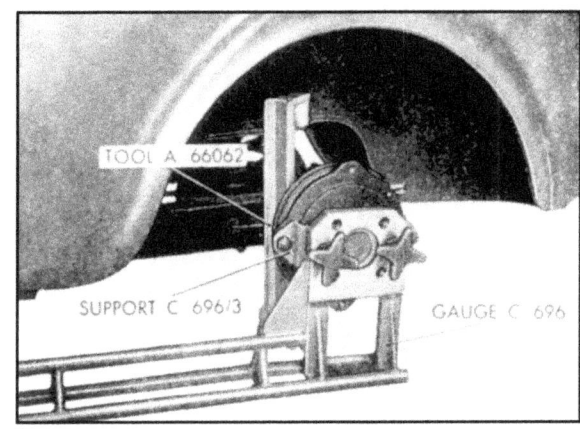

Fig. 261 - Checking left rear wheel toe-in by gauge and tools shown in the figure.

Toe-in is checked after setting wheel plane perpendicular to floor by means of tool A. 66062.

c) Lift rear suspensions by compressing the coil springs and shock absorbers. Screw on the fixture lower shank until the index registers with the mark «Nuova 500» stamped on bracket. In this position the wheel plane is vertical and the center (0, fig. 259) of wheel shaft results at 5.00'' (127 mm) from buffer stop bracket.

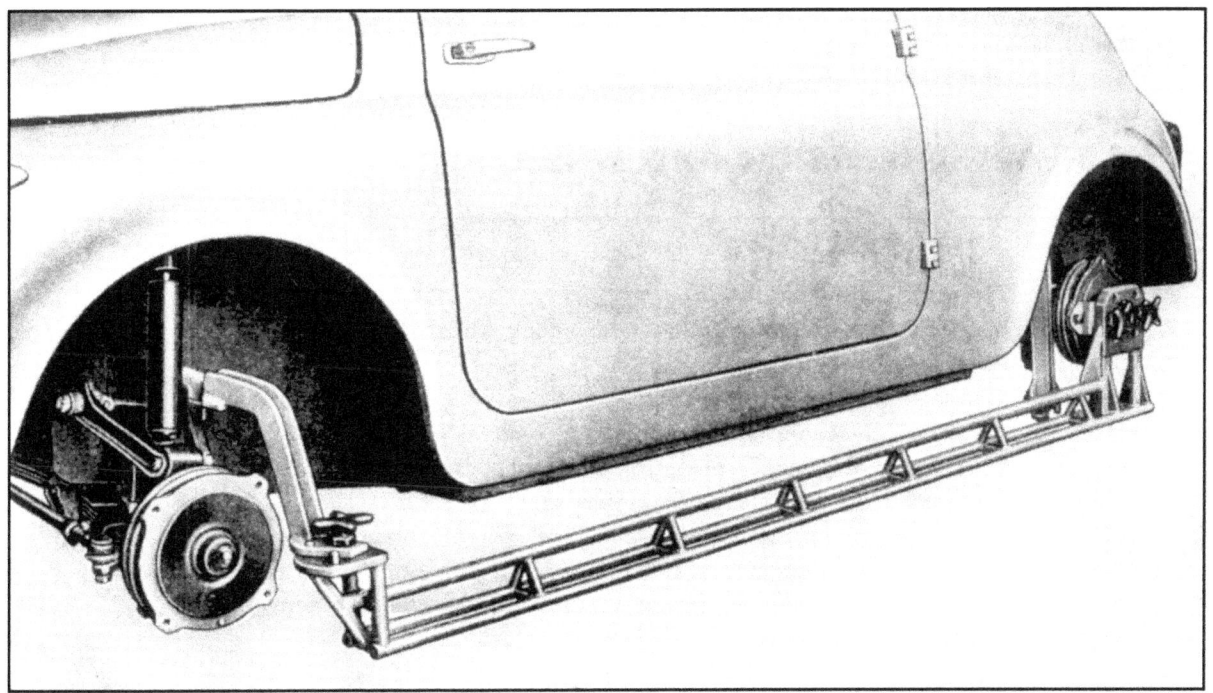

Fig. 262 - Checking left rear wheel toe-in by gauge C. 696, bracket and support C. 696/3 and tool A. 66062 (see also figs. 261 and 263).

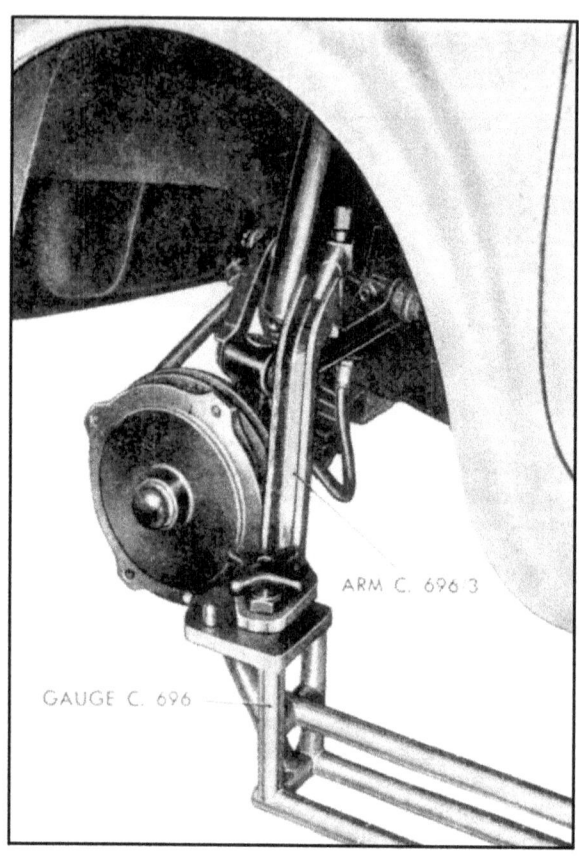

Fig. 263 - Checking left rear wheel toe-in.

With the pin of bracket C. 696/3 .216" (5,5 mm) from the swinging arm pin, rear wheel plane is parallel to car longitudinal centerline. Instead, when the pin of bracket C. 696/3 is in slight contact with the swinging arm pin, rear wheel plane is tilted to car longitudinal centerline by an angle of 0° 10' toeing-in at front.

d) Secure support **C. 696/3** to wheel drum and connect gauge **C. 696** to the support, then tightening the two clamping screws (fig. 261).

e) Apply, at front of gauge **C. 696**, bracket **C. 696/3** (fig. 263).

f) Check that the pin mounted on front end of bracket **C. 696/3** is in touch with front suspension swinging arm pin (fig. 263). If this conditions is not complied with, operate as outlined in g).

As already said a $^{-10'}_{+15'}$ tolerance is permitted, provided such value is the same also for the other rear wheel.

Rear wheels, in fact, must be both in perfect straightahead position or toed-in of the same angle.

When wheel is parallel to car centerline, the pin of bracket **C. 696/3** will be .216" (5,5 mm) apart from the pin of front suspension swinging arm.

g) Back out the swinging arm outer support-to-body mounting screws and position arm in such a way as to obtain the condition described in point f).

After adjustment, tighten the outer support mounting screws to 28.9 to 36.2 ft.lbs (4000 to 5000 kgmm) using a torque wrench. Tighten also the two swinging arm pin nuts (C, fig. 260) to 43.4 to 50.6 ft.lbs (6000 to 7000 kgmm).

Take off gauge **C. 696** with bracket and support **C. 696/3**; repeat the check and adjustment operations on the other wheel, minding that bracket **C. 696/3** must be located in the other position specified.

REAR SUSPENSION AND WHEEL SERVICE EQUIPMENT

A.	8279	Wrench - wheel shaft nut.
A.	10228	Tool device - aiding installation of shock absorber.
A.	40005/1/9	Puller - wheel drums.
A.	56024	Wrench - shock absorber plug.
A.	56030	Wrench - hydraulic shock absorber removal and installation.
A.	66056	Tool - swinging arm « estendblock » removal and installation.
A.	66057	Alignment bar - shims on swinging arm.
A.	66062	Fixture - coil spring compression and wheel retainment in vertical position.
A.	66064	Fixture - swinging arm check-up and adjustment.
A.	95697	Dynamometer - wheel bearing rotation torque measurement.
A.	95697/2	Support - dynamometer A. 95697.
C.	696	Gauge - wheel alignment checking (use with C. 696/3).
C.	696/3	Bracket and support - for wheel alignment gauge (use with C. 696).

REAR SUSPENSION AND WHEEL TIGHTENING REFERENCE

ITEM	Drwg. or Std. Part No.	Thread	Material	Tightening Torque
Swinging arm pin-to-floor nut ...	1/25747/11	12 MB (x1,5)	R 50 Cdt (Pivot bar R 80 Cdt)	43.4 to 50.6 ft.lbs (6.000 to 7.000 kgmm)
Swinging arm support-to-floor screw	832632	10 x 1,25 M	R 80	28.9 to 36.2 ft.lbs (4.000 to 5.000 kgmm)
Hub and brake housing flange-to-swinging arm nut	1/21647/11	10 x 1,25 M	R 50 Cdt (Screw R 80)	43.4 ft.lbs (6.000 kgmm)
Flexible joint-to-rear wheel shaft nut	1/07246/20	18 MB (x1,5)	R 80 (Shaft 38NCD4 Bon)	see page 148
Differential shaft sleeve-to-flexible joint screw	1/60446/21	8 MA (x1,25)	R 80 Cdt	20.3 ft.lbs (2800 kgmm)
Wheel-to-hub screw	990166	10 MA (x1,5)	C 35 R (Bon Cdt)	32.5 to 39.8 ft.lbs (4.500 to 5.500 kgmm)
Rear wheel bearing rotation torque, below				0.36 ft.lbs (50 kgmm)

REAR SUSPENSION AND WHEEL SPECIFICATIONS

Swinging Arms. Connection to body .... Adjustment .... Position of arm for tightening of nuts to mounting pins on body	by « estendblocks » shims wheels vertical
Coil Springs. Free height .... Height under a 904±44 lbs (410±20 kg) load .. Height under a 1268±64 lbs (575±29 kg) load .. Solid height .... Flexibility	8.70'' (221 mm) 5.94'' (151 mm) 4.24'' (123 mm) 3.67'' (93 mm) .3034 in/100 lbs (17 mm/100 kg)
Wheels. Roller bearing adjustment .... Bearing rotation torque, below .... Wheel alignment: toed-in (identical for both rear wheels) Bearing lubrication	by resilient spacer .36 ft.lbs (50 kgmm) 0° 10' $^{- 10'}_{+ 15'}$ FIAT MR grease
Shock Absorbers .... Type .... Diameter (inner cylinder) .... Fluid grade .... Capacity	two hydraulic, telescopic 1.063'' (27 mm) FIAT S. A. I. oil .088 Imp. qts. - .104 U.S. qts. (100 cc ± 5 - 0,090 kg)

HYDRAULIC SHOCK ABSORBERS

Description . . . . page 154
OPERATION . . . . » 154
DISASSEMBLY, INSPECTION, REASSEMBLY . . . . » 155
CHECKING DAMPENING DIAGRAMS . . . . » 156

Description.

Front and rear shock absorbers are of the telescopic, double-acting type.

Main data:
— Working cylinder diameter:
    front . . . . 1.063" (27 mm)
    rear . . . . 1.063" (27 mm)
— Length (between rubber ring shoulders):
    front:
      telescoped-in   8.3464" ± .0787" (212 ± 2 mm)
      telescoped-out 13.1890" ± .0787" (335 ± 2 mm)
      stroke . . . . 4.8425" (123 mm)
    rear:
      telescoped-in   7.0865" ± .0787" (180 ± 2 mm)
      telescoped-out 10.6693" ± .0787" (271 ± 2 mm)
      stroke . . . . 3.5826" (91 mm)
— Fluid capacity:
    front . . . . . . .137 U.S. qts - .112 Imp. qts
                  (130 ± 5 cm^3 - 0,120 kg)
    rear . . . . . . .104 U.S. qts - .088 Imp. qts
                  (100 ± 5 cm^3 - 0,090 kg)

These shock absorbers are also termed «direct acting», since their dampening action takes place directly on suspension without the intermediary of levers.

They are fitted with thermostatic valves ensuring steady dampening action regardless of temperature variations.

Essentially, a shock absorber of this type consists of a cylindrical body formed by two coaxial tubes (14) and (15) (fig. 264), of which the inner one acts as a working cylinder and the outer one as a casing.

The annular interstice between these two elements performs as a fluid reservoir.

A third outer cylinder (13) shields rod (2) from mud and stones.

On top, cylinder body is closed by bush (11), oil seals (5) and (9), and housing (4).

Rod (2) slides through seals (5): its upper end is fixed to body floor and its lower end carries piston (22) on which rebound (26) and inlet (21) valves are arranged.

At bottom, the shock absorber is closed by plug (35) with threaded shank (36) for shock absorber mounting on suspensions.

At cylinder (15), carrier plug (32) is mounted with compression (33) and compensating (30) valves.

Two concentric rows of orifices are provided in piston.

The internal row is blanked underneath by the rebound valve which opens downwards. The external row is blanked by inlet valve which opens upwards.

Hydraulic shock absorbers, both front and rear, (starting from vehicles manufactured in the month of March 1959) are provided with a vapour pocket bleeder from cylinder interior.

The bleeder device consists of a capillary hole (12, fig. 264) interconnecting the inner cylinder (15) with the upper chamber (10), and of a passage tube (16) from upper chamber to fluid reservoir.

Any vapour pockets in pressure cylinder are evacuated past the capillary hole (12) into the chamber (10), whence they flow down, during shock absorber operation, through passage (16) in a light fluid stream and up to top reservoir with the reservoir fluid.

This system definitely does away with any vapour lock is shock absorber hydraulic circuit, which is isolated from air contained in fluid reservoir.

Operation.

The shock absorber described above may be considered as divided in three sections:

— top portion of cylinder above piston (always full of fluid);
— bottom portion of cylinder below piston (always full of fluid);
— fluid reservoir, i. e., the annular interstice between cylinders (14) and (15) (never completely full).

REBOUND PHASE

This is the phase in which shock absorber extends. The fluid above piston finds the external row of orifices (24) closed and is forced through

REAR SUSPENSION AND WHEELS

the internal row (25), thus acting on rebound valve (26) and passing to cylinder lower portion.

During its upward travel the piston produces a vacuum which draws fluid from the reservoir through annular passage (31) of carrier plug (32) and compensating valve (30). The amount of fluid passing from reservoir to cylinder will be volumetrically equal to the portion of piston rod that has slid out.

Therefore in this phase only the rebound and compensating valves are active while the compression and inlet valves are inactive.

COMPRESSION PHASE

In this phase shock absorber telescopes in and the piston travels downwards.

The fluid in the lower chamber lifts inlet valve (21) and part of it passes into cylinder upper portion.

Some of the fluid, instead, rams compression valve (33), and through its orifices (34), passes into the reserve.

The dampening effect in this phase is the result of the displacement of an amount of fluid volumetrically equal to the portion of rod entering the cylinder.

During this phase both the compensating (30) and rebound (26) valves remain closed and only the compression (33) and inlet (21) valves are operative.

Disassembly, Inspection, Reassembly.

Wash outer casing with warm water or kerosene.

Clamp lower shank in a vise and telescope-up outer casing.

Using wrench A. 56024, unscrew upper threaded ring (3).

Remove from vise and take out inner cylinder (15); by a screwdriver inserted in cylinder bottom chamfer, remove lower plug (32) carrying compression and compensating valves.

Push rod into cylinder (15), and clamp upper shank in a vise, unscrew plug (29), remove piston (22) with inlet and rebound valves.

Withdraw rod (2) from cylinder (15) and remove seal gasket, housing, threaded ring, etc.

Wash all components in kerosene or gasoline and then inspect parts carefully to see that:

a) inlet, rebound and compensating valve discs are not deformed;

b) the sliding surfaces of piston, seal ring and compression valve are smooth and are fluid-tight;

c) rebound and compression valve springs and upper spring for seal gasket are not weakened or broken;

d) the two seal gaskets are not worn or damaged; it is advisable to replace them in any case;

SECTIONAL VIEW OF SHOCK ABSORBER

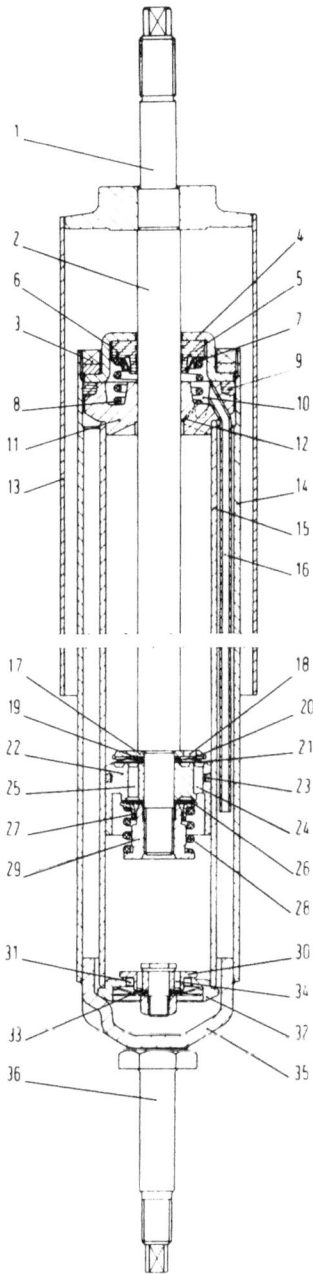

Fig. 264 - Sectional view of shock absorber.

1. Threaded shank, floor mounting. - 2. Rod. - 3. Cylinder upper blanking threaded ring. - 4. Seal housing. - 5. Rod seal. - 6. Tab spring. - 7. Spring cup. - 8. Gasket packing spring. - 9. Casing gasket. - 10. Vapour pocket drain chamber. - 11. Rod guide bush. - 12. Vapour pocket drain capillary hole. - 13. Dust shield. - 14. Casing. - 15. Working cylinder. - 16. Vapour pocket drain passage. - 17. Valve lift limiting disc. - 18. Fluid passage orifice. - 19. Valve lift adjustment washer. - 20. Valve star-shaped spring. - 21. Inlet valve. - 22. Piston. - 23. Compression ring. - 24. Inlet valve holes in piston. - 25. Rebound valve holes in piston. - 26. Rebound valve. - 27. Valve guide cup. - 28. Rebound valve spring. - 29. Piston mounting plug. - 30. Compensating valve. - 31. Compensating valve annular passage. - 32. Compensating-and-compression valve carrier plug. - 33. Compression valve. - 34. Compression valve orifices. - 35. Lower plug. 36. Threaded shank, lower mounting.

e) rod and cylinders are not deformed.

f) air pocket evacuating passage is not plugged. Take care not to kink the passage during disassembly and assembly operations. Replace passage, if damaged;

g) capillary hole (12, fig. 264) is not plugged.

Replace all damaged parts.

To reassemble shock absorber, reverse order of disassembly operations.

Special care shall be taken in refilling the shock absorber.

Fig. 265 - Shock absorber tester A. 76003.

In a graduated cylinder, measure:

— .112 Imp. qts. - .137 U. S. qts. (130 ± 5 cm^3) - front shock absorbers, or

— .088 Imp. qts. - .104 U. S. qts. (100 ± 5 cm^3) - rear shock absorbers

of FIAT-SAI oil.

Then proceed as follows:

Mount piston on rod, insert rod and piston assembly into cylinder (15, fig. 264).

Push piston against bush (11), then, pour fluid up to about 1/2 inch from the edge.

Press fit plug (32) and pour the remaining fluid in the casing (14).

Finally, insert cylinder (15) in casing (14) and tighten upper threaded ring (3).

It is good practice to use tool A. 10228 for shock absorber assembly and disassembly operations.

IMPORTANT - The amount of **FIAT-SAI** oil introduced in shock absorbers, must always correspond exactly to recommendations.

A too high level would not allow the shock absorber to telescope in completely and would cause irreparable damages, while a too low level would reduce the dampening effect and might cause noisy operation.

Checking Dampening Diagrams.

Before disassembling the shock absorber for overhaul, it will be advisable to check its operation on shock absorber tester **A. 76003** (fig. 265) to determine dampening efficiency.

Set up tester for the type of shock absorber to be checked.

To this purpose, and in accordance with the tester instruction book, proceed as follows:

a) Adjust reaction arm length at 9.843" (250 mm) (fig. 266).

b) Adjust test stroke at 3.937" (100 mm), for front shock absorber, and at 3.150" (80 mm), for rear shock absorber (fig. 267).

c) Adjust distance between shock absorber mounting pins by bringing the two indexes in line with the reference marks on plate fitted on tester

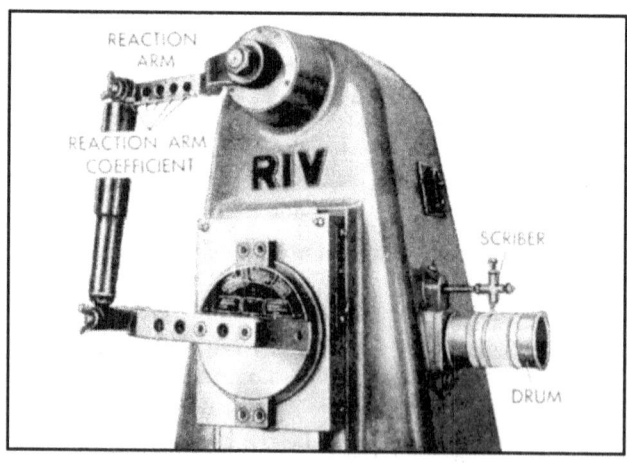

Fig. 266 - Detail of the A. 76003 shock absorber tester head.

slide side (fig. 266) relevant to shock absorber under test.

d) Wind the sheet of paper on the drum and scribe the base line by running the tester unloaded.

Install shock absorber on the tester, making sure that articulations are free. Test must be carried out at room temperature, since the ordinates on the master diagram have been computed according to this test condition.

Let shock absorber complete four or five cycles before tracing the dampening diagram by lowering the scriber to contact the paper sheet rolled on the drum (fig. 266).

Remove the traced paper from drum, place it under the plexiglass master diagram and check shock absorber diagram.

DIAGRAM INTERPRETATION

a) The values of the rebound and compression reactions are referred to the maximum ordinates of the corresponding diagrams.

b) The peak of the curve must be included between the master diagram ordinates.

c) The diagram must be regular and, in the inversion point, must in no spot be parallel to the base line.

After checking operation, disassemble shock absorber, inspect and replace parts as required.

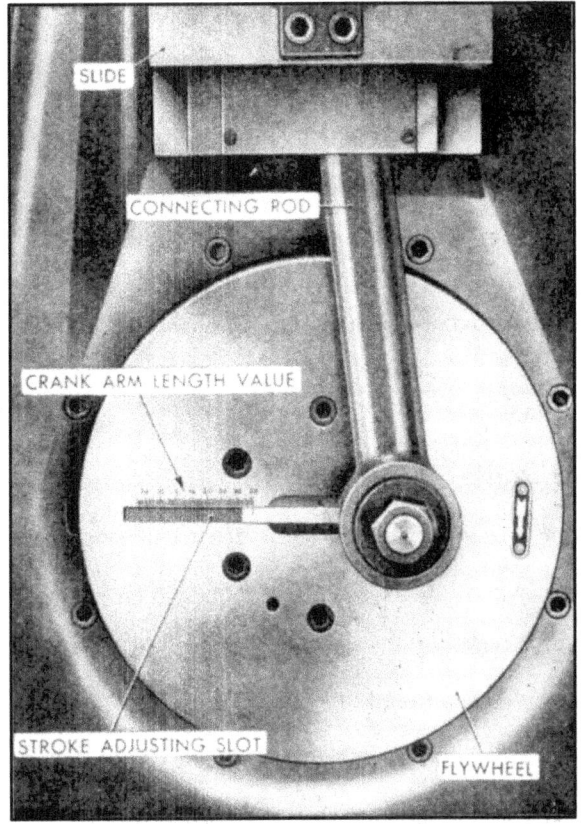

Fig. 267 - Detail of the shock absorber operation tester A. 76003.
In the figure the tester is set for a stroke of 3.937'' (100 mm), suitable for checking front shock absorbers.

TROUBLE DIAGNOSIS AND CORRECTIONS
REAR SUSPENSION AND WHEELS

Irregular or Abnormal Tire Wear.

POSSIBLE CAUSES	REMEDIES
1) Incorrect tire pressure.	1) Tires should be inflated, front and rear, to recommended pressure. Pressure specifications are given on page 187.
2) Wheels out of balance.	2) Inspect and fix as directed on page 187.
3) Wheels off center.	3) Inspect and fix as directed on page 187.
4) Misadjusted brakes.	4) Adjust brakes as outlined on page 178.
5) Weak or broken coil springs.	5) Check spring camber under load and replace spring if not within specifications (page 149), or broken.
6) Excessive load.	6) See load specifications, page 296.
7) Incorrect wheel alignment.	7) Check and adjust rear wheel toe-in as outlined on page 151.

Sag at One Wheel.

POSSIBLE CAUSES	REMEDIES
1) Incorrect tire pressure.	1) Check pressure of tires and inflate as specified on page 187.
2) Weak or broken coil spring.	2) Check spring camber under load and replace spring if not within specifications (page 149), or broken.
3) Wear of shock absorber causes poor dampening action.	3) Overhaul shock absorber and replace worn parts.

Squeaks, Thumps, or Rattles.

POSSIBLE CAUSES	REMEDIES
1) Wheels out of balance.	1) Inspect and fix as directed on page 187.
2) Wheels off center.	2) Inspect and fix as directed on page 187.
3) Misadjusted brakes.	3) Adjust brakes as outlined on page 178.
4) Weak or broken coil springs or spring seats dislodged.	4) Check spring camber under load and replace spring if not within specifications (page 149), or broken. Replace upper and lower rubber seats, if damaged.
5) Wear of shock absorbers causes poor dampening action.	5) Overhaul shock absorbers and replace worn parts.
6) Worn rubber bushings in control arms.	6) Replace bushings by new ones.
7) Poor lubrication of wheel bearings.	7) Proceed as directed on page 148 and under « Maintenance ».

Pull to One Side.

POSSIBLE CAUSES	REMEDIES
1) Incorrect tire pressure.	1) Check pressure of tires and inflate as prescribed on page 187.
2) Misadjusted brakes.	2) Adjust brakes as directed on page 178.
3) Distorted suspension arm.	3) Remove, check on test equipment (see page 146), straighten arm, if possible, and set correctly on installation.

Section 7
STEERING GEAR AND LINKAGE

	Page
SERVICING THE STEERING GEAR	161
STEERING RODS	165
CHECKING FRONT WHEEL TOE-IN	166
TIGHTENING REFERENCE	167
SERVICE EQUIPMENT	167
SPECIFICATIONS	168
TROUBLE DIAGNOSIS AND CORRECTIONS	169

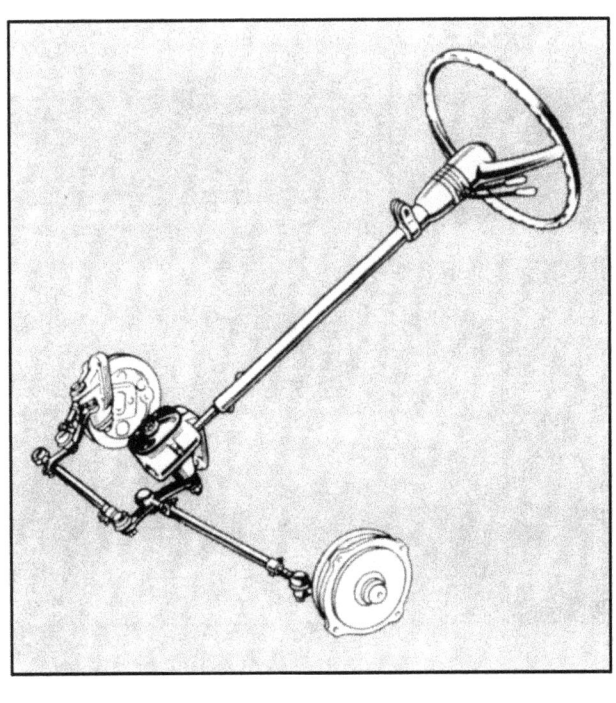

STEERING SYSTEM

Description	page	160
SERVICING THE STEERING GEAR	»	161
Steering Wheel Removal	»	161
Steering Box Removal	»	161
Steering Box Disassembly	»	161
Inspection and Adjustment	»	163
Steering Box Assembly and Installation	»	164
Relay Lever Support	»	165
STEERING RODS	»	165
CHECKING FRONT WHEEL TOE-IN	»	166
TIGHTENING REFERENCE	»	167
SERVICE EQUIPMENT	»	167
SPECIFICATIONS	»	168
TROUBLE DIAGNOSIS AND CORRECTIONS	»	169

Description.

Steering gear is by worm screw and sector with a 26 to 2 ratio.

The steering box is located on front left hand side of dash wall (fig. 268).

The steering gear consists of:

— a pitman arm and a relay lever articulated on a pin supported on the body;

— a central track rod connecting the pitman arm and the relay lever;

— two track rods, connecting respectively the pitman arm and relay lever to knuckle arms.

The steering radius is 14 ft. 1 in (4,30 m).

NOTE - Before carrying out any adjustment of steering gear, check that no other steering component is affected by play or maladjustment; otherwise, proceed first with its adjustment.

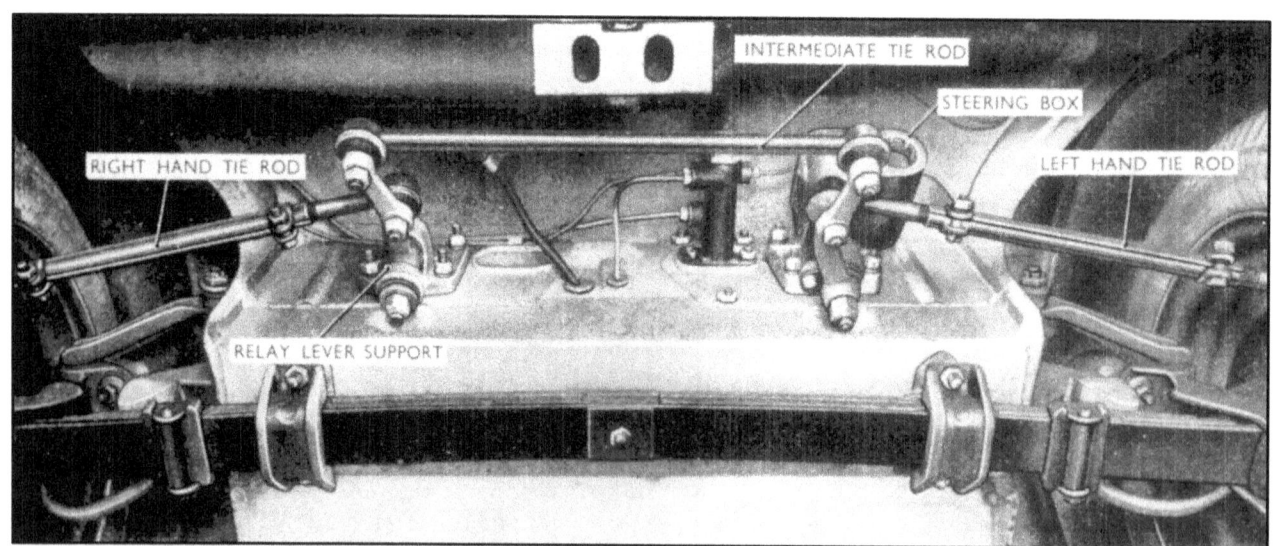

Fig. 268 - Steering box, idler member and steering linkage arrangement on vehicle.

STEERING SYSTEM

SERVICING THE STEERING GEAR

Steering Wheel Removal.

Remove horn control from steering wheel.
Remove cable from push button seat and cable insulating sleeve; then, using wrench **A. 8279**, unscrew steering wheel-to-shaft nut (fig. 269).

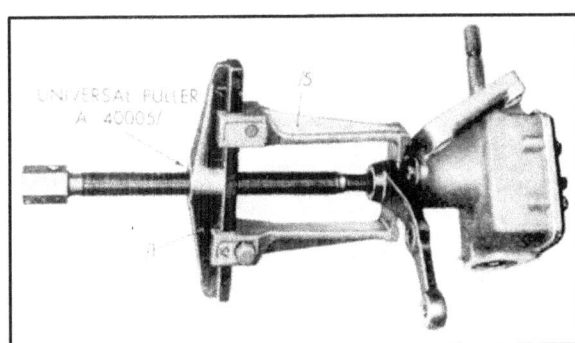

Fig. 270 - Removal of pitman arm by puller A. 40005/1/5.

Secure steering box to servicing support **A. 66032**, remove self-locking nut, and disinsert pitman arm using puller **A. 40005/1/5** (fig. 270).

Remove cotter pin and back out worm screw adjuster and bearing retainer lower sleeve, using wrench **A. 8065** (fig. 271).

After removing lower gasket from sector shaft, back out screw securing the eccentric bush adjusting plate and take off plate and upper seal.

Disinsert worm sector thrust washer and shims.

Remove worm screw by pulling from below (lower bearing outer ring will remain in housing). The two bearing inner rings will remain on worm screw; to take them off, use puller **A. 46019**.

Remove: oil seal with tool **A. 10110** (fig. 273) and then worm screw upper bearing outer ring with tool **A. 66040** (fig. 272).

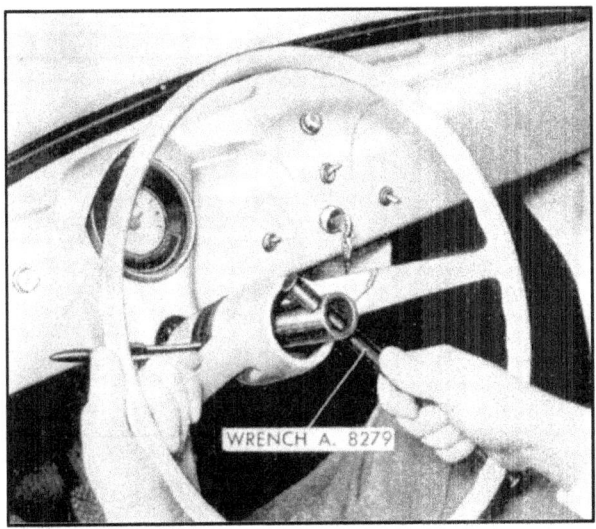

Fig. 269 - Removal of steering wheel mounting nut, using wrench A. 8279.

Steering Box Removal.

Proceed as follows:

Inside car, back off the steering shaft-to-worm screw mounting nut.

From the bottom, remove the two track rod self-locking nuts from pitman arm, then, by tool **A. 46006**, withdraw pins from seats.

Remove steering box-to-body nuts.

Disinsert worm screw from steering shaft and take out steering box.

To install steering box, reverse removal operations; tighten steering box-to-body nuts with 14.5 to 18.1 ft.lbs (2000 to 2500 kgmm) of torque.

Steering Box Disassembly.

Proceed as follows:

Take off cover provided with screw and nut for worm sector adjustment and drain out the oil from the steering box.

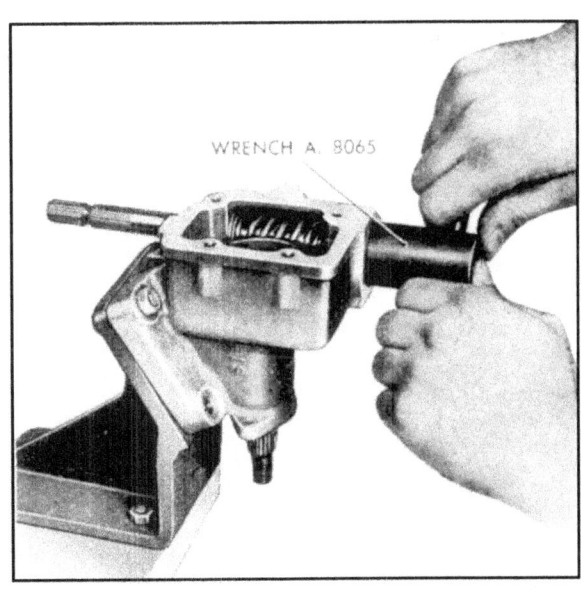

Fig. 271 - Removing adjuster ring by wrench A. 8065.

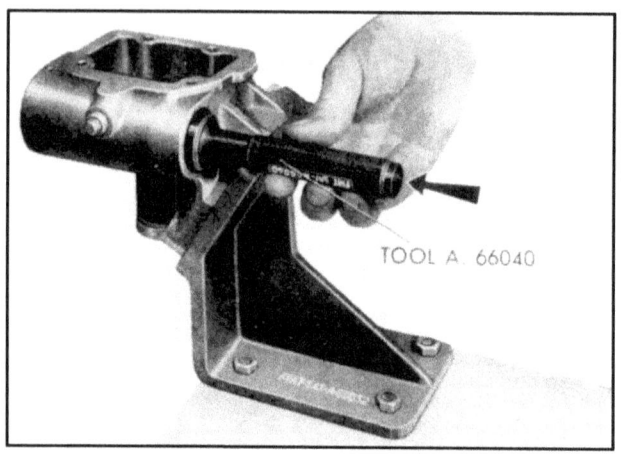

Fig. 272 - Removing upper bearing outer ring by remover A. 66040.

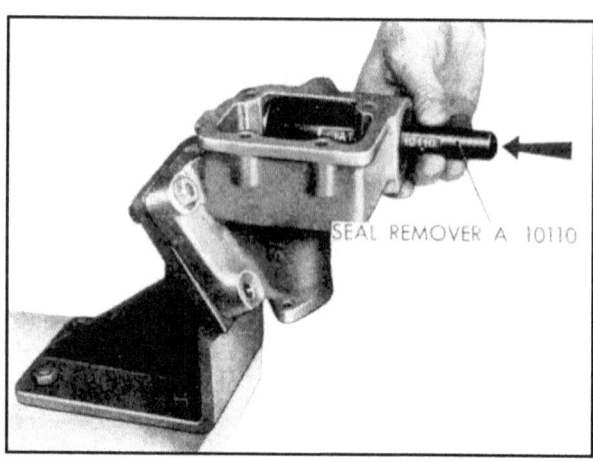

Fig. 273 - Removal of oil seal by tool A. 10110.

Fig. 274 - Layout of steering gear components.

1. Steering wheel and column assembly. - 2. Nut. - 3. Toothed washer. - 4. Plain washer. - 5. Steering column bracket-to-instrument panel screw. 6. Steering column-to-worm screw locking screw. - 7. Lock plate. - 8. Plain washer - 9. Cover screw. - 10. Toothed washer. - 11. Cover. - 12. Gasket. - 13. Pin. - 14. Nut. - 15. Plain washer. - 16. Worm sector adjusting screw. 17. Worm sector and shaft assy. - 18. Worm screw. - 19. Thrust washer.

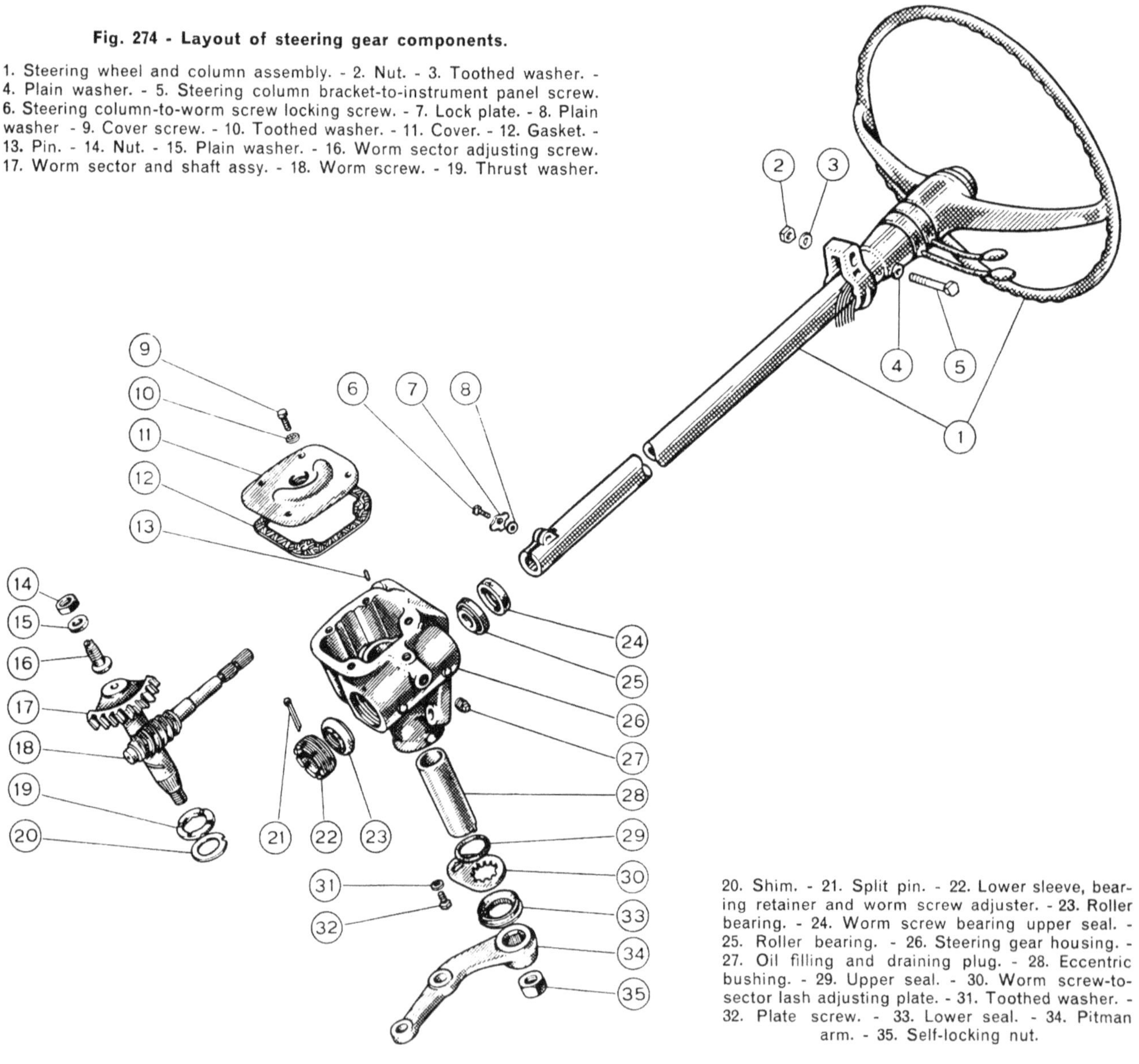

20. Shim. - 21. Split pin. - 22. Lower sleeve, bearing retainer and worm screw adjuster. - 23. Roller bearing. - 24. Worm screw bearing upper seal. - 25. Roller bearing. - 26. Steering gear housing. - 27. Oil filling and draining plug. - 28. Eccentric bushing. - 29. Upper seal. - 30. Worm screw-to-sector lash adjusting plate. - 31. Toothed washer. - 32. Plate screw. - 33. Lower seal. - 34. Pitman arm. - 35. Self-locking nut.

STEERING SYSTEM

Inspection and Adjustment.

Check parts accurately to see that sector teeth and worm screw threads shown no sign of seizing, indents or scoring.

Check contact surfaces to make sure that meshing between the two parts takes place at center; this to have a basis for adjustments during assembly.

Check clearance between eccentric bush (5, fig. 277) and worm sector (11, fig. 277) which must not exceed .0039" (0,10 mm).

Assembly clearance: .00000" to .00165" (0,000 to 0,042 mm).

NOTE - Should eccentric bushing-to-sector shaft clearance exceed .0039" (0,10 mm), install a new bushing.

After installation, ream inner face of bushing using reamer U. 0360/20.

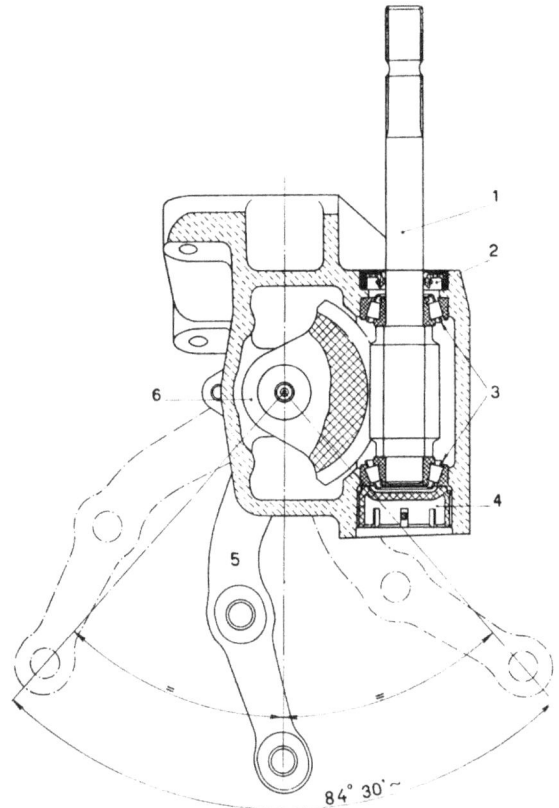

Fig. 276 - Section of steering box, through worm screw.

1. Worm screw. - 2. Seal. - 3. Roller bearing. - 4. Worm screw adjuster and bearing retainer. - 5. Pitman arm. - 6. Worm sector.

Fig. 275 - Steering box cutaway.

It is advisable to check also worm screw centering: max. permissible out-of-true is .00195" (0,05 mm).

As to adjustments to be performed when servicing steering gear, proceed as described below.

If backlash between worm screw and sector is excessive, adjust as follows:

Disconnect pitman arm and relevant seal.

Back out screw (7, fig. 277) fixing adjustment plate (6).

Rotate eccentric bush (5) by the adjustment plate and move sector in toward worm screw.

Secure plate again by using the second fixing hole.

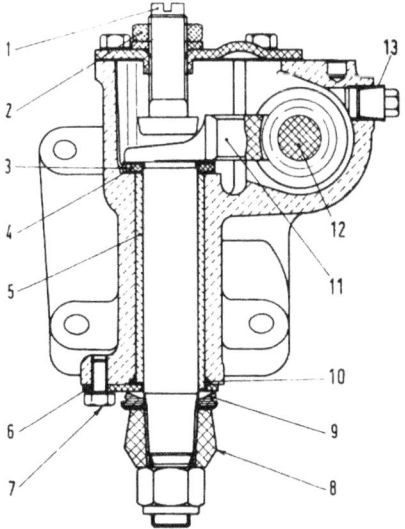

Fig. 277 - Section of steering box, through worm sector.

1. Sector adjustment screw. - 2. Locking nut and plain washer. - 3. Sector thrust washer. - 4. Shim. - 5. Eccentric bush. - 6. Bush adjusting plate. - 7. Plate screw and toothed washer. - 8. Pitman arm. - 9. Sector lower seal. - 10. Upper seal. - 11. Worm sector. - 12. Worm screw. - 13. Oil filler and level plug.

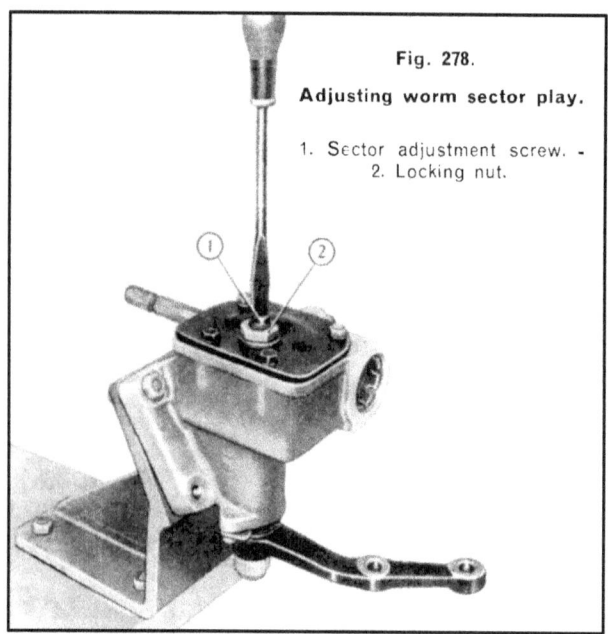

Fig. 278.

Adjusting worm sector play.

1. Sector adjustment screw. - 2. Locking nut.

Should adjusting plate be already fixed in second hole (which would impede repositioning after rotation), remove plate from bush, rotate one or more serrations and secure.

If play in worm screw rollers is excessive, screw up lower adjuster ring (4, fig. 276). Once adjustment is over, adjuster ring must be secured by cotter: to this end, position ring in such a way that hole in steering box lines up with one of the spaces between ring castellations.

As already mentioned, worm screw and sector must mesh in their central portion: if off center, this condition may be corrected by moving sector axially. To do so, add or remove shims (4, fig. 277) below thrust ring of worm sector.

The next adjustment must be carried out by means of adjustment screw (1, fig. 278) on cover, then locking screw by nut (2).

Shims are supplied as spares with .0039" (0,10 mm) thickness.

Both the above adjustments must eliminate any play and backlash in steering gear without rendering steering too stiff.

Replace any seal found damaged.

NOTE - Steering worm and sector are assembled with a touch fit at tooth flank.
Adjustment is made by rotating the worm sector mounting eccentric bushing.

Steering Box Assembly and Installation.

Steering box is assembled by reversing disassembly operations.

Tools to be used:

— **A. 66043** to insert eccentric bush;
— **A. 66046** to install worm screw upper roller bearing inner and outer rings;
— **A. 8065** wrench, for worm screw adjuster ring.

It is essential that before re-assembly, all components be perfectly clean and well lubricated.

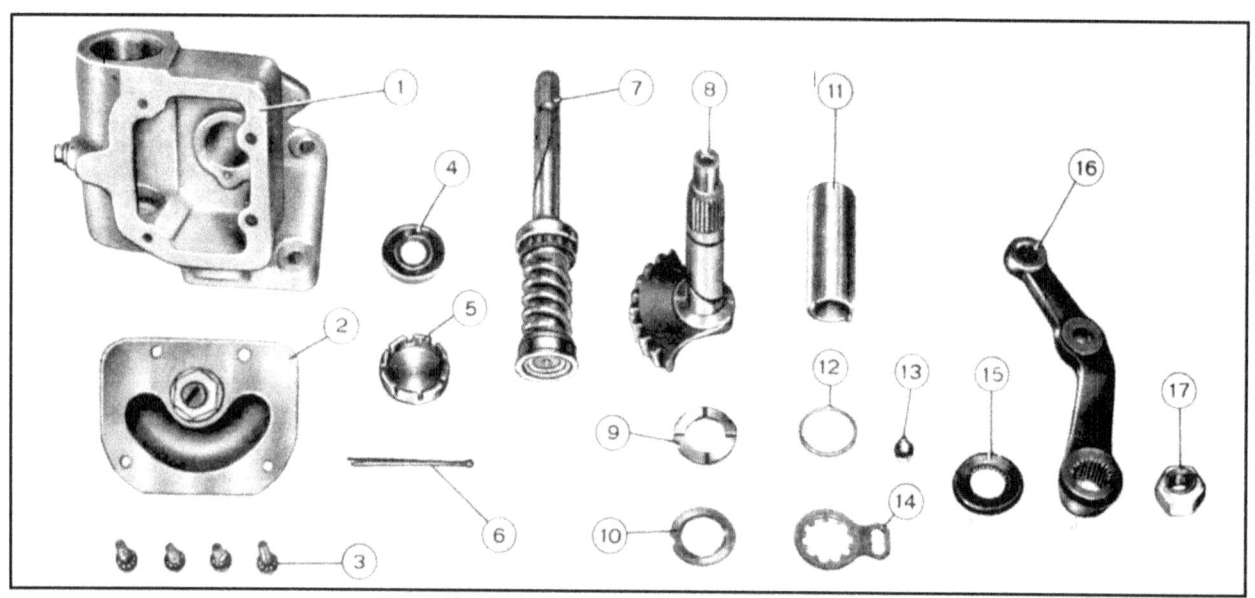

Fig. 279 - Steering box components.

1. Steering box housing. - 2. Cover. - 3. Cover mounting screws and toothed washers. - 4. Worm screw seal. - 5. Adjuster ring - 6. Adjuster ring cotter pin. - 7. Worm screw. - 8. Sector and shaft assy. - 9. Sector thrust washer. - 10. Sector shim. - 11. Eccentric bush. - 12. Upper seal. - 13. Plate screw and toothed washer. - 14. Bush adjusting plate. - 15. Lower seal. - 16. Pitman arm. - 17. Pitman arm mounting nut.

STEERING SYSTEM

Fig. 280 - Securing steering wheel mounting nut.
(Tightening torque: 28.9 to 36.2 ft.lbs — 4000 to 5000 kgmm).

Pitman arm nut must be tightened to 72.3 to 79.6 ft.lbs (10.000 to 11.000 kgmm).

For correct pitman arm positioning on assembly, the sector shaft and the pitman arm are marked with notches, or a tooth is omitted in the sector serration, whereas the pitman arm has a double tooth, which prevents incorrect assembly.

To reinstall the steering gear, reverse the removal procedure outlined on page 161. Steering box-to-body shell mounting nuts should be drawn up with 14.5 to 18.1 ft.lbs (2000 to 2500 kgmm) of torque, using a torque wrench.

Steering wheel mounting nut should be drawn up with 28.9 to 36.2 ft.lbs (4000 to 5000 kgmm) of torque (fig. 280).

Relay Lever Support.

Removal and disassembly of support are not difficult.

If play between pin and bushes is excessive, replace bushes.

Check also wear condition of pin and, if necessary, replace.

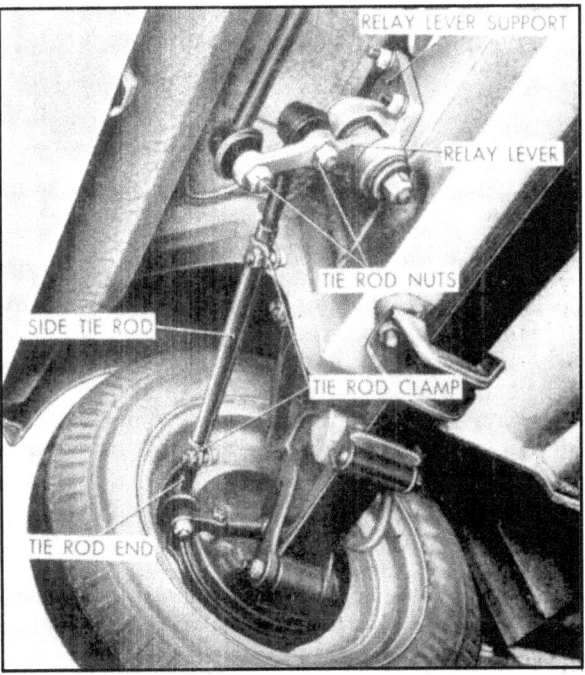

Fig. 282 - Close-up view of steering idler member and right hand side tie rod.

At reassembly, the only particular care to be used is that the pin nut must be tightened to 39.8 to 43.4 ft.lbs (5500 to 6000 kgmm) (after the toe-in has been adjusted and with wheels in straightahead position).

Support-to-body mounting nuts must be tightened to 14.5 to 18.1 ft.lbs (2000 to 2500 kgmm), same as for steering box-to-body nuts.

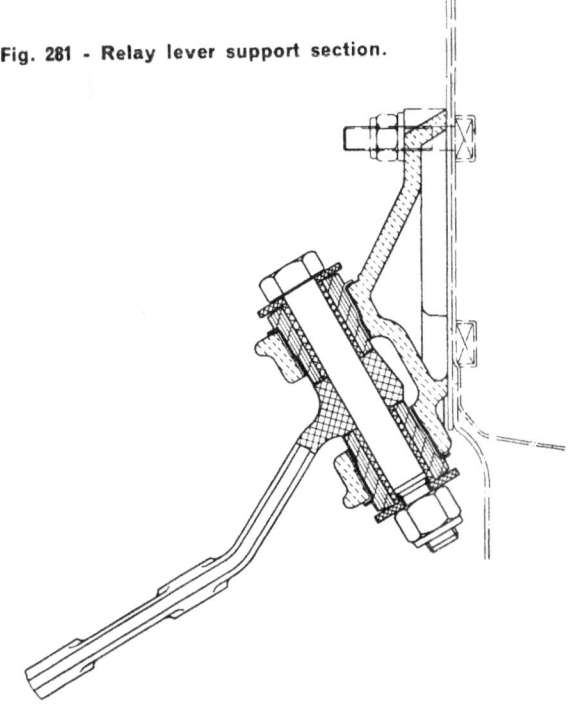

Fig. 281 - Relay lever support section.

STEERING RODS

Steering rods are three: two lateral, adjustable, and one intermediate, non-adjustable.

The two side track rods consist of: two R.H.-threaded and two L.H.-threaded heads, two sleeves

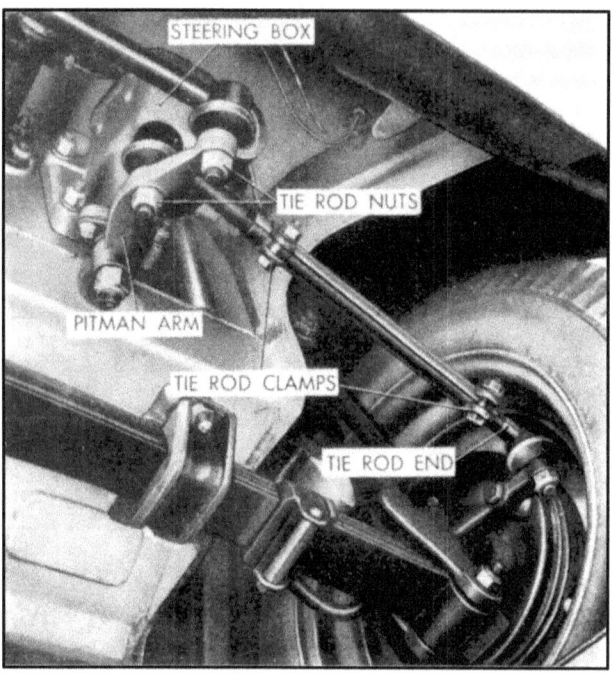

Fig. 283 - Close-up view of steering linkage: pitman arm and left hand side tie rod.

one for right and one for left track rod adjustment), and four locking clamps.

The intermediate steering rod is in a single piece with heads and is not adjustable.

Steering rod end articulations are made up of a ball pin, a socket, a spring, a spring cup, a plug and a gasket.

Front wheel toe-in is adjusted by suitably rotating the two side track rods, as directed in the following chapter.

Removal of steering rods from pitman arm, relay lever and knuckle arms is performed with pullers: **A. 46006** (removal from pitman arm and from relay lever) and **A. 6473** (removal from knuckle arms).

Fig. 284 - Checking front wheel toe-in with gauge **C. 692**.

If excessive play is noticed at articulations, or if ball pin is found damaged, replace the complete head.

Though installation of steering rods is not difficult, maximum care must be taken in reassembly, since steering is fundamental for driver's safety. Tie rod ball pin-to-knuckle arm nuts must be tightened to 18.1 to 21.7 ft.lbs (2500 to 3000 kgmm).

CHECKING FRONT WHEEL TOE-IN

Before starting the check, see that:

— tire pressures are as recommended: 17.1 p.s.i. (1,20 kg/cm^2) at front and 26.3 p.s.i. (1,85 kg/cm^2) at rear;

 steering wheel is at mid-travel and spokes are horizontal;

— wheels are in straightahead position;

— car is in static load conditions or with an orderly load of four passengers.

Fig. 285 - Gauge **C. 692** plunger contact point.

Adjust height of gauge **C. 692** plungers until they coincide with the wheel horizontal centerline, then set plungers against the outer edge of rim rear portion (A, fig. 286) and mark off with chalk.

Next, bring gauge in front of wheels, move car forward and stop when chalk marks line up with gauge plungers (B). Set one plunger in contact with wheel (fig. 285). The gap between the other plunger and the other wheel must be within the recommended .0000" to .0787" (0 to 2 mm) range.

STEERING SYSTEM

NOTE - After measurement, see that points **A** and **B** are equally apart from car centerline.

If toe-in needs correction, slacken the four clamps fixing the sleeves on track rod heads. Rotate sleeves in opposite directions and of an equal amount.

Since sleeves have one right-hand and one left-hand threaded end, when sleeve is turned in one direction both heads are screwed out and when turned in the opposite direction both heads are screwed in.

The result of this is a variation in track rod length.

When a perfect adjustment has been obtained, tighten the four sleeve clamps; with fully tightened clamp nuts, check that expansion slot in the sleeve registers with clamp joint; with fully tightened clamp, joint faces must not be in contact, otherwise the faulty clamp must be replaced.

Finally, when the steering gear is reinstalled, keep the wheels in straightahead position and tighten the relay lever pin nut with 78.2 to 85.3 ft.lbs (5500 to 6000 kgmm) of torque.

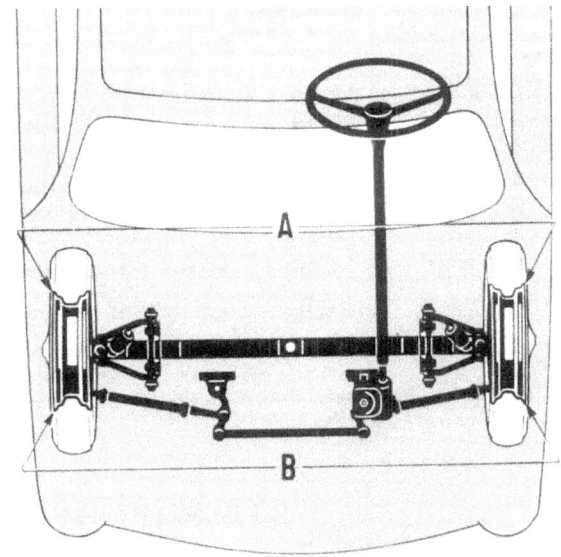

Fig. 286 - Toe-in adjustment check data.

A − B = 0 to .0787" (0 to 2 mm).

STEERING SYSTEM TIGHTENING REFERENCE

ITEM	Drwg. or Std. Part No.	Thread	Material	Tightening Torque
Pitman arm-to-sector shaft nut . . .	1/25748/11	14 MB (x1,5)	R 50 Cdt (Sector 19CN5 Cmt 3)	72.3 to 79.6 ft.lbs (10.000 to 11.000 kgmm)
Relay lever pin nut	1/25747/11	12 MB (x1,5)	R 50 (Pin R 80 Cdt)	39.8 to 43.4 ft.lbs (5.000 to 6.000 kgmm)
Steering box-to-body nut and relay lever support nut	1/61041/11	8 MA (x1,25)	R 50 Cdt (Screw R 80 Cdt)	14.5 to 18.1 ft.lbs (2.000 to 2.500 kgmm)
Tie rod ball pin nut	1/25756/11	10 x 1,25 M	R 50 Cdt (Pin R 100 Bon)	18.1 to 21.7 ft.lbs (2.500 to 3.000 kgmm)
Steering wheel nut	743601	18 MB (x1,5)	R 50 Cdt (Shaft C 12 tube)	28.9 to 36.2 ft.lbs (4.000 to 5.000 kgmm)

STEERING SYSTEM SERVICE EQUIPMENT

A. 6473   Puller - steering rod head pins (single).
A. 8065   Wrench - adjuster ring.
A. 8279   Wrench - steering wheel nut.
A. 10110   Drift rod - worm screw seal.
A. 40005/1/5   Puller - steering control relay lever.

(continued)

Steering System Service Equipment (*continued*).

A.	46006	Puller - steering rod head pins (paired).
A.	46019	Puller - worm screw roller bearing inner ring.
A.	57033	Wrench - steering box oil level inspection plug.
A.	66032	Support - steering mechanism servicing.
A.	66040	Remover - steering box upper roller bearing outer ring.
A.	66043	Installer and remover - worm sector shaft bushing.
A.	66046	Installer - worm screw roller bearing inner and outer ring.
C.	692	Gauge - front wheel toe-in check.
U.	0360/20	Reamer - worm sector shaft bushing.

STEERING SYSTEM SPECIFICATIONS

Steering gear type	worm screw and roller
Ratio	26 to 2
Worm screw bearings	taper roller
Linkages	with relay lever
Side track rods	adjustable by threaded ends
Intermediate rod	with incorporated ends
Sector shaft bushing	bronze
Worm screw bearing adjustment	through threaded sleeve adjuster
Worm screw-to-sector lash adjustment	through sector shaft eccentric bushing rotation
Sector shaft bushing I. D.	.7874" to .7882" (20,000 to 20,021 mm)
Sector shaft diameter	.7874" to .7866" (20,000 to 19,979 mm)
Sector shaft-to-sector shaft bushing assembly clearance	.00000" to .00165" (0,000 to 0,042 mm)
Turning radius	14 ft. 1 in (4,30 m)
Wheel steering angles: inner wheel	33º
outer wheel	abt. 25º 40'
Steering wheel turns (lock to lock)	abt. 3.05
Front wheel toe-in (fully laden car)	.0000" to .0787" (0 to 2 mm)
Front track	44.09" (1121 mm)
Wheelbase	72.44" (1840 mm)
Steering gear oil: capacity	.105 Imp. quarts - .124 U.S. quarts (0,120 l. - 0,110 kg)
grade	FIAT W 90 (SAE 90 EP)

STEERING SYSTEM TROUBLE DIAGNOSIS AND CORRECTIONS

Front Wheel Shimmy.

POSSIBLE CAUSES	REMEDIES
1) Incorrect tire pressure.	1) Inspect tire pressure and inflate as recommended on page 187.
2) Incorrect front wheel alignment.	2) Inspect and correct front wheel alignment as outlined on page 136.
3) Loose front wheel bearings.	3) Adjust bearings as outlined on page 135.
4) Wheels out of balance.	4) Inspect and correct as outlined on page 187.
5) Loose steering linkage connections.	5) Inspect, replace damaged parts, if any, and tighten nuts with torque specified on page 167.
6) Loose steering gear or relay lever support at body mountings.	6) Check all mounting nuts for tightness with recommended torque (page 167).
7) Incorrect fitting of steering worm to worm sector.	7) Adjust steering gear as outlined on page 163.

Hard Steering.

POSSIBLE CAUSES	REMEDIES
1) Incorrect tire pressure.	1) Inflate tires to correct pressure as specified on page 187.
2) Incorrect front wheel alignment.	2) Check wheel alignment and adjust as outlined and tabulated on page 136.
3) Incorrect adjustment of steering worm to worm sector.	3) Adjust steering gear as recommended on page 163.

Hard Turning when Stationary.

POSSIBLE CAUSES	REMEDIES
1) Incorrect tire pressure.	1) Check pressure of tires and inflate to correct values as specified on page 187.
2) Incorrect adjustment of steering worm to worm sector.	2) Adjust steering gear as recommended on page 163.

Pull to One Side.

POSSIBLE CAUSES	REMEDIES
1) Incorrect tire pressure.	1) Inspect and inflate tires as specified on page 187.
2) Incorrect front wheel alignment.	2) Inspect and adjust front wheel alignment as specified on page 136.
3) Incorrect front wheel bearing adjustment.	3) Adjust bearings as specified on page 135.
4) Distorted kingpin housing or swinging arms.	4) Disassemble suspension and check kingpin housing on test equipment as outlined under « Front Suspension and Wheels ». Replace kingpin housing, if distorted, and swinging arms which cannot be reshaped correctly.
5) Unequal brake adjustment.	5) Adjust brakes as specified on page 178.
6) Semi-elliptic spring weak or broken.	6) Check spring against data on page 129 and replace damaged or broken spring.

Rattles.

POSSIBLE CAUSES	REMEDIES
1) Loose steering linkage connections.	1) Inspect, replace worn parts, if any, and tighten nuts with torque recommended on page 167.
2) Loose steering gear or relay lever support at body mountings.	2) Check all mounting nuts for tightness with recommended torque (page 167).
3) Semi-elliptic spring weak or broken.	3) Check against data on page 129 and replace damaged or broken spring.
4) Lack of lubrication.	4) Lubricate as specified in maintenance chart (page 286).

Loose Steering.

POSSIBLE CAUSES	REMEDIES
1) Incorrect front wheel bearing adjustment.	1) Adjust as recommended on page 135.
2) Loose steering linkage connections.	2) Inspect, replace worn parts, if any, and tighten nuts with torque recommended on page 167.
3) Loose steering gear mountings.	3) Tighten mounting nuts with recommended torque (page 167).
4) Incorrect adjustment of steering worm to worm sector.	4) Adjust steering gear as recommended on page 163.

STEERING SYSTEM

Jerky Steering.

POSSIBLE CAUSES	REMEDIES
1) Incorrect front wheel alignment.	1) Inspect and adjust as recommended on page 136.
2) Incorrect front wheel bearing adjustment.	2) Adjust as recommended on page 135.
3) Wheels out of balance.	3) Inspect and correct as recommended on page 187.
4) Loose steering linkage connections.	4) Inspect, replace worn parts, if any, and tighten nuts with torque recommended on page 167.
5) Loose or incorrect fitting of worm to sector.	5) Adjust or take up play as recommended on page 163.

Side-to-Side Wander.

POSSIBLE CAUSES	REMEDIES
1) Incorrect tire pressure.	1) Check tire pressure and inflate as specified on page 187.
2) Incorrect front wheel alignment.	2) Check wheel alignment and adjust as specified on page 136.
3) Loose steering linkage connections.	3) Check, replace damaged parts and tighten nuts with torque specified on page 167.
4) Loose steering gear or relay lever support at body mountings.	4) Check all mounting nuts for tightness with recommended torque (page 167).
5) Incorrect fitting of steering worm to worm sector.	5) Adjust steering gear as outlined on page 163.
3) Distorted kingpin housing or swinging arms.	6) Check kingpin housing on test equipment as shown under « Front Suspension » and replace kingpin housing, if distorted, and swinging arms which cannot be reshaped correctly.
7) Semi-elliptic spring weak or broken.	7) Check spring against data on page 129 and replace if damaged or broken.

Tire Squeal on Turns.

POSSIBLE CAUSES	REMEDIES
1) Incorrect tire pressure.	1) Check tire pressure and inflate as specified on page 187.
2) Incorrect wheel alignment.	2) Check and correct as specified on page 136.
3) Distorted kingpin housing or swinging arms.	3) Check kingpin housing on test equipment as shown under « Front Suspension and Wheels »; replace kingpin housing, if distorted, and swinging arms which cannot be reshaped correctly.

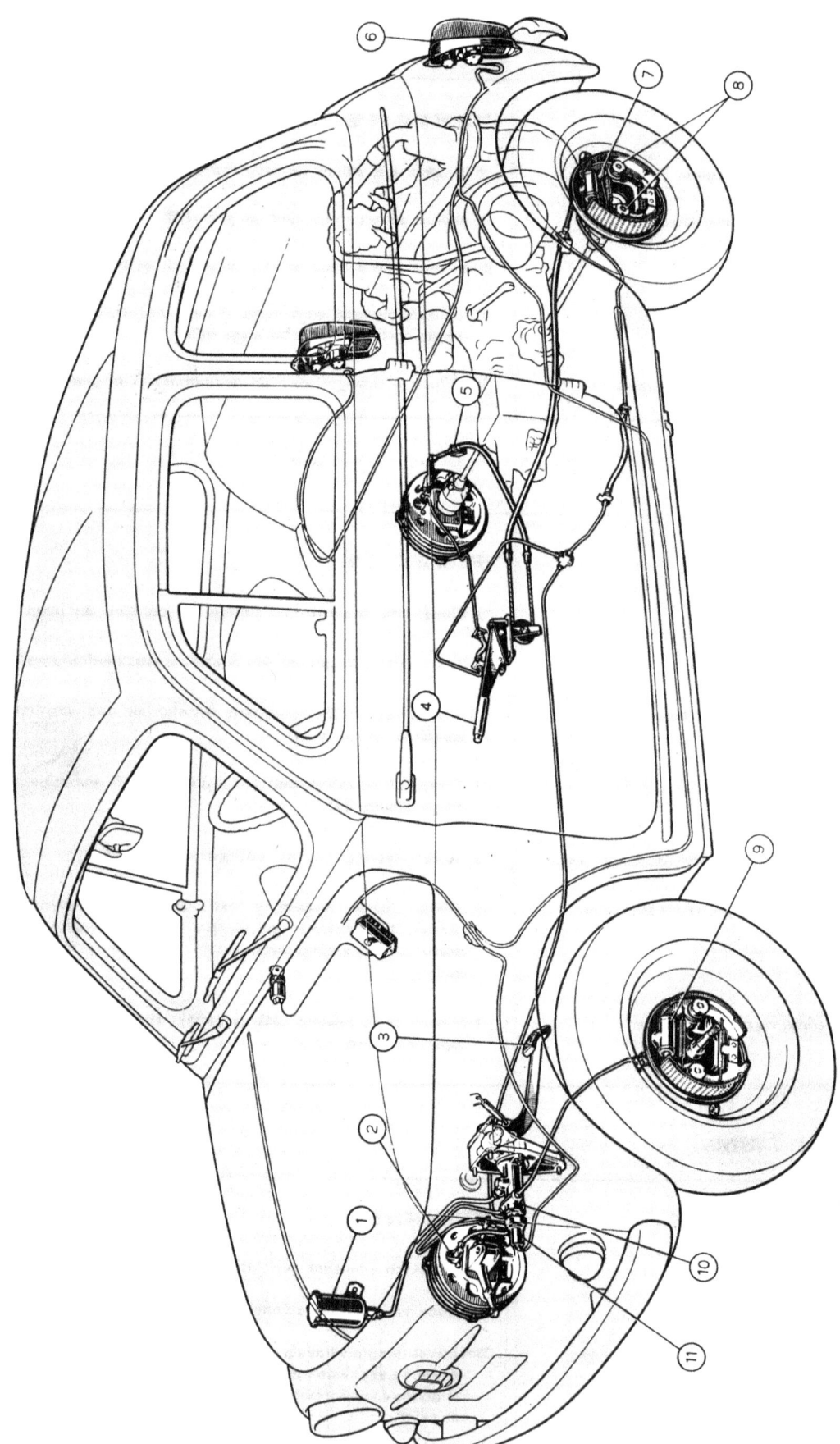

Fig. 287 - Service and rear wheel parking brake system diagram.

1. Brake fluid reservoir. - 2. Bleeder connections. - 3. Service brake pedal. - 4. Hand lever, mechanical parking brake on rear wheels. - 5. Hand lever travel adjustment stretchers. - 6. Stop lamps. - 7. Mechanical brake operating lever. - 8. Shoe clearance self-adjusting device 9. Wheel cylinders. - 10. Master cylinder. - 11. Stop light pressure-operated switch.

Section 8

BRAKES
WHEELS AND TIRES

	Page
HYDRAULIC SERVICE BRAKES	175
HAND PARKING BRAKE	181
BRAKE TIGHTENING REFERENCE	181
BRAKE SERVICE EQUIPMENT	181
BRAKE SYSTEM SPECIFICATIONS	182
HYDRAULIC BRAKE SYSTEM TROUBLE DIAGNOSIS AND CORRECTIONS	183
WHEELS AND TIRES	187

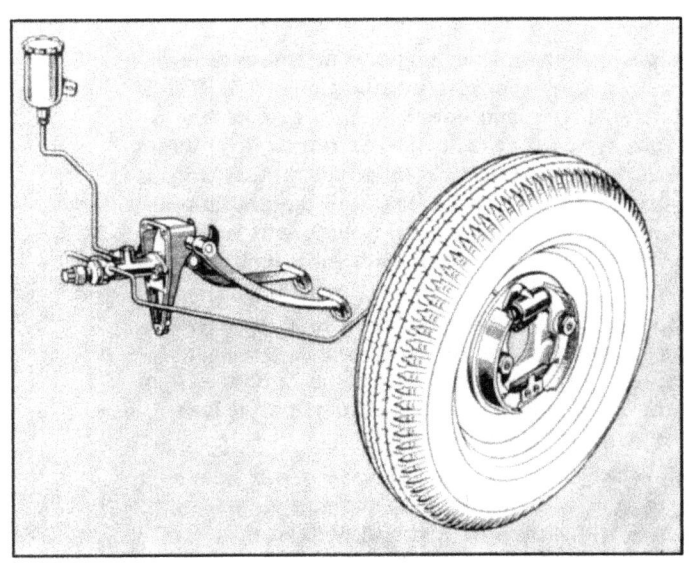

BRAKES

Description	page	174
HYDRAULIC SERVICE BRAKES	»	175
Master Cylinder	»	175
Wheel Cylinders	»	175
Hydraulic System Operation	»	176
Inspecting the Hydraulic System	»	176
Checking Master Cylinder	»	177
Checking Wheel Cylinders	»	178
Self-Adjustment of Brake Shoe Clearance	»	178
Description and Operation of the Self-Adjusting Device	»	178
Inspection and Assembly of the Self-Adjusting Device	»	178
Drums	»	179
Brake Shoe Linings	»	179
Bleeding the Brake System	»	179
Bonding Brake Shoe Linings	»	180
Brake Fluid Reservoir	»	180
HAND PARKING BRAKE	»	181
BRAKE TIGHTENING REFERENCE	»	181
BRAKE SERVICE EQUIPMENT	»	181
BRAKE SYSTEM SPECIFICATIONS	»	182
HYDRAULIC BRAKE SYSTEM TROUBLE DIAGNOSIS AND CORRECTIONS	»	183

Description.

The « New 500 » model is provided with:

— hydraulically operated service brakes on the four wheels;

— mechanically operated parking brake on rear wheels.

Service brakes are of the expanding-shoe type, with linings, and are pedal controlled.

The shoes, of pressed steel sheet, are of the self-centering type; thanks to the particular system (figs. 288 and 295), brake shoes adapt themselves automatically to the drum so that the contact between shoe lining and drum is better and more steady, with an evener wear and longer life of linings.

Furthermore, a shoe-to-drum clearance take up device (as described on page 178) has been incorporated having the purpose of automatically adjusting the brakes, with the result that pedal free travel is kept on constant values.

Parking brake operates mechanically the rear wheel shoes and is controlled by a hand lever on center tunnel, between the two front seats.

The auxiliary hand brake, which should be used as a normal braking means only in emergency and with great caution, has been basically designed for keeping the car at standstill in parking position.

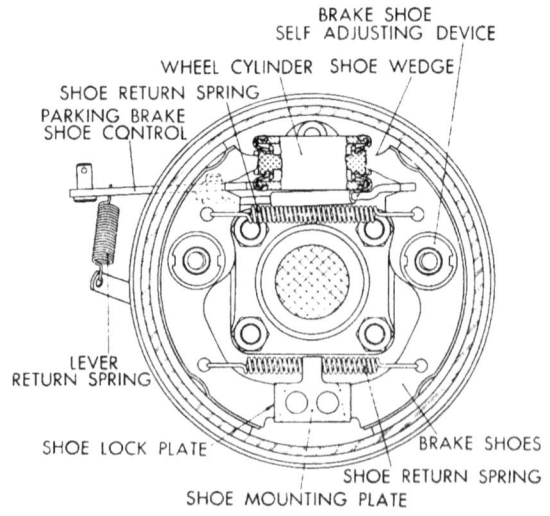

Fig. 288 - Right rear wheel brake assembly.

HYDRAULIC SERVICE BRAKES

Master Cylinder.

The master cylinder is of the floating valve ring type, featuring extremely simple construction, strong components and minimum number of parts.

It operates in the following way (fig. 289):

The brake pedal pushrod exerts pressure directly on master cylinder plunger (9). On feed chamber rear end, sealing is ensured by front rubber valve (18) identical to valve (16). Valve (18) is fitted on a shoulder of plunger (9), and is squeezed between parts (9) and (17) by return spring (4) with a radial pressure sufficient to ensure a tight sealing.

When the master cylinder is at rest, valve (16) has no radial pressure, and, moreover, it is in such a position as to allow master cylinder to be fed through compensating hole (5). Valves (16) and (18) have a toric section; their maximum free diameter is equal to, or slightly larger than, the cylinder diameter; when not under hydraulic pressure, only their outer face mid portion is in contact with the cylinder wall, while the edges clear it.

When hydraulic pressure, combined with spring reaction, comes into play, it causes valve expansion. The contact area is reduced to a minimum and the rounded fluid-side edge ensures good lubrication to sliding surfaces and drag is negligible.

Compensating hole (5) in master cylinder is .0275" (0,7 mm) in diameter. This ensures proper compensation in case of fluid expansion due to drum heating, reduces clogging probabilities by foreign matter having entered the system and improves bleeding by facilitating the expulsion of air bubbles from compression chamber.

Inner diameter of master cylinder is 3/4".

Wheel Cylinders.

The 3/4" I. D. front and rear wheel cylinders (fig. 294) differ only in their connections to brake lines: connections are flexible at front and rigid at rear.

As in master cylinder, sealing is obtained by the rubber seal rings (5, fig. 294) which expand radially under fluid pressure.

Spring (7), resting on thrust cups (6) presses seal rings against plungers (3) acting on shoes through stems (1).

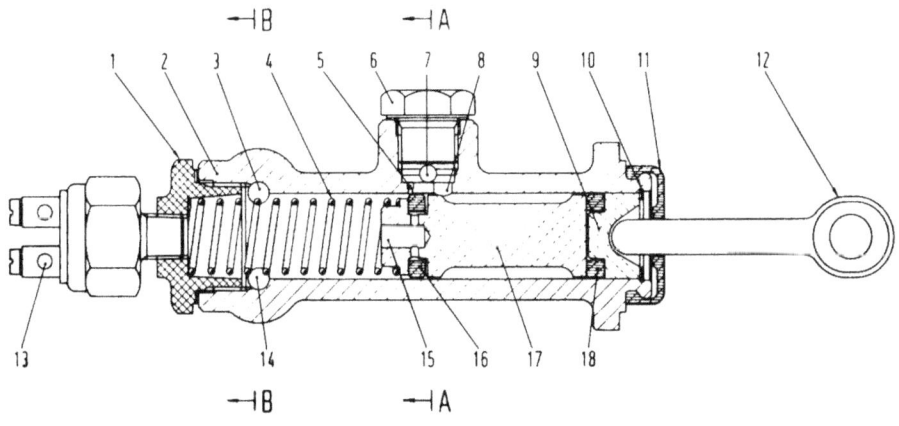

Fig. 289. Master cylinder section.

1. Plug and spring seat. - 2. Body. - 3. Front wheel brake line duct. - 4. Plunger return spring. - 5. Compensating hole. - 6. Plug. - 7. Supply duct. - 8. Fluid inlet hole. - 9. Plunger. - 10. Plunger snap ring. - 11. Boot. - 12. Push rod. - 13. Terminal, stop light switch. - 14. Rear wheel brake line duct. - 15. Holes in floating ring carrier for fluid passage. - 16. Valve. - 17. Valve carrier. - 18. Valve. - 19 and 20. Connection and line from brake fluid reservoir. - 21 and 22. Lines and connections for front wheel brakes. - 23 and 24. Lines and connection for rear wheel brakes.

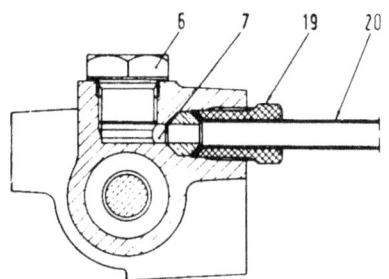

Fig. 290 - Section through arrival connection.

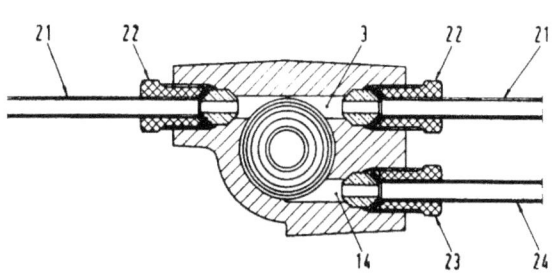

Fig. 291 - Section through connections of front and rear wheel brake lines.

Fig. 292 - Right hand side front wheel brake housing flange, with drum removed.

Hydraulic System Operation.

Through hole (8, fig. 289), the fluid is admitted to master cylinder, seeps through gap between valve carrier ring (17) and master cylinder barrel and, flowing through valve carrier ring holes (15), reaches and fills the system.

By depressing the brake pedal, the plunger is moved forward by pushrod (12).

The forward stroke of plunger (9) and valve carrier (17) brings valve (16) to rest against valve carrier front face. Continuing in its forward movement, valve ring (16) passes over compensating hole (5) and cuts off any communication with the fluid reservoir. Compression of the fluid begins from this instant.

By acting on front and inner faces of valve, it warrants perfect valve sealing even under noticeably high operation pressures.

When pressure reaches the fluid in wheel cylinders (fig. 294) it forces plungers (3) apart and through the plunger stems actuates the brake shoes.

In wheel cylinders, seal rings (5), also when at rest, are axially compressed by cups (6) under the action of spring (7). Rings are under the radial and axial action of hydraulic pressure so that their sealing ability is improved as pressure increases.

After releasing the pedal, the combined action of both brake shoe and master cylinder plunger return springs sends the fluid back to master cylinder and all parts resume their original position, so that free intercommunication between the system and the reservoir is restored.

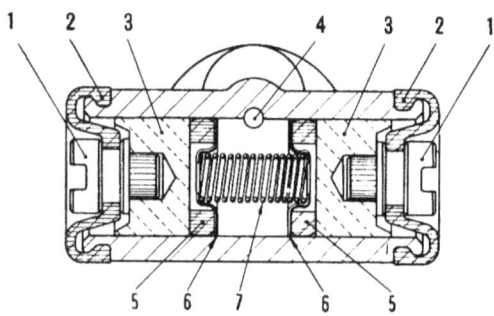

Fig. 294 - Wheel cylinder section.

1. Shoe actuating stems. - 2. Boot. - 3. Plungers. - 4. Fluid inlet hole. - 5. Seal rings. - 6 and 7. Spring thrust cups and plunger reaction spring.

Since no valves proper are fitted in this system, and the communication orifice between system and reservoir is amply dimensioned, bleeding is a very simple and easy operation.

In most cases, to eliminate air or vapor locks in the lines it will suffice to pump brake pedal: air will be drawn into master cylinder and discharged through reservoir vent.

Inspecting the Hydraulic System.

Check that:

1) Metal lines are in tip top condition, i. e., without flattenings and cracks and are away from sharp edges.

2) Hoses have not been fouled with oil or grease which would destroy the rubber.

3) All line fastening clips are secure. If loose, lines may crack as a consequence of vibrations.

4) No fluid leaks are noticeable at connections.

Fig. 293 - Right hand side rear wheel brake housing flange, with drum removed.

BRAKES

Should leaks be detected, tighten connections, being careful not to twist pipes during this operation.

5) The fluid level reaches reservoir filter.

The fluid to be used is the FIAT special blue label brake fluid (or equivalent non-mineral grade) and it must not be contaminated by any other liquid which, if present, would irreparably damage the special rubber gaskets of the system.

Avoid any spilling over body paint of fluid which is a strong solvent.

6) The play between pushrod and master cylinder plunger is .0197" (0,5 mm). This corresponds approximately to a .0984" (2,5 mm) pedal free travel.

Checking Master Cylinder.

Proceed as follows:

— disconnect stop light cables from pressure-operated switch;

Fig. 296 - Front wheel cutaway.

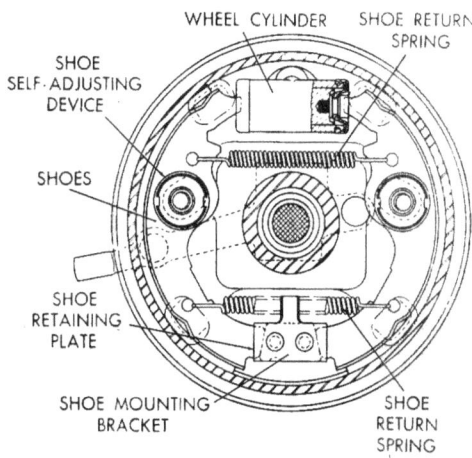

Fig. 295 - Left front wheel brake assembly.

Carefully check master cylinder inner surface and plunger outer surface: they must be absolutely mirror-like and play must not be excessive.

Smoothen out any roughness present on master cylinder inner surface to prevent fluid leaks or excessive wear of seals or plunger.

It goes without saying that smoothening must not appreciably change master cylinder inner diameter. If this diameter cannot be preserved, replace master cylinder body.

Replace seals.

Inspect master cylinder rear end boot: if damaged, replace.

Make sure plunger return spring has not weakened.

Before installation, clean all parts by washing in clean brake fluid. Avoid any contact with mineral oil, gasoline, kerosene or diesel oil which would irreparably damage rubber seals.

Reassemble master cylinder by introducing the parts in reversed disassembly order.

— blank the brake fluid reservoir with a wood plug;

— screw out front and rear wheel cylinder brake fluid delivery line connections (four) at master cylinder;

— remove master cylinder.

To disassemble master cylinder, operate as follows:

— remove plunger end rubber boot from cylinder body;

— take off plunger circlip;

— slide off from inside of cylinder body: plunger, plunger seal, valve-ring carrier, valve-ring and reaction spring;

— remove stop light pressure-operated switch;

— remove cylinder body stop plug and upper plug.

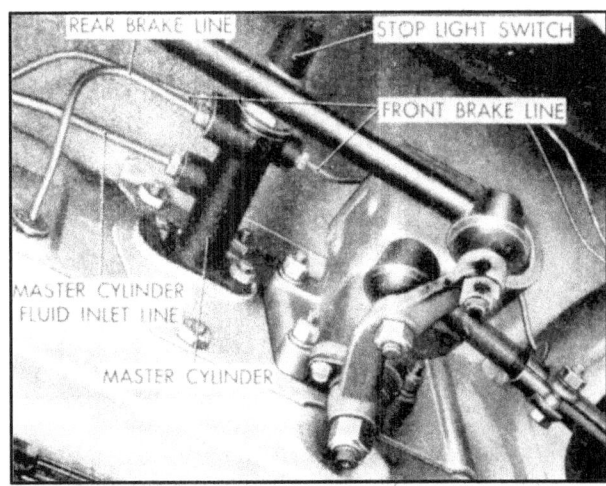

Fig. 297 - Arrangement of master cylinder and related brake lines on car.

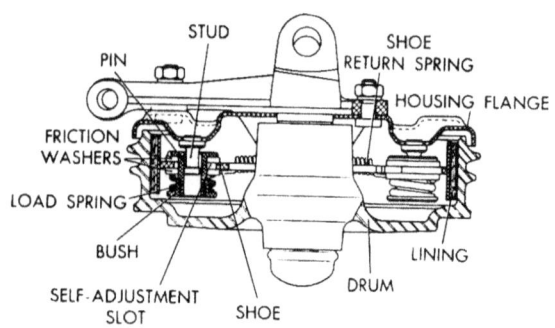

Fig. 298 - Left front wheel brake assembly section through self-adjusting device.

As a lubricant, use exclusively the FIAT special blue label brake fluid.

Also for master cylinder installation on body shell, just reverse the removal procedure.

Checking Wheel Cylinders.

After removing cylinders from brake housing flanges, remove rubber boots (2, fig. 294), on cylinder ends. Plungers, brake shoe stems and seal rings will be pushes out by spring expansion. Remove thrust rings and reaction springs.

Check that barrel and plunger surfaces have a mirror-like finish and show no rough or grainy spots. Replace parts or the assembly, as required.

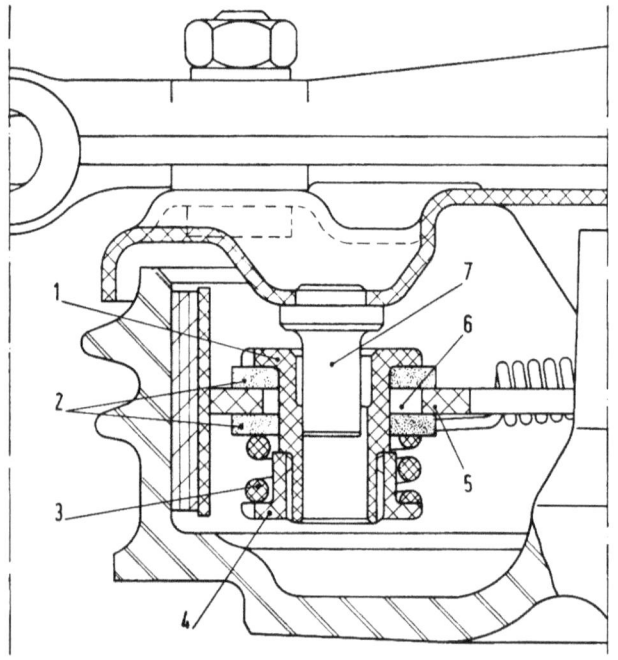

Fig. 299 - Sectional view of a self-adjusting device for automatic brake shoe-to-drum clearance take-up.

1. Pin. - 2. Friction washers. - 3. Load spring. - 4. Bushing. - 5. Shoe. 6. Self-adjustment slot. - 7. Stud.

Check the reaction spring for weakness and thrust washers for distortion: replace spring and washer assembly, if required.

Check, and preferably replace, the seals; inspect also wheel cylinder end boots for damages and replace as required.

Before reassembly, lubricate wheel cylinder parts by immersion in « FIAT special brake fluid (blue label) ».

Self-Adjustment of Brake Shoe Clearance.

The « New 500 » is equipped with a specially designed brake shoe clearance self-adjustment device which eliminates all the manual adjustment operations required before with other types of brake.

In fact, everytime brake pedal is depressed, this device automatically takes up any possible excess clearance developed as a consequence of lining wear.

Description and Operation of the Self-Adjusting Device.

On the side faces of shoe ribs are placed two friction washers in line with an adjustment slot machined in brake shoe (figs. 298 and 299).

The washers are held against shoe by a pin and bush screwed together through the slot with the interposition of a load spring. The pin is hollow and fits on the stud in brake housing flange. A clearance of .0315" (0,8 mm) between pin hole I. D. and stud O. D. permits the necessary displacement of shoes for proper braking under normal conditions without calling into play the self-adjustment device.

When shoe clearance adjustment is no longer as specified, on account of lining wear or improper assembly, the braking action - after overriding the stud-to-pin clearance - will overcome the resistance of friction washers and drag along the shoes into contact with drum.

After releasing the pedal, the action of return springs will be weaker than the friction of adjustment washers on shoes and, therefore, shoes will remain in the new position assumed up to the time when, following a further wear of linings, shoes will again be repositioned by the device.

Inspection and Assembly of the Self-Adjusting Device.

Check the integrity of all components and replace any worn or damaged part.

Before reassembly, it is advisable to check also the efficiency of springs. Their flexibility may be checked with tester **A. 11493** by compression to a height of .374" (9,5 mm). The corresponding load reading on tester should be 97 ± 4.9 lbs (44 ± 2,2 kg).

Reassemble the device as follows:

On support **A. 54002/2**, place the pin of the device.

Then insert: the first friction washer, the shoe, the second friction washer, the load spring and the bushing.

On support, fit wrench **A. 54002/1**, and by exerting a slight pressure to overcome spring load, tighten fully the bush on pin.

Finally, caulk pin and bushing.

Install the shoes on brake housing flange and hook up the two return springs.

Next, move shoes outwards as far as they will go and release: check that during return of shoes the friction washers have stayed put.

Instead, if the return springs have succeeded in changing the position of brake shoes relative to friction washers, it will be necessary to re-check the assembly and, particularly, the return and load springs. In fact, as previously pointed out, the shoe return springs must never affect the self-adjusting device.

Drums.

While servicing the brakes, inspect also the drums: if excessively scored or ovalized, recondition on lathe **M 10** using the spindle and bushes:

— **A. 72202/1/7** on front drums;
— **A. 72202/1/12** or rear drums.

After turning, still on lathe **M 10**, lap the drums to smoothen out any possible tool marks, thus ensuring longer lining life and better braking. In the turning and lapping operations the maximum permissible oversize beyond nominal drum diameter of 6.702" to 6.712" (170,230 to 170,480 mm) is .039" (1 mm).

Never exceed this limit or else both drum strength and braking efficiency would be impaired. The reduction in braking efficiency would result from the increase in shoe expansion travel and the consequent diminished contact pressure.

No adjustment will be required after drum assembly, as the self-adjusting device will take care of adapting shoe position to new drum diameter the first time brake pedal is actuated after servicing.

Brake Shoe Linings.

Check lining thickness and, if found excessively reduced, either replace the shoe or bond a new lining as described on page 180.

Minimum allowable lining thickness for proper operation is .059" (1,5 mm).

Replace linings if found greasy and check drums for oil infiltrations. Remedy, if required.

Fig. 300 - Bleeding the left front wheel brake.

(Use rubber hose A. 10103).

Bleeding the Brake System.

In case the system has been partially drained, during a major overhaul, or when some connections have had to be unscrewed, bleed system as follows:

1) Top up brake fluid reservoir.

2) Fit one end of bleeder hose **A. 10103** on wheel cylinder bleeder screw. Immerse the other hose end in a transparent vessel partially filled with brake fluid (fig. 300).

3) Slacken bleeder screw (1, fig. 301) a few turns and pump pedal repeatedly and quickly; stop pumping when fluid issues in a solid stream without bubbles.

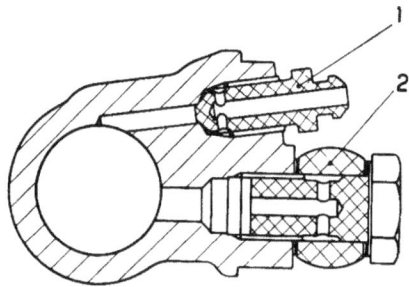

Fig. 301 - Wheel cylinder cross section.

1. Bleeder screw. - 2. Fluid line connection.

4) While keeping brake pedal depressed, tighten bleeder screw and remove bleeder hose.

5) Repeat operations 2, 3 and 4 on the other wheel cylinders.

NOTE - In case brake system has been completely drained, after refilling and before bleeding, proceed as follows:

  a) **Slacken bleeder screws a few turns on all four wheel cylinders.**

  b) **Pump brake pedal and then tighten the screws when fluid begins to issue.**

Should air bubbles continue to issue through bleeder hose ends, though bleeding operation is prolonged, check all connections for air leaks.

If no leaks are found, check master cylinder and wheel cylinder seals for perfect tightness.

NOTE - The bleeding operation of the hydraulic brake system may also be carried out with the bleeding equipment Ap. 5038.

WARNING

To prevent air from being drawn in by master cylinder during the bleeding operation, the fluid level in reservoir must never be allowed to fall under the minimum mark.

If bleeding operations have not been carried out properly, master cylinder plunger travel will be greater than normal and, with pedal fully depressed, a more or less marked sponginess will be felt, depending upon the amount of air that has remained in the system.

In this case, bleeding must be repeated simultaneously on the four bleeder screws.

If brake system of car in question has been in service for long, do not re-utilize the fluid.

The fluid bled into vessels, must be carefully filtered, before re-usage.

BONDING BRAKE SHOE LININGS

Brake linings are bonded on shoes by the « Permafuse » process described in a separate FIAT Service Department publication.

Bonding of lining on shoe is obtained by the interposition of a synthetic resin which is hardened by baking. This process ensures such a bonding of parts that linings cannot be torn off unless they are destroyed.

This is indispensable to prevent unbonding of linings during operation which would cause very serious consequences.

To obtain best results, follow strictly the instructions given in the booklet on the « Permafuse » process which also lists the proper equipment required.

It is important to note that the main feature of « Permafuse » resin (more particularly, the bonding fluid) is represented by its complete drying during the baking process. After vulcanizing, it becomes hard and vitreous, and is hence brittle.

Bubbles on shoe edges after heat treatment (whose brittleness is evidence of a perfect bonding) by solidifying and breaking into extremely hard fragments, will act as a powerful abradant with much damage to linings.

For this reason, removal of all resin residues squeezed out on shoe edges during bonding is of utmost importance and cannot be overemphasized.

This can be easily accomplished with a scraper, chisel, blade or any other suitable tool.

BRAKE FLUID RESERVOIR

It is located in front compartment to the right of fuel tank (fig. 302).

Should the line be detached from it, fluid outlet hole must be blanked by a wooden peg, to be fitted after removing cap and strainer (fig. 302).

Peg length must be such that reservoir cap may be reinstalled. This precaution is essential to prevent the entrance of foreign matter in the reservoir and the absorption of moisture, oil or kerosene vapors by the fluid, whose properties would otherwise be altered and impaired.

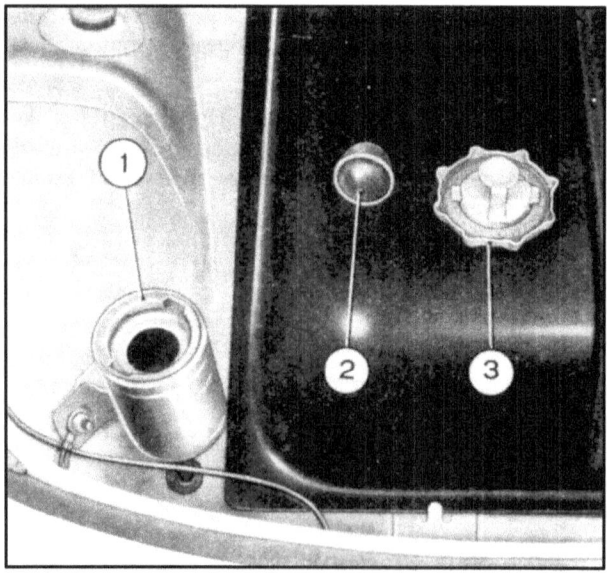

Fig. 302 - Brake fluid reservoir.
1. Reservoir. - 2. Strainer. - 3. Cap, vented.

HAND PARKING BRAKE

The auxiliary parking and emergency brake mechanically operates the rear wheel service brake shoes; control lever is placed on tunnel between seats.

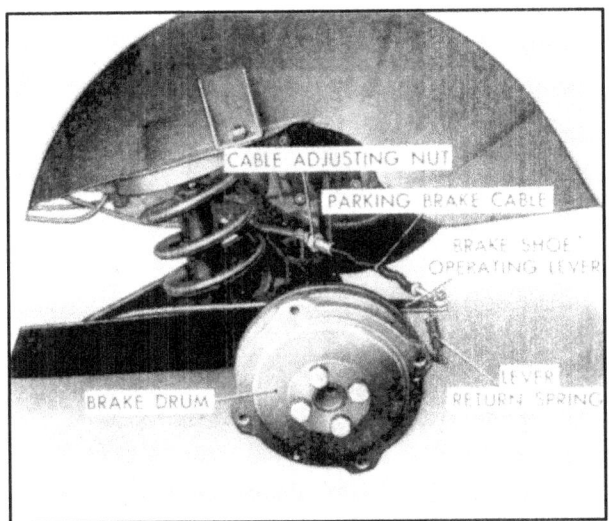

Fig. 303 - Parking brake control at left hand side rear wheel.

The hand lever lower end carries a sheave in which runs a wire rope, whose ends are connected to operating levers on brake housing flanges. When hand lever is pulled, through suitable articulations the operating levers expand brake shoes. Two stretchers are fitted at rope ends.

When brake efficiency needs checking, proceed as follows:

— pull hand lever. If brake is unable to hold car, bring lever to rest position, then pull it up by two ratchet serrations and work on both stretchers (fig. 304).

After adjustment, check that rope stretches sufficiently before hand lever comes to stroke end.

Particular care must be taken in performing this operation as any abnormal tension of rope would also affect the hydraulic brakes on rear wheels, since brake shoes are common to both systems.

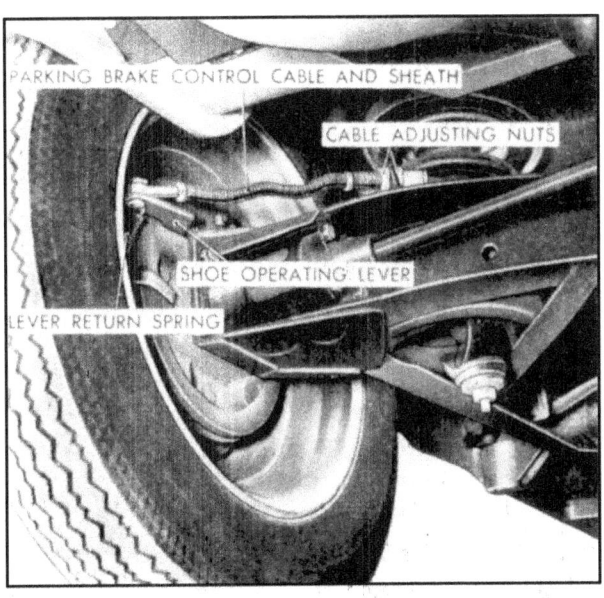

Fig. 304 - Parking brake control and adjusting mechanism at left hand side rear wheel.

BRAKE TIGHTENING REFERENCE

ITEM	Drwg. or Std. Part No.	Thread	Material	Tightening Torque
Brake housing flange-to-steering knuckle nut	1/61008/11	8 MA (x1,25)	R 50 Cdt (Screw R 50)	14.5 ft.lbs (2.000 kgmm)
Brake housing flange-to-swinging arm nut	1/21647/11	10 x 1,25 M	R 50 Cdt (Screw R 80)	43.4 ft.lbs (6.000 kgmm)

BRAKE SERVICE EQUIPMENT

A.	10103	Air bleeder rubber hose.
A.	40005/1/9	Puller - brake drums.
A.	54002/1/2	Installer - self-adjusting device on brake shoes.
A.	64026	Clamping tool - brake lining bonding.
A.	64027	Adapter - brake lining bonding.
A.	72202/1/7	Bushes - front wheel brake drum turning.
A.	72202/1/12	Bushes - rear wheel brake drum turning.
A.	72235	Tools - holding wheel cylinder pistons on assembly.
Ap.	5038	Bleeding equipment - hydraulic brake system.

BRAKE SYSTEM SPECIFICATIONS

Service Brakes:	
Type	hydraulic, self-centering, expanding-shoe
Drum: diameter	6.702" to 6.712" (170,230 to 170,480 mm)
maximum diameter oversize allowance	.0394" (1 mm)
Linings:	
Type of bonding	« PERMAFUSE »
Width	1.181" (30 mm)
Length (developed)	7.09" (180 mm)
Thickness	.1654" to .1772" (4,2 to 4,5 mm)
Shoe-to-drum clearance	take-up self-adjusting device
Self-adjustment device springs:	
Part No.	986339
Wire diameter	.142" (3,6 mm)
Inner diameter	.720" (18,3 mm)
Working coils	1
Total No. of coils	2½
Height	.484" (12,3 mm)
Height, seated	.374" (9,5 mm)
Corresponding load	97±4.9 lbs (44±2,2 kg)
Master cylinder diameter	3/4"
Wheel cylinder diameter	3/4"
Master cylinder plunger-to-pushrod clearance	.0197" (0,5 mm)
Pedal free travel	.0984" (2,5 mm)
Brake fluid:	
Type	FIAT special blue label brake fluid (or equivalent non-mineral grade)
Quantity liters	0,220
kg	0,215
Imp. quarts	.192
U.S. quarts	.232
Hand Parking Brake:	
Type	lever-controlled mechanical expansion of rear wheel brake shoes
Control	by hand lever on center floor tunnel
Wire rope adjustment	by stretchers located on swinging arms, behind brake housing flange

HYDRAULIC BRAKE SYSTEM
TROUBLE DIAGNOSIS AND CORRECTIONS

Locked Brake Pedal.

POSSIBLE CAUSES	REMEDIES
1) Swollen linings because the fluid used is inadequate or contaminated by kerosene, gasoline or mineral oil.	1) Flush the system, replace all rubber parts, refill with new fluid and air bleed the lines.
2) Plungers or valve carriers locked by deposits of fluid, foreign matter, etc.	2) Clean and bleed the system.
3) Master cylinder compensating hole blanked because plunger clearance is misadjusted.	3) Adjust the rod-to-plunger clearance by setting to .0197" (0,5 mm).
4) Clogged compensating hole. No compensation takes place.	4) Disassemble and clean master cylinder.
5) Seized master cylinder piston due to infiltrations of water through rear end because boot has failed or seals are no longer tight.	5) Service the master cylinder, replace the plunger and the boot and/or seals, to prevent water infiltrations.
6) Seized pedal shaft (this is also the cause for hard pedal or locked brakes).	6) Free and smoothen the parts and lubricate.

Spongy Pedal.

POSSIBLE CAUSES	REMEDIES
1) Air in brake system because of imperfect bleeding.	1) Repeat the bleeding operations more accurately.
2) Swollen hose because of deterioration.	2) Replace the hose; bleed the system.
3) Hose swollen under fluid pressure because hose used is of poor quality.	3) Fit new hoses of a quality approved by FIAT and bleed the system.
4) Air in master cylinder on account of insufficient seal tightness.	4) Fit a new valve-ring, checking that the plunger land height is less than ring thickness. Bleed the system.
5) Use of a brake fluid whose boiling point is too low.	5) Change the fluid with the FIAT special blue label fluid (or equivalent non-mineral grade) and bleed the system.
6) Reservoir filler cap vent hole clogged. This promotes a vacuum in master cylinder that sucks in air through rear seal.	6) Clean reservoir filler cap and bleed the system.

Pedal Yields Under Slight Pressure.

POSSIBLE CAUSES	REMEDIES
1) Deteriorated floating valve-ring.	1) Fit a new valve-ring, check that there are no roughness or irregularities in master cylinder and bleed the system.
2) Chips or impurities on valve-ring sealing surfaces.	2) Clean, replace the valve-ring if found deteriorated and bleed the system.
3) Fluid leaks through connections.	3) Tighten connections and, if necessary, replace faulty parts. Bleed the system.
4) Fluid leaks at wheel cylinders.	4) Replace the deteriorated seals and packings. Dry and clean brake shoe linings.
5) Fluid leaks through hoses.	5) Replace the damaged hose, using only FIAT - approved hoses and bleed the system.

Excessive Pedal Free Travel.

POSSIBLE CAUSES	REMEDIES
1) System has not been bled.	1) Bleed the system.
2) Defective self-adjusting device.	2) Reset the device.
3) Fluid level in reservoir is too low.	3) Refill with special FIAT blue label brake fluid (or equivalent non-mineral grade); if required, bleed the system.
4) Master cylinder plunger rod misadjusted.	4) Adjust the rod-to-plunger clearance and set to .0197" (0,5 mm) (this corresponds to a pedal free travel of .0984" - 2,5 mm).
5) Deteriorated rubber seals in master cylinder or in wheel cylinders.	5) Replace the seals and bleed the system.
6) Excessive swelling of hoses because the ones used were of poor quality.	6) Replace by FIAT - approved hoses and bleed the system.
7) Thermal expansion of drums because of excessive overheating.	7) Allow drums to cool off. Check brake shoe linings and drums. Replace damaged parts.

Weak Braking.

POSSIBLE CAUSES	REMEDIES
1) Fluid leakage from wheel cylinders.	1) Dry and clean the brake shoe linings, service the wheel cylinder replacing damaged parts and bleed the system.

Unbalanced Braking.

POSSIBLE CAUSES	REMEDIES
1) Fluid leaks at one wheel cylinder.	1) Dry and clean the brake shoe linings, service the wheel cylinder and bleed the system.
2) Rust corrosion on the edges of a wheel cylinder.	2) Eliminate rust and replace the boots.
3) Seized plunger in one wheel cylinder.	3) Service the wheel cylinder, replace the plunger and bleed the system.
4) Hose obstructed because the inner pipe has swollen or is clogged (if the brakes on one axle are excluded, weak braking may result).	4) Replace or clean the pipe and bleed the system.
5) Obstructed flow in metal pipe which has flattened or is clogged (if the brakes on one axle are excluded, weak braking may result).	5) Replace or clean the pipe and bleed the system.
6) Defective self-adjusting device.	6) Reset the device.

Shoes Drag Permanently on Drums.

POSSIBLE CAUSES	REMEDIES
1) Weak return springs.	1) Replace the springs.
2) Brake pedal has no free travel.	2) Adjust the rod-to-plunger clearance and set to .0197" (0,5 mm).
3) Seized master cylinder plunger.	3) Service the master cylinder, replace the plunger and bleed the system.
4) Excessive tension on parking brake cable.	4) Adjust cable as outlined on page 181.
5) Master cylinder flooded because compensating hole is clogged.	5) Service the master cylinder, replace the valve-ring if swollen or deteriorated, clean the compensating hole and bleed the system.

Excessive Effort Required on Pedal to Operate Shoes.

POSSIBLE CAUSES	REMEDIES
1) Swollen rubber seals because the fluid used is inadequate or contaminated by kerosene, gasoline or mineral oil (this may also cause a permanent drag of shoes on brake drum).	1) Flush the system, replace rubber parts, refill with new brake fluid, and bleed the system.

Brakes Locked Even After Releasing the Pedal.

POSSIBLE CAUSES	REMEDIES
1) Weak or broken return springs.	1) Replace inefficient springs.
2) Clogged master cylinder compensating hole.	2) Clean and bleed the system.
3) Rubber seals swollen or stuck because of contamination by kerosene, mineral oil, gasoline, etc.	3) Flush the system, replace all rubber parts, refill with new brake fluid and bleed the system.

Reduced Pedal Free Travel.

POSSIBLE CAUSES	REMEDIES
1) Master cylinder compensating hole blanked on account of misadjusted plunger rod.	1) Adjust the rod-to-plunger clearance and set to .0197" (0,5 mm).
2) Master cylinder compensating hole clogged by impurities.	2) Clean and bleed the system.
3) Master cylinder compensating hole clogged by a swollen valve-ring.	3) Flush the system, replace the valve-ring, refill with new fluid and air-bleed the lines.

Brakes Chatter.

POSSIBLE CAUSES	REMEDIES
1) Drum out of round.	1) Turn the drum on lathe and lap it to eliminate out of round.
2) Linings glazed or worn.	2) Replace linings.
3) Oil or grease on linings.	3) Replace linings.
4) Loose housing flange.	4) Tighten brake housing flange nuts with the torque specified on page 181.
5) Detached linings.	5) Replace linings.

WHEELS AND TIRES

WHEEL BALANCE	page 187
TIRE INFLATING PRESSURE	» 187
TIRE WEAR	» 187
CHANGING THE WHEELS	» 188

Wheels are of the disc type, size . . 3½ x 12"
Tires are of the low pressure type, size 125-12

Wheel Balance.

Balancing of the wheel with tire is very important in order that wobbling of front wheels is avoided, since this could affect steering performance and shorten tire life.

It is therefore extremely important to check the wheels and eliminate all possible causes of unbalance.

The causes that may affect wheel balance are:

a) wheel lateral runout, which may be caused by bumps or abnormal lateral strain;

b) out-of round of wheel due to eccentricity either of rim or tire;

c) static unbalance, due to uneven distribution of weight with respect to rotation axis.

The first two causes may be easily detected by putting into rotation first the rim alone and then the wheel and tire against a scriber.

If runout and out-of-round are not substantial, no repairs are necessary; otherwise remedies shall be taken as required.

As to point c), perform balancing on electronic balancer **A. 76002** which ensures best results in the shortest possible time and with very simple operations.

For the use of the balancer, follow the instructions contained in the handbook accompanying every machine.

Tire Inflating Pressure.

Check pressure with cold tires.

Check that tire pressures correspond closely to the specified values, since too high pressures cause uncomfortable riding and excessive wear of tire tread central portion while too low pressures bring about rapid tread wear. Also, care for even inflation of all tires, because tires inflated at different pressures affect road holding qualities and stability of car.

	Front	Rear
Low load	17.1 p.s.i. (1,20 kg/cm²)	28.8 p.s.i. (1,60 kg/cm²)
Full load	17.1 p.s.i. (1,20 kg/cm²)	26.3 p.s.i. (1,85 kg/cm²)

Tire Wear.

Abnormal wear of tires may occur on different areas of tread, as follows:

a) Front tires show an excessive wear only on one side of the tread: check camber. If it is correct, wear must be ascribed to the habit of negotiating curves at high speeds.

b) Tires show a wear particularly remarkable on both sides of tread rather on center portion: tires are inflated at a pressure lower than prescribed. Under such condition the tread side surfaces are supporting most of the load, while center portion is deflected upwards.

c) Tires show wear on tread center portion: tires are inflated at a pressure higher than prescribed. Under such condition tread central portion is supporting most of the load.

d) Too much wear on tread inner end of both wheels: toe-out is the possible cause; check and adjust toe-in as required.

e) Remarkable wear on tread outer end of both wheels: excessive toe-in, correct to specified value.

f) One front tire shows wear on tread inner end and the other on outer end: steering is maladjusted and causes an excessive toe-in on one wheel, and toe-out on the other.

Check wheel alignment and see that steering and suspension components are not deformed.

NOTE - To ensure uniform wear of all tires, change wheels in criss cross fashion every 3,000 miles (5.000 km).

CHANGING THE WHEELS

To obtain best results, follow this procedure:

a) If possible, place car on level ground and, to prevent any accidental movement of car while jacked up, lock rear wheels with the parking brake.

b) Remove the wheel cover by loosening center mounting screws.

Using the speed handle, slacken about one turn the four wheel fixing screws.

c) Place jack nub in bracket (fig. 305) under body floor, then jack up until wheel to be removed clears ground.

d) Undo and remove the four fixing screws. Pull off wheel.

e) Fit spare wheel. The wheel location dowel on brake drum must fit into the hole provided on wheel disc. Insert wheel fixing screws and tighten uniformly in criss-cross sequence.

f) Lower car and disinsert jack nub from bracket under floor.

g) **Tighten down wheel fixing screws in alternate fashion with 32.5 to 39.8 ft.lbs (4500 to 5500 kgmm) of torque, using a torque wrench.**

Refit wheel covers and secure with center fixing screw.

Fig. 305.

Jacking up the car.

Section 9

AIR CONDITIONING CHASSIS TIGHTENING REFERENCE

	Page
CAR AIR CONDITIONING	191
GENERAL CHASSIS TIGHTENING REFERENCE	193

9

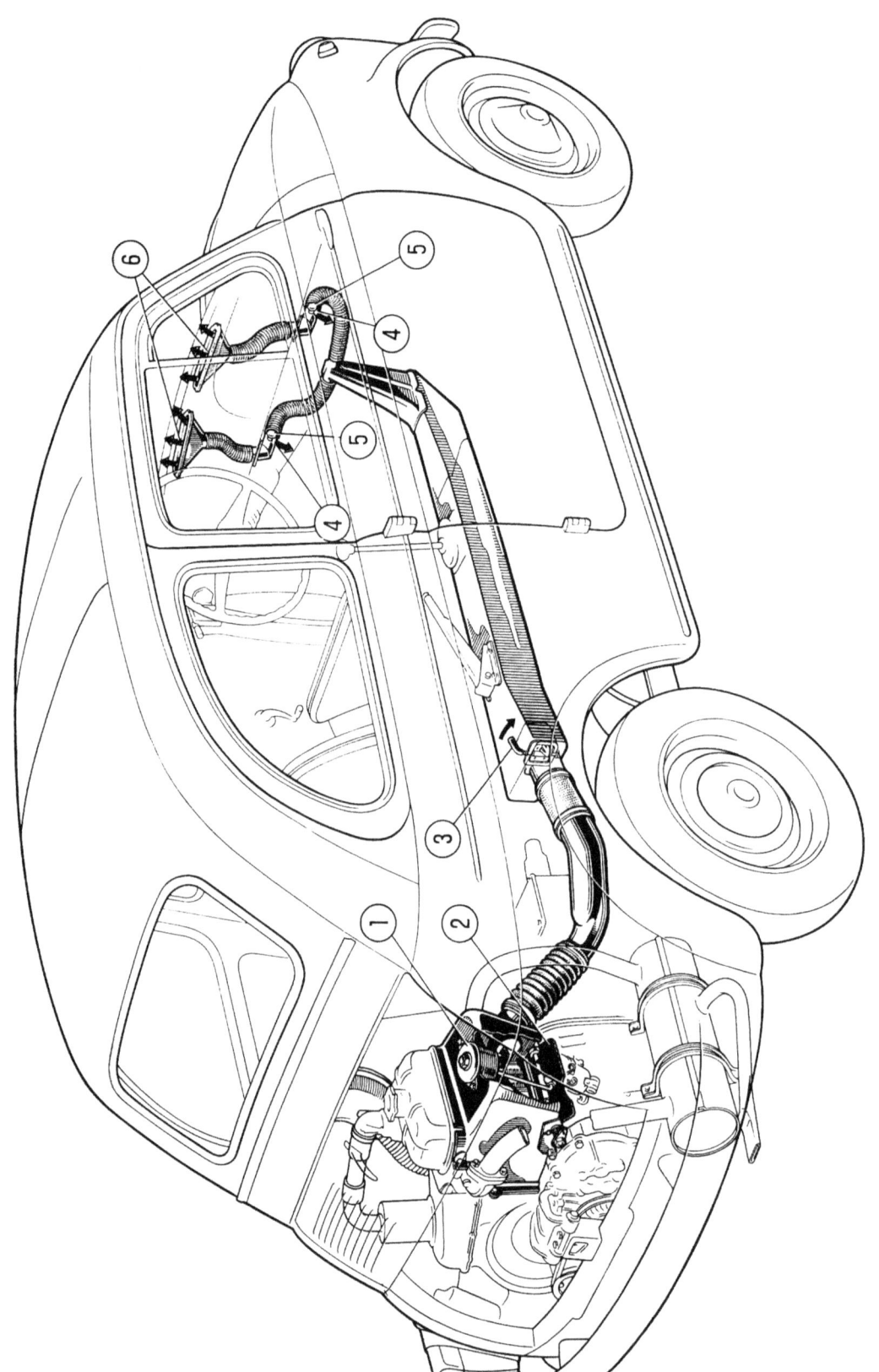

Fig. 306 - Phantom view of car heating system.

1. Thermostat controlling shutter. - 2. Shutter, engine cooling air outlet. - 3. Lever, heater hand control. - 4. Warm air outlet slots. - 5. Demister valve control knobs. - 6. Windshield demister diffusers.

NOTE - The car may be also equipped, optionally, with a heating booster as shown in fig. 309.

CAR AIR CONDITIONING

Ventilation	page 191
Heating	» 191
Inspection	» 191
Windshield Demisting	» 191
GENERAL CHASSIS TIGHTENING REFERENCE	» 193

Ventilation.

Air conditioning in car interior is obtained by suitably adjusting swivel ventilator panes on doors.

Moreover, when door drop glasses are cranked part way or all the way down, admission of outside air is increased to a remarkable extent, affording better ventilation in car interior.

Fig. 307 - Inner view of door on side opposite to steering wheel; ventilation panel.

Heating.

This is accomplished by re-circulation of warm air from the engine cooling system through engine cowling.

A hose (see fig. 306) conveys warmed air from engine cowling to center tunnel on floor, where air flows out through two slots being cut on windshield air delivery hoses.

Air admission can be adjusted by turning to the right the lever controlling the tunnel throttle valve at rear seat.

Model 500 is optionally equipped with a heating booster to fill particular requirements.

This device consists of a casing on front exhaust pipe being connected to engine cowling and warmed air passage tunnel. Thus, air flowing to car interior is heated to a higher temperature (see fig. 309).

Inspection.

Check that the lever, lever spring and butterfly valve hinge have not been deformed: repair or replace as required. Check the ducting to tunnel as well as upper and lower hoses for soundness: replace if they are damaged.

Windshield Demisting.

Two air hoses with throttle valves for air flow control, are relayed from a casing in front of center floor tunnel. Hoses are connected to two air diffusers which are set on instrument panel and parallel to windshield glass.

When throttle valves (see 5, fig. 306) are operated through two control knobs, warmed air is streamed directly on to windshield glass, to prevent windshield misting, frosting or icing.

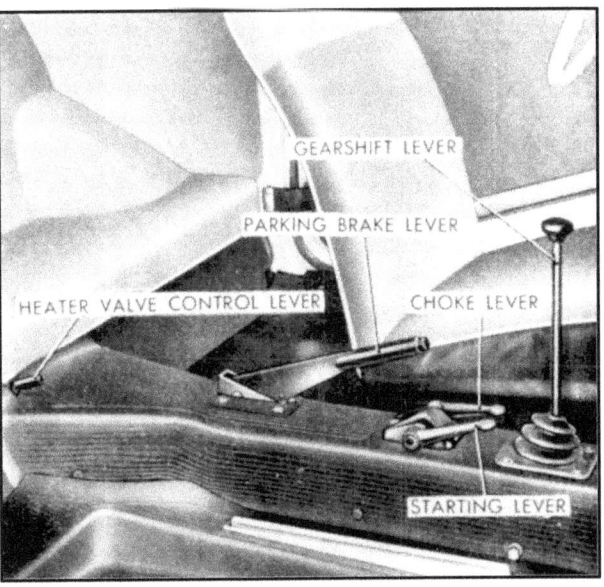

Fig. 308 - Hand controls on center floor tunnel.

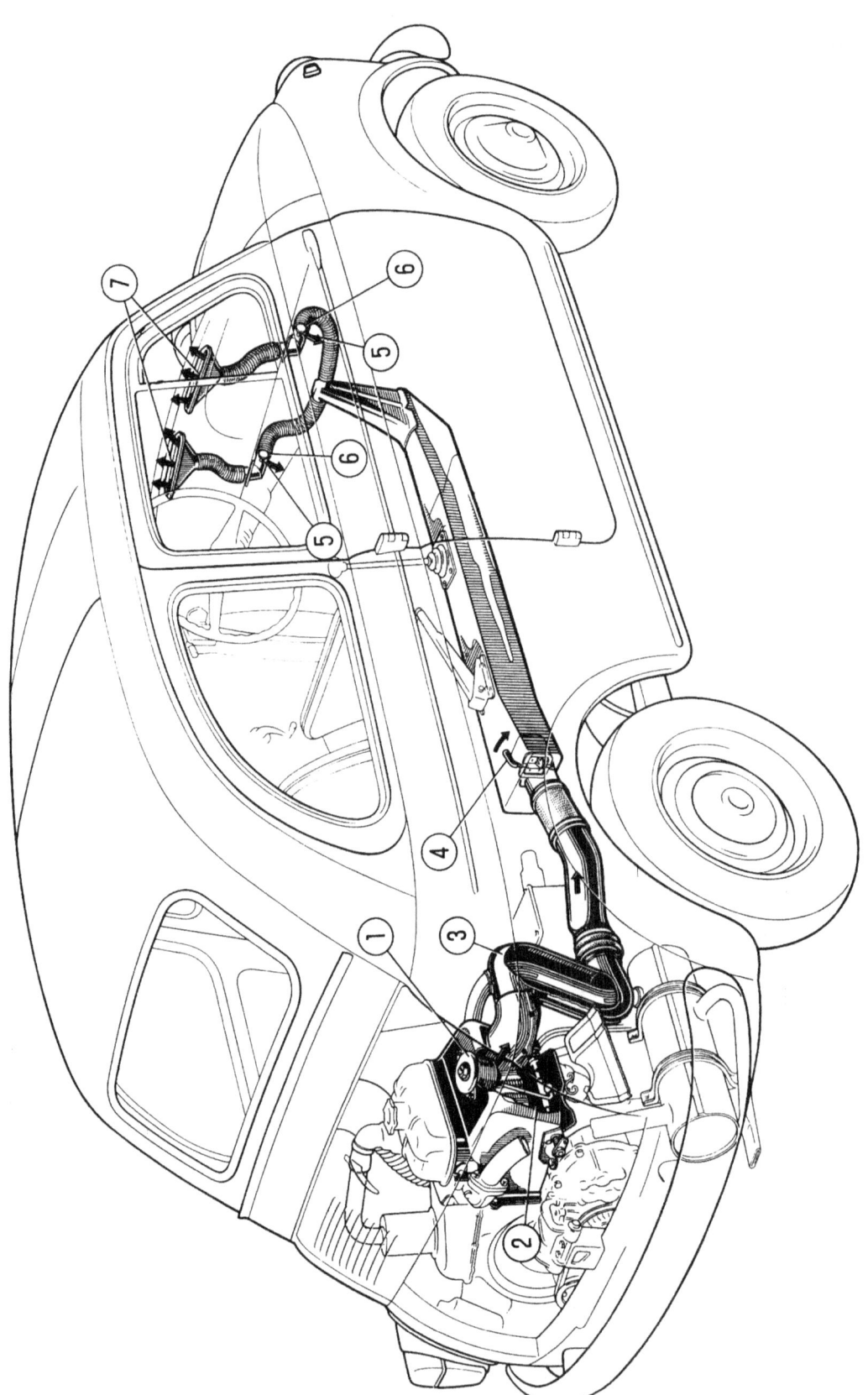

Fig. 309 - Phantom view of car heating system, boosted type.

1. Thermostat controlling shutter. - 2. Shutter, engine cooling air outlet. - 3. Car interior heater booster. - 4. Lever, heater hand control. - 5. Warm air outlet slots. - 6. Demister valve control knobs. - 7. Windshield demister diffusers.

GENERAL CHASSIS TIGHTENING REFERENCE

ITEM	Drwg. or Std. Part No.	Thread	Material	Tightening Torque
Primary shaft gear nut	1/08019/11	14 MC (x1)	R 50 Cdt (Shaft 14CN5 Cmt5)	18.1 to 25.3 ft.lbs (2.500 to 3.500 kgmm)
Layshaft (with bevel pinion) gear nut	1/07934/11	14 MB (x1,5)	R 50 Cdt (Shaft 14CN5 Cmt5)	28.9 to 36.2 ft.lbs (4.000 to 5.000 kgmm)
Ring gear-to-differential case screw	891596	8 MA (x1,25)	R 100	23.1 ft.lbs (3.200 kgmm)
Differential bearing housing-to-gearbox nut	1/61008/11	8 MA (x1,25)	R 50 Cdt (Stud R 50 Cdt)	13 ft.lbs (1.800 kgmm)
Gearbox casing and bell housing-to-engine nut	1/21647/11	10 x 1,25 M	R 50 Cdt (Stud R 50 Cdt)	27.5 ft.lbs (3.800 kgmm)
Gearbox-differential carrier assembly -to-engine nut	1/61008/11	8 MA (x1,25)	R 50 Cdt (Stud R 100)	18.1 to 21.7 ft.lbs (2.500 to 3.000 kgmm)
Front swinging arm-to-body mounting pin rubber bushing nut . . .	1/07933/11	12 MB (x1,5)	R 50 Cdt (Pin C 40 Bon)	28.9 to 36.2 ft.lbs (4.000 to 5.000 kgmm)
Leaf spring-to-body floor nut . . .	1/21647/11	10 x 1,25 M	R 50 Cdt (Screw C 21 R)	28.9 ft.lbs (4.000 kgmm)
Kingpin housing-to-front swinging arm nut	1/25745/11	10 x 1,25 M	R 50 Cdt (Screw R 80 Cdt)	39.8 to 43.4 ft.lbs (5.500 to 6.000 kgmm)
Brake housing flange - to - steering knuckle nut	1/61008/11	8 MA (x1,25)	R 50 Cdt (Screw R 50)	14.5 ft.lbs (2.000 kgmm)
Leaf spring-to-kingpin housing nut .	1/25745/11	10 x 1,25 M	R 50 Cdt (Screw R 80 Cdt)	28.9 ft.lbs (4.000 kgmm)
Front swinging arm-to-body nut . .	1/21647/11	10 x 1,25 M	R 50 Cdt (Screw C 21 R)	28.9 ft.lbs (4.000 kgmm)
Front wheel bearing steering knuckle nut	980498 4042887	14 MB (x1,5)	R 50 (Steering knuckle 38 NCD 4 Bon)	21.7 ft.lbs (3.000 kgmm) see page 135
Rear swinging arm pivot bar-to-body floor nut	1/25747/11	12 MB (x1,5)	R 50 Cdt (Pivot bar R 80 Cdt)	43.4 to 50.6 ft.lbs (6.000 to 7.000 kgmm)

(continued)

General Chassis Tightening Reference (continued).

ITEM	Drwg. or Std. Part No.	Thread	Material	Tightening torque
Rear swinging arm support-to-body floor screw	832632	10 x 1,25 M	R 80	28.9 to 36.2 ft.lbs (4.000 to 5.000 kgmm)
Hub and brake housing flange-to-rear swinging arm nut	1/21647/11	10 x 1,25 M	R 50 Cdt (Screw R 80)	43.4 ft.lbs (6.000 kgmm)
Flexible joint-to-rear wheel shaft nut	1/07246/20	18 MB (x1,5)	R 80 (Shaft 38 NCD 4 Bon)	see page 148
Axle shaft sleeve-to-rear wheel flexible joint screw	1/60446/21	8 MA (x1,25)	R 80 Cdt	20.3 ft.lbs (2.800 kgmm)
Steering wheel nut	743601	18 MB (x1,5)	R 50 Cdt (Shaft C 12 tube)	28.9 to 36.2 ft.lbs (4.000 to 5.000 kgmm)
Steering box and relay lever support -to-body nut	1/61041/11	8 MA (x1,25)	R 50 Cdt (Screw R 80 Cdt)	14.5 to 18.1 ft.lbs (2.000 to 2.500 kgmm)
Pitman arm-to-worm sector nut . .	1/25748/11	14 MB (x1,5)	R 50 Cdt (Sector 19CN5 Cmt3)	72.3 to 79.6 ft.lbs (10.000 to 11.000 kgmm)
Tie rod ball stud-to-lever nut . . .	1/25756/11	10 x 1,25 M	R 50 Cdt (Stud R 100 Bon)	18.1 to 21.7 ft.lbs (2.500 to 3.000 kgmm)
Relay lever pin nut	1/25747/11	12 MB (x1,5)	R 50 Cdt (Pin R 80 Cdt)	39.8 to 43.4 ft.lbs (5.500 to 6.000 kgmm)
Wheel-to-hub stud	990166	10 MA (x1,5)	C 35 R Bon Cdt	32.5 to 39.8 ft.lbs (4.500 to 5.500 kgmm)

Section 10
ELECTRIC SYSTEM

	Page
BATTERY	196
GENERATOR	199
GENERATOR REGULATOR	213
STARTER	227
IGNITION SYSTEM	236
LIGHTING SYSTEM	244
GAUGES AND CONTROLS	252

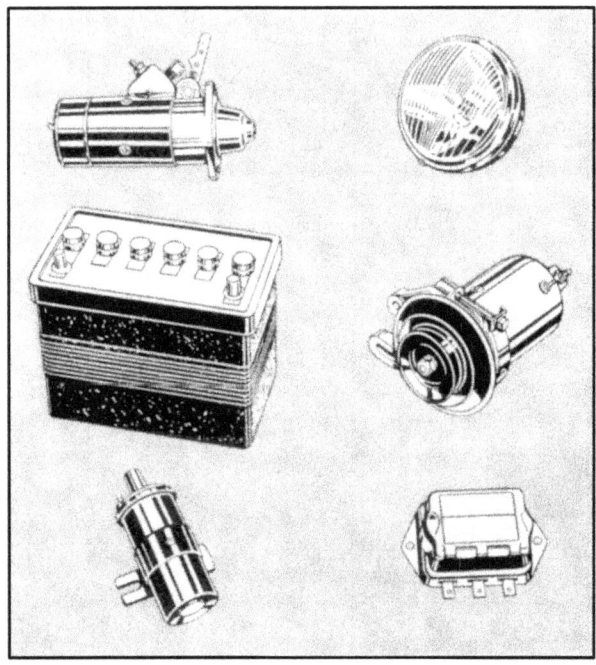

BATTERY

SPECIFICATIONS . . . . page 196
INSPECTION AND UPKEEP . . . . » 196
RECHARGING BATTERY WITH EXTERNAL MEANS . . . . » 199

Specifications.

« New 500 » Model is equipped with a battery having the following specifications:

— Tension . . . . 12 V
— Capacity (at 20 hrs discharge rate) 32 Amp/hr
— Length . . . . 9.252" (235 mm)
— Width . . . . 5.236" (133 mm)
— Height . . . . 7.795" (198 mm)
— Weight (w/electrolyte) abt. 30.4 lbs (13,8 kg)

Location: ahead of fuel tank in front compartment, right side (fig. 310).

The battery connectors are sunk in sealant; this design feature improves insulation and reduces current leaks to ground, corrosion, etc.

NOTE - Starting from car serial number 172311 a new type of battery has been fitted. See relevant specifications on page 311.

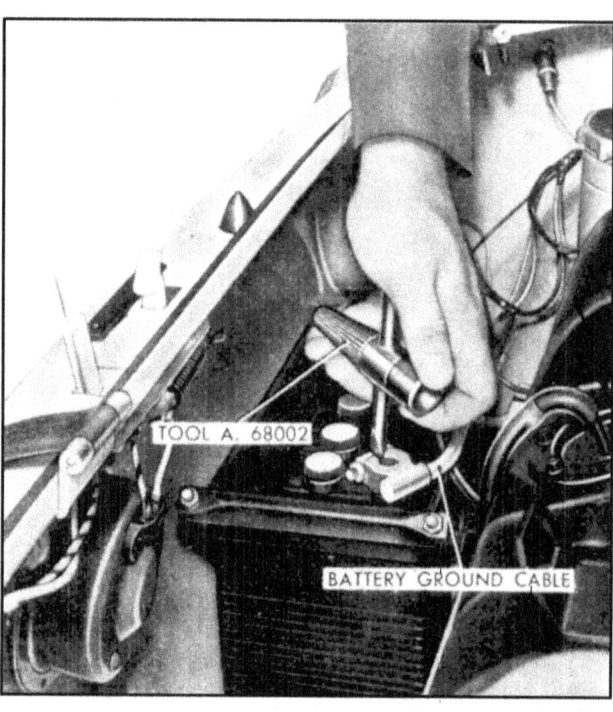

Fig. 311 - Slackening clamps from battery posts by tool A. 68002.

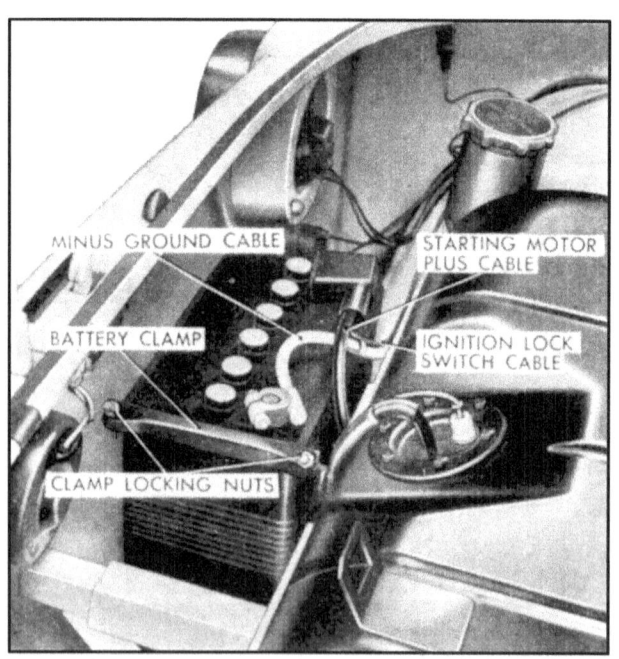

Fig. 310 - Battery arrangement.

Inspection and Upkeep.

1. - Access to battery.

Raise front compartment lid and back out the two battery hold-down frame nuts.

2. - Cleaning.

The battery must always be clean and dry, especially its top.

Use a hard brush and keep out dust or other foreign matter from cells.

Check that sealing compound around battery cell covers has not cracked (with consequent electrolyte leaks). Electrolyte should never spill over battery because highly corrosive. In case leaks have already occurred and some parts are corroded, clean and coat with acidproof paint all serviceable damaged parts and replace the unserviceable ones.

3. - Posts and terminal clamps.

To unscrew or tighten terminal clamp nuts **do not use pliers or hammers** but the specially provided wrenches.

To free clamp, never grab and rotate the cable but use tool **A. 68002** (fig. 311). Jerking the cable stresses and may crack the ebonite cell cover or may tear cable off clamp, thus causing electrolyte dispersion paths, with consequent damages.

Any corroded terminals, clamps or cables must be replaced.

Corrosion reduces the section of conductor, resulting in increased conductor ohmic resistance. This causes a noticeable voltage drop at terminal clamps of starter, whose output will be reduced and starting will not always be successful.

To clean terminals and clamps, use tool **A. 68002** (figs. 312 and 313).

Well clean terminals and clamps must be coated with pure ropy vaseline. Particular attention must be devoted to the lower end of terminals and clamps where acid is more likely to be present.

Do not use grease, because it reacts with the electrolyte which, in form of a fine spray, issues from plugs with the naturally developed gases and forms conductive salts (green or bluish) which cause current dispersions and favour corrosion of terminals, clamps and connectors.

Always use pure ropy vaseline.

If vaseline is not pure, reactions may occur as in the case of grease. If not ropy, it may soften excessively when heated, fall on battery cover and soften also the cover sealing compound.

It is also important not to use vaseline too liberally: a thin uniform coating will do.

After the cleaning and vaseline-coating operations, fix clamps securely on battery posts to reduce contact resistance.

4. - Electrolyte level.

Check level periodically. During battery operation, water is the only element that evaporates. Consequently, only distilled water must be added to top up battery and never any acid.

Electrolyte level must be kept constantly above separators, but not above a given height. Separators must never be allowed to emerge from electrolyte.

NOTE - Distilled water should be added into six battery elements using automatic filler **A. 13021** (fig. 314).

Refills must always be effected with battery cold (68° F - 20° C) and at rest, and up to a level above separators of:

— $3/16''$ (5 mm), when battery is charged 100%;
— $1/8''$ (3 mm), when battery is in normal operating condition.

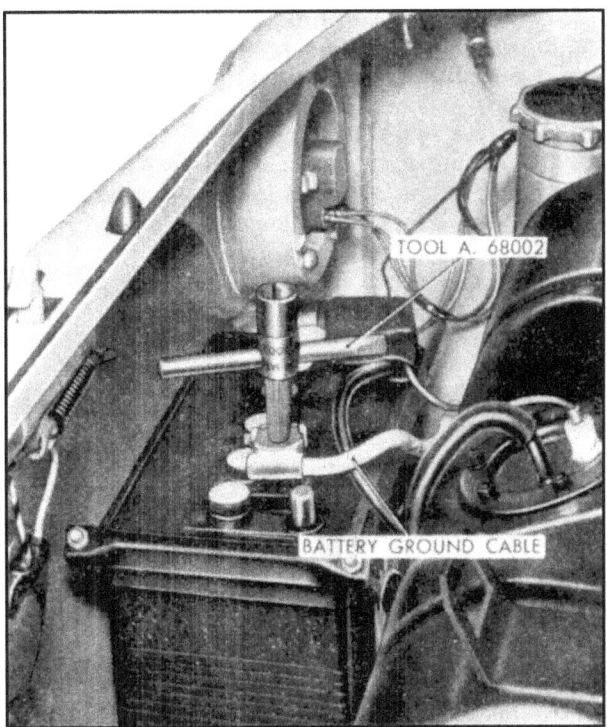

Fig. 312 - Cleaning battery posts by tool A. 68002.

This, because during operation the state of charge ranges between 2/3 (density about 1.23) and 3/4 (density about 1.25) of full charge.

The above levels must never be exceeded to prevent the overflowing of electrolyte from plug vent holes when the battery is subject to heavy charge rates, such as on long runs.

To check on electrolyte level, use a $3/16''$ to $5/16''$ (5 to 8 mm) dia. glass tube inserted through plug seat down to separator top edge. Blank tube upper

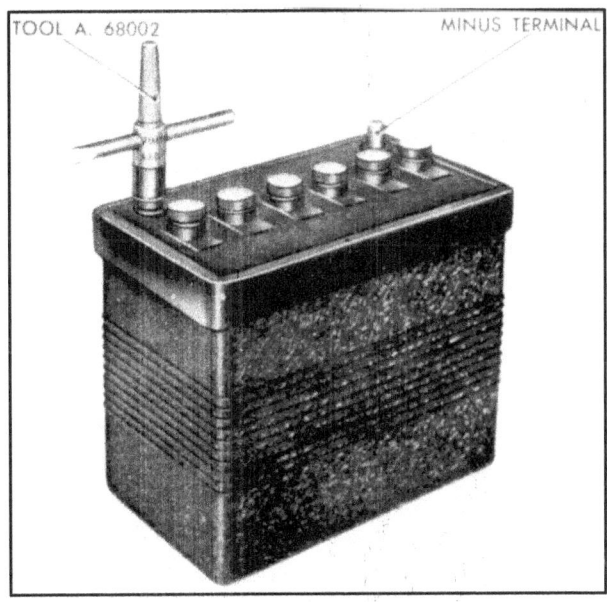

Fig. 313 - Cleaning battery cable clamps by tool A. 68002.

end with a finger, lift tube out of cell, and check height of solution drawn up by tube. Reference marks on tube bottom end will facilitate level readings.

Electrolyte level must be checked at 1500 mile (2500 km) intervals or every 15 days if car is in garage. If car is not used for a long time, battery must receive proper maintenance care (recharging, topping up, etc.).

Should electrolyte level in one cell be found lower than in the others, check cell for cracks since this indicates a leak has occurred.

Fig. 314 - Setting electrolyte level in battery elements by adding distilled water through automatic filler A. 13021.

5. - Checking the state of charge.

The state of charge is determined by measuring the electrolyte specific gravity. The charge measurement by the high-discharge method (Voltmeter individual cell tester) should never be adopted, since cells tested may be damaged seriously and current consumption is very high.

The electrolyte gravity is proportional to the state of charge. Relationships are:

SPECIFIC GRAVITY*	STATE OF CHARGE
1.28	Fully charged
1.25	Three-fourths charged
1.22	One-half charged
1.19	One-fourth charged
1.16	Barely operative
1.11	Completely discharged

(*) Specific gravity of batteries for export to U.S.A. and Canada should be 1.27 ± 0.005 at 77° F (25° C), with fully charged battery.

IMPORTANT - Take hydrometer readings away from battery, because any electrolyte (which contains sulphuric acid) dripping onto battery will cause corrosion, current dispersions, etc.

To check specific gravity, use the accurate hydrometer **C. 852**. Readings should be taken at eye level on float graduated stem, with free float and tube held vertical. Once reading has been taken, return the electrolyte to the cell from which it had been sucked into hydrometer.

Specific gravity readings should never be taken under these conditions:

a) incorrect electrolyte level;

b) too warm or too cold electrolyte: temperature should be 68°±9° F (20°±5° C);

c) soon after topping up (wait until acid solution in electrolyte is uniform: if battery is dicharged, wait a few hours);

d) soon after repeated engine starts: also in this case, wait until acid dispersion is uniform;

e) bubbling electrolyte: wait until all bubbles sucked in hydrometer with the solution have come up into empty portion of tube.

If the following conditions are found:

— cell gravity readings more than 0.02 apart;

— excessively high specific gravity: 1.30;

— low specific gravity: 1.22;

and at the same time an excessive overheating of battery during regular operation (more than 18° F [10° C] above ambient temperature), take the battery for repair to one of the Battery Manufacturer's Shops.

When car is not used for a long time, recharge periodically once a month. Recharge must be carried out with low current (4 Amps max) until a lively « boiling » is noticed in all cells.

On FIAT cars, **fitted with voltage regulators, the battery does not require a periodical recharge during operation, inasmuch as the car recharging system is sufficient to keep battery in perfect efficiency.**

If battery runs down during operation (the long standing periods during which battery is self-discharged should naturally not be taken into account), this indicates abnormal operating conditions, the most commonly encountered ones being:

I) Improper recharging system operation (generator and regulator). - See the instructions outlined for generator and regulating units on the following pages.

II) Current dispersion caused by defective insulation in car system. - This is a rather frequent case, especially when car owner adds on his own

ELECTRICAL

initiative some new users (special horns, fog lamps, etc.), in which case the tampers with the electric system and faulty insulations are very likely to occur.

If a megohmmeter is available, check insulation by placing the instrument between the disconnected battery positive cable and ground (all users totally excluded). Even in the worst test conditions (wet car, etc.) an insulating resistance reading of less than 10,000 Ohms should not be recorded.

A quick check can be carried out using a milliammeter: arrange it in series between battery positive cable clamp and terminal, and make sure that indicated current (without any users inserted in the circuit) is not greater than 1 milliampere.

NOTE - Before connecting or disconnecting the positive clamp from battery terminal, always disconnect the negative cable (grounded on frame) from battery.

III) **Addition of users by the car owner.** - A given proportionate margin is possible with the charging system. Therefore, provided given limits are not exceeded, the addition of a few users can be tolerated.

IV) **Use of car on short runs, with frequent stops and repeated use of 4th gear at very low speeds.** - Because starter is used often, battery discharges quickly. Generator supplies no output or develops only a part of the power it should because its r.p.m. rate is too low.

It will suffice to tell car owner to run car in low gear when travelling at reduced speeds: the generator will then operate at a normal recharging rate.

V) **Sulphated battery with shorted or «open» cells.**

Recharging Battery with External Means.

Bearing in mind the aforementioned recommendations, recharging the battery by rectifiers or motor-generator converter unit will be necessary only when car is not used for a long time or when the abnormal operating conditions outlined in points 5 I), II), III), IV) have occurred.

Remember the following:

a) after removal from car, clean well the battery, especially its top;

b) check electrolyte level;

c) insert battery in the charging circuit and methodically check, at intervals, the state of charge using a hydrometer;

d) clean battery once more, before installation on car.

GENERATOR

DESCRIPTION	page 199
OPERATION	» 202
BENCH TESTING INSTRUCTIONS	» 203
TROUBLE SHOOTING INSTRUCTIONS	» 204
SERVICING	» 207
SPECIFICATIONS	» 210

Description.

« New 500 » Model is equipped with generator **DSV 90/12/16/3 S** having the following characteristics:

— Nominal tension . . . . 12 Volts
— Maximum continued operation output (ammeter limit) . . . . . . 16 Amperes
— Maximum current output . . . . 22 Amperes
— Maximum power, continued operation . . . . 230 Watts
— Maximum power . . . . 320 Watts
— 22 Ampere current output speed, at 68° F (20° C) . . . . 3050 to 3200 r.p.m.
— Max. steady speed . . . . 9000 r.p.m.

DSV 90/12/16/3S GENERATOR

SECTION A-A

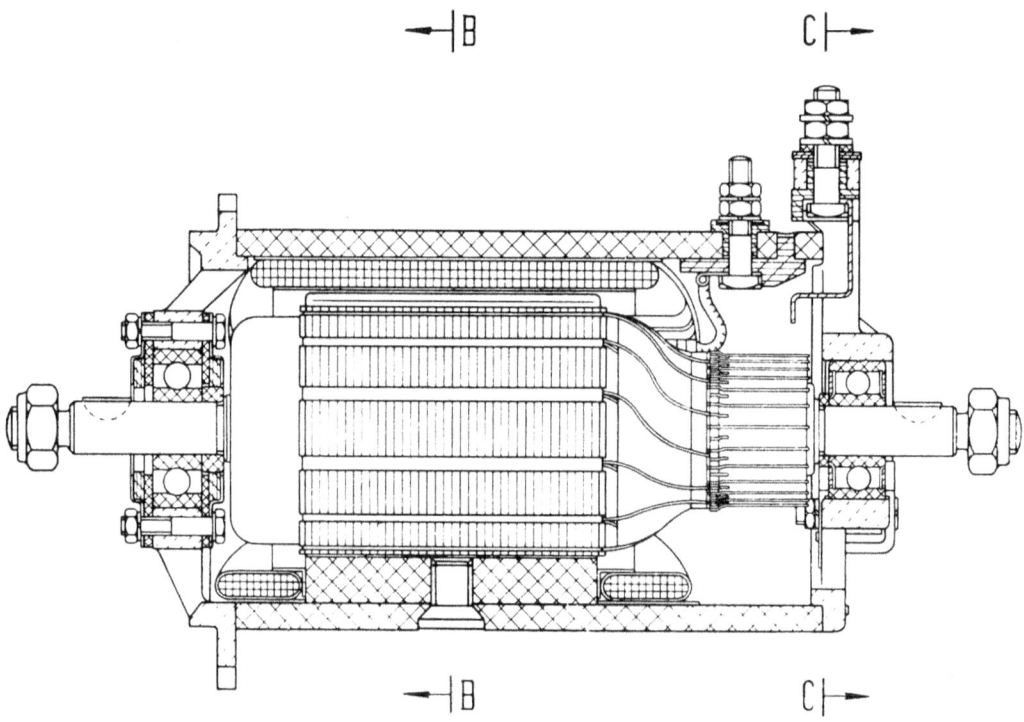

Fig. 315 - Longitudinal section.

SECTION B-B

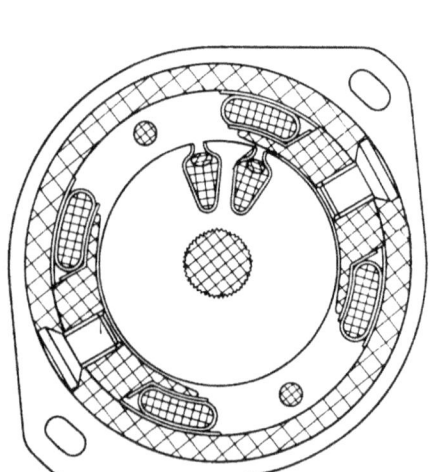

Fig. 316 - Cross section through armature and pole shoes.

SECTION C-C

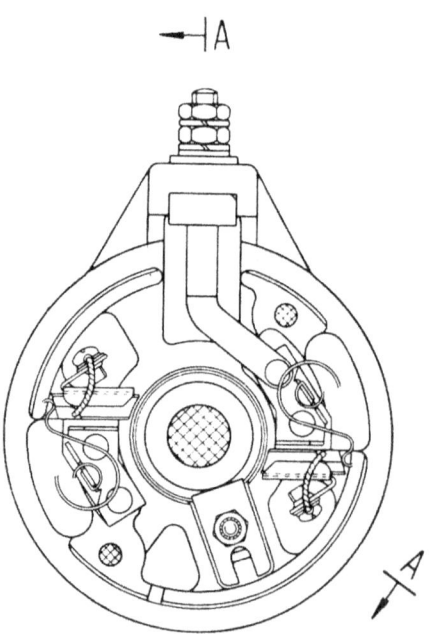

Fig. 317 - Commutator end head.
« Reaction » type brush holders are visible.

— Initial charging speed at 12 Volts and 68° F (20° C) *1710 to 1860 r.p.m. **1710 to 1790 r.p.m.

— 16 Ampere current output speed, at 68° F (20° C) *2550 to 2800 r.p.m. **2550 to 2700 r.p.m.

— Rotation . . . . . clockwise, commutator end
— Two-pole, shunt field winding.
— Separate regulator assembly (FIAT GN 1/12/16).
— Engine-to-generator drive ratio (with new belt) 1.74

The armature is mounted on two ball bearings.

The drive end bearing is force-fitted in head and its outer ring is locked by two retainers screw-mounted on head.

The bearing inner race remains fast on shaft owing to the lateral pressure exerted by the blower hub secured by self-locking nut. The race face opposite to hub face rests against the shaft shoulder through an interposed spacer.

The commutator end bearing is floating both in head seat and on shaft.

To prevent rotation, the outer race (which might be dragged along by the friction of the rubber seals ensuring the life lubrication of bearing) is clamped by a suitable collar that, though preventing the rotation, leaves the race free to slide axially in its seat.

The collar consists of two clamps held together by bolt, nut and lockwasher. The bolt fits into a hole in generator head and prevents the rotation of the collar clamping the bearing outer race.

The assembly may slide axially in order to permit the bearing to adapt itself to the varying operating conditions and to the thermal expansion of armature shaft.

The bearing inner race remains fast on shaft owing to the lateral pressure exerted by the pulley hub which is secured to the shaft by a self-locking nut. Pressure is maintained by a shoulder surface on shaft.

The heads are fastened to frame by two tie rods passing between the two pole shoes.

Commutator end head is provided with brush holders of the « reaction » type (fig. 319).

This design feature, with respect to « radial type » brush holders, remarkably reduces the vibration of brushes in their holders and hence the jumping of brushes on commutator during generator operation. Furthermore, with brush section on par, the brush contact surface on commutator increases.

---

* For generators with armature package disc teeth .1732" (4,4 mm) in length (early type).

** For generators with armature package disc teeth .1969" (5 mm) in length.

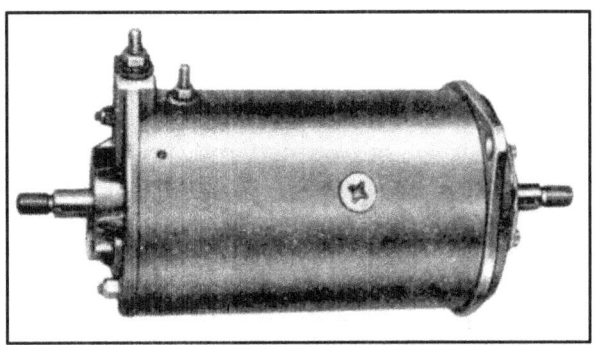

Fig. 318 - FIAT generator DSV 90/12/16/3 S.

As a result, the following advantages are obtained:

— less sparking and wear of brushes, with added life;

NOTICE

Instant damage is caused to regulator if terminal 67 of generator is connected to terminal 51 of regulator and, consequently, terminal 51 of generator is connected to terminal 67 of regulator.

— less overheating and wear of commutator, with added life;

— less excitation current in generator, resulting in longer life of voltage regulator and current regulator contacts.

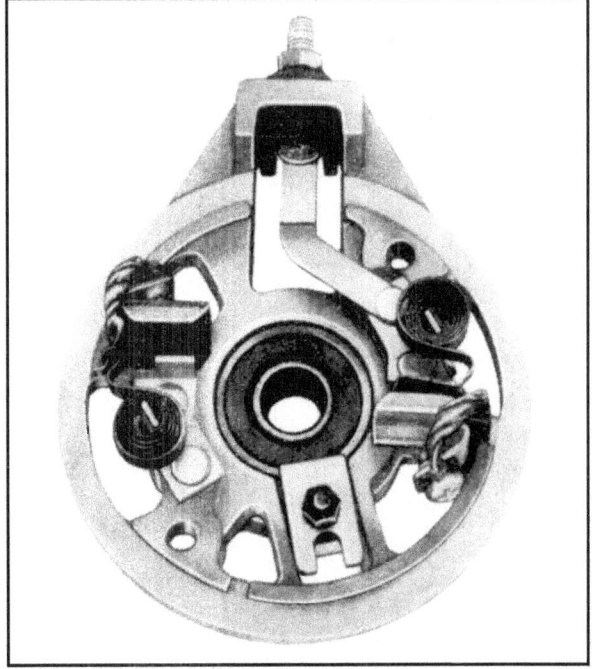

Fig. 319 - Commutator end head of generator DSV 90/12/16/3 S.

« Reaction » type brush holders.

Internal generator windings are efficiently cooled by the fan and drive pulley, forming a single unit. Air enters through the openings on the commutator end head and is circulated by the fan.

The generator is provided with the two following numbered terminals:

— Terminal 51 applied and suitably insulated on commutator end head: connected to positive

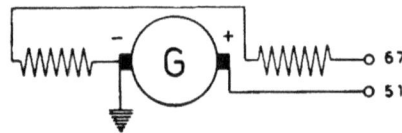

Fig. 320 - Generator wiring diagram.

brush. Terminal axis perpendicular to generator axis.

— Terminal 67 applied and suitably insulated on generator frame: connected to one end of field winding. Terminal axis perpendicular to generator axis.

Terminals 51 and 67 must be connected with the regulator terminals bearing the same numbers.

Operation.

When generator connected with its regulator is set into operation, the voltage increases gradually with r.p.m. rate, but there is no output as long as cutout contacts remain open.

As voltage within generator reaches 12.6 ± 0.2 volts, cutout contacts close and current flows to battery and users.

As outlined in detail under the heading « Generator Regulator », the current regulator of the FIAT GN 1/12/16 regulator assembly fitting this generator, is « thermally stabilized ».

The amount of current delivered depends upon battery state of charge and power of users.

Proper current and voltage regulation is provided by the current and voltage regulators incorporated with the cutout.

Thanks to this feature, the limiting current of a cold regulator (at the beginning of operation, after a sufficently long inactivity period), is higher than maximum steady output of generator. Therefore, if current draw from electrical units is heavy, the generator may be overloaded.

The generator, however, can withstand this overload because it, too, is at the beginning of operation and not yet « thermally stabilized », i.e. its windings are still at ambient temperature.

As both regulator and generator warm up due to heat transfer from windings, current regulator reduces (within 20-30 minutes) the limiting current until it reaches a value that the generator can withstand safely in continuous operation. This value varies with ambient temperature and is reached when the unit is thermally « soaked » at rated operation temperature.

It ensues that the overload cannot cause dangerous temperatures within the generator since, as generator temperature increases, the load decreases.

The temporary initial operation in overload of generator permits a quicker battery charging when charge level is lowest due to a difficult cold start or when the car is operated in town with frequent stops and starts and recharge periods are very short.

As said above, the limiting current value with thermally stabilized regulator is variable with ambient temperature.

Therefore in winter the limiting current is lower than in summer.

As a result there will be lesser heat dissipation of generator in winter and better uniformity of generator temperature in both seasons.

However the in-and-out power balance in the system is not compromised as the average current consumption is lower in summer time.

The generator must work exclusively with its own regulator.

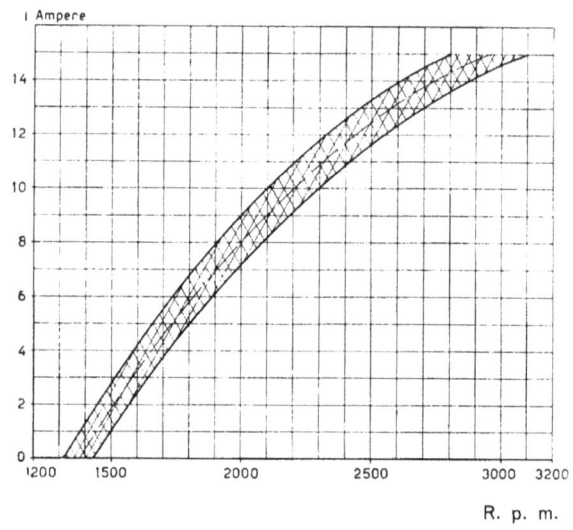

Fig. 321 - Output curve of warm generator R 90-180/12-2500 Spec. (up to engine No. 056195). - Steady 12 V tension.

Therefore, we warn against connecting terminal 67 directly to terminal 51 during generator tests on bench, or on engine, since under such conditions the generator would perform simply as a shunt excited generator in which voltage increases progressively with the increase in generator speed and induces a field current so strong that the field winding might burn.

BENCH TESTING INSTRUCTIONS

Check generator efficiency by carrying out the mechanical and electrical tests described below.

Operation Tests.

Follow strictly the procedure outlined for each test, making sure that all instruments and gauges are available for prompt use.

Testing generator as a motor (at 68° F - 20° C).

This is the first and simplest test for a quick generator check.
Wire up according to diagram fig. 322.

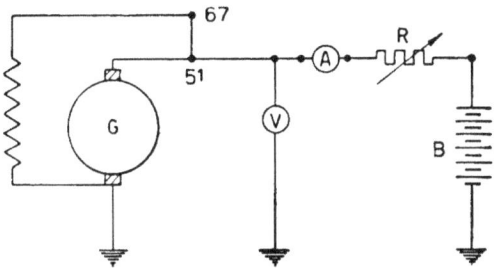

Fig. 322 - Wiring diagram for testing generator as a motor.
G. Generator. - V. Voltmeter, 15 V scale. - A. Ammeter, 10 A scale. - B. Battery capable of supplying a voltage slightly above 12 V during a discharge of 5 A. - R. Plate type rheostat for regulating the battery voltage, 100 A capacity, variable resistance of 0.2 to 20 Ω.

Feed generator with a 12 V d.c. supply and check that current draw is 5 ± 0.5 A and speed 1500 ± 100 r.p.m.

Output test at 12 V steady tension (at 68° F - 20° C).

NOTICE - Prior to plotting the output curve, make sure that brushes are thoroughly seated in commutator bore.

Install generator on test bench and couple it with a motor whose speed may be varied at will by small degrees.
Wire up according to diagram fig. 323.
Before starting the test, run generator, without fan, for half an hour at 4500 r.p.m., delivering a 5 ± 0.5 A - 14 V current to a resistor. Stop motor.
Disconnect load rheostat.
Start generator and speed up gradually until voltmeter reading is 12 volts; at this point, determine generator speed by a revolution counter.
This represents the cut-in speed at 12 volts output (origin of curve on abscissa axis).

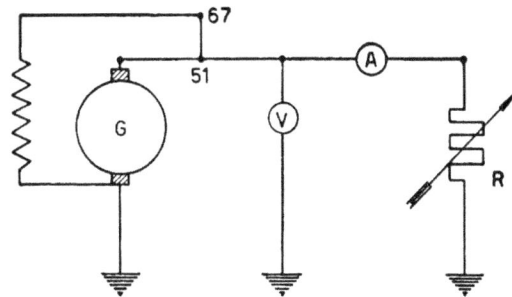

Fig. 323 - Wiring diagram for the determination of the ampere/revolution output curve at a steady 12 V voltage (68° F - 20° C).
G. Generator. - V. Voltmeter, 15 V scale. - A. Ammeter, 25 A scale. - R. Plate type rheostat, 100 A capacity, variable resistance of 0.20 to 20 Ω.

Stop generator and connect load rheostat.
While driving generator at steady speed in different increments, adjust load rheostat to ensure a constant 12 V output at each given r.p.m. rate; at the same time, read he value of current supplied. Each determination will give a point of the output curve.
Note that readings must be taken in a very short period of time, since the curve extends beyond generator nominal power and currents higher than those of the nominal output range impose an overload that generator cannot withstand for long without overheating, with consequent failure of insulations.
The curve plotted by points must lie within the limits indicated in the shaded area shown in fig. 324.

Ohmic Resistance Test.

Resistance at 68° F (20° C) must be 0.145 ± 0.01 Ω for the armature and $8 ^{+0.1}_{-0.3}$ Ω for field winding.
Field winding ohmic resistance may be deter-

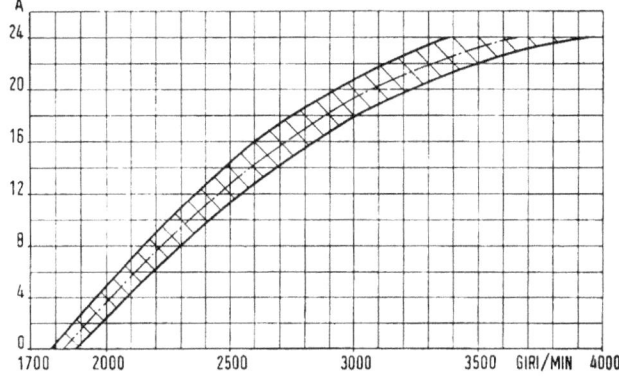

Fig. 324 - Output curve of warm generator DSV 90/12/16/3 S (from engine No. 056196).

GIRI/MIN = R. P. M.

mined with assembled generator, by simply measuring the resistance between terminal 67 and ground.

The recommended measurement method is that of the Volt/Ampere ratio in which a sufficiently high voltage is applied and measured, together with the current drawn by the winding. The ratio of applied voltage to drawn current gives the ohmic resistance, according to the formula: $\frac{V}{I} = R$.

Alternatively, a Wheatstone bridge may be used, provided it is sufficiently accurate.

Determining armature winding resistance is more difficult on account of the low value involved and, therefore, must be made only in exceptional cases, provided proper equipment is available.

In this case proceed as follows:

— solder two wire lengths on the faces of two commutator segments 180° apart;

— apply 2 to 2.5 volts and measure with accuracy the current drawn (Volt and Ampere readings).

Resistance R (in Ohms) is still given by $\frac{V}{I}$.

Mechanical Characteristics Check Data.

1) Brush hold-down springs load must be 1.3 to 1.6 lbs (0,60 to 0,72 kg).

2) Maximum commutator out-of-round (on rubbing surface): not more than .0004" (0,01 mm).

3) Commutator mica must be undercut at least .04" (1 mm) throughout its entire length and width.

TROUBLE SHOOTING

Troubles in battery charging system may originate from:

a) generator;

b) other components of system.

Before inspecting generator for faults, make sure that no other component in the system is responsible for the trouble.

To detect the trouble, observe the charge indicator which may give the following indications:

1. By inserting and rotating lock switch key to ignition ON position, the indicator lights up. It normally goes out when engine reaches the predetermined r.p.m. rate.

This is a sign that generator is efficient.

2. By inserting and rotating the key to ignition ON position, the indicator lights up. It goes out only at a fairly high engine r.p.m. rate.

Generator is faulty and defects may be:

2.1. Short-circuited coils in field winding.

2.2. Field winding, or **jumper between the two field windings**, grounded on frame.

2.3. Large number of armature coils shorted.

These irregularities cause a complete alteration of the cut-in and max. output speed rates which shift to increasingly higher values in proportion to the severity of short circuits.

WARNING - Troubles 2.1 and 2.2 must be remedied as soon as detected since they are liable to render unserviceable the entire recharging system, owing to the abnormally high excitation current induced, whose value increases because of the reduction in field winding resistance.

The voltage regulator contacts are required to cut a current higher than the rated one and, therefore, are quickly damaged.

This condition will ultimately result in the unserviceability of the entire regulating unit.

On the other hand, when replacing a regulating unit with oxidized contacts, before setting recharging system into operation, again check the generator (points 2.1, 2.2, 2.3) and repair or replace accordingly, or else also the new regulator might be damaged in a short time.

2.4. Insulating coat (grease, etc.) between contacts of voltage regulator or current regulator. This results in increased resistance between said contacts and hence in reduced excitation current. Also this trouble causes an increase in generator cutting-in speed and maximum output speed.

3) By inserting and rotating the key to the ignition ON position the indicator lights up but does not go out even with engine running at high r.p.m. rates.

Defects may be:

3.1. Broken connection between terminal 67 of generator and terminal 67 of regulator.

3.2. Heavily oxidized or dirty contacts of either voltage or current regulators.

3.3. Inner regulator connections to terminals 67 and 51 unsoldered or broken.

3.4. Connection to terminal 51 of regulator broken.

3.5. Broken field winding.

3.6. Grounded armature winding.

3.7. Broken armature winding.

3.8. Grounded field winding.

3.9. Worn brushes not contacting commutator, or commutator coated with an insulating film (grease, oxide, etc.).

3.10. Cutout which does not close (e. g., magnetizing coil broken).

In this case, at a given speed, generator voltage equalizes battery voltage and the indicator goes out; then (the charging circuit being broken), at a higher r.p.m. the generator voltage reaches the no-load adjustment value of voltage regulator (15 V) and the indicator burns again feebly on account of the difference in generator over battery voltage.

3.11. Though cutout armature lowers, contacts do not close the circuit, being excessively worn or heavily oxidized.

Also in this case consequences are as outlined in point 3.10.

4) By inserting and rotating the key clockwise to the ignition ON position, the indicator does not light up, even when engine is speeded up.

Check first the indicator bulb and replace if defective. Check also contact of bulb base with holder. If bulb is efficient, causes for trouble may be:

4.1. Open circuit between generator terminal 51 and regulator terminal 51.

4.2. Open circuit between regulator terminal 51 and plug-in connection of red indicator in instrument cluster.

4.3. Open circuit between plug-in connection « INTER » in instrument cluster and red indicator.

4.4. Open circuit between instrument cluster plug-in connection « INTER » and plug-in connection « 15/54 » of ignition lock switch.

4.5. Open circuit inside ignition lock switch.

4.6. Open circuit between plug-in connection « 30 » of ignition lock switch and plug-in connection « 30 » of fuseholder.

4.7. Open circuit between plug-in connection « 30 » of fuseholder and plus clamp of battery.

5) By inserting and rotating the key clockwise to the ignition ON position, the indicator lights up. After starting and speeding up the engine, the indicator goes out but when the engine reaches and exceeds a given r.p.m. rate the indicator lights up again feebly.

This is not an indication of troubles in the recharging system but, rather, that **the indicator bulb is faulty**, i. e., the bulb begins to light up at a too low voltage.

In fact, at the indicator circuit terminal points there is a small voltage differential - due to the normal voltage drops along the circuit - when generator supplies a rather high current (discharged battery, users « ON »).

If the bulb begins to light up when tension is too low, its filament will glow feebly. To remedy this trouble, fit a new indicator bulb which will begin to light up at a voltage of 1.1-1.5 V.

This voltage may easily be checked using a suitable potentiometer and a 2-Volt scale voltmeter.

NOTE - If the above case is met, check the following:

a) The tightening of clamp 30 of generator regulator.

b) The proper coupling of plug-in connections located in the section of circuit between regulator terminal 30 and terminal 30 of ignition lock switch.

Said checks are important because the loosening of regulator terminal 30 or the inadequate coupling of plug-in connections (weakened inserts, etc.) cause an increase in voltage drops along the circuit, so that the lamp lights up too soon.

TROUBLE SHOOTING HINTS

Should conditions under point 2 occur, check generator for defects indicated in 2.1, 2.2 or 2.3.

Note that:

1) Troubles of points 2.1 and 2.2 may be detected by a resistance measurement on field winding. The resistance value must be as specified under « Ohmic Resistance Test » (page 203), or $8 \, ^{+0.1}_{-0.3}$ Ohms.

The measurement is made by connecting the tester outlets respectively to terminal 67 and ground (fig. 325).

Under conditions of point 2.1 it is more reliable to use a shorted coil detector, if available. High frequency detectors are the most recommended, but to use them the field windings must be removed from frame.

2) The defect stated under 2.3 causes, besides the trouble indicated in 2), also a commutation trouble in correspondence with the segments connected to shorted coils.

The increased brush wear, due to a worsened commutation, is accompanied by damages to the

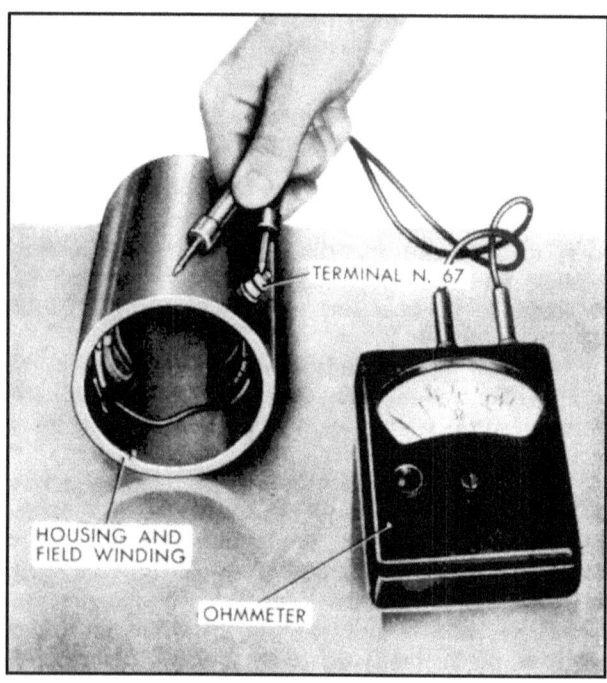

Fig. 325 - Using an ohmmeter to check generator field winding.

involved commutator segments (sinking). This condition further contributes to brush wear.

For shorted coils detection, an armature tester as test benches are equipped with (fig. 326) may be used, but its sensitivity is limited to two or more shorted coils.

After checking generator, check also regulating unit for the reasons stated in point 2) as outlined under « Regulator Bench Testing Instructions », page 218.

3) If conditions correspond to those under point 3), first check the regulator and, if found efficient, single out by elimination the defective item among those indicated in points 3.1 and 3.4 through 3.9 inclusive.

4) If conditions are those of point 4, generator is not faulty. Therefore, check the other items listed in sub-paragraphs of point 4).

5) Possible troubles in generator may also be the quick wear of brushes and damaged commutator. These defects may not be easily detected during operation, at any rate not until brushes are almost worn out. However, a careful inspection of commutator and brushes may prevent further harm.

Causes of this type of trouble may be:

a) loose commutator segments;
b) inadequate quality of brushes;
c) some shorted armature coils.

The defect mentioned in a) seldom occurs and is due to some segment having worked loose under the combined action of centrifugal force and heating-and-cooling cycles. The segments are displaced radially and, by protruding beyond commutator surface, cause an imperfect contact of brushes which cannot follow the commutator irregularities

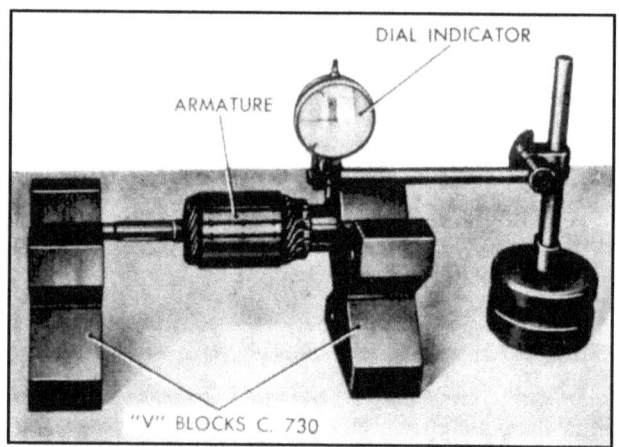

Fig. 327 - Checking commutator out-of-round.

It must not exceed .00039" (0,01 mm).

by inertia with consequent heavy arcing. Furthermore, this actually mills the brushes. The defect may easily be detected by a dial indicator (fig. 327), as follows.

Support generator armature. Rest the dial indicator plunger on the two edges of commutator surface not rubbed by brushes and, by rotating slowly the armature, determine maximum out-of-round points and their location. If segments are properly seated, out-of-round must not exceed .00039" (0,01 mm).

The fault quoted in b) causes an alteration in commutation and, consequently, an abnormal wear of both commutator and brushes.

Use of genuine FIAT brushes (supplied by the Spare Parts Department) will minimize troubles from this source.

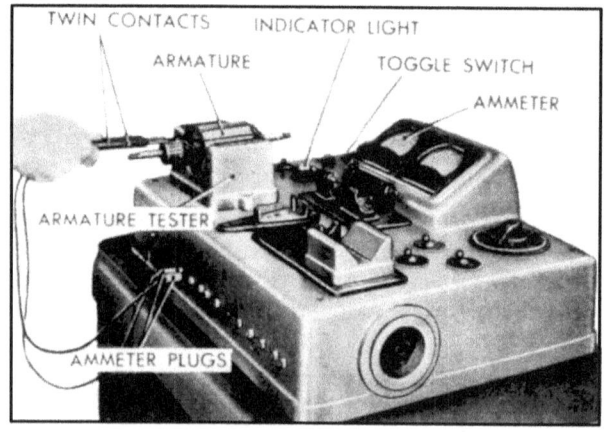

Fig. 326 - Testing the armature on bench, using a twin contact tester.

In correspondence with an open coil the ammeter reading will be zero.

ELECTRICAL

Trouble c), though not causing an appreciable increase in cut-in and output speeds of generator, and therefore not easily detectable during operation, induces commutation alterations and spot-damaging of commutator.

To single out shorted coils, use a high frequency tester, inserting a voltmeter between segments. Under normal generator operation conditions, life of brushes should range on some 18,000 miles (30.000 km).

GENERATOR SERVICING

A. - The only repairs that may be carried out by Service Station personnel are:

— commutator re-turning;

— repairs of broken or unsoldered field winding connections.

B. - Any other failed part must be replaced.

Disassembly of Generator.

Undo the pulley self-locking nut and slide the pulley off the armature shaft.

Undo the fan self-locking nut and slide the fan off the armature shaft.

Remove the two Woodruff keys on armature shaft.

Unscrew thru bolt nuts and pull out the bolts.

Partially disinsert the commutator end head to the point where brushes are still seated on commutator. Using the special tool provided, relieve load of springs on brushes by arranging spring ends on brush sides.

Brushes will thus be locked in their holders and cannot be chipped by striking against armature shaft during commutator end head removal.

Next pull out completely the commutator and fan end heads, and the armature.

Now, the generator has been dismantled into the following component assemblies:

— commutator end head;
— armature;
— frame;
— fan end head.

To remove ball bearings from heads and field winding from frame, proceed as follows:

COMMUTATOR END HEAD

Back out the ball bearing outer race stop bracket mounting screw nut.

Take out stop brackets and ball bearing.

FAN END HEAD

Back out the ball bearing retainer mounting screw nuts.

Remove the retainers and the seals. Using the special tool provided, take out the ball bearing.

FRAME

After disconnecting one end of the field winding from terminal 67 and the other end from ground

Fig. 328.
DSV 90/12/16/3 S generator components.

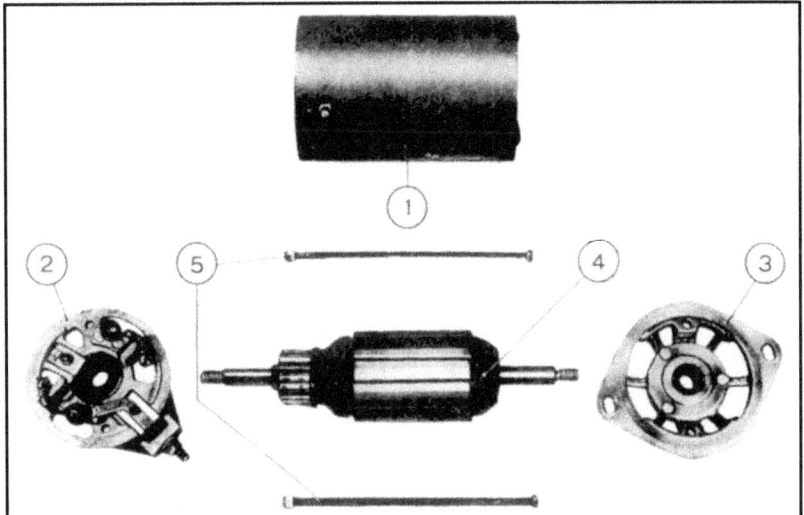

1. Frame. - 2. Commutator end head. - 3. Fan end head. - 4. Armature. - 5. Through bolts.

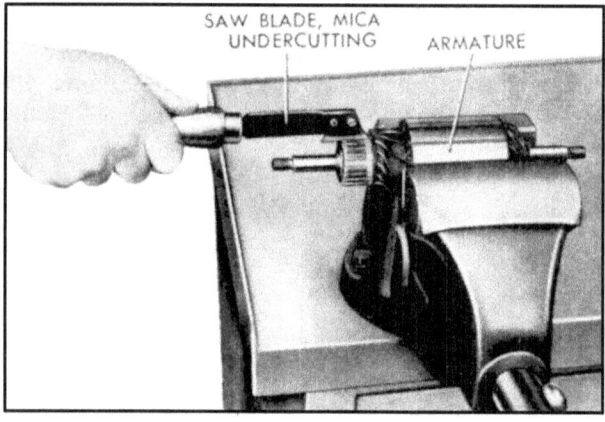

Fig. 329 - Undercutting the mica of a commutator by means of a saw blade.

(in the latter case, remove first the hollow-stem rivet securing wire end on frame), take off the field winding by undoing the outer screws fixing the pole shoes.

COMMUTATOR RE-TURNING

The armature assembly must be placed on a lathe and suitably centered, as it is not possible to hold the armature shaft between lathe centers.

This centering must be perfect because commutator out-of-round must not exceed .00039" (0,01 mm) (fig. 327).

After re-turning undercut the mica using a saw blade (fig 329).

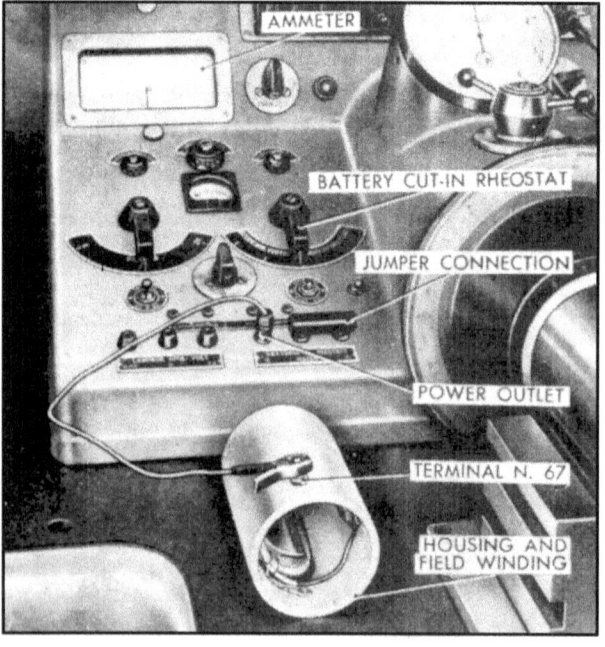

Fig. 330 - Checking generator field winding on test bench.

Broken Field Winding, with Shorted or Grounded Coils.

Repair only if trouble consists in unsoldered or broken connections. In all other cases replace winding with a **genuine one**.

Do not attempt to build a winding since windings are made of a copper wire coated with special insulating material (vinyl acetate) and require, for winding, soldering, impregnation, etc., **special treatment and equipment covered by suitable Process Standards**.

Field winding inspection (fig. 330) may be carried out using the bench for current feed and instrument reading.

Heat new winding to 122° F (50° C) before installation, to render it slightly flexible, thus facilitating its seating under pole shoes.

Pole shoes must be well set against frame and their screws fully tightened, so as to restore original air gap.

After reassembly, check that pole shoe inner diameter is 2.2952" to 2.2991" (58,3 to 58,4 mm).

If diameter departs from above figures, it is an indication that assembly is incorrect.

In this case, the whole operation must be repeated. **Never ream pole shoes.**

Shorted, Grounded or Open Armature Coil.

If this winding is damaged or shorted in its coils, it cannot be repaired by Service Stations for the same reasons as given for the field winding but must be replaced as an assembly with the armature.

Brush Replacement.

Only genuine FIAT spares must be used. Brushes with different hardness or composition characteristics would impair commutator life and affect generator and regulator operation adversely.

The use of unsuitable brushes determines poor commutation, followed by accelerated wear rate of commutator segments and brushes, remarkable voltage drops between commutator and brushes and a marked excitation current increase.

Under these conditions the voltage and current regulator contacts of the generator regulator are crossed by a current higher than normal.

This higher current causes material transfer between contacts, generally of voltage regulator, forming build-up on one contact and pit in the other.

The following two cases may be met:

1) The transfer of material between contacts continues to occur until the pitted tungsten contact

is pierced through. The build-up on the other contact will then touch the support of the pierced-through contact.

Since the support is of iron, arcing in the contact area causes an immediate local oxidation.

Consequently, the two contacts are insulated and the regulating resistance remains in the excitation circuit of the generator that is no longer able to supply any current.

2) The transfer of material between contacts welds them together. Under this condition, the voltage regulator cannot do its part of work (it no longer adjusts voltage) and the voltage may rise to excessively high values whereby the generator will supply high current even when battery has reached the « fully charged » condition. A result of this is an overcharging of battery which consequently will be quickly and irreparably damaged.

Also the life of users in car electric system is reduced, particularly the lamps.

Summing it all up, the use of unsuitable brushes, besides a poor life of brushes and quick wear of commutator, also means damages to the generator regulator and, sometimes, to battery on account of overcharging.

Inspection.

Independently of the repair or replacements effected, before reassembling the generator:

a) blow all carbon dust from components;

b) with a dry rag, clean brush holders and commutator end head from all grease and carbon dust;

c) with a dry rag, clean commutator, especially between segments.

Do not use emery cloth or sand paper, or even cloths soaked in oil, gasoline or solvents of any kind;

d) pack up ball bearings with FIAT Jota 3 grease;

e) check brush pressure for specifications given under « Mechanical Characteristics Check Data ».

NOTE - Do not use lubricants other than specified, unless of equivalent grade.

Reassembly.

Reverse disassembly operations.

A few reminders for a correct assembly:

— the commutator end ball bearing outer race stop bracket mounting screw nut must be tightened to .80 ft.lbs (110 kgmm);

— the pulley and fan-to-generator armature shaft self-locking nuts must be tightened to 14.5 ft.lbs (2000 kgmm).

After reassembly, repeat generator operation checks proceeding as directed under « Generator Bench Testing », page 203.

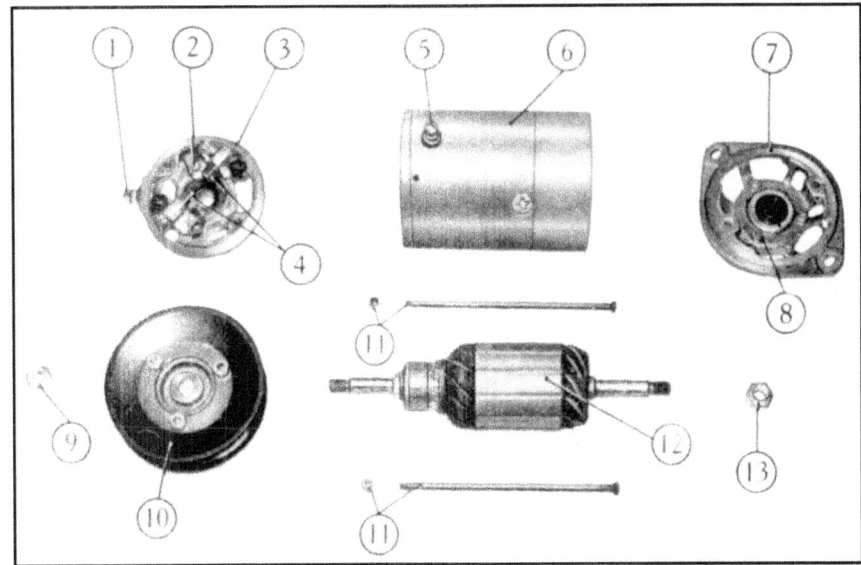

Fig. 331 - Components of generator R 90-180/12-2500 Spec. (up to engine No. 056195).

1. Terminal 51. - 2. Bearing outer ring retainment terminal nut. - 3. Commutator end head. - 4. Brushes. - 5. Terminal 67. - 6. Frame. - 7. Blower end head. - 8. Bearing retainer nuts and screws. - 9. Pulley retainment nut. - 10. Pulley. - 11. Head mounting tie rods and nuts. - 12. Armature. - 13. Blower retainment nut.

GENERATOR SPECIFICATIONS
(from engine No. 056196)

Type	DSV 90/12/16/3 S
Nominal tension	12 Volts
Max. continued operation output (ammeter limit)	16 Amperes
Max. current output	22 Amperes
Max. steady power	230 Watts
Max. power	320 Watts
Initial charging speed at 12 Volts and 68° F (20° C)	1710 to 1860 r.p.m. (*) 1710 to 1790 r.p.m. (**)
16 A. max. output delivery speed, at 68° F (20° C)	2550 to 2800 r.p.m. (*) 2550 to 2700 r.p.m. (**)
22 A. max output delivery speed, at 68° F (20° C)	3050 to 3200
Max. steady speed	9000 r.p.m.
Rotation, drive end	clockwise
Poles	2
Field winding	shunt
Regulator, separate	FIAT GN 1/12/16
Drive ratio (new belt), engine-to-generator	1.74
Pole shoe I. D.	2.2952" to 2.2991" (58,3 to 58,4 mm)
Brush part No.	4034356
Bench Testing Data.	
— Testing generator as a motor (at 68° F - 20° C):	
Feed voltage	12 V
Current draw	5 ± 0.5 Amps
Speed	1500 ± 100 r.p.m.
— Output test (at 68° F - 20° C):	
Steady voltage	12 V
Speed for abt. 30 minutes	4500 r.p.m.
Current delivery to resistor, at 14 Volts	5 ± 0.5 Amps
After bringing generator to operation temperature by running generator at the above specified speed and time rates, at a steady 12 V tension, read the values of the current output at every generator speed increment.	
— Ohmic resistance test (at 68° F - 20° C):	
Armature resistance	$0,145 \pm 0.01$ Ohms
Field winding resistance	$8 \, {}^{+0.1}_{-0.3}$ Ohms
— Mechanical characteristics test:	
Load of spring on new brushes	1.3 to 1.6 lbs (0,600 to 0,720 kg)
Commutator maximum out-of-round	.00039" (0,01 mm)
Mica undercut depth	.0394" (1 mm)
Lubrication.	
Ball bearings	FIAT Jota 3 Grease

(*) Refers to generators with armature package disc teeth .1732" (4,4 mm) in length (early type).
(**) Refers to generators with armature package disc teeth .1969" (5 mm) in length.

ELECTRICAL

GENERATOR SPECIFICATIONS
(up to engine No. 056195)

Type	R 90-180/12-2500 Spec.
Nominal tension	12 Volts
Max. continued operation output	180 Watts
Max. steady current output (ammeter limit)	13 Amps
Poles	2
Field winding	shunt
Regulator	separate
Cutting-in speed (at 68° F - 20° C)	1300-1380 r.p.m.
Speed at which generator reaches max. continued operation output (tension: nominal; temperature: 68° F - 20° C)	2250-2400 r.p.m.
Max. steady speed	7500 r.p.m.
Rotation, viewed from commutator end	clockwise
Engine-to-generator drive ratio (with new belt)	1.74
Pole shoes I. D.	2.3192" to 2.3259" (58,91 to 59,08 mm)
Armature outside diameter	2.2814" to 2.2834" (57,95 to 58 mm)
Part No. of brushes	879210

Bench Testing Data.

— Testing generator as a motor (at 68° F - 20° C):

Feed voltage	12 V
Current draw	4 to 4.5 Amps
Speed	1050 ± 50 r.p.m.

— Output test (at 68° F - 20° C):

Steady voltage	12 V
Speed for abt. 30 minutes	3750 r.p.m.
Current delivery to resistor (at 14 Volts)	5 ± 0.5 Amps

After bringing generator to operation temperature by running generator at the above specified speed and time rates, read, at a steady 12 V tension, the values of the current output at every generator speed increment.

— Ohmic resistance test (at 68° F - 20° C):

Armature resistance	0.31 ± 0.01 Ohms
Field winding resistance	6.4 ± 0.2 Ohms

— Mechanical characteristics test:

Load of springs on new brushes	1.3 to 1.6 lbs (0,600 to 0,720 kg)
Brush-to-brush holder clearance — crosswise	.0039" to .0118" (0,1 to 0,3 mm)
Brush-to-brush holder clearance — lengthwise	.0118" to .0236" (0,3 to 0,6 mm)
Commutator maximum out-of-round	.00039" (0,01 mm)
Mica undercut depth	.0394" (1 mm)

Lubrication.

Ball bearings	FIAT Jota 3 Grease

FIAT R 90-180/12-2500 Spec. GENERATOR

SECTION A-A

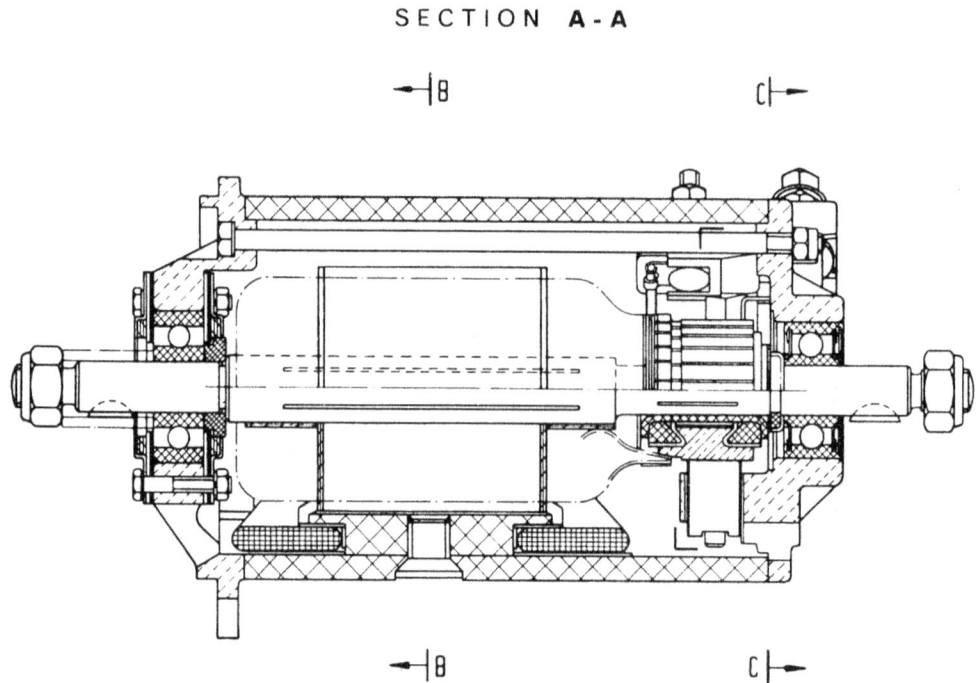

Fig. 332 - Longitudinal section.

SECTION B-B

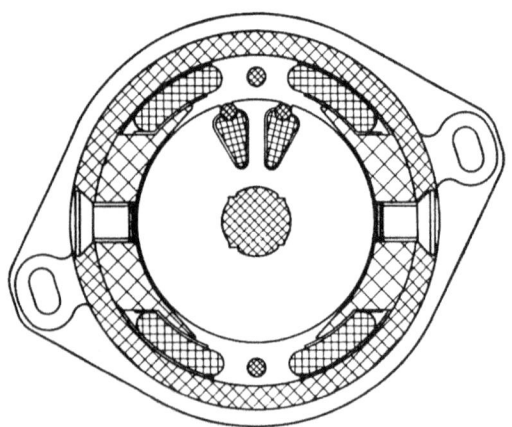

Fig. 333 - Generator sectioned through the frame, pole shoes and windings.

SECTION C-C

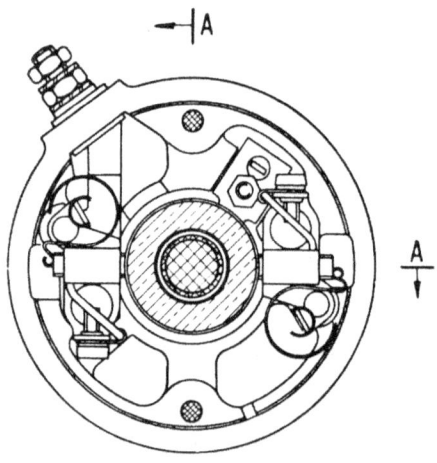

Fig. 334 - Section of generator through commutator and view of commutator end head.

ELECTRICAL

GENERATOR REGULATOR

DESCRIPTION	page 213
OPERATION	» 214
BENCH TESTING INSTRUCTIONS	» 218
TROUBLE SHOOTING INSTRUCTIONS	» 220
SERVICING	» 221
SETTING THE REGULATOR ASSEMBLY	» 223
GN 1/12/16 REGULATOR CHECKING AND SETTING DATA	» 225
OPERATION TEST AND SEALING	» 226
A/4-180/12 REGULATOR CHECKING AND SETTING DATA	» 226

Description.

The GN 1/12/16 regulator to suit « New 500 » Model consists of three separate units: voltage regulator, current regulator, cutout relay (three-core regulator).

NOTE - Up to engine No. 056195 regulator type A/4-180/12 has been installed. Check-up and setting data relevant to this assembly are chartered on page 226.

Voltage regulator and current regulator relays (fig. 336) consist of a « U » shaped body one of whose arms is bent to form a flange, while the other adjustment arm provides a stop for the hinge spring.

The « U » shaped body is secured to frame by

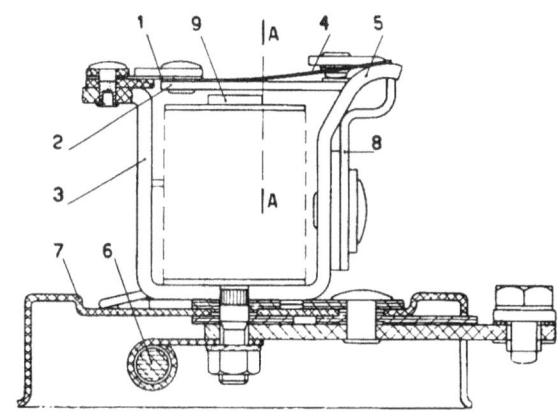

Fig. 336 - Voltage regulator and current regulator for regulator assembly GN 1/12/16.

1. Hinge spring (steel and bimetal for current regulator and bimetal for voltage regulator). - 2. Armature. - 3. Body. - 4. Adjusting spring. - 5. Adjustment arm. - 6. Voltage regulator resistance. - 7. Base. - 8. Stationary contact blade spring. - 9. Core.

the core threaded shank and carries, on the flanged end, an armature supported by a « hinge » spring (steel leaf and bimetal leaf overimposed in current regulator and bimetal leaf in voltage regulator).

In turn, the armature carries the movable contact.

Fixed contacts of both voltage and current regulators are mounted on two blade springs secured to a single bracket riveted to the « U » shaped adjustment arm.

The design of the two fixed contact carrier blade springs is such as to permit the adjustment of the contact position by suitably bending the blade springs.

The cutout is similar in design to the other two relays (fig. 337).

The hinge spring is bi-metallic, same as for the voltage regulator.

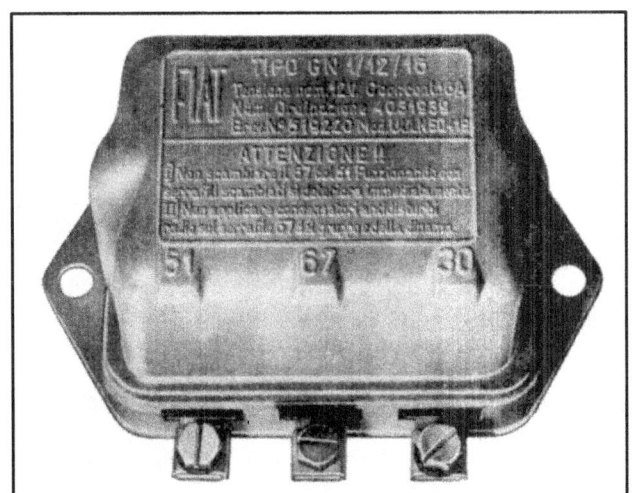

Fig. 335 - Regulator GN 1/12/16 with cover (terminal numbers are clearly visible).

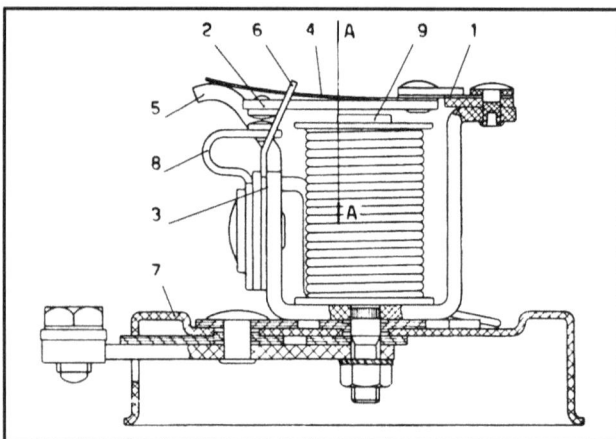

Fig. 337 - Cutout of regulator GN 1/12/16.

1. Bi-metallic hinge spring. - 2. Armature. - 3. Body. - 4. Adjustment spring. - 5. Adjustment arm. - 6. Armature stop. - 7. Base. - 8. Stationary contact blade spring. - 9. Core.

All armatures are provided with blade springs, so that their tension may be adjusted to the setting value.

This adjustment is obtained by suitably bending the adjustment arms.

The voltage regulator coil consists of a fine wire winding with a great number of turns, shunt-connected to generator.

The cutout coil consists of a fine wire winding with a great number of turns, shunt-connected to generator, and of a winding consisting of a few turns of heavy wire, connected in series with the generator charge circuit (cutout series winding).

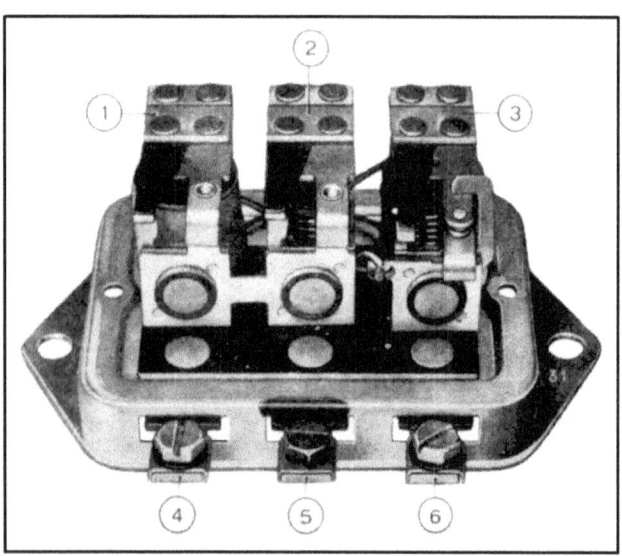

Fig. 338 - Regulator assembly GN 1/12/16.

Front view.

1. Voltage regulator body and armature plate. - 2. Current regulator body and armature plate. - 3. Cutout body and armature plate. - 4. Terminal 51. - 5. Terminal 67. - 6. Terminal 30.

The current regulator coil consists of a few turns of heavy wire series-connected with the generator charge circuit.

The base has three terminals, to which the various cables are connected, and two mounting flanges.

Terminal numbers are stamped on cover:

— No. 51 - connection to generator positive terminal;

— No. 67 - connection to generator field winding;

— No. 30 - connection to electric devices.

The regulator cover is secured to base through the interposition of a rubber gasket, which seals the unit against dust and moisture.

A regulating resistors is fitted under the base, and is secured by the voltage regulator and current regulator relay core threaded shanks.

Operation.

At low speeds generator voltage is not sufficient to induce a current strong enough to create in the voltage regulator and cutout relays a magnetic field capable of attracting the armatures.

At this time no current flows through the current regulator winding which, therefore, is not energized.

Under these conditions all armatures are at rest, so that contacts of cutout are open and those of voltage and current regulators are closed.

As generator speed increases, voltage and current rise until, at a given value, the cutout relay is energized enough to pull the armature, thus closing the contacts. This allows a flow of current to circulate from positive brush to users and to positive battery terminal and then to generator negative brush at which it closes the circuit.

This current flows through the series winding of cutout and produces a magnetizing action, which adds to that of the shunt winding, and then passes also in the current regulator winding.

In the cutout, the effect of this current is that of assisting in keeping more strongly closed the contacts.

However, current regulator contacts do not yet open since the current must still rise to higher values, as specified below.

Normally, if after cutout has closed the generator voltage continues to increase, on reaching the voltage regulator setting value the contacts of this relay will open.

As these contacts open due to the magnetic pull exerted on the armature by the cores of the shunt winding, the regulating resistor is automatically inserted in the generator field circuit.

This reduces the field current and, hence, the voltage of the generator and causes the voltage regulator contacts to close; from this instant the field current increases again and, consequently, also the generator voltage rises.

This cycle is repeated many times a second so that the voltage variations result imperceptible and voltage is maintained at the rated values.

When either the current drawn by users exceeds a given limit or battery is in a low state of charge, a heavy output is required of the generator.

With this current the magnetic pull on the current regulator armature becomes so strong that, by overcoming armature spring load, it forces down the armature and closes the contacts.

This causes also the insertion of the regulating resistor in the generator field circuit, producing the same effects described above for the voltage regulator, so that current is kept within controlled limits.

Should the current output exceed said limits, the current regulator armature will vibrate continuously, taking the place of the voltage regulator armature that, therefore, will remain inoperative.

In other words, it limits the generator current output, while the voltage regulator controls and maintains tension within the setting limits, so that it supplies to both battery and generator the right amount of power needed to meet operational requirements.

In the case the generator output value falls below the value of the current stored in battery, a «reverse» current will flow back from battery to generator. But this current will circulate in a reverse direction in the series windings of both the current regulator and cutout. This will have no effect on the current regulator, which will not be energized enough to pull down the armature, but on the cutout core it will produce a demagnetizing action with consequent release of the armature and opening of contacts. This way the current flow from battery to generator will be cutout, thus preventing discharge of the battery.

As hinted in the previous chapter, the voltage regulator and cutout relay have a bi-metal hinge-spring and the current regulator is provided with a dual hinge-spring consisting of a steel leaf and a bi-metal leaf set the one upon the other.

As far as the voltage regulator and cutout relay are concerned, the purpose of the bi-metal hinge spring is the thermal compensation of voltage.

In fact, when relay temperature varies, the ohmic resistance of windings varies accordingly and, along with these two factors, also the current absorption of the shunt winding and the magnetic pull on armature are changed.

Precisely, ohmic resistance increases with temperature increase, while magnetic pull becomes weaker and, consequently, the setting voltage (contact opening in voltage regulator, and contact closing in cutout) increases.

To compensate for the weakened magnetic pull, the hinge spring is bi-metallic and is arranged in such a way as to gradually relieve the load of adjustment spring as temperature increases.

In the case of the voltage regulator this is a «thermal overcompensation», namely, the bi-metallic spring action is greater than required to keep voltage temperature steady as ambient temperature varies.

It follows that when ambient temperature increases (summer), the voltage regulator setting voltage is slightly reduced.

The contrary happens when ambient temperature decreases (winter).

This «thermal overcompensation» is necessary, since the voltage of a battery, in which current flows, decreases as electrolyte temperature increases, and vice-versa. On the other hand, the electrolyte temperature is affected by ambient temperature.

Should voltage regulator setting tension not suit ambient temperature conditions of battery, the following troubles would occur:

— with high ambient temperature, setting voltage would become excessive and the battery would be compelled to store too high a current - after reaching the normal charge level - and would «boil» with consequent damages to plates;

— with low ambient temperature, setting voltage would be too low and the battery would fail to reach a correct state of charge.

The task of the dual hinge spring in the current regulator is that of permitting the **thermal correction of the limiting current (thermally stabilized regulator).**

The spring consists of a steel leaf and a bi-metallic lamina placed one on top of the other and is so arranged as to reduce gradually the reaction of return springs as temperature increases. By this provision the pull of current regulator armature will decrease as temperature increases and the limiting current will therefore be higher with cold regulator and lower with warm regulator.

Purposes are the following:

— at the beginning of operation, after a sufficiently long inactivity period (at least 2 hours), the regulating unit is not «thermally stabilized», i. e., it is at ambient temperature.

Under these conditions the limiting current is higher than maximum permissible generator continuous current and, therefore, if current draw from users is heavy, the generator may be overloaded. The generator, however, can withstand this overload beacause it too is at the beginning of operation and not yet thermally stabilized, i. e., its windings are still at ambient temperature. As both regulator and generator warm up, the action of the bi-metallic lamina reduces (within 20-30 minutes) the limiting current until it reaches a value that the generator may withstand safely in continuous operation. This value varies with ambient temperature and is reached when the unit is thermally «soaked» at rated operation temperature. It ensues that the overload cannot cause dangerous temperatures within the generator since, as generator temperature increases, the load decreases.

The temporary initial operation in overload of generator permits a quicker battery charging when charge level is lowest due to a difficult cold start or when the car is operated in town with frequent stops and starts and recharge periods are very short.

— As said above, the limiting current value with thermally stabilized regulator is variable with ambient temperature. In fact, under these conditions the bi-metallic lamina temperature will be higher

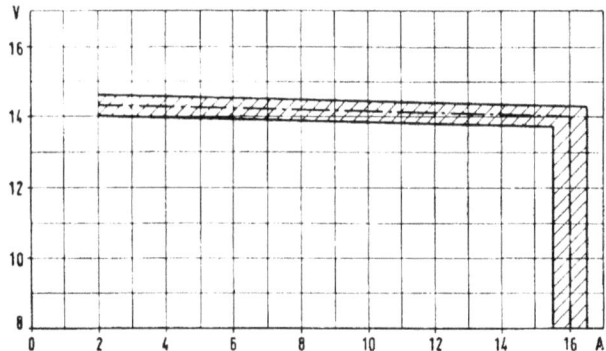

Fig. 339 - Characteristic V-Amp curves on battery of GN1/12/16 regulator.

Temperature: 122° ± 5° F (50° ± 3° C). - Generator speed: 4500 r.p.m.

or lower depending on ambient temperature, so that limiting current will be higher at lower ambient temperatures and lower at higher ambient temperatures. Also, the limiting current will be higher in winter and lower in summer with consequent lesser heat dissipation of generator in winter and better uniformity of generator temperature in both seasons.

Fig. 339 shows the characteristic curve of the regulating unit. In the diagram the area where the two strips meet indicates the limit of operation between voltage regulator and current regulator.

As it is apparent from the characteristic curve, current remains constant up to a given voltage and then decreases rapidly.

It is just because of this feature that the A/4 regulators, by exploiting in full the generator output capacity, assist in keeping the battery in the best state of charge, even under the most severe service, as required on vehicles whose engines are started very frequently or when there is a great number of users.

In the particular case that a generator operates with a battery almost totally discharged, the regulator will provide for the maximum flow of current to the battery until this has reached a high state of charge (about 14 volts).

As the battery reaches the correct level of charge, the voltage regulator enters into operation to maintain voltage around 14.5 volts, thus determining a rapid decrease in the charging current (provided no users are switched on which draw heavily from the battery). This way, the battery reaches full charge with no risk of being damaged.

When battery is fully charged, the current levels off at a few amperes and there remains, thus maintaining the battery well charged and without causing excessive electrolysis, positive grid sulphation, overheating, damages to separators, etc.

It should be noted that in the case of a battery fully charged left at rest for some time (whereby its voltage drops approximately to the nominal value - 12 Volts, i. e. 2 Volts per cell), when generator resumes delivery the output values will not be those corresponding to the end of charge, but considerably higher, since the battery does not reach full voltage immediately. Under these conditions, only the current regulator will operate. However, as the battery voltage rises, the current diminishes and the voltage regulator takes over, to maintain tension within the rated limits.

In other words, the charging cycle is repeated but in a much shorter time.

WARNING

1. - Connections to terminals 67 and 51 of regulator should **never** be interchanged, otherwise the regulator would **immediately become unserviceable**, since (see figs. 340-341) the current supplied by generator would flow from generator terminal 51 to regulator terminal 67 through the voltage and current regulator contacts. The effects are readily evident: as soon as generator voltage increases, it causes the voltage regulator contacts (or current regulator contacts, depending on battery state of charge or on the amount of current drawn by users) to open, and since under these conditions the contacts are requested to break the entire current supplied by generator instead of merely inserting a resistance in the circuit), a heavy arcing will occur, with consequent melting of material, oxidation and charring of contacts, etc.

In a short time this will cause the welding of contacts.

The trouble in this situation is that the unit, though operating abnormally and supplying a reduced voltage, will continue to operate just the same, and a repairman not amply versed in such problems or not provided with proper facilities, may not

ELECTRICAL

become aware of the incorrect connection until after unit failure due to welding of contacts. This trouble causes also the generator field winding to burn.

It should be noted that under these conditions an incorrectly wired unit would be damaged even if operated for a few seconds only, since the contacts overheat, undergo transfer and become oxidized.

It follows that though rewiring connections correctly and restoring normal regulator operation, contacts are irreparably damaged and very soon pitting and build-up will occur (if an initial melting has taken place which primes the phenomenon), or oxidation will become so heavy as to insulate contacts.

Attention is drawn on the fact that the troubles originating from a wrong connection of terminals 67 and 51 are not peculiar to this type of regulator but are common to all types of vibrating regulators, whichever are the construction and the wiring diagram.

Keep in mind that the unit must operate exclusively with its own generator if long life and satisfactory operation of the unit is expected.

If regulator is not used with the generator for which it has been designed, or vice-versa, such condition will result in irregular operation, inadequate performance and poor contact life characteristics.

2. - Be careful not to mishandle the unit during assembly and disassembly operations. This recommendation holds also for regulators in storage. Handle regulators always very gently to avoid damages to the more delicate parts.

3. - When installing regulator on test bench, insert an insulating sheet between regulator base and support on which the unit is mounted. During tests, the regulator must be mounted vertically, with terminals lowermost.

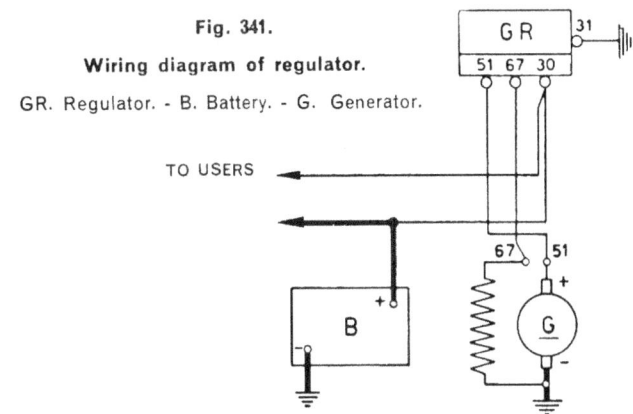

Fig. 341.
Wiring diagram of regulator.
GR. Regulator. - B. Battery. - G. Generator.

4. - During tests wire up generator, regulator, battery and ground, according to the diagrams given further on. **Make sure terminal 51 of generator is connected to terminal 51 of regulator and terminal 67 of generator is connected to terminal 67 of regulator. If connections are interchanged the regulator would be immediately ruined, as explained above.**

5. - Connection between regulator base (31) and ground must be such as to ensure a perfect electrical contact, otherwise regulator remains inoperative (no current would pass in shunt windings) and generator voltage would reach values so high as to burn the generator windings and damage seriously the voltage and current regulator contacts.

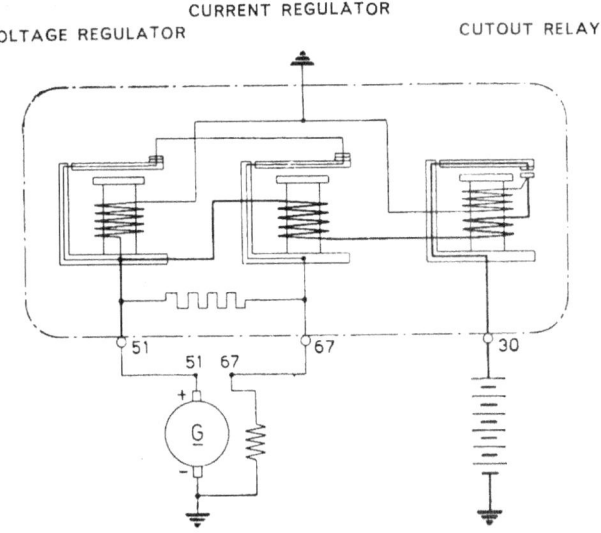

Fig. 340 - Wiring diagram of regulator GN 1/12/16.

IMPORTANT

Never insert radio interference suppression condensers of any capacity between:

— terminal 67 and ground;

— terminals 67 and 51, both on generator and on regulator.

If condensers are inserted between said terminals, regulator contacts will be damaged in a very short time.

Normally, regulators do not cause radio interference.

If this recommendation is disregarded, **the regulator will be damaged**, as explained above.

BENCH TESTING INSTRUCTIONS

To check the efficiency of GN 1/12/16 type regulator, proceed as follows:

On a test bench, install a FIAT DSV 90/12/16/3 S generator.

Couple this generator to a motor whose speed may be varied at will in small increments.

Prepare all instruments and devices required to test cutout, voltage and current regulators in accordance with the diagrams and instructions given hereunder.

NOTE - Due to the fact that test bench gauges are subject to being upset from vibrations and the difficulty of detecting any fault in bench circuits, it is good practice to use portable gauges to check the generator regulator, by setting the generator-regulator-gauges wiring circuit through outside electrical connections, which can be inspected more easily.

WARNING

Reliable results can be obtained only if tests are run under the exact conditions specified for each single test.

Checking Cutout.

1. - **Closing voltage** (ambient temperature: 77°±18° F [25°±10° C]).

   1-1. Wire as shown in diagram (fig. 342).

   1-2. Initially the unit must be at ambient temperature of 77°±18° F (25°±10° C).

   1-3. Operate the unit with no load, at ambient temperature of 77°±18° F (25°±10° C) for 15-18 minutes, with cover installed and with voltage of:

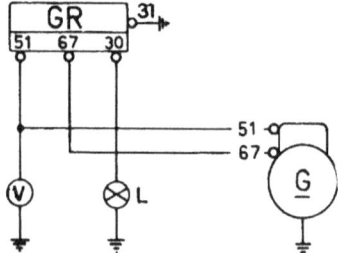

Fig. 342 - Wiring diagram for checking the cutout closing voltage.

GR. Regulator GN 1/12/16. - G. Generator FIAT DSV 90/12/16/3 S. - V. Voltmeter, 20 V scale (0.5% accuracy). - L. 12 V, 3 to 5 W bulb.

— 16.5 V for initial temperatures of 59° to 68° F (15° to 20° C).

— 15 V for initial temperatures of 68° to 95° F (20° to 35° C).

This way, the thermal stabilization of the unit is obtained, i. e., the temperature of both the cutout shunt windings and bi-metallic springs increases due to heat developed by the windings and reaches the « operative value ».

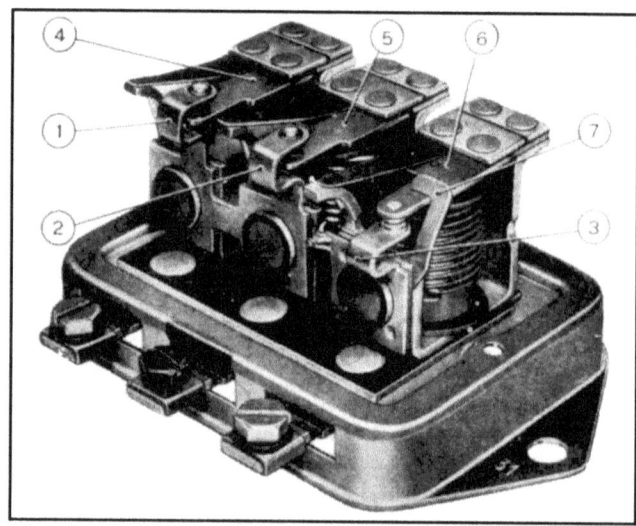

Fig. 343 - Regulator assembly GN 1/12/16.

Perspective view from cutout side.

1. Voltage regulator stationary contact carrier arm. - 2. Current regulator stationary contact carrier arm. - 3. Cutout stationary contact carrier arm. - 4. Voltage regulator armature. - 5. Current regulator armature. - 6. Cutout armature. - 7. Cutout armature stop.

Thermal stabilization is necessary because initially there is a « transient voltage » of some minutes before the setting voltage stabilizes on a steady value, and if this condition is not observed results are liable to be erroneous.

1-4. Soon after reaching thermal stabilization, start the generator, increase its speed gradually and check on voltmeter the value of cutout contact closing voltage. Take reading at the instant at which test lamp glows. Closing contact voltage should be 12.6±0.2 V.

2. - **Reverse current** (ambient temperature: 77°±18° F [25°±10° C]).

This check must be performed soon after the closing voltage test, so that thermal stabilization remains unaltered (point 1-3).

   2-1. Wire as shown in diagram (fig. 344).

   2-2. Speed up generator to 4500 r. p. m. for

ELECTRICAL

5 minutes, making sure voltmeter reads at least 14.5 V, then gradually reduce generator r.p.m.

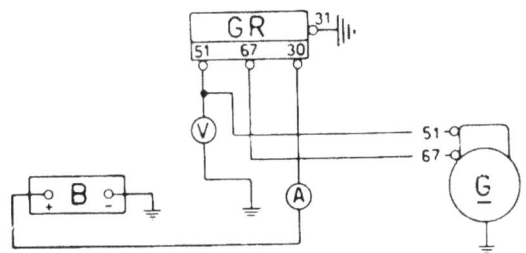

Fig. 344 - **Wiring diagram for checking the reverse current of cutout.**

GR. Regulator GN 1/12/16. - G. Generator FIAT DSV 90/12/16/3 S. - B. Battery, 50 Ah, fully charged. - A. Ammeter, asymmetrical scale 10-0-15 A. - V. Voltmeter, 20 V scale (0.5% accuracy).

2-3. The ammeter needle, at first indicating a given charging current, will gradually move to zero and then shift to the other side of the scale to indicate reverse current value. By still reducing generator speed, the reverse current reading will increase to a given value and then abruptly fall to zero (cutout contacts have opened).

This limit indicates max. reverse current value which must not exceed 16 Amp.

NOTE - To obtain the max. reverse current possible, the reduction in generator speed must be so quick as not to give battery voltage sufficient time to drop excessively (10 seconds). Should it be desired to repeat the test, to avoid erroneous readings which may result from residual magnetism in cutout, wait until generator stops and then re-start.

Checking Voltage Regulator.

Regulating voltage, with half load, on battery (ambient temperature: $122^\circ \pm 5^\circ$ F [$50^\circ \pm 3^\circ$ C]).

Wire as shown in diagram (fig. 345).

1. **Operate regulator in ambient temperature of $122^\circ \pm 5^\circ$ F ($50^\circ \pm 3^\circ$ C) for 30 minutes**, by supplying a current half that of regulated current which is 16 ± 0.5 Amperes.

For this test, the thermostat oven Ap. 5014 should be available, so that regulator can be maintained at the above specified temperature (fig. 346).

2. Soon after this test, keeping regulator always at $122^\circ \pm 5^\circ$ F ($50^\circ \pm 3^\circ$ C), stop generator and start it again, increasing its speed gradually up to 4500 r.p.m.

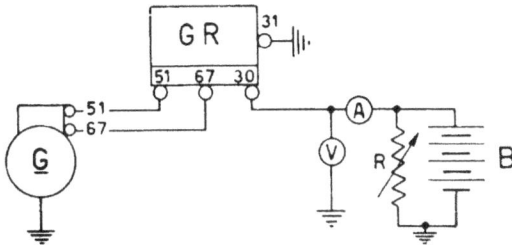

Fig. 345 - **Wiring diagram for checking the current and voltage regulators.**

GR. Regulator GN 1/12/16. - G. Generator FIAT D 90/12/16/3. - V. Voltmeter, 20 V scale (0.5% accuracy). - A. Ammeter, 20 A scale (to check voltage regulator) and 40 A scale (to check current regulator). - R. Rheostat, 25 A. 3 Ω. - B. Battery, 50 Ah, fully charged.

3. Adjust rheostat R for a generator output corresponding to half-load current, that is 8 ± 2 Amps.

Fig. 346 - **Checking and setting voltage regulator and current regulator.**

1. Regulator assembly. - 2. Voltmeter. - 3. Ammeter. - 4. Thermostat oven Ap. 5014. - 5. Generator D 90/12/16/3.

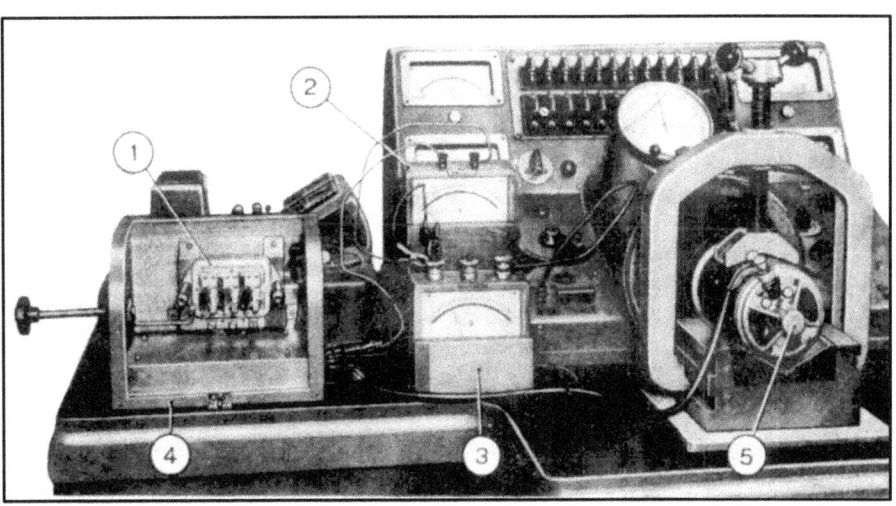

Generator assembly is put in thermostat oven Ap. 5014 and is wired up with outside electrical circuits, which can be easily checked, and portable gauges.

4. With this generator output, voltage should be 14.2±0.3 V.

NOTE - To check current and voltage regulator, use a **D 90/12/16/3** generator, fitted with its rotor.

Checking Current Regulator.

Regulated current on battery.

Wire in accordance with the same diagram as for voltage regulator.

The regulated current on battery must be checked immediately after testing the half-load regulated voltage (on battery) of the voltage regulator.

1. Instruments are the same as used in determining half-load regulated voltage, excepting the ammeter which must have a 40 Amp scale.

2. Insert maximum rheostat resistance.

3. Operate the regulator in the oven at 122°±5°F (50°±3° C) for 30 minutes with regulator-controlled current (reduce resistor **R** of rheostat until current is steady and voltage drops) and 13 Volt tension.

4. Check current for a steady delivery (that is operation temperature).

5. Stop the generator, restart and speed it up to 4500 r.p.m. Check that the regulated current value corresponds to specified 16±0.5 Amperes.

By still reducing the resistance, the current shall remain constant. The voltage, instead, with the decrease in resistance should drop to as low as 12 V.

TROUBLE SHOOTING INSTRUCTIONS

1. - Low recharging rate with fully charged battery.

This indicates that generator-regulator operation is normal.

2. - High recharging rate with fully charged battery.

This condition discloses that voltage regulator does not control generator output as it should. A high recharging rate on a fully charged battery damages the battery and the ensuing high voltage is detrimental to users.

Possible causes are:

a) Voltage regulator setting too high.
b) Faulty voltage regulator windings.
c) Short circuit, between generator positive terminal and field winding.

This impedes a normal insertion of resistance in generator field circuit when voltage regulator contacts open.

d) Insufficient generator-to-regulator connection through ground.

e) High temperature. This reduces battery emf reaction to the charge, meaning that battery receives a high recharging current even if regulator rated voltage is correct.

f) Welding of voltage regulator or of current regulator contacts.

If this trouble is not ascribable to high temperatures, detect the cause by disconnecting cable terminal 67 from regulator, while generator operates at average speed.

The following conditions may be experienced:

1. Output keeps on high level.

If so, there will be a short circuit between plus terminal and field winding of generator, as already hinted at c) above.

2. Output drops to nil.

If so, defect lies in regulator. Inspect regulator as hinted in previous items a) - b) - d) - f).

NOTE - It may happen that generator output remains very high even after a long recharge period, though temperature is not excessive and regulator operation is correct.

In this case the trouble is not due to regulator but to battery being «aged», i.e., it no longer takes the charge and its voltage cannot rise beyond a given limit, whereby generator output cannot decrease.

This trouble is quite frequent and is to be ascribed to poor maintenance, sulphation or misuse of battery.

3. - Discarged battery and high recharging rate.

This indicates that generator-regulator operation is correct.

NOTE - It may happen that, although the generator-regulator system is operating regularly, as the engine is started and revved up to a certain speed, the generator charge light goes out and then glows feebly.

This is not an indication of troubles in the charging system, but merely a consequence of a faulty bulb which has a low lighting voltage.

ELECTRICAL

As a matter of fact, when the generator delivers a certain amount of current (battery discharged, users in), a small power differential occurs at the circuit ends, due to normal voltage drops in the circuit.

If the lighting voltage of the bulb is too low, the bulb filament glows feebly.

To remove this trouble, just replace the indicator bulb by another having the lighting voltage of 1.1 to 1.5 Volts (12 Volt bulb) or of 2 to 2.5 Volts (24 Volt bulb).

To check lighting voltage, use a potentiometer and a voltmeter with a 3 Volt scale.

4. - **Discharged battery and low recharging rate, or no recharge at all.**

Possible causes are:

a) loose connections, faulty cables;

b) defective battery;

c) high resistance of charging circuit;

d) low setting of voltage or current regulators;

e) oxidized contacts in voltage or current regulators;

f) other defects in generator.

If a) is not the cause, proceed as follows:

To detect whether battery is the cause of trouble, replace it with a fully discharged but efficient battery.

If generator output reaches maximum value, the replaced battery was faulty.

If trouble does not disappear, find out whether the fault originates in generator or in regulator, by temporarily short circuiting regulator terminals 67 and 51 and increasing generator speed.

If the output, which was zero or very low, rises to a given value, the trouble is due to one of the following causes:

a) low voltage or current regulator settings;

b) oxidized voltage or current regulator contacts. This oxidation causes an excessive resistance in generator field circuit and, consequently, the output is very low or even zero;

c) accidental resistance or interruptions in generator field circuit (in the regulator, connections or windings).

No output, instead, reveals a faulty generator.

5. - **Windings damaged from overheating, cutout overheated connections and contacts.**

This may be due to inversion of generator polarity.

An inversion of polarity rapidly overheats the cutout and current regulator series windings by inducing a very high reverse current in the generator-regulator-battery circuit (in fact, generator emf and battery emf add up on a low resistance circuit). Overheating involves and damages also the other circuits. Also the current carrier spring, the connections and cutout contacts overheat.

To re-polarize the generator, temporarily connect terminal 51 to terminal 30 on regulator with a jumper.

Before connecting the jumper, make sure all connections between generator and battery are as they should be.

A brief flash of current will thus flow through generator field and re-polarization will take place.

REGULATOR SERVICING

As a rule a defective regulator should be replaced. Limit repairs to very exceptional cases.

If a repair has to be made on regulator, follow strictly these directions:

Before unit is unsealed, check regulator as directed under « Trouble Shooting » and make perfectly sure that the repair is really necessary and worthwhile.

When servicing a faulty regulator, absolutely abstain from disassembling, replacing or repairing any part of its relays.

Repairs must be limited to the substitution of complete relays besides the resistor or connections between them.

Cover and resistor should be kept in containers which protect them from damage, distortion, grease soiling, foreign matter, etc.

Opening the Regulator.

Loosen the cover-to-base screws and remove the cover and gasket.

CAUTION

Always bear in mind that most troubles, especially the serious ones, like:

— excessive wear or welding of cutout contacts;

— oxidation of voltage and current regulator contacts;

Fig. 347 - Regulator assembly GN 1/12/16.
Rear view.

1. Cutout winding terminal soldered to base. - 2. Voltage regulator winding terminal soldered to base. - 3. Current regulator series winding terminal soldered to voltage regulator frame.

— contact pitting and build-up in voltage regulator and current regulator;

— contact welding in voltage regulator and current regulator;

— short-circuited coils;

— overheating windings;

are often due to causes not ascribable to regulator and which generally originate from troubles in the generator, such as alteration of field winding resistance, use of improper brushes, damaged circuits (wires, etc.).

Especially use of improper brushes brings about a poor commutation, with rapid wear of commutator segments and brushes themselves, high voltage drop between commutator and brushes and remarkable increase of field current.

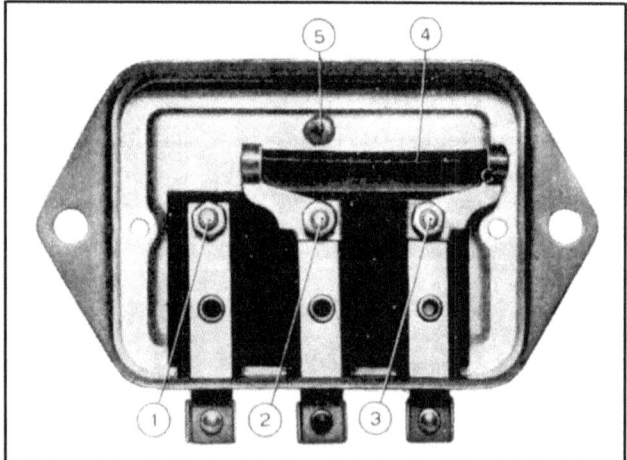

Fig. 348 - Regulator assembly GN 1/12/16.
Bottom view.

1. Nut, cutout fixing. - 2. Nut, current regulator and resistance fixing. - 3. Nut, voltage regulator and resistance fixing. - 4. Resistance. - 5. Soldering on base of cutout and voltage regulator shunt windings.

In such conditions voltage regulator and current regulator contacts are affected by a current which is above the standard value.

This causes stock transfer between contacts, generally in the voltage regulator, with the result that one contact is pitted and the other built up.

Stock transfer will grow until pitting of tungsten contact turns into a hole. Therefore the tip of the built up contact reaches the bracket of the pierced contact.

As the bracket is of iron, sparkling at the contact area will cause local oxidation.

So both above contacts are isolated and the regulating resistance of the unit is all the time in the field winding of the generator, which delivers no output.

As a rule, regulator operation and life are most satisfactory. **For this reason, the serviceman must not simply restore unit to efficiency but should also test generator and the entire recharging system.**

Regulating Resistance Replacement.

If it has been found that the voltage and/or current regulator settings have been altered, namely:

— regulated voltage is low or reduced to negligible values;

— voltage is no longer under control, but rises to high values;

— regulated current no longer ranges within rated limits and is excessive;

the trouble may be ascribed to an open regulating resistor or to an alteration in resistance value, which possibly induces the following damages:

— oxidation of voltage or current regulator contacts (« low » or « very low » no-load voltage);

— welded voltage regulator contacts (uncontrolled voltage reaching very high values);

— welded current regulator contacts (uncontrolled current reaches very high values).

Inspect the resistor and make sure that the wire is neither broken nor disconnected from terminals and that no coils are shorted or with damaged insulation.

In doubtful cases, remove the resistor and test at 68° F (20° C); its value must be 105±3 Ohms.

This operation can be performed without taking off resistor from regulator. Just insert a lintless paper between current and voltage regulator contacts and take the reading across terminals 51 and 67.

If a different value is found, replace resistor by taking off nuts (2 and 3, fig. 348) with lock washers.

The resistor **must not** be repaired. A repair is never satisfactory since special methods and equipment are required. Replace with a new resistor.

Caution. - If the resistor is found damaged, remember that to restore regulator efficiency it will not suffice to simply replace the resistor, but it is **indispensable** to inspect the whole regulator; if any damage is detected, regulator must be replaced.

To reassemble resistor on regulator, refit nuts (2 and 3, fig. 348), being careful not to forget lock washers which must be fitted as before removal. During assembly, do not damage the wire with the screwdriver or wrench.

Subsequently, check armature-to-core air gap of current and voltage regulators, taking the measurement on core edge towards contacts. Gap should equal .0391″ to .0437″ (0,99 to 1,11 mm; axis A-A, fig. 336).

Finally check regulator setting in accordance with the instructions given under « Regulator Setting ».

The above checks are indispensable since the voltage and current regulator cores, and relevant frames, are interconnected and mounted on base by the same nuts that secure the regulating resistor. Therefore, when handling the unit to replace regulating resistor, the arrangement of relays may be altered. For this reason, make sure that, after tightening the nuts, no asymmetry, if any, is left.

In any case, the operation should be performed with maximum care and **regulating resistor mounting nuts should be tightened securely.**

If after adjustment, armature-to-core air gaps are not within specified tolerance, it will be necessary to bend blade spring (8, fig. 336) carrying the stationary contact so as to bring air gap again within recommended limits. During this operation, it is essential to maintain the parallelism of both the movable and stationary contacts, that is to say, the two contacts should touch each other at their centers. This condition should be checked using a magnifying glass.

NOTE - Even if cutout is not involved when regulating resistor is removed, it is always advisable to inspect cutout just the same, checking that:

— armature-to-core air gap, **with contacts closed**, measured at core edge towards contacts (A-A fig. 337) is .0138″ (0,35 mm);

— contact gap, **when open**, is .0177″ ± .0023″ (0,45 ± 0,06 mm).

SETTING THE REGULATOR ASSEMBLY

The adjustment of regulator assembly must be carried out placing the unit upright on bench with terminals lowermost.

WARNING - If the regulator assembly has remained for a certain while in a room below 59° F (15° C) or above 95° F (35° C), prior to proceeding as outlined hereafter, keep the regulator for at least one hour at 77° ± 18° F (25° ± 10° C) room temperature.

Setting Cutout Relay.

Wire as shown in diagram (fig. 349 for GN 1/12/16 and fig. 353 for A/4-180/12).

The setting of instruments before inserting the unit should be:

— P at minimum (Voltmeter reads zero);
— T open;
— R all inserted (max. resistance);
— T_1 open.

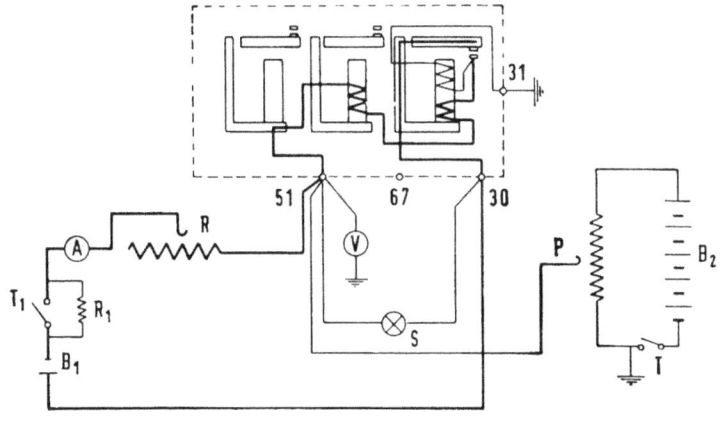

Fig. 349.
Wiring diagram for setting the cutout relay.

(GN 1/12/16 regulator assembly).

B_1. 2-V battery. - B_2. 20-V battery. - A. Ammeter, 20 A scale (1% accuracy). - V. Voltmeter, 20 V scale (0.5% accuracy), directly connected to terminals 31-51. - P. Potentiometer for voltage adjustment, having such a capacity that the current draw of the cutout shunt winding does not cause sensible variations in the voltage readings (voltmeter under no load). - S Test lamp, with 2 V, 3 W bulb, to signal opening and closing of contacts. - R. Rheostat, 4 Ω, 12 A. - R_1. Voltage drop resistor, suitable to allow turning on of S with T_1 open and cutout contacts open.

Setting of instruments before inserting the unit: P. At minimum (voltmeter reads zero). - T. Open. - R. All inserted (max. resistance). - T_1. Open.

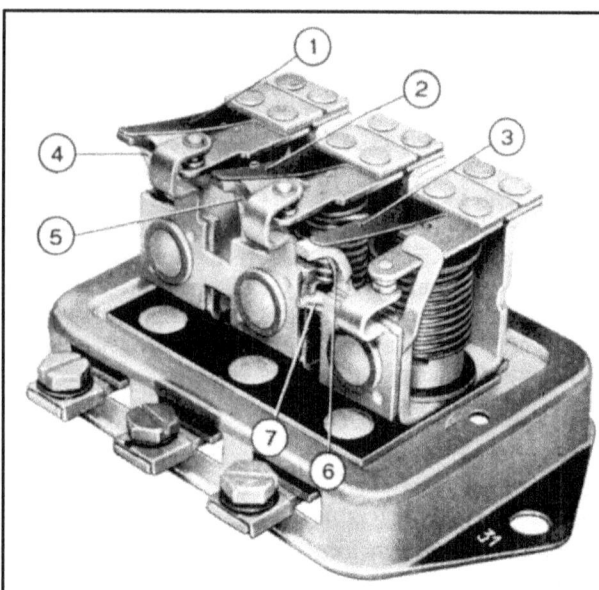

Fig. 350 - Regulator assembly GN 1/12/16.

Perspective view from cutout relay side.

1. Voltage regulator adjusting spring. - 2. Current regulator adjusting spring. - 3. Cutout adjusting spring. - 4. Voltage regulator adjustment arm. - 5. Current regulator adjustment arm. - 6. Cutout adjustment blade spring. - 7. Soldering of cutout shunt and series winding.

1. - **Contact closing voltage** (ambient temperature: $77° \pm 18°$ F [$25° \pm 10°$ C]).

a) Close switch T.

b) Stabilize regulator thermally by feeding current for 15-18 minutes at 16.5 V (obtained by suitably adjusting P) for initial regulator operating temperatures of 59° to 68° F (15° to 20° C), or at 15 V for initial operating temperatures of 68° to 95° F (20° to 35° C).

c) Immediately after stabilizing regulator, bring voltage to 12.6 ± 0.2 V by adjusting P.

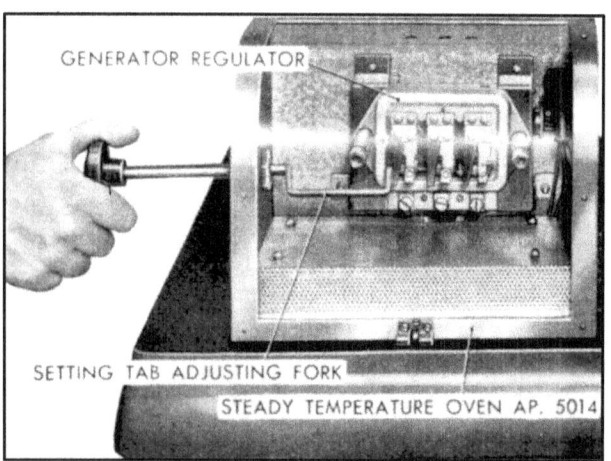

Fig. 351 - Setting the voltage regulator.

To this purpose, the regulator assembly is put in thermostat oven Ap. 5014.

d) Adjust load on setting spring by bending the relevant arm, until pilot lamp S goes out.

e) Reset P to minimum.

f) Again increase voltage by P and check that pilot lamp goes out at the specified voltage.

2. - **Reverse current** (ambient temperature: $77° \pm 18°$ F [$25° \pm 10°$ C]).

This test must be run soon after the closing voltage test, so as to maintain regulator thermal stabilization.

a) With switch T closed, using P bring voltage to 14.5 V. Cutout contacts should be closed, pilot lamp S off.

b) Close T_1.

c) Increase reverse current by means of rheostat R, and check that pilot lamp S glows as contacts part.

Opening may also be unsteady: such condition is evidenced by a slight buzz.

d) Check on ammeter the value of the reverse current causing the opening of contacts: it should not exceed 16 Amps.

e) If reading is unstable, or S lights up at tolerance limit, reset reverse current to the minimum value and repeat operation c).

f) Open switches T and T_1 and again adjust rheostat R and potentiometer P to minimum settings.

Setting Voltage Regulator

(ambient temperature: $122° \pm 5°$ F [$50° \pm 3°$ C]).

NOTE - This test requires the availability of oven **Ap. 5014** within which the regulator can be maintained.

a) Wire as shown in diagram (fig. 352).

b) Load voltage regulator adjusting springs by suitably bending the relevant arm.

c) With the unit in thermostat oven at $122° \pm 5°$ F ($50° \pm 3°$ C) close I, start generator and stabilize regulator thermally by feeding current for 30 minutes at 15 V (obtained by suitably adjusting generator speed).

d) With unit still at 122° F (50° C), stop generator, open I, start generator again and speed it up to 4500 r.p.m.

e) Set voltage regulator adjustment spring load by suitably bending the relevant adjusting arm and by rheostat R so as to have a voltage of 14.2 ± 0.3 V and half-load current of 8 ± 2 Amps.

f) Check steadiness and accuracy of voltage regulator setting by stopping the generator, starting it off again after a short while, and speeding up to 4500 r.p.m.

ELECTRICAL

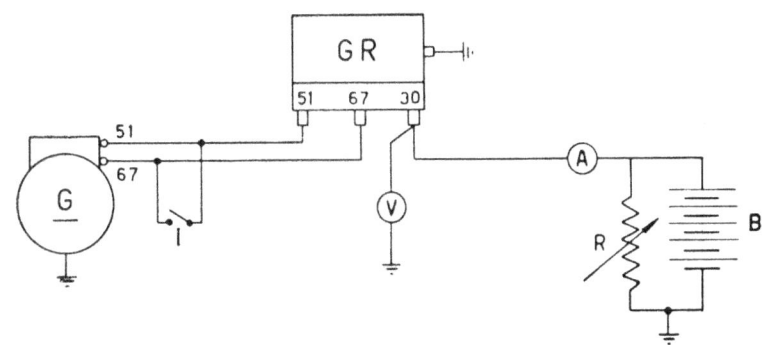

Fig. 352.
Wiring diagram for setting the voltage and current regulators.

GR. Regulator assembly GN 1/12/16. - G. Generator D 90/12/16/3. - V. Voltmeter, 20 V scale (0.5% accuracy). - A. Ammeter, 20 Amp. scale (for voltage regulator), or 40 Amp. scale (for current regulator). - R. Rheostat, 25 Amps., 3 Ohms. - B. 50 Amp/h battery, fully charged. - I. Switch.

Setting Current Regulator

(ambient temperature: $122° \pm 5°$ F [$50° \pm 3°$ C]).

To be performed immediately after adjusting voltage regulator, using the same wire diagram (fig. 352) and instruments, except ammeter, which should have a 40 A scale.

a) With the regulator in thermostat oven at $122° \pm 5°$ F ($50° \pm 3°$ C), close I, start the generator and set its speed and rheostat R for a 13 Volt tension and 16 ± 0.5 Ampere output.

b) Operate in above conditions for 30 minutes with the regulator at $122° \pm 5°$ F ($50° \pm 3°$ C), stop the generator and open I. Again run the generator at 4500 r.p.m.

c) Adjust the load of current regulator setting spring by bending the spring tab, and rheostat R, in order that regulated current and voltage are respectively 16 ± 0.5 Amperes and 13 Volts.

d) Check regulated current for stability and precision by stopping generator and running it again as hinted in step b).

GN 1/12/16 REGULATOR CHECKING AND SETTING DATA

(«New 500» starting from engine No. 056196)

Cutout Relay.	
Feed voltage for thermal stabilization:	
regulator initial { $59° - 68°$ F ($15° - 20°$ C)	16.5 V
operating temperature $68° - 95°$ F ($20° - 35°$ C)	15 V
Closing voltage	12.6 ± 0.2 V
Voltage-contact stroke variation: below	1 V/mm
Reverse current: up to and not above	16 Amps
Air gap (closed contacts)	.0138" (0,35 mm)
Point gap	$.0177" \pm .0023"$ ($0,45 \pm 0,06$ mm)
Voltage Regulator.	
Battery	50 A/h
Half-load current	8 ± 2 Amps
Setting voltage after thermal stabilization in oven at $122° \pm 5°$ F ($50° \pm 3°$ C) for 30 minutes, half-load on battery	14.2 ± 0.3 V
Feed voltage for thermal stabilization	15 V
Air gap	.0391" to .0437" (0,99 to 1,11 mm)
Current Regulator.	
Regulated current on battery	16 ± 0.5 Amps
Voltage for regulated current inspection	13 V
Air gap	.0391" to .0437" (0,99 to 1,11 mm)
Regulating Resistor	105 ± 3 Ω

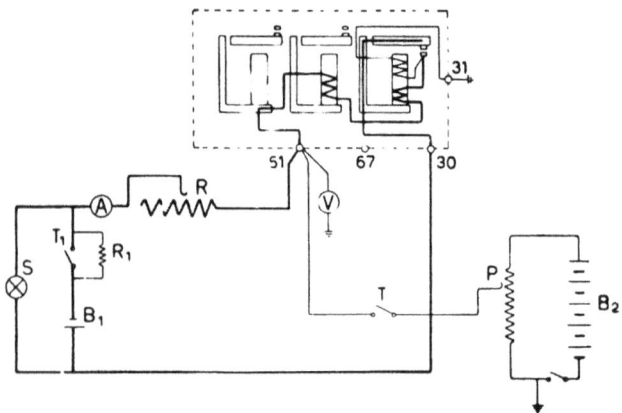

Fig. 353 - Wiring diagram for setting the cutout relay.
(A/4-180/12 regulator assembly).

B_1. 2 V battery. - B_2. 20 V battery. - A. Ammeter, 15 A scale (1% accuracy). - V. Voltmeter, 20 V scale (0.5% accuracy), directly connected to terminals 31-51. - P. Potentiometer for voltage adjustment, having such a capacity that the current draw of the cutout shunt winding does not cause sensible variations in the voltage readings (voltmeter under no load). - S. Test lamp, with 2 V, 3 W bulb, to signal opening and closing of contacts. - R. Rheostat, 4 Ω, 12 A. - R_1. Voltage drop rheostat, suitable to allow turning on of S with T_1 open and cutout contacts open.

Setting of instruments before inserting the unit:
P At minimum (Voltmeter reads zero). T. Open. - R. All inserted (max resistance). - T_1. Open.

OPERATION TEST AND SEALING

After the regulator has been set, close the assembly in a warm condition (see « Warning » below) by fitting cover and gasket, and check as outlined under « Bench Testing Instructions ». Next apply the paint seal.

WARNING

Whenever the unit has been opened and kept open for servicing, it must be operated for a while and the cover fitted only after a suitable warm up period.

Close cover carefully on warm unit and check that rubber gasket between cover and base is properly seated and ensures adequate sealing.

This eliminates the moisture usually deposited on windings and prevents the formation of moisture occurring when cover is applied on a cold unit. If any moisture is trapped in the unit, during operation when the unit is warm moisture will evaporate and deposit on armatures, thus causing highly detrimental oxidation of contacts.

A/4-180/12 REGULATOR CHECKING AND SETTING DATA

(« New 500 » up to engine No. 056195)

Cutout Relay.	
Feed voltage for thermal stabilization:	
regulator initial 59° - 68° F (15° - 20° C)	16.5 V
operating temperature 68° - 95° F (20° - 35° C)	15 V
Closing voltage	12.6 ± 0.2 V
Voltage-contact stroke variation: below	1 V/mm
Reverse current: up to and not above	10 Amps
Air gap (closed contacts)	.0138″ (0,35 mm)
Point gap	.0177″ ± .0023″ (0,45 ± 0,06 mm)
Voltage Regulator.	
Battery	50 A/h
Half-load current	6.5 ± 0.5 Amps
Setting voltage after thermal stabilization in oven at 122° ± 5° F (50° ± 3° C) for 30 minutes, half-load on battery	14.5 ± 0.3 V
Feed voltage for thermal stabilization	15 V
Air gap	.0391″ to .0437″ (0,99 to 1,11 mm)
Current Regulator.	
Regulated current on battery	13 ± 0.5 Amps
Air gap	.0391″ to .0437″ (0,99 to 1,11 mm)
Regulating Resistor	105 ± 3 Ω

STARTER

DESCRIPTION	page 227
OPERATION	» 227
BENCH TESTING INSTRUCTIONS	» 229
TROUBLE SHOOTING INSTRUCTIONS	» 230
SERVICING	» 234
SPECIFICATIONS	» 235

Description.

— Type . . . . FIAT B 76-0,5/12 S
— Tension . . . . 12 Volts
— Nominal power . . . . 0.5 kW
— Rotation (pinion end) . . . counterclockwise
— Pole shoes . . . . four
— Excitation . . . . series

The armature rotates on self-lubricating bronze bushes.

Heads are joined to frame by tie rods passing in the space between pole shoes.

Commutator and brushes may be reached after removing the cover band.

The switch is mounted on frame. As shown in diagram fig. 354, the stationary contact is directly connected to battery; the other contact is connected to one end of field winding, whose other end is wired to the positive brush.

The negative brush is grounded.

The two switch stationary contacts are electrically insulated from grounded parts and are interconnected by a movable contact only when starting control is actuated.

The switch may be inspected after removing the two mounting screws (fig. 365).

The overrunning clutch type drive unit consists of (figs. 355 and 356):

— a pinion, integral with overrunning clutch outer race;

— a hub carrying, on one end, four lugs alternated with four races which, through four rollers, drive the pinion along when the hub rotates in a given direction; the hub slides on armature shaft through a straight spline coupling;

— a sleeve sliding on the hub, and on which the forked lever works;

— a coil spring;

— a sleeve retainer pressed against the sleeve by said spring.

Operation.

When pulling the starter hand lever, through a flexible transmission this operates the lever controlling the pinion engagement with the flywheel.

During this stage two cases may occur:

1) The pinion tooth finds immediately the corresponding space between the ring gear teeth and, assisted by the chamfering provided on the edges, goes into mesh with ring gear. As the shift lever completes its travel, it closes the starter motor switch so that cranking takes place.

2) The pinion tooth finds, instead, a flywheel tooth and cannot mesh.

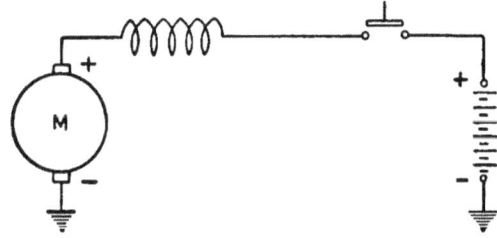

Fig. 354 - Operation diagram of starter B 76-0,5/12 S.

The shift lever, however, completes its travel since the sleeve slides on the hub and compresses the interposed spring.

Under these conditions, the spring, besides allowing the lever rotation, forces also the pinion against the flywheel.

As the lever completes its travel, its closes the starter switch contacts.

The starter is thrown into rotation, driving along the pinion which, forced by the spring, goes into mesh with the ring gear after completing a small angle.

As soon as the engine fires, the starter hand lever must be released.

STARTER B 76-0,5/12 S

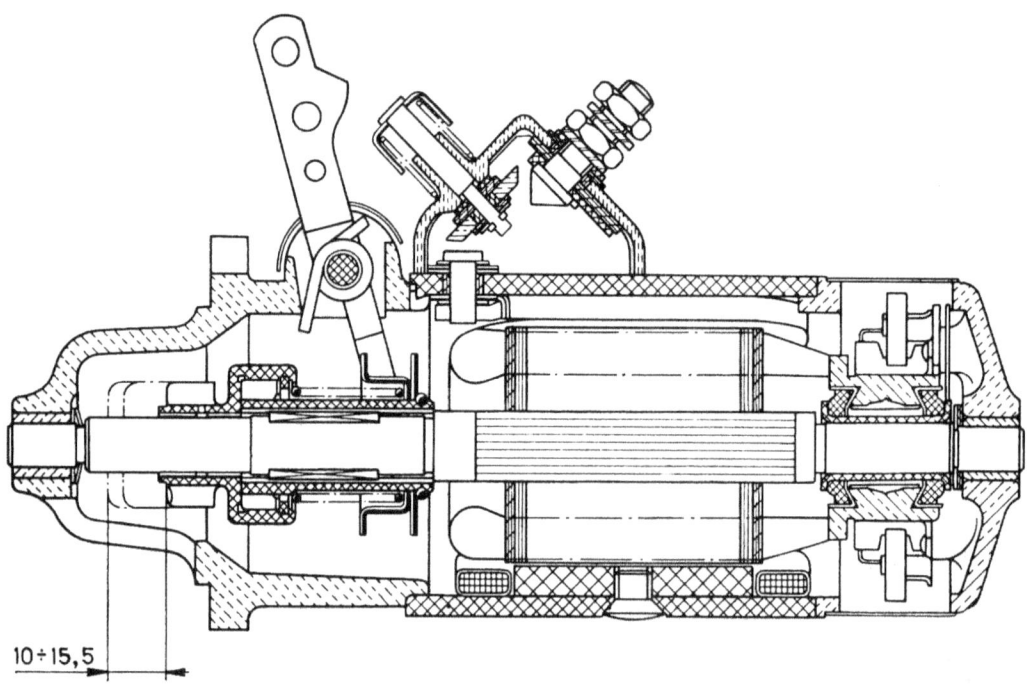

Fig. 355 - Starter assembly longitudinal section.

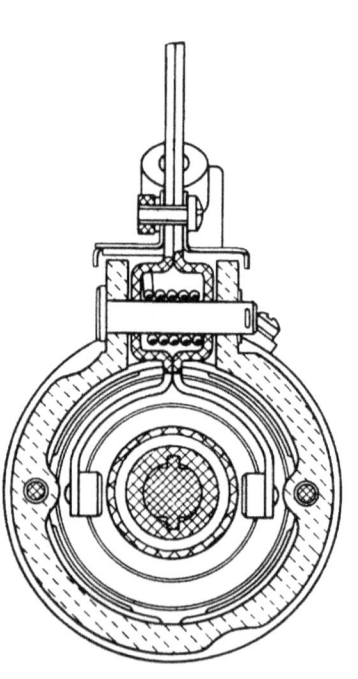

Fig. 356 - Cross section on drive unit.

Fig. 357 - Section through commutator end head, showing the brushes.

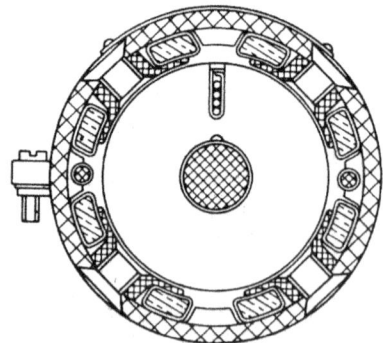

Fig. 358 - Section through pole shoes and armature winding.

ELECTRICAL

This action opens the starter switch contacts, the starter stops, and, under the return spring action, the pinion is unmeshed from ring gear.

Should the hand lever not be immediately released after the engine fires, owing to the high ratio between starter pinion and ring gear, the pinion, and hence the armature, would be spun at terrific speed, with consequent centrifugation of coils and commutator segments. This excessive speed, however, is prevented by the overrunning clutch of the drive unit which allows the pinion to be momentarily driven by the ring gear, while the armature, instead, runs at the normal « no load » speed.

Nevertheless, the engine should never be accelerated during starting, when the pinion is still engaged with the flywheel, to prevent an excessive strain on the overrunning clutch and a premature wear.

The characteristic curves of starter B 76-0,5/12 S are shown in fig. 359.

The performances represented by these curves are obtained using either the specified batteries in the required state of charge and temperature, or any other suitable direct current supply characterized by the voltage-current curve shown in fig. 359.

If the voltage-current characteristic differs, only the torque-current curve will not suffer consider-

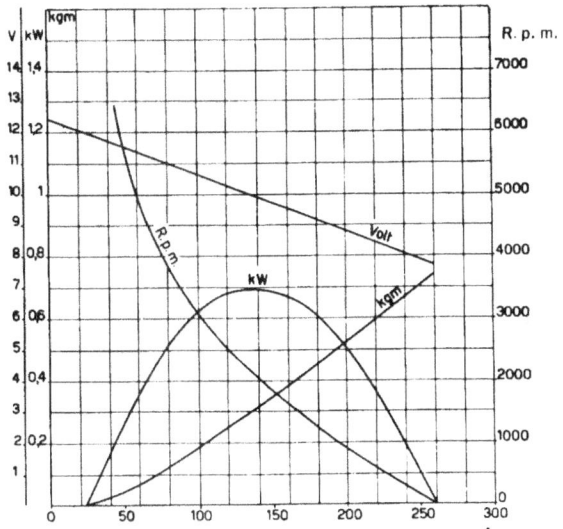

Fig. 359 - Characteristic curves of starter **FIAT B 76-0,5/12 S**. Readings at 68° F (20° C).

able variations, while, on the contrary, the speed will vary along with power and performance.

If a suitable means to obtain the required voltage-current characteristics is not available, the test should be limited to the torque-current curve. Even in this case, results will only be approximate.

BENCH TESTING INSTRUCTIONS

Check starter efficiency by carrying out the mechanical and electrical tests described below. Follow strictly the procedure outlined, making sure that all instruments and gauges are properly adjusted.

1. - Operation test.

Connect starter to a high capacity 12-V battery, so as to avoid current fluctuations during the test.

Adjust rheostat so that to prescribed current absorption there will correspond at starter terminals the exact voltage specified below. This is an essential condition to obtain reliable results which, otherwise, would be true only for the torque (and even in this instance only approximately).

Wire up as per diagram fig. 360.

Install starter on a bench provided with a ring gear (whose ratio to pinion is not less than 10 to 1) and a dynamometric brake. By pushing starter switch lever to travel end, carry out ten 4-second starts at intervals of 30 seconds.

Braking the motor when supplied with a 130 A, 10 V current, the torque should be 2.025 ± .144 ft.lbs (0,28 ± 0,02 kgm) at 2250 ± 100 r.p.m.

2. - Stall torque.

With the same wiring and installation layout described above, lock the ring gear and actuate starter lever. The starter should draw 258 A at a 7.7 ± 0.3 V current and give a 5.28 ± 0.4 ft.lbs (0,73 ± 0,05 kgmm) torque.

3. - No-load test.

Same wiring layout.

Move starter out from ring gear so that pinion

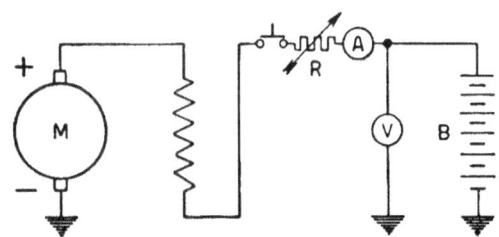

Fig. 360 - Wiring diagram for **B 76-0,5/12 S** starter operation test.

M. Starter. - V. Voltmeter, 15 V scale. - A. Ammeter, 350 Amp. scale. - B. Battery, 32 Ah, 12 V. - R. Rheostat, 200 Amp. capacity.

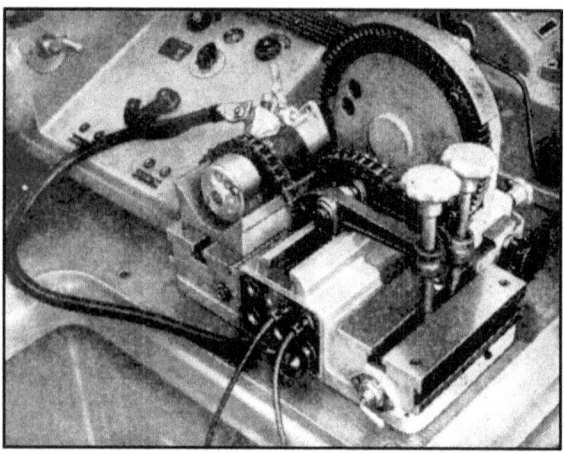

Fig. 361 - Brake test of starter.

cannot mesh even when travelling its full forward stroke.

Actuate starter lever.

With a 12 V current at terminals, the starter should draw no more than 30 Amperes and turn at 8500 ± 1000 r.p.m.

Ohmic Resistance Test.

From the data obtained during the **stall torque test** and by computing the ratio of voltage to drawn current, the starter internal resistance may be directly determined. Its value, with starter at 68° F (20° C), must be 0.03 ± 0.001 Ω.

Mechanical Characteristics Check Data.

1) Brush hold down springs load must be (with new brushes) 2.5 to 2.9 lbs (1,15 to 1,3 kg).

2) Armature shaft axial play must be .0059" to .0256" (0,15 to 0,65 mm).

3) Commutator mica must be undercut at least .04" (1 mm) throughout its entire length and width.

4) The efficiency of drive unit free wheel must be such that the static torque required to rotate the pinion slowly is not greater than .35 in.lbs (0,4 kgcm).

TROUBLE SHOOTING

Operation troubles in starting system may originate from:

— starter;
— other components of system.

First locate the source of trouble, then inspect the starter. Possible troubles are:

1. - On pulling the hand lever, starter fails to function. Causes:

   1.1. Oxidized battery terminals and clamps.
   1.2. Loose starter switch or battery clamps.
   1.3. Dead battery.
   1.4. Excessively worn brushes which do not contact commutator.
   1.5. Starter switch contacts heavily oxidized, worn or insulated by foreign matter.
   1.6. Grounded field or armature windings.
   1.7. Thrown armature or commutator.

2. - On pulling the hand lever, starter rotates very slowly. This trouble is also revealed by a characteristic noise.

   Causes:

   2.1. Worn brushes not contacting commutator.
   2.2. Field or armature windings partially grounded.
   2.3. Oxidized battery terminals and clamps.
   2.4. Loose starter switch or battery clamps.
   2.5. Battery barely operative or with one or more cells damaged (short circuited, sulphated, no longer capable of retaining the charge, etc.).

3. - On pulling the hand lever, starter runs regularly but develops unusual noises.

   Causes:

   3.1. Self-lubricating bushes of both armature and pinion excessively worn.
   3.2. Pinion that does not unmesh from ring gear soon after releasing starter lever.
   3.3. Oxidation of drive unit, particularly of the collar on which the forked lever works, causing the axial displacement of drive unit.

TROUBLE SHOOTING HINTS

4.1. Should conditions under point 1. occur, inspect the system, including battery and starter, so as to single out the faulty component by process of elimination.

4.1.1. First inspect battery posts and clamps (point 1.1) for oxidation. Check that they are evenly coated with pure ropy vaseline. The coating must be renewed at regular intervals. If posts and clamps are oxidized, remove clamps (using exclusively a wrench and, if required, a puller; never pliers or other tools that might damage irreparably the battery). Wipe clean both the posts and the clamps.

Refit and tighten clamps and coat with pure ropy vaseline.

4.1.2. If terminals are not oxidized, check clamp tightening (point 1.2) on both battery and starter.

4.1.3. If connections are found in order, check state of battery charge (point 1.3), using a hydrometer. If electrolyte density is found very low (1.16 or even less), the cause for starter failure is in the battery.

Note, however, that the total battery discharge originates from a faulty insulation at some point which grounds the system. In this case look for the dispersion point which might be located in cables, users, or even within the battery cells.

Though less likely, the trouble may be attributed to the recharging system that may be inspected as directed in the relevant Chapter.

Changing or recharging the battery without locating the discharging cause would be useless.

4.1.4. If inspections relevant to points 1.1, 1.2, 1.3, have unearthed no irregularities, the starter is at fault.

Remove it from car and inspect all its components carefully.

4.1.5. Lack of contact between brushes and commutator due to brush wear (see 1.4) is normal if it occurs after a long period of starter operation.

At maximum starter power, with fully charged battery and normal temperature, brushes may withstand nearly 5000 starts of 2 seconds each before wearing out.

The above conditions, however, are much more severe than those of actual operation, since four or more times the number of starts are actually obtained during normal car service.

In terms of mileage, the life of brushes depends on the type of service in which the vehicle is used. In any case, even with very frequent starts, brushes last for more than 18,000 miles (30.000 km).

If wear is abnormal, it may be due to the causes stated in point 5.3.3. After determining that this is the origin of starter failure, replace brushes.

Note, however, that the commutator may also have suffered damages and must be inspected very carefully.

If wear is normal, commutator may be trimmed by a simple re-turning followed by proper undercutting of the mica (fig. 362). If, instead, wear is abnormal and damages as those quoted under 5.3.2 have been induced, replace the armature.

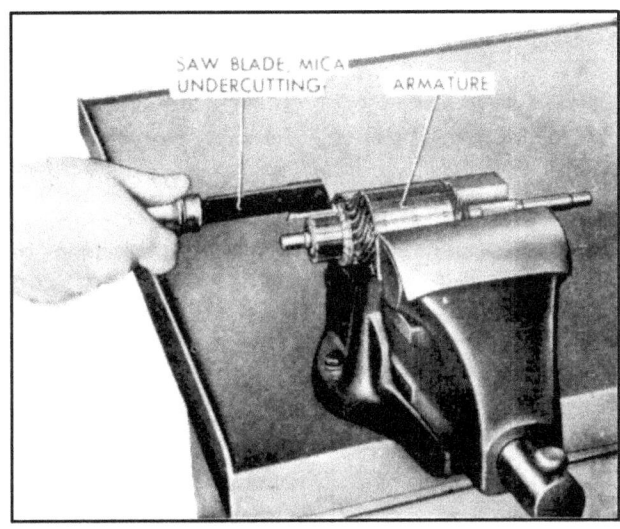

Fig 362 Undercutting insulating mica between starting motor armature segments

4.1.6. After checking that both brushes and commutator are in good condition, inspect starter switch (point 1.5) which may show:

a) **Oxidized contacts**. - It may happen that on account of short circuited coils in the starter windings, the current draw exceeds given values with an ensuing overheating and/or charring of contacts. Reconditioning of contacts is not sufficient to restore starter efficiency. Therefore, inspect the starter to single out the cause of contact oxidation.

b) **Too much worn contacts**. - Remove and replace the switch.

c) **Presence of insulating particles between stationary and movable contacts**. - Disassemble switch and clean contacts.

4.1.7. Possible grounding of field and/or armature windings (point 1.6).

If this trouble is present when the switch is closed, a strong current flow towards ground will occur with considerable risk of damaging switch contacts and cables.

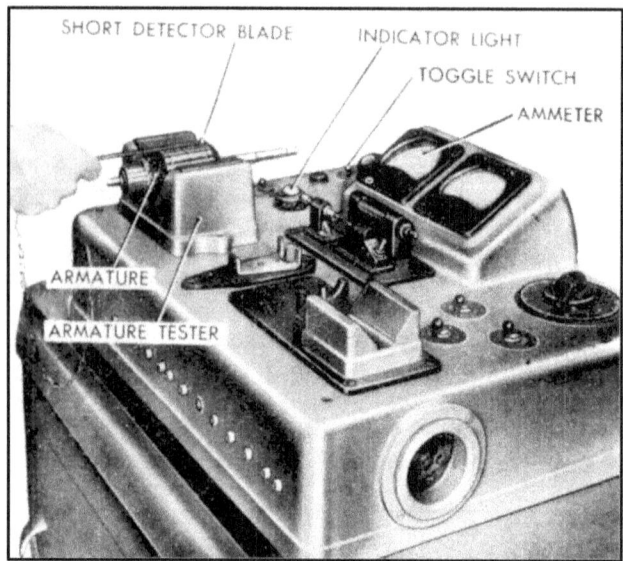

Fig. 363 - Using a blade to test the starter armature on bench.

The blade vibrates when contacting a shorted coil.

Disassemble starter. The grounded point will be readily identified by blackened insulations. If grounding is in the armature, the commutator segments connected to the grounded coils will also be badly damaged.

Replace faulty parts.

4.1.8. Thrown armature (1.7) or commutator. Causes may be:

a) Seizing of overrunning clutch.

b) Loosening of slot stopping wedges or of commutator segments under combined action of centrifugal force and heating-and-cooling cycles.

Trouble b) is normally due to trouble a), but sometimes originates from erroneous starting maneuvers.

During manufacture overrunning clutches are submitted to the static sliding torque, whose value must not exceed .35 in .lbs (0,4 kgcm), as specified under « Mechanical Characteristics Check Data », point 4 (page 230).

The overrunning clutch may be damaged, however, by the following erroneous starting maneuvers:

i) too long meshing of pinion with ring gear after engine has started;

ii) speeding up of the engine before starter control hand lever is released;

iii) defective operation of starting control, such as: seizing of bowden, of tie rod or of levers, weakened springs, etc.

If maneuvers i) and ii) are repeated a number of times, the overrunning clutch overheats, the grease is quickly burnt, rollers and plungers wear, and finally, the whole drive unit seizes.

Under these conditions the pinion can no longer free-wheel and therefore drives along the armature at such a high speed that coils and commutator will be thrown.

This trouble, however, can be prevented if drive units are inspected and overhauled when servicing the starter.

As for loose and missing commutator segments, see point 5.3.2. for probable causes.

4.2. In case trouble 2 occurs, look for the source by following the procedure outlined under 4.1.

4.2.1. For causes indicated under 2.3 and 2.4, see respectively 4.1.1 and 4.1.2.

4.2.2. After ascertaining that connections are in order, check battery and its state of charge (point 2.5).

If electrolyte density is less than 1.22, the battery is 50% discharged and must be recharged.

The battery may have one or more cells damaged, shorted or sulphated, so that it can no longer retain the charge.

Battery must be replaced.

4.2.3. If nothing abnormal is found relevant to 2.3, 2.4, 2.5, the source must be looked for exclusively in the starter according to the following procedure:

4.2.4. Brush wear (point 2.1): see point 4.1.5.

4.2.5. If brushes and commutator are in good condition, inspect armature and field windings (point 2.2), which may have some shorted coils.

By reducing the number of useful coils, the short circuit in armature winding brings about a reduction in starter power. Furthermore, by causing commutation troubles in correspondence with segments connected to shorted coils, the shorting stresses brush wear owing to both the worsened commutations and the damage on commutator (sinking) in correspondence with said segments.

An armature tester may be used to locate shorted coils, though its accuracy does not exceed two shorted coils. More accurate readings may be obtained by using high-frequency detectors in conjunction with a voltmeter connected across segments.

Should the field winding have one or more shorted coils, the starter power would also be noticeably reduced.

Accurate determinations are possible only by removing the field winding and measuring its electrical characteristics with a high-frequency instrument.

4.3. If trouble under point 3 occurs, no check of electric system is required. Possible causes must be looked for in the starter, proceeding as follows:

4.3.1. Remove starter from car and inspect the drive unit and related parts. If the drive unit

ELECTRICAL

or the collar (on which the engagement fork acts) are found oxidized (3.3), lubricate thoroughly with FIAT Jota 2/M grease.

4.3.2. If engagement unit is in working order, check bushes for excessive wear. These bushes are of self-lubricating bronze and require special equipment for press fitting in their seats.

4.3.3. If troubles described in 3.1 and 3.3 are not present, noisiness should be attributed to the faulty operation of the drive unit engagement control (see 3.2).

First, lubricate the splined coupling and the pins of control levers. Check for weakened or oxidized return springs of both switch and levers.

When reinstalling starter on car, check that starting control bowden does not bind in its sheath (due to kinks, twisting, etc.), that it is adequately lubricated and, finally, that when at rest it allows the pinion to clear the flywheel ring gear.

If the bowden is damaged, replace.

5. - Some of the troubles described above cannot be easily detected when starter is installed on car but may be revealed by:

— the operation tests described previously;
— the inspection of starter inner components.

Such troubles may be traced to:

5.1. Poor commutation, accompanied by an excessive brush wear with respect to the period and type of car service.

Possible causes:

5.1.1. Shorted armature winding coils.

5.1.2. Loose commutator segments.

5.1.3. Incorrect grade brushes.

5.2. Reduction in the torque and power developed by the motor.

Possible causes:

5.2.1. Shorted field winding coils.

5.2.2. Shorted armature winding coils.

5.3. If trouble indicated under 5.1. occurs, detect its source as follows:

5.3.1. Check shorted coils (5.1.1) as described in 4.2.5.

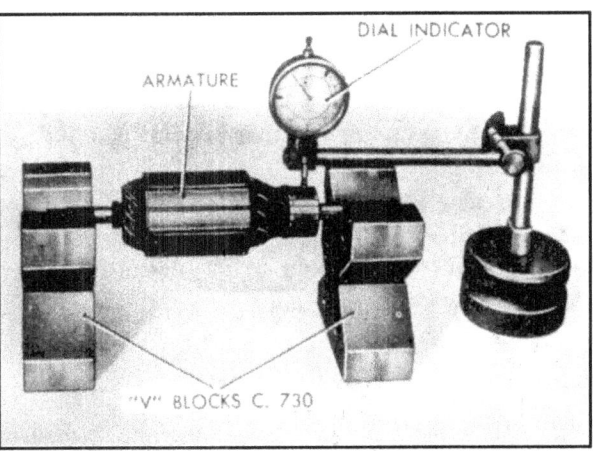

Fig. 364 - Checking starting motor armature commutator for out-of-round.
Run-out should not exceed .00039'' (0,01 mm).

5.3.2. If armature winding is found in order, check commutator.

The defect mentioned in 5.1.2 is normally due to some segments having worked loose under the combined action of centrifugal force and heating-and-cooling cycles. Segments are displaced radially, and protruding beyond the commutator surface, cause an imperfect contact of brushes (which cannot follow the commutator irregularities because of inertia) with consequent heavy arcing. Furthermore, this actually mills the brushes.

In some cases, conditions may be so bad that a loose segment is dislodged by striking against the brushes.

The defect may be easily detected with a dial indicator as follows:

Fix the starter firmly. Rest the dial indicator plunger on the commutator surface not rubbed by brushes, and by rotating the armature slowly, determine the maximum out-of-round points and their location (fig. 364).

If segments are properly seated, out-of-round must not exceed .00039'' (0,01 mm).

5.3.3. If commutator is found undamaged, check brushes. They should be standard FIAT parts.

6. - If trouble corresponds to 5.2.1 or 5.2.2, follow the procedure described under 4.2.5.

STARTER SERVICING

1. - The only repairs that may be carried out by Service Stations are:

— commutator re-turning;
— repairs to field winding connections damaged in insulation, broken or unsoldered.

2. - Any other part must be replaced.

Commutator Re-Turning.

For this operation install on lathe the armature, having care that it rotates on its own shaft axis, so that shaft out-of-round does not add to commutator out-of-round.

Brush Replacement.

Take off cover band and remove old brushes. Fit original FIAT brushes whose hardness and composition is such as to ensure best performance of starter and long life of commutator.

Removal of Armature Assembly.

Remove cover band. Lift brush hold-down springs and take off commutator end head.

Slide off armature assembly from drive unit and from pole shoes. If inspection shows that armature is efficient, re-install the latter by reversing the removal operations.

Before re-installation blow clean the armature, the drive end head and the frame; lubricate the armature shaft splined end with FIAT Jota 2/M grease and wipe well the commutator with a clean cloth free of grease, gasoline or other substances.

Replacing Drive Unit.

Take off armature as described before. Remove drive end head and then withdraw the drive unit from the head by rotating the lever as far as it will go.

Before reassembling the drive unit, lubricate its components with FIAT Jota 2/M grease.

Replacing Starter Switch.

Take off switch by removing the two mounting screws. Install a new switch being careful to tighten well the field winding terminal clamping nuts.

Replacing Field Winding.

Remove armature from frame, free pole shoes by slackening their mounting screws and take off field winding. Heat new winding to 122° F (50° C) to render it slightly flexible, thus facilitating its seating under pole shoes.

Pole shoes must be correctly seated on frame by tightening their mounting screws until the original air gap is restored.

After reassembly check that pole shoe inner diameter is 2.0697" to 2.0768" (52,57 to 52,75 mm).

If diameter departs from the above figures, it is an indication that assembly is incorrect.

In this case, the whole operation must be repeated.

Never ream pole shoes to obtain correct diameter.

Check also that armature diameter is 2.0394" to 2.0413" (51,80 to 51,85 mm).

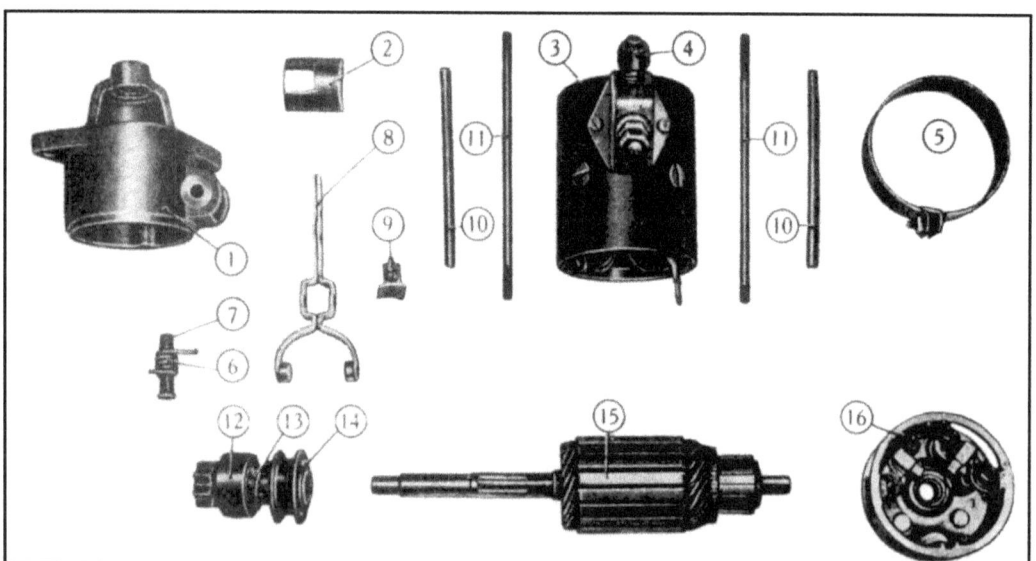

Fig. 365.

Components of starter.

1. Drive end head. - 2. Head shield. - 3. Frame. - 4. Switch. - 5. Commutator cover band. - 6 and 7. Pin and spring for lever 8. - 8. Starting engagement lever. - 9. Head shield. - 10 and 11. Head fixing tie rods and tubes. - 12. Pinion, complete. - 13. Starting engagement spring. - 14. Drive unit sleeve and free wheel hub. - 15. Armature. - 16. Commutator end head.

ELECTRICAL

STARTER MOTOR SPECIFICATIONS

Type	B 76-0,5/12 S
Voltage	12 V
Nominal power	0.5 kW
Rotation (pinion end)	counterclockwise
Pole shoes	4
Field winding	in series
Engagement	by free wheel
Mechanical Data.	
— Pole shoes I.D.	2.0697 to 2.0768 in. (52,57 to 52,75 mm)
— Armature diameter	2.0394 to 2.0413 in. (51,80 to 51,85 mm)
— Part No. of brushes	805581
Bench Test Data.	
— Operation test at 68° F (20° C):	
Current	130 Amp
Torque developed	2 ± .14 ft.lbs (0,28 ± 0,02 kgm)
Speed	2250 ± 100 r.p.m.
Tension	10 Volts
— Stall torque at 68° F (20° C):	
Current	258 Amp
Tension	7.7 ± 0.3 Volts
Torque developed	5.3 ± .36 ft.lbs (0,73 ± 0,05 kgm)
— No-load test:	
Current, up to and not above	30 Amp
Tension	12 Volts
Speed	8500 ± 1000 r.p.m.
— Ohmic resistance during stall torque test, at 68° F (20° C)	0.03 ± 0.001 Ω
Mechanical Characteristics Test.	
Load of spring on new brushes	2.5 to 2.9 lbs (1,15 to 1,30 kg)
— Armature shaft axial play	.0059" to .0256" (0,15 to 0,65 mm)
— Mica undercut depth, up to and not above	.04" (1 mm)
— Drive unit free wheel efficiency: static torque required to rotate pinion slowly, up to and not above	.35 in. lbs (0,4 kgcm)
Lubrication.	
— Drive unit splines	FIAT Jota 2/M grease
— Sleeve-to-engagement lever surfaces	FIAT Jota 2/M grease

IGNITION SYSTEM

DESCRIPTION	page 236
OPERATION	» 236
DISTRIBUTOR	» 236
COIL	» 240
SPARK PLUGS	» 241
TIMING	» 242
IGNITION SYSTEM SPECIFICATIONS	» 243

Description.

The ignition system consists of:

— ignition coil;

— ignition distributor with breaker, centrifugal automatic advance and condenser;

— low and high tension wiring;

— spark plugs;

— a power supply provided by generator-and-battery.

The system is subdivided into two circuits:

— **the low tension circuit** or primary circuit, which includes: the power supply, breaker, condenser and ignition coil primary winding;

— **the high tension circuit** or secondary circuit, which includes: the ignition coil secondary winding, distributor rotor, distributor cap with terminals and central brush, high tension cables and spark plugs.

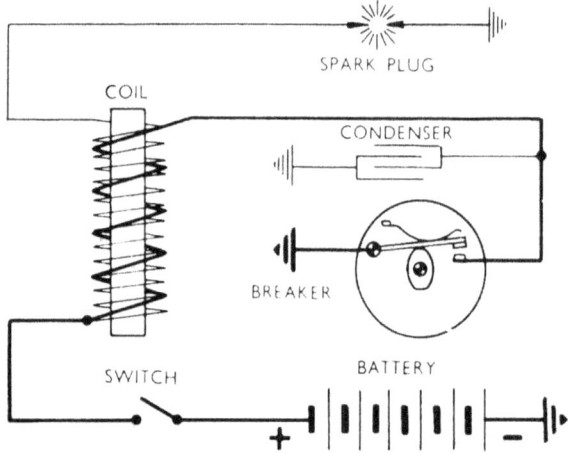

Fig. 366 - Ignition system wiring diagram.

Operation.

The circuit breaker in the distributor interrupts the primary circuit by opening the contacts.

The current flow, broken in the primary winding, does not arc the contact gap because it discharges into the condenser which is connected in parallel to contacts.

Thus, the primary current flow instantly collapses, producing a sudden drop of intensity in the magnetic field.

This collapse induces a voltage surge in the ignition coil secondary winding.

The high e. m. f. is distributed to spark plugs (in firing sequence) by the ignition distributor rotor.

IGNITION DISTRIBUTOR

The automatic advance device, the low-tension circuit breaker, condenser and rotor are all incorporated in this unit.

The automatic advance device consists of a plate carrying two weights, symmetrically hinged on plate at one end, articulated on cam carrier shaft and provided with return springs.

Due to the action of centrifugal force, a more or less high rotational speed moves the weights outwards. Since weights pivot on cam carrier

ELECTRICAL

shaft, the latter moves angularly, resulting in a rotation of cams with respect to distributor drive shaft.

The breaker consists of the cam on drive shaft and of two contacts, one of which is stationary while the other rotates with breaker arm and is provided with rubbing block.

The cam has two lobes to control the opening and closing of contact points. The stationary contact is mounted on an adjustable support to make possible the adjustment of contact gap.

From the ignition coil, the H. T. current reaches the distributor cap central terminal, and through the rotor (which may be considered as a revolving contactor), it is distributed to each of the spark plugs in turn.

Checking the Distributor on Test Bench.

1. - Operation test.

Install distributor on tester and connect it to the variable-speed motor. Wire to an ignition coil and a battery, and connect the two peripheral cap terminals to two terminals of an adjustable point gap spark tester.

Rotate distributor for some minutes in the prescribed direction at a speed of about 2000 r. p. m., keeping the spark tester point gap at 3/16″ (5 mm).

Then, widen gap to 3/8″ (10 mm) and check if any sparking takes place in distributor.

Aside from the particular noise produced, such sparks are revealed either by a drop in intensity or a total lack of one or more sparks at the tester.

2. - Checking the automatic advance curve.

Install distributor on tester and connect to ignition coil, motor and battery as outlined in point 1.

Then, with a jumper, connect one cap terminal to the stroboscope on test bench.

Operate the distributor at a speed of 300 to 400 r. p. m. and, by means of the stroboscope, record the value in degrees at which the spark is induced. Increase distributor r. p. m. and take a second stroboscope reading.

If the increase in r. p. m. is very slight in comparison to that of the preceding test, the stroboscope reading will be the same. Continue to increase the rotational speed and take new readings at every 200 to 300 r. p. m. increment.

The difference between the values now recorded and the previous ones (which were constant) will give in degrees the distributor spark advance.

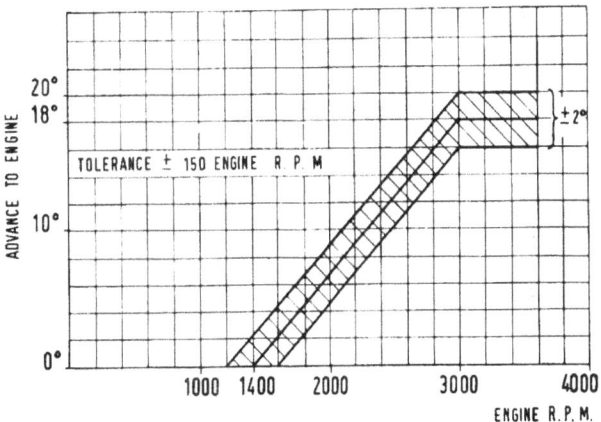

Fig. 367 - Ignition distributor centrifugal advance variations.

Since the distributor rotational speed is half that of engine, the values obtained must be doubled (both the r. p. m. and advance in degrees) to properly plot the diagram of distributor automatic advance-versus-engine and to compare it with figure 367.

It may be gathered from this diagram that maximum angling of centrifugal automatic advance, as referred to engine speed, is 18°±2°.

On « 500 Sports » engine, centrifugal automatic advance is 12°±2° at 4,600 engine r. p. m.

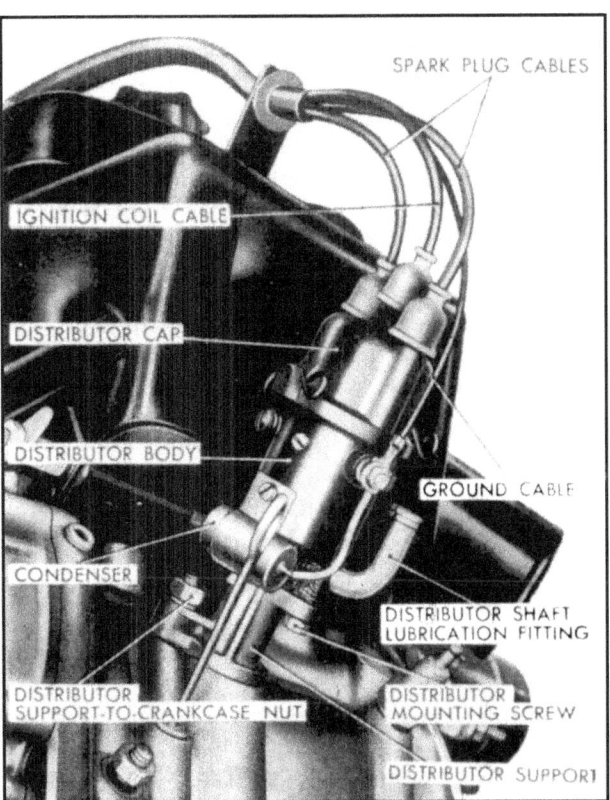

Fig. 368 - Ignition distributor in place on engine.

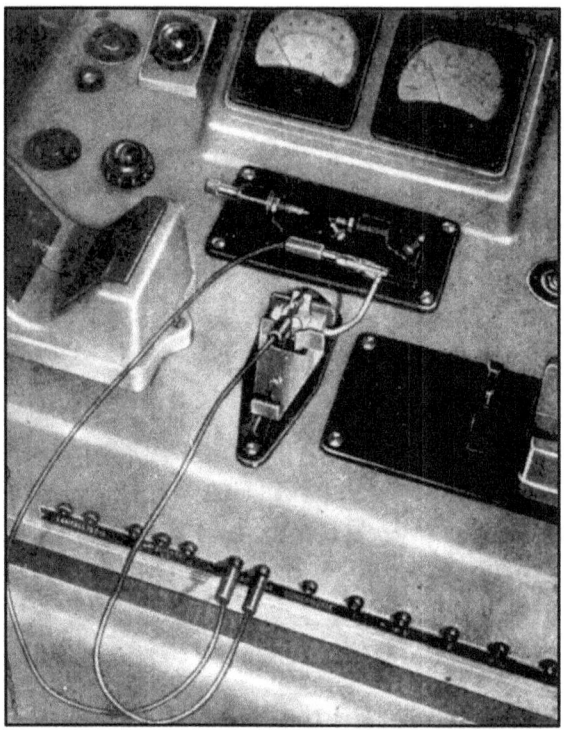

Fig. 369 - Checking a condenser on bench.

3. - Checking the timing.

Install distributor on test bench and remove cap.

Wire to an ignition coil and battery, and insert an ammeter or a test lamp in the primary circuit.

Manually operate the distributor in the specified direction, and on the graduated disc of the stroboscope - in correspondence with the timing mark - read the value in degrees at the instant the contacts snap open.

This instant is revealed by the return to zero of the ammeter needle or by the test lamp going out. Keep rotating the distributor in the same direction until the ammeter needle moves away from zero (the ammeter follows the value of primary current), or the lamp lights up again, indicating that contacts have closed.

At this precise moment, record the value in degrees read in correspondence with the timing mark.

Continue the rotation of distributor and record the new value corresponding to the new re-opening of contacts (lamp goes out or ammeter needle returns to zero).

The difference between the second value and the first one, represents the closing angle value; instead, the difference between the third and the second, is the opening angle magnitude.

These two angles should total 180°±1°.

4. - Checking the breaker contact points opening-closing rate.

Proceed as described for timing in point 3, with the exception that in this case the test must start from the closing position (ammeter registers the primary current or lamp is on).

Then, measure the closing and opening angles which must be, respectively, 78°±3° and 102°±3°.

5. - Checking distributor noises.

No matter at what speed the car is driven, the distributor should not be noisy.

Generally, the presence of marked noises can be attributed to the following sources:

a) contact points pressure lower than 16.75± 1.8 oz (475±50 gr);

b) excessive play between rotor shaft and shaft seat;

c) weakened weight springs.

Trouble a) will also account for a difficult ignition at high speeds.

Instead, higher contact point pressure values will result in a marked wear of contacts, cam and movable contact rubbing block.

In case c) also a consequent alteration in automatic advance will be present and ignition will be advanced on specified r. p. m. rate.

6. - Checking mechanical components.

Contacts should be checked for pitting oxidation and charring.

Ascertain that rotor, cap stationary contacts, H. T. central brush are not worn by more than .0118" (0,3 mm).

Check breaker arm rubbing block. Its wear must not be such as to upset breaker timing by more than 2° with respect to ignition distributor setting.

Using feeler **A. 95117**, check also that contact gap is .0185" to .0209" (0,47 to 0,53 mm) and contact points pressure 16.75±1.8 oz (475±50 gr).

7. - Checking the condenser.

Condenser capacity - measured at a frequency ranging from 50 to 100 Hz. - should be from 0.15 to 0.20 μF.

TROUBLE SHOOTING INSTRUCTIONS

Ignition Failing or Completely Absent.

Possible causes:

a) **Condenser shorted or with low-insulation resistance.**

Voltage built up in the secondary circuit is insufficient to produce sparks, or sparking is poor.

b) **Defective distributor cap (cracks, carbonized inner surface or deposited moisture).**

In this case, current leaks to ground along cracks, burnt paths and moisture.

c) **Cracks, carbon or moisture traces on rotor plastic portion.**

Leaks occur as described in b).

d) **Distributor cap central brush worn or broken, brush spring deformed or burnt.**

Arcing occurs between rotor and central brush, with consequent voltage drop and low tension at spark plug electrodes.

e) **Build-up and pitting on contact points.**

Generally, this is caused by contact points gap being less than specified, due to wear of breaker arm contact carrier lever rubbing block.

Since build-up causes improper opening of primary circuit, the secondary circuit will supply an inefficient spark.

f) **Burnt or oxidized contact points.**

Possible causes:

— excessive resistance in condenser circuit, caused by improper connections or broken cables. In turn, this accounts for poor ignition both when starting or at high speeds;

— oiled or soiled contact surfaces;

— (less frequently) too high setting of regulator (much above max. allowable rate).

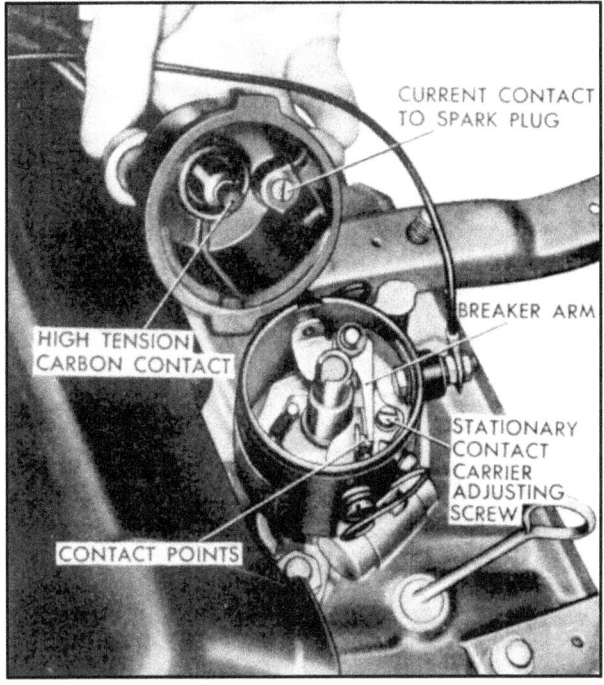

Fig. 370 - Ignition distributor in place on engine with cap lifted out.

The oxidation or burning of contacts determines a high resistance between contact points and hence permanently cuts out the primary circuit with consequent exclusion of the ignition system.

g) **Excessive contact opening.**

The spark is weak, particularly at high speeds, since the closing time of contacts is too brief and the primary current cannot reach the value required for proper operation in such a short interval.

Extremely Advanced Ignition.

This is generally caused by weakened centrifugal weight springs.

INSPECTION AND REPAIR

Replace distributor caps which are cracked or have traces of carbon.

Cap terminals, rotor and breaker contacts (when oxidized, corroded or burnt) can be cleaned with a fine-cut file. Never use emery cloth in these cases.

When terminal and rotor wear exceeds .0118" (0,3 mm), rotor and distributor cap must be replaced.

Also, replace the breaker arm if the rubbing block turns out to be excessively worn. The breaker arm should be replaced by a new one, moreover, when points are worn to such an extent as the gap exceeds the last setting limit of .0209" (0,53 mm), so that the adjustment through the stationary contact carrier screw (fig. 370) is no longer possible.

To adjust the point gap, loosen the stationary contact carrier adjusting screw and move the contact carrier in or out, as required. After the adjustment has been made, use a feeler gauge and check if point gap is within recommended values (.0185" to .0209" - 0,47 to 0,53 mm). Again tighten the contact carrier screw.

If distributor drive shaft play is excessive, replace the ignition distributor.

Weak centrifugal weight springs must be replaced with original spares. When servicing or inspecting the ignition distributor, add **FIAT VS** oil in the oiler wick. With this same oil, wet the cam carrier shaft felt.

IGNITION COIL

The ignition coil consists of a soft iron core around which both primary and secondary windings are wound. These two windings are embedded in insulating compound. The unit is housed in a metal casing provided with a bakelite insulating cap for winding end outlets.

On the coil cap are found two side terminals and a central terminal. The two side terminals constitute the primary winding inlet and outlet, while the central terminal is for secondary winding outlet.

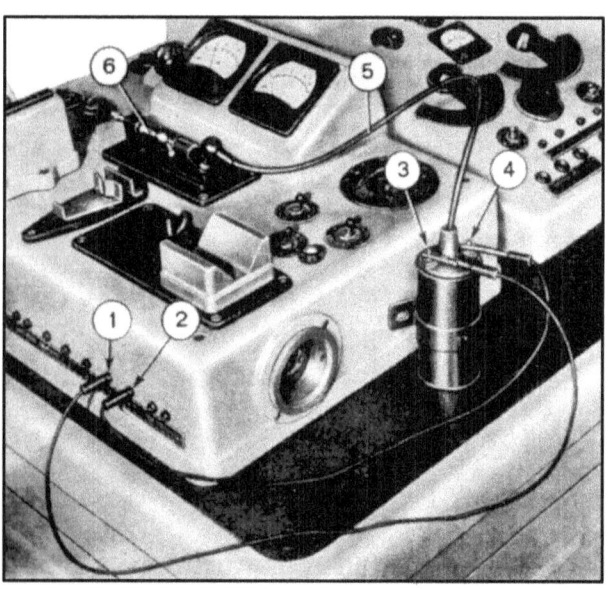

Fig. 371 - Checking an ignition coil on test bench.
1. Breaker. - 2. 12-Volt power socket. - 3. Low tension cable terminal. - 4. Power cord terminal. - 5. High tension cable. - 6. Spark issuing between tester points.

Bench Testing Instructions.

Proceed as follows to check ignition coil efficiency:

1. - Ohmic resistances.

The ohmic resistance of the primary circuit at 68°±9° F (20°±5° C) must not be lower than 3.2 Ohms.

Secondary circuit resistance must instead be 5000±100 Ohms.

2. - Grounding insulation.

Ignition coil must withstand without any sparking, an alternate tension of 500 V r. m. s., 50 Hz, applied for three minutes between one end of the primary winding and the metal casing.

3. - Measuring spark length.

Run the ignition coil with the distributor without using H. T. distribution, and send all sparks to a standard ionising point spark tester for measurement of maximum spark length (see fig. 371).

After the coil has been operating for approximately one hour at a 450 to 500 r. p. m. and is warm, spark length at 12 Volts should be at least 15/32" (12 mm).

4. - Test with shunted spark tester.

Insert a 1 MΩ resistance in parallel with spark tester.

Under these conditions, spark length should not be less than 3/4 the length of the spark obtained in the previous test.

5. - Over-voltage test.

Feed the ignition coil with a 17 V battery at 60 sparks per second, connecting the H.T. lead directly to spark tester with 5/16" (8 mm) spark gap adjustment.

The coil must withstand this test without damage for 15 minutes.

Trouble Shooting and Servicing Instructions.

Possible ignition coil defects are:

a) Open circuits - check this by a simple circuit tester (test lamp, bell tester, etc.).

b) Shorted inner winding turns - check this by measuring the circuit resistance (provided a great number of turns are shorted).

c) Insulating compound squeezed out: this may affect coil insulation.

d) Water leaking in through a defective seal; check this by measuring ground insulation.

e) Loose or dirty connections.

Only in case e) can ignition coil be restored to proper efficiency. In all other cases, coil must be replaced.

SPARK PLUGS

Technical Data.

Thread (metric) . . . . 14 × 1,25 mm

Mark { Model « 500 » . . . . CW 225 N
{ Model « 500 Sports » . CW 250 A

Electrode gap .0197" to .0236" (0,5 to 0,6 mm)

The ceramic insulation consists of a special material (pink colored and called « Sintal ») particularly suitable for this type of spark plugs.

NOTE - Vehicles for export to U.S.A. and Canada are equipped with the following spark plugs:
— Thread (metric): 14 x 1,25;
— Mark: L 7 (Champion);
— Gap: .0236" to .0276" (0,6 to 0,7 mm).

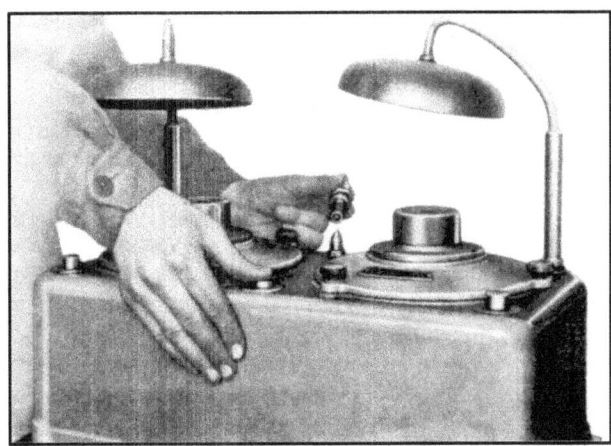

Fig. 373 - Blowing a spark plug after sanding and washing.

Inspection and Repair.

Should ignition troubles and misfiring occur in one or both cylinders, check spark plug condition.

For a perfect cleaning of spark plugs, use the proper Service Center where the spark plug is

Fig. 372 - Sanding a spark plug.
The spark plug is washed in the device to the right.

first sanded (fig. 372), then washed by gasoline under pressure and, finally, blown dry (fig. 373).

Check electrode gap and adjust to .0197" to .0236" (0,5 to 0,6 mm).

To adjust the gap, bend the outer electrode towards the central one; never try to move the central electrode towards the outer one, since this would break the porcelain, with consequent failure of spark plug.

If the porcelain appears black and coated with carbon deposits, pour some alcohol or gasoline in the capsized spark plug and after a while scrub with a wire brush.

After these operations, check spark plugs for gas tightness.

To remove and install plugs on engine, use wrench A. 50022.

Tightness Test.

The tightness test of the parts which compose a spark plug, that is insulator body and center electrode, is made on test bench as shown in fig. 374.

Screw the spark plug on to the Service Center seat, then operate the manual pump lever until a 284 to 356 p.s.i. (20 to 25 kg/cm^2) pressure is obtained.

Fig. 374 - Testing a spark plug for gas tightness.

Using a distributor, pour some drops of oil or kerosene on spark plug (fig. 374).

In the plug is leaky, oil or kerosene will bubble out, most likely between the insulator and metal body.

Electrical Test.

Screw the spark plug, without copper seal, on to the Service Center seat; tightness is assured by the connection seal on seat.

Adjust the tester spark meter point gap at 5/16" (8 mm), then operate the manual pump lever. Take care to push the lever all the way down each time, to have the pressure gauge dial read as tabulated hereafter:

Tester spark meter point gap		Spark plug gap		Tester cell pressure reading					
				Very good plug		Good plug		Faulty plug	
in	mm	in	mm	p.s.i.	kg/cm²	p.s.i.	kg/cm²	p.s.i.	kg/cm²
.315	8	.020	0,5	85	6	71	5	57	4
.315	8	.024	0,6	71	5	57	4	50	3,5

Place the **high tension** cable socket on the spark plug and depress the switch button.

The following conditions may be experienced:

1) Looking through the eye piece, a vivid spark is seen to issue through the plug electrodes; if so, the plug is serviceable.

2) Spark occurs at the meter points. Decrease the tester pressure and see at what pressure spark issues through plug electrodes. To judge on the efficiency of the spark plug under test, compare data with those in the table.

When replacing spark plugs, use exclusively the original ones, or CW 225 N (Model « 500 ») and CW 250 A (Model « 500 Sports »).

NOTE - Some sparks at the meter points can be tolerated.

Should no spark be seen either at the plug or at the meter, this is an indication that the plug insulator is cracked and the spark occurs internally between ground and electrode. As a result, the spark plug is unserviceable.

IGNITION TIMING

This timing is necessary when the distributor shaft and/or camshaft have been removed.

Proceed as follows:

On timing sprocket cover, fit fixture **Ap. 5030/1** as shown in fig. 375. Make sure cylinder No. 1 is in the compression stroke, i. e., with both valves closed. Bring crankshaft to the position in which **the mark** on centrifugal filter cover will line up with the 10° mark on fixture: this corresponds to a 10° static advance B. T. D. C.

Remove distributor cap and rotate drive shaft by hand until rotor points to contact for firing in cylinder No. 1.

In this position contacts are about to snap open (check first if maximum contact distance is .0185" to .0209" - 0,47 to 0,53 mm).

Without disturbing distributor shaft, insert lower coupling on its toothed end, install support and tighten the lock nut. Secure ignition distributor to support with the mounting screw.

To check if ignition distributor is properly timed to engine and if centrifugal automatic advance and total advance angles are as specified (18° and 28°, respectively), proceed as follows:

Connect timing tester Ap. 5030 with a 220-Volt, single-phase power outlet fitted with grounding insert.

The grounding of the tester should be made positively prior to or on plugging in of the tester service cord. **Under any circumstances, never allow the tester to operate without ground connection.**

Connect ground terminal with a bare metal portion of car under test.

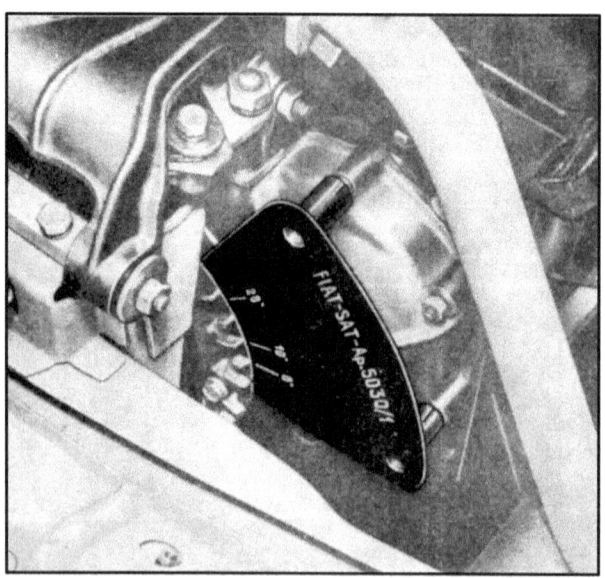

Fig. 375 - Use of fixture Ap. 5030/1 to check ignition timing.

ELECTRICAL

Set strobe light offing adapter between No. 1 spark plug wire and spark plug.

NOTE - Ignition timing of model 500 Sports engine: static advance 10°, automatic advance 12°, total maximum advance 22°.

Chalk off the T.D.C. mark on centrifugal filter cover.

Start the engine and aim the winking light beam on the chalk mark drawn on filter cover. If ignition is timed, **at slow running speed** the mark on filter cover must be seen aligned with the first white line (10°) on the fixture. By speeding up the engine so as to bring the automatic advance into operation, the chalked mark will be seen to move counter-clockwise until, at maximum r. p. m., it will reach the second white mark on fixture (28°).

If fixture **Ap. 5030** is not available, the advance position may be determined as follows:

See that cylinder No. 1 piston is in the compression stroke; rotate crankshaft clockwise so that the cast reference mark on centrifugal filter cover is set .5118″ to .5512″ (13 to 14 mm) ahead of the **arrow** cast on timing sprocket cover. This setting corresponds to a static advance of 10° B.T.D.C.

Then, proceed with the other operations as recommended for ignition distributor timing and mounting.

IGNITION SYSTEM SPECIFICATIONS

	« 500 »	« 500 Sports »
Ignition Distributor.		
Static advance	10°	10°
Centrifugal advace	18° at 3,000 r.p.m.	12° at 4,600 r.p.m.
Breaker contact pressure	16.8±1.8 oz. (475±50 gr.)	
Contact gaps	.0185″ to .0209″ (0,47 to 0,53 mm)	
Condenser capacity at 50-100 Hz	0.15 to 0.20 μF	
Cam carrier shaft felt and oiler lubricant	FIAT VS oil	
Ignition Coil.		
Primary winding ohmic resistance at 68°±9° F (20°±5° C)	≥ 3.2 Ω	
Secondary winding ohmic resistance at 68°±9° F (20°±5° C)	5000±100 Ω	
Ground insulation resistance at 500 V d. c.	≥ 50 MΩ	
Spark Plugs.		
Thread . . . . metric	14 x 1,25 M	
Code	CW 225 N	CW 250 A
Electrode gap	.0197″ to .0236″ (0,5 to 0,6 mm)	
Vehicles for Export to U. S. A. and Canada.		
Thread . . . . metric	14 x 1,25 M	
Code (Champion)	L 7	
Electrode gap	.0236″ to .0276″ (0,6 to 0,7 mm)	

LIGHTING SYSTEM

DESCRIPTION	page	244
HEADLAMPS	»	245
FRONT PARKING AND DIRECTION INDICATOR LAMPS	»	247
NUMBER PLATE LAMP	»	247
REAR PARKING, DIRECTION INDICATOR, STOP LAMPS AND REFLECTOR LENS	»	247
FUSES	»	247
SIDE DIRECTION INDICATOR LAMPS	»	249
REAR VIEW MIRROR LIGHT	»	249
INDICATORS IN THE INSTRUMENT CLUSTER	»	249
LIGHTING SYSTEM - U.S.A. AND CANADA VEHICLES	»	249
Headlamps	»	249
Bulb Specifications	»	250
LIGHTING SYSTEM SPECIFICATIONS	»	251

Description.

The lighting system consists of:

— Two headlamps with double-filament globe bulb (45 Watts for high beam and 40 Watts for low beam).

Headlight shifting is operated through the outer light control switch (1, fig. 376) below steering wheel, after toggle switch (7, fig. 376) at center of instrument panel has been turned on.

— Two front parking and direction indicator lamps below headlights, provided with double-filament globe bulb (5 Watts for parking lights and 20 Watts for winking direction indicator lights) (these lamps have been adopted starting from serial No. 099627).

— Two side direction indicator lamps fitted with 2.5 W tubular bulb (these lamps have been adopted starting from serial No. 099627).

— Number plate lamp with 5-Watt globe bulb.

— Two three-purpose rear lights (parking, winking direction indicators, stop) with reflector lens, are provided with one single-filament 20-W globe bulb (direction) and one double-filament globe bulb (5-W parking and 20-W stop lights).

— High beam indicator (blue light), with 2.5-Watt tubular bulb (this light has been adopted starting from serial No. 099627).

— Winking direction indicator pilot light (green), with 2.5-Watt tubular bulb (this light has been adopted starting from serial No. 099627).

— Courtesy light on rear view mirror, with 3-Watt cylindrical bulb; light is toggle switch controlled.

— Instrument cluster light with 2.5-Watt tubular bulb, controlled by a toggle switch on instrument panel.

— Four warning lights on instrument cluster, each with a 2.5-Watt bulb:

1) No-charge indicator. - 2) Fuel reserve supply indicator. - 3) Low oil pressure indicator. - 4) Parking light indicator.

Fig. 376 - Gauges, controls and signals.

1. External light shifting lever. - 2. Directional signal control lever. - 3. High beam indicator. - 4. Instrument cluster, including: speedometer and mileage recorder, parking light indicator, no-charge indicator, reserve supply indicator, low oil pressure indicator. - 5. Instrument cluster light switch. - 6. Directional signal pilot light. - 7. External light switch. - 8. Windshield wiper switch. - 9. Windshield demisting warmed air diffuser control knobs. - 10. Ignition and services lock switch. - 11. Manual accelerator control. - 12. Accelerator pedal. - 13. Brake pedal. - 14. Clutch pedal. - 15. Horn button. - 16. Front compartment lid catch control.

ELECTRICAL

HEADLAMPS

Removing the Optic Unit and Bulbholder.

The headlamp as a unit may be taken out of fender by slightly pressing the lens and rotating the unit 15° counterclockwise (fig. 377).

The replacement of bulb alone is more easily done from inside front compartment (fig. 378) as follows:

— grab the upper lug of rubber protection cap, pull down and free the bulbholder;

— pull up the bulbholder-to-reflector fastener spring;

— pull out the bulbholder and replace the bayonet coupled bulb.

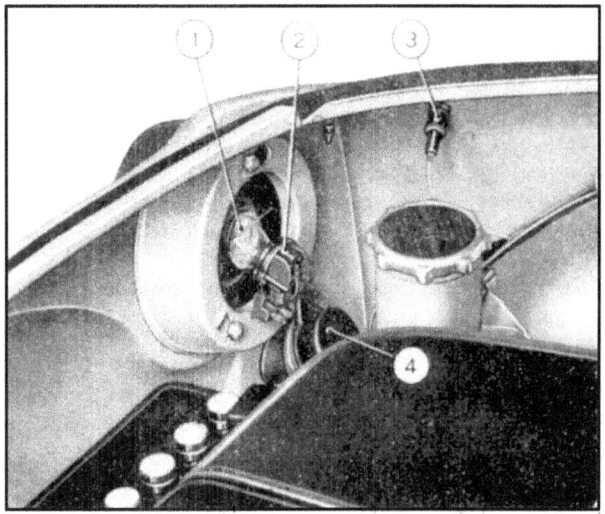

Fig. 378 - Replacement of bulb from inside front compartment.

1. Double-filament bulb. - 2. Bulbholder. - 3. Side direction indicator light. - 4. Bulbholder shield.

Fig. 377 - Replacement of headlamp optic unit.

Press on lens and rotate slightly counterclockwise, as shown by the arrow.

WARNING

Headlamp reflectors are aluminized; therefore, during disassembly, be careful not to soil or touch the reflecting surface with fingers. Should reflector be dusty, clean preferably with an air blast or a feather duster. Never use a cloth, which would impair the reflecting surface brilliancy.

Bulbs must not be replaced by others of a different type or wattage, as this would result, in the first case, in decreased headlamp efficiency, and in the second, in an excessive current consumption greater than the normal generator output, which would cause gradual discharging of the battery.

When simply removing the optic unit, never screw in or out the three rear hexagonal head screws which, besided fixing the unit, also serve for beam aiming. This will spare a re-aiming after headlamp installation.

Aiming.

Headlights should be aimed in a no-load condition.

Check that tires are inflated at the specified pressure.

Place the vehicle on level ground, at 16′ 5″ (5 meters) from a screen in shadow and set perpendicular to vehicle longitudinal centerline (fig. 380).

Jounce the vehicle both sides to set suspensions.

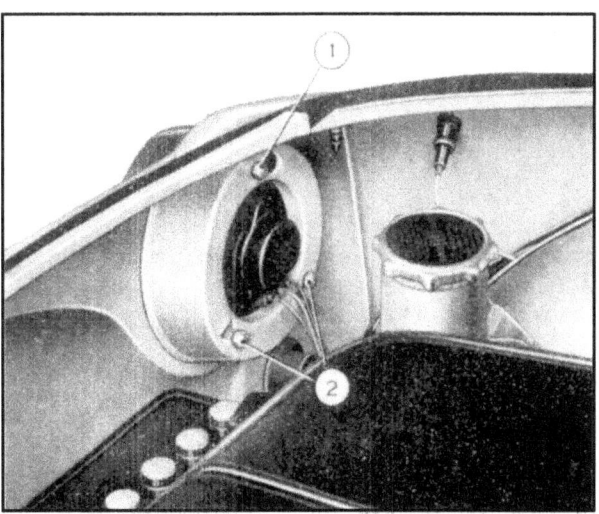

Fig. 379 - Beam aiming screws.

1-2. Headlight pool tilt and divergence setting screws.

On the screen, draw two vertical lines a-a at a distance A from each other corresponding to headlamp center-to-center distance (see table below).

Draw a horizontal line b-b at the heights B indicated in table. The heights vary depending on whether the vehicle suspensions are new or not. Suspensions have practically reached the « set » condition after the vehicle has run about 900/1000 miles (first service voucher).

To check headlight adjustment, switch on low beams and see that:

— the horizontal separation line between lit and unlit areas is on line b-b (fig. 380) and never above it.

Switch on high beams and see that:

— the center point (hot spot) of each light pool is on line a-a or just outside it; a $10\,^{15}/_{64}''$ (26 cm) increase in distance A specification, corresponding to a 3° aggregate beam divergence, is permissible.

In case above conditions are not met, headlamps must be re-aimed as follows.

— To correct the vertical adjustment, turn both lower screws (2, fig. 379) of the same amount and in the same direction, while the upper screw (1) on back side of lamp is turned in the opposite direction.

— To correct the horizontal adjustment, turn the two lower screws (2) in opposite directions without disturbing the upper screw (1).

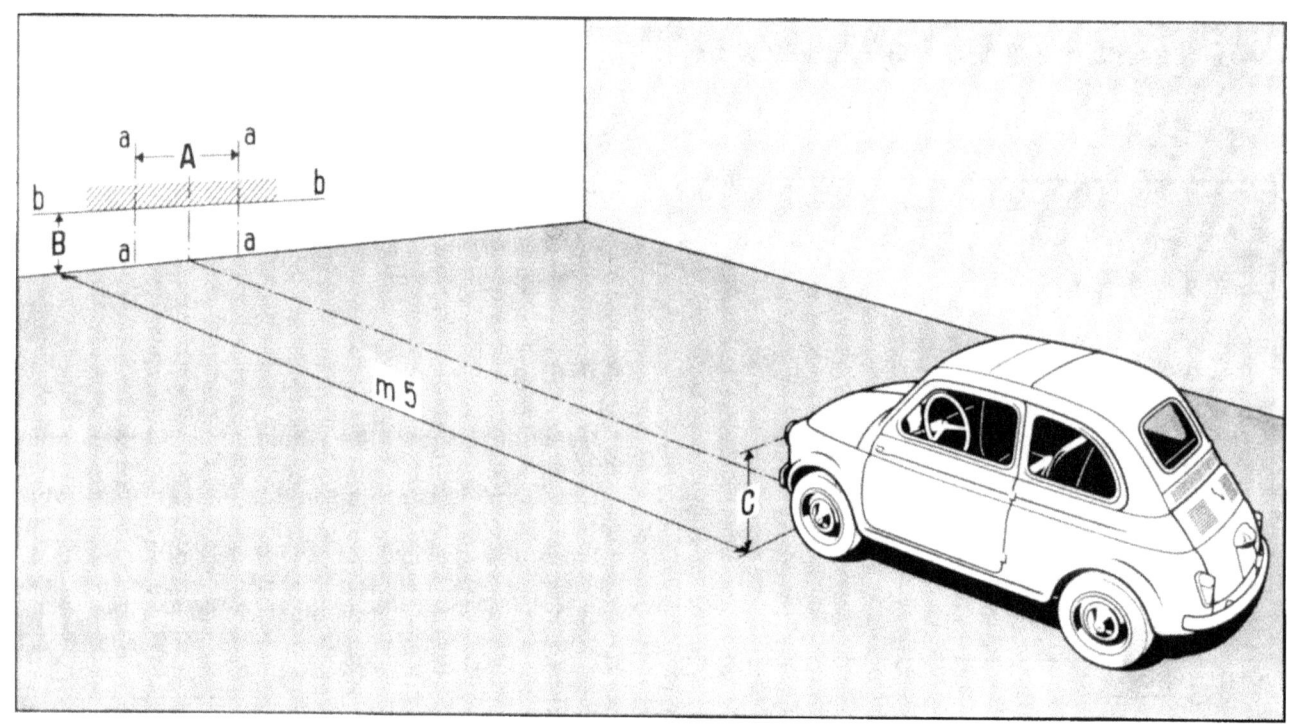

Fig. 380 - Headlamp aiming chart.

HEADLAMP AIMING DATA

VEHICLE TYPE	HEADLAMP TYPE	A	B	
			New Vehicle	Seated Vehicle
New 500	symmetric	$32\,^{11}/_{16}''$ (830 mm)	C minus $1\,^{9}/_{16}''$ (40 mm)	C minus $1\,^{3}/_{8}''$ (35 mm)

A = Headlamp center-to-center distance.

B = Height of beam above ground (separation line of lit and unlit areas), at 16,5'' (5 m) distance.

C = Height of headlamp center above ground, on aiming.

ELECTRICAL

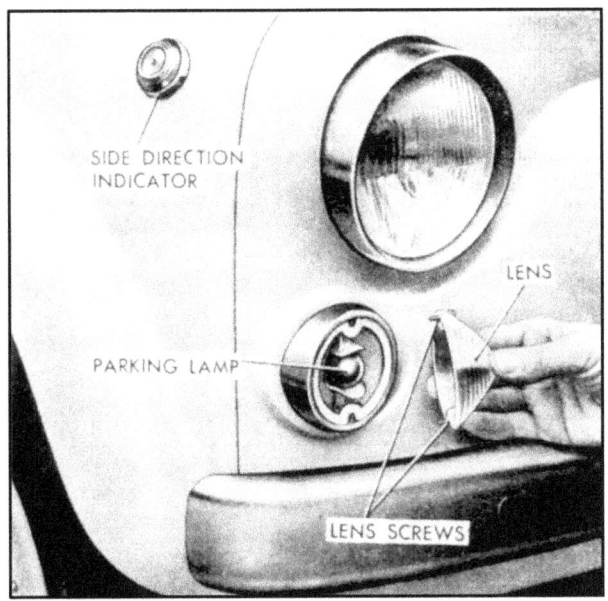

Fig. 381 - Disassembling front parking and direction indicator lamp.

Front Parking and Direction Indicator Lamps.

To replace the double filament bulb (5/20 W), undo the screws (fig. 381) securing the lens to lamp casing; bulb is secured by bayonet coupling.

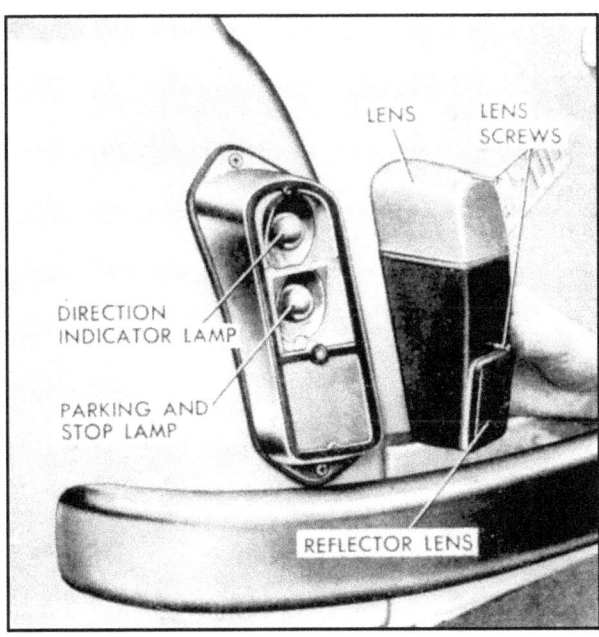

Fig. 382 - Disassembling tail parking, stop, direction indicator lamp and reflector lens.

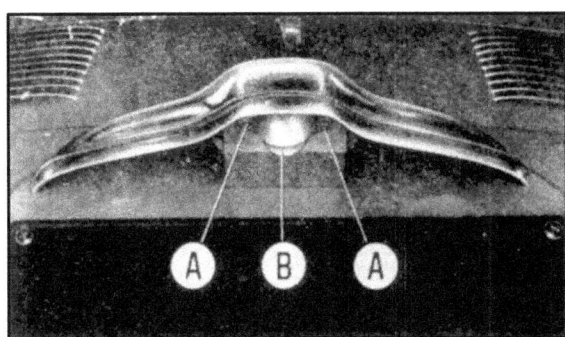

Fig. 383 - Number plate lamp.
A. Lens and light cap mounting screws. - B. Lens.

Number Plate Lamp.

To replace the bayonet-coupled, 5-Watt globular bulb, back out the lens and light cap mounting screws (fig. 383).

Rear Parking, Direction Indicator, Stop Lamps and Reflector Lens.

To replace bulbs, undo the two screws (fig. 382) securing the lens to lamp casing.
Bulbs are fixed by bayonet coupling.

Fuses.

The electric system is protected by six 8-A fuses, located in a box inside the front compartment (fig. 384).

Fig. 384 - Location of electrical system fuses.

1. Fuse No. 30/2. - 2. Fuse No. 30/3. - 3. Fuse No. 56/b1. - 4. Fuse No. 56/b2. - 5. Fuse No. 15/54. - 6. Fuse No. 30.

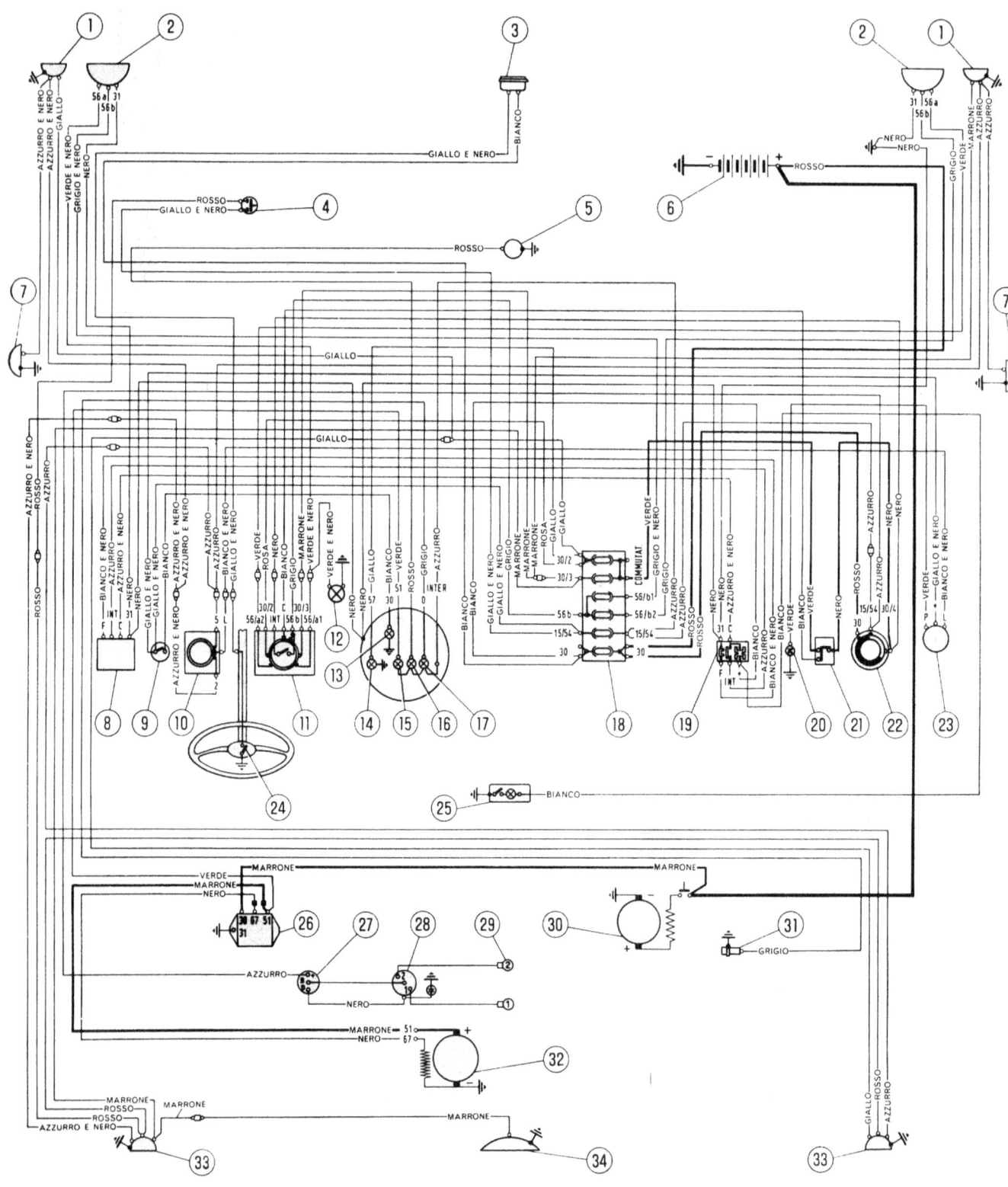

Fig. 385 - Diagram of the electric system with color coded cables.

KEY TO CABLE COLORS

Azzurro = **Blue**	Marrone = **Brown**	Verde = **Green**	Verde e Nero = **Black and Green**
Bianco = **White**	Nero = **Black**	Azzurro e Nero = **Black and Blue**	Grigio e Nero = **Black and Grey**
Giallo = **Yellow**	Rosa = **Rosy**	Bianco e Nero = **Black and White**	Commutat. = **Switch**
Grigio = **Grey**	Rosso = **Red**	Giallo e Nero = **Black and Yellow**	INT-Inter = **Switch**

(Specifications on opposite page)

ELECTRICAL

FUSES (fig. 384)	CONTROLLED CIRCUITS
1 - Fuse No. 30/2	Right headlamp high beam - Left front parking light with indicator - Right rear parking light.
2 - Fuse No. 30/3	Left headlamp high beam with indicator - Right front parking light - Left rear parking light - Number plate light.
3 - Fuse No. 56/b 1	Left headlamp low beam.
4 - Fuse No. 56/b 2	Right headlamp low beam.
5 - Fuse No. 15/54	Winking direction indicators with pilot light - Instrument cluster light - Stop light.
6 - Fuse No. 30	Horn - Windshield wiper - Rear view mirror light.

Before replacing a burnt fuse, look for the cause of blowing. Reference to the wiring diagram (figure 385) will be found most useful.

For better guidance, the complete list of six fuse-controlled circuits is given here above.

Unprotected circuits:

— Generator charge and relevant indicator.
— Ignition.
— Starting.
— Low oil pressure indicator.
— Fuel reserve supply indicator.

Side Direction Indicator Lamps.

To replace the 2.5 W tubular bulb, operate from below fender (3, fig. 378) and slide off bulb holder from rubber socket.

Bulb is secured by bayonet coupling.

Rear View Mirror Light.

To replace the 3-Watt cylindrical bulb, back out the two lamp frame-to-mirror frame mounting screws and pull bulb out of the retaining spring fingers.

Indicators in the Instrument Cluster.

To replace any of these tubular 2.5-Watt bulbs, disinsert bulbholders and then the bayonet-coupled bulbs.

LIGHTING SYSTEM - U.S.A. AND CANADA VEHICLES

The lighting system to suit «Version 140» and «Version 144» vehicles for export to U.S.A. and Canada, includes the lamps and bulbs specified on page 250.

Headlamps.

Removal of Sealed Beam Unit.

To remove the sealed beam unit, proceed as follows:

1) Back out the screw (2, fig. 386) and slide off the rim from its lodging.

2) Using a screwdriver, disengage the four spring fingers (3, fig. 386) retaining the sealed beam unit and mounting ring assembly.

3) Withdraw the sealed beam unit from its seat and slide off the unit tripolar receptacle.

Specifications of fig. 385 (page 248).

1. Front parking and direction indicator lamps. - 2. Headlamps (high and low beams). - 3. Horn. - 4. Stop lights pressure-operated switch. - 5. Fuel reserve supply indicator sending unit. - 6. Battery. - 7. Side direction indicator lamps. - 8. Windshield wiper motor. - 9. Panel light switch. - 10. Directional signal lever switch. - 11. External lighting changeover lever switch. - 12. Higt beam indicator. - 13. Panel light. - 14. Parking lights indicator. - 15. Generator charge indicator. - 16. Fuel reserve supply indicator. - 17. Low oil pressure indicator. - 18. Fuses. - 19. Windshield wiper 3-position switch. - 20. Direction indicator pilot light. - 21. External light switch. - 22. Ignition lock switch. - 23. Flasher unit, direction indicators. - 24. Horn button. - 25. Rear view mirror light. - 26. Generator regulator. - 27. Ignition coil. - 28. Ignition distributor. - 29. Spark plugs. - 30. Starter motor. - 31. Low oil pressure indicator sending unit. - 32. Generator. - 33. Rear parking, stop and direction indicator lamps. - 34. Number plate lamp.

NOTE - Mark ▬ means that the cable is provided with numbered strip or ferrule.

Fig. 386 - Removing lamp rim to service Sealed Beam Units.

1. Rim. - 2. Rim fixing screw. - 3. Unit mounting springs.

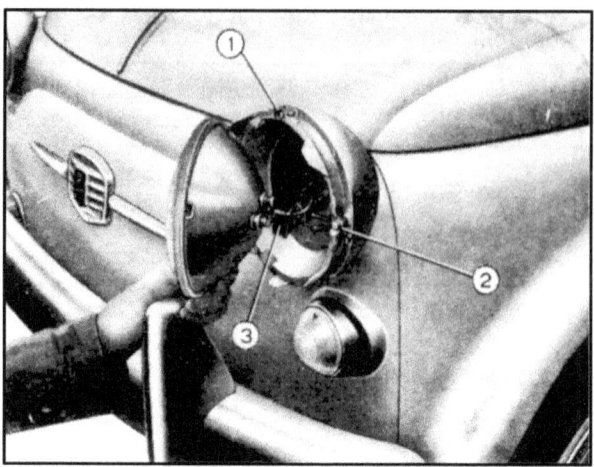

Fig. 387 - Headlamp aiming.

1. Beam vertical aiming adjustment screw. - 2. Beam horizontal aiming adjustment screw. - 3. Headlamp terminal plug.

Aiming.

Using proper wrench, work on two screws (1 and 2, fig. 387). The upper screw (1) is to adjust beam vertically, the lower screw (2) adjusts beam horizontally.

For aiming specifications, comply with S. A. E. headlight aiming Standards.

BULB SPECIFICATIONS

Q.ty	LOCATION	TYPE ORIGINAL EQUIPMENT	TYPE SAE EQUIVALENT
2	Headlamps (high beam and low beam)	« Sealed beam » headlamp unit 5400	

2
2
	Front lamps: direction indicators
	         parking lights
	Tail lamps: stop lights
	         parking lights
		12 V - 5/20 W FIAT Norm. 1/08569/90	No. 1016 - 12.8 V 21/6 Cp

2	Tail lamps: direction indicators	12 V - 20 W FIAT Norm. 1/08562/90	No. 1141 - 12 V - 21W
1	License plate light	12 V - 5 W FIAT Norm. 1/08577/90	No. 89 - 13 V - 6 Cp
1 1 1 1 1 1 1	Instrument cluster light Direction indicator pilot light (green) Headlamp high beam indicator (blue light) Generator charge indicator (red light) Low oil pressure indicator (red light) Reserve supply indicator (red light) Parking light indicator (green light)	12 V - 2.5 W FIAT Norm. 1/08583/90	—
1	Courtesy light	12 V - 3 W FIAT Norm. 1/08595/90	—

ELECTRICAL

LIGHTING SYSTEM SPECIFICATIONS *

Headlamps	2
Double filament globe bulb:	
high beam	45 W
low beam	40 W
Front parking and direction indicator lamps	2
Double filament globe bulb:	
parking	5 W
direction indicator (flashing)	20 W
Side direction indicator lamps	2
Tubular bulb	2.5 W
Rear parking, direction indicator and stop lamps (with reflector lens)	
Globe bulbs:	2
single filament (direction indicators)	20 W
double filament { parking	5 W
stop	20 W
Rear number plate lamp	1
Globe bulb	5 W
Inner lighting:	
Cylindrical bulb incorporated in rear view mirror	3 W
switch: toggle type	on mirror frame
Instrument cluster light:	
Tubular lamp with toggle switch on panel	2.5 W
Indicators - 4 tubular bulbs in instrument cluster, each	2.5 W
Tell-tales on dashboard:	
— direction indicator, green	
— parking light, green } tubular bulb	2.5 W
— high beam, blue	
Fuses, six	8 Amps

(*) For lighting system to suit « Version 140 » and « Version 144 » vehicles, see covering data on pages 249 and 250.

GAUGES AND CONTROLS

INSTRUMENT CLUSTER	page 252
LOCK SWITCH	» 253
FUEL RESERVE SUPPLY INDICATOR SENDING UNIT	» 253
FLASHING DIRECTION INDICATOR SYSTEM	» 253
DIRECTIONAL SIGNAL AND OUTER LIGHTING CHANGE-OVER SWITCH	» 256
WINDSHIELD WIPER	» 259
WINDSHIELD WIPER TOGGLE SWITCH	» 261
HORN	» 261
ELECTRICAL ACCESSORY ITEMS SPECIFICATIONS	» 264

INSTRUMENT CLUSTER

All gauges are clustered in a single instrument mounted on dashboard above steering column, incorporating; parking lamp pilot light, generator charge indicator, fuel reserve supply indicator, low oil pressure indicator, and speedometer with mileage recorder.

Fig. 388 - Instrument cluster.

Parking Lamp Indicator.

Glows (green) when ignition lock switch key is in position 1 or 2 with inserted toggle switch on instrument panel.

Generator Charge Indicator.

Shows red only when ignition is turned ON. Goes out when generator output is sufficient for battery charge (lights off): 12.6±0.2 Volts, engine at 1100 r.p.m. and car road speed (in 4th gear) 14.3 m.p.h. (23 km/h).

Fuel Reserve Supply Indicator.

Shows red only when ignition is turned ON and amount of fuel in tank has dropped to .9-1.3 U.S. gals or .8-1.1 Imp. gals (3,5-5 liters).

Low Oil Pressure Indicator.

Shows red only when ignition is turned ON. Goes out when operating oil pressure reaches 7.1 to 21.3 p.s.i. (0,5 to 1,5 kg/cm²) and opens the sending unit contacts.

With warm engine and an r.p.m. rate below 1000, indicator may light up even if pressure is under control and operation regular.

Speedometer-Mileage Recorder.

Maximum speed limits corresponding to the different gears (I-II-III) (after 1800 miles running-in) are indicated by red spots on dial.

Speedometer drive ratio: 1000 pinion r.p.m. equals 1 km reading on recorder (1 r.p.m. = 1 meter).

Seen from flexible drive shaft end, speedometer drive rotation is counterclockwise.

LOCK SWITCH

This switch (fig. 389) is provided with two keys (one is a spare). Insert and rotate key rightwards (position 1) to control ignition and various service circuits and leftwards (position 2) for night parking (change-over switch lever in position 1) (fig. 391).

With key in position 1, the following circuits are energized: fuel level gauge and relevant reserve supply indicator, generator charge indicator, low oil pressure indicator, direction indicators and their pilot light, stop lights, instrument panel light, headlamps (high and low beams), number plate light and parking lights.

The key may be withdrawn from switch only when set in positions 0 and 2.

Repair.

The lock switch has been designed to warrant long life of components, both electrical and mechanical, and best possible performance and therefore troubles are unlikely to occur.

The switch is of the sealed type and, therefore,

Fig. 389 - Lock switch key positions.

Position 0: all circuits OFF (permits withdrawal of key). Position 1: engine and services ON (key cannot be withdrawn). - Position 2: parking lights ON, with outer lighting switch lever in position 1 (permits withdrawal of key).

should be replaced as a complete unit rather than attempt any repair.

FUEL RESERVE SUPPLY INDICATOR SENDING UNIT

The sending unit has been designed to warrant long life of components, both electrical and mechanical, and best possible performance.

Occasionally check, during refuelings, if the indication of fuel reserve supply is correct: .9-1.3 U. S. gals or .8-1.1 Imp. gals (3.5 to 5 liters).

Possible causes of any irregularity are:

a) burnt reserve supply indicator bulb;

b) interruption of the circuit between sending unit and indicator bulb;

c) distorted sending unit float bracket. In this case, the bulb will light up to indicate a reserve supply of fuel greater or smaller than specified;

d) some damage in sending unit.

Remedies:

a) replace the bulb;

b) restore circuit efficiency;

c) remove sending unit from tank and restore bracket shape to original conditions;

d) the sending unit is of the sealed type and, therefore, should be replaced rather than attempt any repair.

FLASHING DIRECTION INDICATOR SYSTEM

The flashing light directional signal system utilizes the higher wattage filament (20 W) of front parking lamps; at rear, the 20-Watt bulb of parking, direction indicator and stop lamps, and the 2.5-Watt bulb of both side direction indicators.

The system consists of: a directional signal switch, a winking device (flasher unit), the front, side and rear lamps mentioned above and a bulb (2.5 W) incorporated in pilot light.

The directional signal switch is connected to flasher unit and three signal lamp pairs.

The flasher unit (fig. 390) is of the hot wire type and consists of:

— a magnetic core with winding A, in series with lamp circuits, and an additional auxiliary winding - formed of a few turns of wire - in series with the pilot light circuit;

— a main armature A_p which opens and closes intermittently a contact by inserting and disinserting an additional resistor R in the circuit;

— an additional resistor R;

— a secondary armature A_1 that switches on and off the pilot light synchronously with directional signal by closing and opening an auxiliary contact;

— a hot wire f in series with resistor R.

The flasher unit is connected to the directional signal switch and to terminal 15/54 of ignition lock switch through relevant fuse.

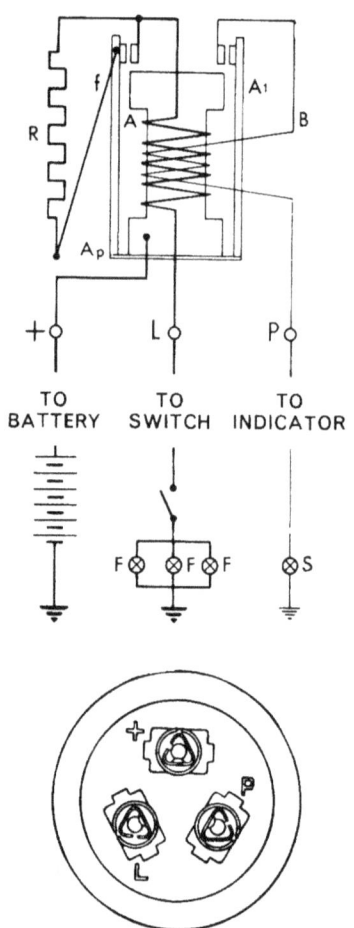

Fig. 390 - (Top) flasher unit operation diagram, for bench testing; (bottom) flasher unit contacts side view.

A. Series winding. - A_p. Main armature. - A_1. Auxiliary armature. - B. Auxiliary winding. - F. Front and rear parking and direction indicator lamps. - L and P. Terminals. - R. Additional resistor. - S. Pilot lamp. - f. Hot wire.

Operation.

In the « neutral » position (direction indicator toggle switch at centre, circuit OFF) current does not flow in any part whatever of the system and the flasher unit armature contacts are open because main armature is held back by stretched wire f in series with resistor R, and the auxiliary armature by the relevant pre-load spring. Therefore, resistor R is inserted and pilot light S is off.

By shifting toggle switch lever (to the right or left), one of the two circuits closes (either the right or the left one).

The current, coming from battery, flows through the main armature A_p, wire f, resistor R, winding A of flasher unit (fig. 390), the front and rear 20-Watt bulb filament, side lamp 2.5-Watt filament and ground. Since flow is limited by resistor R, the current is not sufficient to cause filaments to glow but it does heat wire f which lengthens and allows main armature to close the contact and shorts the wire itself and resistor R.

Then, current increases and filaments glow. Wire f, through which no current now flows, cools off and shortens, and hence opens the main armature contact again, thus inserting resistor R in the circuit.

Current drops, filaments go out, and the cycle is repeated.

The auxiliary contact for the pilot light operates as follows: when current in main circuit increases (phase in which signal lamp bulb filaments glow), winding A attracts auxiliary armature A_1 and closes the contact of pilot light S which will light up and flash with direction indicator lamp signals; when current drops (the higher wattage filaments fade out), the auxiliary armature return spring overcomes the magnetic attraction of winding A, opens contacts of pilot light S, which will go out. The duration of each cycle is less 1 second.

Winding B in series with auxiliary circuit has the purpose of preventing auxiliary armature contacts from damage (welding) in case of short circuit between terminal P and ground. This shorting could take place when, for any reason whatever, clamp P is accidentally connected to ground. Were it not for winding B, this occurrence would originate a marked arcing when contacts open and heavy welding when contacts close, while the fuse cannot interrupt the circuit before contacts become completely stuck together, at which time it would be too late.

As a matter of fact, since one flash takes less than a second, the ON-cycle is too short to blow the direction indicator fuse on account of its thermal inertia.

Thanks to winding B, instead, the short circuit current magnetically locks the auxiliary armature, while its contacts are closed until the fuse blows.

On the other hand, said winding does not affect the regular operation of the flasher unit, when the auxiliary circuit is closed to ground through pilot lamp S, because the current drawn by the latter is so small that it makes the action of winding B negligible.

ELECTRICAL

Since front lamps also function as parking lights (lower wattage filaments), at night the directional signal will overlap the parking light and the turn will be indicated by an intermittent (winking) increase in intensity; in daytime, instead, this indication is given directly by the lamps which go on and off.

Flasher Unit Bench Testing.

This device must be bench-tested according to the operation diagram shown in fig. 390.

The bulbs F, connected in parallel, must have the same power as the one fitted on the car, because the flasher unit is connected in series with these lamps and operation cannot be regular if the load is not the standard one and, what is more, the device is liable to be damaged if the current is too high.

WARNING

Never insert terminal « L » directly to ground without having first connected in series the bulbs specified, or else the flasher unit will be irreparably damaged.

For the same reason terminal « L » must never be shorted to ground nor must there be any short-circuits in all leads from said terminal to bulbs.

The flasher unit must never receive blows of any kind, since the very delicate components could easily be damaged with consequent breakages, misadjustments, etc.

Flasher unit operation characteristics are as follows:

1) At a nominal tension of 12 V and with a nominal bulb load totalling 42.5-Watts, the number of flashing cycles per minute at 68° F (20° C) must be 85 ± 8.

2) Under above conditions, the flasher unit should begin to signal within a second and fade out within 1.5 seconds after the circuit has been closed.

3) The ratio between the light on and off time should range between 0.7 and 1.4.

4) With a tension 1.25 times the nominal one (15 V), at a temperature of 104° F (40° C), the cycles must not exceed 110 per minute.

5) With a tension 0.8 times the nominal one (9.5 V), at a temperature of —4° F (—20° C), the cycles must not be less than 45 per minute.

6) The contact of pilot light must flash the bulb synchronously with the cycles, when both bulbs F are operative.

When one of the two 20-Watt bulbs on the same side fails, the pilot light should not flash; if this occurs, the driver is warned of one of the following faults in the system:

— broken or burnt filament in one of the 20-Watt bulbs;

— faulty contact between one 20-Watt bulb and its socket due to weakening, failure or oxidation of the current carrier spring lamina;

— open circuit between lamp and switch;

— defective grounding of one of 20-Watt bulb lamps.

Trouble Shooting Instructions.

Troubles that may arise during direction indicator operation are many and different in nature.

The following instructions refer both to right and left signalling circuits:

1. - **All lamps are regularly operative but pilot light does not glow.**

Possible causes independent of flasher unit are:

— burnt pilot light bulb;

— broken connection between terminal « P » and pilot light bulb;

— defective contact of pilot bulb in socket.

Possible causes in flasher unit are:

— shorted turns in winding « A »;

— auxiliary contacts oxidized or worn to such an extent that bulb circuit can no longer be closed;

— unsoldering of auxiliary armature « A_1 » movable contact or of fixed contact;

— unsoldering of auxiliary winding « B » end from stationary contact support;

— unsoldering of auxiliary winding « B » end from terminal « P »;

— excessive core-to-auxiliary armature « A_1 » air gap;

— excessive load on auxiliary armature « A_1 » return spring;

— broken auxiliary winding « B ».

2. - **Only one lamp is operative (front or rear) and pilot light does not glow (see point 7 of the preceding chapter).**

Possible causes:

— broken 20-Watt filament in the bulb of the inoperative lamp;

— broken cable between the inoperative lamp and the directional signal switch;

— defective contact between inoperative lamp bulb and socket lamina;

— defective grounding of inoperative lamp.

3. - Lamps (front, rear and pilot light) are all inoperative.

Possible causes independent of flasher unit are:

— blown fuse, caused by a short circuit (see paragraph « Operation »);
— broken main lead between ignition lock switch terminal « 15/54 » and flasher unit plus terminal;
— broken cable between flasher unit terminal « L » and directional signal switch terminal « L »;
— broken cables between directional signal switch and lamps;
— defective grounding of lamps;
— dirty, oxidized or worn directional signal switch contacts;
— both lamps on the same side burnt;
— defective contact with socket, of both lamps on the same side.

Possible causes in flasher unit are:

— resistor « R » broken;
— unsoldering of resistor « R » from main stationary contact support;
— main contacts strongly oxidized;
— unsoldering of main armature « A_p » movable contact or unsoldering of stationary contact from its support;
— winding « A » broken;
— winding « A » end unsoldered from main stationary contact support;
— unsoldering of winding « A » end from terminal « L ».

4. - Direction indicator lamps and pilot light flash with abnormal intermittence or flashing times (on - off) are much different.

The flasher unit is misadjusted; generally, this occurs after the flasher unit receives a blow; less frequently, the cause may be a weakening or breakage of wire « f ».

5. - Indicator lamps and pilot light glow but do not flash.

Causes are located in flasher unit and may be:

— breaking or weakening of wire « f », in which case main contacts remain permanently closed;
— welding of main contacts.

6. - Indicator lamps glow but do not flash; pilot light remains off.

Causes are located in flasher unit and are due to the main winding being directly in contact with the core owing to poor insulation.

In case the cause for trouble is located in the system and not in the flasher unit, repairs do not require any special instructions (replacement of bulbs, cleaning of contacts, proper arrangement of connections, etc.).

Before replacing a burnt fuse, look for the cause, i. e., the short circuit from which the blowing originated. If the short circuit is detected in a portion of lead between terminal « L » of flasher unit and the lamps, install a new flasher unit since most likely the old one is damaged.

To determine whether or not the trouble is in flasher unit when all indications from inspection point to this unit as the source of trouble, check flasher unit on test bench as outlined before.

Flasher units are delicate and, for this reason, cannot be repaired. Therefore, always replace faulty units without even attempting any repairs.

SELF-CANCELLING DIRECTIONAL SIGNAL SWITCH-OUTER LIGHTING CHANGE-OVER SWITCH

Description.

These two switches form a centralized control unit consisting of:

— directional signal switch, which returns automatically to rest position after negotiating the turn, when steering wheel is brought back to straightforward drive position;
— change-over switch, controlling the outer lights (parking, high and low beams) and the headlamp flashes.

The unit is located on steering column, under steering wheel.

Directional Signal Switch.

Is controlled by the upper (shorter) lever (figure 391) of the unit. The lever may take three positions determined by a click, the central position being the neutral. The upward or downward movement of the lever controls a revolving drum which, by establishing proper contacts, sends a pulsating current from flasher unit to front and rear directional lamps on the side of the turn to be negotiated. At the same time the drum brings one of the two triggers to the latching position.

ELECTRICAL

The return of the lever to neutral is automatic with the return of wheels to straightforward drive, and is controlled by a two-lobe cam spring mounted at center of steering wheel.

NOTE - On installation of directional signal switch-outer lighting change-over switch unit, lay a coat of vaseline on the horn control lamina contact, fitted on the unit, and on the contact ring, fitted on steering wheel hub. Do not overstretch cables, otherwise they may be snapped at the stationary contacts.

When the wheels are steered, one of the two lobes catches the drum control trigger which rotates around its fulcrum. The further rotation of the steering shaft causes the trigger disengagement from the lobe and its return to rest position under the action of its load coil spring. The latching mechanism is thus «loaded». Subsequently, when the steering wheel is brought back to straightforward drive position, the spring lobe catches the trigger, which rotates about its fulcrum and exerts a pressure on the inner wall of a seat provided in the drum. Under this pressure the drum revolves and returns to rest position together with the control lever. After this movement, also the trigger frees the spring lobe and returns to rest position.

Change-Over Switch.

Is controlled by the lower (longer) lever (figure 391) which may be set in the following three positions being shifted by a click:

1 - Front and rear parking lamps, and number plate lamp ON.

2 - Headlamp low beam, parking and number plate lamps ON.

3 - Headlamp high beam, parking and number plate lamps ON.

NOTE - Outer lighting change-over switch is energized by operating the outer lighting switch on instrument panel.

Furthermore, by pushing the lever towards the steering wheel, from any lever position excepting No. 2, the flashing of low beams is obtained.

The connection of the electric circuits is obtained by sprung contacts carried on the two revolving drums, and by stationary contacts mounted on the two relevant plastic insulating supports.

Switch Unit Removal.

1) By a screwdriver, pry off the horn push-button at steering wheel center.

2) Disconnect the plug-in contact.

3) Unscrew the steering wheel hold-down nut.

4) Remove steering wheel from shaft.

5) Slacken the bolt securing the steering column support to body.

6) Disinsert all plug-in contacts of the switch unit.

7) Remove the switch unit from steering column.

Switch Unit Installation.

Reverse the removal operations. After installation check that, with steering wheel in straightforward drive position and directional signal switch lever in neutral, the reference index on the outer face of the directional signal switch drum is in line with the index on steering wheel hub.

Fig. 391 - Positions of outer lighting and direction indicator control levers.

Direction indicator control lever (upper): D. Lever in position for right turn signalling; S. Lever in position for left turn signalling. -
Outer lighting switch control lever (lower): I. Parking and number plate lights ON; II. Low beam, parking and number plate lights ON; III. High beam, parking and number plate lights ON.

Trouble Shooting.

Possible causes for faulty operation are:

A) **Directional Signal Switch.**

1. - **The lever does not return automatically to neutral after straightening the wheels.**

The trouble may originate from:

a) defects in the latching mechanism such as:

i) failure or weakening of trigger return spring;
ii) seizing of triggers;
iii) excessive play of triggers on fulcrum pin;
iv) failure of trigger fulcrum pins;
v) deformations of triggers;
vi) excessive wear of trigger rollers.

Any of the above defects calls for the replacement of the complete unit.

b) Failure, weakening or wear of the two-lobe spring fixed at center of steering wheel.

Replace the spring.

2. - Lever rotation clicks not marked or practically inexistent.

The trouble may originate from:

a) Failure of the seat in revolving drum for positioning ball.

b) Wear, or failure, of positioning rack teeth.

In either case, replace the complete unit.

3. - With lever in the upper or lower position, the directional signal flashes occasionally or does not glow at all.

After checking external connections, flasher unit, lamps and bulbs, and all are faultless, the trouble may be due to:

a) Seizure of movable contact in its seat in revolving drum, so that it does not close the circuit on the fixed contacts.

b) Excessive wear of movable and fixed contacts.

c) Failure or weakening of the movable contact load coil spring.

d) Excessive clearance of revolving drum in its seat. This clearance determines an inadequate rocking of revolving drum, such that in some cases the movable contact clears the fixed contacts.

e) Disconnected fixed contact current leads.

In all the above cases, replace the complete unit.

4. - Remarkable effort required to shift the lever or seizing of the lever in any of the three positions.

The trouble may originate from:

Excessive projection of positioning ball (more than its diameter) from its seat. In this case, instead of entering its seat and compressing the load spring, the ball remains squeezed between the seat edge and a tooth of the rack, thus acting as a wedge. This requires a much greater effort to shift the lever and in some cases may also lock the control. Should this occur, replace the complete unit.

B) Outer lighting Change-Over Switch.

1. - While tripping the lever for headlamp flashes, abnormal opening or closing of the circuits takes place.

The trouble may originate from:

a) Excessive clearance of revolving drum in its seat. This clearance, during the above lever shifts, determines an excessive rocking of revolving drum, whereby the movable contacts will not close the circuit with fixed contacts.

b) Excessive wear of movable and fixed contacts.

c) Seizure of the movable contact in its seat in the revolving drum.

d) Failure or weakening of the movable contact coil spring.

In these cases replace the complete unit.

2. - In whichever position the lever is tripped, the headlamp low beams keep staying ON.

The trouble may originate from:

a) Seizure of the flashing control spring contact trigger in its seat.

b) Loss in flashing control movable contact flexibility.

In either case replace the complete unit.

3. - When tripping the lever for headlamp flashes, the low beams are not switched ON.

The trouble may originate from:

a) Failure of the flashing control movable contact.

b) Oxidation of the flashing control movable and fixed contacts.

c) Wear of the flashing control trigger.

d) Wear of flashing control trigger seat surface in revolving drum.

e) Disconnection of fixed contact current leads.

In all the above cases, replace the complete unit.

4. - Lever rotation clicks not marked or practically inexistent.

Causes for trouble and relevant remedies are the same as outlined under point 2. for the Directional Signal Switch.

5. - Remarkable effort required to shift the lever or seizing of the lever in any of its positions.

The cause of this trouble is the same as outlined under 4. for the Directional Signal Switch.
Replace the complete unit.

ELECTRICAL

WINDSHIELD WIPER

It consists of a motor unit that drives wiper blades back and forth through a reduction gearing and linkage. The reduction gear includes a worm screw on armature shaft and a helical pinion. The motor, left blade pivot and linkages are mounted on a sheet metal bracket, conferring the necessary rigidity to the system.

The right blade pivot, instead, is connected to the main drive link.

When assembling the wiper on car, this pivot is fixed directly on the body.

The unit is provided with an automatic parking device ensuring the return of blades to the position where visibility impairments are negligible. Below is a diagram (fig. 392) where the operation of this unit can be seen.

The windshield wiper is controlled by a lever switch which may assume the following three positions:

— **Up (position 1 or « ON »).** - Excited by windings A (series) and B (shunted), the motor runs the wipers at a 50-60 sweeps per min rate.

— **Center (position 0 or « OFF »).** - Blades stop immediately, regardless of their position. All motor windings are excluded.

— **Down (position 2 or « Parking »).** - With switch lever pressed down, blades are automatically parked. In this position also auxiliary winding S is energized. When released, lever snaps back to OFF position.

Winding S is formed by a few coils of heavy wire; it hence has low resistance and high current absorption, such as to produce a strong excitation e. m. f.

Since, as it is known, by strenghtening a d. c. motor magnetic field the motor rotational speed decreases and torque increases, following the insertion of winding S the wiper motor will sensibly reduce the speed of blade sweep, though still retaining a torque such as to enable blades to overcome possible obstacles on the glass (snow, ice, etc.).

Blades will park when switch D, incorporated in motor, is opened by the sliding sector fitted on rotating arm (for diagram simplicity, in fig. 392 said sector is represented as a cam).

The reduction in speed is necessary to prevent the sliding sector from overriding the opening position of switch D, since the latter position corresponds to blades parked against cowl.

This ensures best conditions of visibility.

Bench Testing Instructions.

Windshield wiper unit check data:

By feeding a 14-V current to the motor and by braking with a stall torque of .43 ft.lbs (6 kgcm) - obtained by a friction brake - the following should not be exceeded: a temperature increase of 90° F (50° C), a 60 r.p.m. speed when warm, and a current draw of 1.7 to 1.8 Amp. Stall torque at 14 V must not be less than .5 ft.lbs (70 kgcm) (warm and with shaft locked).

Trouble Shooting Instructions.

If wiper unit operation is faulty, or it does not operate at all, possible causes are:

a) improper assembly on body;
b) irregularities of motor unit.

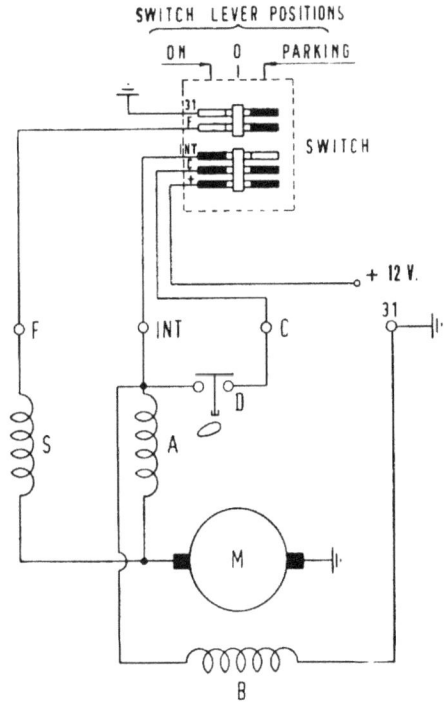

Fig. 392 - Windshield wiper wiring diagram.
A. Series winding. - B. Shunt winding. - D. Switch. - M. Motor. - S. Additional winding. - F. - INT - C = Terminals.

An improper assembly on body may bring about a distortion of wiper mounting bracket.

The consequences of this are abnormal stresses on pivots and linkages resulting in irregular and difficult blade sweep.

In this case, check the unit for proper assembly on body referring to opposite column as a guide.

As to point b), some of the more commonly encountered wiper motor troubles are:

1) **With switch lever pressed down (parking position), the automatic parking of blades does not take place. Instead, blades keep on sweeping at reduced speed.**

The trouble is in this case caused by the sliding sector that fails to open switch D (fig. 392). Check by backing out the four motor cover mounting screws and uncover the sliding sector. If possible, suitably deform the sector to bring it again into contact with the rod tip of switch D.

2) **With switch lever pressed down (parking position), the automatic parking of blades does not take place. Instead, blades stop in whatever position.**

Cause: switch D does not close and, consequently, no current flows between terminals « C » and « INT ». This may be due to foreign matter lodged between the movable contact and the fixed contacts of switch D.

Wash contacts with gasoline and, if necessary, recondition with a very fine clean file.

3) **The motor unit, though operating regularly, is remarkably noisy.**

This is due to abnormal reduction gear operation (out-of-true, tooth defects, excessive wear of pinion or worm, etc.).

Replace the motor unit.

4) **With switch lever pushed up (« ON » position) or pressed down (parking position), the wiper is unoperative.**

After ascertaining that the trouble is not imputable to wiring defects or switch, failure of wiper operation may be due to one of the following causes:

a) Shorted or interrupted windings A/B or S. Replace the motor as an assembly.

b) Broken or unsoldered inner connections. If possible, repair very carefully, due attention being given to the soldering and insulation of contacts.

c) Failure of brush to commutator contact on account of the following causes:

c-1. Excessive brush wear.

c-2. Commutator fouling.

c-3. Locking of brush in brush-holder owing to poor clearance between the two parts.

In case c-1 replace the complete motor unit.

In case c-2 washing the commutator and then polishing it with very fine emery cloth is sufficient.

In case c-3 restore the brush-to-brush holder clearance to correct value.

Instructions for Reassembly of Windshield Wiper on Body.

When reinstalling the unit, follow carefully the sequence and directions given. For partial reassemblies, proceed as instructed in the relevant paragraphs. However, remember that checking also the parts that have not been disassembled is a good practice which will prove useful.

1) Mount wiper on body by fully tightening the nuts fixing the pivots on which arms are fitted. Ensure that rubber sealing bushes between pivots and body are correctly assembled to prevent water infiltrations.

Next, secure mounting bracket lower edge to body by means of the special square bracket. Do not deform mounting bracket to provide proper mating with body surface. Instead, resort to the square bracket which, to this end, is provided with adjusting slots. In this way, linkages will not be bent and will not undergo abnormal stresses during operation.

2) To fit motor unit on mounting bracket there is no particular rule to be followed, excepting: a proper tightening of screws, a correct assembly of the main link on pivot lever, and a proper locking of fastener on pivot lever to prevent its unseating during operation.

3) After having established all electrical connections, taking into due account cable identification markings, switch on and run the motor for a few seconds, at the same time checking all switch positions, including the automatic parking (position 2), so that stopping of the sweep will take place with pivots in parking position which is the one for wiper arm mounting. If no assembly defects are found, check the motor unit. This does not require the removal of wiper unit assembly. To remove motor unit alone, disconnect the motor rotating lever-to-main link connection by taking off, either with fingers or screwdriver, the spring fastener clipped on link pin groove. Then, take off the screws fixing motor on mounting bracket.

If wiper unit operation is noisy, particularly on a dry windshield, it is advisable to replace the complete unit. This noisiness must be ascribed to irregular operation of motor reduction gearing. In time, gears will wear and may seize, or break, thus rendering the unit unserviceable.

4) On pivots (see point 1), install the shims, snap ring, wiper arm, plain washer and lock washer. Then, fully tighten the nuts **with wiper arms parked** (to the left, looking at windshield).

These nuts must be properly and carefully tightened or else blades may become misadjusted and give rise to the previously described trouble of stopping the motor under tension and its sub-

ELECTRICAL

sequent burning, unless switch is immediately turned OFF.

5) Check that wiper arms may be tilted 100° downwards without striking against cowl or front compartment lid.

6) Check that blade pressure on glass is 10.6 to 12.3 oz (300 to 350 grams).

7) Run wiper for approximately two minutes and check for smooth and quiet operation.

WINDSHIELD WIPER TOGGLE SWITCH

The switch may assume the following three positions:

— **Up**: wiper is switched ON even if ignition is OFF (ignition switch not in or in « zero » position).

— **Center**: blades stop immediately in whatever position they are on glass.

— **Down**: blades will automatically park. To obtain this, switch lever must be kept down by finger pressure. As soon as released, lever will snap back to **Center** position.

Trouble Shooting.

The more common troubles that might be met are:

1) Excessive effort needed to operate switch lever.
Cause: seizure of lever in its seat on account of poor lubrication, accumulation of foreign matter, etc.
Remedy: take down switch from instrument panel, wash movable contacts control mechanism in gasoline and lubricate the control lever and its sliding seat, with pure ropy vaseline.

2) One of the two rollers (movable contacts) does not exert sufficient pressure on its stationary contact, thus determining a poor or non-existent electrical circuit.

This is generally attributed to an excessively reduced radial clearance of switch control lever in its seat.

In this case, in fact, the seat of the lever, at whose end is fitted the plastic support guiding the movable contacts, does not permit the support to slide a sufficient amount to evenly distribute the spring load on both movable contacts.

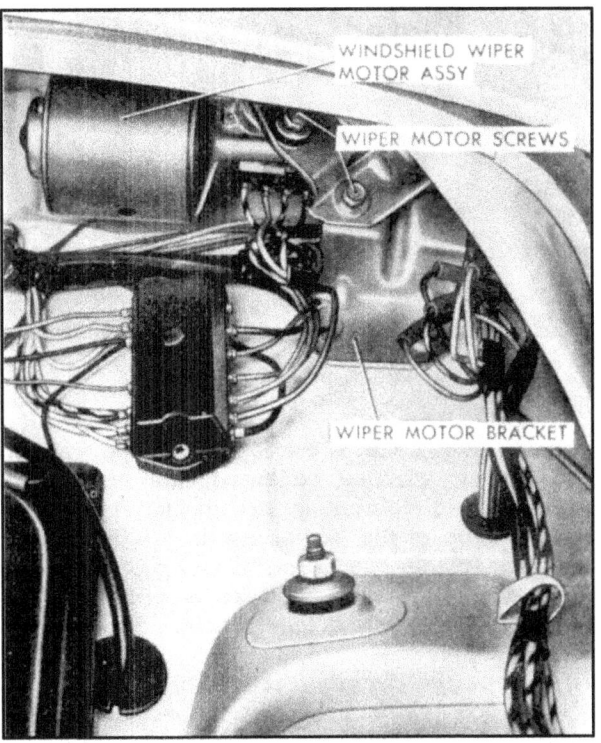

Fig. 393 - Arrangement of windshield wiper unit on vehicle.

Repair.

The switch has been designed to ensure trouble-free operation and maximum possible electrical and mechanical life.

In case of faulty operation not ascribable to cause 1) above, it is advisable to replace the switch as an assembly without attempting any repair.

HORN

The horn circuit comprises: the horn, pushbutton at center of steering wheel and ground (obtained through car body).

One terminal is connected to battery; the other to pushbutton on steering wheel, having the function of closing the circuit through ground.

The horn includes a diaphragm that is caused to vibrate rapidly by an electromagnet. When current flows through the electromagnet winding, the induced magnetic field attracts an armature towards the winding core. The armature is fixed to the horn diaphragm so that a movement of the armature causes a distortion of the diaphragm. At the same time the horn points open so that the

Fig. 394 - Removing horn button.

horn winding circuit is also opened. The magnetic field of the winding collapses, the armature is released, and returns to its original position as the distortion of the diaphragm is relieved. When this takes place, the points close, the winding is again energized, the armature is once more attracted and the cycle is then repeated for a number of times.

The repeated distortion of the diaphragm causes its vibration which produces the warning signal.

Trouble Shooting Instructions.

If horn is inoperative, possible causes are:

1) Damaged horn.

2) Broken connection between battery and horn.

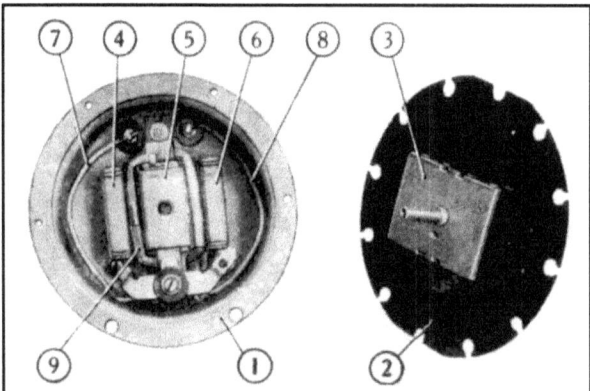

Fig. 395 - Horn (opened).
1. Body. - 2. Diaphragm. - 3. Armature. - 4, 5, 6. Core. - 7. Cable: terminal-condenser-stationary contact. - 8. Cable: terminal-magnetizing coil end. - 9. Magnetizing coil.

3) Broken connection between horn and pushbutton.

4) Damaged pushbutton mechanism.

5) Directional signal and outer lighting change over switch blade contact failing to adhere to steering wheel hub ring contact.

6) Current lead off horn blade contact on directional signal and outer lighting switch.

Damages to horn may be:

1-a) Distorted or broken diaphragm.

1-b) Connections, or inner windings, broken or burnt.

1-c) Electromagnet contact points deteriorated or excessively worn.

In each of these cases replacement of the horn will be necessary.

Fig. 396 - Checking magnetizing coil soundness.

In case 1-c), if wear or deterioration of contacts is not excessive, an adjustment may be made by the adjusting screw after having cleaned the contact points with a fine-cut file.

After adjustment, apply some paint on the screw for a twofold purpose: as a check on any unwanted tamperings and as a seal against possible water infiltrations to horn through screw threads.

In case the horn itself seems to be in perfect order, look for troubles described in points 2), 3) and 4).

The trouble mentioned in point 2) may be checked by means of a jumper connection. That is, connect battery directly to horn and press the pushbutton: if horn signals, the defect will be due to a broken connection between battery and horn.

ELECTRICAL

A similar procedure may be followed for the defect mentioned in point 3).

If even after all these checks no sound is heard, check pushbutton.

It will then be necessary to single out the trouble among the following causes:

4-1) Fixed and movable contacts oxidized or dirty.

4-2) Ring on which lower end of spring rests is oxidized or dirty.

If both defects are noticed, it will be convenient to check that return spring has not weakened through use, since this can bring about improper opening of the circuit with consequent smelting of contacts and their oxidation.

Fig. 398 - Horn sound adjustment.
1-2. Current plugs. - 3. Contact setscrew.

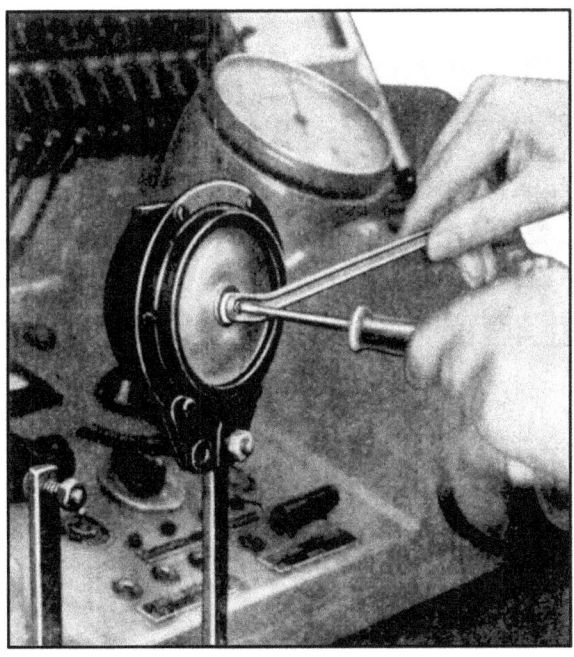

Fig. 397 - Horn sound adjustment.

Obtained by adjusting the armature air gap.

If trouble is to be traced to point 5), causes may be as follows:

5-1. Blade contact weak or broken.

5-2. Blade contact point worn.

5-3. Steering wheel ring contact worn at blade contact point.

In cases 5-1 and 5-2, replace the directional signal and outer lighting change-over switch assembly. In case 5-3, just replace the steering wheel hub ring contact.

If trouble is to be traced to point 6), replace the directional signal and outer lighting change-over switch assembly.

NOTE - Under any circumstances, prior to reassembling, remember recommendations as per «**NOTE**» under «Directional Signal and Outer Lighting Change-over Switch Trouble Shooting» (page 257).

Still to be pointed out is the fact that, at times, even with horn operating and with its components (including the contacts) in good condition, the signal obtained may not be pure and not sufficiently loud: in such cases, the breaker is misadjusted. It will suffice to act conveniently on the adjusting screw until the desired sound is obtained.

Removal and Installation.

No special instructions are required for horn removal and installation.

The only precaution to take is that the rubber gasket bonded to horn body must not be detached.

If horn must be replaced, before installing the new horn, bond on the latter the rubber gasket, with adhesive, in the same position as on the replaced horn.

ELECTRICAL ACCESSORY ITEMS SPECIFICATIONS

Low oil pressure indicator	red light
Signals when engine oil pressure is less than	7.1 to 21.3 p.s.i. (0,5 to 1,5 kg/cm^2)
Generator charge indicator	red light
Signals when:	
Generator voltage is less than	12.6 V
Engine speed, below	1100 r.p.m.
Car speed in 4th gear, below	14.3 mph (23 km/h)
Fuel reserve supply indicator	red light
Signals when the fuel in tank is below	.8 to 1.1 Imp. gals .9 to 1.3 U.S. gals (3.5 to 5 lt)
Direction indicators pilot light.	
Number of cycles per minute of flasher unit with a nominal load of 42.5 W:	
— at a nominal tension of 12 V and at 68° F (20° C)	85 ± 8
— at a tension 1.25 times the nominal one (15 V) and at 104° F (40° C) . . . not above	110
— at a tension 0.8 times the nominal one (9.5 V) and at —4° F (—20° C) . . . not below	45
Windshield wiper unit	crank gear type
Sweeps per minute	50 to 60
Motor unit bench test data:	
Feed voltage	14 V
Stall torque	.43 ft.lbs (6 kgcm)
Stator overheating temperature . . . not above	90° F (50° C)
Speed, when warm . . . not above	60 r.p.m.
Current draw . . . not above	1.8 Amps
Starting torque (with locked shaft), warm, at 14 V . . not below	5 ft.lbs (70 kgcm)
Wiper blade pressure on windshield	10.6 to 12.3 oz. (300 to 350 gr.)
Wiper arm tilting angle	100°

Section 11
BODY

	Page
CONSTRUCTION OF BODY SHELL	267
DOORS	268
GLAZING	271
INNER TRIMMING	273
FRONT COMPARTMENT LID	274
ENGINE COMPARTMENT LID	275
BUMPERS	276
FRONT PANEL ORNAMENT	276
FOLDING TOP	276
SUN ROOF	277
TRIM MOULDINGS AND STRIPS	278
SEATS	278
REPAIRING ACCIDENTED CARS	279
FLOOR ALIGNMENT FIXTURE	280
CAR CARE	283

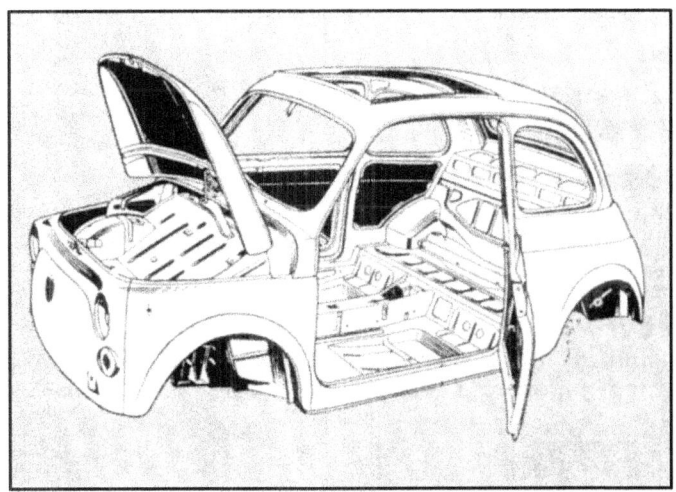

BODY

CONSTRUCTION OF BODY SHELL . . . page	267
Foreword . . . »	267
Spare Parts . . . »	267
DOORS . . . »	268
Weatherstrips . . . »	268
Inner Panellings . . . »	268
Handles and Locks . . . »	268
Window Regulator . . . »	269
Regulator Replacing Instructions . . . »	270
GLAZING . . . »	271
Door Window Drop Glass and Weatherstrip . . . »	271
Door Ventilator . . . »	271
Windshield . . . »	272
Rear Quarter Windows and Back Window . . . »	273
INNER TRIMMING . . . »	273
Felt Pads . . . »	273
Rubber Mats . . . »	273
Imitation Leather Inner Panelling . . . »	274
FRONT COMPARTMENT LID . . . »	274
Lid Ornament Molding . . . »	275
ENGINE COMPARTMENT LID . . . »	275
BUMPERS . . . »	276
FRONT PANEL ORNAMENT . . . »	276
FOLDING TOP . . . »	276
SUN ROOF . . . »	277
TRIM MOULDINGS AND STRIPS . . . »	278
SEATS . . . »	278
Front Seats . . . »	278
Rear Seat . . . »	279
REPAIRING ACCIDENTED CARS . . . »	279
Alignment . . . »	280
Fixture A. 66063 for Body Floor Alignment Inspection . . . »	280
Water and Dust Tightness . . . »	283
CAR CARE . . . »	283
Cleaning the Cloth Upholstery of Seats and Rear Compartment Lining . . . »	283
Cleaning Imitation Leather . . . »	284
Chrome Parts . . . »	284
Glass Panels . . . »	284
Washing the Car . . . »	284

CONSTRUCTION OF BODY SHELL

Foreword.

The compact and sturdy integral body is made up of the following structural assemblies:

1) Floor.
2) Rear floor and wheelboxes.
3) Front framing, dashboard and wheelboxes.
4) Right side panel.
5) Left side panel.
6) Windshield lower frame.
7) Windshield upper frame.
8) Front panel.

These assemblies are joined by electric spot welding.

Body Spare Parts.

Replacement of damaged parts is in many cases more convenient than attempting repairs.

Therefore, spares for those parts that are liable to be damaged or deformed in case of accident are provided for repair or replacement purposes.

List of these spares may be checked on the Body Spares Catalogue.

Small sections may be cut from the new part when damage does not require the integral replacement of the whole part.

NOTE - Parts must be joined by electric spot welding; when a spot welder is not available, an electric arc welder may be used. It is not advisable to use torch welding, since parts may be deformed by heat.

It shall be the repairman's task to judge case by case the extent of the repair. No detailed rules can be given here, since too many are the conditions that may be met. However, it should be kept in mind that the purpose of body repairs is not only that of restoring the car to its original appearance but, and mainly, that of restoring the car to the original sturdiness.

It is easily realized that if the repair has been made with the only purpose of masking the damage, neglecting the structural function of the bodywork, weak spots will develop in time liable to adversely affect the car sturdiness and riding safety.

NOTE - The following descriptions covering some of the major body parts are sufficient to make the operator understand his work, so that he may safely carry out the assembly and disassembly of parts. If damaged parts, of parts whose function is impaired, are found during the vehicle overhaul, it is a good practice to replace such parts.

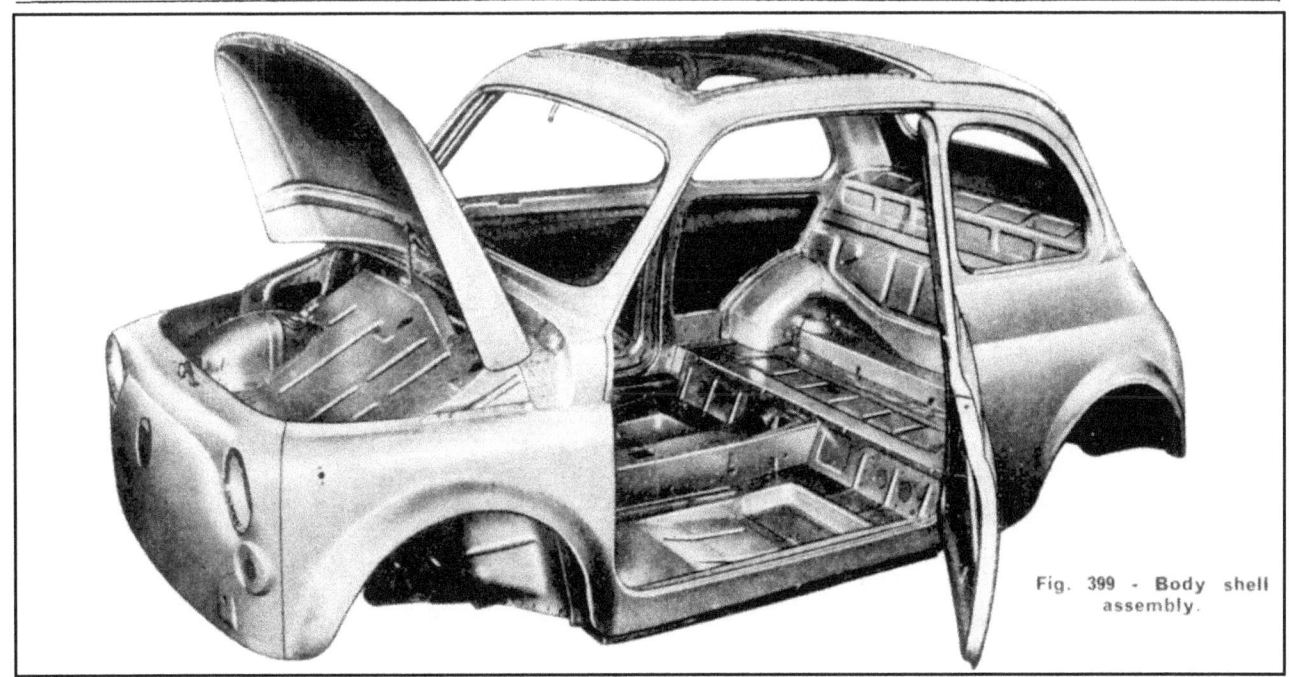

Fig. 399 - Body shell assembly.

DOORS

The two forward-opening doors have welded-on upper and lower hinge halves being joined by articulation pins to the other halves welded on the body. Hinge pins must be fitted with ball head uppermost.

Opening of the door is limited by a rubber check strap fixed by four self-tapping screws (two on door and two on body).

The check strap shall be mounted as follows:

— Put some sealing compound on the check strap mounting holes.

— insert the screws in the plates and in the strap.

— Interpose a washer, one on each screw, between: body and strap, door and strap.

— Lock the screws.

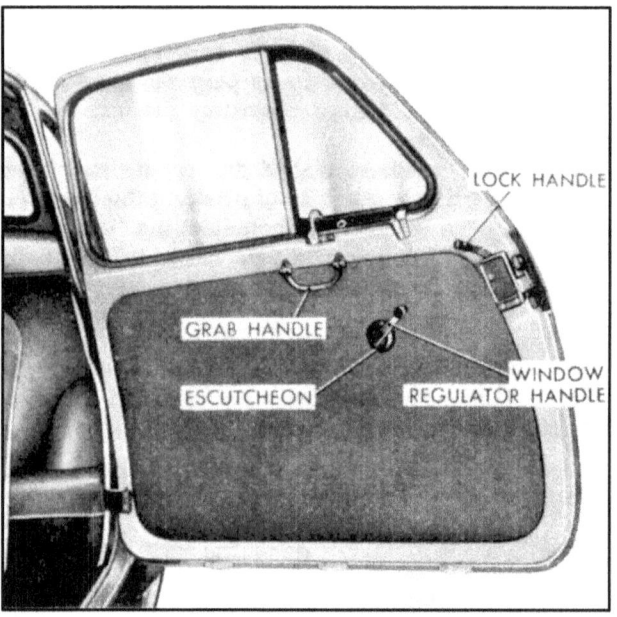

Fig. 400 - Left-hand side door, L. H. D. car.

Weatherstrips.

A one-piece weatherstrip is fitted to the door opening and fixed by « weatherstrip bonding compound ».

To replace it, proceed as follows:

Detach used weatherstrip, clean door opening flange with gasoline and remove rust spots.

Clean new weatherstrips from graphite or talc, used to prevent aging in storage; if necessary, wash with gasoline the side to be bonded, then let it dry.

By a brush, apply a coat of « bonding compound » on the side to be fixed. Let it dry for about 15 minutes (drying time depends upon the type of compound used).

Position rubber weatherstrip on door opening flange without pulling or forcing. The joint should be on down side at lower rear end of door opening.

Apply heavy pressure on weatherstrip starting from center to ends.

On door flange are located two rubber lining lengths: one, some $3\,5/32''$ (8 cm) long, at door lock, and the other, some $27\,5/32''$ (70 cm) long, fits starting from $1\,31/32''$ (5 cm) above upper hinge.

To replace these rubber lining lengths, operate as directed for door opening weatherstrips.

NOTE - Allow time for rubber weatherstrips on both door opening flange and door panel to be well cemented, prior to closing door.

Water leakages are often caused by closing the door too soon.

Inner Panellings.

Imitation leather lined masonite trim panels are fitted on all versions of « New 500 » Model.

Trim panels are secured in the housing below door window by means of four stiff clips at top and seven spring clips at bottom equally spaced around the panel border.

These fasteners are pressure snapped into holes on door framework inner flange.

To assure a better seating of trim panel in door housing, the door framework has been designed with a plate which should be bent down on trim panel after installation.

Prior to installing door trim panel a tarred felt pad should be cemented on door inner flange, in order to avoid that any water leaking in through door window rubber weatherstrips may be absorbed by trim panel.

Handles and Locks.

Doors are provided with locks which may be opened by handles either from inside or outside.

The driver's side door handle is provided with a key controlled lock (fig. 401).

The door on opposite side may be locked from inside by a safety device (figs. 403 and 404) controlled by a lever which may assume the following three positions:

— center, closed (fig. 403);

— forward, open;

— downward, locked (fig. 404).

BODY

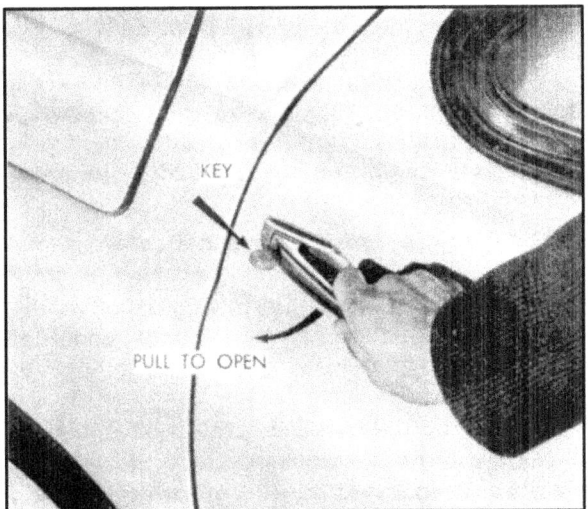

Fig. 401 - Driver's side door handle with key-controlled lock.

When the inner handle is in locked position the door cannot be opened from outside.

A striker plate is fitted on the body to seat lock striker.

Assemble lock as follows:

From outside, mount handle assembly and insert washer on the stud; screw the nut just a few turns to allow lock-to-handle mating at assembly.

Arrange handle dog horizontally, then tighten mounting nut.

Mount the lock, securing with three screws and washers. Fit the plate with two rubber guide blocks fastened by two screws.

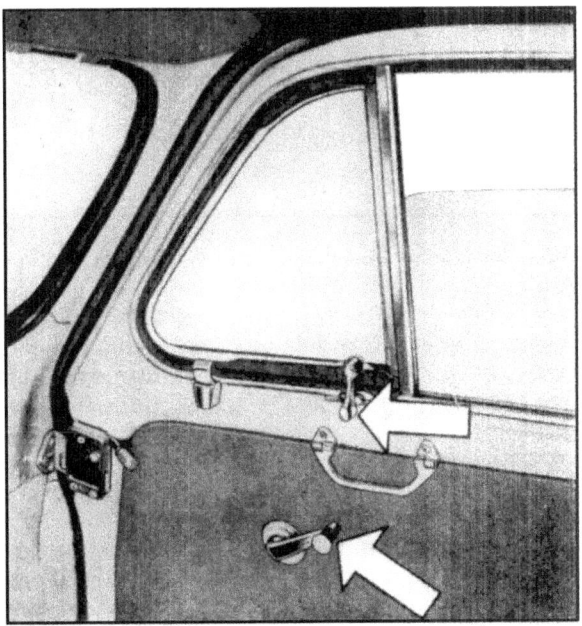

Fig. 402 - Detail of right door.
Upper arrow points to vent wing lock handle. Lower arrow points to window regulator handle.

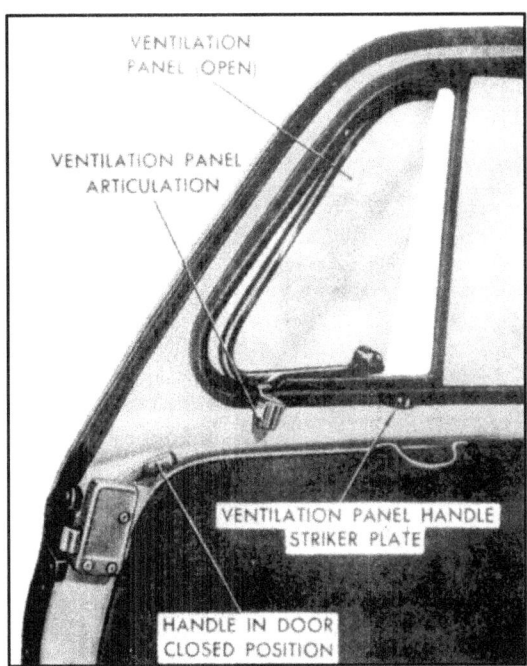

Fig. 403 - Inner view of door on side opposite steering wheel.

Striker plate and shim are secured by three screws.

Window Regulator.

The unit is of the lever type with gear control. The constructional simplicity of this system makes it highly reliable and operation troubles should be very unlikely.

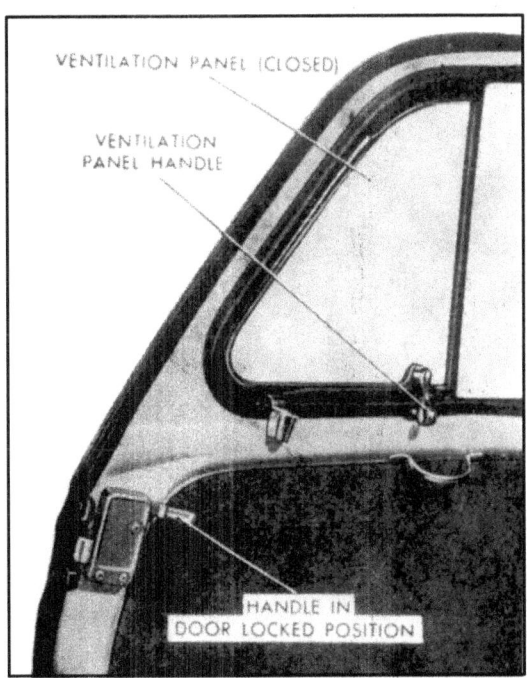

Fig. 404 - Inner view of door on side opposite steering wheel.

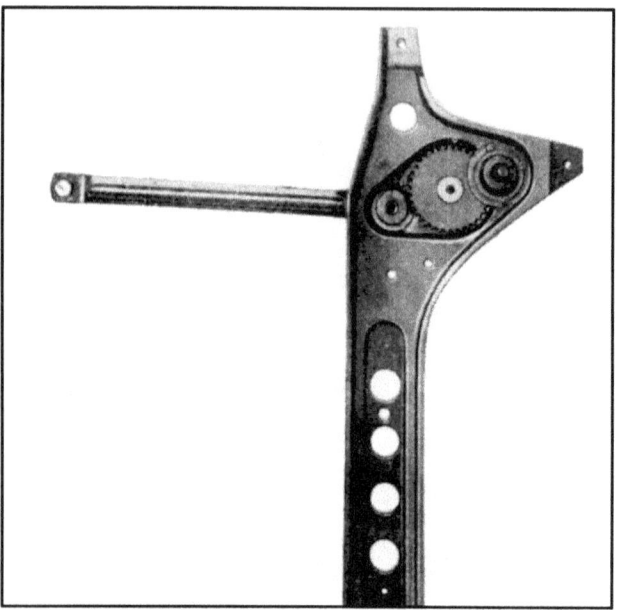

Fig. 405 - Left-hand side door window regulator, viewed from car interior.

The unit consists of a train of gears which transmits the crank movement to the lifting lever with a high reduction ratio. When the crank is rotated, it actuates a pinion integral with its shaft. The pinion is in mesh with a gear, on the hub of which is mounted a second pinion that meshes with the lever toothed sector.

At its end the lever carries a pin fitting in a guide rail adapting the glass. By rotating the crank in one direction or the other the glass is lifted or dropped.

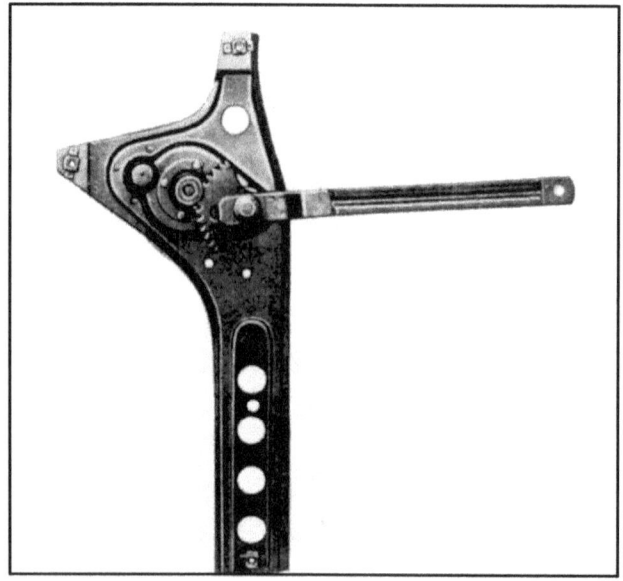

Fig. 406 - Left-hand side door window regulator, viewed from door inside.

Regulator Replacing Instructions.

No separate components of the window regulator are supplied. When worn or damaged, the window regulator must be replaced.

To remove the window regulator, operate as follows:

— Depress the door lining panel so as to reach the crank key. Remove the key and the crank.

— Remove the panel by prying it off with a screwdriver inserted between panel and door frame, being careful to avoid scratching the door paint.

— Detach the intermediate protection lining.

— Remove the screws securing the window regulator to door, tilt the regulator suitably to disinsert the lever pin from the guide and take off the regulator assembly.

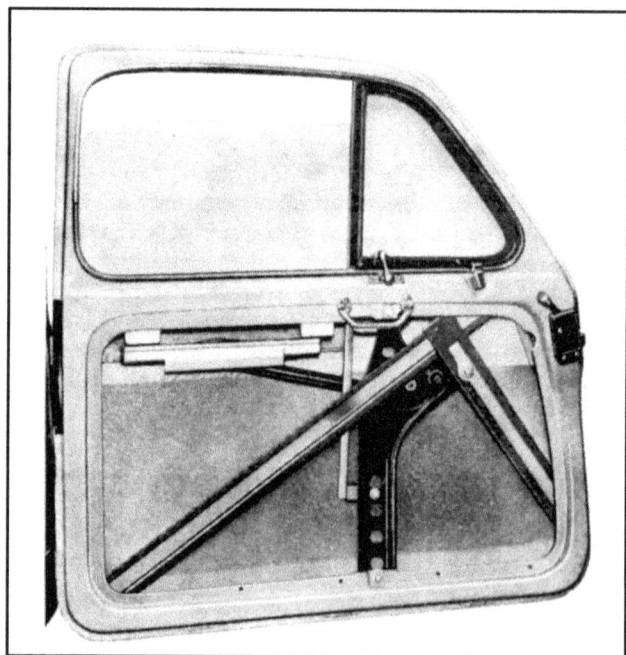

Fig. 407 - Location of window regulator in left-hand side door panel housing.

If a stiffening in the regulator operation is noticed, lubricate carefully the gears and the lever pin guide, checking also that the glass slides freely in its channels. To reinstall the regulator, reverse the removal operations. Before refitting the lining and the door panel, check the regulator for correct operation, i. e., the glass must move up and down without excessive effort on the crank.

After gluing the lining, check that it adheres evenly on door to avoid interference with window regulator operation owing to possible misplacements.

GLAZING

Door Window Drop Glass and Weatherstrip.

Door windows are fitted with swivelling front glass pane and drop rear glass pane.

See following paragraph for swivelling glass pane.

To install the door window drop glass, proceed as follows.

Fit No. 16 clips equally spaced all along the door window flange.

Install the glass runway, by inserting it in the rear and upper side of window groove. Runway will be fastened in place by clips as previously fitted.

Install the glass runway, complete with fabric lining, and secure it to regulator frame on upside with self-threading screws and on down side with bracket, screw, plain washer and spring washer. Gear-type window regulator is secured to door panel with three screws, three plain washers and three toothed washers (see description on a separate paragraph, page 269).

Install window rubber weatherstrips, which are fabric-lined on both inner faces in touch with the glass pane, to avoid that this may be scratched during up and down travel. Lock weatherstrips with clips as previously fitted.

Place the metal joint cap.

Install and arrange in place the drop glass, complete with lower rubber weatherstrip, metal channel and run plate for sliding travel of window regulator arm.

NOTE - « Convertible » version of Model 500 is equipped with stationary type window rear glass. Glass pane secures to the door panel by means of two brackets and screws, spring washers and nuts.

Door Ventilator.

It consists of:
 1) glass;
 2) weatherstrip between glass and chromium plated frame;
 3) chromium plated frame with pin and bracket for upper and lower articulation;
 4) frame control handle;
 5) lining.

To install the ventilator glass, proceed as follows:

Coat the outer edge of glass, on which the chrome plated frame must be installed, with a 50% solution of gasoline and benzol to facilitate glass insertion into frame.

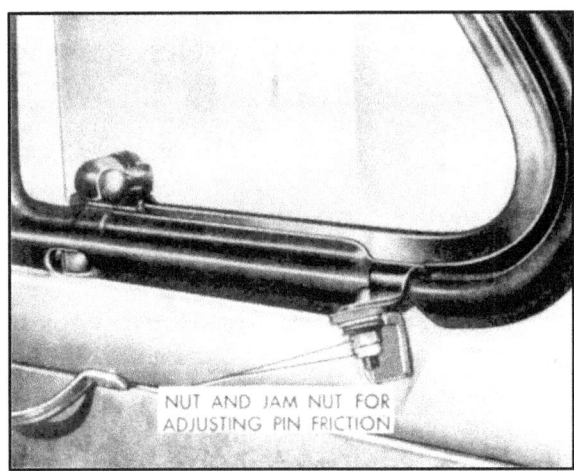

Fig. 408 - Ventilation panel lower articulation.

Position the rubber weatherstrip and press on the chrome plated frame. Slide in the strip length overhanging from frame.

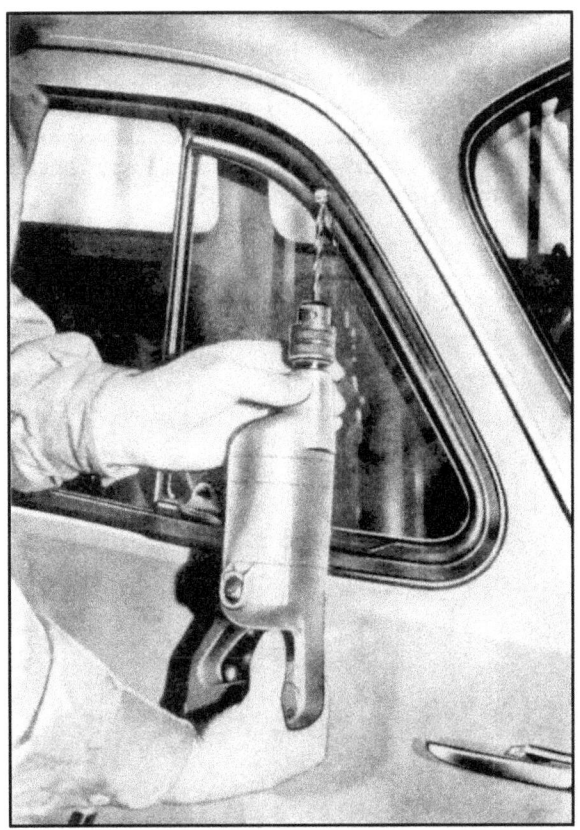

Fig. 409 - Removal of ventilation panel.

First eliminate the upper clenched articulation pin using a portable electric drill.

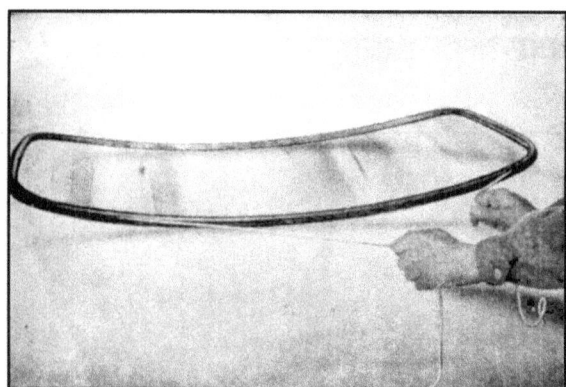

Fig. 410 - Installing draw-cord in windshield glass weatherstrip.

Fig. 412 - Adapting windshield weatherstrip.
Simply pull the draw-cord.

Install the lock handle, which is secured to frame by means of a screw sunk in handle body and two corrugated spring washers being placed between frame and handle.

Prior to installing ventilator pane on door panel, take care to insert metal channels in front post flanges at pane base with the purpose of holding rubber weatherstrip firmly in place.

Install the rubber weatherstrip and arrange it carefully in seat. Weatherstrip is secured by clips on metal channels as installed previously.

Install the handle striker plate and secure it to door channel by means of two self-threading screws.

Insert lower ventilator swivel in door panel-welded bracket, fit reaction spring and secure ventilator assembly through nut, lock nut and plain washer so that it can be freely adjusted in any position without undue clearance (fig. 408).

Fit chrome cover on lower ventilator swivel. Insert upper ventilator swivel in door panel brackets and clench it with special plier, to assure upper ventilator articulation.

Windshield.

It is curved to improve visibility and is provided with weatherstrip.

For assembly, proceed as follows:

— fit weatherstrip on glass;

— insert a draw-cord completely around weatherstrip outer lip. Cord ends shall come out at center of glass lower side (see fig. 410);

Fig. 411 - Positioning the windshield after tilting wiper blades.

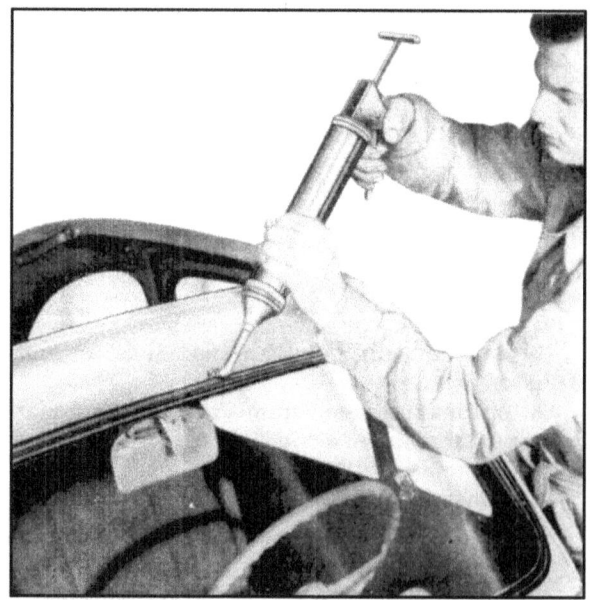

Fig. 413 - Injection of sealing compound between weatherstrip and body, using the gun.

— press windshield assembly against body opening from outside (fig. 411); then, pull cord ends from inside to overlap weatherstrip on body opening lip (fig 412).

Rear view mirror bulb cable, coming out from dashboard right end next to windshield, must be worked into and under the weatherstrip lip all the way around to rear view mirror.

Next, inject some sealing compound under weatherstrip outer lip (fig. 413).

To remove windshield, tilt first wiper arms, then push glass outwards and remove complete windshield assembly (fig. 414).

NOTE - Excess of sealing compound may be removed from glass and weatherstrip by a doctor blade and a cotton flock moistened with sealing compound solvent.

Rear Quarter Windows and Back Window.

Also these glass panes are provided with weatherstrips.

To remove glass, push it outwards.

For assembling, proceed as directed for windshield, inserting a draw-cord completely around, then press against opening and pull cord to overlap weatherstrip lip.

Fig. 414 - Removal of windshield glass.
Simply press out as shown.

Inject some sealing compound under outer lip.
Weatherstrip inner groove must be filled by the sealing compound.

BODY INNER TRIMMING

To deaden mechanical component vibrations and make car inside more comfortable, it has been lined with special sound deadening material.

Tarred Felt Pads.

They are bonded on various sections of the body, as specified below, by a special sound deadening, bonding compound.

They must be placed in the following locations:

a) steering wheel side footboard;
b) side opposite to steering wheel footboard;
c) floor right front end;
d) floor left front end;
e) front wheelboxes.

When bonding compound is applied by a spray gun, mask off control tunnel and seat fixed guide rails.

Vegetal felt pads, matched with tarred felt pads, are applied in the following locations, by means of bonding compound: vertical wall between intermediate and rear floor, bulkhead, rear floor, level panel below back window and rear wheelboxes. Tarred area should contact body metal.

Rubber Mats.

They should be arranged as follows:

a) right front wheelbox;
b) left front wheelbox;
c) right front floor;
d) left front floor;
e) central tunnel.

Front wheelbox mats must be gun sprayed with bonding compound on the lower surface.

Tunnel mat is fixed by rubber studs inserted in the specially drilled holes.

Floor mats are also fixed by eight rubber studs and by two tap rivets located at center of door sill between the two rubber studs.

Imitation Leather Inner Panelling.

Imitation leather panels are located as follows:
- a) rear quarter right side;
- b) rear quarter left side;
- c) right door;
- d) left door.

Panels are secured by clips and spring fasteners. Rear quarter panels are secured by three clips and one spring fastener, to be inserted in the body housing contour flange. Two flexible masonite panels are fitted on rear wheelboxes and secured to body floor through clip retainers.

The installation of door panels has already been described on page 268, under « Doors ».

Two imitation leather-lined foam rubber paddings are fitted on rear body side at quarter windows and secured by spring fasteners. Paddings have been designed to work as buffers.

FRONT COMPARTMENT LID

One-piece and rear hinged at center.

Hinge lower leaf is welded to body upper crossmember, hinge upper leaf is secured to lower leaf by nuts and washers screwed on lid studs.

Leaf connection is obtained by two clenched pins. Lid is held open by a prop inserted in a bracket welded to body and loaded with a spring which has also the task of fastening the prop (fig. 415).

Lid is kept closed by a locking catch. A safety hook is provided to avoid accidental opening.

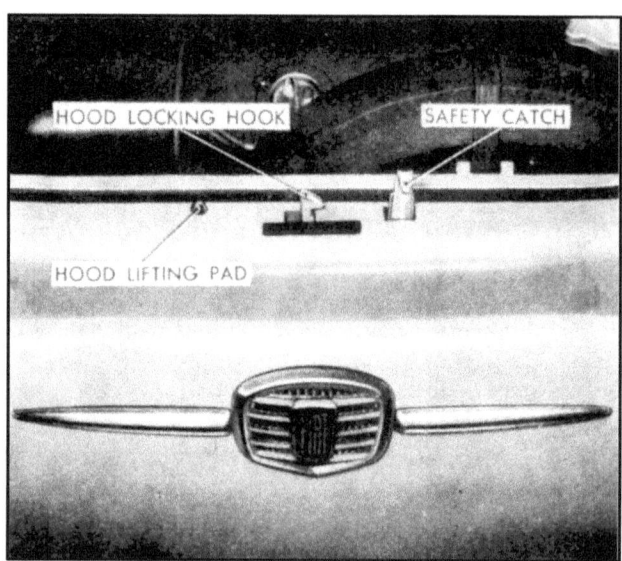

Fig. 416 - Hood lid locking hook, safety catch and lifting pad.

Lid weatherstrip is arranged on front and side flange of front compartment opening.

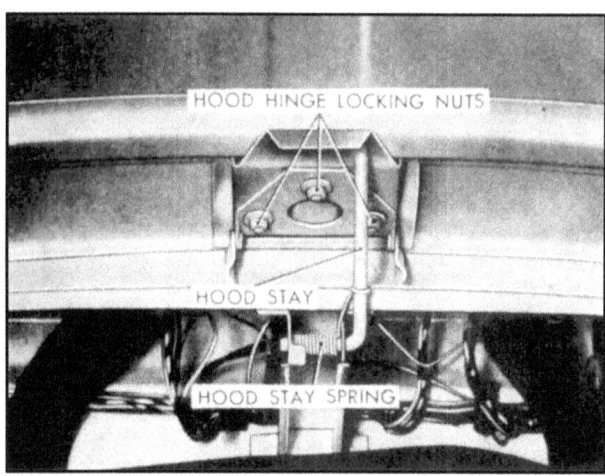

Fig. 415 - Close-up view of hood lid hinge and stay.

The catch release mechanism is controlled by a handle, at left under instrument panel, and connected to a bowden.

The bowden is arranged inside of front compartment and the wire passes through a bracket and is secured to catch.

A return spring is fitted on the catch, and pivots on a clenched pin. To lift the lid, insert fingers and push in the safety catch (fig. 416), which is pivoted on a hollow clenched pin. A spring is provided for catch return. To facilitate disengagement of safety catch, a rubber bumper causes the lid to rise lightly.

Fig. 417 - Hood lid lining and rubber buffers.

BODY

To install weatherstrip, brush the bonding compound on the edge of the opening. Six rubber bumpers are press-fitted on body shell and at both rear ends of front compartment lid.

Lid Ornament Molding.

It is press fitted at center on four slots and secured by clips.

ENGINE COMPARTMENT LID

Opening and closing of lid is controlled by a handle.

Lid opens downwards and pivots on two lower hinges: hinge pin (male) is welded on lid and its socket (female) is welded to body rear lower crossmember.

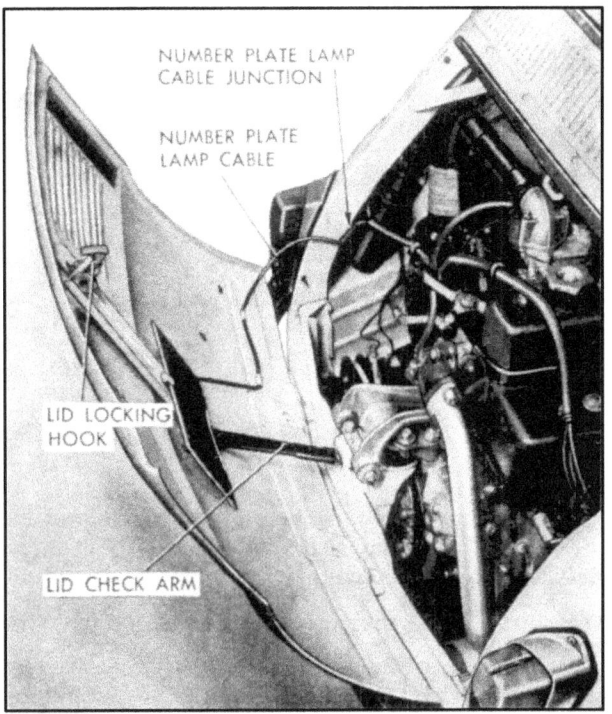

Fig. 419 - Engine compartment lid (opened).

Fig. 418 - Engine compartment lid in closed position.

To take off lid, proceed as follows:

— disinsert number plate lamp cable plug-in terminal (fig. 419);
— unhook the check strap by suitably orienting the retaining crosspiece;
— back out the right pin self-locking nut;
— exert a slight pressure on lid right side (towards the left).

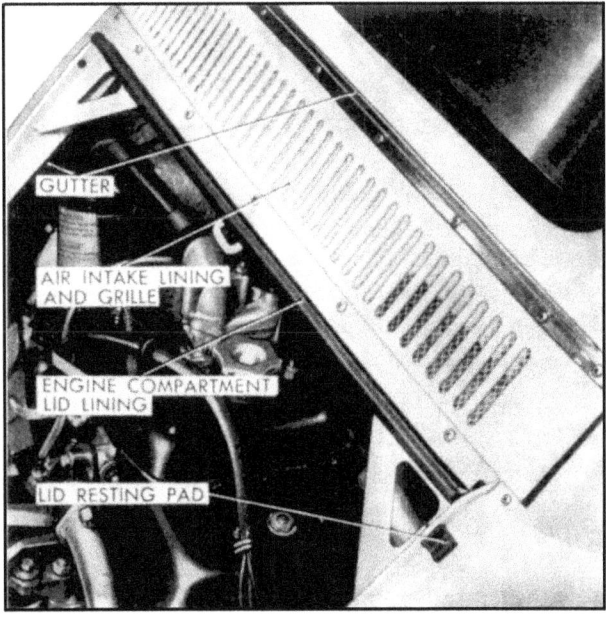

Fig. 420 - Close-up view of engine air intake grille and engine compartment lid lining.

BUMPERS

Fig. 421 - «New 500», front end view.

Front and rear bumpers are of the single-bar type.

At rear, bumper is mounted on body cross-member. Bumpers are secured by two bolts with the interposition of metal-lined rubber spacer pads.

By allowing slight bumper flexibility, especially on lateral bumps, the rubber pads absorb slight shocks and protect the body.

To take off bumpers, back out their mounting nuts from inside front and engine compartments, then remove the plain and lock washers.

Front and rear bumpers to suit vehicles for export to U.S.A. and Canada are of the reinforced type and include, beside a blade, two guards. Two threaded pins welded to guards secure bumpers to body brackets, with the interposition of two metal spacers.

FRONT PANEL ORNAMENT

The ornament (fig. 421) centrally mounted on body front panel, consists of a central FIAT nameplate and two side moldings.

To install the ornament, proceed as follows:

Position one of the two side moldings and insert its mounting lug and stud in panel slot and hole, respectively.

Place central plate on panel and insert its side wing under the molding tip.

Fit the other side molding with its tip on the other central plate wing.

Hold the parts so mounted against the panel and, from inside front compartment, place the plain and lock washers on the studs. Next, fit and screw in the nuts.

FOLDING TOP

The folding top assembly consists of:

a) imitation-leather top with vinylite back window;

b) front end frame, complete with the two handles and catches; movable bow articulated on frame side rails;

c) three stiffening bows fixed by chromium-plated buttons and tipped with rubber blocks;

d) front molding for top mounting on frame;

e) rear molding for top mounting on engine cooling air intake body panel;

f) roller top retaining strap (figs. 422 and 423).

When installing the top, remember the following:

a) The top rear molding is secured by ten

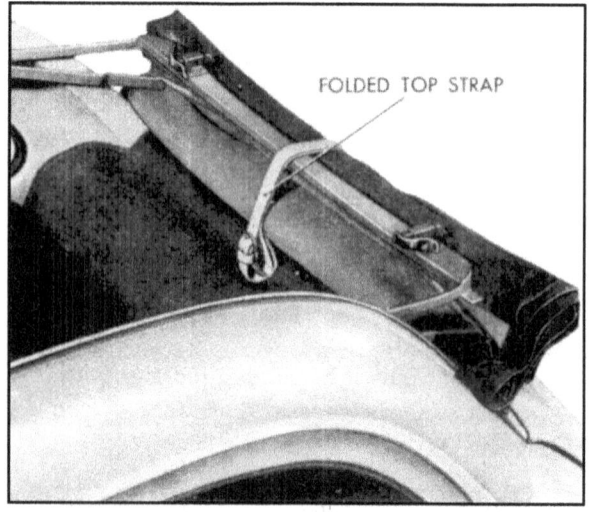

Fig. 422 - Folded top retainment belt strap.

screws, six self-tapping and four standard, so located:

— one long, self-tapping screw at each end;

— two standard screws, at center;

— two standard screws, next to the long self-tapping screws;

— four self-tapping screws, two on each side between the standard screws.

Said screws also secure the upper end of the engine air intake panel to body.

b) After having fixed the rear molding, spread the complete top all the way to the front. Make sure articulated bow is located between the second and third stiffening bows. Then, by special screws, fix the frame rails to the upper inner ends of body side panels.

Fig. 423 - Arrangement of rolled top.
This should be done carefully to prevent damaging the vinylite back window. Roll must never obstruct engine air intake slots.

SUN ROOF

« New 500 » Sun Roof version differs from Convertible version in the top arrangement. Sun Roof consists of a rear metal panel or dome and a front imitation-leather covering which works as a collapsible top.

On dome panel is installed the weatherstrip-surrounded back window and the following items are cemented: a plastic lining, a foam rubber strip at upper front end and two rubber welts on sides to prevent water leakage.

The dome panel is secured laterally to body shell by means of four screws, four plain washers

Fig. 425 - « Sun Roof » top in locked position.

and four spring washers, and at rear by means of nine self-threading screws which provide a mounting also for engine air intake grille and gutter.

The collapsible top is made up as follows:

a) an imitation-leather lining;

b) a metal framing having a front cross member, on which control handles and top front latch strikers

Fig. 424 - « Sun Roof » top in unlatched position.

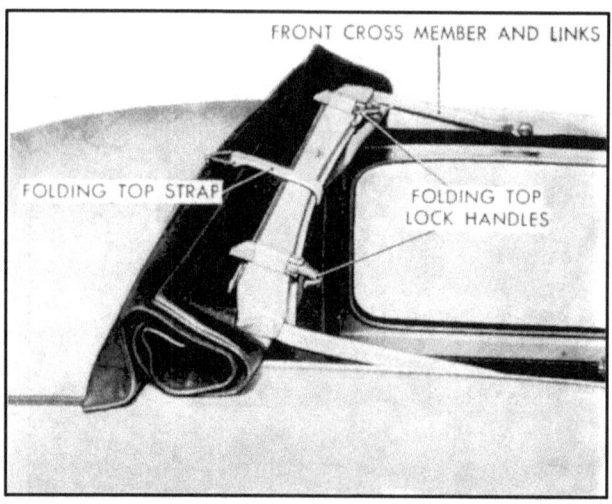

Fig. 426 - « Sun Roof » top in collapsed and fastened position.

are fitted, and a movable bow riveted to top lining and provided with rubber pads for top rest on body;

c) a front moulding for top lining mounting on framing cross member;

d) a rear moulding for top lining mounting on dome panel;

e) a top lining retaining strap, secured to front end of dome through a bridge bracket;

f) a bracket for strap hooking-up with top lining in folded position.

For Sun Roof assembly, proceed as follows:

— install dome panel on body shell;

— position the collapsible top assembly and secure it at rear to dome panel through eight rivets;

— stretch the top covering to closed position and secure both framing side arms to body shell rails, through special screws.

TRIM MOULDINGS AND STRIPS

Trim mouldings and strips on side panels, doors and below doors are secured by means of clips or spring fasteners which snap into openings drilled on applicable parts.

It is good practice to lock fasteners in their holes using « Vibradamp » cement.

SEATS

Front Seats.

The two front bucket seats consist of a one-piece tubular frame with imitation-leather or cloth padded cushion and back. Additional comfort is provided by a number of rubber bands hooked across frame under the cushion and a sheath covering on the seat back.

Seat frame bottom front ends are provided with sliding guides running in guide rails fixed on floor. Sliding guides are articulated on frame tubes to permit forward tilting of seats and facilitate access to rear compartment (fig. 427).

Two rubber pads provide the cushioning of seat frame on guide rails (figs. 427 and 428).

The seat adjustment control lever is fitted on frame right tube to permit unlocking of seats (turn lever rightwards) and their relocation to suit personal comfort (fig. 428).

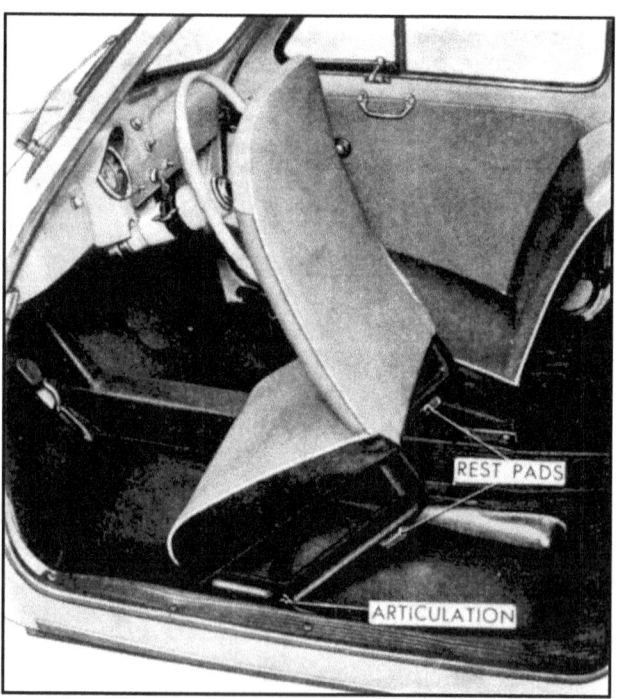

Fig. 427 - Front seat tilted forward to facilitate access to rear compartment.

BODY

Rear Seat.

The rear seat consists of a foam rubber cushion and back. Seat back is cemented to rear floor and body shell bulkhead.

Rear seat lining is of fabric and imitation leather, and includes also a masonite floor which is fitted below back window.

The seat lining is held in place by four self-threading screws, two of which secure the floor below back window and two the lining at back bottom.

Fig. 428 - Front seat position adjuster arrangement.

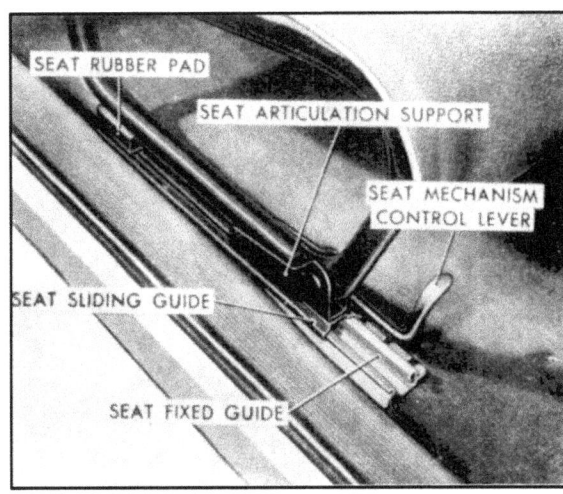

REPAIRING ACCIDENTED CARS

The damages a car may undergo in an accident may be different in nature and severity.

For this reason it is rather difficult to give specific and detailed instructions on body repair, covering the many possible cases, as each blow and/or bump may lead to given deformations which must be eliminated in accordance with the best method suggested by the type of damage.

A thorough knowledge of body construction and welding seams is however an essential condition before any repair of body parts is attempted.

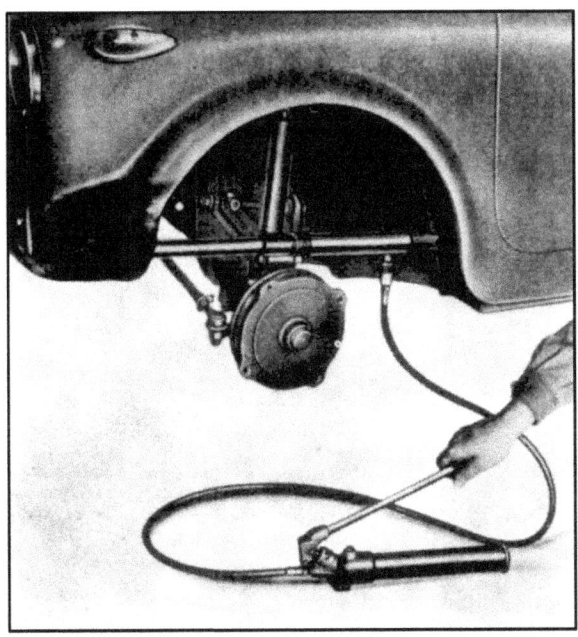

Fig. 329 - Application of the hydraulic hand-operated jack for front fender straightening.

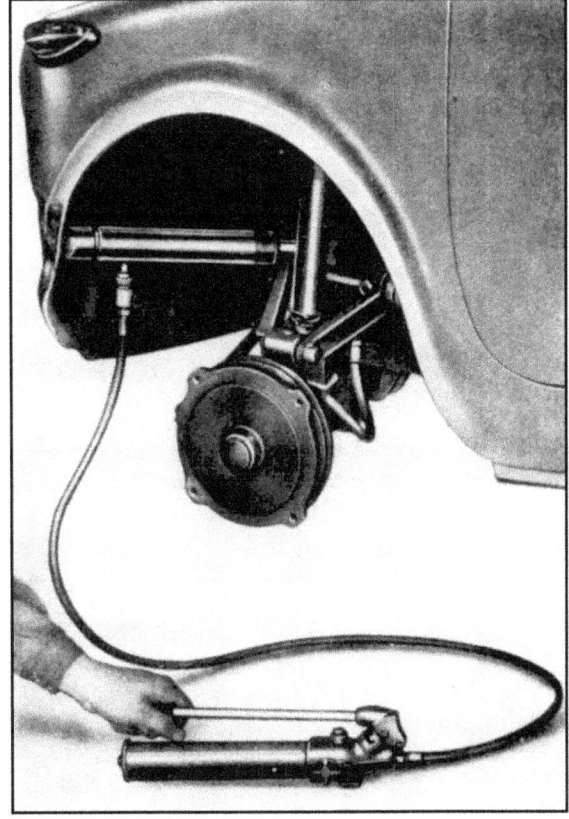

Fig. 430 - Application of the hydraulic hand-operated jack for front fender straightening.

In most of such cases it will be necessary to remove some parts in order to gain access to the distorted items for performance of straightening and aligning operations.

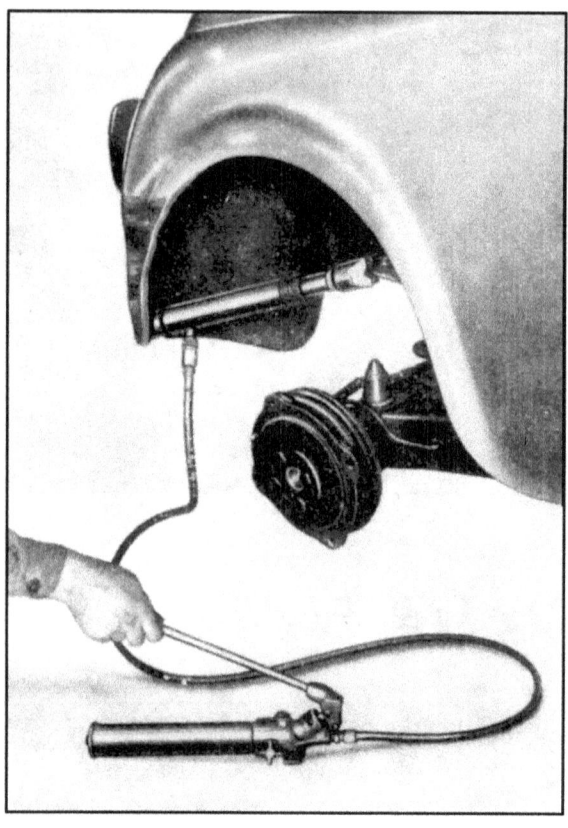

Fig. 431 - Application of the hand-operated hydraulic jack for rear fender straightening.

Position of jack is changed as required to obtain progressive action.

If body is very badly damaged, it will be advisable to take off all easily removable inner panellings. This will provide a clearer vision of parts during repair and alignment operations at the same time facilitating measurements, checks and the application of hydraulic jacks for panel straightening and squaring (figs. 429, 430 and 431).

Alignment.

The car is of the integral construction type and, therefore, the floor is in a single unit with body, as shown in fig. 399.

On a bumped car first check the alignment of front and rear wheels. Any misalignment will be revealed by a lack of parallelism between front and rear wheel axes or between front and rear wheel track widths.

It is essential to check that the misalignment is not due to distortion of front and rear swinging arms, of track rods, etc.

If misalignment is caused by deformations of body panels, these must be reshaped and the mounting points of mechanical units of floor must be rechecked, using the reference data given in fig. 435 or the specially designed fixture **A. 66063** (fig. 434).

Body floor must be checked very accurately and any deformation must be fully corrected until floor alignment and squareness will correspond to the data given in figure 435 and fixture **A. 66063** will fit on floor in the manner described and illustrated in the following paragraphs.

FIXTURE A. 66063 FOR BODY FLOOR ALIGNMENT INSPECTION

To check floor alignment and the position of front and rear suspension mountings for correct location, use fixture **A. 66063** illustrated in figures 432, 433 and 434.

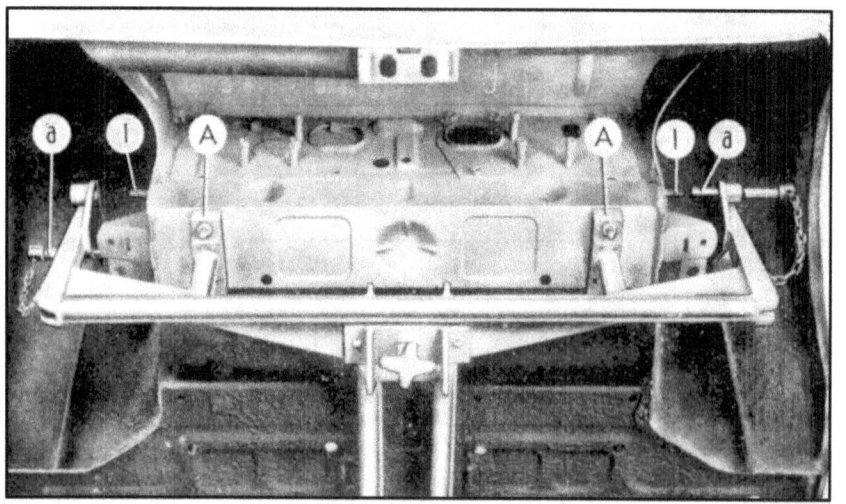

Fig. 432.

Checking floor front end by fixture A. 66063.

A. Brackets, attachment of fixture to leaf spring mounting studs. - 1. Swinging arm pin mounting studs. - a. Fixture hollow pins.

Hollow pins « a » must fit on studs « 1 ».

Fig. 433.

Checking floor rear end by fixture A. 66063.

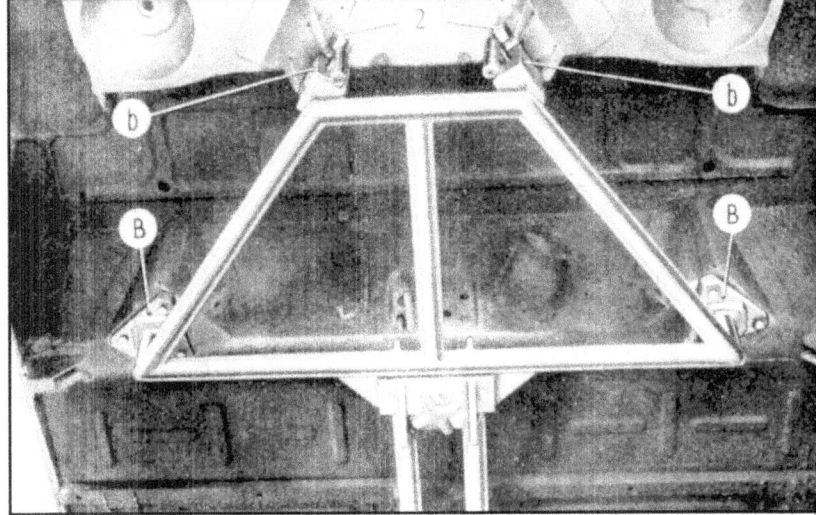

B. Brackets, attachment of fixture to rear swinging arm outer supports. - b. Articulations of fixture that must fit into pins «2». - 2. Pins, swinging arms inner mounting on floor.

Fixture front end checks the mounting position of leaf spring and swinging arm pin fixing studs.

The rear end checks the position of rear swinging arm mountings.

The central part joins the fixture front and rear end and serves to check floor alignment.

To check alignment, proceed as follows:

Position fixture front end of floor and fix its two brackets (A, fig. 432) on leaf spring mounting studs; then, check alignment of the two fixture side arm hollow pins (a, fig. 432) with right and left swinging arm pin mounting studs (1, fig. 432).

Position fixture rear end on floor and fix its outermost ends to mounting holes (B, fig. 433) of rear suspension swinging arm outer supports. The two fixture articulated joints (b, fig. 433) must be inserted into the pins (2, fig. 433) placed in swinging arms inner mounting brackets.

After having carried out the above two checks, install fixture central part. Fixture front and rear ends are provided with centering dowels (C and D, respectively) in which central part of fixture must be inserted and fixed by two clamp-screw knobs (E, fig. 434).

If not difficulty is encountered in installing the fixture on floor and check points coincide (« 1 » and

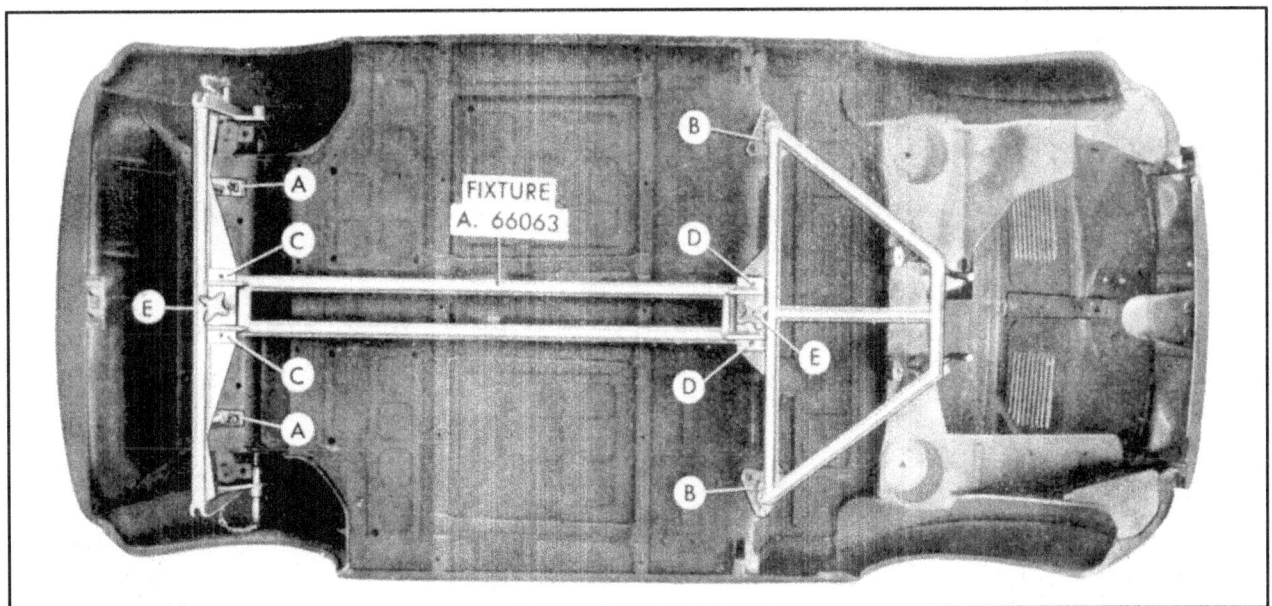

Fig. 434 - Checking alignment of floor and front and rear suspension mountings with fixture A. 66063.

A. Brackets, attachment of fixture to leaf spring mounting studs. - B. Brackets, attachment of fixture to rear swinging arms outer supports. - C and D. Pins, fixture central portion centering on front and rear elements. - E. Clamp-screw knobs, joining the three fixture elements.

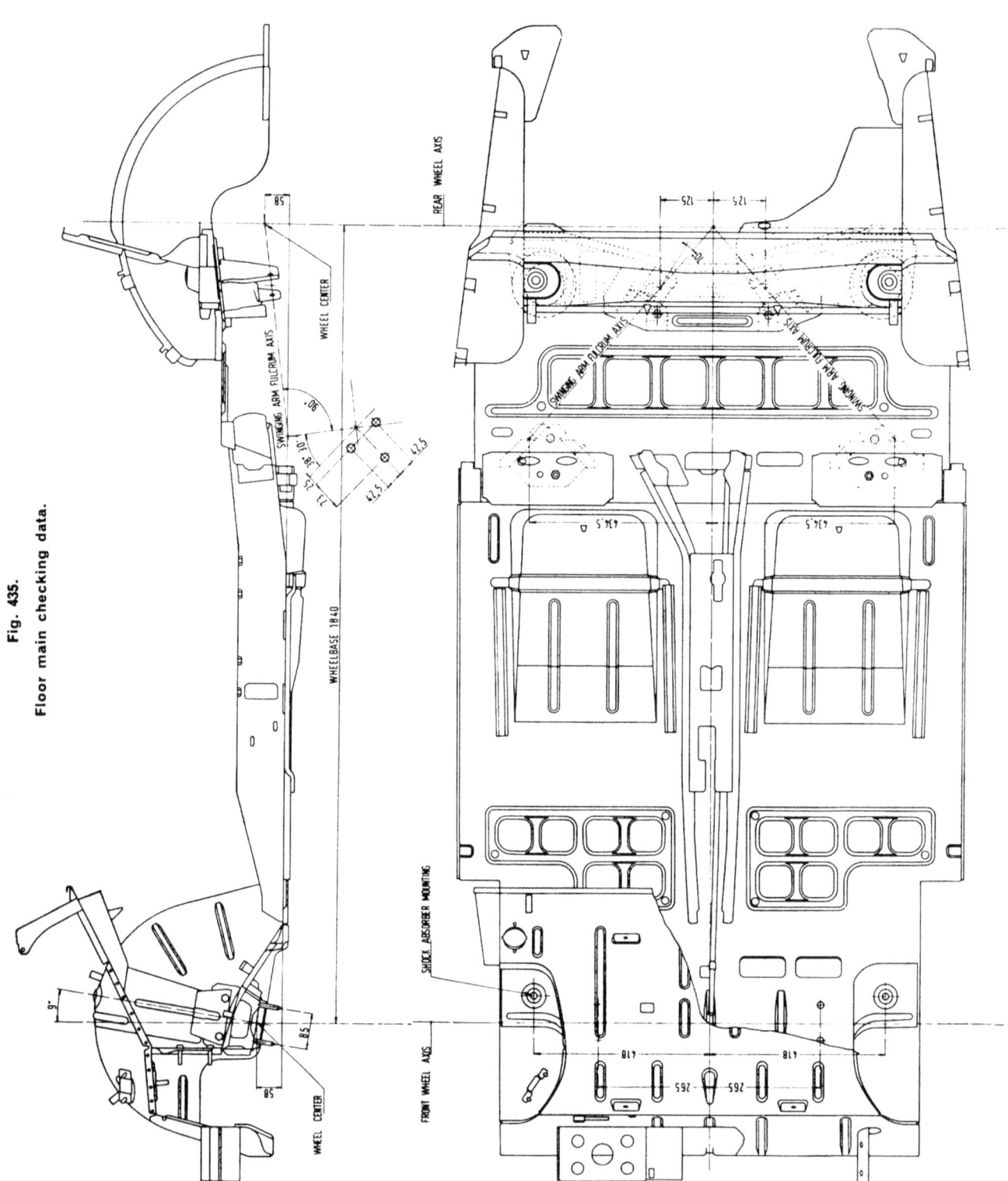

Fig. 435. Floor main checking data.

BODY

«a», fig. 432 at front; «2» and «b», fig. 433 at rear), it is an indication that floor has not undergone any deformation and is aligned.

If misaligned, proceed with the necessary corrections.

To straighten out or reshape deformed body or floor parts, use the specially designed equipment shown in fig. 430 which includes a pump-controlled hydraulic jack.

Floor and body panel straightening are operations that call for a thorough knowledge of the construction of parts involved and the know-how required to quickly locate joint areas and welding seams.

Water and Dust Tightness.

Ater body repairs and before re-installation of inner panellings, inspect accurately all points (joints and welds) where water and dust infiltrations are likely to occur. In case any of such points are found faulty, remedy by sealing compound applied with a suitable gun.

CAR CARE

Cleaning the Cloth Upholstery of Seats and Rear Compartment Lining.

A periodical cleaning based on specially devised methods is a «must» to ensure long life and preserve the attractive appearance of upholstery cloth.

Dust and dirt blown into the car when windows are open settle on the upholstery and tend to wear the cloth causing an unsightly appearance. For this reason, it is extremely important to do some rather frequent cleaning (about every 15 days), shortening this interval as the car accumulates mileage.

Wipe off dust using a brush or, better still, use the household vacuum cleaner, if available.

To remove ordinary soiling of the upholstery cloth, proceed as follows:

— lukewarm water and a neutral soap should be used, applying to surface on a piece of clean cloth or brush, wiping in the direction of upholstery nap rather than against it;

— repeat the operation using only a clean damp cloth and no soap;

— when upholstery cloth is dry, brush back against nap to restore a «fresh», fluffy look.

To obtain good results, stains must be removed in the least possible time after they are made, because spots that are allowed to remain for long on cloth will set and their removal will be very difficult, if not impossible.

Some types of stains call for specific spot removers. Use those of reliable repute and follow label instructions.

Fig. 436.

« New 500 » Sun Roof.

Cleaning Imitation Leather.

Never use oil, paints or ammonia solutions.

The cause for any alteration or loss of imitation leather softness or luster, should generally be ascribed to the use of unsuitable or harmful cleaners.

To keep imitation leather clean, simply wash with a soap-sudded moist clotch. Then, wipe clean with a moist cloth and no soap.

Finally, rub with a clean dry cloth and stop when original luster is restored.

Chrome Parts.

To preserve the enduring finish of chrome parts, wash periodically using a cloth dampened with kerosene, dry, and rub with a cloth moistened in fluid oil. Next, remove any trace of oil using a clean woolen cloth.

This procedure will not alter the brilliancy of chromium-plated parts and will preserve them from the detrimental action of atmospheric agents like climate dampness or saline air.

Glass Panels.

Glass panels must be cleaned with a chamois or rag: in either case utmost cleanliness is an essential condition, inasmuch as if already used to clean the car, they might be soiled with dust or contain sand. This foreign matter is abrasive and will eventually scratch glass panels to the point where perfect visibility is impaired.

Washing the Car.

Body will call for washing at variable intervals depending on driving conditions.

If a car washing tunnel is not available, proceed as follows:

Using an ordinary garden hose (with nozzle), wash first the bottom of car, including the wheels. If required, caked road grime should be softened with a sponge. Do not allow the water spout to strike wheel paint finish too violently.

Wash all body panels with running water, moderating the pressure of the water spout. Complete the washing with a sponge, rubbing gently at first to prevent scratching the finish with the entrained dirt (rinse sponge often) and then more vigorously, using plently of running water all the time.

Dry car thoroughly with a clean chamois. No trace of water must remain on the finish.

To prevent damages to windshield wiper during the washing operation, pass the sponge or chamois under wiper blades which must be lifted and tilted towards cowl: never displace blades angularly.

If after washing and drying with chamois the original luster of the finish is not restored, use one of the many polishing compounds of good commercial grade. A slight amount of color showing up on the cloth while polishing should not be cause for alarm as this is a natural condition having no consequence on the luster and life of the finish.

Grease, oil and tar stains on the body finish may be removed with some gasoline followed by an immediate wiping with a dry cloth.

Fig. 437.

« New 500 » Convertible.

Section 12

MAINTENANCE
TOOL EQUIPMENT
CAR SPECIFICATIONS

	Page
MAINTENANCE	286
LUBRICANT SPECIFICATIONS	287
TOOL EQUIPMENT	288
TOOL KIT	290
«NEW 500» SPECIFICATIONS	291

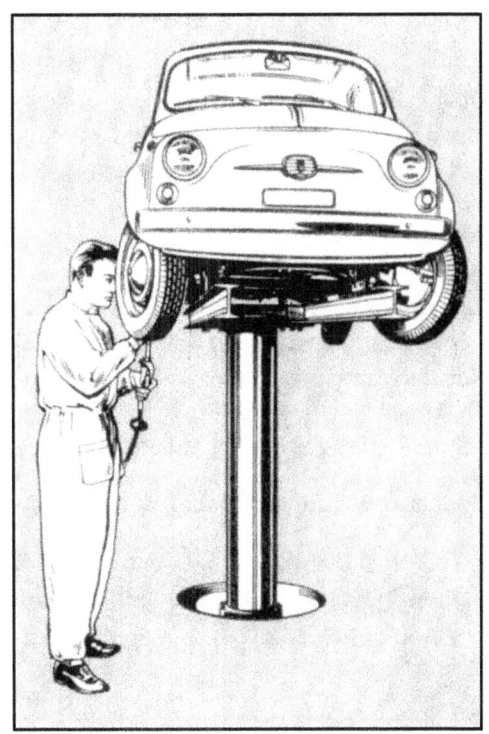

12

MAINTENANCE

OPERATIONS	Miles	6.000	12.000	18.000	25.000	31.000	37.000	44.000	50.000
	Km	10.000	20.000	30.000	40.000	50.000	60.000	70.000	80.000

LUBRICATION

1. Lubricate ignition distributor		★	★	★	★	★	★	★	★
2. Check gearbox-differential unit oil level		★	★		★	★		★	★
3. Replace oil in gearbox-differential unit				★			★		
4. Lubricate generator ball bearings					★		★		
5. Lubricate starter free wheel					★		★		
6. Lubricate door hinges			★		★		★		★

Every 300 miles (500 km): Check oil level in sump.

Every 1500 miles (2.500 km): Inject grease in lubricators.

Every 6000 miles (10.000 km): Replace oil in sump.

CHECKS AND INSPECTIONS

1. Replace air cleaner cartridge		★	★	★	★	★	★	★	★
2. Check ignition distributor breaker contacts		★	★	★	★	★	★	★	★
3. Clean spark plugs and check gap		★	★	★	★	★	★	★	★
4. Clean carburetor filter		★	★	★	★	★	★	★	★
5. Check brake fluid level		★	★	★	★	★	★	★	★
6. Check tappet clearance		★	★	★	★	★	★	★	★
7. Check and adjust front wheel bearing play			★		★		★		★
8. Check and adjust rear wheel bearing play					★		★		
9. Clean and lubricate battery terminals and clamps and check tension		★	★	★	★	★	★	★	★
10. Check generator and starter brushes for wear					★		★		
11. Tighten all bolts and nuts fixing units to body			★		★		★		★

Every 300 miles (500 km): Check tire pressure.

Every 1500 miles (2.500 km): Check electrolyte level in battery.

Every 6000 miles (10.000 km): Road test car.

FIAT LUBRICANT SPECIFICATIONS

FIAT VS 40 Oil for engine (above 86°F - 30°C) (SAE 40)	Flash point (in open cup) Pour point Viscosity at 132°F (50°C) } Engler units / Kinematic cSt Viscosity at 212°F (100°C) } Engler units / Kinematic cSt	min 464°F (240°C) max 17.6°F (−8°C) 11.4 to 12.6 86.6 to 95.6 min 2.22 min 14
FIAT VS 30 Oil for engine (above 32°F - 0°C) (SAE 30)	Flash point (in open cup) Pour point Viscosity at 132°F (50°C) } Engler units / Kinematic cSt Viscosity at 212°F (100°C) } Engler units / Kinematic cSt	min 456°F (230°C) max −0.4°F (−18°C) 8 to 9 60.8 to 68.4 min 1.92 min 10.90
FIAT VS 20 Oil for engine (32° to 5°F - 0° to −15°C) (SAE 20)	Flash potin (in open cup) Pour point Viscosity at 132°F (50°C) } Engler units / Kinematic cSt Viscosity at 212°F (100°C) } Engler units / Kinematic cSt	min 428°F (220°C) max −0.4°F (−18°C) 4.7 to 5.5 35 to 41.3 min 1.58 min 7.20
FIAT VS 10 W Oil for engine (below 5°F - −15°C) (SAE 10 W)	Flash point (in open cup) Pour point Viscosity at −0.4 F (−18°C) } Engler units / Kinematic cSt Viscosity at 132°F (50°C) } Engler units / Kinematic cSt Viscosity at 212°F (100°C) } Engler units / Kinematic cSt	min 404°F (200°C) max −13°F (−25°C) max 330 max 2500 2.7 to 3.3 18.5 to 23.7 min 1.38 min 4.80
FIAT W 90 Oil (SAE 90 EP)	Flash point (in open cup) Viscosity at 132°F (50°C) } Engler units / Kinematic cSt	min 374°F (190°C) 14.5 to 15.5 110.2 to 118
FIAT Jota 1 Grease	Drop point (Ubbelohde) Worked penetration Soap base	min 356°F (180°C) 310 to 340 $\frac{mm}{10}$ Lithium
FIAT Jota 2 M Grease	Drop point (Ubbelohde) Worked penetration Soap base	min 356°F (180°C) 265 to 295 $\frac{mm}{10}$ Lithium with molybdenum sulphide
FIAT Jota 3 Grease	Drop point (Ubbelohde) Worked penetration Soap base	min 374°F (190°C) 220 to 250 $\frac{mm}{10}$ Lithium
FIAT MR Grease	Drop point (Ubbelohde) Worked penetration Soap base	min 356°F (180°C) 235 to 250 $\frac{mm}{10}$ Lithium
Special FIAT blue label brake fluid	Heavy Duty non-mineral type	—

SPECIAL SERVICE TOOLS

This list does not include tools and sets of general use, but merely special tools, some of which are common with other car Models.

Therefore, for a thorough knowledge of all tool equipment recommended for maintenance work, see the «Service Tool Catalogue» issued by FIAT Service Dept.

For reasons of standardization, the catalogue number of some tools has been varied. In the text and illustrations of this manual, tools are identified with the previous numbering.

The following list reports, in the first column, the old number of tools, and in the second column, the covering up-to-date number.

Previous Number	New Number	Description
		ENGINE
Arr. 2074	A. 60512	Adapter, engine and engine-gearbox-differential unit removal and installation (use with hydraulic jack).
Arr. 2077	A. 60516	Hook, engine and engine-gearbox-differential unit lifting and moving.
Arr. 2205/2	A. 22205/7	Arms, engine mounting on rotating stand.
A. 8262	A. 50033	Wrench, valve-to-rocker clearance adjustment.
A. 8262 bis	A. 50053	Wrench, rocker adjustment screw lock-nuts.
A. 10114	A. 60182	Installer and remover, piston ring.
A. 11475	A. 94069	Grinding stone carrier spindle, valve seat grinding.
A. 11478	A. 94056	Grinding stone, valve seats.
A. 11479	A. 94057	20° cutter, valve seat width narrowing.
A. 11482	A. 94058	Cutter carrier spindle, valve seat refacing.
A. 11489	A. 94059	Pilots, set of, valve seat refacing cutters.
A. 40006/1/2	A. 40006/1/2	Puller, clutch shaft pilot bushing.
A. 40014	A. 40014	Puller, cylinder head.
A. 50022	A. 50087	Wrench, spark plugs.
A. 50040	A. 50040	Wrench, holding pulley during removal and installation of generator and fan.
A. 50089	A. 50089	Socket (13 mm), rocker arm nut locking.
A. 60000	A. 60027	Tool, cylinder reaming (modified).
A. 60017	A. 60017	Tester, valve seat tightness.
A. 60018	A. 60018	Plug, spark plug seat blanking, valve tightness test.
A. 60041	A. 60041	Fixture, cylinder head support during decoke.
A. 60077	A. 60077	Reamer, small end bushing.
A. 60084	A. 60084	Remover and installer, engine valve.
A. 60152	A. 60152	Fixture and bushing, crankshaft mounting on grinder.
A. 60153	A. 60153	Punch, valve guide installation and removal.
A. 60154	A. 60154	Installer, pistons.
A. 60155	A. 60213	Fixture, connecting rod bushing installation and removal.
A. 60156	A. 60156	Tool, cylinder retaining (engine on rotating stand).
A. 60157	A. 60212	Tool, piston pin installer and remover.
A. 60158	A. 60158	Base plate, cylinder head support, valve removal and installation.
A. 60159	A. 94030	75° cutter, intake and exhaust valve seats refacing.
A. 60161	A. 60161	Tool, flywheel retainment during installation on crankshaft.
A. 60162	A. 60162	Gauge, with connection, engine oil pressure.
A. 60257	A. 60257	Installers, set of 4, standard and oversize pistons (engine 110 D. 000).
A. 68001	A. 76001	Installer, spark plugs.
A. 72020 bis	D. 15166	Covers, engine protection during car wash.
Ap. 5030	Ap. 5030	Tool, engine timing.
Ap. 5030/1	Ap. 5030/1	Fixture, ignition timing.
C. 110	A. 95110	Feeler gauge, tappet clearance adjustment (.0039" - 0,10 mm).
C. 111	A. 95111	Feeler gauge, tappet clearance adjustment (.0059" - 0,15 mm).
C. 316	A. 95316	Feeler gauges, set of, piston-to-cylinder clearance inspection.

(continued)

TOOL EQUIPMENT

Special Service Tools (continued).

Previous Number	New Number	Description
C. 645	A. 95645	Fixture, engine dead center inspection.
C. 672	A. 95672	Ring gauge, cylinder bore dial indicator calibration.
C. 673	A. 95673	Graduated sector, engine timing checks.
U. 0307	A. 90307	Expansion reamer, piston pin bore and connecting rod small end bush.
U. 0310	A. 90310	Reamer, valve guide bore.
U. 0334	A. 90334	Reamer, crankshaft support dowel holes.
U. 0338/1	A. 90338/1	Reamer, tappet guide bore (1st oversizing).
U. 0338/2	A. 90338/2	Reamer, tappet guide bore (2nd oversizing).
I. 31790	A. 60208	Hose, connection to exhaust silencer during engine tune-up.
I. 31790/2	A. 60209	Connection, hose-to-exhaust silencer during engine tune-up (use with A. 60208).
CLUTCH-GEARBOX AND DIFFERENTIAL UNIT		
Arr. 2076	A. 70508	Adapter, gearbox-differential unit support during removal and installation (use with hydraulic jack).
Arr. 2206/7	Arr. 22206/7	Support, gearbox-differential unit securing to rotating stand Arr. 2204.
A. 42013	A. 45013	Puller, final drive pinion roller bearing inner ring.
A. 52022	A. 55022	Wrench, differential bearing adjuster.
A. 62023	A. 70023	Tool, clutch centering on flywheel at installation.
A. 62028	A. 70028	Drift rod, differential case roller bearing outer ring removal and installation.
A. 62036	A. 70036	Fixture, determination of bevel drive pinion shim thickness (use with C. 689).
A. 62037	A. 70037	Shaft, final drive pinion and bearing assembly measurement to determine the thickness of pinion shim (use with dial gauge).
A. 62038	A. 70038	Fixture, clutch installation and adjustment.
A. 62039	A. 95708	Tool, pinion-to-ring gear backlash check.
A. 62040	A. 70040	Tool (with support for A. 95697 dynamometer mounting), differential bearing rotation torque checks.
A. 62041	A. 70041	Fixture, final drive pinion retainment during nut tightening.
A. 95697	A. 95697	Dynamometer, differential bearing rotation torque.
C. 689	A. 95690	Dial gauge, to be used with tools for determination of bevel pinion shim thickness.
FRONT AND REAR SUSPENSION		
A. 10228	A. 74019	Adapter, hydraulic shock absorber assembly.
A. 56024	A. 57024	Wrench, front and rear shock absorber plug.
A. 56030	A. 57030	Wrench, shock absorber removal and installation.
A. 66016	A. 74016	Installer and remover, bushes on kingpin housing.
A. 66054	A. 74054	Tool, front suspension arm retainment during elastic bush removal (use with universal puller A. 40005/1/5).
A. 66056	A. 74056	Tool, front suspension spring «estendblock», kingpin housing and rear suspension arm removal and installation.
A. 66057	A. 74057	Pin, rear suspension swinging arm shim mounting.
A. 66058	A. 74058	Installer, bushes in front suspension swinging arm.
A. 66061	A. 74061	Fixture, front leaf spring installation (static load).
A. 66062	A. 74052	Tools, pair of, coil spring compression and rear wheels retainment in vertical position.
A. 66064	A. 74064	Fixture, rear suspension swinging arm check and adjustment.
A. 90316	A. 90316	Reamer, kingpin housing bushes.
C. 1004	A. 96004	Fixture, kingpin housing alignment.

(continued)

Special Service Tools (continued).

Previous Number	New Number	Description
		HUBS AND WHEELS
A. 6511	A. 47026/1	Puller, wheel hub outer and inner bearing outer cup.
A. 8279	A. 57005	Wrench, rear wheel drive shaft nut.
A. 40005/1/9	A. 40005/1/9	Puller, wheel drum.
A. 46023	A. 47023	Remover, front wheel hub caps.
A. 66059	A. 74059	Installer, front wheel hub caps.
A. 95697	A. 95697	Dynamometer, rear wheel bearing rotation torque measurement.
A. 95697/2	A. 95697/2	Support for dynamometer A. 95697, rear wheel bearing rotation torque measurement.
C. 696	Ap. 5110/1/2	Gauge, rear wheel alignment checking (use with C. 696/3).
C. 696/3	Ap. 5110/4	Bracket and support, for rear wheel alignment checking gauge (use with C. 696).
		STEERING SYSTEM
A. 6473	A. 47002	Puller, steering rod head pins (separate).
A. 8065	A. 57003	Wrench, steering box adjuster.
A. 8279	A. 57005	Wrench, steering wheel retainment nut.
A. 10110	A. 74017	Drift rod, worm screw seal.
A. 40005/1/5	A. 40005/1/5	Puller, pitman arm.
A. 46006	A. 47006	Puller, steering rod head pins (paired).
A. 46019	A. 47019	Puller, worm bearing cone.
A. 57033	A. 57033	Wrench, steering box oil level inspection plug.
A. 66032	A. 74032	Bracket, steering box servicing.
A. 66040	A. 74040	Drift rod, worm upper bearing cup removal.
A. 66043	A. 74043	Installer, sector bush.
A. 66046	A. 74046	Drift rod, worm bearing cone and cup installation.
U. 0360/20	A. 90360/20	Reamer, worm sector bushing.
		BRAKES
A. 10103	A. 72206	Hose, brake system bleeding.
A. 54002/1/2	A. 56102/1/2	Wrench and fixture, clearance self-adjuster installation on brake shoes.
A. 64026	A. 72226	Clamping tool, brake shoe lining bonding.
A. 64027	A. 72227	Adapter, brake shoe lining bonding.
A. 722202/1/7	A. 72202/1/7	Bushes, front wheel brake drum turning.
A. 72202/1/12	A. 72202/1/12	Bushes, rear wheel brake drum turning.
A. 72235	A. 72235	Tools, wheel cylinder piston holding on wheel cylinder installation.
		BODY
A. 66063	A. 74063	Gauge, body floor checking.

TOOL KIT

The set of wrenches and tools allotted for servicing operations the Owner can do himself, is contained in a bag located in front compartment, above fuel tank.

Bag, containing:

— Wrench, double end, 8 x 10 mm;
— Wrench, double end, 13 x 17 mm;
— Cutting pliers;
— Punch, straight;
— Screwdriver;
— Wrench, socket, for spark plugs;
— Speed handle;
— Jack.

CAR SPECIFICATIONS

GENERAL SPECIFICATIONS OF « NEW 500 » MODEL

SUN ROOF SEDAN
CONVERTIBLE SEDAN } with engine 110.000

SPORTS SEDAN - with engine 110.004

SUN ROOF SEDAN - Version 140
CONVERTIBLE SEDAN - Version 140 } with engine 110.040

SPORTS SEDAN - Version 144 with engine 110.044

ENGINE

	110.000 110.040	110.004 110.044
No. of cylinders, vertical, in-line	2	
Bore	2.5984″ (66 mm)	2.6535″ (67,4 mm)
Stroke	2.7559″ (70 mm)	
Displacement	29.23 cu.in. (479 cm³)	30.48 cu.in. (499,5 cm³)
Compression ratio	7 to 1	8.6 to 1
Max. power (with fan, without silencer)	16.5 HP	21 HP
at	4400 r.p.m.	4600 r.p.m.
Max. torque (with fan, without silencer)	20.25 ft.lbs (280 kgcm)	25.32 ft.lbs (350 kgcm)
at	3,500 r.p.m.	
Max. power, S.A.E. standards	21 HP	25 HP

Fig. 438 - Front view of engine assembly.

Cylinder block with aluminum crankcase; separate cast-iron cylinders.
Aluminum cylinder head with valve seat inserts.
Crankshaft on two supports.
Aluminum-tin alloy main bearings, force-fitted in two supports.
Steel connecting rods of the babbitt-metal-lined thin-wall type, bronze small-end bushing.
Aluminum alloy pistons.
Power plant support: one spring-cushioned mounting at center of rear cross member and two front rubber mountings on transmission sides.

Valve Gear.

Overhead valves, controlled by camshaft through tappets, pushrods and rockers.
Camshaft chain-driven by crankshaft.
Timing data:

— Engines 110.000 and 110.040:

	Early-type	Late-type
Tappet clearance adjustment, for valve timing: intake	.0177″ (0,45 mm)	.0177″ (0,45 mm)
exhaust	.0177″ (0,45 mm)	.0150″ (0,38 mm)
Intake { opens: B.T.D.C.	20°	9°
closes: A.B.D.C.	50°	70°
Exhaust { opens: B.B.D.C.	50°	50°
closes: A.T.D.C.	20°	19°
Final tappet operation clearance adjustment, cold engine: intake and exhaust	.0039″ (0,10 mm)	.0059″ (0,15 mm)

— Engines 110.004 and 110.044:

Tappet clearance adjustment, for valve timing: intake and exhaust . . . . . .0154″ (0,39 mm)

Intake { opens: B.T.D.C. . . . . 25°
closes: A.B.D.C. . . . . 51°
Exhaust { opens: B.B.D.C. . . . . 64°
closes: A.T.D.C. . . . . 12°

Final tappet operation clearance adjustment, cold engine: intake and exhaust . . .0059″ (0,15 mm).

Fuel Feed

by camshaft-controlled mechanical diaphragm pump. Fuel tank in front compartment: capacity about 5.5 U.S., 4.6 Imp. Gals (21 lt).
Air intake through cleaner with silencer.
Recommended gasoline: 83 Oct. rating (Res. Meth.) for 110.000 and 110.040 engines; 92 Oct. rating (Res. Meth.) for 110.004 and 110.044 engines.

Weber 26 IMB1 carburetor for 110.000 and 110.040 engines and 26 IMB 3 carburetor for 110.004 and 110.044 engines, with gradual-action starting device.

Carburetor setting data:

	26 IMB 1	26 IMB 3
Body diameter	1.0236" (26 mm)	
Primary Venturi dia.	.8268" (21 mm)	.8661" (22 mm)
Main jet diameter	.0441" (1,12 mm)	.0492" (1,25 mm)
Idling jet diameter	.0177" (0,45 mm)	
Choke jet diameter	.0354" F 5 (0,90 mm F 5)	
Air bleed diameter	.0925" (2,35 mm)	
Needle valve diameter	.0492" (1,25 mm)	

Lubrication.

Forced oil circulation by camshaft-driven gear-type pump.
Centrifugal oil filter; oil pressure relief valve.
Low oil pressure indicator.
Normal lubrication pressure: 35.5 to 42.6 p.s.i. (2,5 to 3 kg/cm^2).
Engine oil filler cap on cylinder head cover.
Oil dip stick on engine right hand side.

Cooling.

Air, forced, by centrifugal blower and conveyor.
Air outlet by shutter-controlled thermostat:
— shutter opening begins . . 158° to 165° F (70° to 74° C)
— shutter wide open . . . . 178° to 189° F (81° to 87° C)

Fig. 439 - Cut-away view of centrifugal oil filter, oil pump, tappets and ignition distributor.

Power Plant Suspension.

At front, by a floor-mounted support having two adjustable rubber pads on gearbox sides.
At rear, by swinging arm secured to crankcase and body rear cross member, with rubber pad and reaction spring.

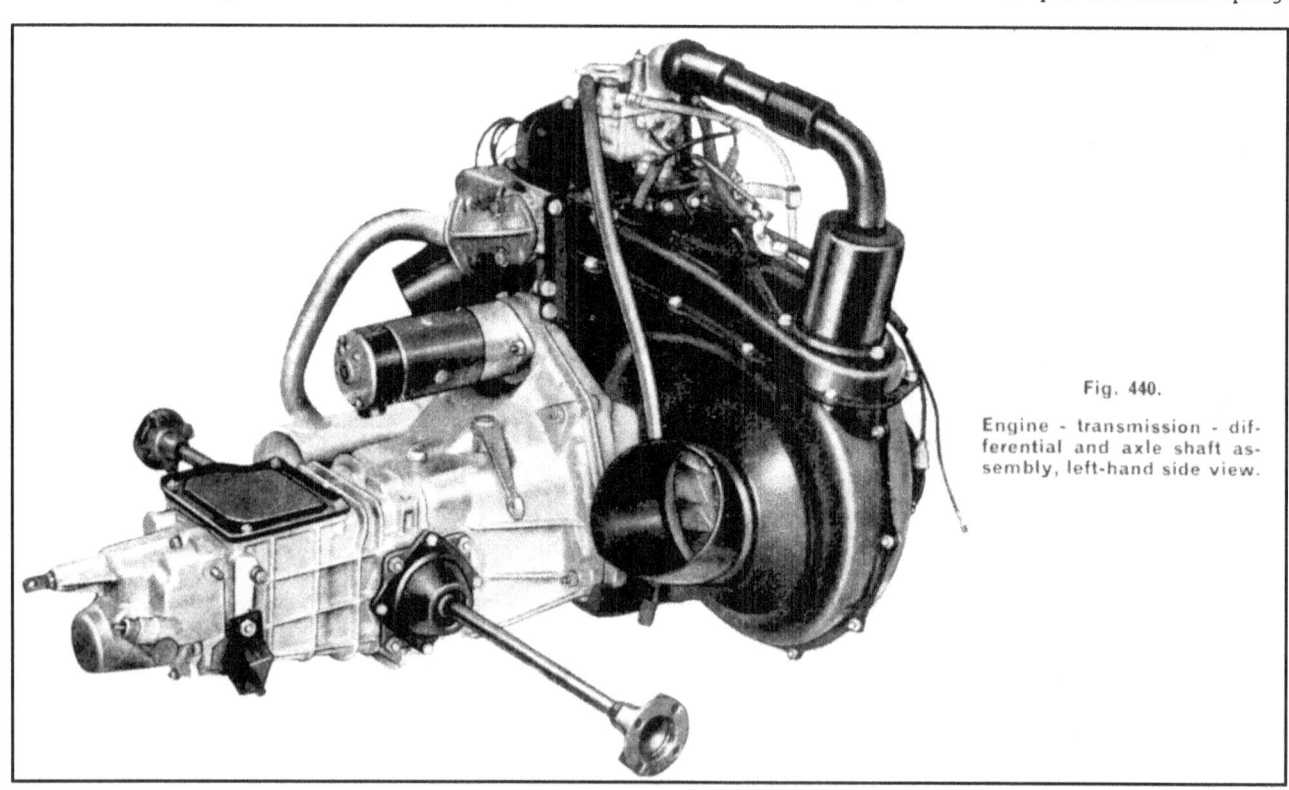

Fig. 440.

Engine - transmission - differential and axle shaft assembly, left-hand side view.

CAR SPECIFICATIONS

Ignition

by battery, coil and camshaft-driven distributor.

Static advance . . . . 10°

Automatic advance:
- engines 110.000 and 110.040 . . . . 18°
- engines 110.004 and 110.044 . . . . 12°

Breaker point gap . . . . . .0185" to .0209" (0,47 to 0,53 mm)

Spark plugs:
- diameter and pitch . . . . 14 x 1,25 mm

engine 110.000
- type . . . . CW 225
- gap . . . . .0197" to .0236" (0,50 to 0,60 mm)

engine 110.004
- type . . . . CW 250 A
- gap . . . . .0197" to .0236" (0,50 to 0,60 mm)

engines 110.040 and 110.044
- type . . . . Champion L 7
- gap . . . . .0236" to .0276" (0,60 to 0,70 mm)

Starting

by electric motor mounted on gearbox casing; starter control lever on tunnel.

POWER TRAIN

Clutch.

Single-plate, dry.
Annular friction linings.

Gearbox and Differential.

Incorporated in a single unit, with three-section aluminum casing.

Four forward speeds and reverse; 4th speed is an overdrive; constant mesh second, third and fourth speeds with quick-shift front-teeth synchronizers.

Control by hand lever on tunnel, between seats.

Gear ratios:
- 1st . . . . 3.27 to 1
- 2nd . . . . 2.06 to 1
- 3rd . . . . 1.30 to 1
- 4th . . . . 0.87 to 1
- Reverse . . . . 4.13 to 1

Differential and final drive gears incorporated in gearbox.

Final drive ratio:
- « 500 » . . . . 8 to 41
- « 500 Sports » . . . . . . 8 to 39

Drive

is transmitted to rear wheels through two swing half axle shafts.

Frame:

consists of floor framing, integral with the body.

SUSPENSION - STEERING - BRAKES

Front Suspension:

wheels independently sprung, with transversal leaf spring; hydraulic, telescopic shock absorbers.

Hydraulic, telescopic shock absorbers: I. D. 1.063" (27 mm)

Front end geometry (fully laden):

Camber (at rim) . . . . . .1969" to .2362" (5 to 6 mm) (1"±20')

Caster . . . . 9°±1°

Rear Suspension:

wheels independently sprung, with coil springs and hydraulic, telescopic shock absorbers.

Hydraulic, telescopic shock absorbers: I. D. 1.063" (27 mm)

Rear end geometry (fully laden):

Rear wheel alignment: wheel plane parallel to ground and tilted to car centerline by an angle of 0° 10' toeing-in in driving direction (a $^{-10'}_{+15'}$ tolerance is permitted).

Steering.

LHD; RHD optional.

Control by worm screw and helical sector: ratio 2 to 26

Independent steering rods to each wheel.

Minimum turning circle diameter . . about 28 ft 3" (8,60 m)

Front wheel toe-in (laden car) .0000" to .0787" (0 to 2 mm)

Hydraulic Service Brakes.

On all four wheels, of the expanding-shoe type, controlled by pedal through master cylinder and wheel cylinders.

Drum diameter . . . . 6.6929" (170 mm)

Lining width . . . . 1.1811" (30 mm)

Master cylinder diameter . . . . 3/4"

Wheel cylinder diameter . . . . 3/4"

Sheet steel self-centering shoes.

Shoe-to-drum clearance self-adjusting device.

Mechanical Parking Brake.

On rear wheels.

Controlled by lever on tunnel between seats.

Steel rope, with two tension adjustment stretchers.

Wheels and Tires.

Disc wheels, with rims type . . . . 3 1/2 x 12'

Low pressure tires . . . . 125-12"

Tire pressure:
- front
  - low load . . . . . 17.1 p.s.i. (1,20 kg/cm²)
  - full load . . . . . 17.1 p.s.i. (1,20 kg/cm²)
- rear
  - low load . . . . . 22.8 p.s.i. (1,60 kg/cm²)
  - full load . . . . . 26.3 p.s.i. (1,85 kg/cm²)

ELECTRIC SYSTEM

Tension . . . . 12 Volts

Generator.

FIAT DSV 90/12/16/3 S, belt driven from crankshaft, maximum steady output . . . . 230 Watts
Cut-in speed (lights out):
- engine, abt . . . . 1100 r.p.m.
- car in top gear . . . . 14.3 m.p.h. (23 km/h)

Generator Regulator.

Type GN 1/12/16.
Voltage regulator, cut-out and current regulator in a single unit.

Battery:

capacity at 20-hr discharge rate . . . . 32 Ah
Location: in front compartment, ahead of fuel tank.

Starter.

FIAT B 76-0,5/12 S: power . . . . 0,5 kW
Controlled by hand lever on tunnel. Pinion provided with overunning clutch.

Horn: electric, controlled by button on steering wheel hub.

Windshield wiper: electric, twin-arm, with three position switch, on instrument panel.

Self-cancelling direction indicator and outer light lever switch below steering wheel, with flashing pilot light.

Ignition lock switch: key operated; controls also outer lighting

Instrument cluster light switch: on instrument panel.

Instrument cluster (five indications).

Courtesy light switch: on rear-view mirror.

Fuses: six, 8 Amp; within easy reach from front compartment.

Bulbs (*).

Location	Type	Wattage (12 Volts)
Headlamps:		
high beam	spherical,	45
low beam	double filament	40
Front lamps:		
direction indicators	spherical,	20
parking lights	double filament	5
Tail lamps:		
stop lights	spherical,	20
parking lights	double filament	5
direction indicators	spherical	20
Side direction indicators . . .	tubular	2.5
Number plate lamps	spherical	5
Courtesy light	cylindrical	3
Instrument cluster light		
Direction indicators pilot light .		
Generator charge indicator . .		
Low oil pressure indicator . . .	tubular	2.5
Fuel reserve supply indicator .		
Parking light indicator		
High beam indicator		

(*) For lighting equipment to suit « 140 and 144 Version » cars, see specifications on page 249.

Fig. 441.
« New 500 » Sports Sedan.

BODY

Two-door, four seater integral bodied sedan.

Sun roof or convertible top. Sports version is supplied with all-metal or sun roof.

Sunk-in headlamps.

Curved safety-glass windshield.

Front compartment, with rear-hinged lid and central longitudinal moulding, housing fuel tank, battery, spare wheel, horn, brake fluid reservoir, tool kit, wiper motor and fuses. Lid open by prop.

Rear-hinged doors. Windows with front ventilator pane and rear drop, crank-operated pane. Driver's side door locked by key. Safety lock on opposite door. Horizontal outer handles.

Fixed-pane rear quarter windows.

Black rubber weatherstrips for windshield, door window, rear quarter window and back window (Sun Roof).

One-bow imitation leather folding top (Sun Roof), or three-bow imitation leather collapsible top with vinylite back window

Engine compartment, with bottom-hinged removable lid, centrally mounted number plate and lamp; finned aeration slots.

Front and rear polished aluminum bumpers.

Foldable and adjustable tubular frame bucket front seats. Upholstery: cloth and imitation leather or all-leather.

Bench-type rear seat with padded cushion and back. Upholstery: cloth and imitation leather or all-leather.

Fluted-rubber mat on floor, floor sides, front wheelboxes and control passage tunnel.

Imitation-leather panelling underbelt and on doors.

Pressed sheet steel instrument panel, painted to match body finish. Glove compartment welded to dashboard.

Rear-view mirror with incorporated light.

Adjustable sun visors.

Unlined body inner parts painted to match body finish. Internal headlining. Front ornament and mouldings on door, rear panel and below door.

PERFORMANCES

Maximum speed, after run-in (1,800 miles - 3.000 km):

« 500 »

low gear	15.5 m.p.h. (25 km/h)
2nd gear	24.9 m.p.h. (40 km/h)
3rd gear	40.4 m.p.h. (65 km/h)
high gear	abt 59 m.p.h. (95 km/h)

« 500 Sports »

low gear	16.2 m.p.h. (26 km/h)
2nd gear	27.3 m.p.h. (44 km/h)
3rd gear	43.5 m.p.h. (70 km/h)
high gear	above 65.2 m.p.h. (105 km/h)

Climbable gradient, with good roads and run-in engine:

« 500 », under full load (4 people):

low gear	20%
2nd gear	12%
3rd gear	6.5%
high gear	3.5%

« 500 Sports », under full load (2 people plus 154 lbs - 70 kg luggage):

low gear	28%
2nd gear	17%
3rd gear	9%
high gear	5%

Fig. 442.
« New 500 » Sun Roof, 140 Version.

DIMENSIONS

Overall length (with bumpers) . . . 116.93" (2970 mm) (*)
Maximum width . . . . 52.05" (1322 mm)
Maximum height (unladen) . . . . . . 52.16" (1325 »)
Wheelbase . . . . 72.44" (1840 »)
Front track (on ground) . . . . 44.13" (1121 »)

Rear track (on ground) . . . . 44.69" (1135 mm)
Ground clearance (laden) . . . . . . 5.31" (135 »)

(*) Version 140 and 144 . . . . 121.06" (3075 mm)

WEIGHTS

Curb weight (with replenishments, spare wheel, tool kit and accessories):
— Sun Roof . . . . 1102 lbs (500 kg)
— Convertible . . . . 1080 lbs (490 kg)
— Sports Car . . . . 1124 lbs (510 kg)
— Sun Roof, Version 140 . . . . . . 1113 lbs (505 kg)
— Convertible, Version 140 . . . . . 1091 lbs (495 kg)
— Sports Car, Version 144 . . . . . 1135 lbs (515 kg)

Useful load: « 500 » . . . . 4 people
« 500 Sports » 2 people plus 154 lbs (70 kg) luggage

Total weight, full load:
— Sun Roof . . . . 1720 lbs (780 kg)
— Convertible . . . . 1698 lbs (770 kg)
— Sports Car . . . . 1587 lbs (720 kg)
— Sun Roof, Version 140 . . . . . . 1731 lbs (785 kg)
— Convertible, Version 140 . . . . . 1709 lbs (775 kg)
— Sports, Version 144 . . . . 1598 lbs (725 kg)

Load distribution (Sun Roof):
front axle . . . . 706 lbs (320 kg)
rear axle . . . . 1014 lbs (460 kg)

Section 13

500 D - 500 Type 110 F
500 STATION WAGON

500 D SEDAN (Type 110 D)
500 STATION WAGON (Early type)

	Page
GENERAL INFORMATION	299
MAIN FEATURES	303
MAIN SERVICING DIRECTIONS	319
ENGINE	319
FUEL SYSTEM	331
CLUTCH	337
TRANSMISSION AND DIFFERENTIAL	339
FRONT SUSPENSION AND WHEELS	345
REAR SUSPENSION AND WHEELS	353
STEERING SYSTEM	358
BRAKES	361
ELECTRIC SYSTEM	365

500 SEDAN (Type 110 F)
500 STATION WAGON (Late type)

	Page
GENERAL INFORMATION	373
SPECIFICATIONS AND SERVICE PROCEDURES	377

NOTES

500 D SEDAN (Type 110 D)
500 STATION WAGON (up to serial N° 141706)

GENERAL INFORMATION

MAIN SPECIFICATIONS OF VEHICLES	500 D	500 Station Wagon
DIMENSIONS		
Length, overall, with bumpers	116.93" (2,970 mm)	125.39" (3,185 mm)
Width, overall	52.05" (1,322 mm)	52.09" (1,323 mm)
Height, overall, no load	52.16" (1,325 mm)	53.31" (1,354 mm)
Ground clearance of loading platform (no load)	—	21.85" (555 mm)
Rear door opening: height	—	28.54" (725 mm)
width, bottom	—	32.28" (820 mm)
width, top	—	28.54" (725 mm)
GENERAL DATA		
Wheelbase	72.44" (1,840 mm)	76.38" (1,940 mm)
Tread, front, on ground	44.13" (1,121 mm)	44.13" (1,121 mm)
Tread, rear	44.69" (1,135 mm)	44.53" (1,131 mm)
Turning circle	338.58" (8,600 mm)	338.58" (8,600 mm)
WEIGHTS		
Curb weight (with replenishments, spare wheel, tool kit and accessories)	1,102 lbs (500 kg)	1,224 lbs (555 kg)
Payload	4 people plus 88 lbs (40 kg)	4 people plus 88 lbs (40 kg)
Payload beside the driver (with rear seat back folded down and load uniformly distributed on the loading floor)	—	551 lbs (250 kg)
Weight at full load	1,808 lbs (820 kg)	1,929 lbs (875 kg)
PERFORMANCES		
Maximum speeds at full load on level road, with surface in good condition, after the run-in period (1,800 miles - 3,000 km):		
— first gear	14.3 mph (23 km/h)	14.3 mph (23 km/h)
— second gear	24.9 mph (40 km/h)	24.9 mph (40 km/h)
— third gear	40.4 mph (65 km/h)	40.4 mph (65 km/h)
— fourth gear, over	59 mph (95 km/h)	59 mph (95 km/h)
Maximum climbable gradients at full load with surface in good condition, after the run-in period (1,800 miles - 3,000 km):		
— firts gear	26 %	22 %
— second gear	13 %	11.5 %
— third gear	7 %	6 %
— fourth gear	3.5 %	3 %
— reverse	36 %	30 %

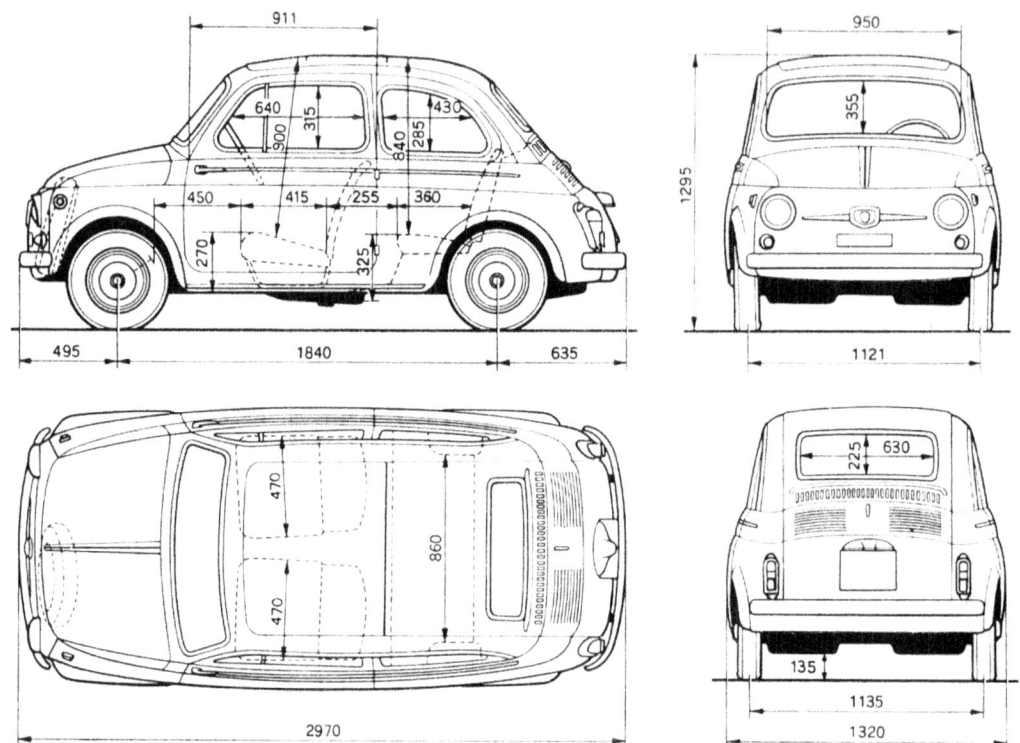

Fig. 1. - Principal dimensions of Model « 500 D » (in mm).
The overall height is intended with an unladen car.

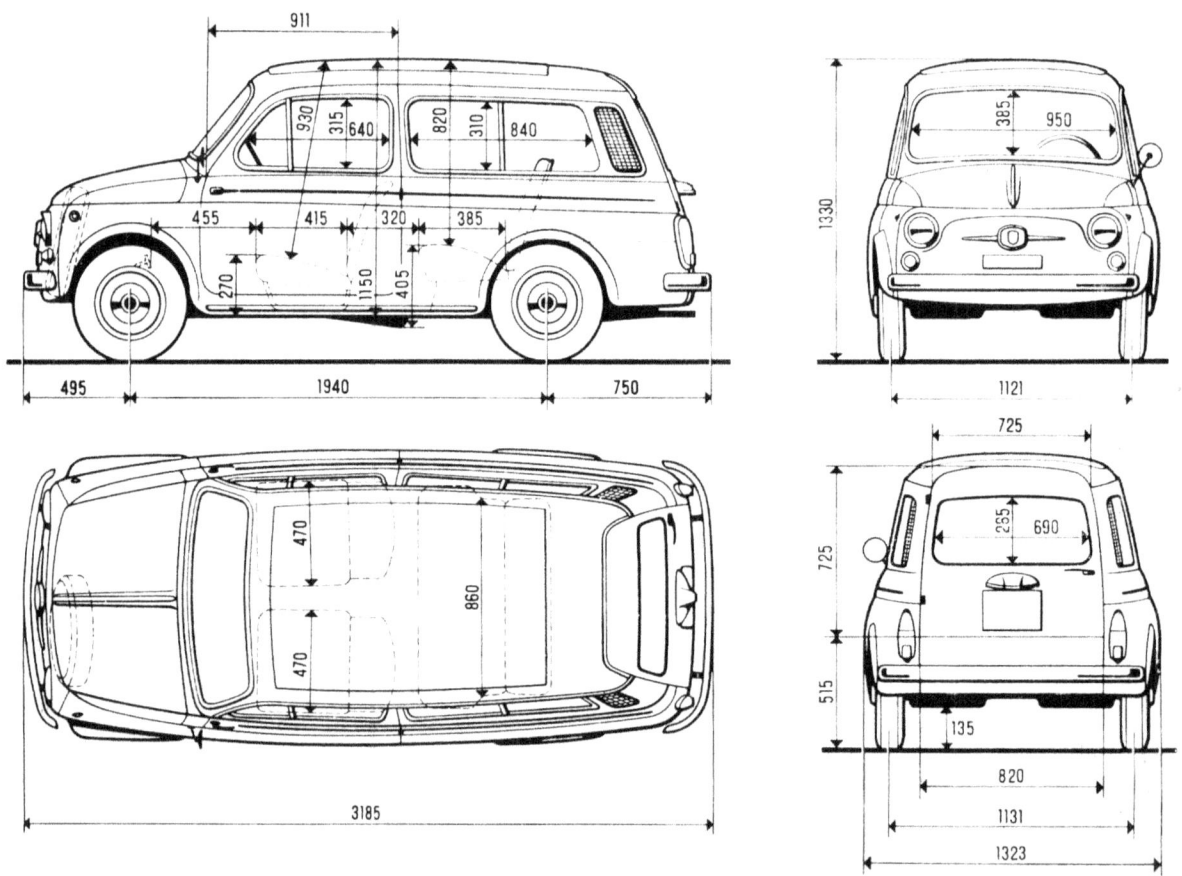

Fig. 2. - Principal dimensions of Model « 500 Station Wagon » (in mm).
The overall height and the height of loading floor are intended with a laden vehicle.

SPECIFICATIONS AND FEATURES

CAPACITIES

UNIT	Quantity				FILL-IN
	Imp. Units	U.S. Units	lt	kg	
Fuel tank............	4.6 gals	5.5 gals	21	—	Gasoline: 83 Oct. Rat. (Res. Method)
Oil pan (^{1})...........	1.54 qts	1.85 qts	1.75	1.6	FIAT oil (^{3})
Gearbox and differential ..... Steering gear	.97 qts .105 qts	1.16 qts .124 qts	1.1 0.12	1.00 0.11	FIAT W 90/M oil (SAE 90 EP)
Hydraulic brake circuit	.194 qts	.232 qts	0.22	0.22	FIAT blue label brake fluid for hydraulic brakes
Hydraulic shock absorbers: — front, each .... — rear, each	 .112 qts .038 qts	 .137 qts .104 qts	 0.13 0.10	 0.12 0.09	 FIAT S.A.I. oil FIAT S.A.I. oil
Windshield washer bag	(^{2})	(^{2})	—	(^{2})	Mixture of water and cleaner

(^{1}) Total capacity of oil pan, lines, oil filter and crankshaft: 1.859 G.B. qts - 2.22 U.S. qts (1.900 kg) for Model 500 D and 2.06 G.B. qts - 2.48 U.S. qts (2.100 kg) for 500 Station Wagon. The amount shown in the table is the requirement for periodical oil changes.

(^{2}) 1.32 G.B. pts - 1.59 U.S. pts (0.75 kg) of pure water with 0.6 oz (17 grs) solution in summer or with 1.2 oz (34 grs) solution in winter.

(^{3}) Recommended oil grades:

LOWEST ANTICIPATED OUTDOOR TEMPERATURE	FIAT Service MS (*) Oil Supplement 1 oils which fill MS sequence requirements	FIAT Multigrade Oil (*)	LOWEST ANTICIPATED OUTDOOR TEMPERATURE	FIAT Service MS (*) Oil Supplement 1 oils which fill MS sequence requirements	FIAT Multigrade Oil (*)
Below —15° C (5° F) (minimum) .... Between 0° and —15° C (32° to 5° F) (minimum) .	**VS 10 W** (SAE 10 W) **VS 20 W** (SAE 20 W)	— 10 W - 30	Above 0° C (32° F) (minimum) .... Above 30° C (86° F) (average)	**VS 30** (SAE 30) **VS 40** (SAE 40)	20 W - 40

(*) **Warning:** above FIAT oils are or the detergent type: do not top up with oils of different grade or make. When changing to a detergent oil, flush the engine thoroughly.

CAUTION! Starting from engine No. 200784 the total capacity of oil pan, lines, oil filter and crankshaft is 2.64 G.B. qts - 3.17 U.S. qts (3.00 lt - 2.65 kg). The capacity of the oil pan for periodical oil changes is 2.20 G.B. qts - 2.65 U.S. qts (2.5 lt - 2.3 kg).

Fig. 3. - Model « 500 D » Sunroof.

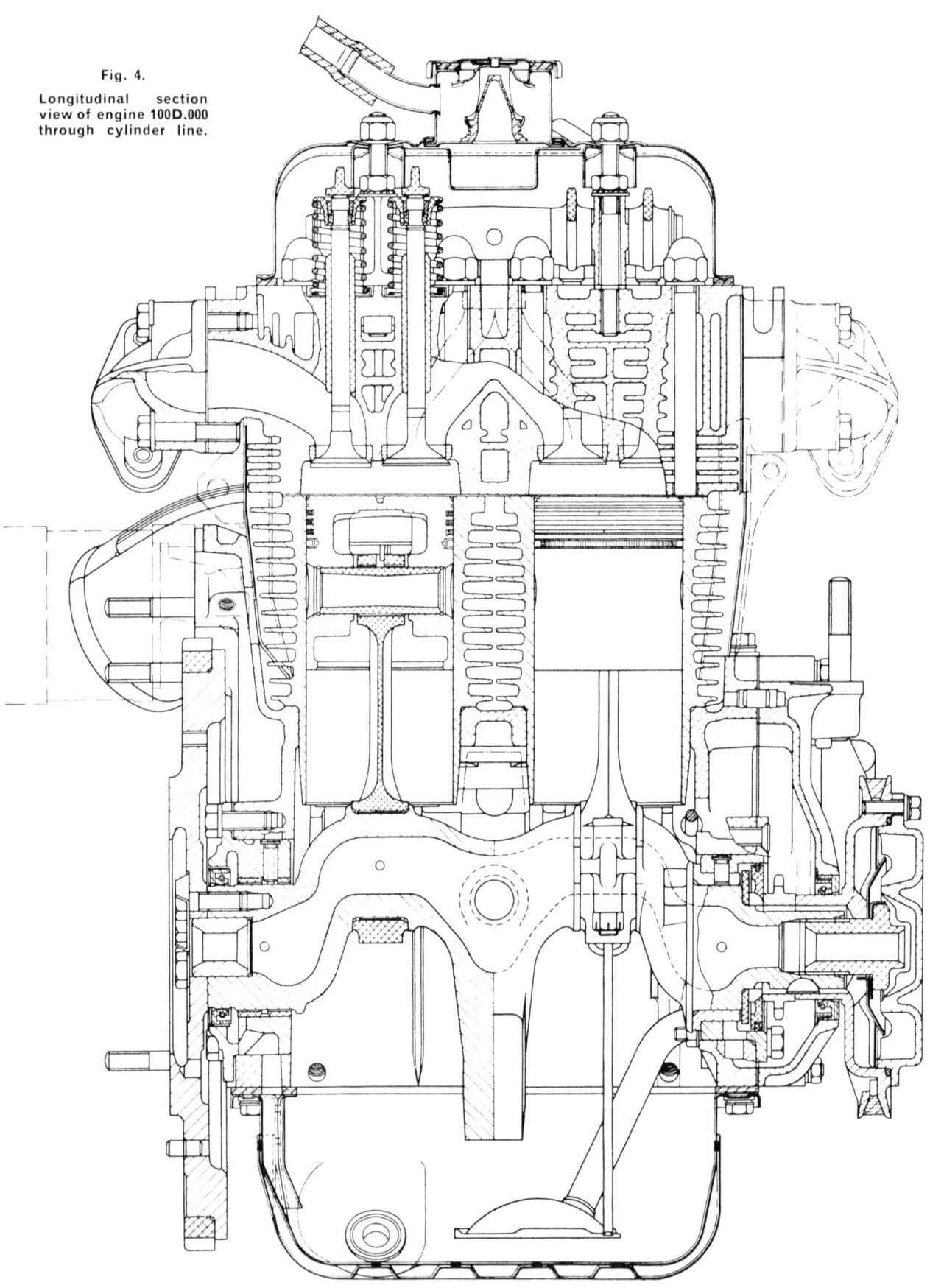

Fig. 4. Longitudinal section view of engine 100D.000 through cylinder line.

MAIN FEATURES

Engine

The engine powering the « 500 D » has two cylinders in line **arranged vertically** and the engine powering the « 500 Station Wagon » has two cylinders in line **arranged horizontally.**

Engine types:
- 500 D 110D.000
- 500 Station Wagon 120.000

The principal characteristics of these engines are shown in the table on foot of page.

The **cylinder block** is formed by two cast-iron **cylinders** with cooling fins. The bottom of cylinders fits into proper seats machined in **crankcase** which is of aluminum and carries 8 studs on which are inserted the cylinders and the aluminum **cylinder head** with cast-iron valve seat inserts.

Crankshaft is of special cast iron and is supported by two bush-type bearings. At center the crankshaft is provided with a counterweight and is hollow to provide a passage for the lube oil to main and con rod bearings, camshaft and rocker shaft.

Connecting rods are of steel with **thin wall bearing halves** on big end and bronze **bushes** in small end.

Pistons, of aluminum, are taper-oval-shaped with maximum diameter at bottom of skirt, at right angle to piston pin. Pistons are fitted with four **rings** of which: one compression at top, two standard oil scrapers and one sideslotted oil scraper.

The piston pin bore is .0984" (2.5 mm) off center with respect to piston centerline, on the side opposite the skirt expansion split.

Piston pin is of steel and retained in piston bosses by two circlips.

Fig. 5. - Cutaway view of engine type 110D.000.
The air cleaner and blower are clearly shown.

Cylinder head is finned to provide a larger heat dissipation surface and carries the **intake and exhaust manifolds**. Intake manifolds join into a single central flange which mounts the carburetor. Exhaust manifolds are parallel to engine centerline: two pipes at manifold ends take exhaust gases to the muffler.

ENGINE TYPE	110D.000	120.000
No. and arrangement of cylinders (in line)	two, vertical	two, horizontal
Bore	2.654" (67.4 mm)	2.654" (67.4 mm)
Stroke	2.755" (70 mm)	2.755" (70 mm)
Displacement	30.48 cu.in (499.5 cc)	30.48 cu.in (499.5 cc)
Compression ratio	7.1	7.1
Maximum horsepower (with fan, without silencer)	17.5 HP	17.5 HP
Maximum horsepower, S.A.E. rating	22 HP	21.5 HP
at	4,400 rpm	4,600 rpm

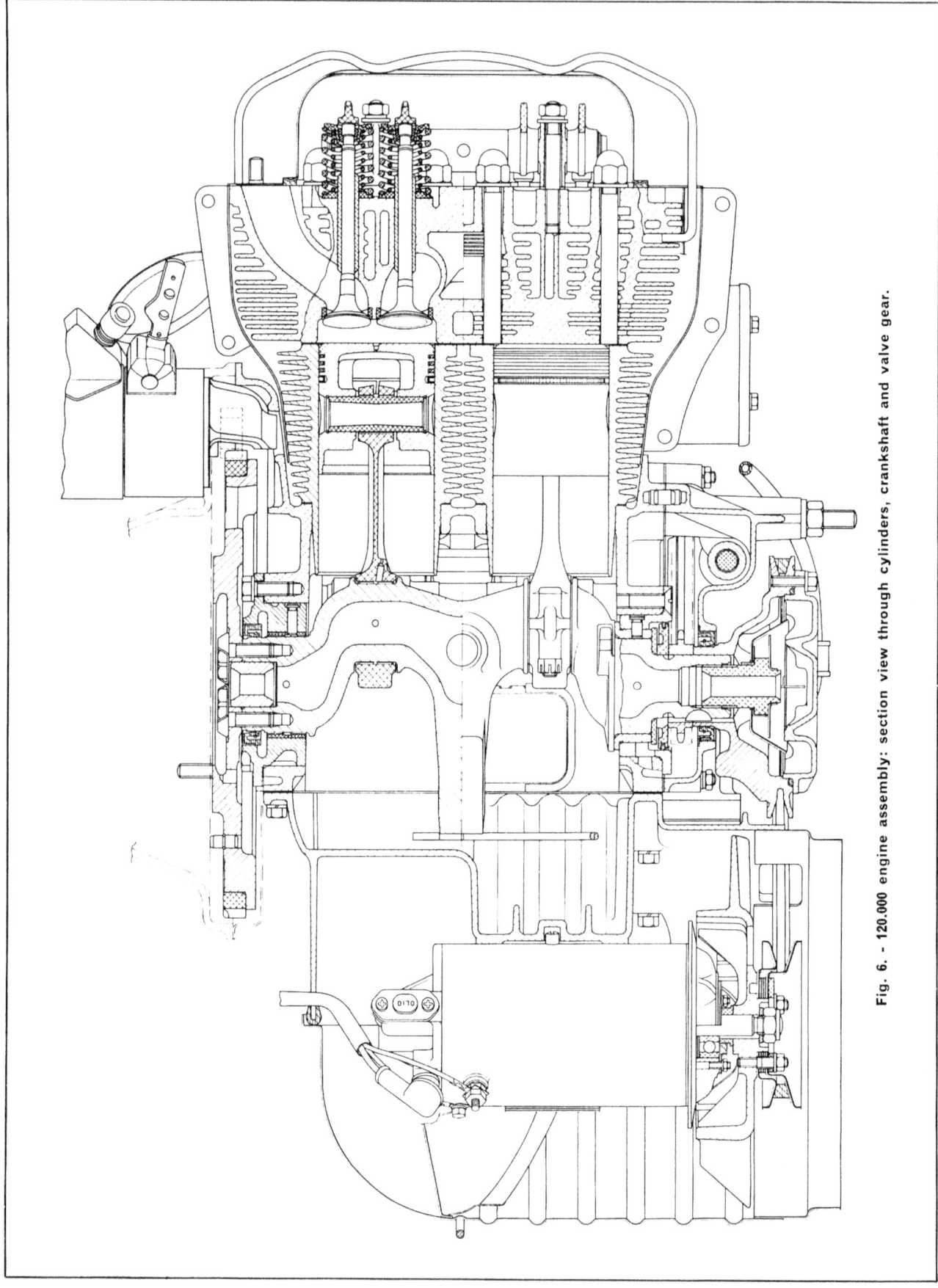

Fig. 6. - 120.000 engine assembly: section view through cylinders, crankshaft and valve gear.

SPECIFICATIONS AND FEATURES

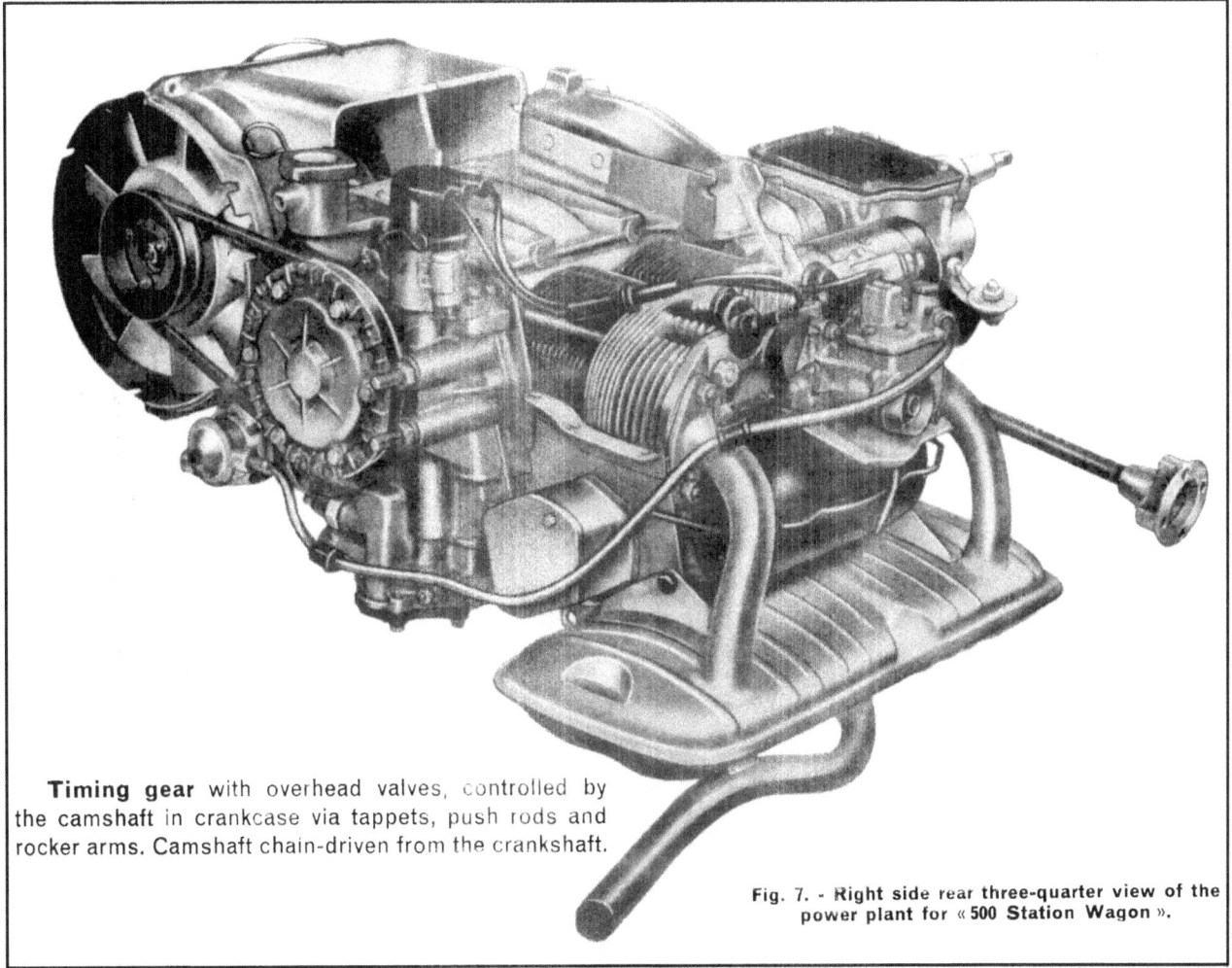

Timing gear with overhead valves, controlled by the camshaft in crankcase via tappets, push rods and rocker arms. Camshaft chain-driven from the crankshaft.

Fig. 7. - Right side rear three-quarter view of the power plant for « 500 Station Wagon ».

Valve timing data are the following:

- Intake { opens . . . . 25° B.T.D.C.
  closes . . . . 51° A.B.D.C.
- Exhaust { opens . . . . 64° B.B.D.C.
  closes . . . . 12° A.T.D.C.
- Tappet clearance, for valve timing check: intake and exhaust . . . . .0154" (0.39 mm)
- Tappet clearance, **with a cold engine**: intake and exhaust . . . . .0059" (0.15 mm)

FUEL FEED

By mechanical diaphragm pump actuated through a pushrod by a lobe on camshaft.

The following carburetor types are used:

— 500 D . . . . Weber 26 IMB 4
— 500 Station Wagon . . . . Weber 26 OC

SETTING DATA OF CARBURETORS	500 D	500 Station Wagon
	Weber 26 IMB 4	Weber 26 OC
Body barrel bore	1.024" (26 mm)	1.024" (26 mm)
Choke tube	.827" (21 mm)	.787" (20 mm)
Main jet	.044" (1.12 mm)	.041" (1.05 mm)
Idling jet	.018" (0.45 mm)	.018" (0.45 mm)
Starting jet	.035" (0.90 mm)	.031" (0.80 mm)
Air correction jet	.093" (2.35 mm)	.083" (2.10 mm)
Needle valve (cushioned)	.049" (1.25 mm)	.049" (1.25 mm)
Emulsion tube	F 8	F 15
Float level	.276" (7 mm)	.295" (7.5 mm)

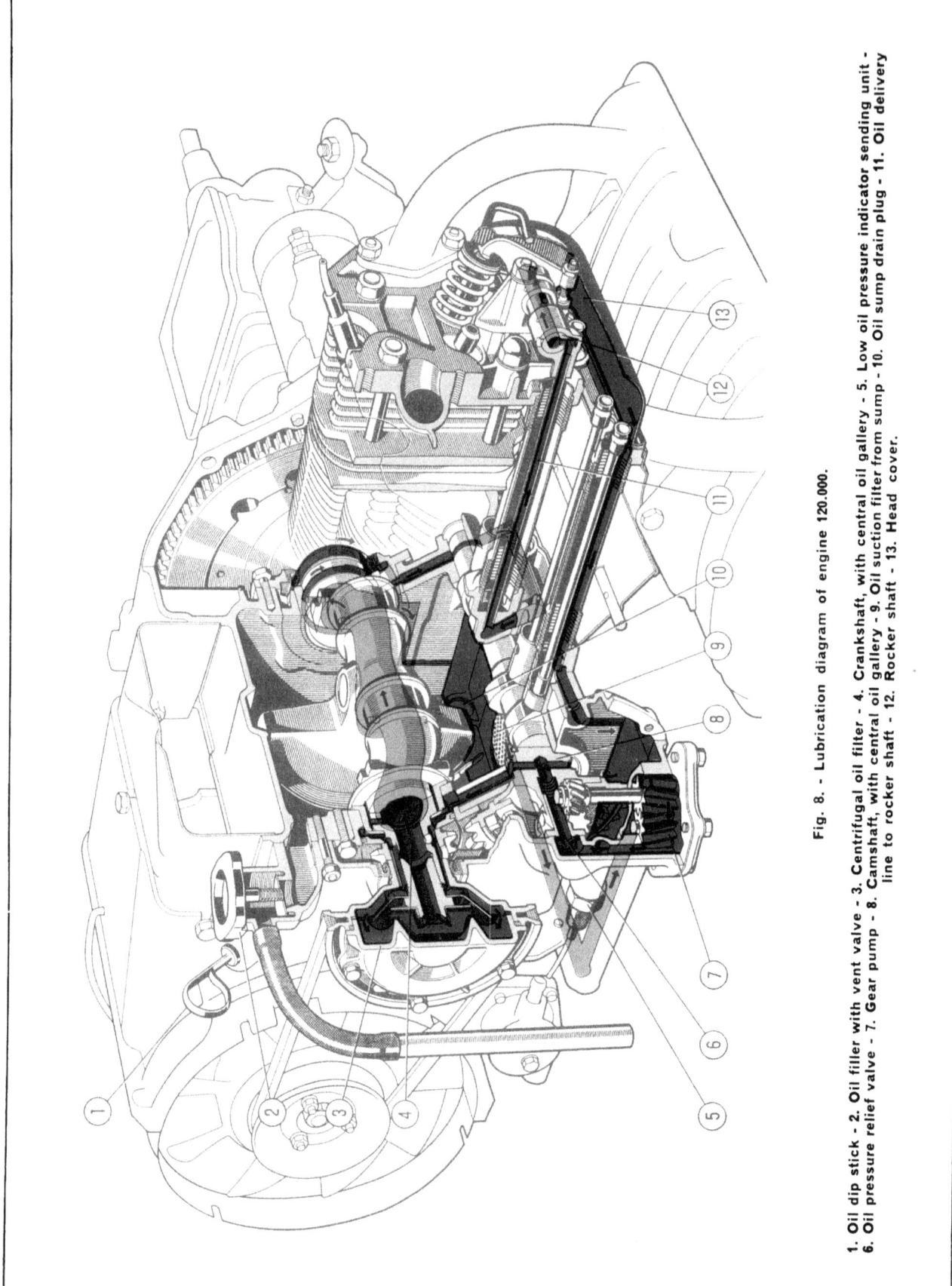

Fig. 8. - Lubrication diagram of engine 120.000.

1. Oil dip stick - 2. Oil filler with vent valve - 3. Centrifugal oil filter - 4. Crankshaft, with central oil gallery - 5. Low oil pressure indicator sending unit - 6. Oil pressure relief valve - 7. Gear pump - 8. Camshaft, with central oil gallery - 9. Oil suction filter from sump - 10. Oil sump drain plug - 11. Oil delivery line to rocker shaft - 12. Rocker shaft - 13. Head cover.

The 26 IMB 4 carburetor is of the downdraft type and the 26 OC carburetor of the horizontal draft type. Both carburetors are single barrel, with starting device (choke) controlled by a lever on floor tunnel; pleated paper cleaner at air intake.

The fuel tank, located in front compartment, has a capacity of 4.6 Imp. gals - 5.5 U.S. gals (21 liters).

LUBRICATION

Pressure metered flow lubrication activated by a gear pump. Oil pressure relief valve at the camshaft. Lube oil strained by a centrifugal filter at the crankshaft.

A red light on the instrument cluster warns the driver of the low oil pressure through a sending unit.

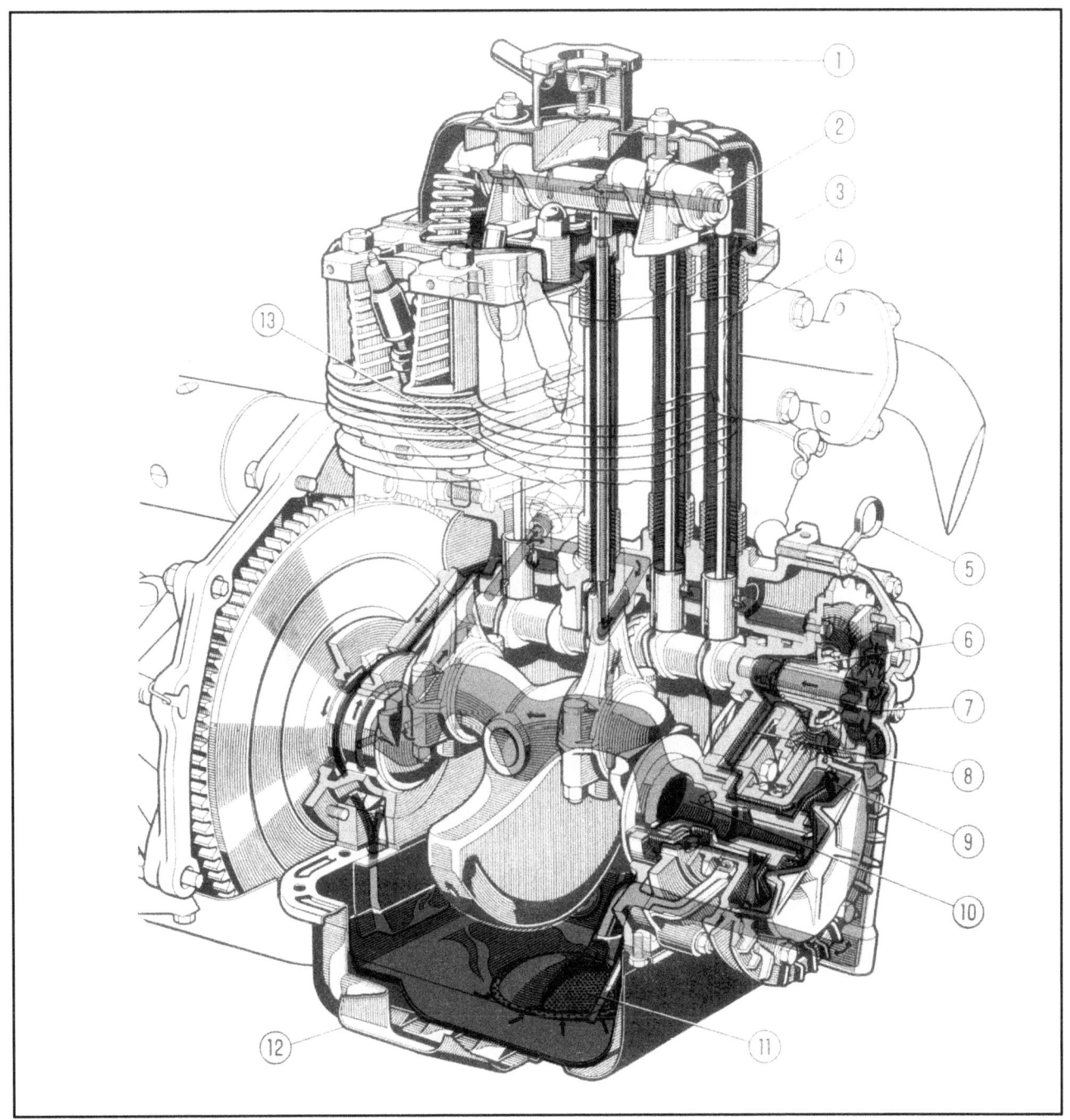

Fig. 9. - Lubrication diagram of engine 110D.000.

1. Oil filler with vent valve - 2. Rocker shaft - 3. Line, oil delivery to rocker shaft - 4. Ducts, cylinder head oil drain - 5. Level indicator rod - 6. Oil pressure relief valve - 7. Gear pump - 8. Oil duct to centrifugal filter - 9. Centrifugal oil filter - 10. Crankshaft with central oil gallery - 11. Oil pump suction screen filter - 12. Sump cooling air conveyor - 13. Low oil pressure indicator sending unit.

The oil pump is driven by a pair of spur gears in mesh at camshaft end in Model 500 D. The engine of 500 Station Wagon features an oil pump actuated by the ignition distributor which, in turn, is driven off the camshaft via a pair of helical gears.

Standard oil pressure: 35.6 to 42.7 psi - 2.5 to 3 kg/cm² (25 to 30 meters of water).

The 500 Station Wagon shows the engine oil filler on the timing gear cover and the dip stick at the rear end of the sump. In Model 500 D engine the oil filler is located on the head cover and the oil dip stick on the right-hand side of the crankcase (as viewed from the vehicle direction of drive).

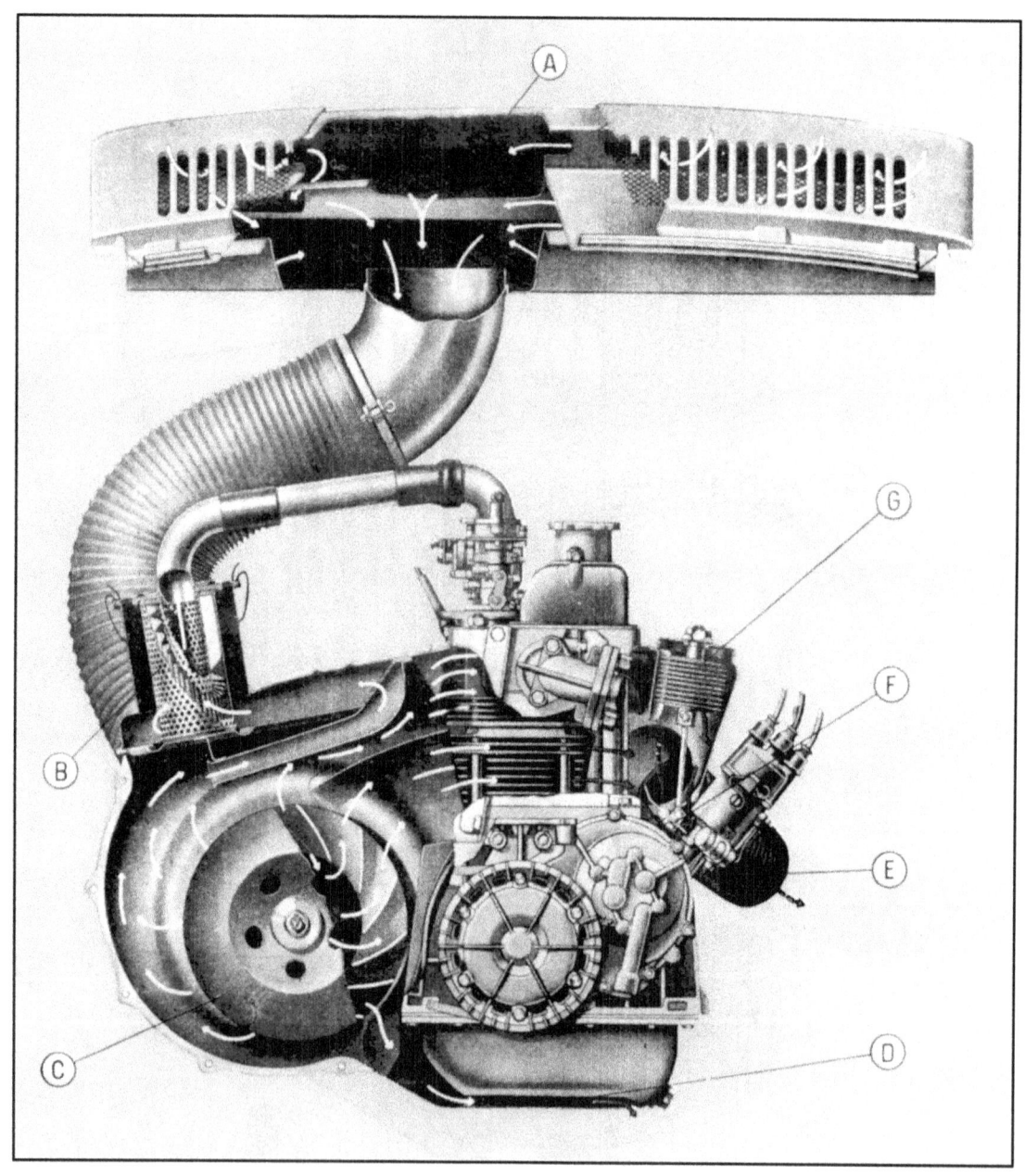

Fig. 10. - Cooling air circulation system of engine 110D.000.

A. Engine cooling air intake - **B.** Carburetor air suction cleaner - **C.** Centrifugal fan and air conveyor - **D.** Oil pan cooling air passage - **E.** Warmed air admission hose to car interior - **F.** Engine air outlet control shutter, wide open position (at 178° to 189° F - 81° to 87° C; shutter starts opening at 158° to 165° F - 70° to 74° C) - **G.** Air outlet thermostat.

COOLING

Air cooled engine. Air circulation is promoted and governed by means of the following:

Model 500 D:
— a centrifugal blower and air conveyor;
— a thermostat controlling the air draft shutter:
  — shutter starts opening 158° to 165° F (70° to 74° C)
  — shutter wide open . . 178° to 189° F (81° to 87° C)

Model 500 Station Wagon:
— a linear blower housed in engine baffles and cowling;
— a thermostat controlling the air draft shutter:
  — shutter starts opening 178° to 185° F (81° to 85° C)
  — shutter wide open . . 196° to 207° F (91° to 97° C)

IGNITION

by battery, camshaft-driven distributor. Ignition coil.

Static advance . . . . 10°
Automatic advance (to engine):
— 500 D . . . . 18°
— 500 Sation Wagon . . . . 28°
Breaker contact gap . .019" to .021" (0.47 to 0.53 mm)
Spark plugs:
— diameter and pitch (metric) . . . . 14 x 1.25 mm
— gap { Marelli . . . .020" to .024" (0.5 to 0.6 mm)
        { Champion . . .024" to .028" (0.6 to 0.7 mm)
— type { 500 D . . . . CW 225 N
        { 500 Sation Wagon . . . Marelli CW 260 N
                                  Champion L 5

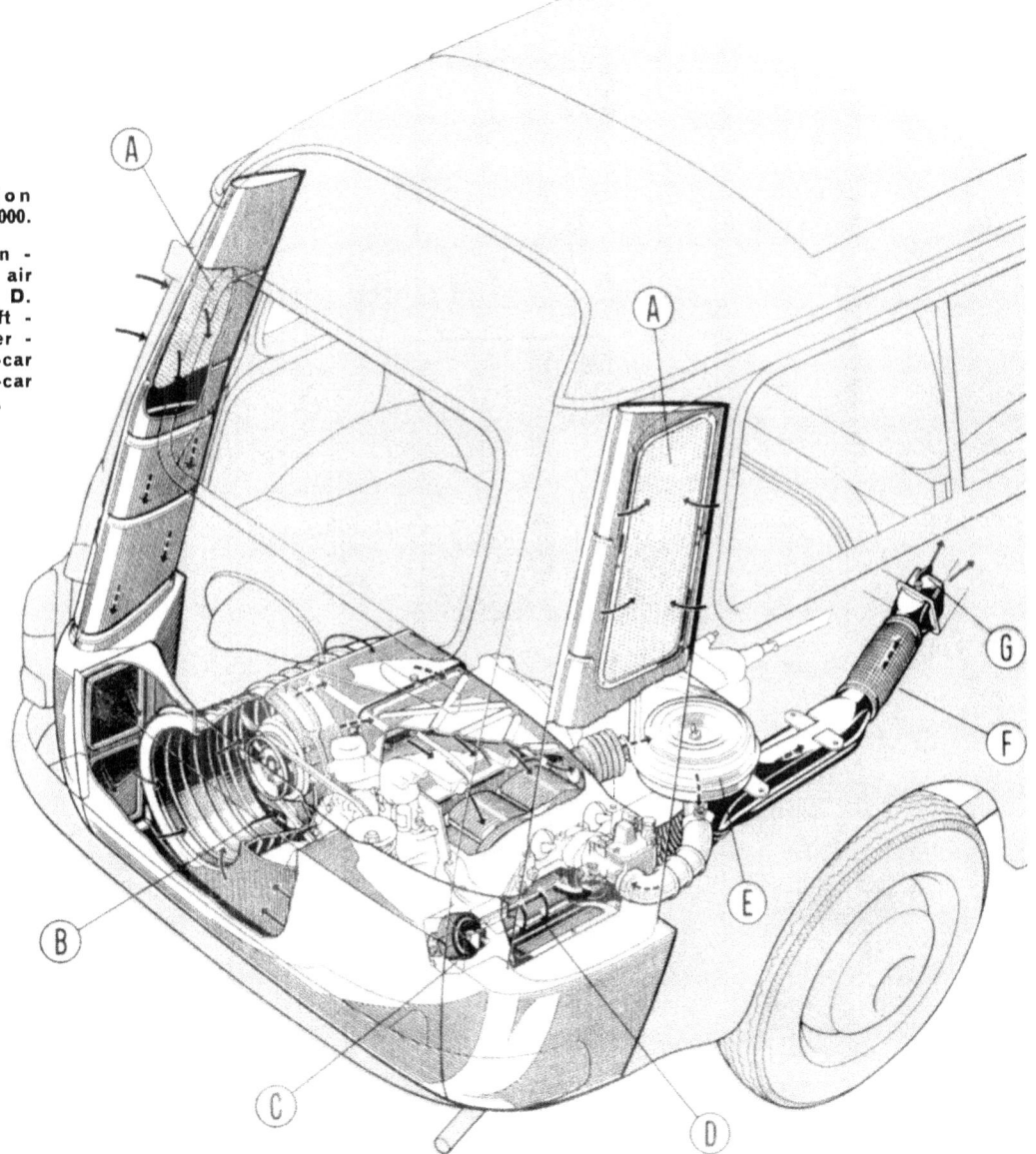

Fig. 11.

Cooling air circulation system of engine 120.000.

A. Air intakes - **B.** Fan - **C.** Thermostat, engine air draft shutter control - **D.** Shutter, engine air draft - **E.** Carburetor air cleaner - **F.** Duct, warmed air-to-car interior - **G.** Lever, air-to-car interior valve control.

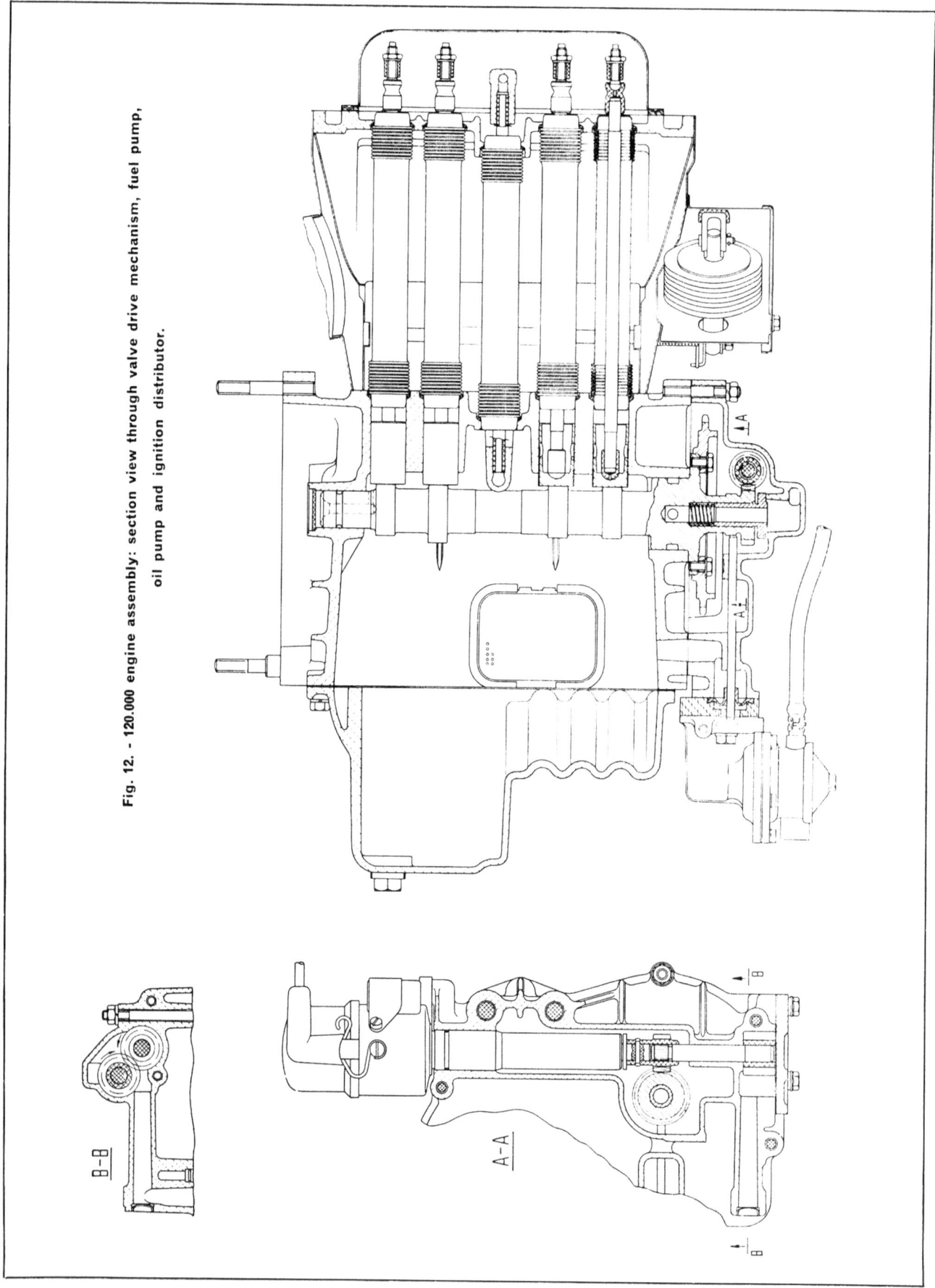

Fig. 12. - 120.000 engine assembly: section view through valve drive mechanism, fuel pump, oil pump and ignition distributor.

STARTING

by electric motor attached to the transmission case. Gearshift lever on floor tunnel.

POWER PLANT MOUNTINGS

Front: the mounting, attached to the underbody, is fitted with two adjustable rubber pads on transmission sides.

Rear:
- 500 D, a swinging arm, attached to the crankcase and to the lower rear body cross member, is fitted with a rubber pad and reactionary spring.
- 500 Station Wagon, a stationary arm is attached to the crankcase and to the lower rear body cross member, with a compounded (spring and rubber) supporting pad in between.

Running Gear

CLUTCH

Single plate, dry, with damper rings.
Outer diameter of linings . . . 5.512" (140 mm)
Pedal free travel . 1.378" to 1.575" (35 to 40 mm)
Pressed graphite thrust ring.

TRANSMISSION AND DIFFERENTIAL

Incorporated in a single unit, with three-section aluminum casing.

Four forward speeds and reverse; 4th speed is an overdrive; constant mesh second, third and fourth speeds with quickshift front-teeth synchronizers.

Gearshift by hand lever on tunnel, between seats.

Gear ratios:
- 1st . . . . 3.70 to 1
- 2nd . . . . 2.06 to 1
- 3rd . . . . 1.30 to 1
- 4th . . . . 0.87 to 1
- Reverse . . . . 5.14 to 1

Differential and final drive gears incorporated in transmission case:

Final drive ratio . . . . 5.125 to 1 (8/41)

Power drive is transmitted to rear wheels by means of two axle shafts, which are connected to differential through slip joints and to wheel shaft through flexible joints.

FRONT SUSPENSION

Independent wheel front suspension, with upper control arms.

Transversal semi-elliptic spring: connection is provided to underbody at two points through rubber pads and to both pillar ends through « estendblocks » and pivot pins.

Fig. 13.
Power plant of Model « 500 D ».

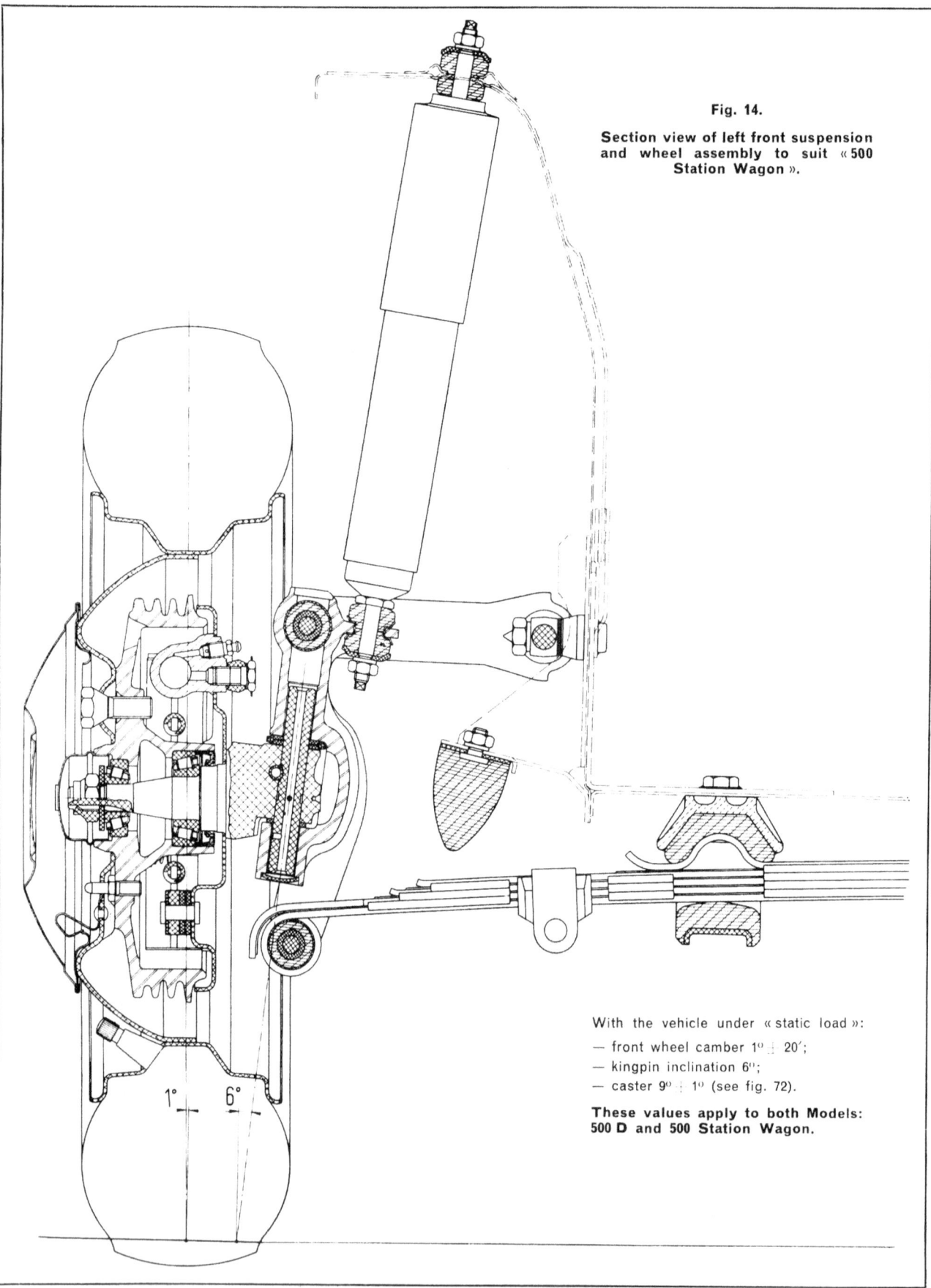

Fig. 14.

Section view of left front suspension and wheel assembly to suit «500 Station Wagon».

With the vehicle under «static load»:
— front wheel camber 1° ± 20′;
— kingpin inclination 6°;
— caster 9° ± 1° (see fig. 72).

These values apply to both Models: 500 D and 500 Station Wagon.

SPECIFICATIONS AND FEATURES

Spring action integrated by two hydraulic, telescoping, double-acting shock absorbers.

Camber, at wheel rim
(fully laden) . . . . . .197" to .236" (5 to 6 mm)
($1° \pm 20'$)

Caster . . . . $9° \pm 1°$

Shock absorber inner
cylinder bore . . . . . 1.063" (27 mm)

REAR SUSPENSION

Independent wheel rear suspension. Coil springs and control arms attached to underbody through «estendblocks» and pivot pins.

Spring action integrated by hydraulic, telescoping, double-acting shock absorbers.

Rear end geometry (static load):
wheel plane parallel to ground and tilted to car centerline by an angle of 0° 10' toeing-in in driving direction (a —10' and +15' tolerance is permitted).

Shock absorber inner cylinder bore 1.063" (27 mm)

STEERING GEAR

LHD standard, RHD optional.
Gear control by worm and sector.

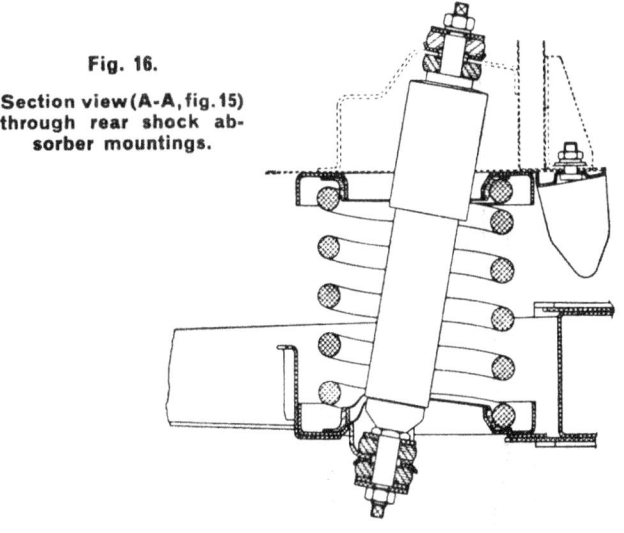

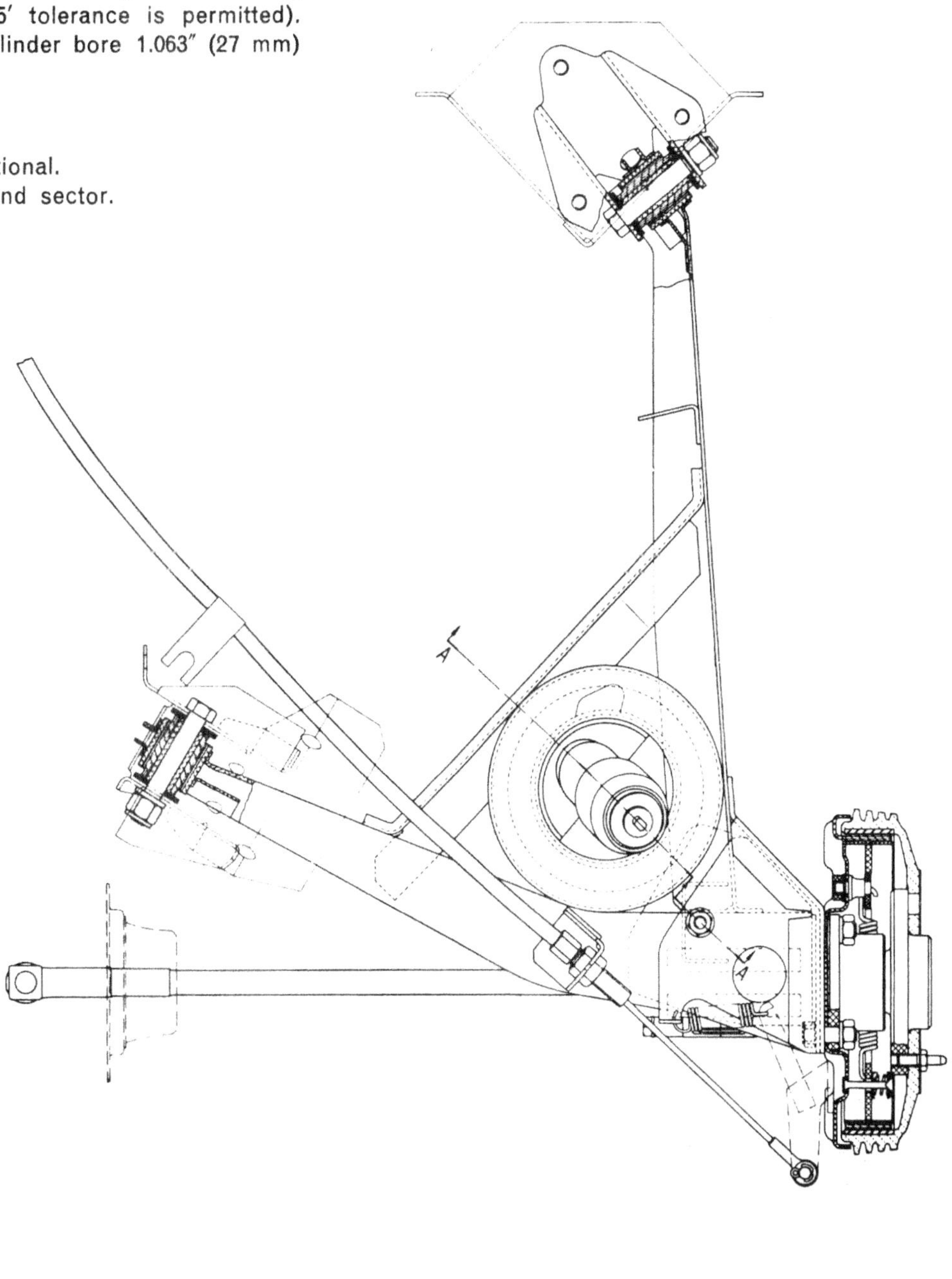

Fig. 16.

Section view (A-A, fig. 15) through rear shock absorber mountings.

Fig. 15.

Right rear suspension assembly: section views through control arm pivot pins and brake drum («500 Station Wagon»).

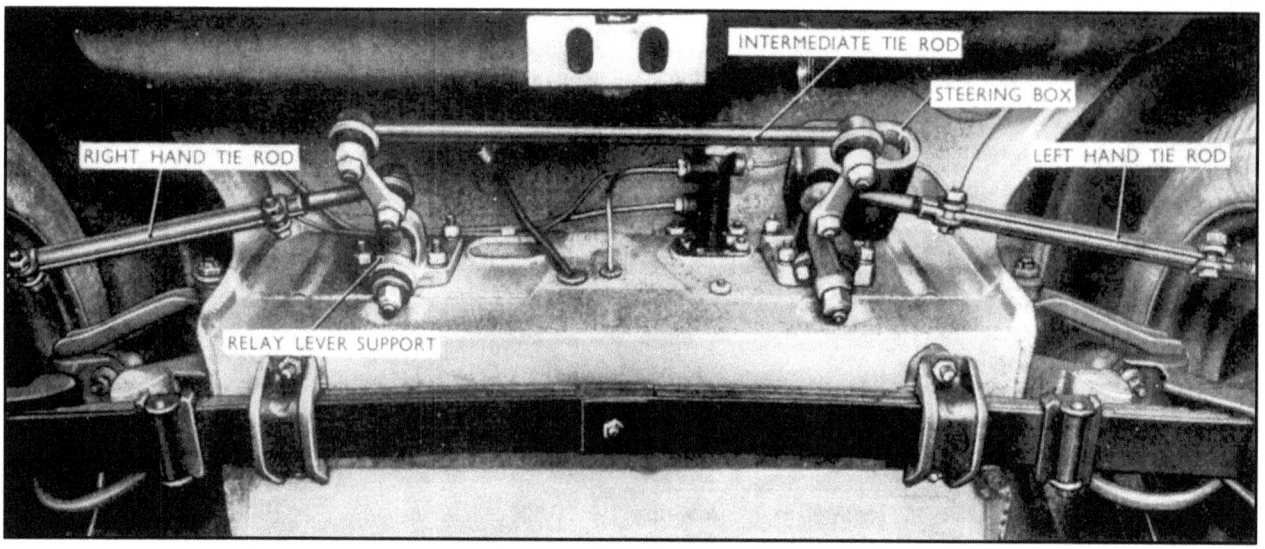

Fig. 17. - View of steering linkage assembly, Model « 500 D ».

Idler arm and steering rods independent to each wheel.

Worm-to-sector ratio .	13 to 1 (2/26)
Turning circle	28' 3" (8.60 m)
Front wheel toe-in (full load)	.000" to .079" (0 to 2 mm)

BRAKES

Service.

On all four wheels, of the expanding-shoe type, controlled by pedal through master cylinder and wheel cylinders attached to housing flanges.

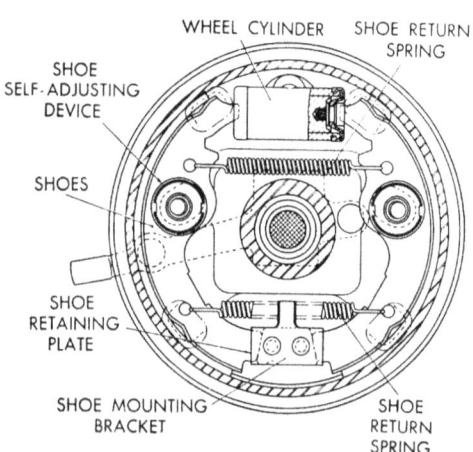

Fig. 18. - Section view of left front wheel, Model « 500 D ».

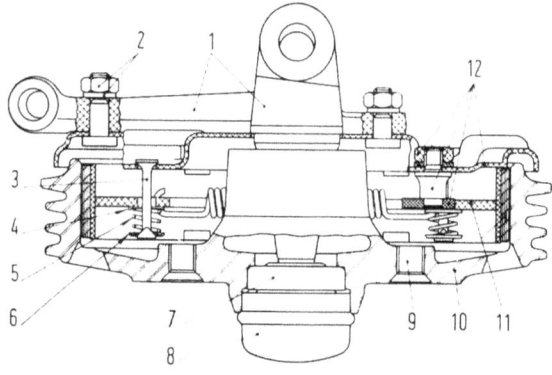

Fig. 19. - Section view through left front wheel brake assembly (« 500 Station Wagon »).

1. Steering knuckle - 2. Nut with washer, fixing the housing flange to steering knuckle - 3. Pin - 4. Inner cup - 5. Shoe guide spring - 6. Outer cup - 7. Bearing on knuckle - 8. Cup - 9. Wheel fixing thread - 10. Drum - 11. Shoe - 12. Housing flange, complete with adjusting cam and nut.

Brake shoe type:

— 500 D: sheet metal, self-centering, with shoe-to-drum clearance self-adjusting device.

— 500 Station Wagon: sheet metal, self-centering, with cams for adjusting shoe-to-drum clearance, which should be .010" (0.25 mm) at adjusting cams.

Drum (500 D	6.693" (170 mm)
diameter (500 Station Wagon . .	7.283" (185 mm)
Shoe lining width	1.181" (30 mm)
Master cylinder bore	3/4"
Front and rear wheel cylinder bore	3/4"

SPECIFICATIONS AND FEATURES

Emergency and Parking Brake.

On rear wheels.
Controlled by ratchet lever on tunnel between seats.
Steel rope, with two tension adjustment stretchers.

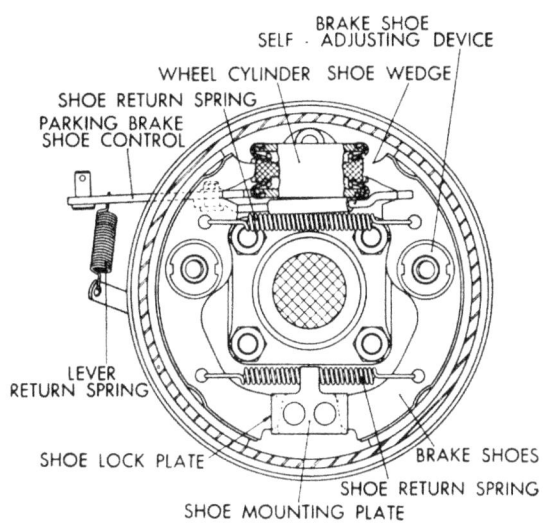

Fig. 20. - Section view of right rear wheel, Model « 500 D ».

WHEELS AND TIRES

Disc wheels, with rim . . . . 3 1/2 x 12″
Low pressure tires:

	500 D	500 Station Wagon
— CEAT . .	125-12 DR 52-4 Ply	125-12 DR 52-6 P.R.
— PIRELLI .	125-12 Rolle 4 p.r.	125-12 Rolle 6 P.R.
— PIRELLI .	125-12 Sempione	125-12 C-SDS
— MICHELIN	125-12-4 P.R.	

Tire pressure:

		500 D		500 Station Wagon	
		psi	kg/cm²	psi	kg/cm²
— low load	front . .	17.1	1.20	17.1	1.20
	rear . . .	22.8	1.60	27.0	1.90
— full load	front . .	17.1	1.20	17.1	1.20
	rear . . .	25.6	1.85	29.9 (*)	2.10 (*)

(*) Rear wheel inflation pressure, for transportation of goods under full load: 34.1 psi (2.40 kg/cm²).

FRAME

The floor framing is totally integrated in the body structure.

Electric System

Tension . . . . 12 Volts

BATTERY

Capacity (at 20-hr discharge rate) . . . . 32 A/hr
Location: in front compartment.
Dimensions:

	Early-type		Late-type	
	in	mm	in	mm
— Length	9.252	235	9.331	237
— Width	5.236	133	5.472	139
— Height (above terminals)	7.795	198	8.858	225
	lbs	kg	lbs	kg
— Weight (with electrolyte)	30.4	13.8	32.6	14.8

Late-type batteries have been adopted starting from the 500 Station Wagon with serial number 004369.

GENERATOR

FIAT DSV 90/12/16/3 S, belt driven from crankshaft, maximum steady output . . . 230 Watts

Cut-in speed (lights off):

— 500 D { engine, abt . . . . 1,050 r.p.m.
         { car in top gear 12.7 m.p.h. (20.5 km/h)

— 500 S. W. { engine, abt . . . . 1,200 r.p.m.
            { car in top gear 15.5 m.p.h. (25 km/h)

GENERATOR REGULATOR

Type GN 2/12/16.
Voltage regulator, cut-out and current regulator in a single unit.

STARTING MOTOR

FIAT B 76-0,5/12 S: power . . . . 0.5 kW
Controlled by hand lever on floor tunnel. Pinion provided with overunning clutch.

FUSES

Six, 8-Amp fuses, located in the dash wall, front compartment side.

INSTRUMENTS AND CONTROLS

Key-type ignition switch, also energizing warning lights.
Instrument cluster light switch.
Outer lighting master switch.
Interior light switch on rear view mirror; jam-type switch on driver's side door pillar for courtesy light.
Interior and engine compartment light switch built in light socket (500 Station Wagon only).
Windshield wiper switch.
Five-purpose instrument cluster.
Self-cancelling outer light and direction indicator lever switch, under steering wheel. Flasher unit.
Horn in front compartment, with control push button on wheel.
Twin-arm electric windshield wiper.
Stop light jam switch.
Low oil pressure indicator sending unit.
Reserve supply indicator tank unit.
Direction indicator tell-tale light.
High beam tell-tale light.

BULBS

DESCRIPTION	TYPE	Wattage (12 Volts)
Headlamps: high beam	globular, double filament	45
low beam		40
Front lamps: direction indicators	globular, double filament	20
parking lights		5
Tail lamps: stop lights	globular, double filament	20
parking lights		5
direction indicators	globular	20
Side direction indicators	tubular	3
Number plate lamp	globular	5
Courtesy light	cylindrical	5
Interior light (S.W. only)	cylindrical	5
Instrument cluster light		
Direction indicators pilot light		
Generator charge indicator		
Low oil pressure indicator	tubular	3
Fuel reserve supply indicator		
Parking light indicator		
High beam indicator		

Body

500 D Sedan, four-seat, two-door.

500 Station Wagon, four-seat, three-door: two side doors and one back.

Unitized body construction.

Fixed-type windshield with curved safety glass.

Front compartment, with rear-hinged lid and central longitudinal moulding, housing fuel tank, battery, spare wheel, tool kit and luggage. Lid open by prop.

Rear-hinged doors: windows with front ventilator pane and rear drop, crank-operated pane. Driver's side door locked by key. Safety lock on opposite door. Horizontal outer handles. Inner grab handles for shutting doors.

Back door (Station Wagon only): single panel, left-hinged with key lock and fixed window pane.

Rear quarter doors with safety glass: one, fixed pane for Model 500 D, two panes, one fixed and one sliding, for Station Wagon.

Rear window with safety glass.

Black rubber weatherstrips for windshield, rear quarter window and back window.

Bright metal trim mouldings for door windows and rear quarter windows (Station Wagon).

Bright metal trim mouldings on side panels.

SPECIFICATIONS AND FEATURES

Medallion and metal strips on front of car.
Roof:
— 500 D: folding, imitation leather lined front section; fixed, sheet metal rear section.
— 500 Station Wagon: imitation leather folding top.

Engine compartment lid (Model 500 D only) to gain access to power plant: centrally arranged license plate and side louvers for engine cooling. Bright metal name plate on left-hand side.

Front license plate arranged at center, down side.

Rear license plate (Station Wagon) arranged at center of back door, down side.

Bumpers, front and rear, of chromium plated steel sheet.

Bucket front seats, folding and adjustable. Upholstery: cloth and imitation leather or all-leather (500 D); all-leather upholstery for Station Wagon.

Bench-type rear seat providing accomodation for two passengers; folding seat back to increase luggage space. Upholstery: cloth and imitation leather or all-leather (500 D); all-leather upholstery for Station Wagon.

Fluted-rubber mats on floor, floor sides, front wheel-housings, control passage tunnel and rear seat back.

Foot wells behind front seat for better accomodation of rear passengers.

Imitation leather trim panels underbelt and on door panels.

Instrument panel of pressed steel sheet, painted to match the car tone and wadded on bottom; utility shelf under the instrument panel; instrument cluster on driver's side, switches and controls at center of panel.

Body inner framing: exposed portion painted to match the car tone.

Ash receiver on top center of the instrument panel.

Rear view mirror at center of header panel above the windshield. The Station Wagon is fitted with an additional rear view mirror on left front pillar post.

Two sun visors, adjustable, above the windshield.

Rear side head rest paddings and headlining (500 D).

Side strap hangers (Station Wagon).

Access to engine compartment by insulating material-lined, front hinged panel which performs also as load space floor (Station Wagon).

Engine air intake through two ducts on rear side body corners; the intake mouthing, behind the rear quarter window, is covered by a stainless steel net with bright metal rim (Station Wagon).

Windshield washer pump.

CAR AIR CONDITIONING

Summer ventilation: open ventipanes, winding or sliding glasses.

Winter heating: use the engine warmed air by turning the shutter open. Heating at front through two delivery hoses blowing against the windshield; two openings on floor tunnel provide heating at rear (Station Wagon only).

Windshield demisting: warmed air is admitted to the windshield past two slots on the instrument panel.

Fig. 21. - Three-quarter front view of « 500 Station Wagon ».

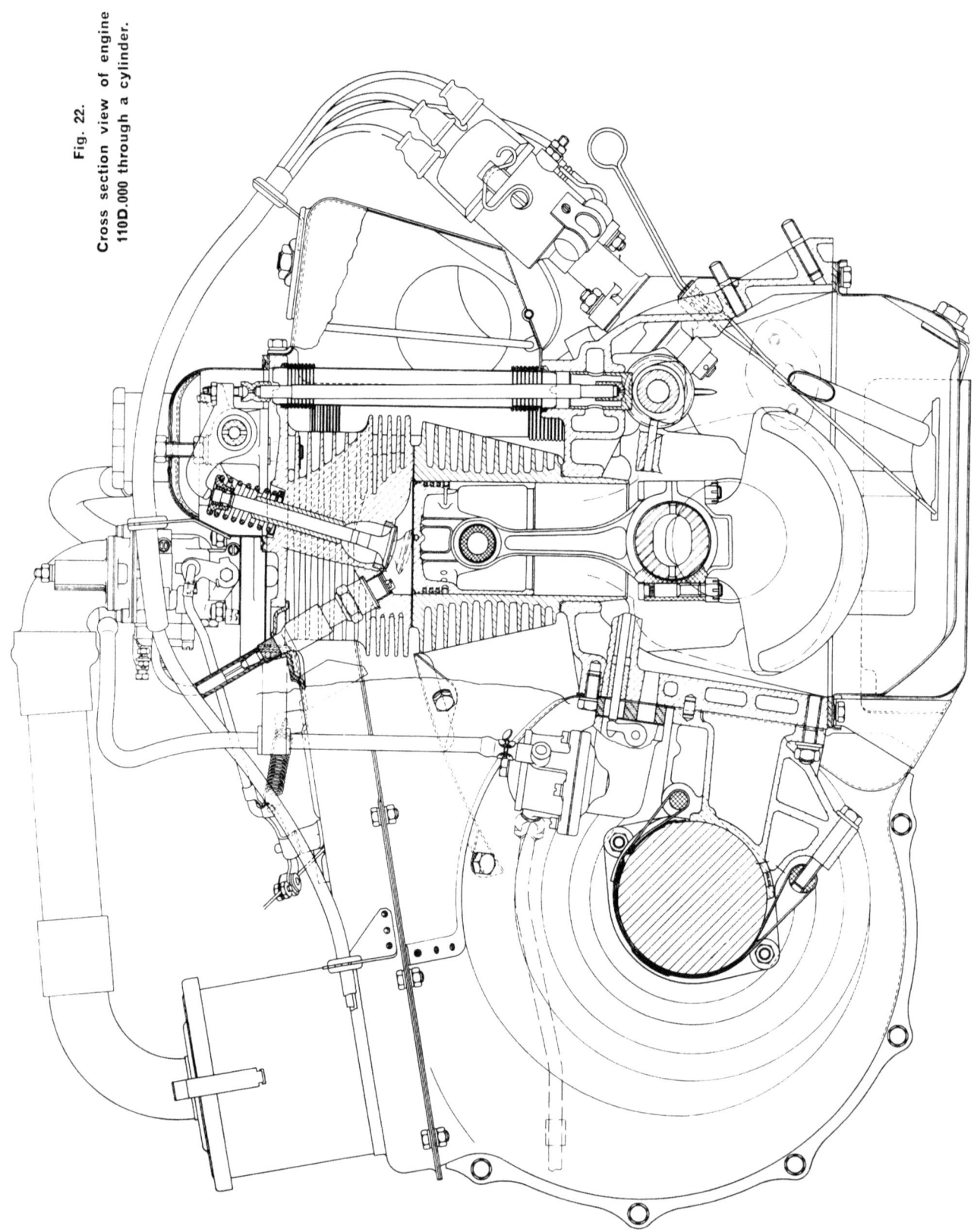

Fig. 22. Cross section view of engine 110D.000 through a cylinder.

MAIN SERVICING DIRECTIONS

Engine

CYLINDERS

The cast-iron cylinders are selected and graded in three classes based on bore diameters: A, B and C. These letters are punched on cylinder top (fig. 23).

To check the bore, measurements must be taken at two different barrel heights, both lengthwise and crosswise (fig. 23).

The 2nd measurement (lower) (fig. 23) must be taken higher than 1.1811″ (30 mm) from cylinder bottom edge.

NOTE - On cylinder barrel lower band (marked « 30 mm » in the drawing) a max. runout of $^{+.0002''}_{-.0006''}$ ($^{+0.005}_{-0.015}$ mm) is allowed with respect to specified inner diameter.

PISTONS

Like cylinders, the oval-shaped pistons are selected into classes A-B-C based on skirt diameter measured at right angles to piston pin.

Pistons are also graded in classes of the same weight within ± .09 oz (2.5 gr).

Each engine must be fitted with pistons belonging to the same class.

Piston skirt diameters:
— at skirt top:
 Class A: 2.6498″ to 2.6502″ (67.305 to 67.315 mm)
 Class B: 2.6502″ to 2.6506″ (67.315 to 67.325 mm)
 Class C: 2.6506″ to 2.6510″ (67.325 to 67.335 mm)
— at skirt bottom:
 Class A: 2.6524″ to 2.6528″ (67.370 to 67.380 mm)
 Class B: 2.6528″ to 2.6532″ (67.380 to 67.390 mm)
 Class C: 2.6532″ to 2.6536″ (67.390 to 67.400 mm)

Pistons and cylinders of the same class must have the following fit clearances (measured at right angles to pin):
— at skirt top   .0033″ to .0041″ (0.085 to 0.105 mm)
— at skirt bottom .0008″ to .0016″ (0.020 to 0.040 mm)

NOTE - For all other data covering the matching of rings to grooves and pins to bosses, see Table on page 32.

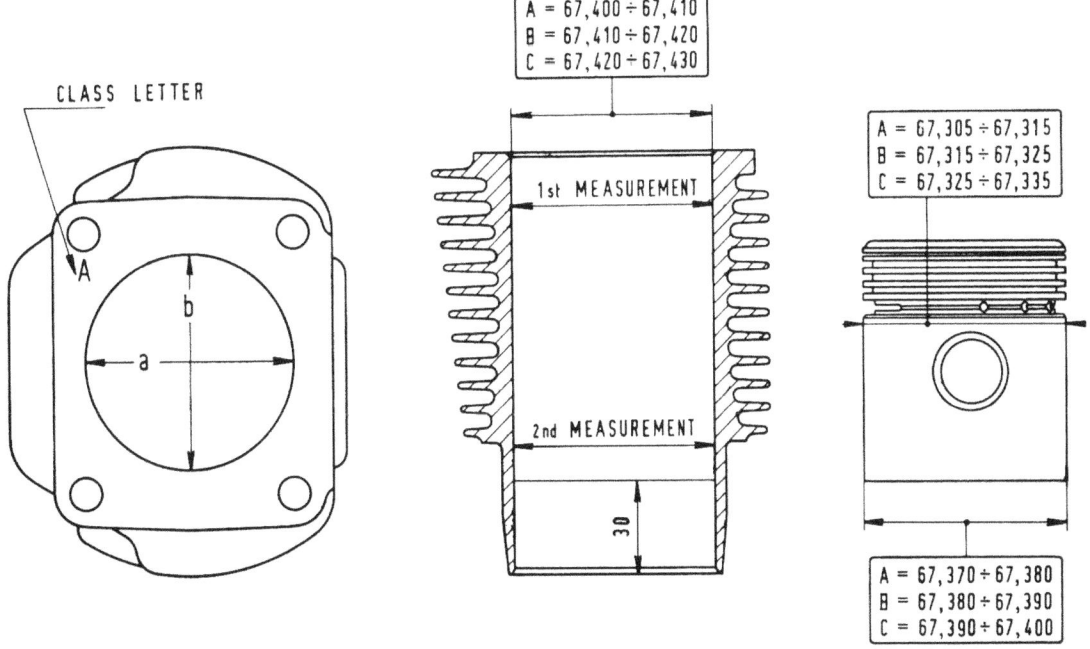

Fig. 23. - Main checking data (in mm) of cylinders and pistons of engines 110D.000 and 120.000.

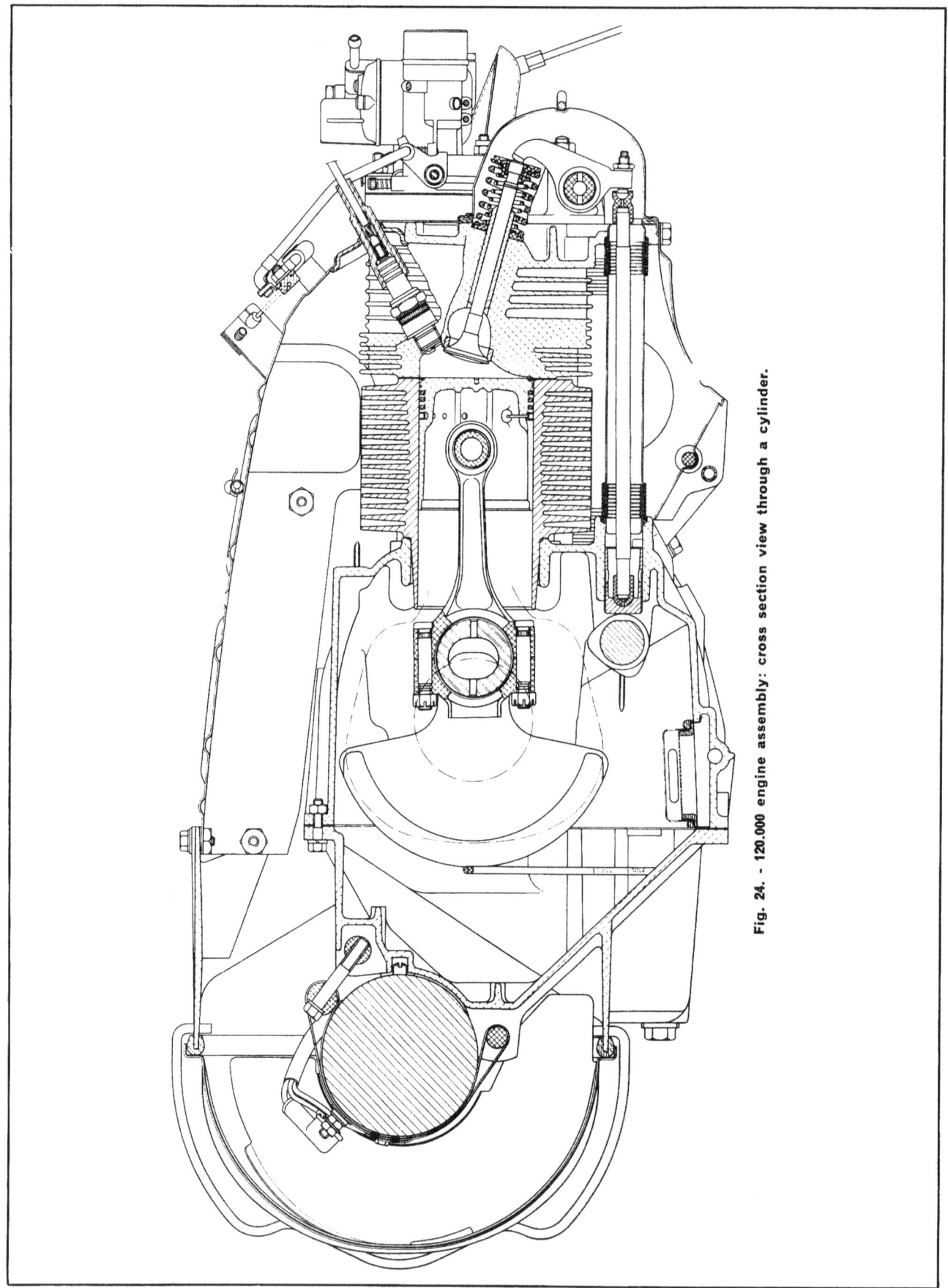

Fig. 24. - 120.000 engine assembly: cross section view through a cylinder.

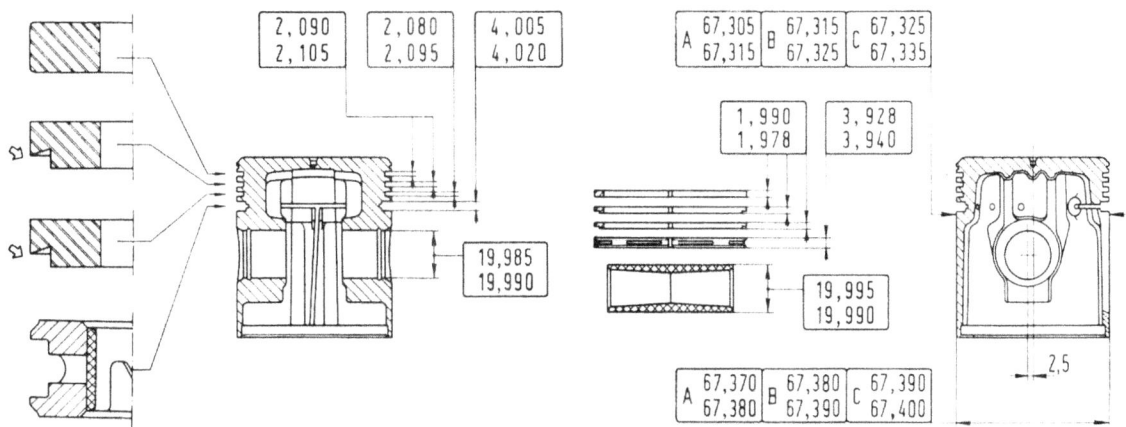

Fig. 25. - Critical dimensions of pistons, piston pins and rings to suit engines 110D.000 and 120.000 (in mm).

Replacement piston oversize range: .0079"-.0157"-.0236" (0.2-0.4-0.6 mm). Piston rings, too, come in this oversize range, with the exception of the radial-cut oil ring; which was previously fitted in the place of the slotted oil scraper ring; the radial-cut oil ring came only in the .0157" (0.4 mm) oversize.

Fig. 25 shows the arrangement of rings in piston grooves.

A pinch fit of .0000" to .0004" (0.000 to 0.010 mm) is specified between the piston pin and its boss in piston. The piston pin is supplied also .0079" (0.2 mm) oversize on outer diameter.

CONNECTING RODS AND ROD BEARINGS

Prior to assembling connecting rods to pistons, check the alignment of connecting rods at small and big end. Maximum misalignment, measured 4.92" (125 mm) apart from rod centerline, is ± .0020" (0.05 mm).

Thin-wall bearings should not be adapted or reworked for any reason; if they are badly pitted or worn, replace them.

Connecting rod bearing halves are supplied in standard size and undersizes.

Use of the « Plastigage » calibrated strip (fig. 27), type PG-1 and PR-1, is recommended to check clearance between connecting rod bearings and journals.

THICKNESS OF CONNECTING ROD BEARING HALVES

Standard	Undersizes			
	.01" (0.254 mm)	.02" (0.508 mm)	.03" (0.762 mm)	.04" (1.016 mm)
.0604" (1.534 mm)	.0654" (1.661 mm)	.0704" (1.788 mm)	0.754" (1.915 mm)	.0804" (2.042 mm)
.0607" (1.543 mm)	.0657" (1.670 mm)	.0707" (1.797 mm)	.0757" (1.924 mm)	.0807" (2.051 mm)

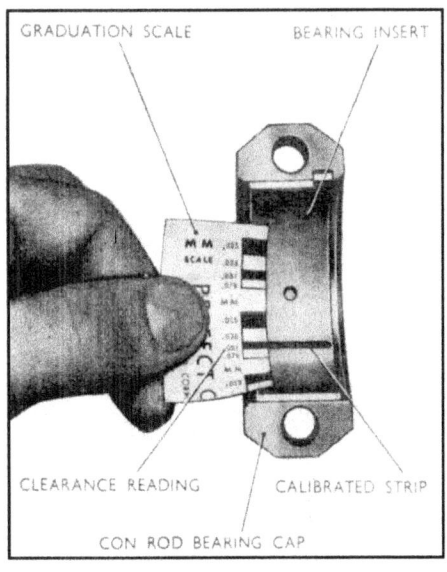

Fig. 26. - Checking con rod bearing insert-to-journal clearance by comparing width of flattened « Plastigage ».

CALIBRATED STRIP

Fig. 27. - « Plastigage » calibrated strip for checking connecting rod bearing-to-journal clearance, and envelope with graduation scale.

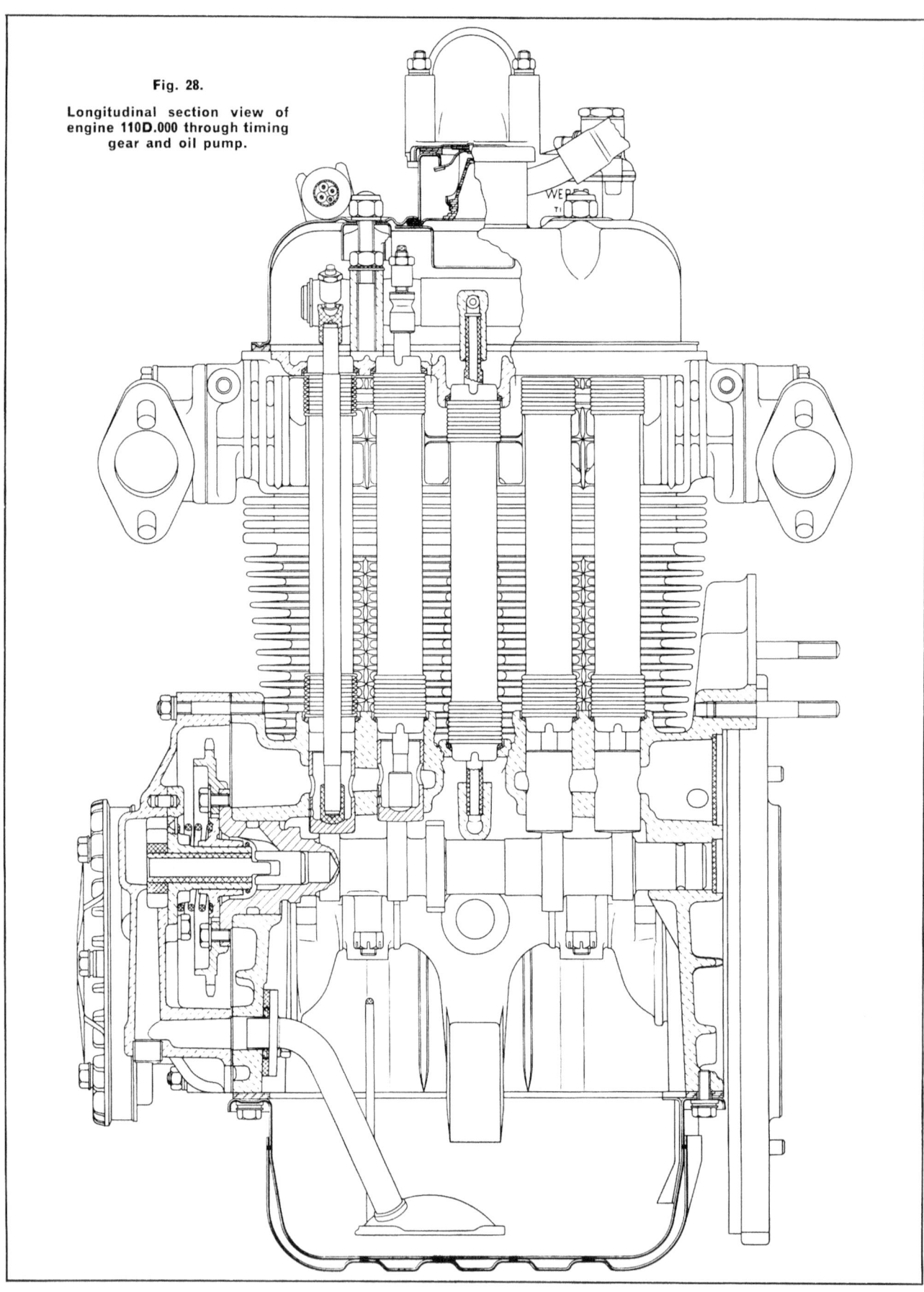

Fig. 28.

Longitudinal section view of engine 110D.000 through timing gear and oil pump.

To determine the amount of clearance between the journal and the bearing shell, compare the width of the flattened «Plastigage», at its widest point, with the graduations on the envelope (fig. 26).

The assembly clearance of connecting rod bearing shells to crankshaft journals should be .0004" to .0024" (0.011 to 0.061 mm).

SMALL END BUSHINGS

During the engine overhaul, if the small end bushing has been replaced by a new one, use care to mill a slot in it in line with the groove machined on rod small end.

Use a cutter having a thickness of .1181" (3 mm) and a diameter of 2.1654" (55 mm); after the milling operation, the cutter center should be 1.378" (35 mm) apart from the bushing bore axis.

The purpose of the slot milled is to ensure a good lubrication between the bushing and piston pin.

Recommended assembly clearance of piston pin to small end bushing: .0002" to .0006" (0.005 to 0.016 mm).

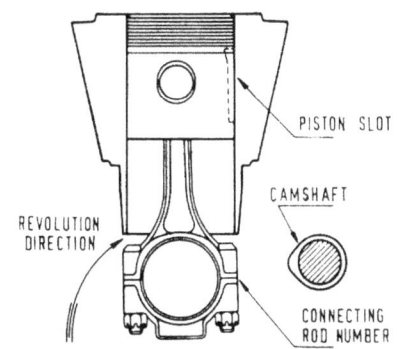

Fig. 30. - Diagram showing the correct position of connecting rod-piston assembly on engine 110D.000.

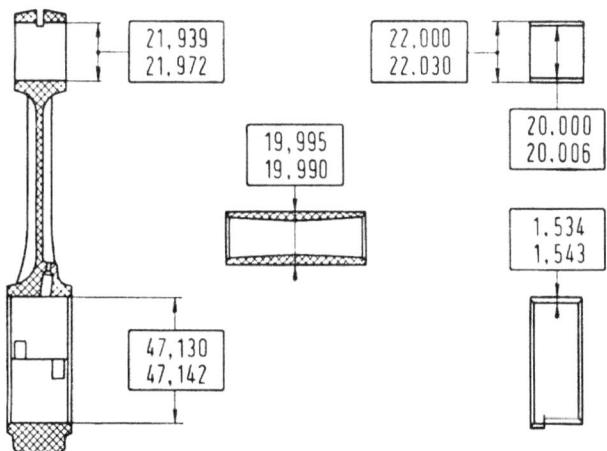

Fig. 29. - Critical dimensions of connecting rods, rod bearings, bushings and piston pins (in mm).

CONNECTING ROD-PISTON ASSEMBLY AND INSTALLATION

The connecting rod should be assembled to the piston, and the assembly of two parts installed in engine, as follows:

— the number stamped on connecting rod stem and cap must face the piston expansion split;

— the piston expansion split and the connecting rod number must face the camshaft;

— the connecting rods must be tied to the crankshaft so that the rod No. 1 is facing to the valve gear side and the rod No. 2 to the flywheel side.

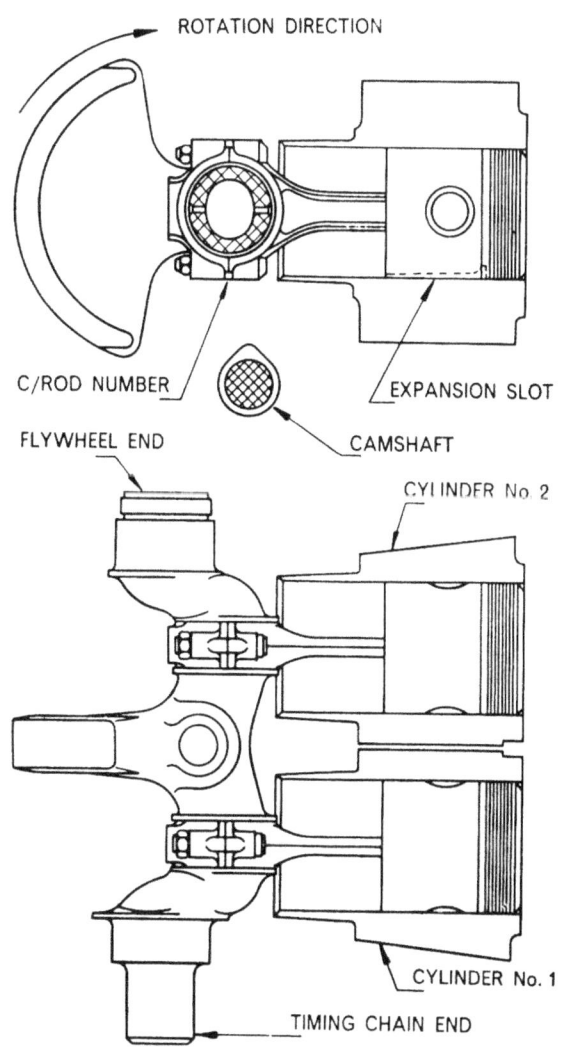

Fig. 31. - Diagram showing the correct position of connecting rod-piston assembly on engine 120.000.

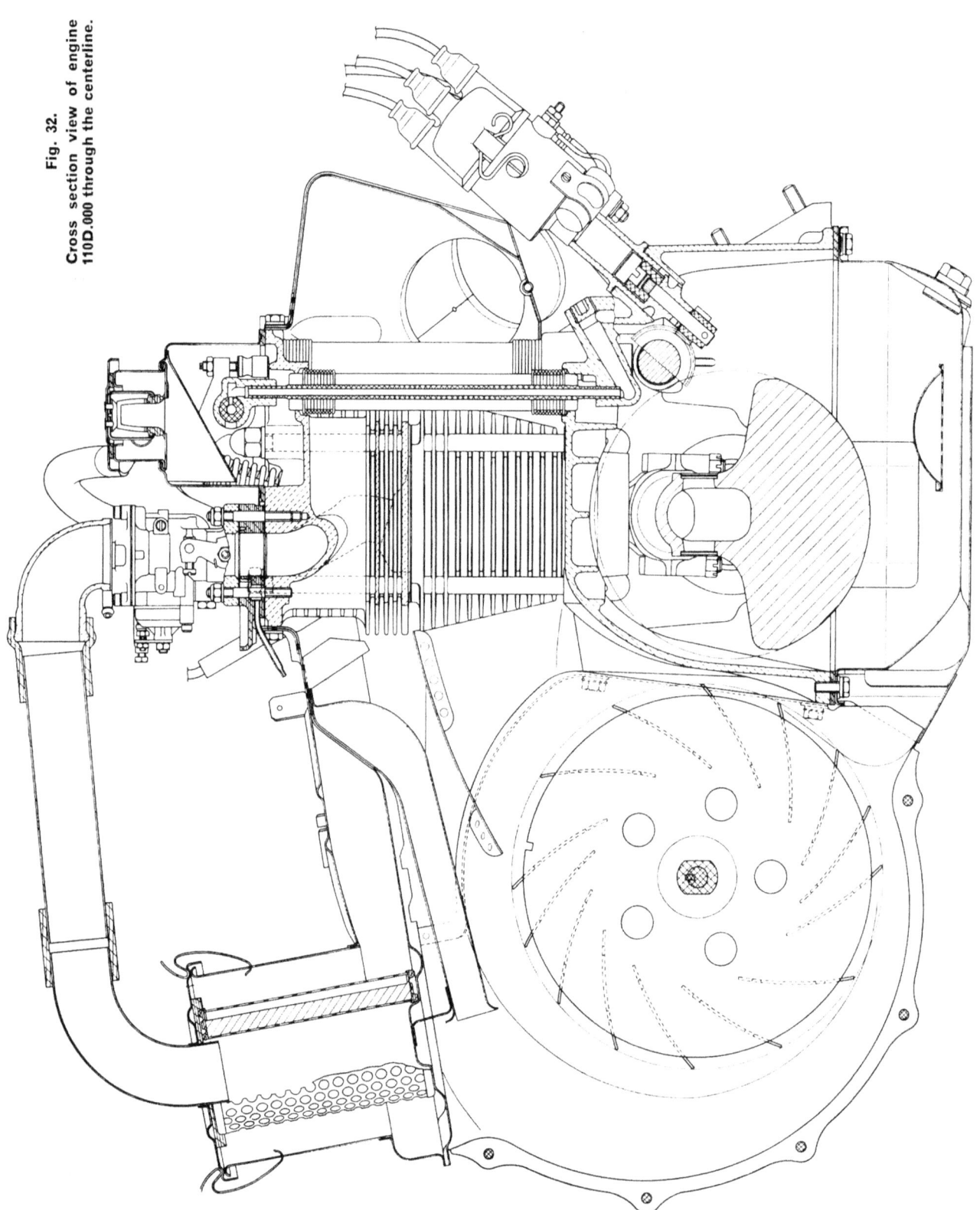

Fig. 32. Cross section view of engine 110D.000 through the centerline.

SERVICE PROCEDURES: ENGINE

CRANKSHAFT AND BEARINGS

If the main and connecting rod bearing journals must be ground, gauge them with an outside caliper to determine the diameter to which they should be reduced. In this connection recall that the clearances of parts are the following:
— between the main bearing journal and the main bearing shell: .0012" to .0026" (0.030 to 0.065 mm);
— between the connecting rod bearing journal and the rod bearing shell: .0004" to .0024" (0.011 to 0.061 mm).

MAIN BEARING I. D.

Standard	Undersizes				
	.0079" (0.2 mm)	.0157" (0.4 mm)	.0236" (0.6 mm)	.0315" (0.8 mm)	.0394" (1 mm)
2.1268" (54.020 mm) to 2.1274" (54.035 mm)	2.1189" (53.820 mm) to 2.1195" (53.835 mm)	2.1110" (53.620 mm) to 2.1116" (53.635 mm)	2.1031" (53.420 mm) to 2.1037" (53.435 mm)	2.0953" (53.220 mm) to 2.0959" (53.235 mm)	2.0874" (53.020 mm) to 2.0880" (53.035 mm)

CONNECTING ROD HALF BEARING THICKNESS

Standard	Undersize			
	.01" (0.254 mm)	.02" (0.508 mm)	.03" (0.762 mm)	.04" (1.016 mm)
.0604" (1.534 mm) to .0607" (1.543 mm)	.0654" (1.661 mm) to .0657" (1.670 mm)	.0704" (1.788 mm) to .0707" (1.797 mm)	.0754" (1.915 mm) to .0757" (1.924 mm)	.0804" (2.042 mm) to .0807" (2.051 mm)

CRANKSHAFT JOURNAL DIAMETERS

Standard	Undersizes				
	.0079" (0.2 mm)	.0157" (0.4 mm)	.0236" (0.6 mm)	.0315" (0.8 mm)	.0394" (1 mm)
2.1248" (53.970 mm) to 2.1256" (53.990 mm)	2.1169" (53.770 mm) to 2.1177" (53.790 mm)	2.1091" (53.570 mm) to 2.1098" (53.590 mm)	2.1012" (53.370 mm) to 2.1020" (53.390 mm)	2.0933" (53.170 mm) to 2.0941" (53.190 mm)	2.0854" (52.970 mm) to 2.0862" (52.990 mm)

CRANKPIN DIAMETERS

Standard	Undersizes			
	.01" (0.254 mm)	.02" (0.508 mm)	.03" (0.762 mm)	.04" (1.016 mm)
1.7328" (44.013 mm) to 1.7336" (44.033 mm)	1.7228" (43.759 mm) to 1.7236" (43.779 mm)	1.7128" (43.505 mm) to 1.7136" (43.525 mm)	1.7028" (43.251 mm) to 1.7036" (43.271 mm)	1.6928" (42.997 mm) to 1.6936" (43.017 mm)

While grinding the crankshaft, pay utmost care to shaping the arm shoulder fillets, the values of which should be kept within the specifications given in figs 33, 34 and 35.

CRANKARM FILLET RADII

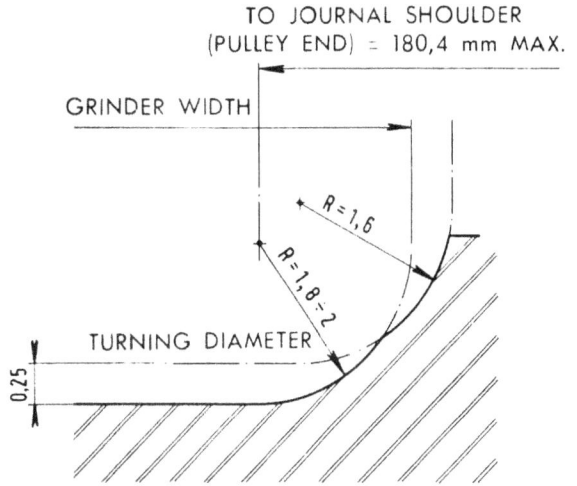

Fig. 33. - Fillet specifications at main bearing journal shoulder, flywheel end.

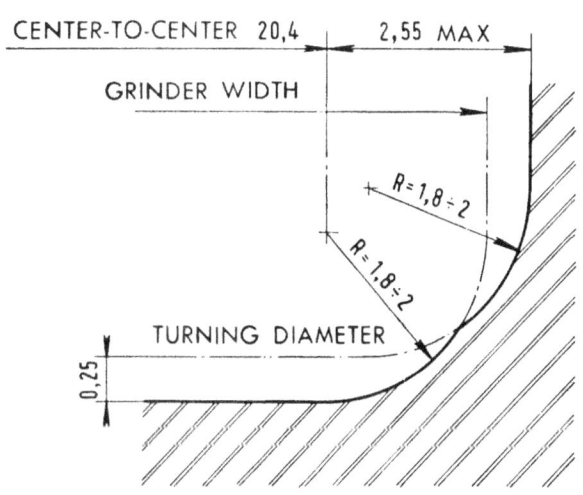

Fig. 34. - Fillet specifications at connecting rod bearing journal shoulders.

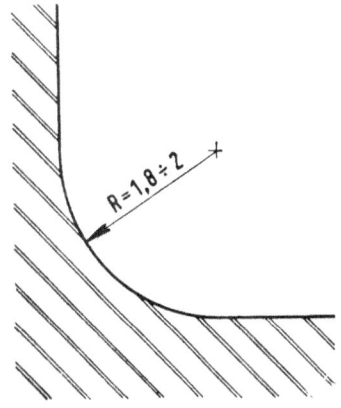

Fig. 35. - Fillet specifications at main bearing journal shoulder, pulley end.

CYLINDER HEAD - VALVES - VALVE GUIDES AND SPRINGS

Critical dimensions of the cylinder head, valves, valve guides and springs are tabulated on page 33.

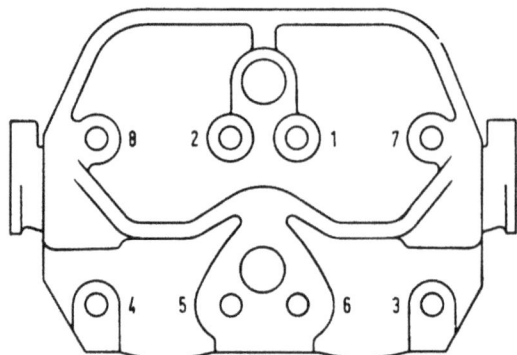

Fig. 37. - Cylinder head stud nut tightening sequence.

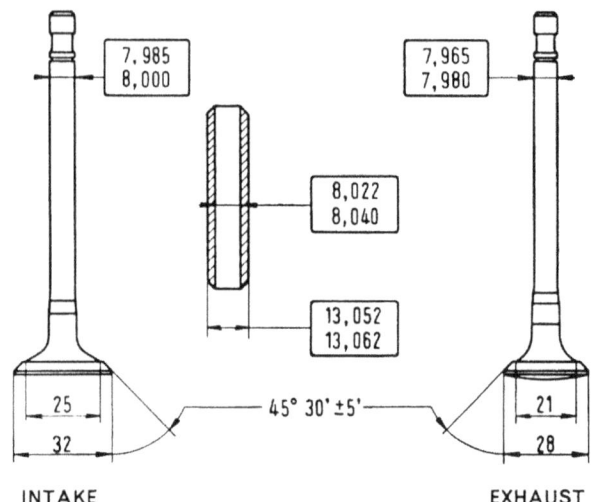

Fig. 36. - Critical dimensions of intake and exhaust valves and guides (in mm).

Tightening the cylinder head stud nuts should be made, using a torque wrench, in the order shown in fig. 37 and in two distinct passes:

— 1st pass: tighten nuts with a torque not exceeding 18.1 ft. lbs (2,500 kgmm);

— 2nd pass: tighten nuts with the recommended torque of 23.9 ft. lbs (3,300 kgmm).

VALVE GEAR

Valve timing and tappet clearance data are outlined on page 9.

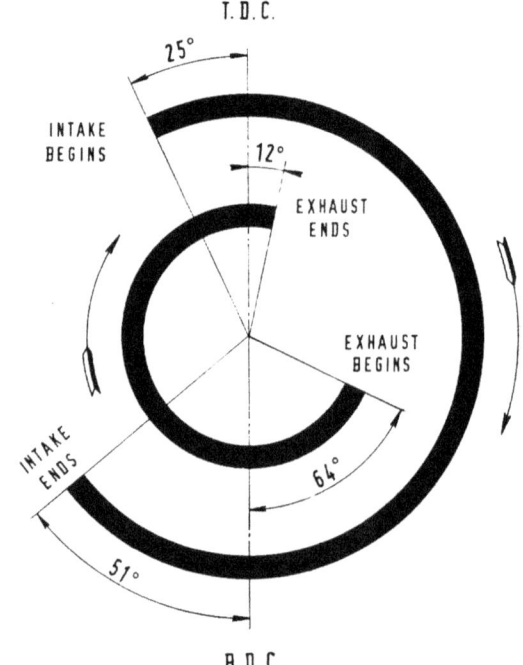

Fig. 38. - Valve timing diagram.

Valve timing data refer to an increased tappet clearance of .0154" (0.39 mm).

ASSEMBLY DATA AND FIT SPECIFICATIONS

CYLINDER AND CRANKCASE

	in	mm
Cylinder bores — Class A	2.6535 to 2.6539	67.400 to 67.410
Cylinder bores — Class B	2.6539 to 2.6543	67.410 to 67.420
Cylinder bores — Class C	2.6543 to 2.6547	67.420 to 67.430
Cylinder O.D. in the centering area on crankcase	2.9523 to 2.9498	74.970 to 74.924
Cylinder seat diameter on crankcase	2.9528 to 2.9540	75.000 to 75.030
Fit of cylinders in crankcase seats	.0012 to .0042	0.030 to 0.106
Camshaft bushing seat diameter:		
— chain end	1.6939 to 1.6954	43.025 to 43.064
— flywheel end	.8669 to .8682	22.020 to 22.053

CONNECTING RODS - C/ROD BEARINGS AND BUSHINGS

	in	mm
Connecting rod bearing seat diameter	1.8555 to 1.8560	47.130 to 47.142
Connecting rod small end bushing seat diameter	.8637 to .8650	21.939 to 21.972
Connecting rod standard bearing thickness	.0604 to .0675	1.534 to 1.543
Connecting rod bearing undersizes	.0100-.0200-.0300-.0400	0.254-0.508-0.762-1.016
Connecting rod small end bushing O.D.	.8661 to .8673	22.000 to 22.030
Connecting rod small end bushing bore (to be obtained after press-fitting)	.7874 to .7876	20.000 to 20.006
Piston pin-to-bushing clearance	.0002 to .0006	0.005 to 0.016
Bushing-to-connecting rod small end (pinch fit at all times)	.0011 to .0036	0.028 to 0.091
Connecting rod bearing-to-crankpin clearance	.0004 to .0024	0.011 to 0.061

CRANKSHAFT - MAIN AND ROD BEARINGS

	in	mm
Standard main bearing journal diameter	2.1256 to 2.1248	53.990 to 53.970
Main bearing I.D.	2.1268 to 2.1274	54.020 to 54.035
Main bearing undersize range	.0079-.0157-.0236-.0315-.0394	0.2-0.4-0.6-0.8-1.00
Fit clearance: main bearing-to-journal	.0012 to .0026	0.030 to 0.065
Standard con rod bearing journal diameter	1.7328 to 1.7336	44.013 to 44.033
Con rod bearing seat diameter	1.8555 to 1.8560	47.130 to 47.142
Thickness of standard con rod bearing insert	.0604 to .0675	1.534 to 1.543
Connecting rod bearing undersize range	.0100-.0200-.0300-.0400	0.254-0.508-0.762-1.016
Fit clearance: con rod bearing-to-journal	.0004 to .0024	0.011 to 0.061

PISTONS - PINS - RINGS

	Engine 120.000 from No. 017001 and Engine 110 D.000	
	in	mm
Standard piston diameter, measured at right angle to pin:		
— at skirt top — Class A	2.6498 to 2.6502	67.305 to 67.315
Class B	2.6502 to 2.6506	67.315 to 67.325
Class C	2.6506 to 2.6510	67.325 to 67.335
— at skirt bottom — Class A	2.6524 to 2.6528	67.370 to 67.380
Class B	2.6528 to 2.6532	67.380 to 67.390
Class C	2.6532 to 2.6536	67.390 to 67.400
Piston pin boss bore	.7868 to .7870	19.985 to 19.990
Groove widths — 1st groove	.0823 to .0829	2.090 to 2.105
2nd groove	.0823 to .0829	2.090 to 2.105
3rd groove	.0819 to .0825	2.080 to 2.095
4th groove	.1577 to .1583	4.005 to 4.020
Piston oversize range	.0079-.0157-.0236	0.2-0.4-0.6
Standard piston pin diam.	.7872 to .7870	19.995 to 19.990
Piston pin oversize	.0079	0.2
Piston-to-cylinder fit clearances, at right angle to pin:		
— at skirt top	.0033 to .0041	0.085 to 0.105
— at skirt bottom	.0008 to .0016	0.020 to 0.040
Piston pin-to-boss bore (pinch fit at all times)	0 to .0004	0 to 0.010
Piston ring thicknesses:		
— compression ring - 1st groove	.0783 to .0779	1.990 to 1.978
— oilscraper rings - 2nd-3rd grooves	.0783 to .0779	1.990 to 1.978
— slotted oilscraper ring - 4th groove	.1551 to .1546	3.940 to 3.928
— radial-cut oilscraper ring (early type) - 4th groove	.1547 to .1535	3.93 to 3.90
Piston ring oversize range:		
— 1st, 2nd, 3rd rings	.0079-.0157-.0236	0.2-0.4-0.6
— 4th ring slotted	.0079-.0157-.0236	0.2-0.4-0.6
radial-cut (early type)	.0157	0.4
Ring-to-piston groove land fit clearances:		
— 1st ring	.0039 to .0050	0.100 to 0.127
— 2nd ring	.0039 to .0050	0.100 to 0.127
— 3rd ring	.0035 to .0046	0.090 to 0.117
— 4th ring slotted	.0026 to .0036	0.065 to 0.092
radial-cut	.0030 to .0047	0.075 to 0.120
Piston ring end gap (rings in barrel):		
— 1st, 2nd, 3rd ring	.0098 to .0157	0.25 to 0.40
— 4th ring slotted	.0079 to .0138	0.20 to 0.35
radial-cut	none	
Maximum weight difference between either piston of a set	± .09 oz	± 2.5 gr

CYLINDER HEAD - VALVES AND VALVE GUIDES

	in	mm
Valve guide seat diameter in cylinder head	.5118 to .5125	13.000 to 13.018
Valve guide O.D.	.5139 to .5143	13.052 to 13.062
Valve I.D. (press fitted)	.3158 to .3165	8.022 to 8.040
Valve guide to cylinder head (pinch fit at all times)	.00134 to .00244	0.034 to 0.062
Valve stem diameter intake	.3144 to .3150	7.985 to 8.000
exhaust	.3136 to .3142	7.965 to 7.980
Valve stem-to-guide fit clearance: intake	.00087 to .00217	0.022 to 0.055
exhaust	.00165 to .00295	0.042 to 0.075
Valve seat inclination angle on cylinder head	45° ± 5′	
Valve face inclination angle	45° 30′ ± 5′	
Intake valve head max. diameter	1.2598	32
Exhaust valve head max. diameter	1.0630	28
For a complete revolution, guided by stem, T.I.R. with plunger on face center	.00079	0.02

VALVE SPRINGS

Engine and Valve Type	Working Turns No.	Inside Diameter		Wire Diameter		A		B				C				Minimum Permissible Load to B	
		in	mm	in	mm	in	mm	in	mm	lb	kg	in	mm	lb	kg	lb	kg
120.000 inner spring	5	.905	23	.146	3.7	1.846	46.9	1.516	38.5	42.1 ±1.8	19.1 ±0.8	1.185	30.1	84.2 ±3.7	38.2 ±1.7	28.7	13
outer spring	7	.598	15.2	.102	2.6	1.583	40.2	1.398	35.5	13.4 ±.7	6.1 ±0.3	1.067	27.1	37.5 ±1.8	17 ±0.8	8.8	4
110 D.000	7¼	.760	19.3	.126	3.2	2.252	57.2	1.594	40.5	52.0 ±2.6	23.6 ±1.2	1.240	31.5	80.2 ±4.0	36.4 ±1.8	43	19.5

A = free length   B = seated length   C = Minimum length, working spring

CAMSHAFT AND CAMSHAFT SEATS

	in	mm
Camshaft journal diameter:		
— timing gear end	1.6919 to 1.6929	42.975 to 43.000
— flywheel end	.8653 to .8661	21.979 to 22.000
Camshaft seat diameter:		
— timing gear end	1.6939 to 1.6954	43.025 to 43.064
— flywheel end	.8669 to .8682	22.020 to 22.053
Camshaft journal-to-seat fit clearance:		
— timing gear end	.00098 to .0035	0.025 to 0.089
— flywheel end	.00079 to .0029	0.020 to 0.074

PUSHRODS - ROCKERS - ROCKER SHAFT AND SUPPORTS

	in	mm
Pushrod seat bore in crankcase	.8662 to .8670	22.003 to 22.021
Standard pushrod O.D.	.8660 to .8652	21.996 to 21.978
Pushrod oversizes	.00197-.00394	0.05-0.10
Pushrod-to-seat clearance	.00028 to .00169	0.007 to 0.043
Rocker shaft support bore	.7089 to .7096	18.005 to 18.023
Rocker shaft diameter	.7087 to .7082	18.000 to 17.988
Rocker shaft-to-support clearance	.00020 to .00138	0.005 to 0.035
Rocker bore	.7093 to .7104	18.016 to 18.043
Rocker-to-shaft clearance	.00063 to .00217	0.016 to 0.055

ENGINE TIGHTENING REFERENCE

DESCRIPTION	Part No.	Thread Pitch	Material	Tightening Torque
Main bearing support-to-crankcase screw	1/60435/20	M 8 x 1,25	R 80	15.2 ft.lbs (2,100 kgmm)
Flywheel-to-crankshaft screw	1/60436/30	M 8 x 1,25	R 100	23.1 ft.lbs (3,200 kgmm)
Connecting rod bearing cap screw self-locking nut	1/25664/20	M 8 x 1	R 80 (screw R 100)	23.9 ft.lbs (3,300 kgmm)
Rocker arm support-to-cylinder head stud nut	1/61008/11	M 8 x 1,25	R 50 Cdt (stud R 80)	15.2 ft.lbs (2,100 kgmm)
Cylinder head-to-crankcase stud nut	1/21647/11	M 10 x 1,25	R 50 Cdt (stud R 100 Cdt)	23.9 ft.lbs (3,300 kgmm)
Cylinder head-to-crankcase stud cap nut	1/40549/11	M 10 x 1,25	R 50 Cdt (stud R 100 Cdt)	23.9 ft.lbs (3,300 kgmm)
Driven gear-to-crankshaft screw	1/09794/20	M 6 x 1	R 80	6.5 ft.lbs (900 kgmm)
Generator and fan drive pulley hub screw	987109	M 24 x 1,5	R 50	108.5 ft.lbs (15,000 kgmm)
Drive pulley cover screw	1/38236/21	M 6 x 1	R 80 Cdt	5.8 ft.lbs (800 kgmm)
Fan-to-generator self-locking nut	1/25756/11	M 10 x 1,25	R 50 Cdt (shaft R 80)	25.3 ft.lbs (3,500 kgmm)
Pulley-to-generator self-locking nut	1/25756/11	M 10 x 1,25	R 50 Cdt (shaft R 80)	14.5 ft.lbs (2,000 kgmm)
Commutator end bearing cup stop clamp screw nut (Engine 100 D.000)	1/07940/14	M 4 x 0,7	R 50 Snt (screw R 50 Snt)	.8 ft.lbs (110 kgmm)
Exhaust silencer-to-cylinder head screw (Engine 120.000)	1/60436/21	M 8 x 1,25	R 80 Cdt	18.1 ft.lbs (2,500 kgmm)
Spark plugs	4012866 4064003 4065417	M 14 x 1,25	—	18.1 to 21.7 ft.lbs (2,500 to 3,000 kgmm)

Fuel System

CARBURETOR

The Weber carburetor type 26 IMB 4, to suit the engine 110D.000 is of the downdraft design; the Weber carburetor type 26 OC, to suit the engine 120.000, is of the horizontal draft design.

Both these carburetors are fitted with a progressive-action starting device which enables the driver to suit the mixture richness to the most varied conditions of starting, until the engine has reached the rated operation temperature.

The dampened needle valve ensures a smooth engine running since, thanks to its dampening device, it is not affected by vibrations and, therefore, keeps steadily constant the level in carburetor bowl.

The diagrammatic views in figs. 39 and 41 clearly show the operation of subject carburetors; in addition, the following is a detailed description of the starting device which is also illustrated in figures 40 and 42.

Starting Device.

This progressive-action device (choke) has the function of ensuring **proper engine cold starting**. It is controlled by means of the lever placed behind the gearshift lever and must be gradually set back to rest position as engine is reaching the rated operation temperature.

WEBER CARBURETOR 26 IMB 4.

The starting device (fig. 40) is made up of valve (33) actuated by the lug of rocker (36) connected, through a suitable shaft, to control lever (38).

By pulling the device control to stroke end, through lever (38) and rocker (36), valve (33) is lifted from its seat and brought to the « fully open » position (diagram « A », figure 40).

Under these conditions valve (33) closes air hole (27) and mixture hole (29) and uncovers mixture orifices (30) (32) [which communicate with starting jet (46) through duct (26)] and air holes (35).

With valve (33) partially opened, hole (29) may communicate with carburetor throat, through the valve central slot, duct (28) and hole (31) drilled in Venturi (21) in correspondence with the restriction.

With throttle (19) in idling speed position, the vacuum of engine cranked by the starter causes the fuel contained in the recess of jet (46), in the jet and in reserve well (45) to be emulsioned with the air coming from holes (43) and (44).

Through duct (26) and holes (30) and (32) the mixture arrives - simultaneously with air from holes (35) - past the throttle through duct (34), thus permitting prompt starting of the engine.

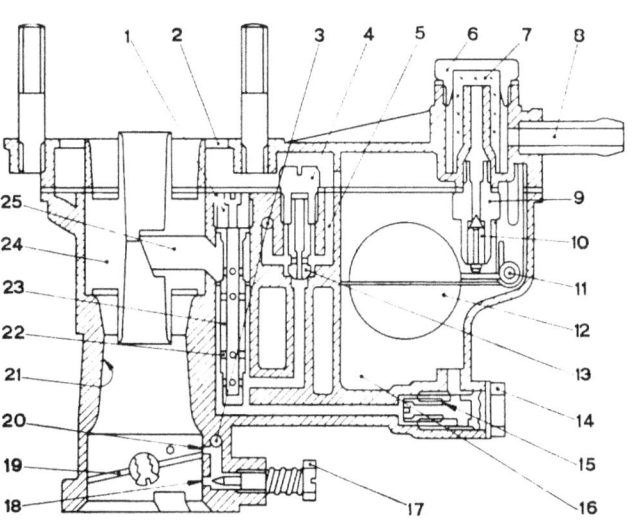

Fig. 39. - Diagrammatic section view of Weber 26 IMB 4 carburetor.

1. Air corrector jet - 2. Air inlet - 3. Idle speed mixture duct - 4. Idle speed jet holder - 5. Idle speed air orifice - 6. Filter cover - 7. Filter - 8. Fuel inlet connection - 9. Needle valve seat - 10. Needle - 11. Float pivot - 12. Float - 13. Idle speed jet - 14. Main jet holder - 15. Main jet - 16. Bowl - 17. Idle speed mixture adjustment screw - 18. Idle speed mixture orifice - 19. Throttle - 20. Transition hole - 21. Primary Venturi (not interchangeable) - 22. Emulsion orifices - 23. Emulsion well - 24. Secondary Venturi (not interchangeable) - 25. Main nozzle.

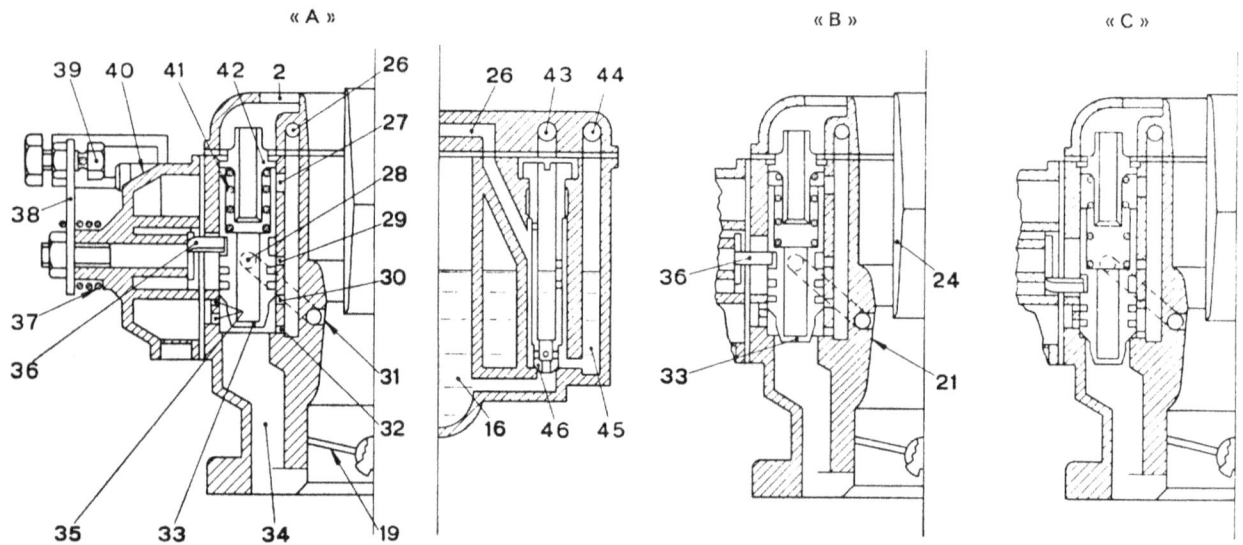

Fig. 40. - Diagrammatic section views of 26 IMB 4 Weber carburetor starting device.

2. Air inlet - 16. Bowl - 19. Throttle - 21. Primary Venturi - 24. Secondary Venturi - 26. Mixture duct - 27. Mixture leaning air orifice - 28. Transition duct - 29. Transition mixture orifice - 30. Starting mixture orifice - 31. Transition orifice - 32. Starting mixture orifice - 33. Starting valve - 34. Mixture duct - 35. Starting device air orifices - 36. Rocker - 37. Lever return spring - 38. Starting device control lever - 39. Control wire screw - 40. Cover with support for starting device control bowden - 41. Starting valve spring - 42. Spring casing - 43. Starting jet emulsion air orifice - 44. Air emulsion reserve well orifice - 45. Starting reserve well - 46. Starting jet.

A. Choke fully inserted - B. Choke partially inserted - C. Choke disinserted.

After engine firing the device delivers a mixture whose fuel/air ratio is such as to permit regular running of engine while still cold. But, as the engine warms up, this mixture would be excessive and too rich; therefore, it becomes necessary to exclude gradually the device as the engine is reaching the rated operation temperature. During this maneuver, valve (33) slowly uncovers hole (27) which permits a greater amount of air to enter through spring guide hole (42) (to weaken the mixture) while, by closing progressively holes (30) and (32) and air holes (35) also the amount of mixture is reduced (see diagram « B », fig. 40).

Hole (29), duct (28), and hole (31), drilled in Venturi (21), have the task of permitting a regular progression of acceleration also with cold engine. By opening throttle (19) to speed up the engine the vacuum acting on duct (34) is reduced. This would cause a reduction in the amount of fuel delivered through said duct (34), with consequent irregular running of the engine, but, through hole (31), duct (28) and hole (29) (from which air is drawn when throttle is closed), some mixture is sucked in by the vacuum formed in the restriction of the Venturi consequent to the opening of the throttle and this compensates for the reduction in delivery through duct (34).

When the starting device is excluded, valve (33) covers also hole (29) and prevents the entrance of mixture (diagram « C », fig. 40).

WEBER CARBURETOR 26 OC

Referring to the operation diagram fig. 42, the fuel from bowl (23) reaches starting jet (37) through duct (35).

By pulling the choke lever (31) to stroke end, valve (30) is lifted from its seat and brought to the « fully open » position (diagram « A », fig. 42). Under these conditions valve (30) uncovers both starting mixture ducts (28) and (29).

With throttle in idling speed position, the vacuum of engine cranked by the starter causes the fuel contained in the recess of jet (37), in the jet and in reserve well (36) to be emulsioned with the air coming from air jet (38).

Through ducts (28) and (29) the mixture arrives — simultaneously with air from holes (34) — past the throttle, thus permitting prompt starting of the engine.

SERVICE PROCEDURES: FUEL SYSTEM

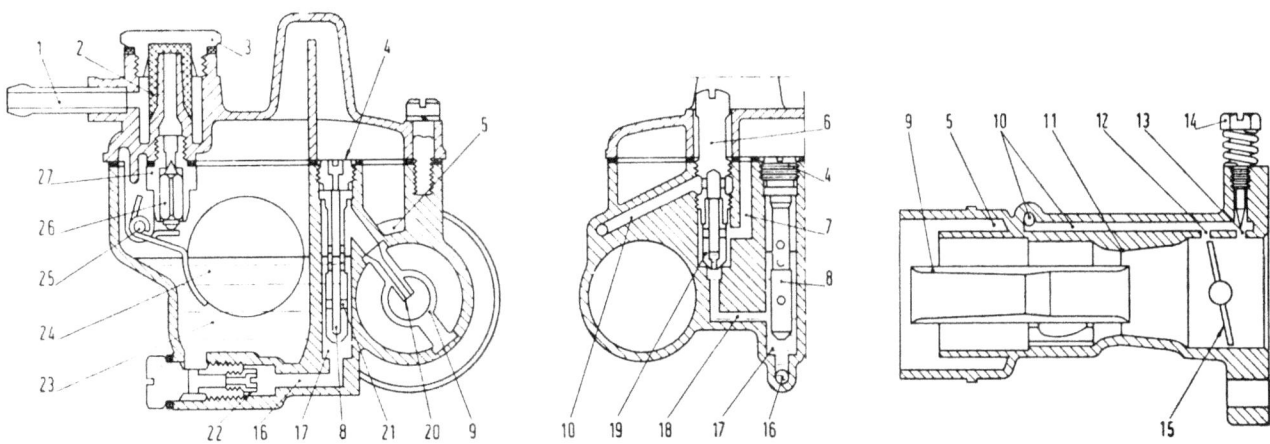

Fig. 41. - Diagrammatic section views of 26 OC Weber carburetor.

1. Fuel inlet connection - 2. Filter gauze - 3. Filter inspection plug - 4. Air corrector jet - 5. Air intake - 6. Idle speed jet holder - 7. Idle air duct - 8. Emulsion tube - 9. Secondary Venturi - 10. Idle mixture duct - 11. Primary Venturi - 12. Progression hole - 13. Idle orifice to duct - 14. Idle mixture adjustment screw - 15. Throttle - 16. Bowl-to-well duct - 17. Emulsion tube housing well - 18. Well-to-idle jet duct - 19. Idle speed jet - 20. Nozzle - 21. Emulsion orifices - 22. Main jet - 23. Bowl - 24. Float - 25. Float pivot - 26. Valve needle - 27. Needle valve.

After engine firing the device delivers a mixture whose fuel/air ratio is such as to permit regular running of engine while still cold. But, as the engine warms up, this mixture would be excessive and too rich: therefore, it becomes necessary to exclude gradually the device as the engine is reaching the rated operation temperature.

During this maneuver, valve (30) gradually blanks mixture duct orifice (28) so as to weaken the mixture while, by closing progressively duct (29), it also reduces little by little the amount of mixture delivered by carburetor (see diagram « B », fig. 42).

When the starting device is excluded, valve (30) covers hole (29) and prevents the entrance of mixture (diagram « C », fig. 42).

Choke Use Directions.

To avail yourself of all the advantages the progressive-action starting device may offer, use it as follows:

ENGINE STARTING

Cold start: fully throw in the device (position « A », figs. 40 and 42); after engine fires push the control part way in.

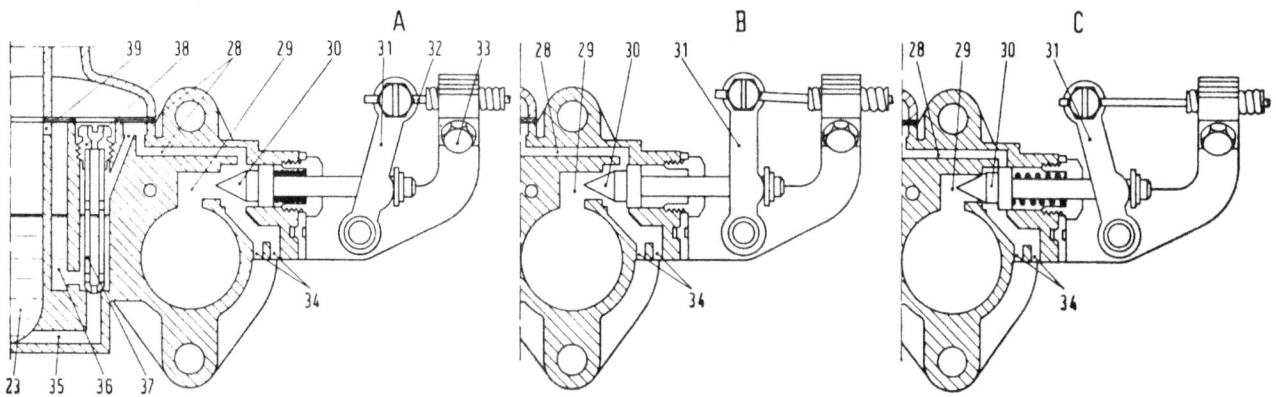

Fig. 42. - Diagrammatic section views of 26 OC Weber carburetor through the starting device.

23. Bowl - 28. Starting mixture duct - 29. Starting mixture duct - 30. Starting valve - 31. Starting device control lever - 32. Starting device control wire - 33. Bowden fixing screw - 34. Emulsion air orifices - 35. Bowl-to-starting jet duct - 36. Starting reserve well - 37. Starting jet - 38. Starting air corrector screw - 39. Reserve well emulsion air slot.

A. Choke fully inserted - B. Choke partially inserted - C. Choke disinserted.

Warm starts: throw in the device only partially (position « B », figs. 40 and 42).

ENGINE WARM-UP

During engine warming-up period, even with car running, push home gradually the starting device lever through successive stages so as to supply the engine with a supplementary amount of mixture as strictly necessary for a regular and smooth engine operation (position « B », figs. 40 and 42).

NORMAL CAR DRIVING

As soon as the engine has reached the rated operation temperature, exclude completely the starting device by bringing the control lever to position « C », (figs. 40 and 42).

Idle Speed Adjustment.

Idling speed is adjusted by throttle setscrew and mixture setscrew. Throttle screw allows of adjusting the throttle opening: conical mixture setscrew has the purpose of metering the amount of mixture coming from idling speed passage, which will then blend with the air flowing past the throttle that, in idle speed setting, leaves a gap between its edges and the throat walls.

This makes possible a rating of mixture best suited to engine requirements and smooth operation.

Always adjust idling speed with engine running and warm by first setting throttle to minimum opening by throttle setscrew so as to ensure steady operation.

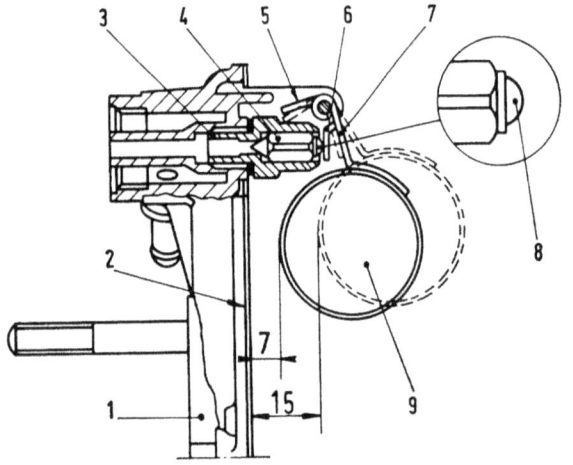

Fig. 43. - Float level setting diagram - Weber carburetor type **26 IMB 4**.

1. Carburetor cover - 2. Cover gasket - 3. Needle valve - 4. Valve needle - 5. Lug - 6-7. Arms - 8. Needle ball - 9. Float.

7 = .2756" - 15 = .5906"

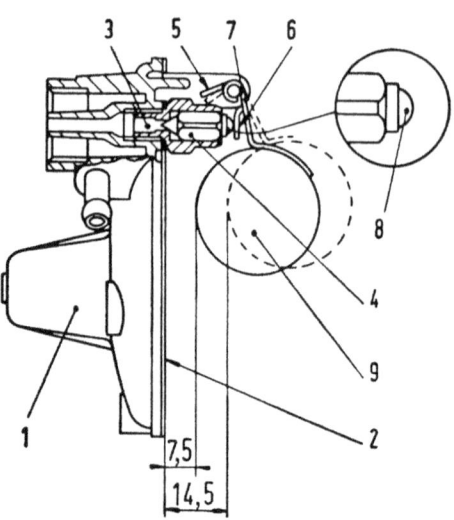

Fig. 44. - Float level setting diagram - Weber carburetor type **26 OC**.

7,5 = .2953" - 14,5 = 5709"

1. Carburetor cover - 2. Cover gasket - 3. Needle valve - 4. Valve needle - 5. Lug - 6-7. Arms - 8. Needle ball - 9. Float.

Next, by turning mixture setscrew in or out, set mixture richness to the most suitable ratio for said throttle opening, thus accomplishing a fast and steady idling; reduce minimum throttle opening some more, by throttle setscrew, until best idling speed is obtained.

NOTE - For the setting data of carburetors, see the table page 9.

Setting Float Level in Bowl.

To set the float level in the carburetor bowl, proceed as follows:

a) Check that needle valve (3, figs. 43 and 44) is screwed tight in its seat.

b) Keep carburetor cover (1) upright or else the weight of float (9) would lower ball (8) fitted on needle (4).

c) Check that with cover held vertical and float arm (6) in slight contact with ball (8) of needle (4), the float is .2756" (7 mm) (engine 110 D.000 fig. 43) or .2953" (7.5 mm) (engine 120.000, fig. 44) away from cover with gasket (2) flat against cover face.

d) Check the float travel: at travel end the float should be respectively .5906" (15 mm) and .5709" (14.5 mm) from the cover face; if necessary, bend lug (5) as required.

SERVICE PROCEDURES: ENGINE TEST

e) If float (9) is not correctly positioned, bend float arm (7) until the correct adjustment is obtained. See that arm (6) is perpendicular to needle (4) axis and does not show rough spots or indents which might impair free sliding of the needle.

f) Check that float (9) rotates freely around ist pivot pin.

CAUTION!

Should replacement of the needle valve (3, figs. 43 and 44) be required, make sure first that the new valve is screwed tight in its lodging with a new seal interposed. This will mean that the level check must be repeated.

TEST RANGE OF REBUILT ENGINES

A rebuilt engine should be submitted to a proper testing range on bench; when doing so, comply with the following data.

Test Speed Rate - rpm	Time - Min.	Brake Load
500	15'	no load
2,000	15'	half load
2,000	5'	full load
Grand total	35 minutes	

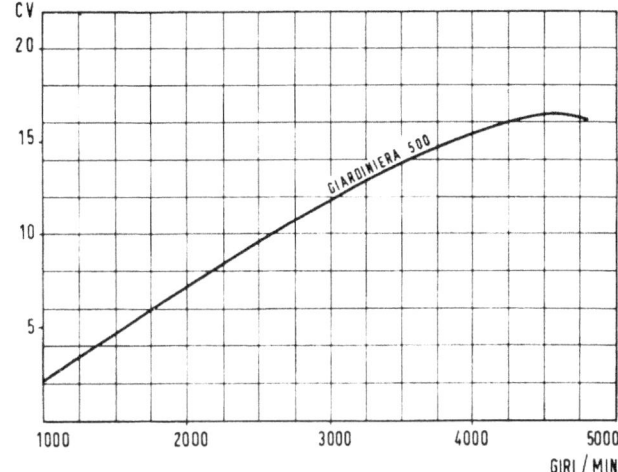

Fig. 46. - Bench power curve of 120.000 engine.
Giardiniera 500 — 500 Station Wagon - GIRI/MIN = R.P.M. - CV = H.P.

When bench testing a rebuilt engine, use care not to run it to top speed limits in an effort to reach the power specified in power charts.

Engine break-in will be completed by the Owner who is bound not to drive the car beyond the speed rates recommended for the initial use.

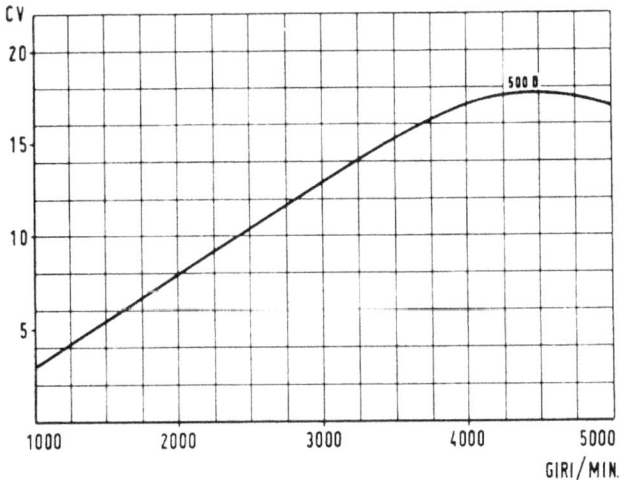

Fig. 45. - Bench power curve of 110 D.000 engine.
GIRI/MIN = R.P.M. - CV = H.P.

NOTICE - Power curves shown in figs. 45 and 46 are minimum specifications for a run-in engine with fan and without exhaust silencer.

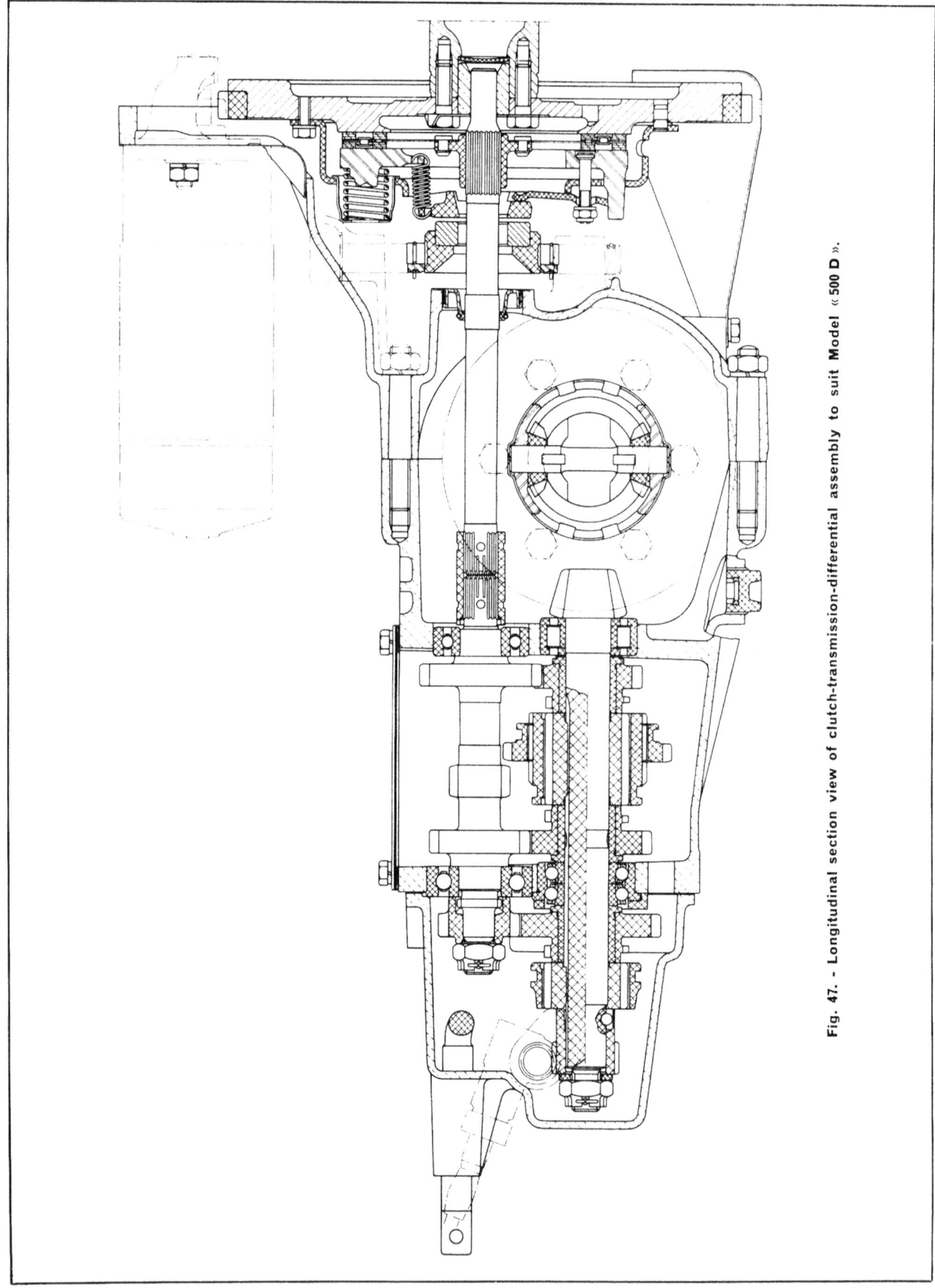

Fig. 47. - Longitudinal section view of clutch-transmission-differential assembly to suit Model « 500 D ».

Clutch

ADJUSTING CLUTCH PEDAL TRAVEL

The clutch needs no care as far as the routine maintenance is concerned. In fact the tip height adjustment of three withdrawal levers, and, consequently, of the lever carrier ring, is made in production where the lever mounting nuts are clenched down on mounting bolts; therefore any misadjustment of withdrawal levers can only be the result of wear and tear.

Clutch pedal must have a free travel of $1\,{}^{3}/_{8}"$ to $1\,{}^{9}/_{16}"$ (35 to 40 mm). Should any correction be required, turn in or out the release lever control tie rod which is adjustable.

After adjustment, lock by nut and jam nut (see fig. 48).

ADJUSTING CLUTCH WITHDRAWAL LEVERS

If the clutch assembly has been dismantled and all components overhauled, including pressure springs which must be tested against data tabulated on page 42, use care, on assembly, to adjust the withdrawal levers in height.

Secure the clutch cover to a supporting plate, with a ring .5413" to .5433" (13.75 to 13.80 mm) thick between

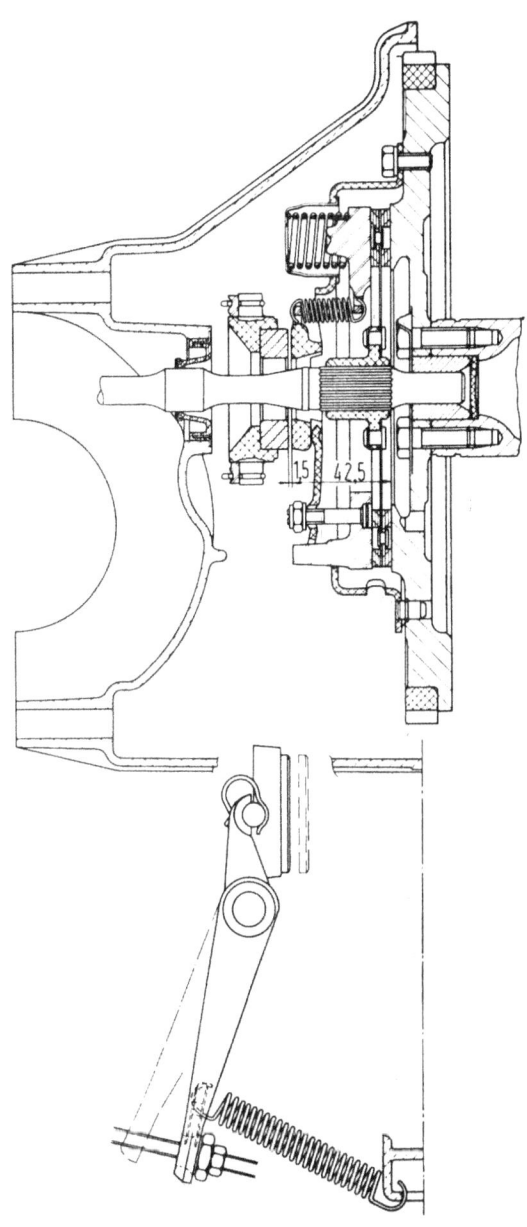

Fig. 49. - Sectional view of clutch assembly to suit « 500 Station Wagon ».

The clearance (.0059" - 1.5 mm) to be obtained through the adjustment of clutch withdrawal levers, applies also to Model « 500 D ».
42,5 = 1.6732"

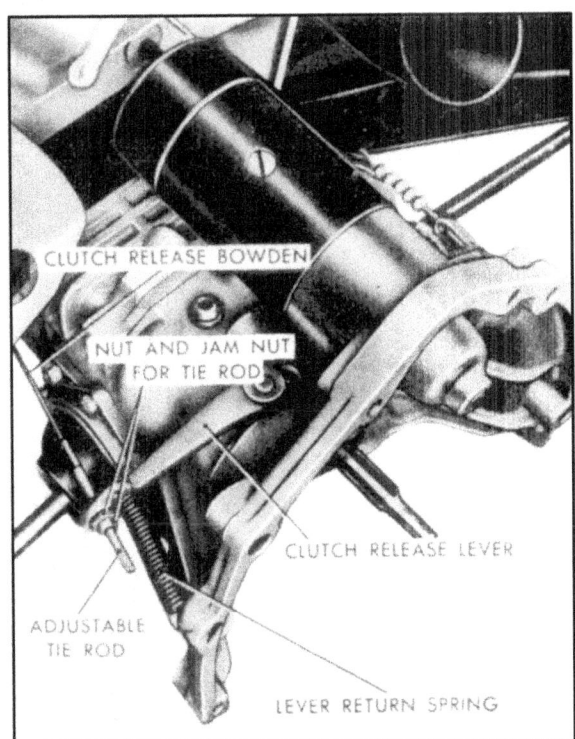

Fig. 48. - Clutch controls and adjusting mechanism.

the pressure plate and the cover plate; set the height of three withdrawal levers for the lever tips to be 1.9094" (48.5 mm) apart from the supporting plate.

With the clutch in place on engine, the distance from the bottom face of withdrawal levers and the flywheel will turn out to be, therefore, 1.6732" (42.5 mm) (fig. 49). As a matter of fact, the net result of subtracting the two figures above (1.9094"—1.6732"-48.5—42.5 mm) is the thickness of the flywheel, which is located between the mounting face of the clutch cover and the resting face of the driven plate.

NOTE - On assembly of clutch, lubricate the following parts with **FIAT Jota 3 grease:**

— pressure plate: boss outer faces;
— clutch cover: withdrawal lever fulcrum;
— withdrawal lever stop nuts: lever contact face;
— withdrawal lever carrier ring: lever contact face.

CLUTCH SPECIFICATIONS

Type	Single plate, working dry
Driven plate hub	Elastic
Driven plate facings of	Ferodo
Facing O. D.	5.51" (140 mm)
Facing I. D.	3.78" (96 mm)
Clutch pressure springs:	
Part. No.	4058334
Wire diameter	.1142" (2.9 mm)
Spring O. D.	.9213" (23.4 mm)
Number of working turns	$5\,^3/_4$
Total number of turns	$7\,^1/_4$
Free length	1.5945" (40.5 mm)
Seated length	.9646" (24.5 mm)
Corresponding load	57.3 ± 2.6 lbs (26 ± 1.2 kg)
Minimum load	48.5 lbs (22 kg)
Lever carrier ring springs:	
Part No.	891319
Wire diameter	.0394" (1 mm)
Spring O. D.	.3740" (9.5 mm)
Number of working turns	$10\,^1/_2$
Free length	.7677" (19.5 mm)
Seated length	1.1811" (30 mm)
Corresponding load	4.8 ± .4 lbs (2.2 ± 0.2 kg)
Pedal free travel	$1\,^3/_8$" to $1\,^9/_{16}$" (35 to 40 mm)
Distance of the upper face of withdrawal lever carrier ring from the clutch cover supporting plate (with a ring .5413" to .5433" - 13.75 to 13.80 mm - thick placed between the pressure plate and the cover plate)	1.9094" (48.5 mm)

Transmission and Differential

In case the transmission and differential assembly must be major overhauled, follow the general procedures for checking single components specified for the car Models of previous construction. In this page are shown some sectional views of transmission details.

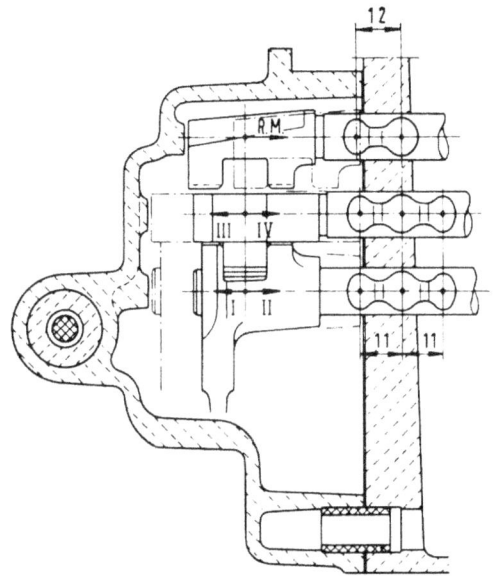

Fig. 50. - Detail of transmission section with indication of striker rods stroke.

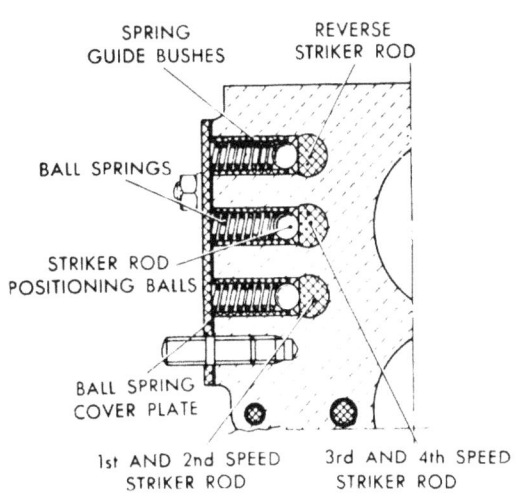

Fig. 52. - Detail of transmission section through striker rod positioning ball springs.

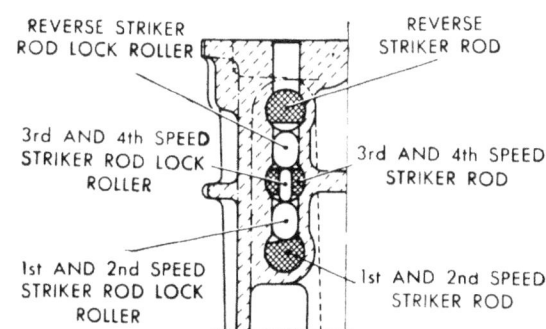

Fig. 53. - Detail of transmission section through striker rod location rollers.

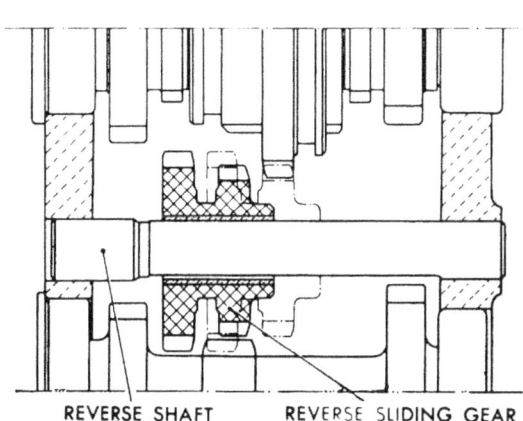

Fig. 51. - Detail of transmission section through reverse sliding gear.

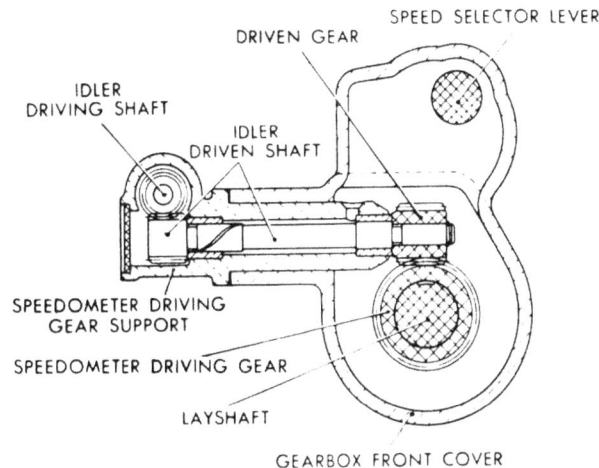

Fig. 54. - Detail of transmission section through speedometer drive gears.

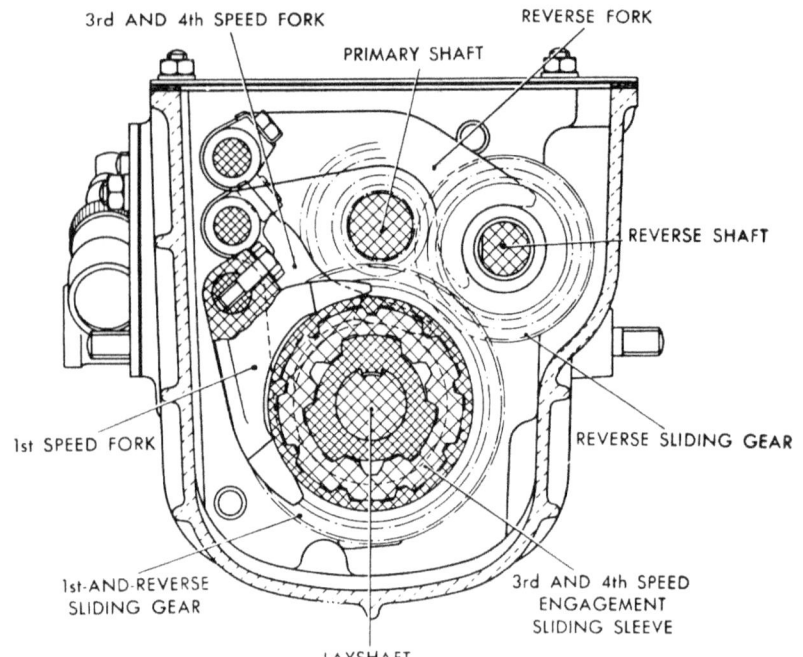

Fig. 55.

Transmission cross section through 3rd and 4th speed engagement sleeve.

NOTE - When the transmission is being rebuilt, it is good practice to go over the gear forks for engagement of first, second, third and fourth, and reverse speed, and check them for the absence of distorsions and a snug fit in relevant gear or sliding sleeve seats.

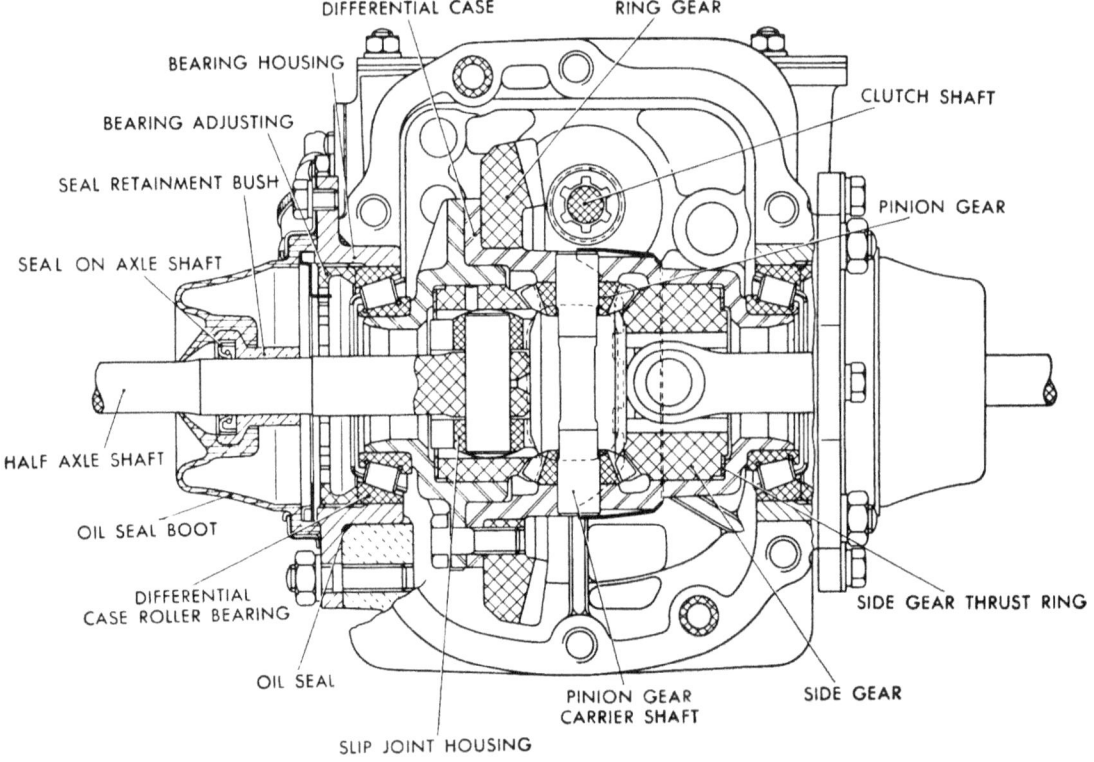

Fig. 56. - Cross section of transmission-differential assembly through differential case.

Adjusting Final Drive Gear Set.

To adjust the pinion mesh with the ring gear, painstakingly follow the procedure outlined hereafter.

The correct positioning of the pinion is obtained by varying the thickness and the amount of the shims which are located between the shoulder of rear roller bearing and the 4th speed driven gear bushing (fig. 47).

Specific tools and fixtures have been designed to facilitate calculations and measurements, thanks to which a simplified formula for figuring the shim pack thickness has been obtained.

The formula for figuring the shim thickness is the following:

$$S = 0.90 + a - (b + c)$$

where:

- **S** = Shim thickness;
- **0.90** = Standard coefficient;
- **a** = Value read on the dial indicator **A. 95690** applied to fixture **A. 70036** (fig. 57);
- **b** = Value stamped on pinion stem (fig. 62);
- **c** = Value read on dial indicator (fig. 60) corresponding to the difference between height of tool **A. 70037** (fig. 59) and the sum of the thicknesses of the items to be installed on pinion and included between front bearing inner shoulder and rear bearing outer shoulder.

Carry out the following steps:

Determining the value of « a »:

— Install the front ball bearing on the transmission

Fig. 58. - Reading value « a » on dial gauge A. 95690.

case and secure it by means of the bearing retaining plate.

— Install the fixture **A. 70036** (fig. 57).
— Fit the dial gauge **A. 95690** (fig. 57) after setting both gauge scale pointers at zero.
— Move to and fro, horizontally, the gauge support and note the gauge readings; stop the gauge in the position where the pointers indicate the minimum value (fig. 58).

This reading represents « a » (fig. 57).

Determining the value of « c »:

— Insert the following items on tool **A. 70037** which has been set on a surface plate: 3rd speed driven

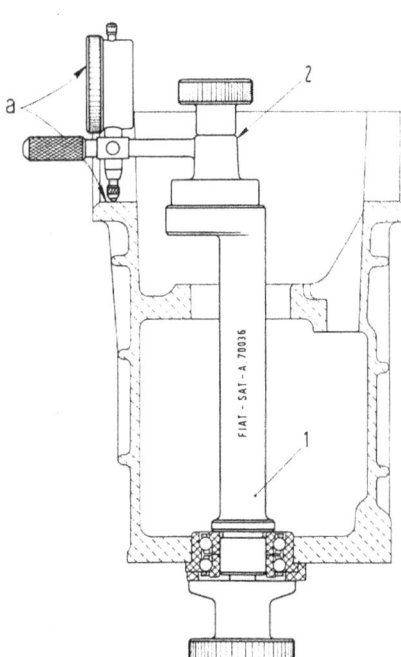

Fig. 57. - Diagram showing the position of tools for determining the value of « a ».

1. Dummy pinion, tool A. 70036 - **2.** Support with dial gauge, tool A. 95690.

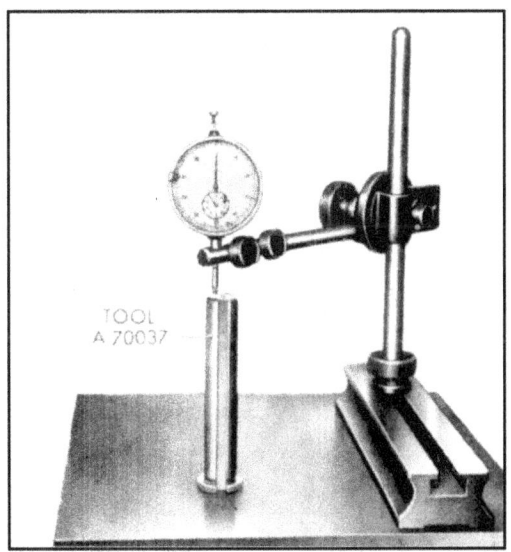

Fig. 59. - Setting dial gauge at zero on tool A. 70037.

Fig. 60. - Reading value « c » on dial indicator.

gear bushing, 3rd and 4th speed gear engagement sleeve hub, 4th speed driven gear bushing and drive pinion roller bearing inner race (fig. 60).

— Set a dial gauge at zero on tool **A. 70037** (fig. 59).

— Rest the dial gauge plunger on the roller bearing inner race and take a reading at the dial (fig. 60).

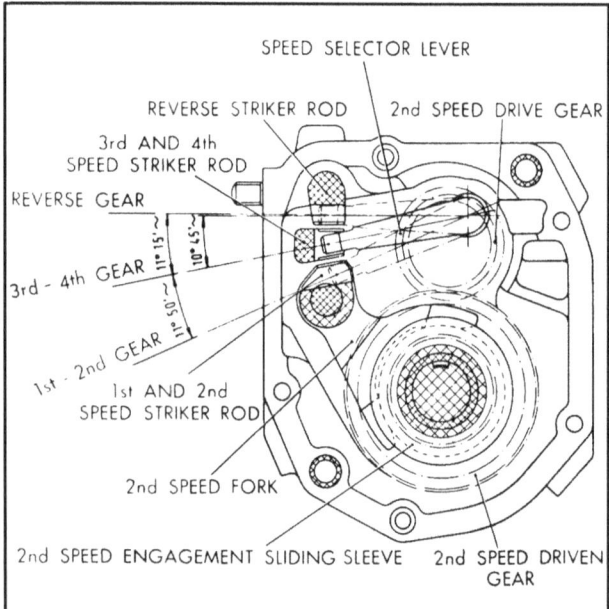

Fig. 61. - Cross section of transmission through striker rods, with the indication of the gear selector lever angular displacements.

This reading represents « c ».

The value « b » is stamped in production on pinion stem (fig. 62).

After the value of « a », « b » and « c » has been determined, figure the thickness of the shim pack by developing the formula outlined above.

Bevel pinion shims are supplied for replacement in the following thicknesses: .0039" and .0059" (0.10 and 0.15 mm).

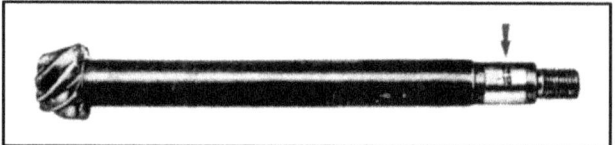

Fig. 62. - Layshaft with final drive pinion.

The arrow points to the numer (14) for correct mating with ring gear and to the centesimal figure (—10) for accurate meshing position of pinion and gear.

Adjusting Ring Gear-to-Pinion Backlash and Checking Differential Bearing Rotation Torque.

To check ring gear-to-pinion backlash, use fixture **A. 95643**; touch the dial indicator plunger to the ring gear (fig. 63).

Then proceed as follows:

— using wrench **A. 55022**, screw in both side adjusters to abut on bearings;

Fig. 63. - Checking and adjusting pinion-to-ring gear backlash.

Backlash should be .0031" to .0047" (0.08 to 0.12 mm).

SERVICE PROCEDURES: TRANSMISSION-DIFFERENTIAL

— affix tool **A. 70040** on either axle shaft, so to lock shaft against the differential case (fig. 63);

— hold the pinion in position using tool **A. 70041** and manually rotate the axle shaft, which is integral with the ring gear, as far as the gear backlash will allow so.

The backlash reading on the indicator dial should be .0031″ to .0047″ (0.08 to 0.12 mm).

To correct the gear backlash, move the ring gear toward or away from the pinion by working evenly on adjuster nuts (fig. 63).

Next check the bearing rotation torque as follows:

— fit dynamometer **A. 95697** to tool **A. 70040** which has been positioned as shown in fig. 64;

— rotate the axle shaft a few turns, to set bearings;

— check the rotation (not starting) torque on dynamometer: it should be 1.01 ± .07 ft.lbs (14 ± 1 kgcm).

To correct the rotation torque, screw in both adjuster nuts evenly, using care not to affect the gear backlash.

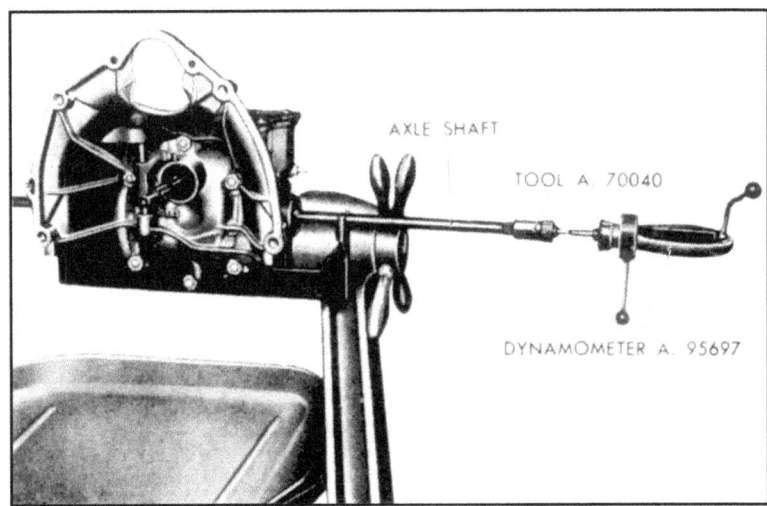

Fig. 64.

Checking differential case roller bearing rotation torque, using dynamometer A. 95697 mounted on tool A. 70040.

Rotation (not starting) torque, should be 1.01 ± .07 ft.lbs (140 ± 10 kgmm).

TRANSMISSION-DIFFERENTIAL ADJUSTMENT AND TIGHTENING REFERENCE

ITEM	Part Number	Thread Pitch	Material	Tightening Torque
Primary shaft gear nut.	1/08019/11	M 14 x 1	R 50 Cdt Shaft 14 CN 5 Cmt 5	18.1 to 25.3 ft.lbs (2,500 to 3,500 kgmm)
Layshaft gear nut	1/07934/11	M 14 x 1,5	R 50 Cdt Shaft 14 CN 5 Cmt 5	28.9 to 36.2 ft.lbs (4,000 to 5,000 kgmm)
Ring gear-to-differential case screw . .	891596	M 8 x 1,25	R 100	23.1 ft.lbs (3,200 kgmm)
Differential bearing housing-to-transmission case nut	1/61008/11	M 8 x 1,25	R 50 Cdt Stud R 50 Cdt	13.0 ft.lbs (1,800 kgmm)
Transmission case and support-to-engine nut	1/21647/11	M 10 x 1,25	R 50 Cdt Stud R 50 Cdt	27.5 ft.lbs (3,800 kgmm)
Transmission-differential support assembly-to-engine nut.	1/61008/11	M 8 x 1,25	R 50 Cdt Stud R 100	18.1 to 21.7 ft.lbs (2,500 to 3,000 kgmm)
Differential roller bearing rotation torque (not break-away)				1.01 ± 0.07 ft.lbs (140 ± 10 kgmm)
Final drive pinion-gear backlash				.0031″ to .0047″ (0.08 to 0.12 mm)

TRANSMISSION-DIFFERENTIAL SPECIFICATIONS

Speeds	4 forward and one reverse
Primary shaft	integral with 1st, 3rd, 4th and reverse speeds drive gear cluster
Bearings	two
Type	ball
Layshaft	integral with final drive pinion
Bearings front	ball type, double row
Bearings rear	cylindrical roller
Type of gears:	
drive, 2nd, 3rd, 4th speed	helical, constant meshed
driven, 2nd, 3rd, 4th speed	with dogs for quick engagement
drive and driven, 1st and reverse	straight spur gears
Gear ratios:	
1st gear	3.70 to 1
2nd gear	2.06 to 1
3rd gear	1.30 to 1
4th gear	0.87 to 1
Reverse	5.14 to 1
Final drive gear	helical
Reduction ratio	8 to 41
Ratio to wheels:	
1st gear	18.96 to 1
2nd gear	10.59 to 1
3rd gear	6.66 to 1
4th gear	4.48 to 1
Reverse	26.33 to 1
Differential case bearings	2
Type	taper roller
Adjustment	by adjusters
Rotation torque (not break-away)	1.01 ± .07 ft.lbs (140 ± 10 kgmm)
Final drive pinion and ring gear	mated
Gear backlash	.0031" to .0047" (0.08 - 0.12 mm)
Pinion positioning	by shims
Lube oil:	
grade	FIAT W 90/M (SAE 90 EP)
capacity qts	(U.S.) 1.16 - (Imp.) .97
capacity lt	1.100
capacity kg	1.000

Front Suspension and Wheels

SEMI-ELLIPTIC SPRING

Semi-elliptic spring testing data are summarized in tables below and main leaf oscillations shown in figs. 65 and 66.

FRONT LEAF SPRING, LOADED AT CENTER

Position	Load P		Camber		Give-in from pos. 2		Deflection rate between pos. 2 and pos. 3	
	lbs	kg	in	mm	in	mm	in/100 lbs	mm/100 kg
2	220.5	100	5.3936 ± .2362	137 ± 6	—	—	2.23 ± .10	125 ± 6
3	441	200	± —	—	4.9212 ± .2362	125 ± 6		

NOTE - When testing the spring never exceed 441 lbs (200 kg) load.

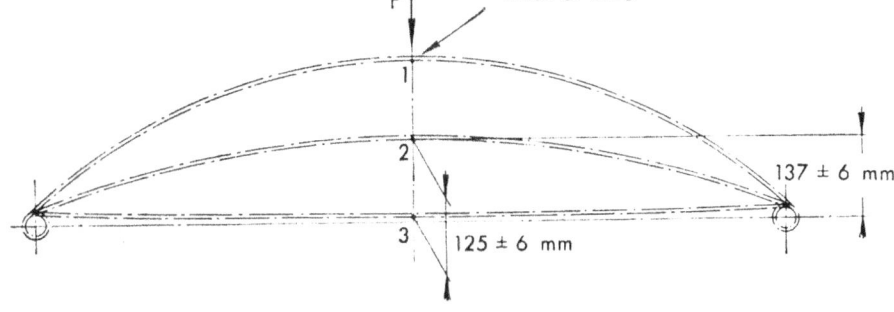

Fig. 65.
Oscillation diagram of centrally loaded spring.

137 ± 6 mm = 5.3936" ± .2362".
125 ± 6 mm = 4.9212" ± .2362".

FRONT LEAF SPRING, INSTALLED ON CAR

	Position	Load P		Camber		Give-in from pos. 1		Deflection rate between pos. 1 and pos. 3	
		lbs	kg	in	mm	in	mm	in/100 lbs	mm/100 kg
1	Initial load for checking deflection rate ...	220.5	100	—	—	—	—		
2	Static load ...	297.6	135	1.1023 ± .1181	28 ± 3	—	—	1.55 ± 07	87 ± 5
3	Final load for checking deflection rate ...	330.7	150	—	—	1.7125 ± .0984	43.5 ± 2.5		
4	Bottoming load ...	451.9	205	—	—	—	—		

NOTE - Spring specifications are intended at assembly conditions, i. e., with pre-compressed rubber pads and without bumpers. Give-in check-up must be carried out by loading both eyes simultaneously.

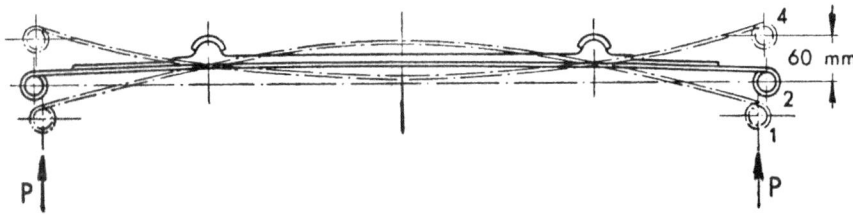

Fig. 66.
Oscillation diagram of spring installed on car.

60 mm = 2.3622".

SWINGING ARMS

The swinging arm pin nuts (5, fig. 73) should be tightened with the arm well lined up with the pin holes (for screws 7, fig. 73).

This is to avoid that rubber bushings may be submitted to undue stresses during movement of swinging arms.

KINGPIN HOUSING

To avoid undue stresses on the kingpin housing «estendblock», it is mandatory that the kingpin housing-to-swinging arm pin nut is tightened with the arm and the housing set at an angle of some 95" (fig. 67). The torque specified for the pin nut is given in the table page 54.

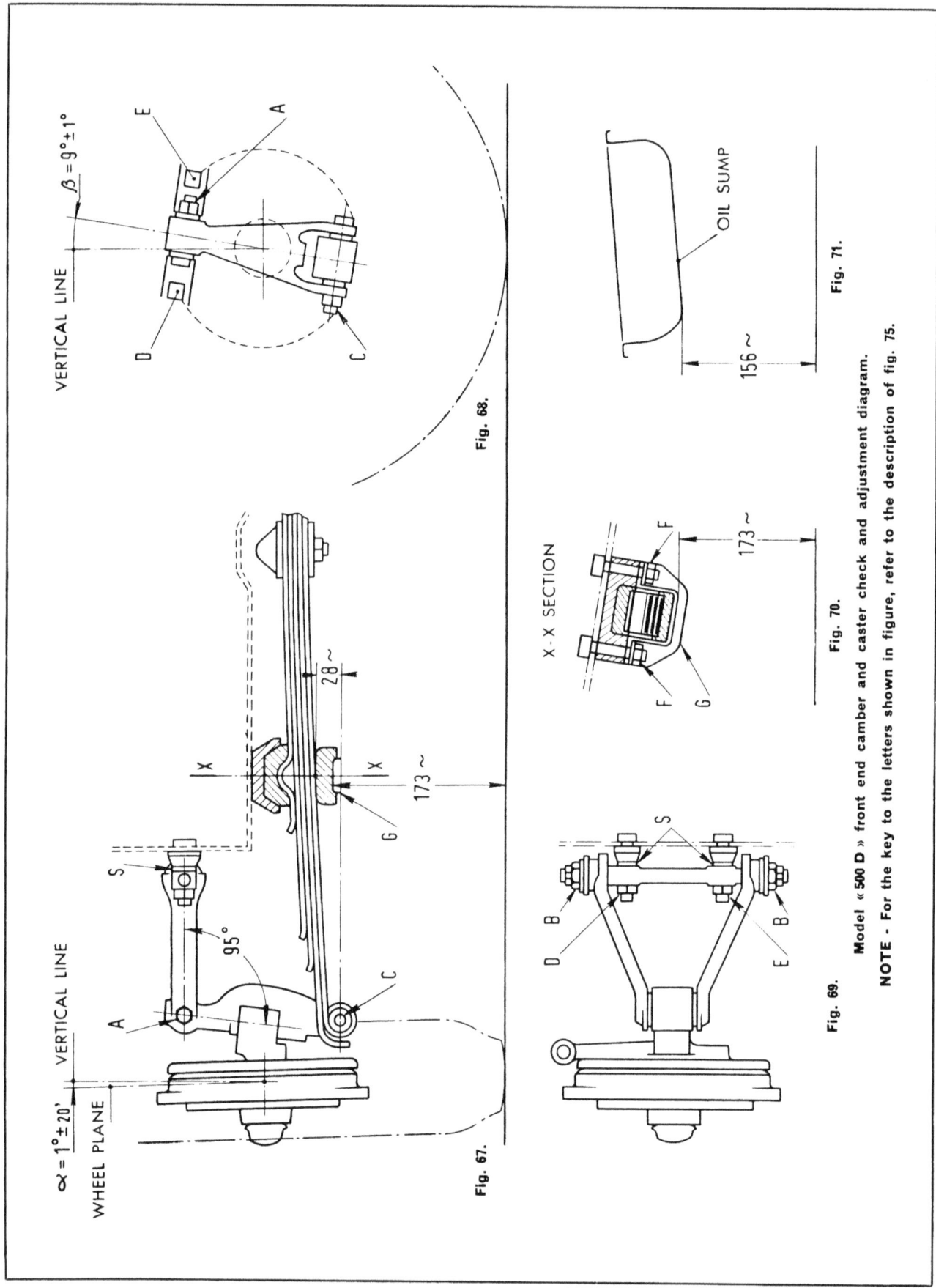

Model «500 D» front end camber and caster check and adjustment diagram.
NOTE - For the key to the letters shown in figure, refer to the description of fig. 75.

FRONT SUSPENSION ASSEMBLY AND INSTALLATION

Proceed as follows.

Install the leaf spring on fixture **A. 74061** (fig. 74) and load it with the proper screw of the fixture until the index « Mod. 500 » appears below cross beam lower edge.

In this position the spring attains the « full static load » setting same as on car; the camber in correspondence with plane X-X (figs. 67 and 75) is approximately 1.10″ (28 mm).

Insert the spring so set and provided with upper elastic supports on the studs projecting from body bottom.

Fit the two support lower caps with elastic pads and screw on the stud nuts to a torque of 28.9 ft.lbs (4,000 kgmm), using a torque wrench.

Work on bench and assemble as follows:

— the steering knuckle to kingpin housing interposing the two upper thrust rings, the snap ring and the lower packing ring of such thickness as to take up any play between knuckle and kingpin housing, provided the free movement of the knuckle is not impaired;

— the brake housing flange assembly on steering knuckle and draw up nuts with 14.5 ft.lbs (2 kgm) of torque;

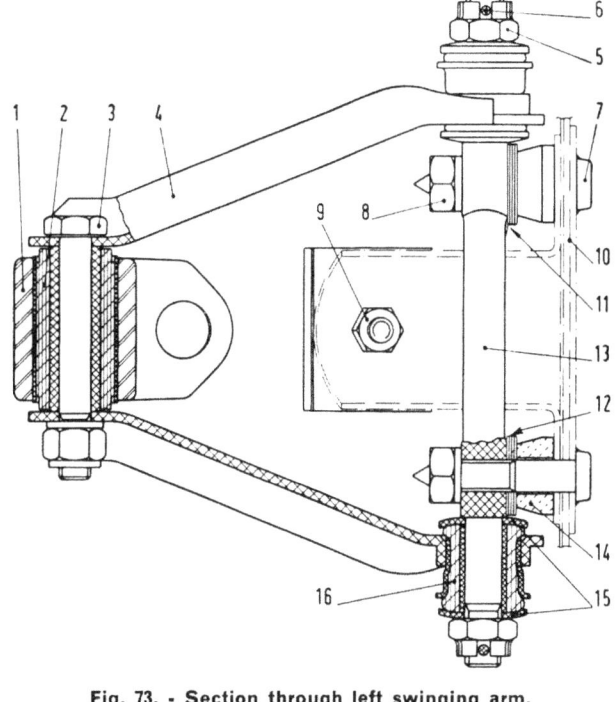

Fig. 73. - Section through left swinging arm.

1. Kingpin housing - 2. Estendblock - 3. Pin, swinging arm to kingpin housing - 4. Half arm - 5 and 6. Nut and split pin - 7. Screw, welded on body - 8. Nut, mounting, pin 13 to body - 9. Rubber buffer mounting nut - 10. Body panel - 11 and 12. Camber and caster adjustment shims - 13. Pin, swinging arm to body - 14. Spacer - 15. Cups for rubber bushing - 16. Rubber bushing.

— the roller bearings and the seal on drum-hub;

— the drum-hub on steering knuckle;

— the nut with washer securing the wheel hub to the steering knuckle;

— the cap to the hub.

NOTE - The installation and adjustment procedure of bearings is outlined in detail in the next paragraph (page 53).

NOTE - For correct inspection of front end geometry, tires should be inflated with the recommended pressure and the steering wheel set for straight forward drive (horizontal spokes).

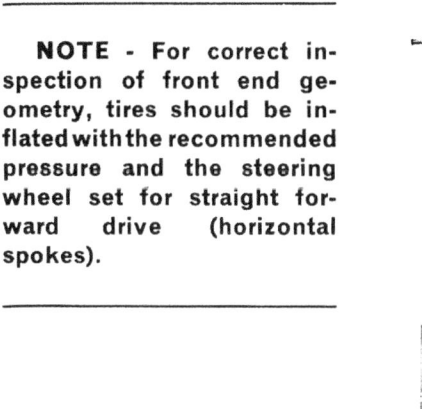

Fig. 72.

Front suspension: section through steering knuckle and leaf spring mounting at kingpin.

Caster: 9° ± 1°

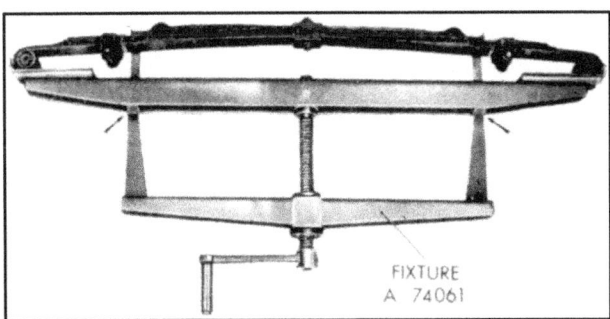

Fig. 74. - Leaf spring position under « full static load » on fixture A. 74061.

Arrows point to the reference marks for correct spring compression.

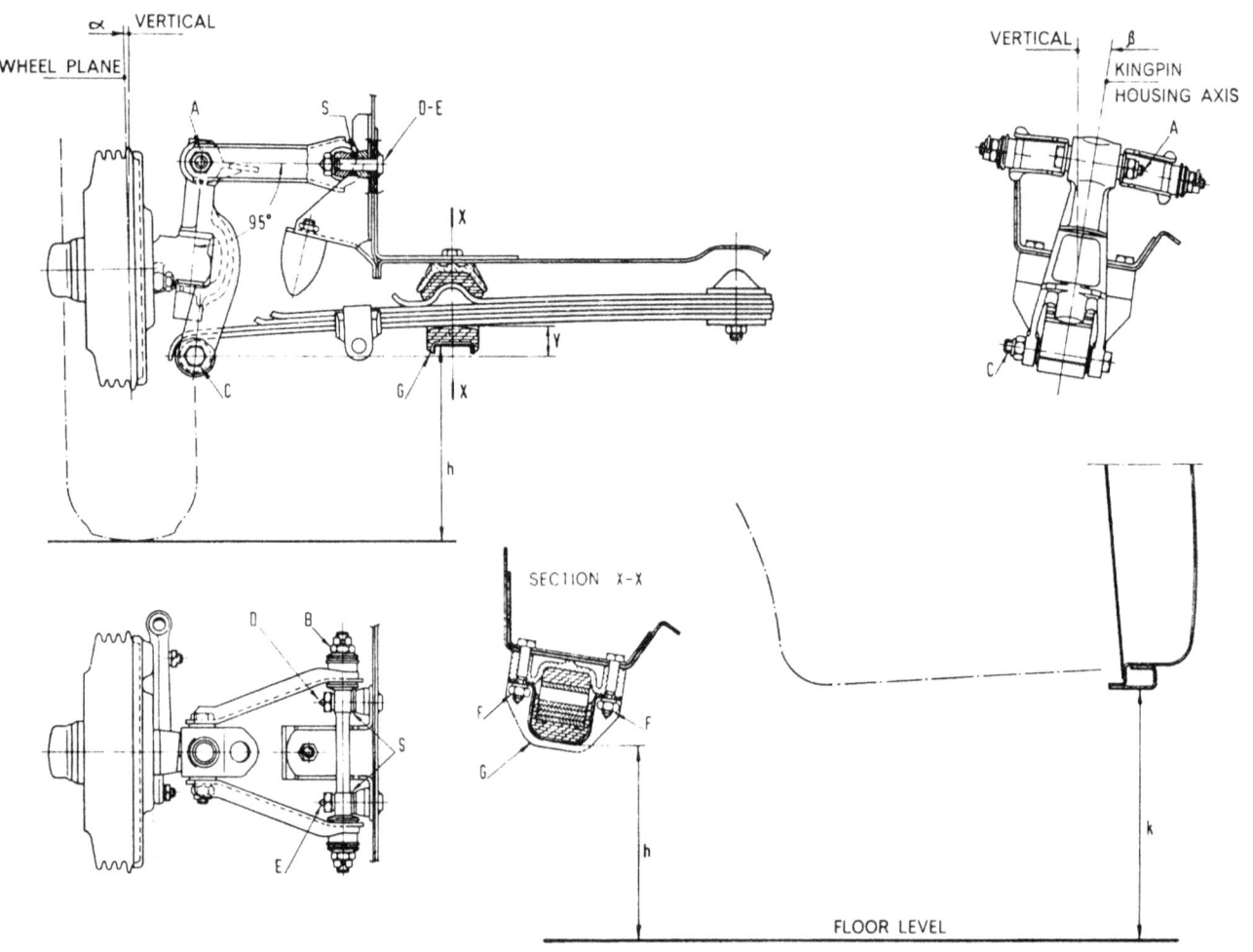

Fig. 75. Front end camber and caster checking and adjusting diagram - « 500 Station Wagon ».

A. Nut and screw, swinging arm to kingpin housing - **B.** Nuts, bolt to swinging arm - **C.** Screw and nut, semi-elliptic spring to kingpin housing - **D. and E.** Studs, swinging arm to body panel - **F.** Nuts, semi-elliptic spring to underbody - **G.** Caps, semi-elliptic spring mounting - α. Camber - β. Caster - **S.** Camber and caster shims.

Specifications, for vehicle under « static load »:

$\alpha = 1° \pm 20'$ $\quad\quad$ $y = 1.10''$ (28 mm) $\quad\quad$ $k = 8.90''$ (226 mm)
$\beta = 9° \pm 1°$ $\quad\quad$ $h = 6.81''$ (173 mm)

Connect now the swinging arm to the wheel assembly, set as above.

The nut must be screwed onto the pin (A, figs. 67 and 75) by arranging the parts as outlined under « Kingpin Housing ». Recommended torque of nut: 39.8 to 43.4 ft.lbs (5.5 to 6 kgm).

Insert the swinging arm pin on the two studs welded on body sides so as to support the suspension/wheel assembly.

Connect kingpin housing to spring eye by inserting the pin and tightening the self-locking nut to 28.9 ft.lbs (4 kgm). **The semi-elliptic spring should be all the time under « static load », properly « set » by fixture A. 74061, as hinted earlier. This point should be particularly stressed, due to the presence of «estend-blocks », the function of which might be impaired, otherwise.**

Slide off the swinging arm and insert spacers and shims (S, figs. 69 and 75) on studs, seeing that the resulting thickness is the same as found at disassembly; again attach the swinging arm.

Screw on the nuts securing the pin to body and tighten to 28.9 ft.lbs (4 kgm).

Install the shock absorber.

Remove fixture **A. 74061**, compressing the leaf spring, then connect steering rods and brake fluid lines.

After installing the suspension (description covers both wheel sides), check and adjust camber and caster angles as directed on page 54.

SERVICE PROCEDURES: FRONT SUSPENSION AND WHEELS

Front Wheels.

Up to the serial No. 444047 (Model 500 D) and the serial No. 085337 (500 Station Wagon), the wheel hub was secured to the steering knuckle by means of a nut with split pin.

On these vehicles, the recess between either bearing should be liberally packed with FIAT MR 3 grease; the lock nut should be tightened to 21.7 ft.lbs (3 kgm), backed out by 60° at least, and then locked with the split pin.

Starting from the serial No. 444048 (Model 500 D) and the serial No. 085338 (500 Station Wagon), the front wheel bearings are secured to the hub by means of nuts, which are locked to the steering knuckle through a staking, instead of a split pin, as previously.

When servicing the hubs, it is therefore necessary to free the nut with a punch before undoing; **the nut shall be discarded and replaced by a new one.**

LUBRICATION INSTRUCTIONS

When mounting the roller bearings, lubricate with FIAT MR 3 grease.

Bearings.

The bearings must not be installed without lubricant.

Before installation on steering knuckles, the space between cage and inner race of the bearings must be packed with grease.

Wheel hub.

The hub shall not be completely filled but the amount of grease should be such as to guarantee a thorough lubrication of the outer bearing and be distributed on the outskirts of the pocket between the bearing outer races.

Recommended amount of grease for the wheel hub:
— Model 500 D . . . . .7 oz (20 gr)
— 500 Station Wagon . . . . 1 oz (30 gr)

Hub cap.

The cap need not be completely filled but the amount of grease shall be such that the space between cap and outer bearing results fully packed after mounting the cap on the hub.

Recommended amount of grease for the hub cap:
— Model 500 D . . . . .35 oz (10 gr)
— 500 Station Wagon . . . . .9 oz (25 gr)

ADJUSTMENT INSTRUCTIONS

Torque wrenches must be accurate within ± 5%.

Before securing the hub make sure the nut screws in freely, then tighten to a 14 1/2 ft.lbs (2 kgm) torque while rocking the wheel hub 4 or 5 times to guarantee proper setting of bearings; at this point, undo the nut completely and finally tighten to a torque of 5.1 ft.lbs (700 kgmm).

Subsequently, the nut shall be backed out by 30°. For this operation punch a mark (B, fig. 76) on the nut washer at a point corresponding to the center of one of the six flats of the nut, then unscrew the nut until the adjacent corner (A, fig. 76) comes in alignment with the punch mark.

Once the nut has been slackened as required, lock it in that position by staking its collar with plier tool **A. 74128** into the groove machined in the steering knuckle threaded end, then rock again the hub.

The hub end play must be .0010" to .0039" (0.025 to 0.100 mm).

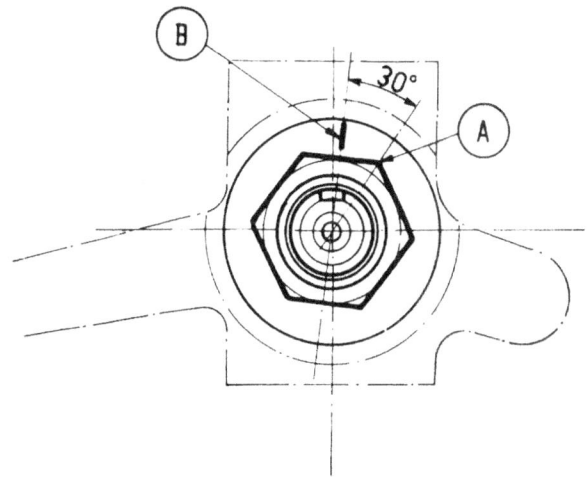
Nut drawn up with 5.1 ft.lbs (700 kgmm).

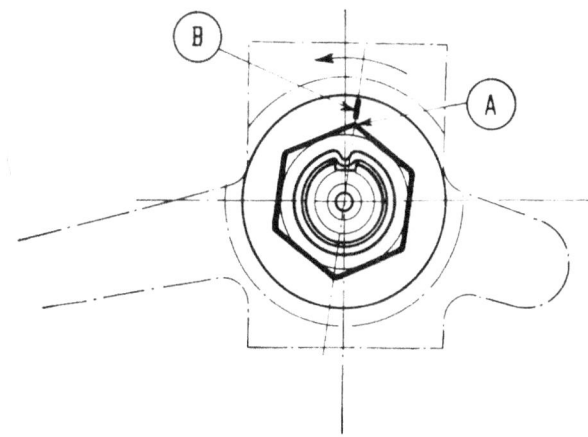
Backing out the nut by 30°.

Fig. 76. - Locking and adjusting front wheel hubs.
A. Corner of the nut - B. Mark on nut washer.

Figure illustrates adjustment of left front hub. To adjust the right hub the procedure should be carried out in reverse order because the nut is left-hand threaded.

END PLAY CHECK

This play can be checked, with the wheel either down or on for 500 Station Wagon, whereas for Model 500 D it is necessary to take the wheel down as the steering knuckle end cannot be reached otherwise.

Check with wheel down.

After removing the hub cap, push the brake drum axially and fully towards car, apply a dial indicator with magnetic base plate to the flat area of the brake drum.

Place the indicator plunger onto the steering knuckle end and zero the instrument; pull the brake drum outwards then read on the indicator dial the amount of hub end play.

Check with wheel on (500 Station Wagon only).

After removing the wheel cover and hub cap, undo a wheel screw then fix bracket **A. 74029** to rim by said screw. Push the wheel axially and fully towards car then apply on bracket the dial indicator with magnetic base plate and proceed according to previous description reading the end play on the dial.

NOTE

When only the hub adjustment is necessary, first replace the nut, then adjust as directed above.

Hub end play should be adjusted only when it exceeds .005" (0.13 mm).

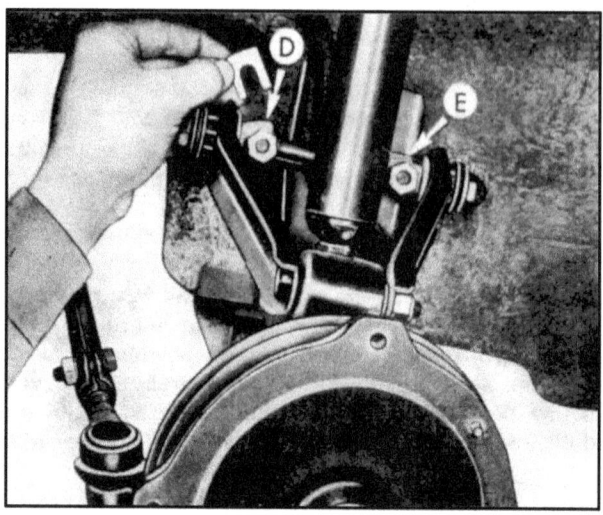

Fig. 77. - Adding shims to adjust front end camber and caster. D. and E. Points where shims should be fitted.

Checking and Adjusting Camber and Caster.

Front end geometry angles, as referred to the condition of « static load », are the following:
— camber . . . . 1° ± 20'
— caster . . . . 9° ± 1°

FRONT SUSPENSION AND WHEELS TIGHTENING REFERENCE

ITEM	Part No.	Thread Pitch	Material	Tightening Torque
Leaf spring-to-body nut	1/21647/11	M 10 x 1,25	R 50 Cdt Screw C 21 R	28.9 ft.lbs (4,000 kgmm)
Kingpin housing-to-swinging arm nut .	1/25745/11	M 10 x 1,25	R 50 Cdt Screw R 80 Cdt	39.8 to 43.4 ft.lbs (5,500 to 6,000 kgmm)
Brake housing flange-to-steering knuckle nut	1/61008/11	M 8 x 1,25	R 50 Cdt Screw R 50	14.5 ft.lbs (2,000 kgmm)
Leaf spring-to-kingpin housing nut . . .	1/25745/11	M 10 x 1,25	R 50 Cdt Screw R 80 Cdt	28.9 ft.lbs (4,000 kgmm)
Swinging arm-to-body nut	1/21647/11	M 10 x 1,25	R 50 Cdt Screw C 21 R	28.9 ft.lbs (4,000 kgmm)
Wheel-to-hub screw: — « 500 D »	990166	M 10 x 1,5	C 35 R Bon Cdt	32.5 to 39.8 ft.lbs (4,500 to 5,500 kgmm)
— « 500 Station Wagon »	4080533	M 12 x 1,5	C 35 R Bon Cdt	43.4 to 50.6 ft.lbs (6,000 to 7,000 kgmm)

SERVICE PROCEDURES: FRONT SUSPENSION AND WHEELS

NOTE - The « static load » implies the following conditions: a distance between the semi-elliptic spring mountings G and the floor level of some 6.81" (173 mm) (figs. 67 and 75); a distance between the lowermost portion of the sump and the floor level of some 6.14" (156 mm) for **Model 500 D** (fig. 71); concerning **500 Station Wagon**, the distance between the center rear bracket, for jacking up the vehicle, and the floor level should be of some 8.90" (226 mm) (k, fig. 75).

Camber (α, figs 67 and 75) and caster (β, figs. 68 and 75) angles are adjusted by working on the amount of shims (S, figs. 69 and 75) between the swinging arm pin and the spacers at body studs.

To increase caster angle (β), shift shims (S) from rear screw (E, fig. 77) to front screw (D); to reduce caster, proceed in reverse direction.

To increase camber angle (α), add shims (S) at both screws (D and E, fig. 77); to reduce camber, remove shims.

The addition or removal of the same quantity of shims at both screws (D and E) permits camber adjustment without disturbing caster.

FRONT SUSPENSION AND WHEELS SPECIFICATIONS

Leaf Spring	1
Leaves	1 main and 4 auxiliary
Camber, with set spring	1.1023" ± .1181" (28 ± 3 mm) under a 297.6 lbs (135 kg) load
Bushings for connection to kingpin housing	« estendblock »
Connection to underbody	by 2 supports with rubber pads
Position of spring to tighten the pin nut for connection to kingpin housing	static load setting
Swinging Arms	2 (4 half-arms)
Connection to body	by pin and rubber bushings
Position of arm to pin holes for pin nut tightening	on the same plane
Kingpin Housings	
Connection to leaf spring and to swinging arm	by « estendblock »
Kingpin angle	6°
Caster	9° ± 1°
Caster adjustment	by shims (.0197" - 0.5 mm thk)
Position of kingpin housing with respect to swinging arm plane for tightening the pin nut	95°
Steering Knuckles	
Steering knuckle-to-kingpin housing play adjustment	by packing rings: thkss .0977" to .098" (2.482 to 2.50 mm) oversize range: 1.004" - 1.024" - 1.043" - 1.063" - 1.083" - 1.103" (2.55 - 2.60 - 2.65 - 2.70 - 2.75 - 2.80 mm) undersize range: .965" - .945" (2.45 - 2.40 mm)
Wheels	
Camber	1° ± 20'
Camber adjustment	by shims .02" (0.5 mm) thk
Toe-in	.0" to .0787" (0 to 2 mm)
Toe-in adjustment	by adjustable sleeves on track rods
Bearing lubrication	FIAT MR 3 grease
Hydraulic Shock Absorbers	2
Type	telescopic
Diameter (working cylinder)	1.063" (27 mm)
Fluid	FIAT S. A. I. oil
Capacity	.112 Imp. qts - .137 U.S. qts 7.93 ± .3 cu in. (130 ± 5 cc - 0.120 kg)

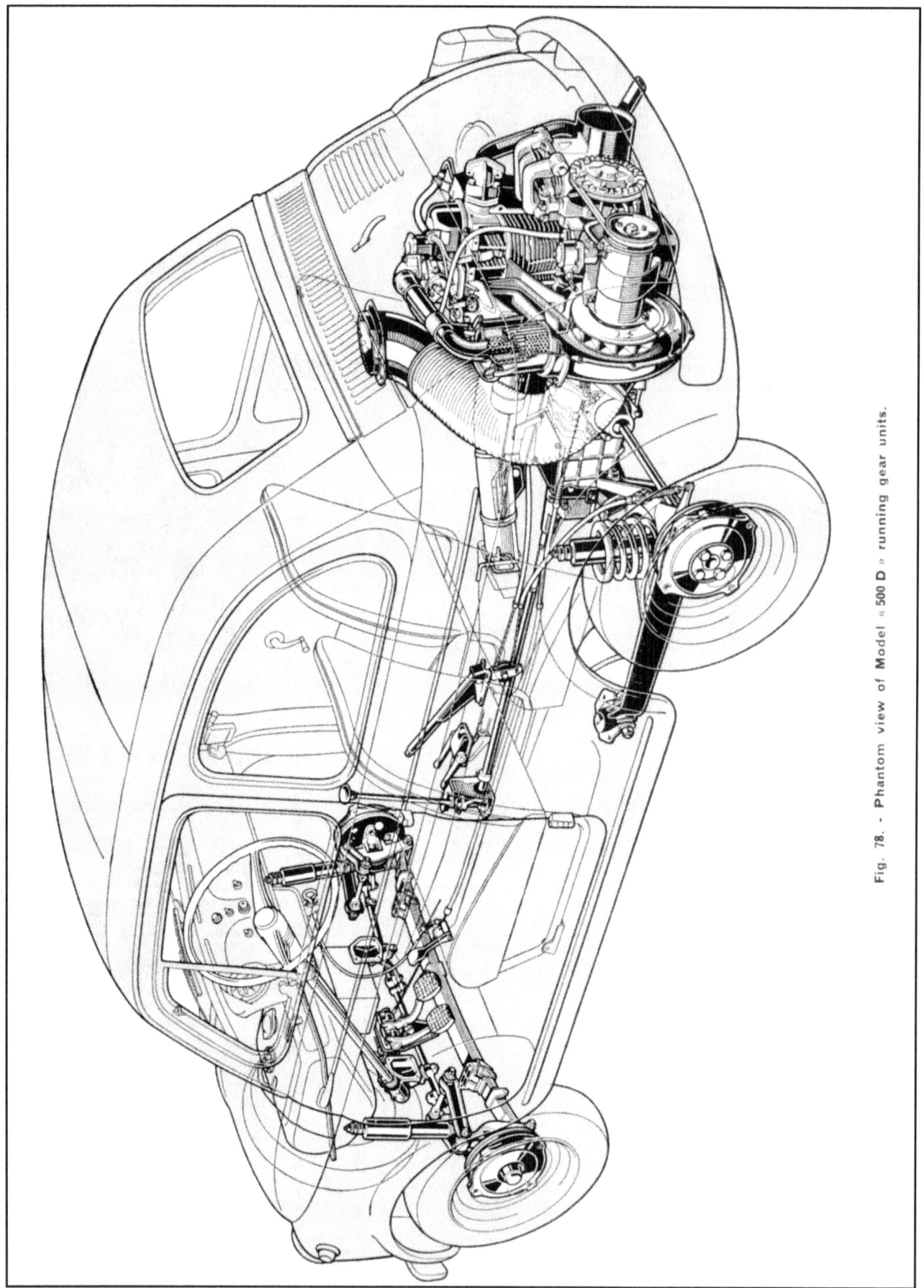

Fig. 78. - Phantom view of Model «500 D» running gear units.

Rear Suspension and Wheels

ADJUSTING WHEEL BEARINGS

To avoid excessive play or stiffening of bearings on rotation, the nut securing the flexible joint to the wheel shaft hub should be tightened gradually, so that the bearing rotation torque does not exceed .36 ft.lbs (5 kgcm).

To check the rotation torque, proceed as follows.

Install support **A. 95697/3** on wheel drum. Insert the shank (2, fig. 79) of dynamometer **A. 95697** in support and grasp lever (3).

Move the needle (4) to register .36 ft.lbs (5 kgcm) on dynamometer scale, as shown in fig. 79 and, using the lever (6), rotate the dynamometer and the wheel shaft some turns, clockwise.

During rotation, check that the needle (5) does not go beyond the setting index (4).

If the rotation torque proves to be over .36 ft.lbs (5 kgcm), which indicates high bearing preload, remove the wheel shaft and replace the resilient spacer by a new one.

Next repeat the rotation torque test.

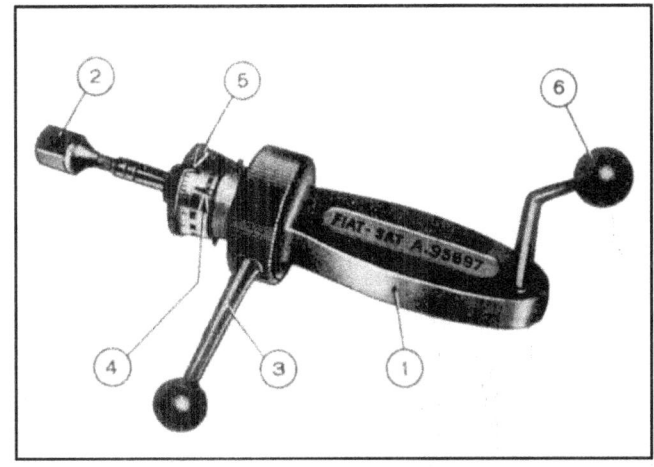

Fig. 79. - Bearing rotation torque dynamometer.

1. Dynamometer A. 95697 - 2. Dynamometer shank to insert in item A. 95697/3, fitted to wheel drum - 3. Dynamometer grip lever - 4. Rotation torque setting index - 5. Adjustable needle - 6. Dynamometer operating lever.

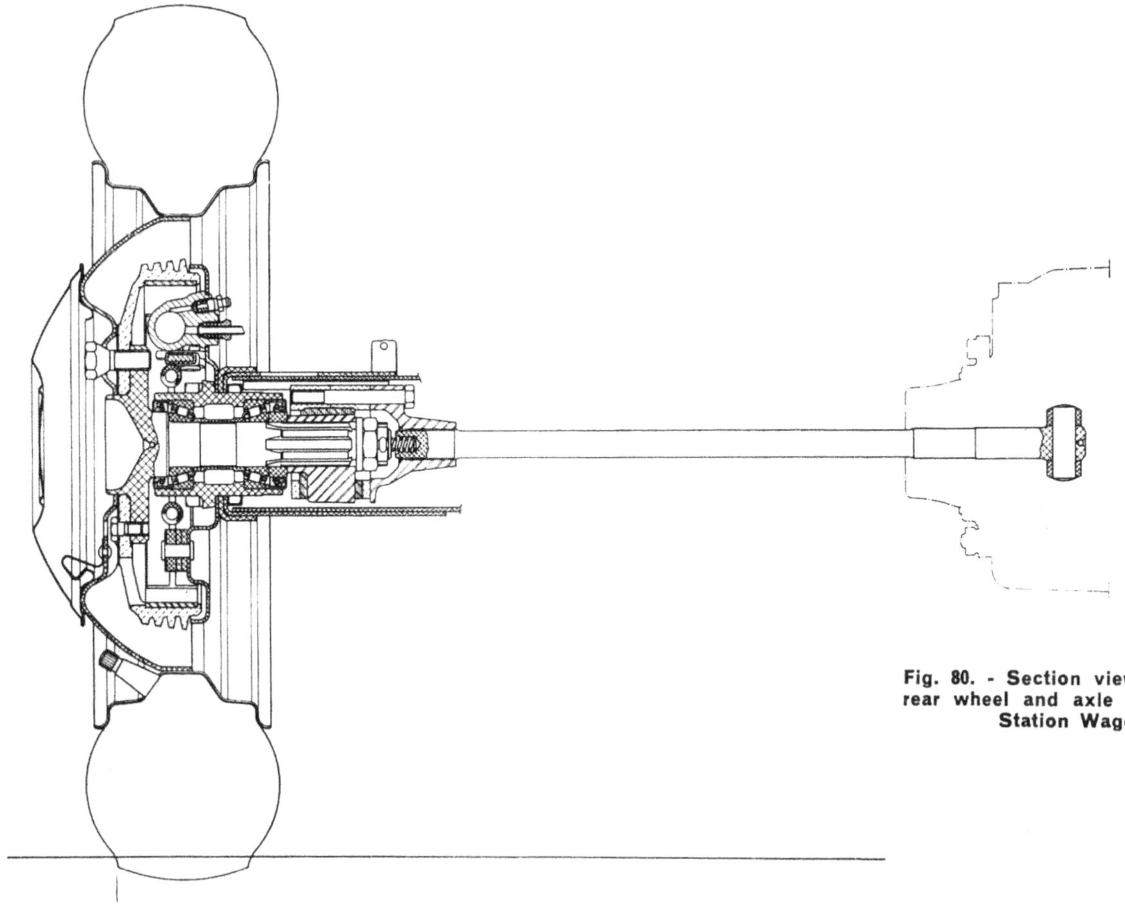

Fig. 80. - Section view of left side rear wheel and axle shaft of « 500 Station Wagon ».

CHECKING AND ADJUSTING REAR WHEEL GEOMETRY

After the rear suspension has been replaced, check and, if necessary, adjust the rear wheel geometry.

Preparatory to these operations:

— tires should be inflated to the recommended pressure;

— the car body should be lowered so that the rear wheels are set at right angle to the floor level; this condition is obtained when: the lowermost portion of the sump is some 6.61" (168 mm) apart from floor level, for Model 500 D (fig. 81), or the center rear bracket for jacking up the vehicle is some 8.90" (226 mm) from floor level, for 500 Station Wagon (k, fig. 83).

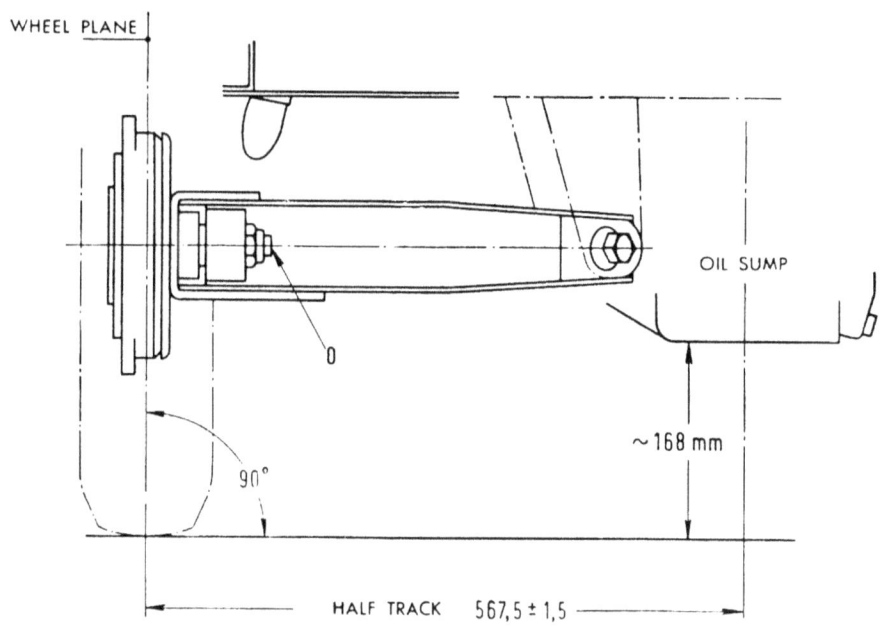

Fig. 81.

Position of rear suspension and of vehicle for rear wheel toe-in inspection and adjustment (Model « 500 D »).

~ 168 mm = abt 6.61"
567,5 ± 1,5 = 22.342" ± .059"

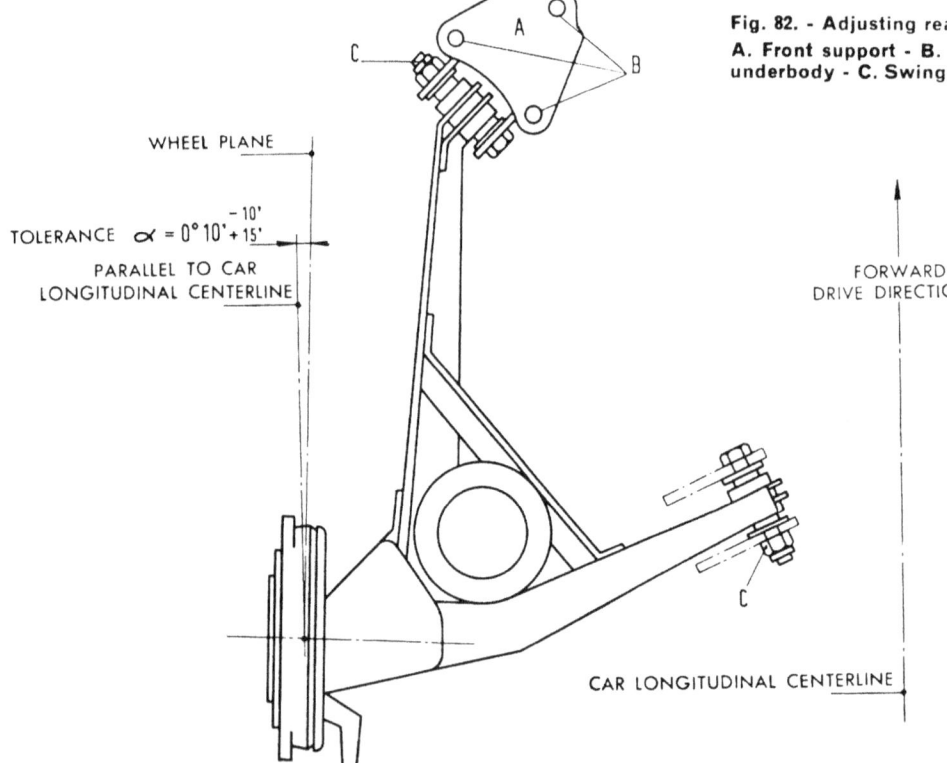

Fig. 82. - Adjusting rear wheel toe-in on Model « 500 D ».
A. Front support - B. Screw holes for fixing support to underbody - C. Swinging arm pin nuts - α. Wheel toe-in angle.

To adjust rear wheel geometry, use clearance existing between the support holes **A** and body mounting screws **B**. Screws **B** must be tightened to 28.9 to 36.2 ft.lbs (4 to 5 kgm). Nuts **C** must be tightened to 43.4 to 50.6 ft.lbs (6 to 7 kgm) after adjustment has been carried out. (These directions and specifications are also applicable to 500 Station Wagon).

SERVICE PROCEDURES: REAR SUSPENSION AND WHEELS

With the vehicle set as above, check the wheel geometry:

— the wheel plane should be tilted to car centerline by an angle of $0°\ 10'\ ^{-10'}_{+15'}$ toeing in at front (figs. 82 and 84);

— the wheel plane should be:

a) 22.342" ± .059" (567.5 ± 1.5 mm) apart from car centerline (half-track), for Model 500 D;

b) 22.264" ± .059" (565.5 ± 1.5 mm) apart from car centerline (half-track), for 500 Station Wagon;

— to adjust the wheel toe-in, take profit of the clearance existing between the support holes (A, figs. 82 and 84) and the mounting screws (B) at body.

After the wheel geometry has been corrected, tighten the screws (B) fixing the front support (A) and the nuts (C) of swinging arm pins, securely.

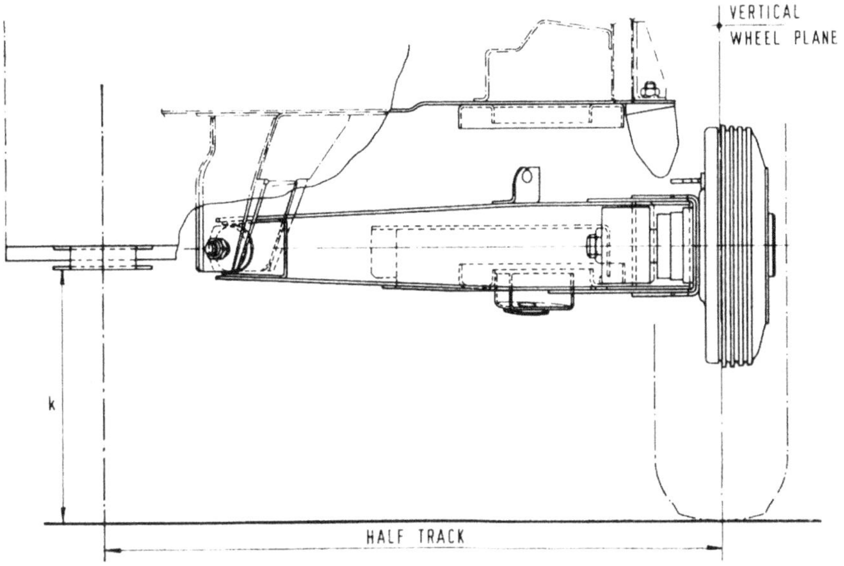

Fig. 83. - Position of rear suspension for rear wheel toe-in inspection and adjustment («500 Station Wagon»).

k. Distance of center rear bracket, for jacking up the vehicle, from floor level (some 8.90" - 226 mm).

Half-track = 22.264" ± .059" (565.5 ± 1.5 mm).

NOTA - Recall that the toe-in angle (α, figs. 82 and 84) **will vary by $0°\ 10'$ under a movement of some 7/32" (5.5 mm) measured at 72.476" (1.84 m) from wheel center for Model 500 D, and at 76.413" (1.94 m) from wheel center for 500 Station Wagon.**

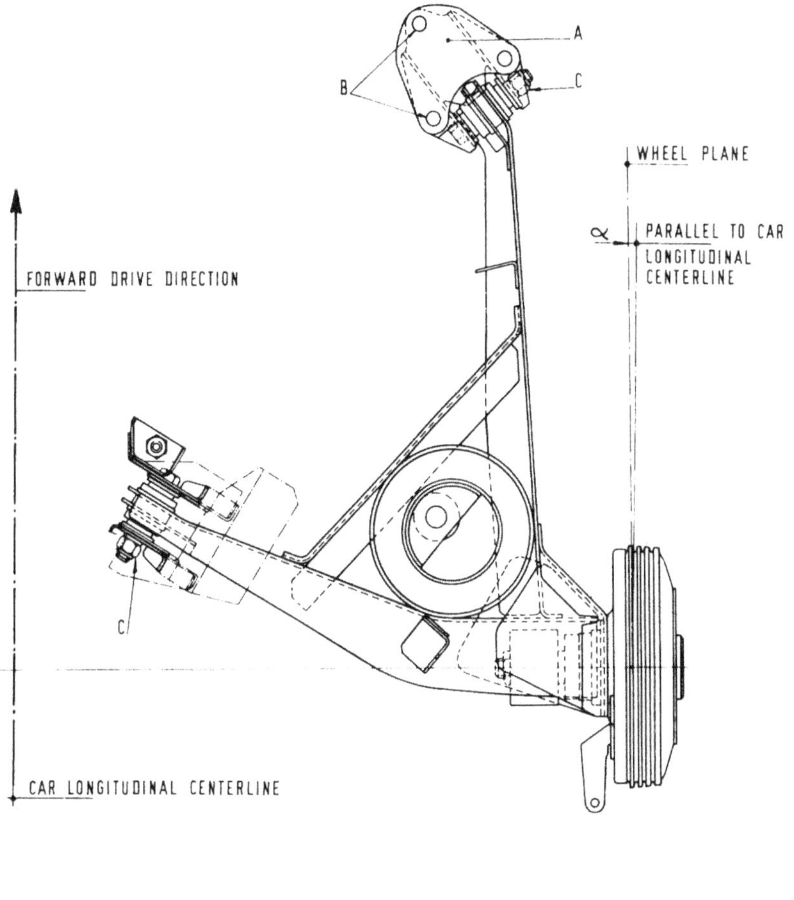

Fig. 84. - Adjusting rear wheel toe-in on «500 Station Wagon».

A. Front support - **B.** Screw holes for fixing support to underbody - **C.** Swinging arm pin nuts - α. Wheel toe-in angle ($0°\ 10'\ ^{-10'}_{+15'}$).

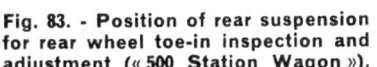

REAR SUSPENSION AND WHEELS TIGHTENING REFERENCE

ITEM	Part No.	Thread Pitch	Material	Tightening Torque
Swinging arm pin-to-underbody nut . .	1/25747/11	M 12 x 1,5	R 50 Cdt Pivot bar R 80 Cdt	43.4 to 50.6 ft.lbs (6,000 to 7,000 kgmm)
Swinging arm support-to-underbody screw	832632	M 10 x 1,25	R 80	28.9 to 36.2 ft.lbs (4,000 to 5,000 kgmm)
Hub and brake housing flange-to-swinging arm nut	1/21647/11	M 10 x 1,25	R 50 Cdt Screw R 80	43,4 ft.lbs (6,000 kgmm)
Flexible joint-to-rear wheel shaft nut .	1/07246/20	M 18 x 1,5	R 80 Shaft 38 NCD 4 Bon	see page 57
Axle shaft sleeve-to-flexible joint screw	1/60446/21	M 8 x 1,25	R 80 Cdt	20.3 ft.lbs (2,800 kgmm)
Wheel-to-hub screw:				
— Model « 500 D »	990166	M 10 x 1,5	C 35 R Bon Cdt	32.5 to 39.8 ft.lbs (4,500 to 5,500 kgmm)
— 500 Station Wagon	4080533	M 12 x 1,5	C 35 R Bon Cdt	43.4 to 50.6 ft.lbs (6,000 to 7,000 kgmm)
Rear wheel bearing rotation torque, not above				0.36 ft.lbs (50 kgmm)

REAR SUSPENSION AND WHEELS SPECIFICATIONS

Swinging Arms.		
Connection to underbody	by « estendblocks »	
Adjustment	shims	
Position of arm for tightening nuts to mounting pins on underbody	wheels vertical	
Coil Springs.	500 D	500 Station Wagon
Free height	8.70" (221 mm)	8.74" (222 mm)
Height under 904 ± 44 lbs (410 ± 20 kg) of load	5.94" (151 mm)	—
Height under 1,102 ± 55 lbs (500 ± 25 kg) of load	—	6.38" (162 mm)
Height under 1,268 ± 64 lbs (575 ± 29 kg) of load	4.24" (123 mm)	—
Height under 1,631 ± 82 lbs (740 ± 37 kg) of load	—	5.24" (133 mm)
Solid height	3.67" (93 mm)	4.09" (104 mm)
Deflection rate	.3034 in/100 lbs (17 mm/100 kg)	.2132 in/100 lbs (12 mm/100 kg)
Wheels.		
Roller bearing adjustment	by resilient spacer	
Bearing rotation torque, not above	.36 ft.lbs (5 kgcm)	
Wheel alignment: toe-in (identical for both rear wheels) . .	$0°\ 10'\ ^{-10'}_{+15'}$	
Bearing lubrication	FIAT MR grease	
Shock Absorbers.	two	
Type	hydraulic, telescopic	
Diameter (working cylinder)	1.063" (27 mm)	
Fluid grade	FIAT S. A. I. oil	
Capacity	.088 Imp. qts - .104 U.S. qts (100 ± 5 cc - 0.090 kg)	

HYDRAULIC SHOCK ABSORBERS

These shock absorbers, which equip both the **front** and **rear** suspension, are also termed « direct acting », since their dampening action takes place directly on suspension without the intermediary of levers.

Rear shock absorbers differ from front ones as far as size, setting and capacity is concerned (see table).

Hydraulic shock absorbers, both front and rear, are provided with a vapour pocket bleeder from cylinder interior.

The bleeder device consists of a capillary hole (12, fig. 85) interconnecting the working cylinder (15) with the upper chamber (10), and of a passage tube (16) from upper chamber to fluid reservoir.

Any vapour pockets in pressure cylinder are evacuated past the capillary hole (12) into the chamber (10), whence they flow down, during shock absorber operation, through passage (16) in a light fluid stream and up to top reservoir with the reservoir fluid.

This system definitely does away with any vapour lock in shock absorber hydraulic circuit, which is isolated from air contained in fluid reservoir.

SHOCK ABSORBER SPECIFICATIONS

Front Shock Absorbers	
Part number	4048307
Working cylinder bore	1 1/16" (27 mm)
Length (between rubber grommet shoulders) telescoped in . . .	8.346" ± .079" (212 ± 2 mm)
telescoped out . . .	13.189" ± .079" (335 ± 2 mm)
Stroke	4.842" (123 mm)
FIAT S.A.I. fluid capacity	.112 G.B.qts - .137 U.S.qts (130 ± 5 cc - 0.120 kg)
Rear Shock Absorbers	
Part number:	
— Model « 500 D » . . .	4044425
— 500 Station Wagon .	4059006
Working cylinder bore	1 1/16" (27 mm)
Length (between rubber grommet shoulders) telescoped in . . .	7.086" ± .079" (180 ± 2 mm)
telescoped out . . .	10.669" ± .079" (271 ± 2 mm)
Stroke	3.583" (91 mm)
FIAT S.A.I. fluid capacity	.088 G.B.qts - .104 U.S.qts (100 ± 5 cc - 0.090 kg)

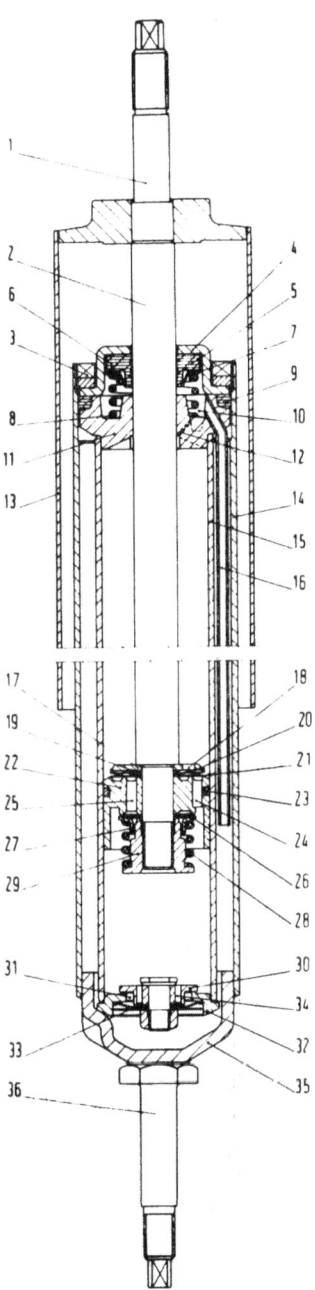

Fig. 85. - Sectional view of shock absorber.

1. Threaded shank, floor mounting - 2. Rod - 3. Cylinder upper blanking threaded ring - 4. Seal housing - 5. Rod seal - 6. Tab spring - 7. Spring cup - 8. Gasket packing spring - 9. Casing gasket - 10. Vapour pocket drain chamber - 11. Rod guide bushing - 12. Vapour pocket drain capillary hole - 13. Dust shield - 14. Casing - 15. Working cylinder - 16. Vapour pocket drain passage - 17. Valve lift limiting disc - 18. Fluid passage orifice - 19. Valve lift adjustment washer - 20. Valve star-shaped spring - 21. Inlet valve - 22. Piston - 23. Compression ring - 24. Inlet valve holes in piston - 25. Rebound valve holes in piston - 26. Rebound valve - 27. Valve guide cup - 28. Rebound valve spring - 29. Piston mounting plug - 30. Compensating valve - 31. Compensating valve annular passage - 32. Compensating-and-compression valve carrier plug - 33. Compression valve - 34. Compression valve orifices - 35. Lower plug - 36. Threaded shank, lower mounting.

Steering System

ADJUSTING STEERING GEAR

After assembly, or during routine maintenance, adjust the steering gear as follows.

If backlash between worm screw and sector is excessive, work on wormshaft eccentric bushing:

Disconnect pitman arm and relevant seal.

Back out screw (7, fig. 86) fixing adjustment plate (6).

Rotate eccentric bushing (5) by the adjustment plate and move sector in toward worm screw.

Secure plate again using the second fixing hole.

Should adjusting plate be already fixed in second hole, remove plate from bushing, advance one serration and secure.

If play in worm screw rollers is excessive, screw up lower adjuster ring (4, fig. 88). Once adjustment is over, adjuster ring must be secured by cotter pin: to this end, position ring in such a way that hole in steering housing lines up with one of the spaces between ring castellations.

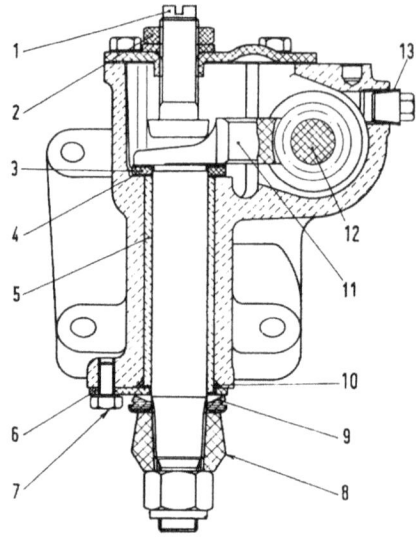

Fig. 86. - Section view of steering gear, through worm sector.

1. Sector adjusting screw - 2. Locking nut and plain washer - 3. Sector thrust washer - 4. Shim - 5. Eccentric bushing - 6. Bushing adjusting plate - 7. Plate screw and toothed washer - 8. Pitman arm - 9. Sector lower seal - 10. Upper seal - 11. Worm sector - 12. Worm screw - 13. Oil filler and level plug.

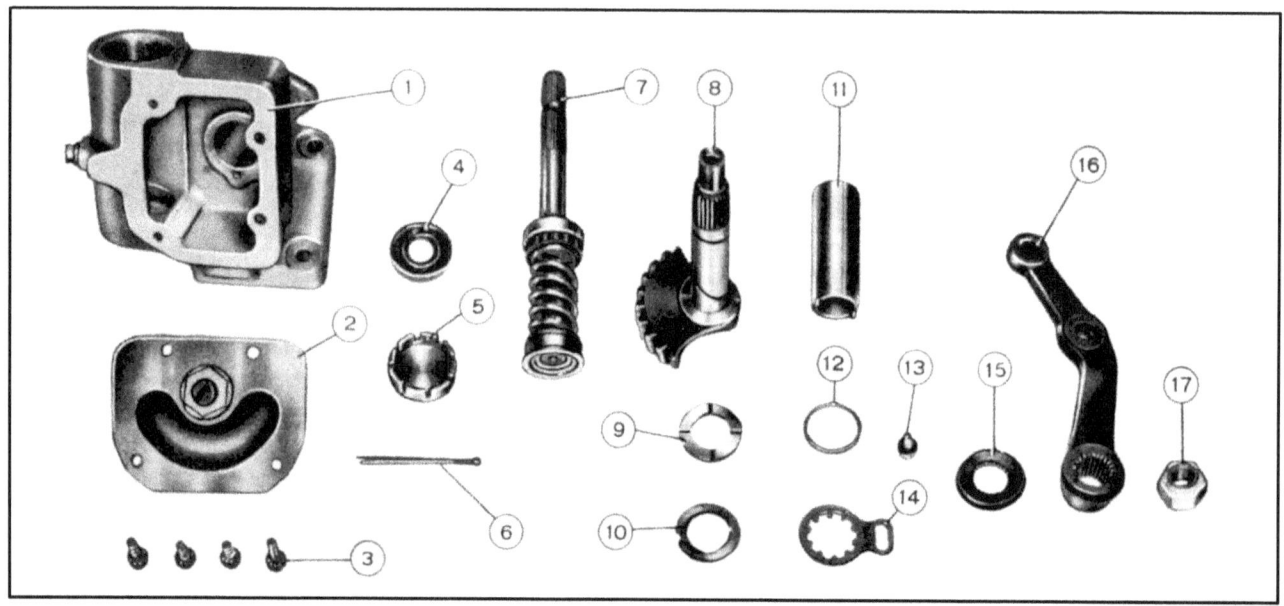

Fig. 87. - Steering gear components.

1. Steering housing - 2. Cover - 3. Cover mounting screws and toothed washers - 4. Worm screw seal - 5. Adjuster ring - 6. Adjuster ring cotter - 7. Worm screw - 8. Sector and shaft assy - 9. Sector thrust washer - 10. Sector shim - 11. Eccentric bushing - 12. Upper seal - 13. Plate screw and toothed washer - 14. Bushing adjusting plate - 15. Lower seal - 16. Pitman arm - 17. Pitman arm mounting nut.

SERVICE PROCEDURES: STEERING

Worm screw and sector must mesh in their central portion: if off center, this condition may be corrected by moving sector axially. To do so, add or remove shims (4, fig. 86) below thrust ring of worm sector.

Shims are supplied as spares with .0039" (0.10 mm) thickness.

The next adjustment must be carried out by means of adjustment screw (1, fig. 86) on cover, then locking screw by nut (2).

Both the above adjustments should correct any play and backlash in steering gear without rendering steering too stiff.

NOTE - Prior to going over the steering gear for adjustment, see whether the steering linkage shows any irregularity: in the affirmative, adjust the steering linkage, first of all.

CHECKING AND ADJUSTING FRONT WHEEL TOE-IN

Before starting this check, make sure that the following conditions are complied with:

— tires inflated with recommended pressure (page 19);
— steering wheel in mid-travel position with spokes horizontal;
— wheels in straightahead position, or symmetrical to car centerline;
— car under full load.

Move the car some yards on so that the suspension may set up regularly. Toe-in measurements should be taken at the same point of wheel rim: measure at **A** (fig. 89), then back up the car to bring points **A** to the position **B**, and measure again. The value obtained at **A** should be equal to or greater than **B** within .0079" (2 mm).

Steering rods are adjustable in length: loosen clamps and screw in or out rod adjusting sleeves.

Next to toe-in adjustment, make sure that the expansion slot in the sleeve registers with the clamp joint; with the clamp fully tightened, there should be always a gap between joint faces.

NOTE - Care should be taken to tighten the idler arm pin nut only after the toe-in adjusting operation and with the wheels set for straight ahead drive.

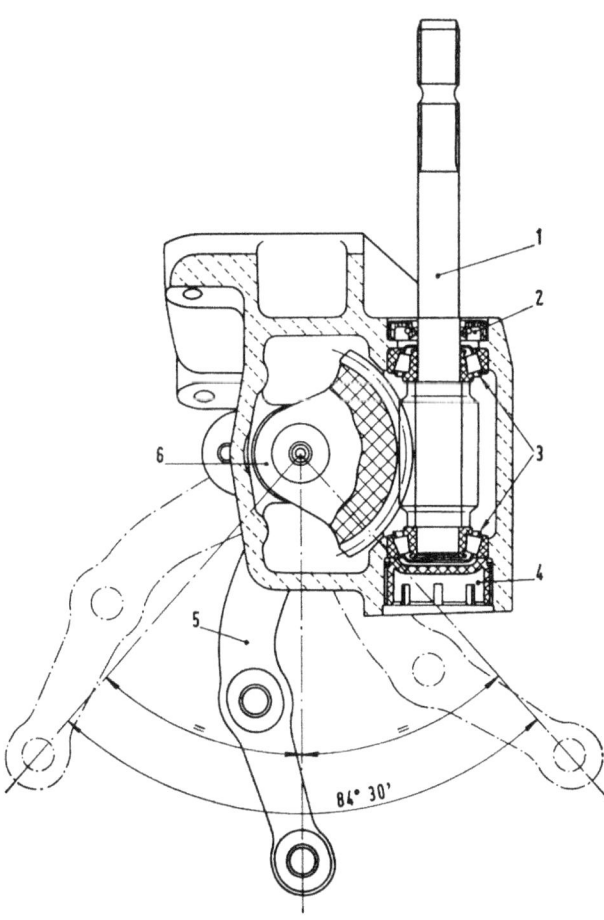

Fig. 88. - Section view of steering gear, through worm screw.
1. Worm screw - **2.** Seal - **3.** Roller bearing - **4.** Worm screw adjuster and bearing retainer - **5.** Pitman arm - **6.** Worm sector.

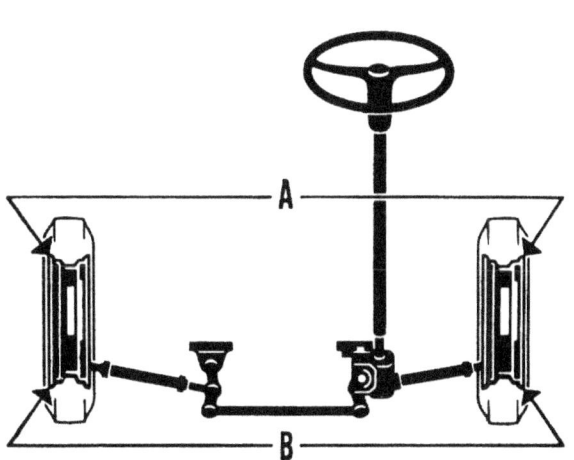

Fig. 89. - Front wheel toe-in checking diagram.
A — B = .000" to .079" (0 to 2 mm).

STEERING SYSTEM TIGHTENING REFERENCE

ITEM	Part No.	Thread Pitch	Material	Tightening Torque
Pitman arm-to-sector shaft nut	1/25748/11	M 14 x 1,5	R 50 Cdt Sector 19 CN 5 Cmt 3	72.3 to 79.6 ft.lbs (10,000 to 11,000 kgmm)
Idler arm pin nut (*)	1/25747/11	M 12 x 1,5	R 50 Cdt Pin R 80 Cdt	39.8 to 43.4 ft.lbs (5,500 to 6,000 kgmm)
Steering gear-to-body nut and relay lever support nut	1/61041/11	M 8 x 1,25	R 50 Cdt Screw R 80 Cdt	14.5 to 18.1 ft.lbs (2,000 to 2,500 kgmm)
Tie rod ball pin nut	1/25756/11	M 10 x 1,25	R 50 Cdt Pin R 100 Bon	18.1 to 21.7 ft.lbs (2,500 to 3,000 kgmm)
Steering wheel nut	743601	M 18 x 1,5	R 50 Cdt Shaft C 12 tube	28.9 to 36.2 ft.lbs (4,000 to 5,000 kgmm)

(*) To be tightened after toe-in adjustment and with wheels set for straight ahead drive.

STEERING SYSTEM SPECIFICATIONS

Steering gear type	worm screw and roller
Ratio	26 to 2
Worm screw bearings	taper roller
Worm screw bearing adjustment	through threaded sleeve adjuster
Worm screw-to-sector clearance adjustment	through sector shaft eccentric bushing rotation
Side track rods	adjustable by threaded ends
Intermediate tie rod	with incorporated ends
Turning radius	14 ft. 1 in (4.30 m)
Wheel steering angles: inner wheel . . . . outer wheel	33° abt. 25° 40'
Steering wheel turns (lock to lock)	abt. 3.05
Front wheel toe-in (fully laden car)	.000" to .079" (0 to 2 mm)
Front track	44.09" (1,121 mm)
Wheelbase { 500 D . . . . 500 Station Wagon	72.44" (1,840 mm) 76.38" (1,940 mm)
Steering gear oil: capacity . . . . grade	.105 Imp. quarts - .124 U.S. quarts (0.120 lt - 0.110 kg) FIAT W 90 (SAE 90 EP)

Brakes

Self-Adjusting Device of Brake Shoe Clearance on Model «500 D».

Model «500 D» is equipped with a specially designed brake shoe clearance self-adjusting device which does away with any manual adjustment operation.

In fact, everytime brake pedal is depressed this device automatically takes up all possible excess clearance developed in consequence of lining wear.

On the side faces of shoe ribs are placed two friction washers in line with an adjustment slot machined in brake shoe (fig. 91).

The washers are held against shoe by a pin and bushing screwed together through the slot with the interposition of a load spring.

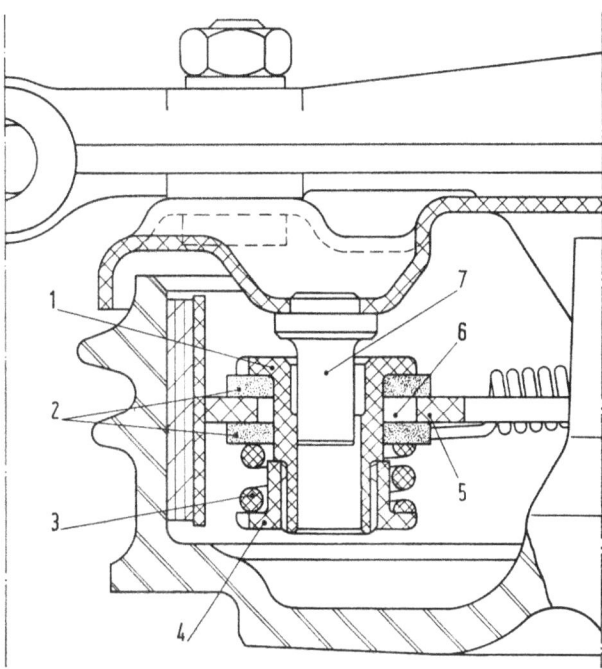

Fig. 91. - Sectional view of a self-adjusting device for automatic take-up of brake shoe-to-drum clearance.

1. Pin - 2. Friction washers - 3. Load spring - 4. Bushing - 5. Shoe - 6. Self-adjustment slot - 7. Stud.

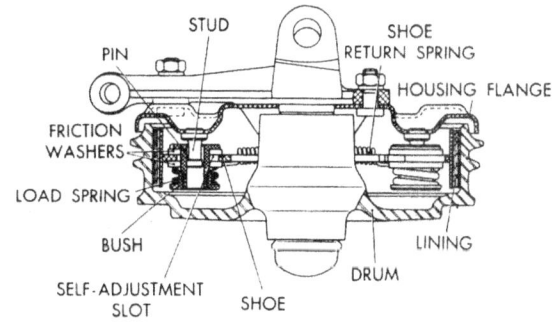

Fig. 90. - Left front wheel brake assembly section through self-adjusting device (Model «500 D»).

The pin is hollow and fits on the stud in brake housing flange. A clearance of .0315" (0.8 mm) between pin hole and stud permits the necessary displacement of shoes for proper braking under normal conditions without calling into play the self-adjustment device.

When shoe clearance adjustment is no longer as specified, on account of lining wear or improper assembly, the braking action - after overriding the stud-to-pin clearance - will overcome the resistance of friction washers and drag along the shoes into contact with drum.

After releasing the pedal, the action of return springs will be weaker than the friction of adjustment washers on shoes and, therefore, shoes will remain in the new position assumed up to the time when, following a further wear of linings, shoes are again repositioned by the device.

Fig. 92. - Left side rear wheel without brake drum (Model «500 D»).

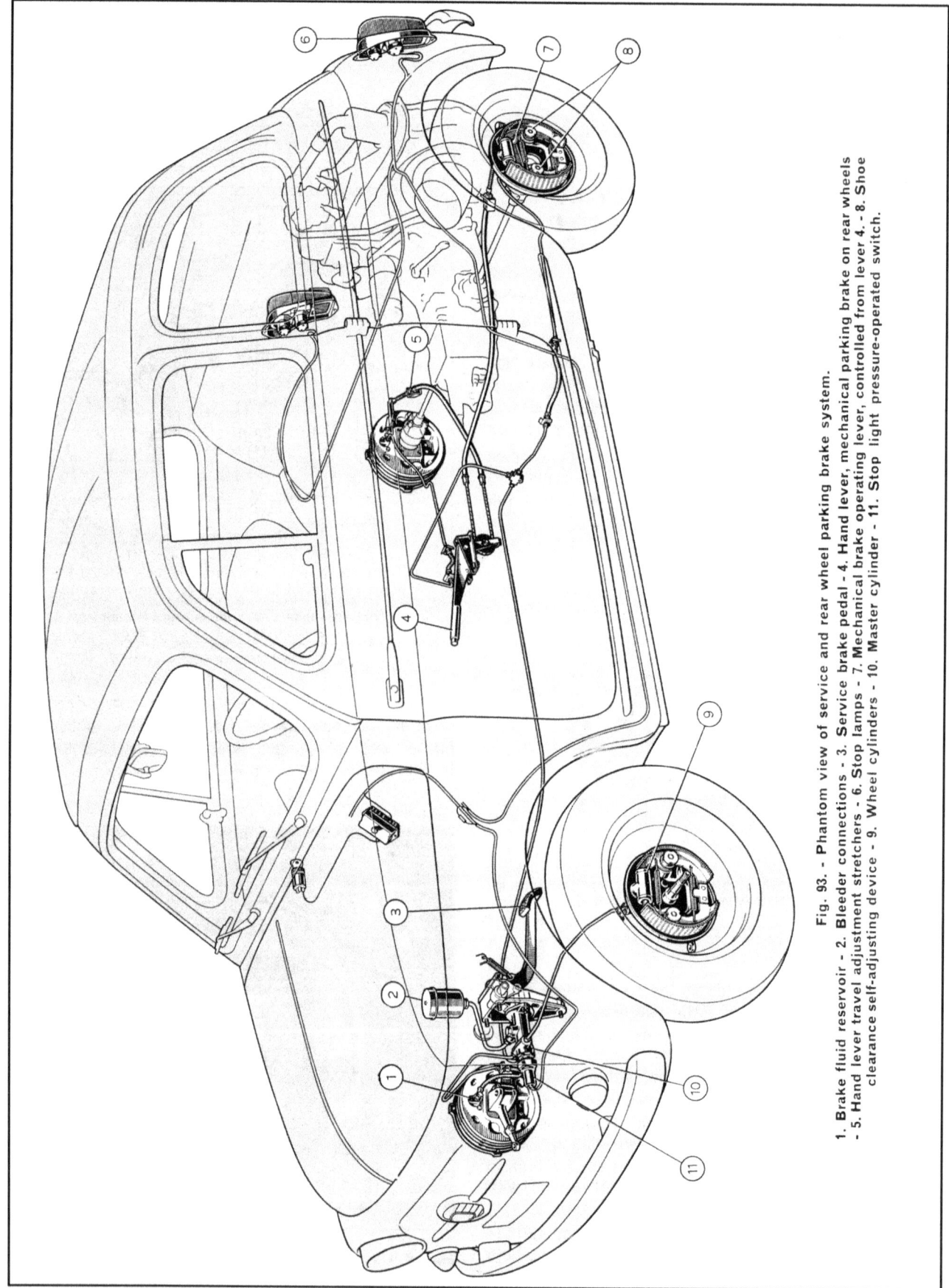

Fig. 93. - Phantom view of service and rear wheel parking brake system.

1. Brake fluid reservoir - 2. Bleeder connections - 3. Service brake pedal - 4. Hand lever, mechanical parking brake on rear wheels - 5. Hand lever travel adjustment stretchers - 6. Stop lamps - 7. Mechanical brake operating lever, controlled from lever 4. - 8. Shoe clearance self-adjusting device - 9. Wheel cylinders - 10. Master cylinder - 11. Stop light pressure-operated switch.

SERVICE PROCEDURES: BRAKES

Adjusting Brake Shoe Clearance on «500 Station Wagon».

The «500 Station Wagon» is equipped with expansion type brakes having self-centering shoes and adjusting cams.

To adjust shoe-to-drum clearance, proceed as follows:

— depress the brake pedal so as to force shoes against the drum;

— keeping shoes in this position, turn in the nuts of adjusting cams (fig. 96) until cams (3, fig. 94) are brought to contact of shoes;

— back out cam nuts by some 20°;

— release the brake pedal and see that the wheel revolves freely.

Replace shoe assemblies if linings are worn to half their original thickness.

NOTE - Turning out cam nuts by 20° corresponds to a clearance of .0098" (0.25 mm) between brake shoes and drum at adjusting cams; this clearance can be gauged through drum openings, after removing the wheel.

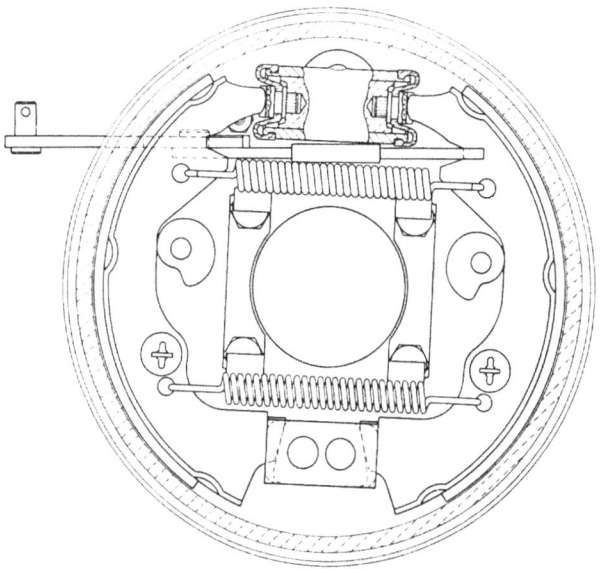

Fig. 95. - Section view of right side rear brake assembly («500 Station Wagon»).

MANUAL BRAKE

To adjust the manual brake ratchet lever travel (which should be made after the shoe clearance setting on «500 Station Wagon»), take the ratchet lever to rest position, then pull it up by two ratchet serrations and work on both stretchers at rear wheel brakes (fig. 96).

Next to the travel adjustment of ratchet lever, again check the shoe clearance setting as far as the Station Wagon is concerned.

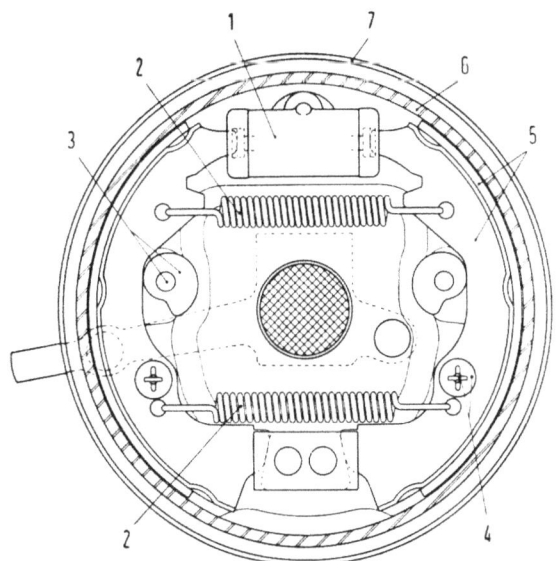

Fig. 94. - Section view of left side front brake assembly («500 Station Wagon»).

1. Wheel cylinder - 2. Shoe return spring - 3. Adjusting cams - 4. Shoe guide pin - 5. Shoe with lining - 6. Drum - 7. Housing flange.

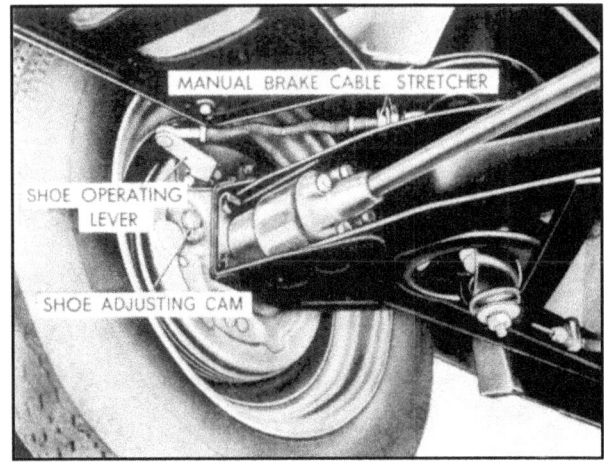

Fig. 96. - Manual brake control and shoe adjusting cam at left side rear wheel of «500 Station Wagon».

BRAKE SYSTEM SPECIFICATIONS

Service Brakes:	
Type	hydraulic, self-centering, expanding-shoe
Drum diameter « 500 D »	6.702" to 6.712" (170.230 to 170.480 mm)
Drum diameter « 500 Station Wagon »	7.2929" to 7.3043" (185.240 to 185.530 mm)
Turning drums: maximum diameter oversize allowance	.0394" (1 mm)
Linings:	
Type of bonding	« PERMAFUSE »
Width	1.181" (30 mm)
Shoe-to-drum clearance « 500 D »	take-up self-adjusting device
Shoe-to-drum clearance « 500 Station Wagon »	.0098" (0.25 mm), by adjusting cams
Self-adjustment device springs (Model « 500 D »):	
Part No.	986339
Wire diameter	.142" (3.6 mm)
Inner diameter	.720" (18.3 mm)
Working coils	1
Total No. of coils	2 1/2
Height	.484" (12.3 mm)
Height, seated	.374" (9.5 mm)
Corresponding load	97 ± 4.9 lbs (44 ± 2.2 kg)
Master cylinder diameter	3/4"
Wheel cylinder diameter	3/4"
Master cylinder plunger-to-pushrod clearance	.0197" (0.5 mm)
Pedal free travel	.0984" (2.5 mm)
Brake fluid:	
Type	FIAT special blue label brake fluid (or equivalent non-mineral grade)
Circuit capacity Imp. quarts	.194
Circuit capacity U.S. quarts	.232
Circuit capacity liters	0.220
Circuit capacity kg	0.220
Manual Parking Brake:	
Type	lever-controlled mechanical expansion of rear wheel brake shoes
Control	by ratchet lever on center floor tunnel
Wire rope adjustment	by stretchers located on swinging arms, behind brake housing flanges

Electric System

BATTERY

The battery equipping Model «500 D» and «500 Station Wagon» from serial No. 004369, is fitted with a particular type of cell cover which incorporates a «level sight». This is visible after removing the plug.

Such new design of the cell filler neck makes the electrolyte topping up operation much easier.

The cell is correctly filled when the electrolyte level reaches the brim of the filler neck lower opening (fig. 97).

FUSES

There are six 8-Ampere fuses, located in front compartment (fig. 98).

Before replacing a blown fuse, trace and remove the origin of blowing.

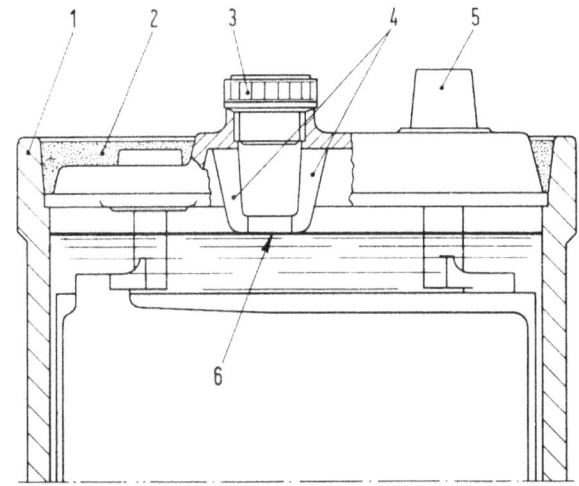

Fig. 97. - Cross section view of battery at a filler neck fitted with electrolyte level sight.
1. Battery container - 2. Sealing compound - 3. Cell plug - 4. Filler neck with vent slots - 5. Terminal post - 6. Electrolyte level sight on filler neck.

Fuse	PROTECTED CIRCUITS
1 No. 30/2	Right headlamp high beam. Front left parking lamp. Rear right parking light. Front parking lamps indicator. Number plate lamp.
2 No. 30/3	Left headlamp high beam - Front right parking lamp - Rear left parking light. High beam indicator.
3 No. 56/b1	Left headlamp low beam.
4 No. 56/b2	Right headlamp low beam.
5 No. 15/54	Direction indicators and pilot light. Panel light. Stop lights. Windshield wiper.
6 No. 30	Horn. Lamp in rear view mirror. Rear inner lamp («Station Wagon» only).

NOTE - The following circuits are not fuse-protected: battery charge and indicator, ignition and starting, low oil pressure indicator, fuel reserve supply indicator.

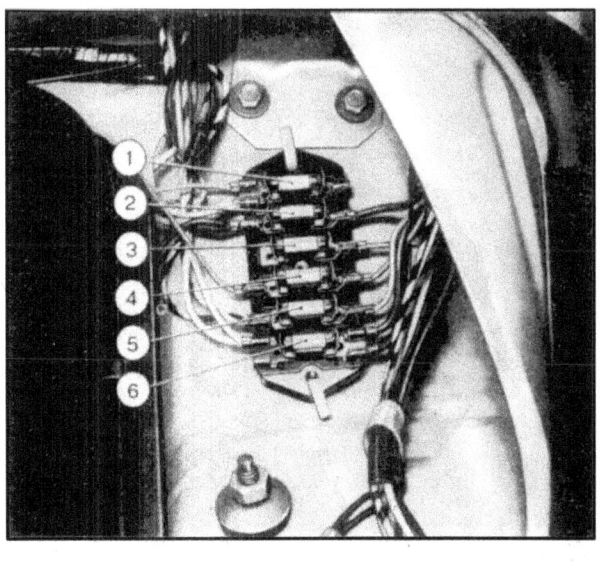

Fig. 98. - Fuses.
1. Fuse 30/2 - 2. Fuse 30/3 - 3. Fuse 56/b1 - 4. Fuse 56/b2 - 5. Fuse 15/54 - 6. Fuse 30.

FIAT GENERATOR TYPE DSV 90/12/16/3 S

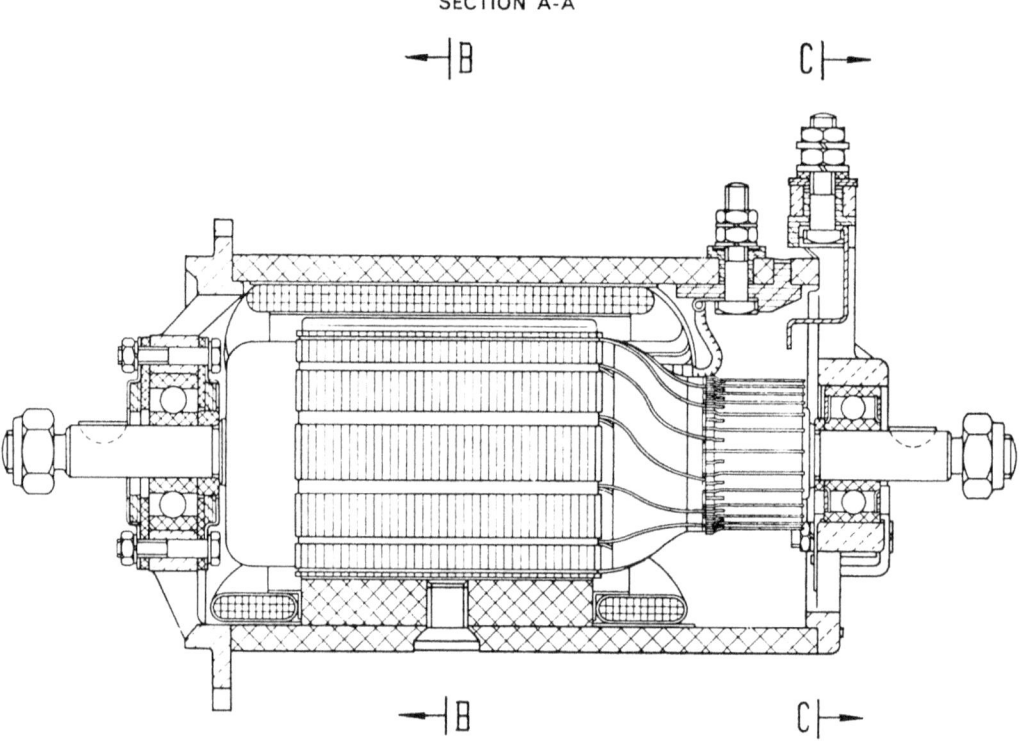

Fig. 99. - Longitudinal section view of generator assembly.

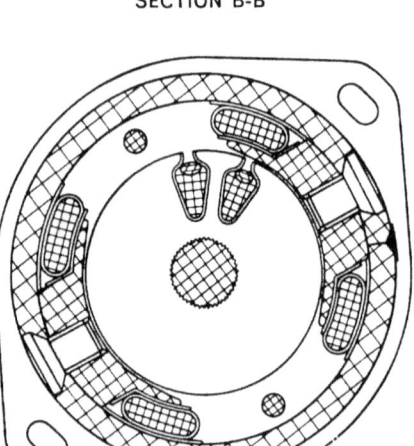

Fig. 100. - Section view through frame, pole shoes and windings.

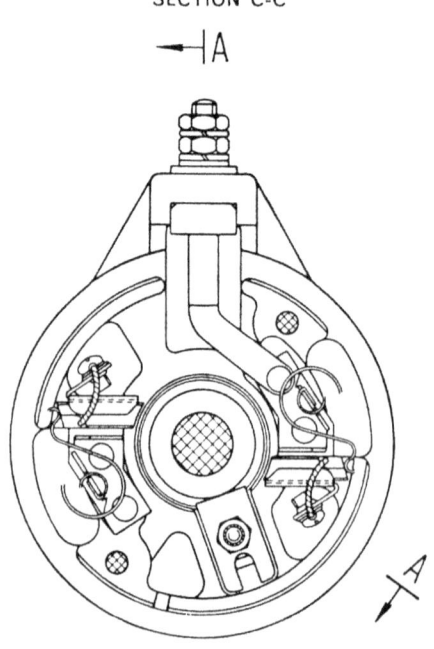

Fig. 101. - Cross section and side view of commutator end head.

SERVICE PROCEDURES: ELECTRICAL

FIAT GENERATOR TYPE D 90/12/16/3 F

(Fitted on Mod. 500 S.W.)

SECTION A-A

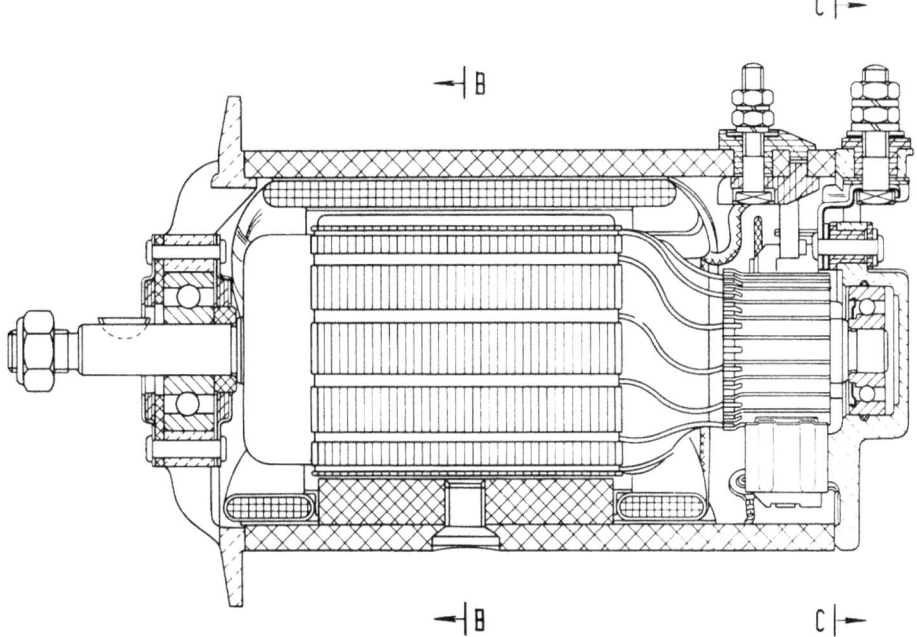

Fig. 102 - Longitudinal section of generator assembly.

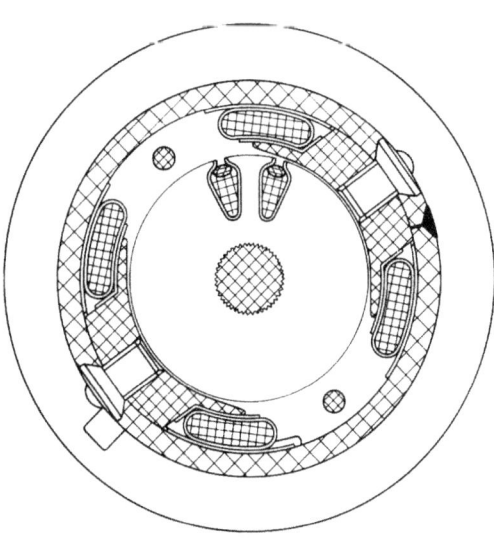

Fig. 103 - Section through frame, pole shoes and windings.

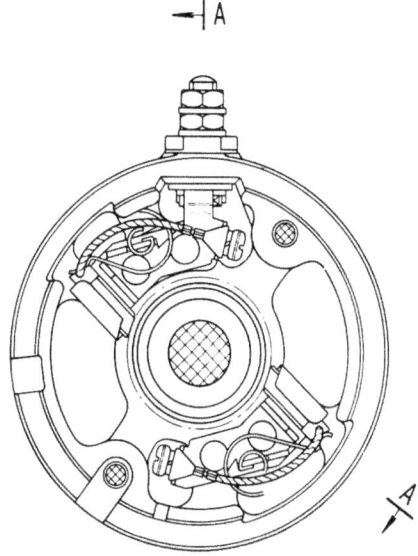

Fig. 104. - Cross section and view of commutator end head.

GENERATOR SPECIFICATIONS

Type { Sedan	DSV 90/12/16/3 S
Type { Station Wagon	D 90/12/16/3 F
Nominal tension	12 Volts
Max. continued operation output (ammeter limit)	16 Amperes
Max. current output	22 Amperes
Max. steady power	230 Watts
Max. power	320 Watts
Initial charging speed at 12 Volts and 68° F (20° C)	1710 to 1860 r.p.m. (*) 1710 to 1790 r.p.m. (**)
16 A. max. output delivery speed, at 68° F (20° C)	2550 to 2800 r.p.m. (*) 2550 to 2700 r.p.m. (**)
22 A. max output delivery speed, at 68° F (20° C)	3050 to 3200
Max. steady speed	9000 r.p.m.
Rotation, drive end	clockwise
Pole shoes	2
Field winding	shunt
Regulator, separate	FIAT GN 2/12/16
Drive ratio (new belt), engine-to-generator	1.74
Pole shoe I.D.	2.2952" to 2.2991" (58.3 to 58.4 mm)
Brush part No.	4034356

Bench Testing Data.

— Testing generator as a motor (at 68° F - 20° C):	
Feed voltage	12 V
Current draw	5 ± 0.5 Amps
Speed	1500 ± 100 r.p.m.
— Output test (at 68° F - 20° C):	
Steady voltage	12 V
Speed for abt. 30 minutes	4500 r.p.m.
Current delivery to resistor, at 14 Volts	5 ± 0.5 Amps
After bringing generator to operation temperature by running generator at the above specified speed and time rates, at a steady 12 V tension, read the values of the current output at every generator speed increment: each reading will be a point of the generator output curve shown in fig. 102.	
— Ohmic resistance test (at 68° F - 20° C):	
Armature resistance	0.145 ± 0.01 Ohms
Field winding resistance	$8 ^{+0.1}_{-0.3}$ Ohms
— Mechanical characteristics test:	
Load of spring on new brushes	1.3 to 1.6 lbs (0.600 to 0.720 kg)
Commutator maximum out-of-round	.00039" (0.01 mm)
Mica undercut depth	.0394" (1 mm)

Lubrication.

Ball bearing, drive end head	FIAT MR 3 Grease

(*) Refers to generators with armature package disc teeth .1732" (4.4 mm) in length (early type).
(**) Refers to generators with armature package disc teeth .1969" (5 mm) in length.

GN 2/12/16 REGULATOR CHECKING AND SETTING DATA

Cutout Relay.	
— Feed voltage for thermal stabilization:	
regulator initial 59° - 68° F - (15° - 20° C)	16.5 V
operating temperature 68° - 95° F (20° - 35° C)	15 V
— Closing voltage	12.6 ± 0.2 V
— Voltage-contact stroke variation: below	1 V/mm
— Reverse current: not above	16 Amps
— Air gap (closed contacts)	.0138" (0.35 mm)
— Point gap	.0177" ± .0023" (0.45 ± 0.06 mm)
Voltage Regulator.	
— Battery	50 A/h
— Half-load current	8 ± 0.5 Amps
— Setting voltage after thermal stabilization in oven at 122° ± 5° F (50° ± 3° C) for 30 minutes, half-load on battery	14.2 ± 0.3 V
— Feed voltage for thermal stabilization	15 V
— Air gap	.0391" to .0437" (0.99 to 1.11 mm)
Current Regulator.	
— Regulated current on battery	16 ± 1 Amps
— Voltage for regulated current inspection	13 V
— Air gap	.0391" to .0437" (0.99 to 1.11 mm)
Regulating Resistor	85 ± 5 Ohms
Additional Resistor, serially connected to voltage regulator	17 ± 1 Ohms

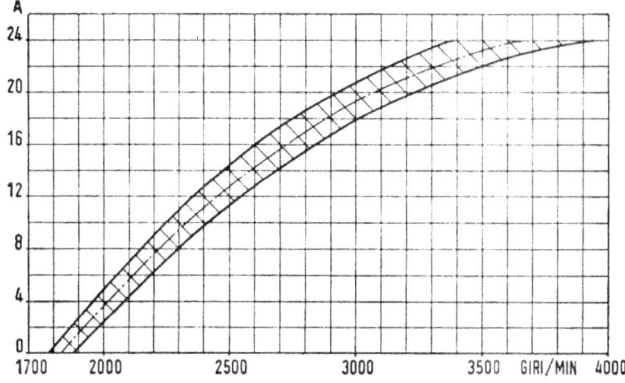

Fig. 105. - Warm output curve of generator DSV 90/12/16/3 S.
GIRI/MIN = R.P.M.

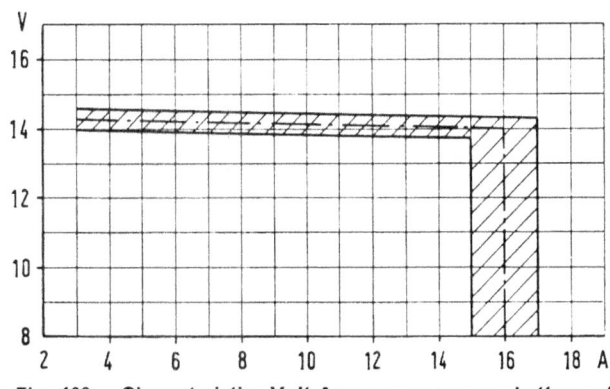

Fig. 106. - Characteristic Volt-Ampere curve on battery of GN 2/12/16 regulator.
Room temperature: 122° ± 5° F (50° ± 3° C) - Generator speed: 4,500 r.p.m.

IGNITION SYSTEM SPECIFICATIONS

Ignition Distributor.	
Static advance	10°
Centrifugal advance « 500 D »	18°
« 500 Station Wagon »	28°
Breaker contact pressure	16.8 ± 1.8 oz (475 ± 50 gr)
Contact gap	.0185" to .0209" (0.47 to 0.53 mm)
Condenser capacity at 50-100 Hz	0.15 to 0.20 µF
Cam carrier shaft felt and oiler lubricant	engine oil
Ignition Coil.	
Primary winding ohmic resistance at 68° ± 9° F (20° ± 5° C), not below	3.2 Ohms
Secondary winding ohmic resistance at 68° ± 9° F (20° ± 5° C)	5,000 ± 100 Ohms
Ground insulation resistance at 500 V d. c., not below	50 M Ohms
Spark Plugs.	
Thread diameter and pitch .... metric	M 14 x 1.25
Type « 500 D »	Marelli CW 225 N
« 500 Station Wagon »	Marelli CW 260 N
	Champion L 7
Point gap Marelli	.0197" to .0236" (0.5 to 0.6 mm)
Champion	.0236" to .0276" (0.6 to 0.7 mm)

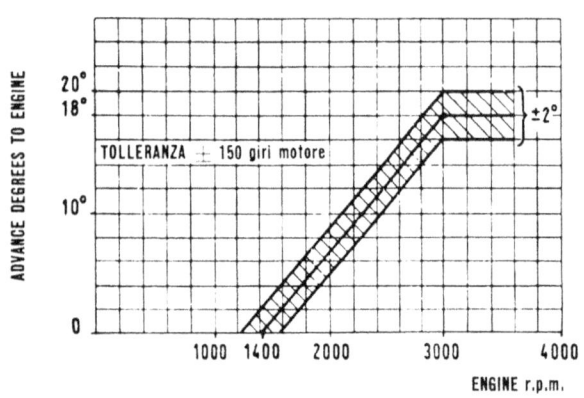

Tolleranza ± 150 giri motore = *Tolerance ± 150 r.p.m. of engine*

Fig. 107. - **Ignition distributor centrifugal advance variations (Model «500 D»).**

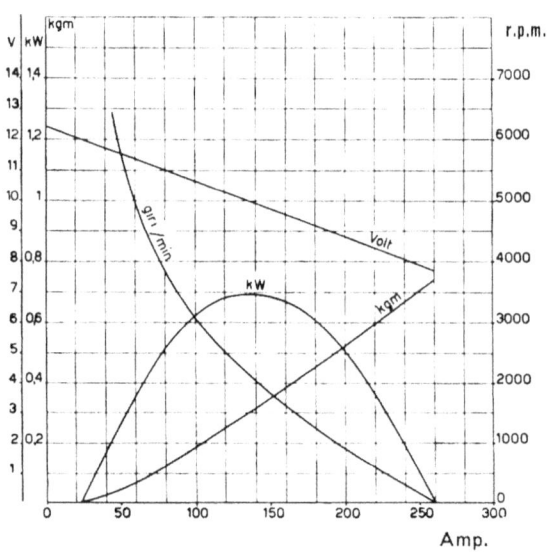

Fig. 108. - **Characteristic curves of starting motor B 76-0,5/12 S.**

FIAT STARTING MOTOR TYPE B 76-0,5 12 S

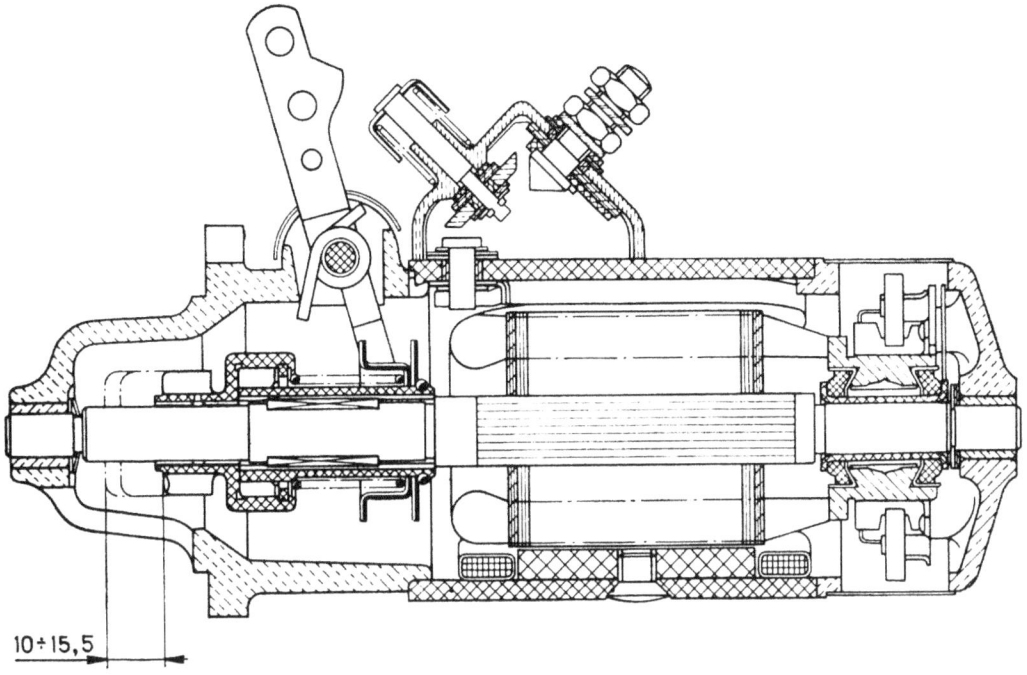

Fig. 109. - Longitudinal section view of starter assembly.
10 ÷ 15,5 = .3937" to .6102".

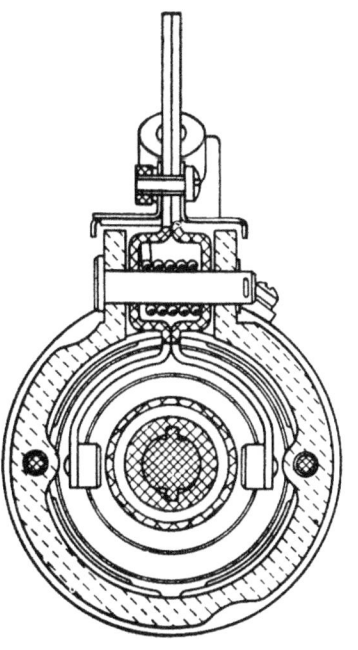

Fig. 110. - **Cross section view through drive unit.**

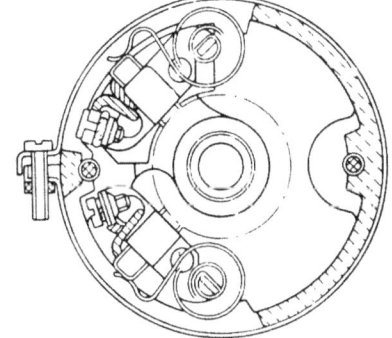

Fig. 111. - Section view through commutator end head, showing brushes.

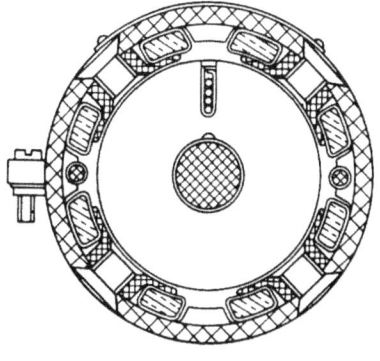

Fig. 112. - Section view through pole shoes and armature winding.

STARTING MOTOR SPECIFICATIONS

Type	B 76-0,5/12 S
Voltage	12 V
Nominal power	0.5 kW
Rotation (pinion end)	counterclockwise
Pole shoes	4
Field winding	serially connected
Engagement	by overrunning clutch
Pole shoes I.D.	2.0697 to 2.0768 in. (52.57 to 52.75 mm)
Armature diameter	2.0394 to 2.0413 in. (51.80 to 51.85 mm)
Part No. of brushes	805581

Bench Test Data.

— Operation test at 68° F (20° C):

Current	130 Amp
Torque developed	2 ± .14 ft.lbs (0.28 ± 0.02 kgm)
Speed	2,250 ± 100 r.p.m.
Tension	10 Volts

— Stall torque at 68° F (20° C):

Current	258 Amp
Tension	7.7 ± 0.3 Volts
Torque developed	5.3 ± .36 ft.lbs (0.73 ± 0.05 kgm)

— No-load test at 68° F (20° C):

Current, not above	30 Amp
Tension	12 Volts
Speed	8,500 ± 1,000 r.p.m.
— Ohmic resistance during stall torque test, at 68° F (20° C)	0.03 ± 0.001 Ohms

Mechanical Characteristics Test.

— Load of springs on new brushes	2.5 to 2.9 lbs (1.15 to 1.30 kg)
— Armature shaft axial play	.0059" to .0256" (0.15 to 0.65 mm)
— Mica undercut depth, not above	.04" (1 mm)
— Drive unit free wheel efficiency: static torque required to rotate pinion slowly, not above	.35 in. lbs (0.4 kgcm)

Lubrication.

— Drive unit splines	FIAT Jota 2/M grease
— Sleeve-to-engagement lever surfaces	FIAT Jota 2/M grease

SERVICE PROCEDURES: ELECTRICAL

AIMING HEADLIGHTS

Headlight aiming operation should be made in a **no-load condition**.

Check that tire inflation pressure corresponds to specifications.

Locate the car on a level floor, 16' 5" (5 m) apart from an opaque white screen in the shade and ensure that the car centerline is at right angles to the screen surface.

Jounce the car both sides to set suspensions.

Draw a pair of vertical lines (a-a, fig. 113) on the screen at a distance A = 32.68" (83 cm) apart, representing the distance between lamp centers. An increase of 10.24" (26 cm) in distance A is tolerated (corresponding to an aggregate beam divergence of 3°).

Then draw a horizontal line (b-b) at heights B shown in the table, according to whether the vehicle is new or with renewed suspensions (not yet settled) or the vehicle is settled. A vehicle is settled in practice when it has already run the mileage specified for the first coupon service (900 to 1,200 miles - 1,500 to 2,000 km).

To aim the headlights, proceed as follows:

— Switch on the dipped lights; the horizontal line of demarcation between the dark area and the illuminated zone should not override the horizontal line b-b (fig. 113).

— Switch on the full lights; the centerpoint of the zone of highest intensity (hot spot) of each lamp should fall on the corresponding line a-a, or slightly outside it, within permitted limits.

If the lamp vertical adjustment must be corrected, work simultaneously on both lower screws in the same direction and on the upper screw in opposite direction. These screws are located at the rear of the lamp and access can be gained from inside the front compartment.

If the lamp horizontal adjustment must be corrected, work on two lower screws in opposite directions and do not disturb the upper screw.

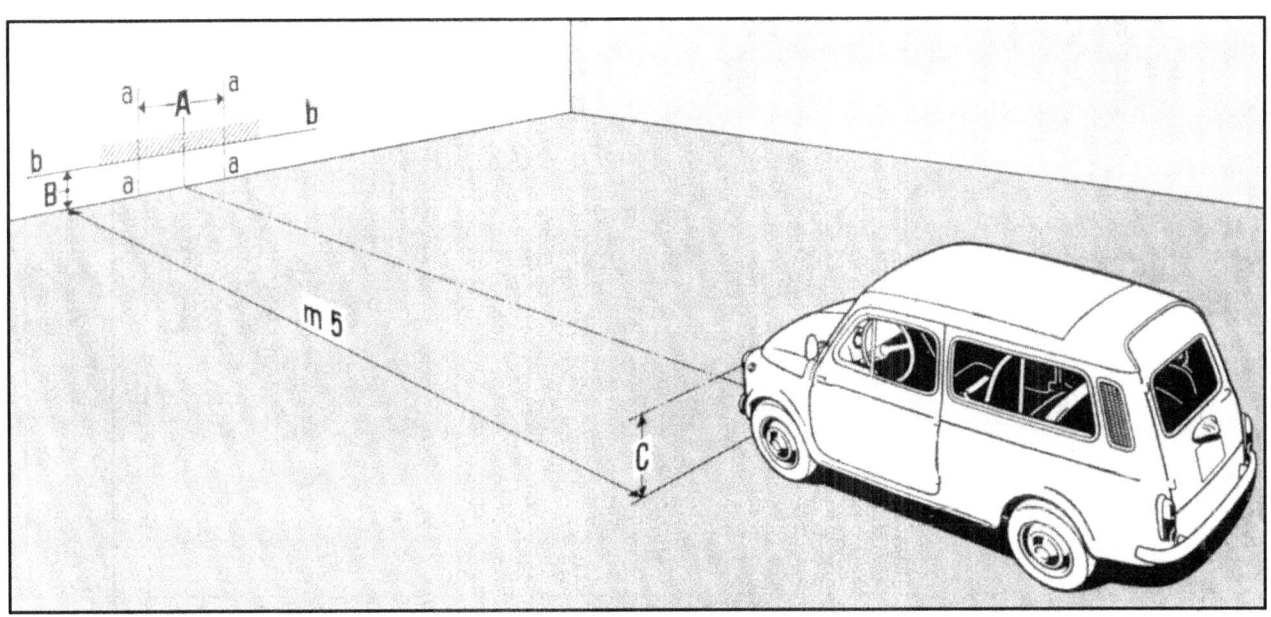

Fig. 113. - Headlight aiming diagram.

A. = Distance between lamp centers - B. = C minus figure shown in table - C = height of lamp centers from ground.

m 5 = 16'5"

HEADLIGHT AIMING DATA

Vehicle Model	A	B		Note
		New Vehicle	Settled Vehicle	
« 500 D »	32.68" (830 mm)	C minus 1.57" (40 mm)	C minus 1.38" (35 mm)	An increase in distance A of 10.24" (260 mm) is tolerated.
« 500 Station Wagon »	32.68" (830 mm)	C minus 2.95" (75 mm)	C minus 1.57" (40 mm)	

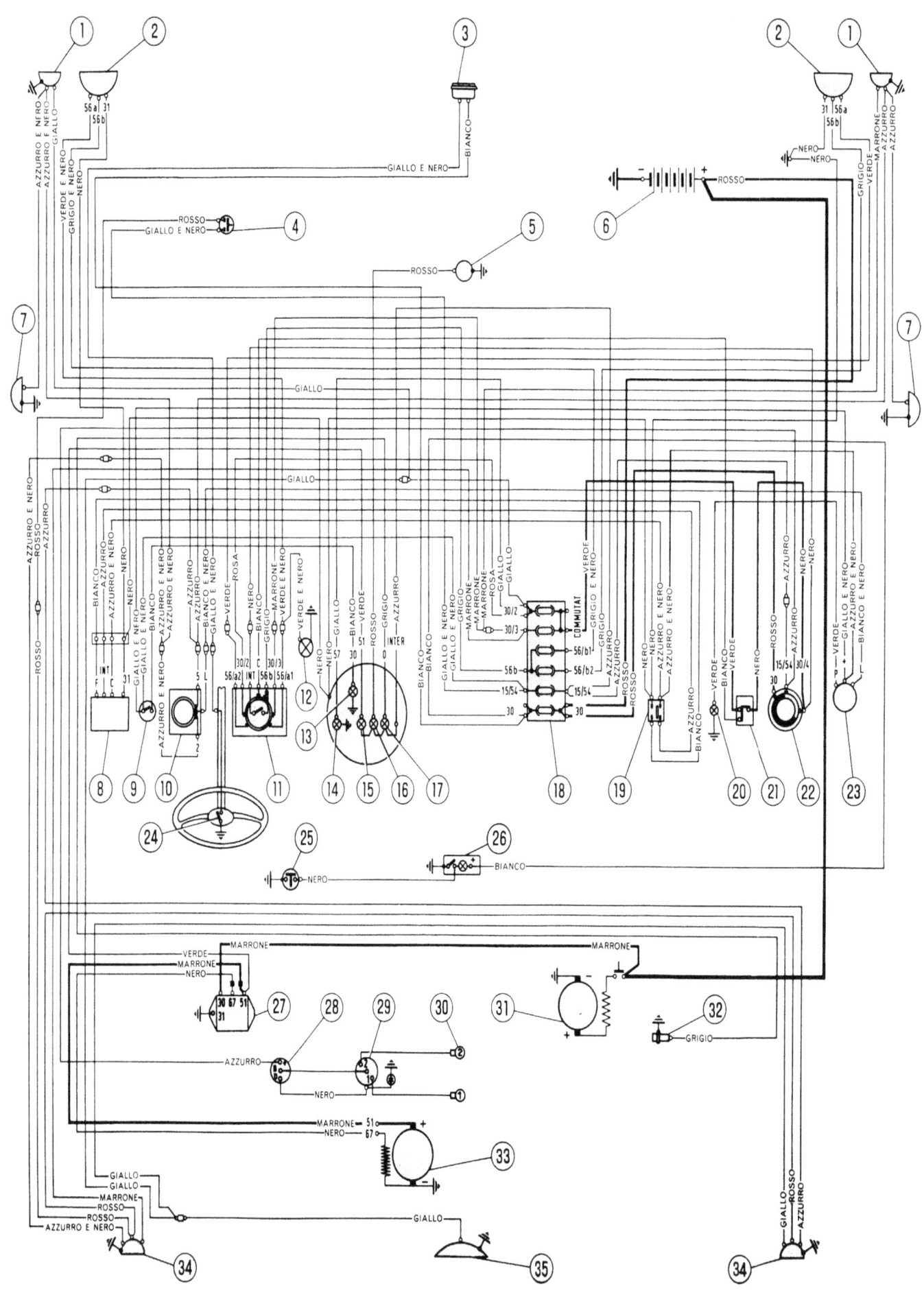

Fig. 114. - Wiring diagram - Model « 500 D ».

1. Front parking and direction indicator lamps.
2. Headlamps (high and low beams).
3. Horn.
4. Stop light pressure-operated switch.
5. Fuel reserve supply indicator sending unit.
6. Battery.
7. Side direction indicators.
8. Windshield wiper motor.
9. Panel light switch.
10. Direction indicator switch.
11. Outer lighting change-over switch.
12. High beam indicator.
13. Panel light.
14. Parking light indicator.
15. Generator charge indicator.
16. Fuel reserve supply indicator.
17. Low oil pressure indicator.
18. Fuses.
19. Windshield wiper switch.
20. Direction indicator pilot light.
21. Outer lighting master switch.
22. Key type switch for ignition and warning lights.
23. Flasher unit (direction indicators).
24. Horn button.
25. Jam-type switch on driver's side door pillar, for light 26.
26. Rear view mirror light.
27. Generator regulator.
28. Ignition coil.
29. Ignition distributor.
30. Spark plugs.
31. Starter motor.
32. Low oil pressure indicator sending unit.
33. Generator.
34. Rear parking, stop and direction indicator lamps.
35. Number plate lamp.

NOTE - Mark ▬ means that cable is provided with numbered strip or ferrule.

KEY TO CABLE COLORS

Azzurro = **Blue**	Giallo = **Yellow**	Marrone = **Brown**
Bianco = **White**	Grigio = **Grey**	Nero = **Black**
Rosa = **Pink**	Verde = **Green**	
Rosso = **Red**	INT-INTER = **Switch**	

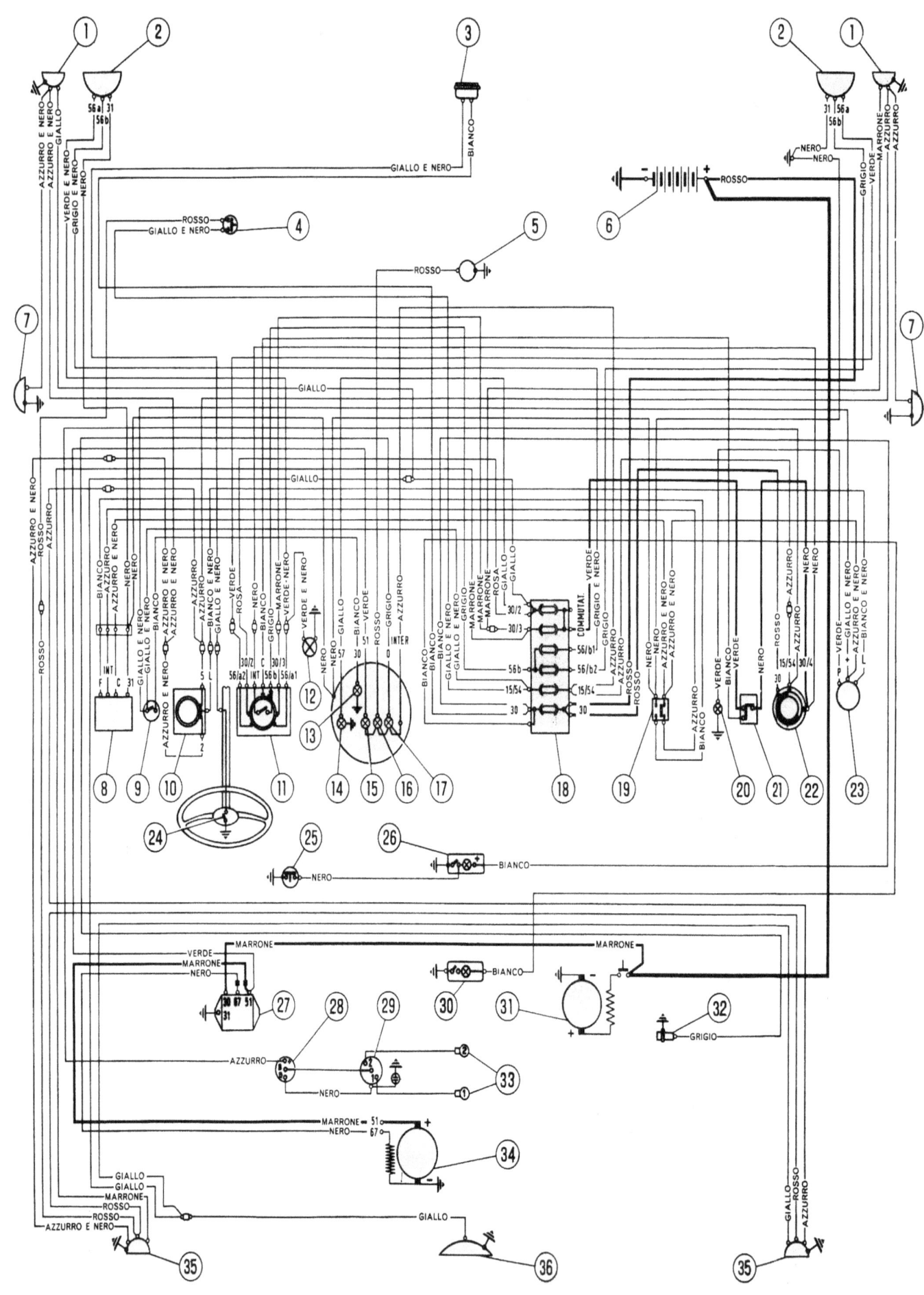

Fig. 115. - Wiring diagram - « 500 Station Wagon ».

1. Front parking and direction indicator lamps.
2. Headlamps (high and low beams).
3. Horn.
4. Stop light pressure-operated switch.
5. Fuel reserve supply indicator sending unit.
6. Battery.
7. Side direction indicators.
8. Windshield wiper motor.
9. Panel light switch.
10. Direction indicator switch.
11. Outer lighting change-over switch.
12. High beam indicator.
13. Panel light.
14. Parking light indicator.
15. Generator charge indicator.
16. Fuel reserve supply indicator.
17. Low oil pressure indicator.
18. Fuses.
19. Windshield wiper switch.
20. Direction indicator pilot light.
21. Outer lighting master switch.
22. Key type switch for ignition and warning lights.
23. Flasher unit (direction indicators).
24. Horn button.
25. Jam-type switch on driver's side door pillar, for light 26.
26. Rear view mirror light.
27. Generator regulator.
28. Ignition coil.
29. Ignition distributor.
30. Inner lamp (also illuminates engine compartment).
31. Starter motor.
32. Low oil pressure indicator sending unit.
33. Spark plugs.
34. Generator.
35. Rear parking, stop and direction indicator lamps.
36. Number plate lamp.

NOTE - Mark ▬ means that cable is provided with numbered strip or ferrule.

KEY TO CABLE COLORS

Azzurro = **Blue**	Giallo = **Yellow**	Marrone = **Brown**
Bianco = **White**	Grigio = **Grey**	Nero = **Black**
Rosa = **Pink**	Verde = **Green**	
Rosso = **Red**	INT-INTER = **Switch**	

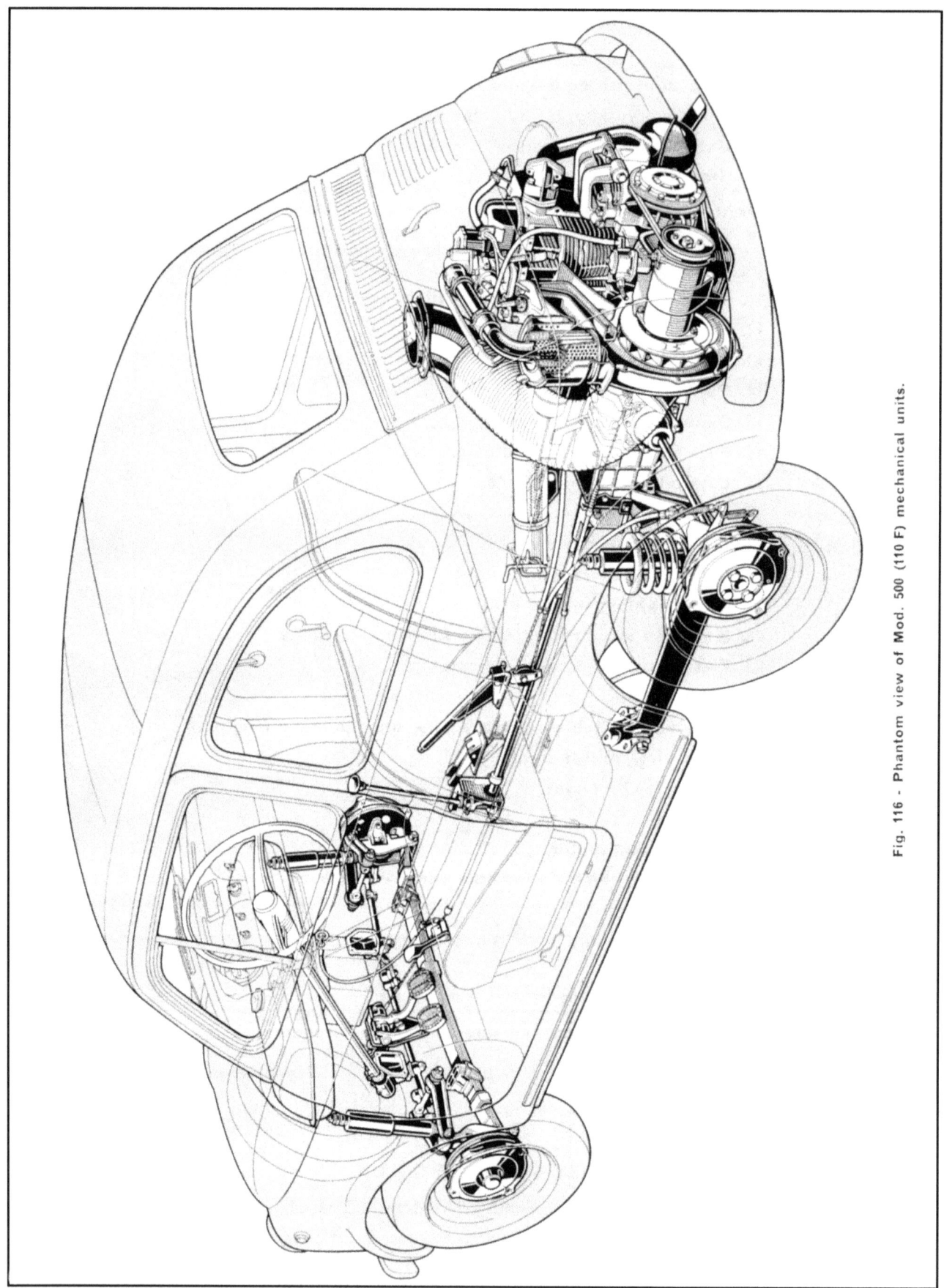

Fig. 116 - Phantom view of Mod. 500 (110 F) mechanical units.

500 SEDAN (Type 110 F)
500 STATION WAGON (from serial N° 141707)

DIFFERENCES FROM MODELS OF PREVIOUS CONSTRUCTION

Engine.

SEDAN

— Unit: varied type code (formerly 110 D.000, now 110 F.000).
— Recirculation device of blow-by gases.
— Heating system safety device.
— Cylinder head: reinforced at the mounting area of exhaust manifold and modified to suit the new safety device.
— Valve springs: two (one inner and one outer) for each valve.
— Cylinders: redesigned to suit the heater safety device.
— Flywheel: adapted for diaphragm spring clutch mounting.
— Starter ring gear: with different tooth pattern.
— Air cleaner container: of larger dimensions.
— Accelerator control: redesigned relay link.

STATION WAGON

— Recirculation device of blow-by gases.
— Heating system safety device.
— Cylinder head: modified to suit the new safety device.
— Cylinders: redesigned to suit the heater safety device.
— Flywheel: adapted for diaphragm spring clutch mounting.
— Starter ring gear: with different tooth pattern.

Chassis.
SEDAN AND STATION WAGON

— Clutch: diaphragm spring type (6.1" - 155 mm diam.).
— Clutch control: redesigned to incorporate thrust ball bearing.
— Differential, final drive, axle shafts: redesigned.
— Slip joints: redesigned those at wheel end.
— Rear control arms: redesigned.
— Rear springs: redesigned.
— Foot and manual accelerator control: redesigned.
— Fuel tank: new long shaped type with screw filler plug and breather valve.
— Front wheel cylinders: 7/8" diam. instead of 3/4" (Sedan only).

Electrical Equipment and Body.

SEDAN

— Starting motor: mounted at three points, different drive pinion tooth pattern.
— Front parking lamps: of new design.
— License plate lamps: of new design.
— Rear tail lamps: of new design.
— Headlamps: asymmetrical low beam type.
— Windshield wiper: modified wiper arms.
— Instrument cluster: of new design.
— Dashboard switches and indicators: rearranged.
— Doors: front hinged, with snap type handles and triple latch.
— Windshield: extended in height.
— Folding top: center catched.
— Air scoop for engine cooling: modified.
— Manual accelerator control: relocated.
— Sound deadening: improved between engine and passenger compartments.

STATION WAGON

— Starting motor: mounted at three points, different drive pinion tooth pattern.
— Front parking lamps: of new design.
— Headlamps: asymmetrical low beam type.
— Instrument cluster: of new design.
— Dashboard switches and indicators: rearranged.
— Folding top: center catched.
— Manual accelerator control: relocated.

500 SEDAN (110 F) - 500 STATION WAGON

GENERAL INFORMATION

	Sedan	Station Wagon
PERFORMANCES		
Maximum speeds at full load on level road, with surface in good condition, after run-in period (1,800 miles - 3,000 km):		
first gear, abt	14 mph (23 km/h)	14 mph (23 km/h)
second gear, abt	25 mph (40 km/h)	25 mph (40 km/h)
third gear, abt	40 mph (65 km/h)	40 mph (65 km/h)
fourth gear, over	59 mph (95 km/h)	59 mph (95 km/h)
reverse, abt	10 mph (17 km/h)	10 mph (17 km/h)
Maximum climbable gradients at full load with surface in good condition, after run-in period (1,800 miles - 3,000 km):		
first gear, abt	26 %	22 %
second gear, abt	13 %	11.5 %
third gear, abt	7 %	6 %
fourth gear, abt	3.5 %	3 %
reverse, abt	36 %	30 %
Weights		
Curb weight (with replenishments, spare wheel, tool kit and accessories)	1,146 lbs (520 kg)	1,235 lbs (560 kg)
Payload	4 people plus 88 lbs (40 kg)	4 people plus 88 lbs (40 kg) 1 person plus 550 lbs (250 kg) *
Weight at full load (four people plus 88 lbs - 40 kg)	1,852 lbs (840 kg)	1,940 lbs (880 kg)
Axle partition of weight (four people plus 88 lbs - 40 kg) front	816 lbs (370 kg)	705 lbs (320 kg)
rear	1,036 lbs (470 kg)	1,235 lbs (560 kg)

(*) Load uniformly distributed on the loading floor (rear seat back folded down).

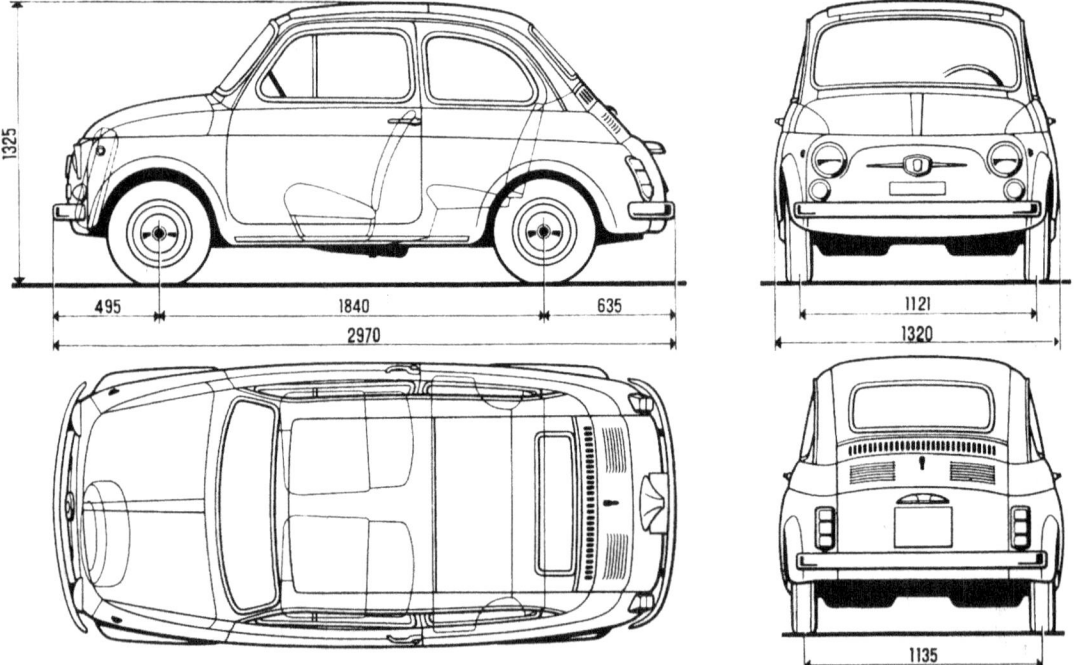

Fig. 117. - **Leading dimensions of 500 Sedan (in mm).**
The overall height applies to an unladen vehicle.

GENERAL INFORMATION

CAPACITIES

UNIT	Quantity				FILL-IN
	Imp. Units	U. S. Units	lt	kg	
Fuel tank.	4.84 gals	5.81 gals	22	—	Gasoline
Oil sump (¹)	2.20 qts	2.65 qts	2.5	2.25	FIAT oil (³)
Transmission and differential . . .	.97 qts	1.16 qts	1.1	1.00	FIAT W 90/M oil (SAE 90 EP)
Steering gear	.105 qts	.124 qts	0.12	0.11	
Hydraulic brake circuit	.194 qts	.232 qts	0.22	0.22	FIAT blue label brake fluid
Hydraulic shock absorbers: front, each . .	.112 qts	.137 qts	0.13	0.12	FIAT S.A.I. oil
rear, each . .	.096 qts	.117 qts	0.11	0.10	
Windshield washer bag	.88 qts	1.05 qts	1.00	—	Mixture of water and FIAT D.P./1 fluid (²)

(¹) Total capacity of oil sump, lines, oil filter and crankshaft: 2.38 G.B. qts - 2.86 U.S. qts (2.4 kg). The amount shown in the table is the requirement for periodical oil changes.
(²) In summer add 30 c.c. to each liter of water; in winter, for temperatures down to 14° F (—10° C) use a 50% solution of D.P./1 fluid. For temperatures below 14° F (—10° C) fill with D.P./1 fluid undiluted.
(³) Recommended oil grades:

OUTDOOR TEMPERATURE		FIAT Unigrade oil	FIAT Multigrade oil
		Detergent oils with low ash content, type MS, level MIL-L-2104 B (*)	
Below —15° C (5° F) minimum		VS 10 W (SAE 10 W)	—
Between —15° C (5° F) and 0° C (32° F), minimum		VS 20 W (SAE 20 W)	10 W - 30
Above 0° C (32° F), min.	Below 35° C (95° F), max	VS 30 (SAE 30)	20 W - 40
	Above 35° C (95° F), max	VS 40 (SAE 40)	

(*) **Warning:** do not top up with oils of different grade or make.

TIRE PRESSURES

	Front				Rear			
	Sedan		S. W.		Sedan		S. W.	
	psi	kg/cm²	psi	kg/cm²	psi	kg/cm²	psi	kg/cm²
Standard tires								
— Low load	18.5	1.3	17.1	1.2	22.8	1.6	27.0	1.9
— Full load transport. of passengers	18.5	1.3	17.1	1.2	27.0	1.9	29.9	2.1
transportation of goods .	—	—	17.1	1.2	—	—	34.1	2.4
Radial ply tires	15.6	1.1	—	—	22.8	1.6	—	—

Fig. 118.
500 Sedan, Sunroof.

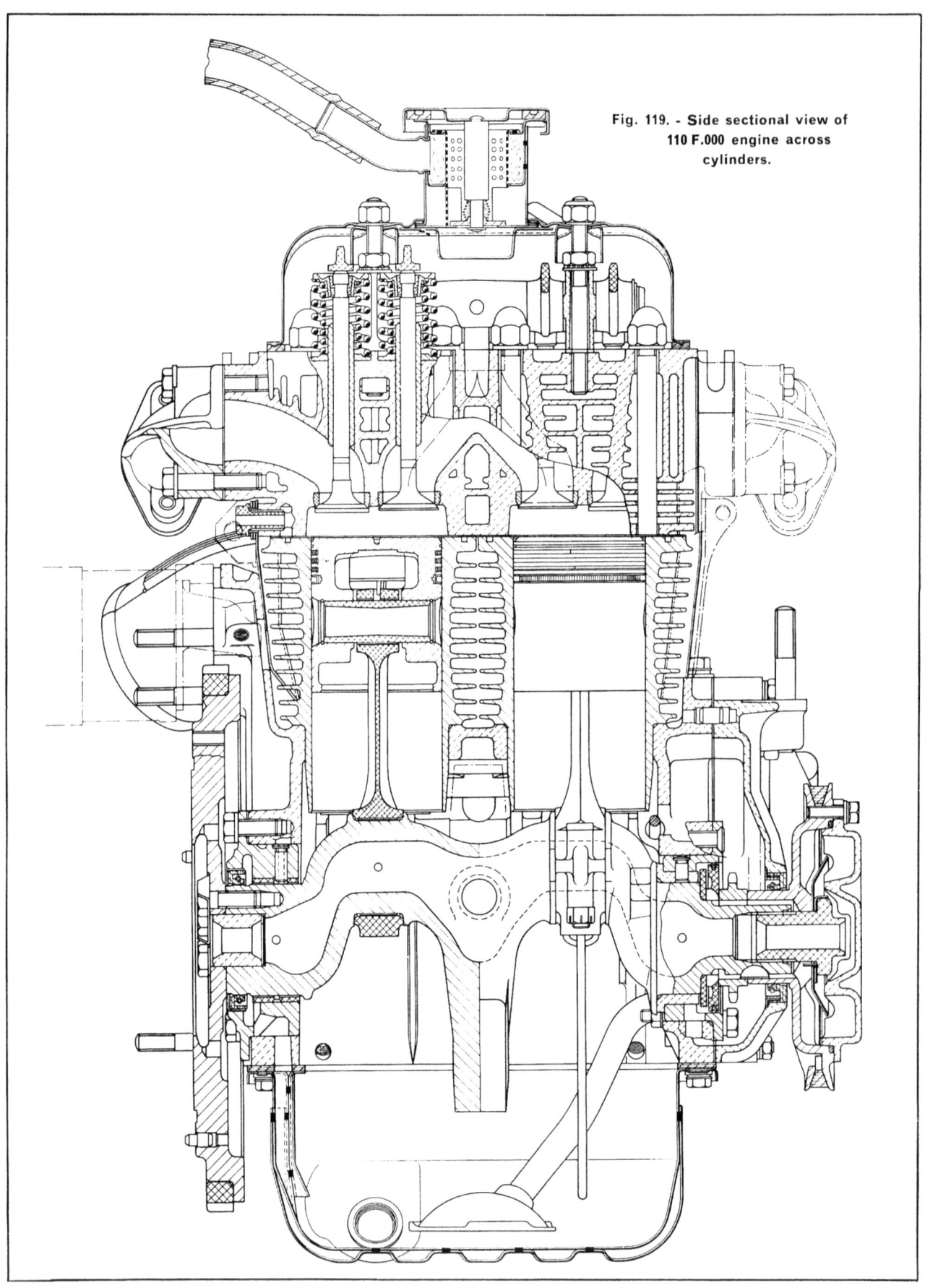

Fig. 119. - Side sectional view of 110 F.000 engine across cylinders.

SPECIFICATIONS AND SERVICE PROCEDURES

Engine

MAIN SPECIFICATIONS OF ENGINE

	Sedan Type 110 F	Station Wagon Type 120
Engine type	110 F.000	120.000
Cycle and strokes	Otto, four-stroke	Otto, four-stroke
No. of cylinders, in line	two, vertical	two, horizontal
Bore	2.654" (67.4 mm)	2.654" (67.4 mm)
Stroke	2.755" (70 mm)	2.755" (70 mm)
Displacement	30.48 cu.in (499.5 cc)	30.48 cu.in (499.5 cc)
Compression ratio	7.1	7.1
Maximum horsepower (DIN)	18	17.5
at	4,600 rpm	4,600 rpm
Maximum horsepower (SAE)	22	21.5
at	4,600 rpm	4,600 rpm
Maximum torque (DIN)	22.4 ft.lbs (310 kgcm)	21.7 ft.lbs (300 kgcm)
at	3,000 rpm	3,000 rpm
Maximum torque (SAE)	26.0 ft.lbs (360 kgcm)	26.0 ft.lbs (360 kgcm)
at	3,500 rpm	3,200 rpm
Taxable horsepower (Italy)	6	6
Timing	valves-in-head	valves-in-head

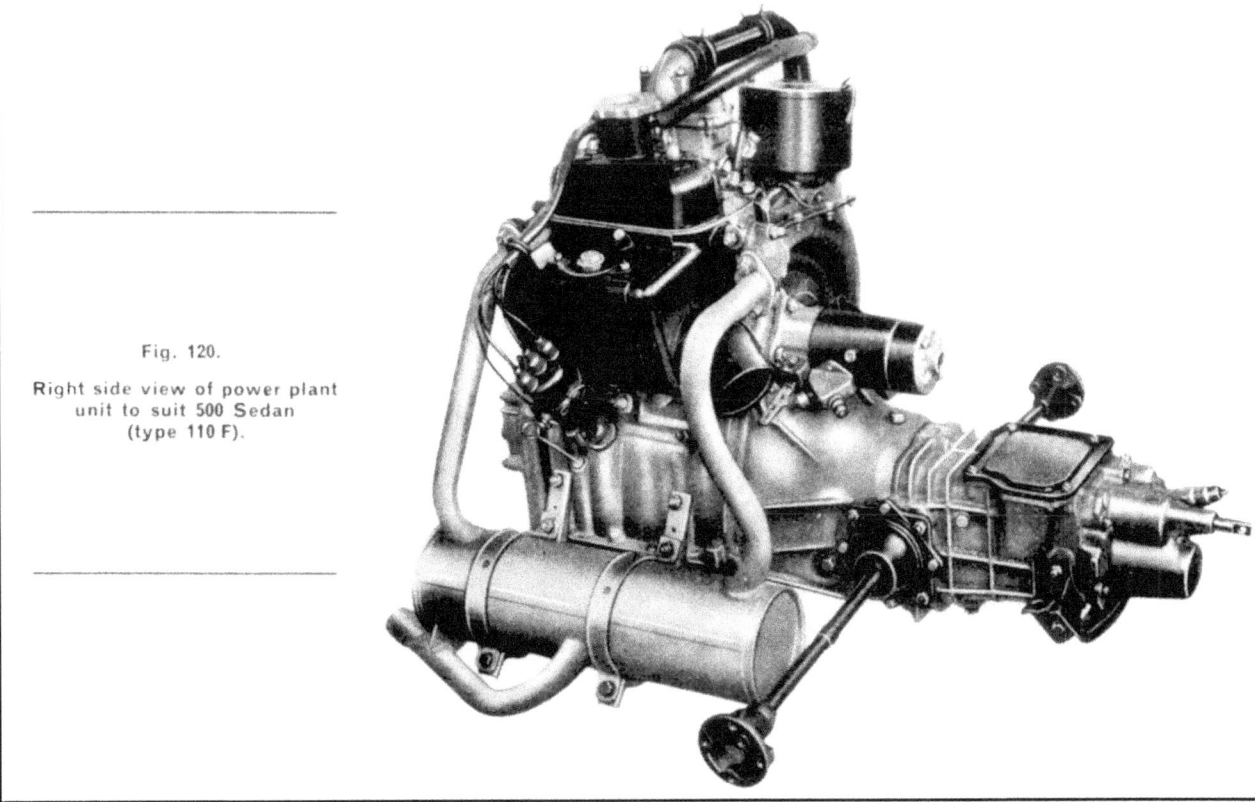

Fig. 120.

Right side view of power plant unit to suit 500 Sedan (type 110 F).

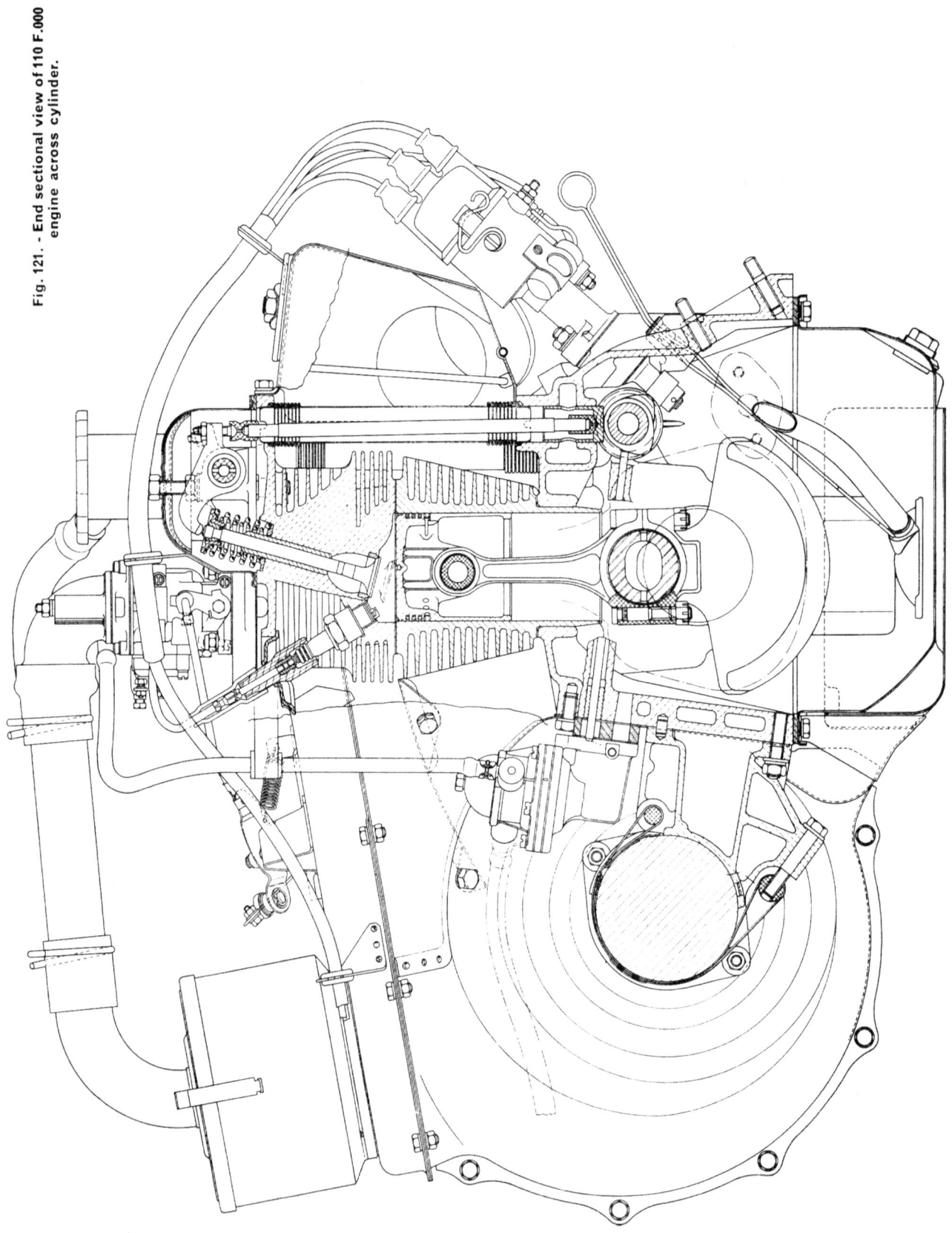

Fig. 121. - End sectional view of 110 F.000 engine across cylinder.

SERVICE PROCEDURES: ENGINE

110 F.000 ENGINE VALVE SPRINGS

Spring Type	Part. N°	Working Turns	Total Turns	Inside Diameter	Wire Diameter	A	B		C		Minimum Load Referred to B
Inner Spring	4015443	7	8.5	.5984" (15.2 mm)	.1024" (2.6 mm)	1.5827" (40.2 mm)	1.3976" (35.5 mm)	13.4 lbs (6.1 kg)	1.0669" (27.1 mm)	37.5 lbs (17 kg)	11 lbs (5 kg)
Outer Spring	4143378	5	6.5	.9055" (23 mm)	.1457" (3.7 mm)	1.8465" (46.9 mm)	1.5157" (38.5 mm)	42.1 lbs (19.1 kg)	1.1850" (30.1 mm)	84.2 lbs (38.2 kg)	33.1 lbs (15 kg)

A = Free height.   B - C = Checking height and load.

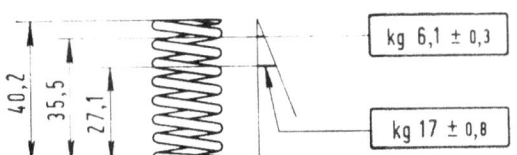

Fig. 122. - Main checking data of inner valve spring for engine 110 F.000.

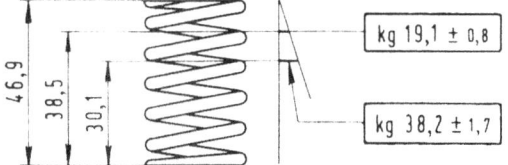

Fig. 123. - Main checking data of outer valve spring for engine 110 F.000.

Fig. 124. - Front view of Sedan engine compartment.

NOTE - Arrow points to the hollow screw for exhaust of gases to the atmosphere in case of accidental failure of the head gasket.

BLOW-BY GASES RECIRCULATION DEVICE

Engine 110 F.000

All the blow-by gases and oil vapours forming in the engine are conveyed to the head cover (1, fig. 125) recess.

Hence they are ported into the pipe (5) via the breather valve (2), rigidly tied to the oil filler cap (3), and the strainer (4) in the filler neck.

Gases and oil vapours from the pipe (5) are then sucked back into the duct (9) connecting the air cleaner (6) to the carburetor (7).

So they are not let out to the atmosphere.

NOTE - The oil vapour strainer (4, fig. 125) and the flame trap (8) can be easily removed from their seats for cleaning or replacement.

Engine 120.000

Starting from engine N° 288156 oil vapours, instead of being exhausted to the atmosphere, have been conveyed to the air cleaner; hence they are sucked back into combustion chambers.

In order to avoid that an excessive amount of oil vapours may be taken along with vapours, with consequent increase in oil consumption, a diaphragm has been fitted in the duct in front of the breather valve (2); this diaphragm consists of a filter gauze (11) and a movable partition (10).

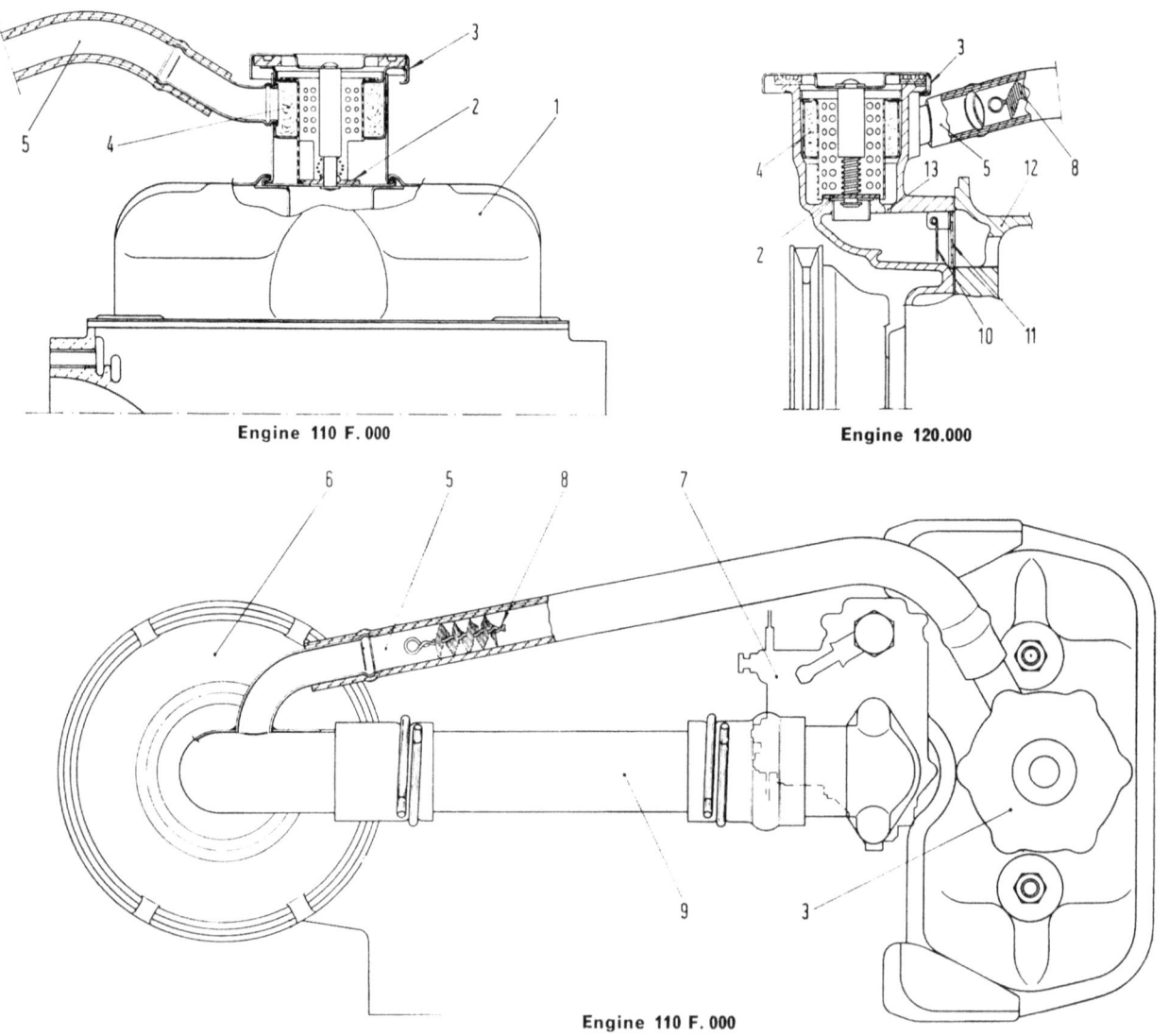

Fig. 125. - Diagram of blow-by gases recirculation device.

1. Head cover - 2. Blow-by gases and oil vapours breather valve - 3. Oil filler cap - 4. Strainer - 5. Pipe - 6. Air cleaner - 7. Carburetor - 8. Flame trap - 9. Air suction pipe, air cleaner to carburetor - 10. Movable partition - 11. Filter gauze - 12. Crankcase - 13. Exhaust duct.

HEATING SYSTEM SAFETY DEVICE

Engines 110 F.000 and 120.000

In order to avoid that engine gases may leak into the heating system as a result of the accidental failure of the head gasket, a safety device has been designed for exhaust of these gases to the atmosphere.

The safety device consists of:
- a square section circular seat (1, fig. 126) formed in the upper face of the cylinder;
- a duct in the cylinder head;
- a pierced screw (3) for each cylinder.

Engine gases are exhausted to the atmosphere from the circular seat in cylinder past the duct (2) and the pierced screw (3).

The screw (3) is also to secure the conveyor.

Fig. 126. - Diagram of the heating system safety device (Sedan and Station Wagon).

1. Circular seat in cylinders - 2. Head ducts - 3. Pierced screws.

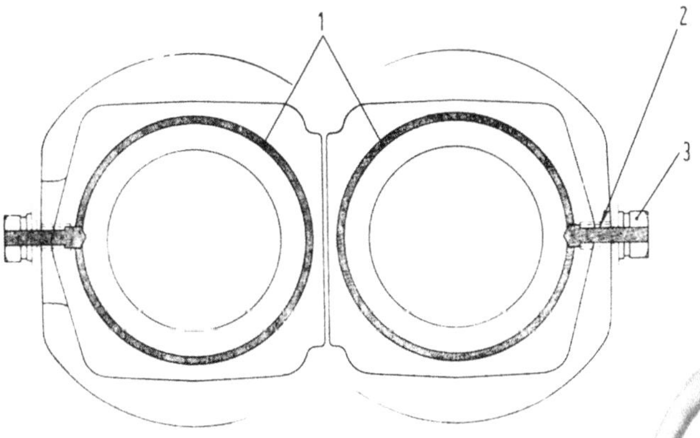

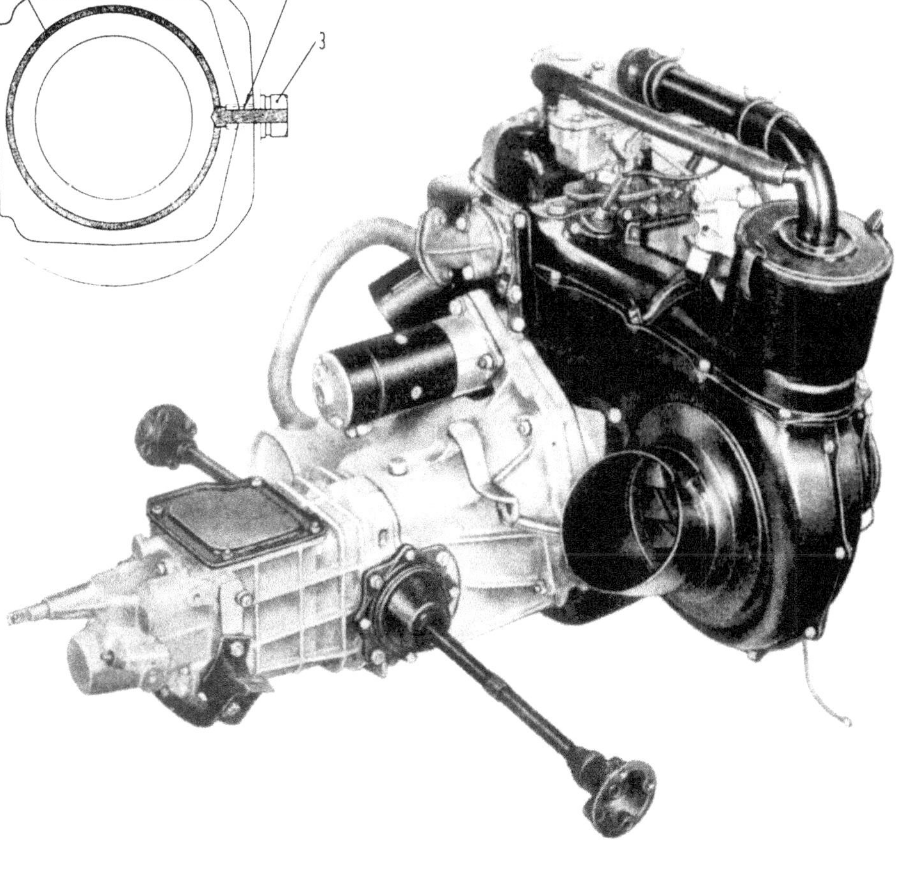

Fig. 127.

Left side view of the power plant to suit 500 Sedan.

Fuel System

AIR CLEANER

Engine 110 F.000

To take down the air cleaner, disengage both spring hooks (2, fig. 128) and lift out the cover (4) by turning it inward with the pipe (5).

The replacement of the filter element should be made every 6,000 miles (10,000 km) or at shorter intervals if it turns out to be clogged from driving on dusty roads.

Fig. 129. - Cut-away view of the engine incorporating the blower.

Fig. 128. - Removing the air cleaner.

1. Filter housing - 2. Spring hooks - 3. Filter element - 4. Cover - 5. Air suction pipe, hoses and clamps - 6. Recirculation pipe for blow-by gases and oil vapours.

FUEL TANK

Sedan and Station Wagon.

The fuel tank is arranged in the front compartment (fig. 130).

It is secured to the dash by means of clamping bands.

To remove the fuel tank from the front compartment just back out both screws which secure the front ends of the clamping bands to the dash; screws are evidenced by arrows in fig. 130.

Fuel tank capacity: 4.84 Imp. gals - 5.81 U.S. gals (22 lt). The fuel recommended is: regular gasoline.

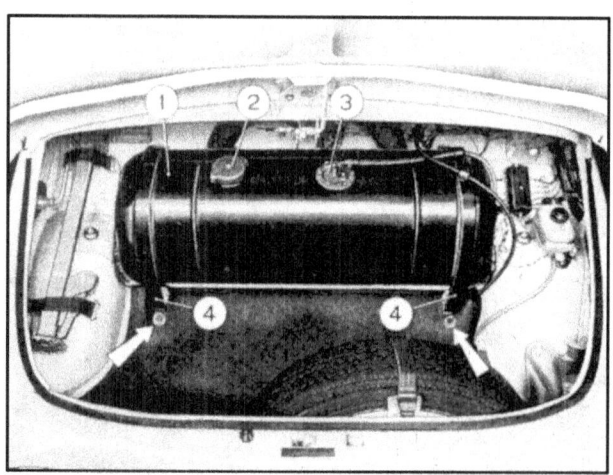

Fig. 130. - Location of the fuel tank in Sedan front compartment.

1. Fuel tank - 2. Filler cap with vent valve - 3. Fuel suction pipe and reserve supply indicator tank unit - 4. Tank clamping bands.

NOTE - Arrows point to fuel tank clamping band screws.

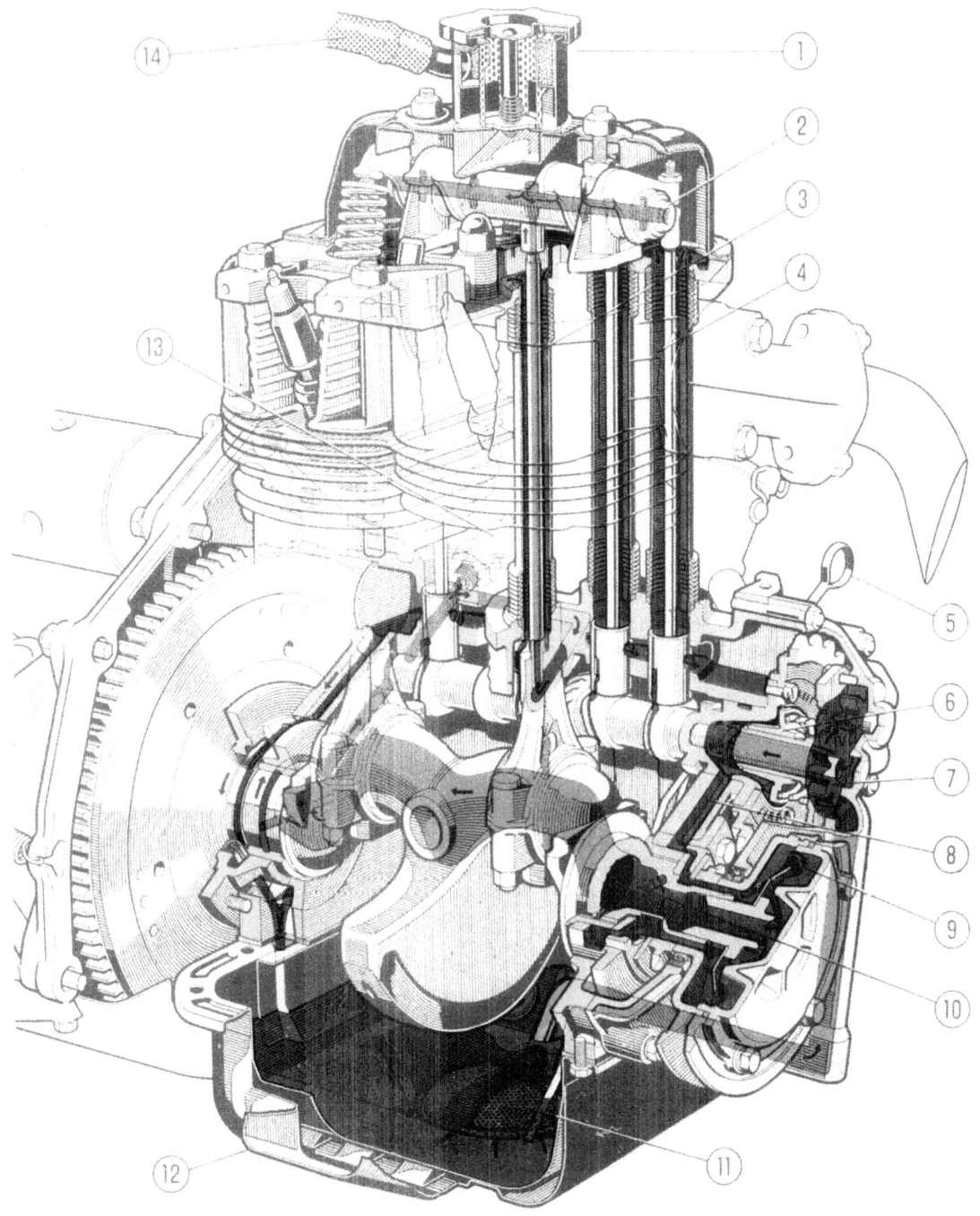

Fig. 131. - 110 F.000 engine lubrication diagram.

1. Oil filler with vent valve and strainer for blow-by gases and oil vapours - 2. Rocker shaft - 3. Line, oil delivery to rocker shaft - 4. Ducts, cylinder head oil drain - 5. Level indicator rod - 6. Oil pressure relief valve - 7. Gear pump - 8. Oil duct to centrifugal filter - 9. Centrifugal oil filter - 10. Crankshaft with central oil gallery - 11. Oil pump suction screen filter - 12. Sump cooling air conveyor - 13. Low oil pressure indicator sending unit - 14. Pipe to air cleaner for recirculation of blow-by gases and oil vapours in engine.

Clutch

Sedan and Station Wagon.

Single plate, dry, with diaphragm pressure spring. This type of clutch differs from the conventional clutch design because the pressure coil springs and all throwout mechanism components (release levers, eyebolts, struts, etc.) have been replaced by a single diaphragm spring.

The new system entails the following advantages:

— the clutch is not apt to slip, even though driven plate linings are worn extensively, thanks to the special shape and placement of the diaphragm spring, which keeps the force on pressure plate unaltered;

— the load on clutch pedal will be practically the same, whereas in the conventional coil spring clutch the load increases in proportion with the pedal travel.

INSPECTION

Position the clutch cover assembly on a base plate in the place of the flywheel, with a lining .311″ (7.9 mm) thick between cover and plate (corresponding to the thickness of the driven plate). Work the clutch mechanism through four full throwout strokes by applying a load of some 181 lbs (82 kg) on release flange, as shown by arrow **F** (fig. 133).

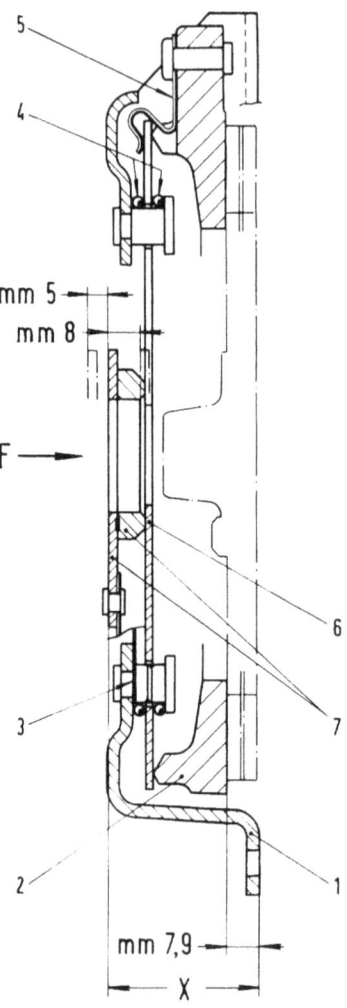

Fig. 133. - Clutch cover assembly inspection diagram.

1. Clutch cover - 2. Pressure plate - 3. Clutch release flange plate - 4. Diaphragm spring rings - 5. Diaphragm spring retainer plate - 6. Diaphragm spring - 7. Clutch release flange.

X   = 1.463″ ± .043″ (37.15 ± 1.1 mm).
F   = direction of clutch release flange movement.
mm 8 = .315″ = release travel.
mm 5 = .197″ = maximum allowance for driven plate lining wear.
  mm 7,9 = .311″.

Fig. 132. - Using tool **A. 70085** to center the driven plate on engine **110 F.000**.

1. Clutch assembly - 2. Tool A. 70085 - 3. Flywheel.

In this condition, check that:

— with a withdrawal travel of .315″ (8 mm) (fig. 133), the pressure plate is .071″ (1.8 mm) out;

— the distance **X** (fig. 133) is 1.463″ ± .043″ (37.15 ± 1.1 mm).

NOTE - Should results be other than above specified, replace the clutch cover assembly by a new one.

INSTALLING CLUTCH ON FLYWHEEL

Before installing the clutch, check the condition of the clutch shaft pilot bushing.

Lubricate the bushing with KG 15 grease.

On installation, position the driven plate with the raised path of hub toward the transmission.

Also, lubricate the contact faces of the driven plate with clutch shaft, on installation.

Prior to tightening clutch mounting screws on flywheel, center the driven plate by means of tool **A. 70085** (2, fig. 132). Clutch mounting screw torque: 5.8 to 7.2 ft.lbs (0.8 to 1 kgm).

NOTE - While handling the clutch for service or carriage, avoid grasping at the release flange, which might be damaged.

ADJUSTING PEDAL TRAVEL

The free travel of clutch pedal is 19/32" to 1 3/16" (15 to 20 mm), corresponding to a clearance of .059" (1.5 mm) (fig. 135) between the throwout sleeve and ring.

Should pedal free travel be less than specified as a result of the wear of the driven plate, restore the original

Fig. 134. - Clutch throwout mechanism to suit 500 Sedan.

1. Clutch throwout yoke - 2. Yoke return spring - 3. Rod nut and counternut - 4. Adjustable rod - 5. Clutch throwout cable.

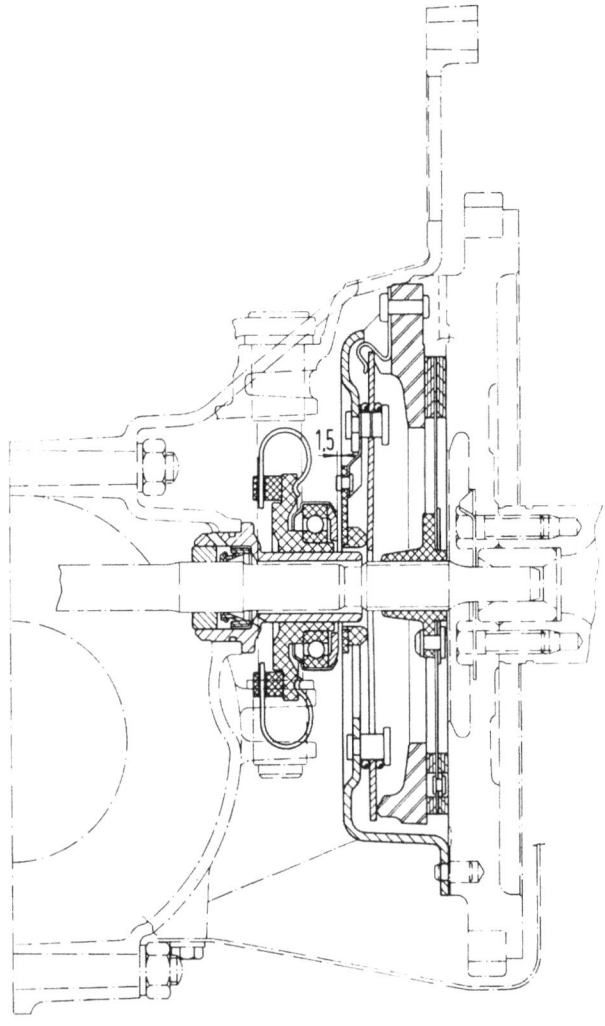

Fig. 135. - Side sectional view of clutch and throwout mechanism (Sedan).

Value .059" (1.5 mm) refers to the clearance to be obtained through the adjustment of clutch throwout yoke rod (4, fig. 134).

operating conditions (.059" - 1.5 mm clearance) by working on the adjustable rod (4, fig. 134) of throwout yoke.

WARNING

When removing the transmission, avoid resting the clutch shaft against the clutch release flange, lest the flange supporting plates may be cocked.

The clutch assembly to suit the Station Wagon differs from the Sedan clutch design outlined above as far as the yoke return spring is concerned; the clutch shaft is fitted with one bushing.

CLUTCH SPECIFICATIONS

Type	single plate, dry
Throwout mechanism	diaphragm spring
Driven plate	with friction linings
Lining O.D.	6.102" (155 mm)
Lining I.D.	4.488" (114 mm)
Runout of driven plate linings	.0098" to .0157" (0.25 to 0.40 mm)
Clutch pedal free travel, corresponding to a clearance of .059" (1.5 mm) between friction ring and throwout sleeve	19/32" to 1 3/16" (15 to 20 mm)
Clutch release flange travel, corresponding to a pressure plate distance of .071" (1.8 mm)	.315" (8 mm)

CLUTCH TIGHTENING REFERENCE

ITEM	Part No.	Thread Diam. and Pitch	Material	Recommended Torque
Clutch mounting screws	1/38243/21	M 6 x 1	R 80 Znt	5.8 to 7.2 ft.lbs (0.8 to 1 kgm)

Transmission - Differential

Sedan and Station Wagon.

The design modifications which this assembly has undergone are clearly shown in figures 136 and 137.

The transmission and differential assembly to suit the Station Wagon differs from the Sedan one as far as the transmission-to-engine mounting plate and the bell housing are concerned.

NOTE - The clutch shaft and three countershaft bushings, too, have been modified.

Fig. 136. - Modified items in transmission-differential assembly.

1. Reverse shifter shaft - **2.** Third and fourth shifter shaft - **3.** First and second shifter shaft - **4.** Countershaft-pinion (and ring gear) - **5-7.** Transmission-differential case - **6.** Housing - **8.** Clutch shaft.

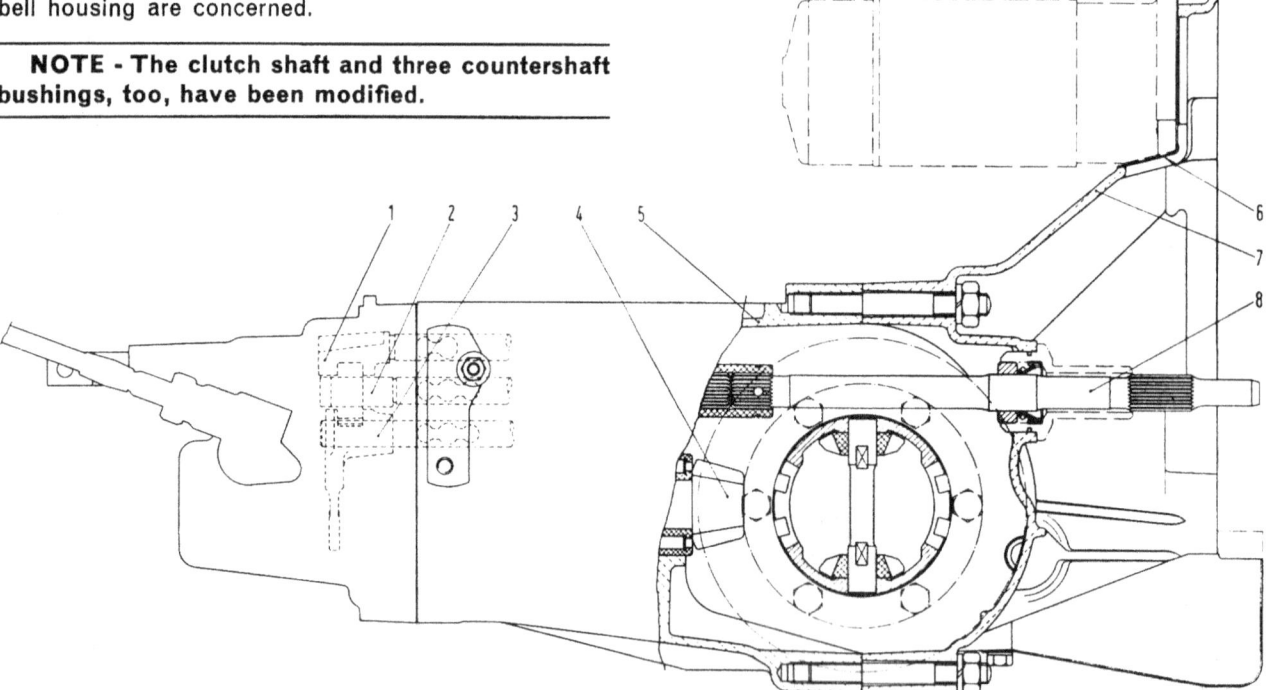

SERVICE PROCEDURES: SUSPENSION AND WHEELS

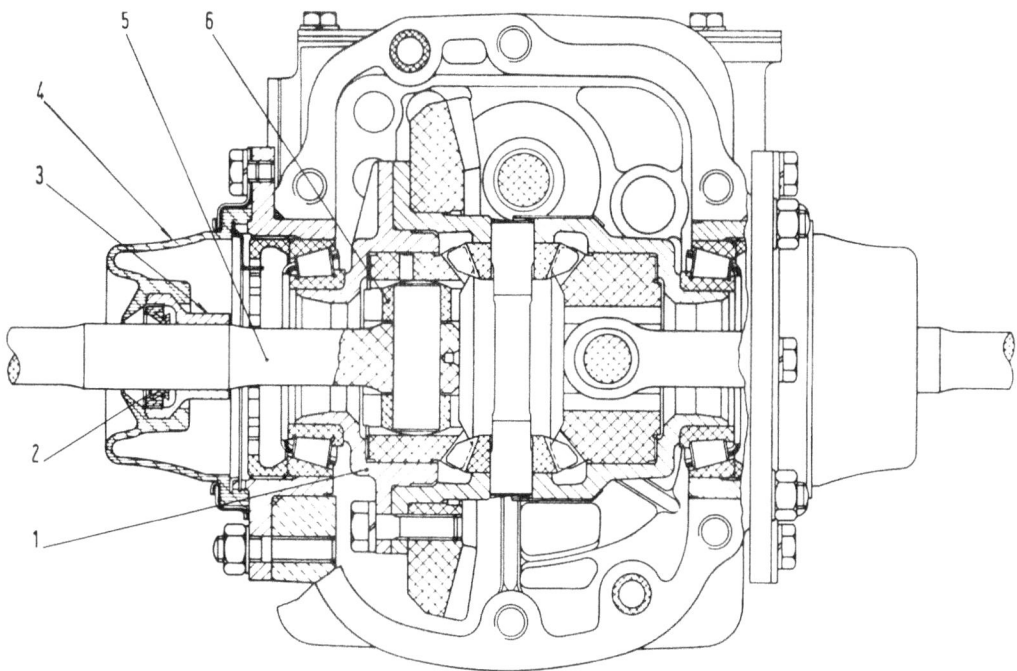

Fig. 137 - End sectional view of transmission - differential assembly.

The items having undergone design modifications, besides those shown in fig. 136, are the following: **1. Differential case and final drive gears - 2. Seal - 3. Bushing - 4. Oil boot - 5. Axle shaft - 6. Joint casing.**

Suspensions and Wheels

Fig. 138. - Rear suspension assembly in place on vehicle (Sedan).

Fig. 139. - Left side rear suspension and wheel assembly (Sedan).

Sedan and Station Wagon.

The modifications involving the wheel side flexible joint and the rear control arm are evidenced in figures 138, 139 and 140. The specifications of the new design rear coil spring are tabulated in the adjacent column.

COIL SPRING SPECIFICATIONS

	in	mm
Sedan		
Free height	8.62	219
Height under a load of 904±44 lbs (410 ± 20 kg)	5.83	148
Height under a load of 1,268 ± 64 lbs (575 ± 29 kg)	4.72	120
Solid height	3.66	93
Deflection rate	.3034/100 lbs	17/100 kg
Station Wagon		
Free height	8.66	220
Height under a load of 1,102 ± 55 lbs (500 ± 25 kg)	6.30	160
Height under a load of 1,631 ± 82 lbs (740 ± 37 kg)	5.20	132
Solid height	4.09	104
Deflection rate	.2132/100 lbs	12/100 kg

NOTE - Wheel alignment should be checked in the following conditions:

— Tires at the correct inflation pressure (normal load).
— Steering wheel and road wheels in the straight ahead position.
— Car in running order with a load corresponding to 4 persons (617 lbs - 280 kg).

Wheel alignment data are as follows:

Front suspension

— Camber . . . . $1° ± 20'$
   Measured at wheel rim . . . . .20'' to .24'' (5 to 6 mm)
— Caster . . . . $9° ± 1°$
— Toe-in { Sedan . . . . 0 to .07'' (0 to 2 mm)
           Station Wagon . . . . . . 0 to .04'' (0 to 1 mm)

Rear suspension

— Camber { Sedan . . . . $0° 25' ± 30'$
           Station Wagon . . . . . $1° 40' ± 30'$
— Toe-in . . . . 0 to .16'' (0 to 4 mm)

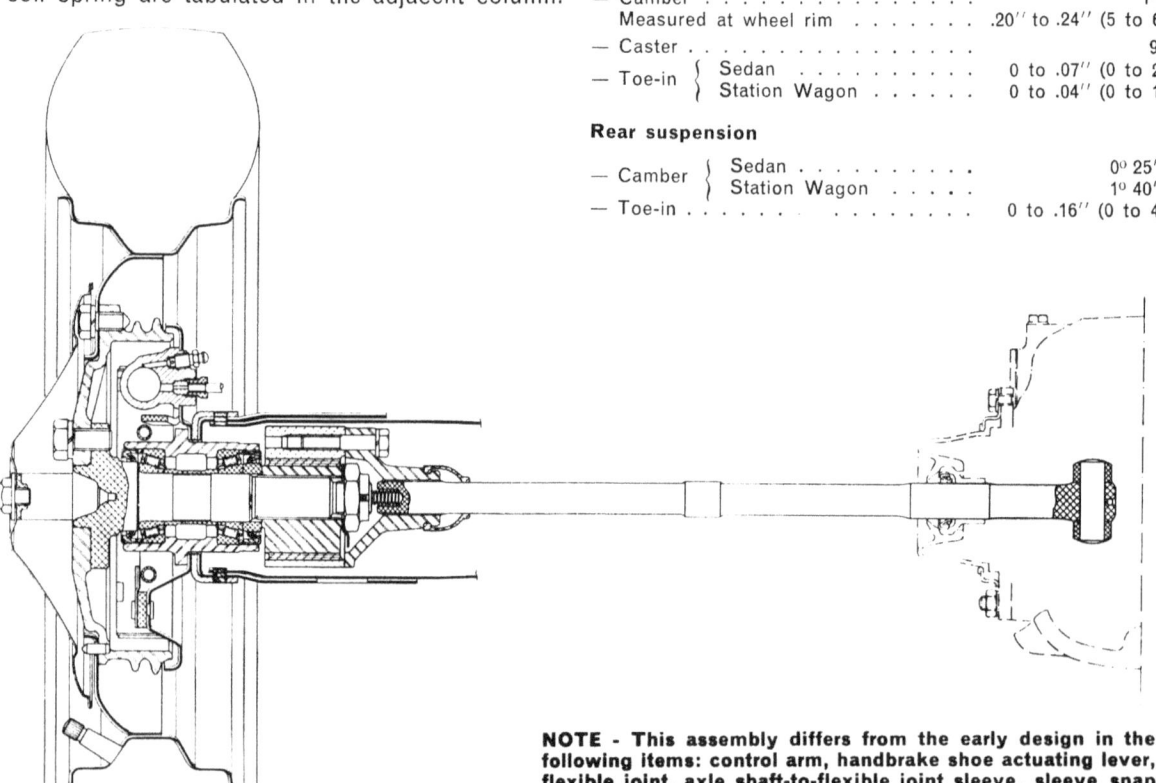

NOTE - This assembly differs from the early design in the following items: control arm, handbrake shoe actuating lever, flexible joint, axle shaft-to-flexible joint sleeve, sleeve snap ring, axle shaft and joint casing.

Fig. 140. - Sectional view of right side rear wheel and axle shaft (Sedan).

Electric System

HEADLIGHTS

Sedan and Station Wagon.

Headlights are of asymmetrical low beam type.
Headlights should be focussed in a **no-load** condition, as follows.

Check that tires are inflated with the recommended pressure (see chart on page 377).

Locate the car on a level floor, 16′ 5″ (5 m) apart from an opaque, white screen vertically in the shade and make sure that the car centerline it at right angle to the screen face.

Jounce the car both sides to set suspensions.

Draw two vertical lines a-a on the screen (fig.141). These lines should be equally spaced from the perpendicular to the car centerline and $32\,^{11}/_{16}$″ (830 mm) apart (A), which distance corresponds to the headlight center-to-center distance.

Draw a horizontal line b-b on the screen at the height from ground specified in the aiming chart on foot of this page.

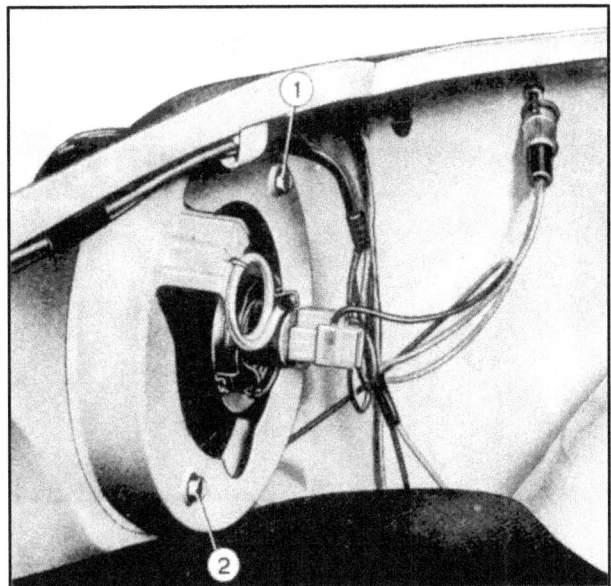

Fig. 142. - Aiming asymmetrical low beam headlights.
1. Screw for vertical beam adjustment - 2. Screw for horizontal beam adjustment.

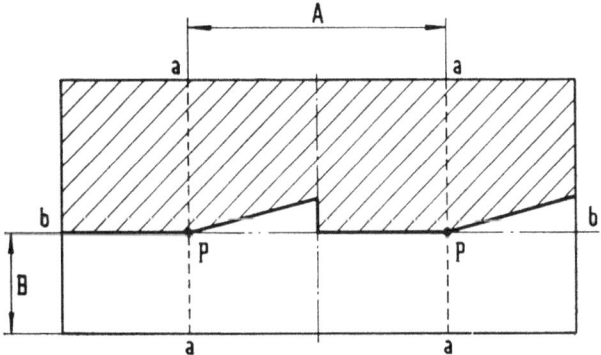

Fig. 141. - Headlight aiming screen.

To aim headlights, switch on the low beam and work on the screw (1, fig.142) for vertical adjustments, and on the screw (2) for horizontal adjustments, until the following conditions are obtained:

— the horizontal separation line between the unlit and lit areas should be on line b-b (fig.141);

— the upward slanting (some 15º) separation lines should start from or just outside the meeting points **P** of vertical lines a-a with the horizontal line b-b (fig.141).

An outward shift of the meeting point **P** to the maximum extent of 1º 30′ ($= 5\,^{1}/_{8}$″ - 130 mm) is permissible.

HEADLIGHT AIMING CHART (FIG. 141)

Type of Vehicle	A	B		NOTE
		New Vehicle	Settled Vehicle	
« Sedan »	$32\,^{11}/_{16}$″ (830 mm)	C minus $1\,^{9}/_{16}$″ (40 mm)	C minus $1\,^{3}/_{8}$″ (35 mm)	A $10\,^{1}/_{4}$ (260 mm) increase in distance A specification is permissible.
« Station Wagon » . .	$32\,^{11}/_{16}$″ (830 mm)	C minus $2\,^{15}/_{16}$″ (75 mm)	C minus $1\,^{9}/_{16}$″ (40 mm)	

A = Headlight center-to-center distance - B = C minus figure shown in chart - C = Ground clearance of headlight center.

NOTE - A vehicle is settled in practice when it has run the mileage specified for the first free service.

500 SEDAN (110 F) - 500 STATION WAGON

Fig. 143. - Instruments and controls (500 Sedan).

1. Change-over switch for outer lighting and light flashes - 2. Directional signal switch - 3. Directional signal indicator - 4. Speedometer-odometer and indicators for parking lights, no-charge, fuel reserve supply, low oil pressure - 5. High beam indicator - 6. Instrument cluster light switch - 7. Ash receiver - 8. Windshield wiper switch - 9. Lock switch for ignition, also energizing starting and warning lights circuits - 10. Outer lighting master switch - 11. Manual accelerator control - 12. Windshield washer pump control - 13. Front compartment release handle.

NOTE - To avoid odometer meddling, a brass seal is applied to one of two instrument frame-to-surround screws on the rear side of the instrument cluster (4, fig. 143).

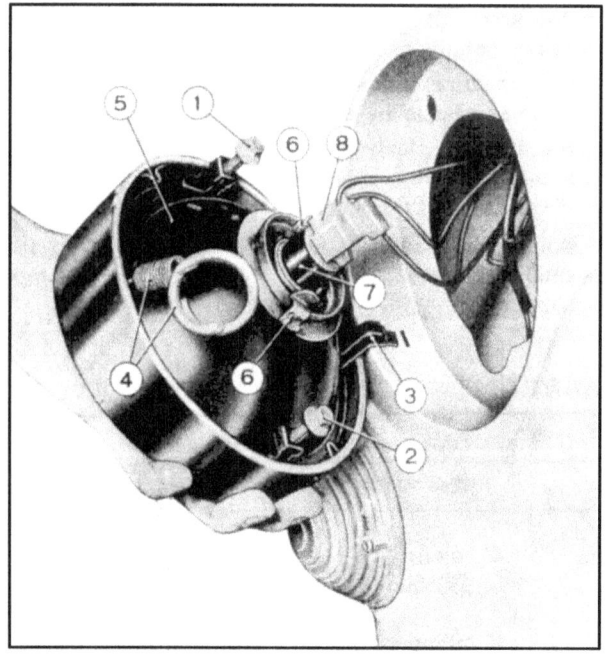

Fig. 144. - Headlamp removal.

1. Screw for vertical beam adjustment - 2. Screw for horizontal beam adjustment - 3. Headlamp locating hook - 4. Headlamp retaining ring and spring - 5. Lamp unit - 6. Bulb spring retainers - 7. Bulb - 8. Junction block.

Fig. 145. - Sedan wiring diagram.

1. Front parking and directional signal lights - 2. High and low beam headlights - 3. Side directional signal lights - 4. Fuses - 5. Horn - 6. Battery - 7. Stop light pressure-operated switch - 8. Fuel reserve supply indicator sending unit - 9. Directional signal flasher unit - 10. Wiper motor - 11. Courtesy light jam switch on driver's side door pillar - 12. Directional signal switch - 13. Horn button - 14. Change-over switch for outer lighting and light flashes - 15. Directional signal indicator - 16. Instrument cluster light - 17. Parking light indicator - 18. No-charge indicator - 19. Fuel reserve supply indicator - 20. Low oil pressure indicator - 21. High beam indicator - 22. Instrument cluster light switch - 23. Map light in rear view mirror - 24. Outer lighting master switch - 25. Key type ignition switch, also energizing starting and warning lights circuits - 26. Windshield wiper switch - 27. Generator regulator - 28. Generator - 29. Starting motor - 30. Ignition coil - 31. Spark plugs - 32. Ignition distributor - 33. Low oil pressure indicator sending unit - 34. Rear tail, stop and directional signal lights - 35. License plate light.

Note. - The mark ■ means that the cable is fitted with numbered strip or ferrule.

CABLE COLOUR CODE

Azzurro = **Blue**	Grigio = **Grey**	Rosa = **Pink**
Bianco = **White**	Marrone = **Brown**	Rosso = **Red**
Giallo = **Yellow**	Nero = **Black**	Verde = **Green**
Azzurro-Nero = **Black and blue**		
Bianco-Nero = **Black and white**		
Giallo-Nero = **Black and yellow**		
Grigio-Nero = **Black and grey**		
Verde-Nero = **Black and green**		
Commut. - INT. = **Switch**		

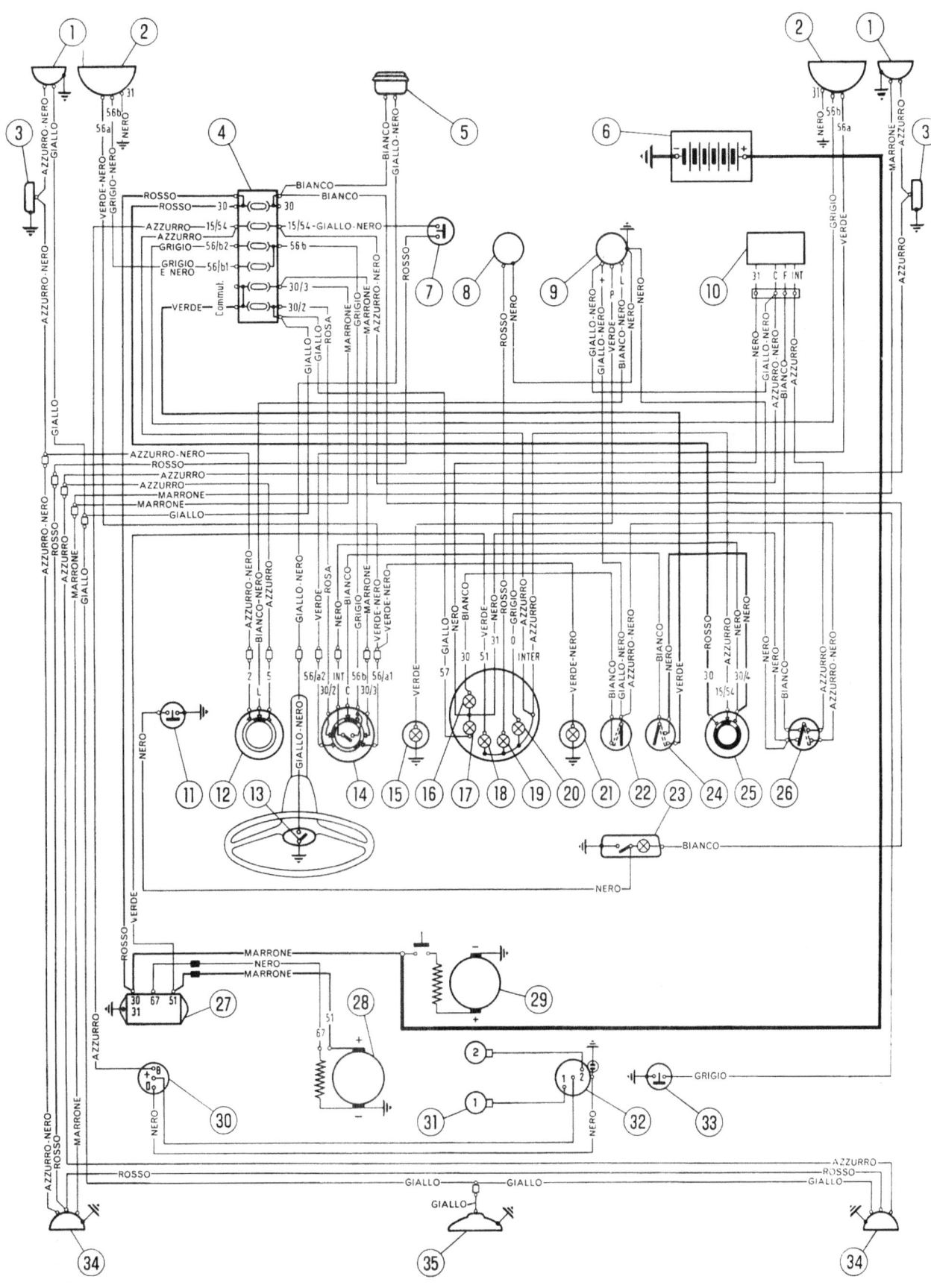

Fig. 145. - **Sedan wiring diagram.**

NOTE - The wiring diagram covering the 500 Station Wagon differs for the presence of an additional inner lamp at rear being wired with the fuse No. 30.

Body

The main modifications introduced to the body structure of 500 Sedan are evidenced in figures 146, 147, 148 and 149.

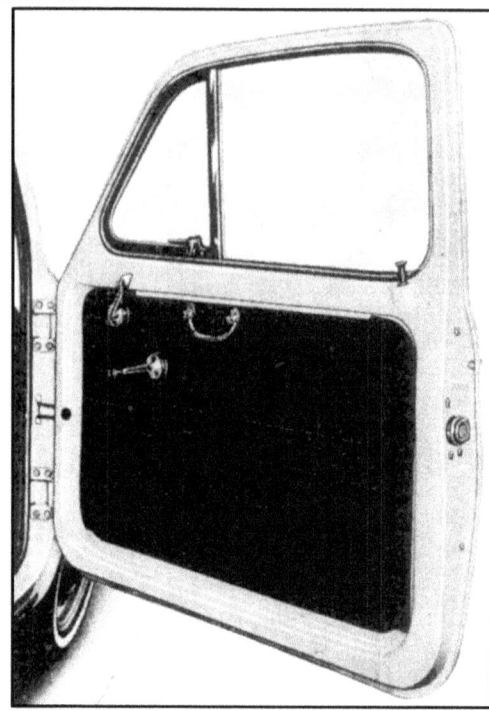

Fig. 146.- Sedan right side door, front-hinged. Door latch is of the triple acting type.

NOTE - Both side door handles are fitted with a key-type lock which operates from the outside.

Locking the door from the car interior by means of the catch pressure button is possible with a shut door only. Avoid depressing the catch button with an open door: as a matter of fact the catch does not work under such conditions and, moreover, damage to the lock may result.

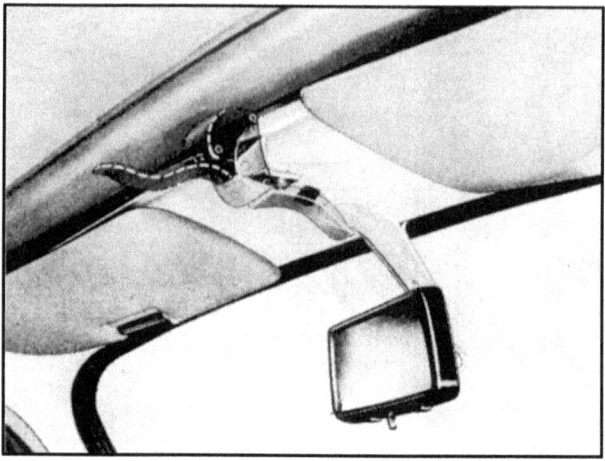

Fig. 147. Center catch of Sedan and Station Wagon folding top. Dotted lines evidence the folding top control handle in open position.

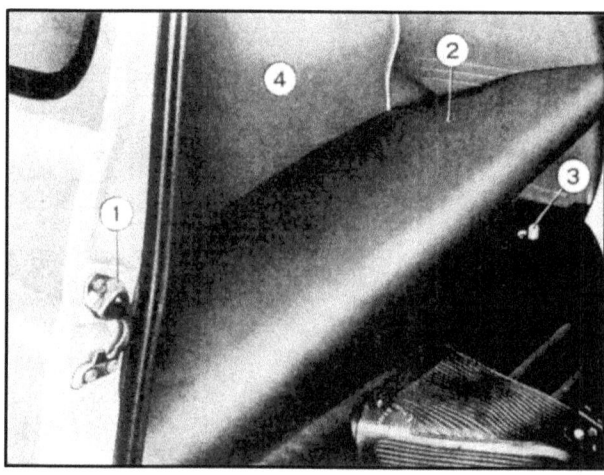

Fig. 148. Sedan rear seat, with removable cushion and reclining back.
1. Striker plate for triple acting door latch - 2. Seat cushion - 3. Dowels (two) for seat cushion location - 4. Seat back.

Fig. 149. Sedan 500, Sun Roof; side doors are hinged at front.

New design tail and stop lights are also featured.

MOD. 500 L SEDAN

DIFFERENCES FROM MOD. 500 (110 F) SEDAN

Chassis.
— Steering wheel with perforated metal spokes.
— Tires:
  Standard . . . . 125-12 (4 p.r.)
  Radial ply 125 SR-12

Electrical.
— New design instrument cluster, containing the fuel gauge, the direction indicator repeater and the headlamp high beam indicator.
— New fuse box.

Body.
— Protection bars on front and rear bumpers.
— New design wheel caps.
— Bright plastic mouldings on roof gutters.
— Windshield and back window with bright plastic rim.
— New FIAT name plate on front end.
— New model name on rear lid.
— Instrument board upholstered with plastic material.
— New design and arrangement of inside door handles; act on handle to open doors and pull the rigid map case to close them.
— Better appearance front seats.

  All cars are equipped with seats with adjustable backs, operated by a lever under the seats.

— New upholstery and trim on doors and seats.
— Rigid map cases on door panels.
— Utility shelf on tunnel.
— Floor mats in moquette and rubber.

Fig. 150 - Mod. 500 L Sedan.

Fig. 151. - Interior view, front compartment.

Fig. 152. - Left side door.

GENERAL CHARACTERISTICS

397

Fig. 153 - Arrangement of controls and indicators.

1. Instrument cluster. - 2. Instrument cluster light switch. - 3. Outside lights switch. - 4. Ashtray. - 5. Windshield wiper switch. - 6. Hand accelerator. - 7. Ignition key switch. - 8. Windshield washer pump. - 9. Hood release lever. - 10. Headlamp beam changeover switch lever. - 11. Direction indicator switch lever. - 12. Clutch pedal. - 13. Brake pedal. - 14. Accelerator pedal. - 15. Gear lever. - 16. Starting motor lever. - 17. Choke lever. - 18. Hand brake lever.

Fig. 154. - Instrument cluster.

1. Fuel gauge. - 2. Speedometer. - 3. Direction indicator arrow repeater. - 4. Mileage reeoster. - 5. Low oil pressure indicator. - 6. Headlamp high beam indicator. - 7. Parking light indicator. - 8. No-charge indicator. - 9. Low fuel indicator.

FUSES

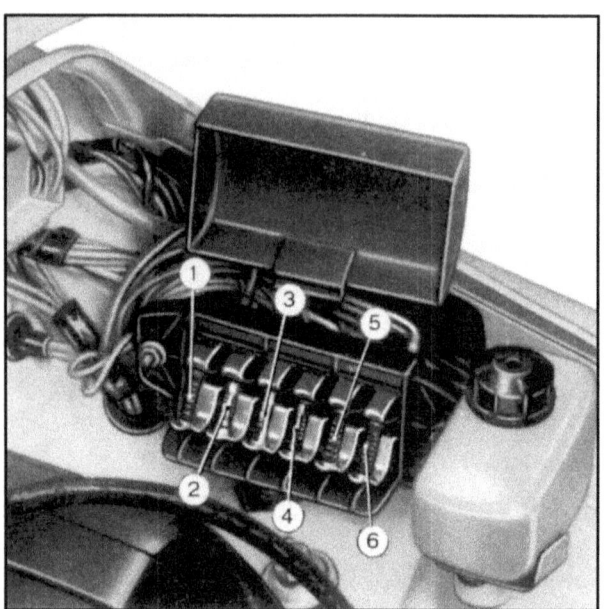

Fig. 155. - Arrangement of fuses.

Six 8-amp. fuses are provided. Unprotected circuits: battery charging circuit and warning light, ignition and starting circuit.

FUSES	CIRCUITS PROTECTED
A/1	— Horn. — Light in rear view mirror.
B/2	— Direction indicators and repeater. — Low oil pressure warning light. — Fuel gauge and low fuel warning light. — Windshield wiper. — Rear stop lights.
C/3	— Right side low beam.
D/4	— Left side low beam.
E/5	— Left side high beam and indicator. — Front right parking light. — Rear left parking light. — Instrument cluster light.
F/6	— Right side high beam. — Front left parking light and indicator. — Rear right parking light. — Number plate light.

Fig. 156 - Wiring diagram of Mod. 500 L Sedan.

1. Front parking and direction lights. - 2. High and low beam headlamps. - 3. Horn. - 4. Battery. - 5. Side direction indicators. - 6. Stop light hydraulic switch. - 7. Fuel gauge sending unit. - 8. Direction indicator flasher. - 9. Windshield wiper motor. - 10. Fuses. - 11. Push-button switch on driver's side door for light 28. - 12. Change-over switch for direction indicators. - 13. Horn push button. - 14. Change-over switch for outside lights and signal flasher. - 15. Fuel gauge. - 16. Low fuel indicator (red light). - 17. Electric cable connections. - 18. No-charge indicator (red light). - 19. Direction indicator repeater (green light). - 20. Parking light indicator (green light). - 21. Headlamp high beam indicator (blue light). - 22. Low oil pressure warning light (red). - 23. Instrument cluster light. - 24. Instrument cluster light switch. - 25. Outside light switch. - 26. Ignition switch controlling other circuits. - 27. Windshield wiper switch. - 28. Interior light, built in rear view mirror. - 29. Generator regulator. - 30. Generator. - 31. Starting motor. - 32. Ignition coil. - 33. Spark plugs. - 34. Ignition distributor. - 35. Low oil pressure indicator sending unit. - 36. Rear parking, stop and direction lights. - 37. Number plate light.

NOTE - The symbol — means that the cable has a numbered sheath or tube.

GENERAL CHARACTERISTICS

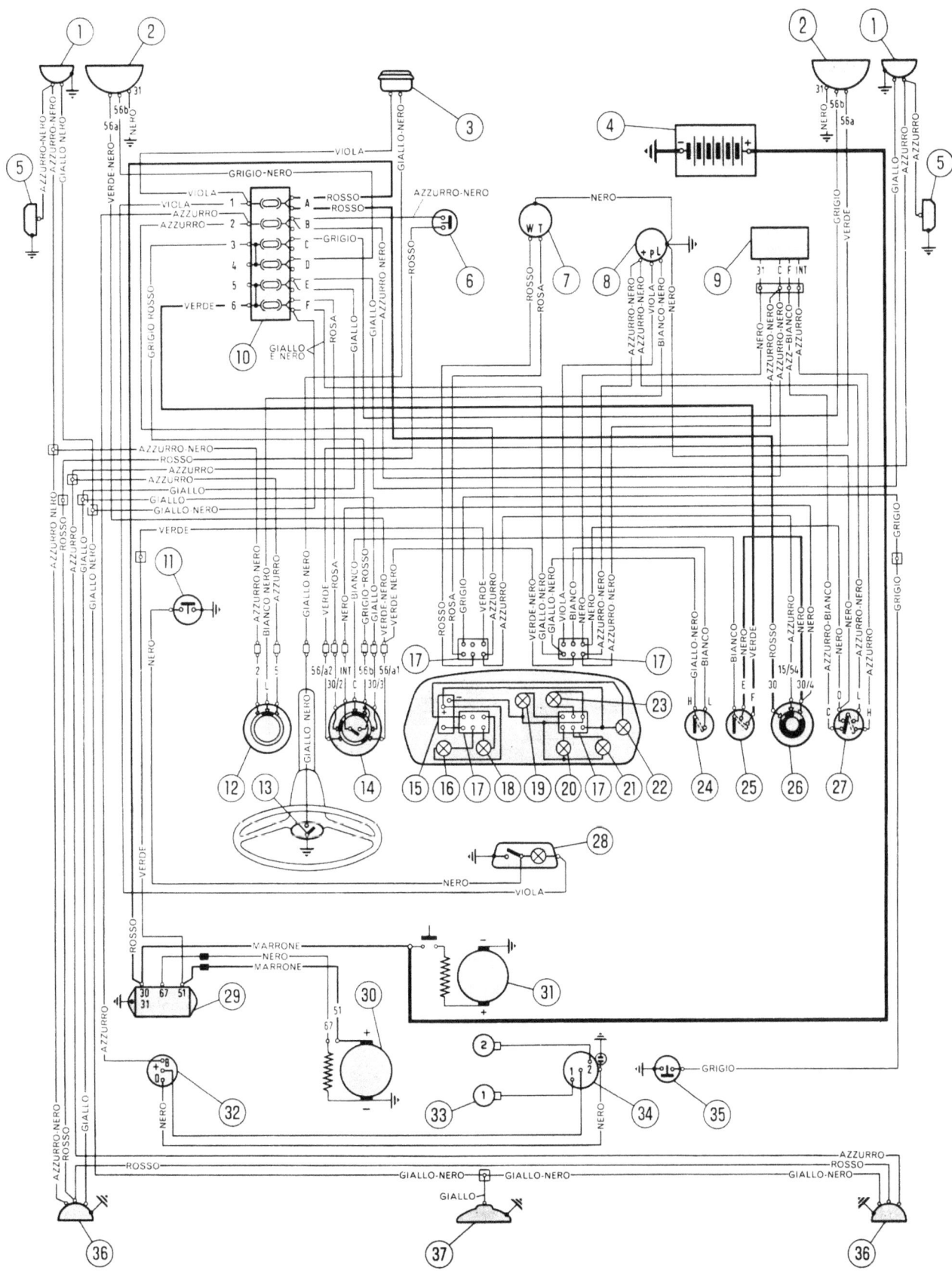

Fig. 156. - Wiring diagram of Mod. 500 L Sedan.

500 L SEDAN

Fig. 157 - Mod. 500 L Sedan.

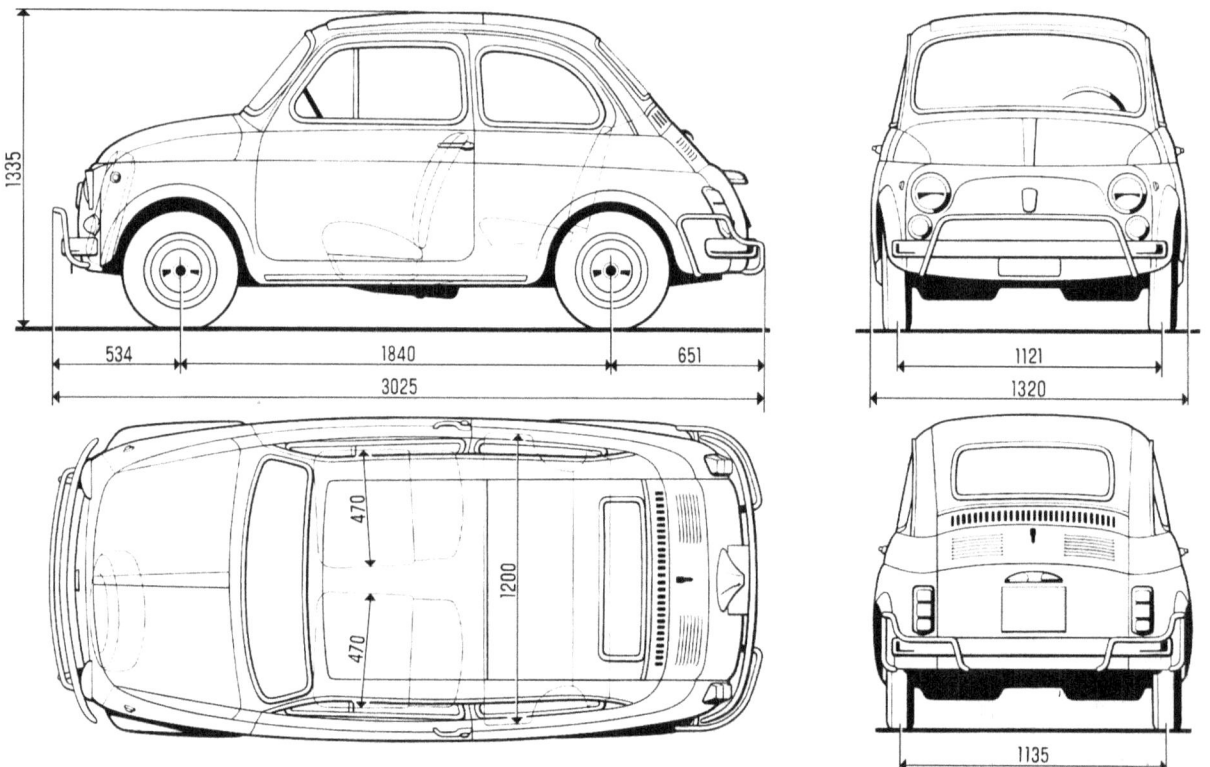

Fig. 158 - Main dimensions of Mod. 500 L Sedan (metric).

The height is for the car unladen.

VELOCEPRESS MANUALS - MOTORCYCLE

1930'S BRITISH MOTORCYCLE CARBS & ELEC COMPONENTS (BOOK OF)
1930'S BRITISH MOTORCYCLE ENGINES (OVERHAUL & MAINTENANCE)
1930'S BRITISH MOTORCYCLE GEARBOXES & CLUTCHES (BOOK OF)
AJS 1932-1948 SINGLES & TWINS 250cc THRU 1000cc (BOOK OF)
AJS 1945-1960 SINGLES 350cc & 500cc MODELS 16 & 18 (BOOK OF)
AJS 1955-1965 SINGLES 350cc & 500cc (BOOK OF)
ARIEL 1932-1939 PREWAR MODELS (BOOK OF)
ARIEL 1933-1951 (WORKSHOP MANUAL)
ARIEL 1939-1960 4 STROKE SINGLES (BOOK OF)
ARIEL 1958-1964 LEADER & ARROW (BOOK OF)
BMW R26 R27 (1956-1967) FACTORY WORKSHOP MANUAL
BMW R50 R50S R60 R69S (1955-1969) FACTORY WORKSHOP MANUAL
BSA BANTAM ALL MODELS FROM 1948 ONWARDS (BOOK OF)
BSA SINGLES & V-TWINS UP TO 1927 (BOOK OF)
BSA SINGLES & V-TWINS UP TO 1935 (BOOK OF)
BSA SINGLES & V-TWINS 1936-1939 (BOOK OF)
BSA SINGLES & V-TWINS 1936-1952 (BOOK OF)
BSA OHV & SV SINGLES 250-600cc 1945-1954 (BOOK OF)
BSA OHV & SV SINGLES 250cc 1954-1970 (BOOK OF)
BSA OHV SINGLES 350 & 500cc 1955-1967 (BOOK OF)
BSA TWINS 1948-1962 (BOOK OF)
BSA TWINS 1962-1969 (SECOND BOOK OF)
DOUGLAS 1929-1939 PREWAR ALL MODELS (BOOK OF)
DOUGLAS 1948-1957 POSTWAR ALL MODELS FACTORY SHOP MANUAL
DUCATI 160cc, 250cc & 350cc OHC MODELS FACTORY SHOP MANUAL
HONDA 50 ALL MODELS UP TO 1970 INC MONKEY & TRAIL (BOOK OF)
HONDA 90 ALL MODELS UP TO 1966 (BOOK OF)
HONDA 125-150cc TWINS C/CS/CB/CA FACTORY WORKSHOP MANUAL
HONDA 250-305 TWINS C/CS/CB FACTORY WORKSHOP MANUAL
HONDA C100 SUPER CUB FACTORY WORKSHOP MANUAL
HONDA C110 SPORT CUB 1962-1969 FACTORY WORKSHOP MANUAL
HONDA TWINS & SINGLES 50cc THRU 305cc 1960-1966 (BOOK OF)
HONDA TWINS ALL MODELS 125cc THRU 450cc UP TO 1968 (BOOK OF)
J.A.P. ENGINES 1927-1952 & MOTORCYCLES 1934-1952 (BOOK OF)
LAMBRETTA 1947-1957 ALL 125 & 150cc MODELS (BOOK OF)
LAMBRETTA 1957-1970 LI & TV MODELS (SECOND BOOK OF)
MATCHLESS 1931-1939 ALL MODELS 250cc THRU 990cc (BOOK OF)
MATCHLESS 1945-1956 350 & 500cc SINGLES (BOOK OF)
MATCHLESS 1955-1966 350 & 500cc SINGLES (BOOK OF)
NEW IMPERIAL ALL SV & OHV FROM 1935 ONWARDS (BOOK OF)
NORTON 1932-1939 PREWAR MODELS (BOOK OF)
NORTON 1932-1947 (BOOK OF)
NORTON 1938-1956 (BOOK OF)
NORTON 1955-1963 MODELS 19, 50 & ES2 (BOOK OF)
NORTON 1955-1965 DOMINATOR TWINS (BOOK OF)
NORTON 1957-1970 TWINS FACTORY WORKSHOP MANUAL
NSU PRIMA 1956-1964 ALL MODELS (BOOK OF)
NSU QUICKLY 1953-1963 ALL MODELS (BOOK OF)
PANTHER 1932-1958 LIGHTWEIGHT MODELS 250 & 350cc (BOOK OF)
PANTHER 1938-1966 HEAVYWEIGHT MODELS 600 & 650cc (BOOK OF)
RALEIGH MOPEDS 1960-1969 (BOOK OF)
RALEIGH MOTORCYCLES 1919-1933 (BOOK OF)
ROYAL ENFIELD 1934-1946 SINGLES & V TWINS (BOOK OF)
ROYAL ENFIELD 1937-1953 SINGLES & V TWINS (BOOK OF)
ROYAL ENFIELD 1946-1962 SINGLES (BOOK OF)
ROYAL ENFIELD 1958-1966 250cc & 350cc SINGLES (SECOND BOOK OF)
ROYAL ENFIELD 736cc INTERCEPTOR FACTORY WORKSHOP MANUAL
RUDGE 1933-1939 (BOOK OF)
SUNBEAM 1928-1939 (BOOK OF)
SUNBEAM 1946-1957 S7 & S8 (BOOK OF)
SUZUKI 50cc & 80cc UP TO 1966 (BOOK OF)
SUZUKI T10 1963-1967 FACTORY WORKSHOP MANUAL
SUZUKI T20 & T200 1965-1969 FACTORY WORKSHOP MANUAL
TRIUMPH 1935-1939 PREWAR MODELS (BOOK OF)
TRIUMPH 1935-1949 (BOOK OF)
TRIUMPH 1937-1951 (WORKSHOP MANUAL)
TRIUMPH 1945-1955 FACTORY WORKSHOP MANUAL
TRIUMPH 1945-1958 TWINS (BOOK OF)
TRIUMPH 1956-1969 TWINS (BOOK OF)
VELOCETTE 1925-1970 ALL SINGLES & TWINS (BOOK OF)
VESPA 1951-1961 (BOOK OF)
VESPA 1955-1963 125 & 150cc & GS MODELS (SECOND BOOK OF)
VESPA 1955-1968 GS & SS (BOOK OF)
VESPA 1963-1972 90, 125 & 150cc (THIRD BOOK OF)
VILLIERS ENGINE UP TO 1959 INC. 3 WHEELERS (BOOK OF)
VILLIERS ENGINE UP TO 1969 (BOOK OF)
VINCENT 1935-1955 (WORKSHOP MANUAL)

VELOCEPRESS TECHNICAL BOOKS – MOTORCYCLE

CATALOG OF BRITISH MOTORCYCLES (1951 MODELS)
INDIAN PONYBIKE, BOY RACER & PAPOOSE ILL PARTS LIST & SALES LIT
MOTORCYCLE ENGINEERING (P.E. Irving)
SPEED AND HOW TO OBTAIN IT (Motor Cycle Magazine UK)
TUNING FOR SPEED (P.E. Irving)

VELOCEPRESS MANUALS - THREE WHEELER'S

BSA THREE WHEELER (BOOK OF)
VINTAGE MORGAN THREE WHEELER (BOOK OF)

VELOCEPRESS MANUALS - AUTOMOBILE

AUSTIN-HEALEY 6-CYLINDER WORKSHOP MANUAL
AUSTIN-HEALEY SPRITE & MG MIDGET WORKSHOP MANUAL 1958-1971
BMW 600 LIMOUSINE FACTORY WORKSHOP MANUAL
BMW 600 LIMOUSINE OWNERS HAND BOOK & SERVICE MANUAL
BMW 2000 & 2002 1966-1976 WORKSHOP MANUAL
BMW ISETTA FACTORY WORKSHOP MANUAL
CORVAIR 1960-1969 WORKSHOP MANUAL
CORVETTE V8 1955-1962 WORKSHOP MANUAL
FIAT 500 FACTORY WORKSHOP MANUAL 1957-1973
JAGUAR E-TYPE 3.8 & 4.2 SERIES 1 & 2 WORKSHOP MANUAL
JAGUAR MK 7, 8, 9 & XK120, 140, 150 WORKSHOP MANUAL 1948-1961
METROPOLITAN FACTORY WORKSHOP MANUAL
MGA & MGB OWNERS HANDBOOK & WORKSHOP MANUAL
MG MIDGET TC, TD, TF & TF1500 WORKSHOP MANUAL
PORSCHE 356 1948-1965 WORKSHOP MANUAL
PORSCHE 912 WORKSHOP MANUAL
TRIUMPH TR2, TR3, TR4 1953-1965 WORKSHOP MANUAL
VOLKSWAGEN TRANSPORTER, TRUCKS & WAGONS 1950-1979 WSM
VOLVO 1944-1968 ALL MODELS WORKSHOP MANUAL

VELOCEPRESS TECHNICAL BOOKS - AUTOMOBILE

FERRARI 250/GT SERVICE AND MAINTENANCE
FERRARI GUIDE TO PERFORMANCE
FERRARI OWNER'S HANDBOOK
FERRARI TUNING TIPS & MAINTENANCE TECHNIQUES
HOW TO BUILD A FIBERGLASS CAR
HOW TO BUILD A RACING CAR
HOW TO RESTORE THE MODEL 'A' FORD
MASERATI OWNER'S HANDBOOK
OBERT'S FIAT GUIDE
PERFORMANCE TUNING THE SUNBEAM TIGER
SOUPING THE VOLKSWAGEN
SOLEX CARBURETORS (EMPHASIS ON UK & EU AUTOMOBILES)
SU CARBURETORS (EMPHASIS ON UK AUTOMOBILES)
WEBER CARBURETORS (EMPHASIS ON ALFA & FIAT)

VELOCEPRESS BOOKS & GUIDES - AUTOMOBILE

ABARTH BUYERS GUIDE
COMPLETE CATALOG OF JAPANESE MOTOR VEHICLES
FERRARI 308 SERIES BUYER'S AND OWNER'S GUIDE
FERRARI BERLINETTA LUSSO
FERRARI BROCHURES AND SALES LITERATURE 1946-1967
FERRARI BROCHURES AND SALES LITERATURE 1968-1989
FERRARI OPP, MAINTENANCE & SERVICE H/BOOKS 1948-1963
FERRARI SERIAL NUMBERS PART I - ODD NUMBERS TO 21399
FERRARI SERIAL NUMBERS PART II - EVEN NUMBERS TO 1050
FERRARI SPYDER CALIFORNIA
HENRY'S FABULOUS MODEL "A" FORD
MASERATI BROCHURES AND SALES LITERATURE

VELOCEPRESS BOOKS – RACING

CARRERA PANAMERICANA - MEXICAN ROAD RACE (BOOK OF)
DIALED IN - THE JAN OPPERMAN STORY
IF HEMINGWAY HAD WRITTEN A RACING NOVEL
LE MANS 24 (THE BOOK THAT THE FILM WAS BASED ON)
VEDA ORR'S NEW REVISED HOT ROD PICTORIAL

AUTOBOOKS WORKSHOP MANUALS & BROOKLANDS ROAD TEST PORTFOLIOS

FOR A COMPLETE LISTING OF THE AUTOBOOKS & BROOKLANDS TITLES THAT WE CURRENTLY HAVE AVAILABLE, PLEASE VISIT OUR WEBSITE.

www.VelocePress.com

Please visit our website

www.VelocePress.com

for a complete up-to-date list of titles, descriptions, and secure online ordering using PayPal.

www.ingramcontent.com/pod-product-compliance
Lightning Source LLC
Chambersburg PA
CBHW060243240426

43673CB00047B/1870